JN261342

Copyright © 2003 A.D.A. EDITA Tokyo Co., Ltd.
3-12-14 Sendagaya, Shibuya-ku, Tokyo 151-0051, Japan
All rights reserved. No part of this publication may be reproduced,
stored in a retrieval system, or transmitted, in any form or by any means,
electronic, mechanical, photocopying, recording, or otherwise,
without permission in writing from the publisher.

The drawings of Frank Lloyd Wright are
Copyright © The Frank Lloyd Wright Foundation 2003
Text Copyright © The Frank Lloyd Wright Foundation 2003
Copyright of photographs © 2003 GA photographers: Yukio Futagawa &
Associated Photographers

The red square with FRANK LLOYD WRIGHT in block letters is a
registered trademark belonging to The Frank Lloyd Wright Foundation.
The Frank Lloyd Wright Foundation grants permission for
A.D.A. EDITA Tokyo to use the mark in its block.

"GA" logotype design: Gan Hosoya

ISBN4-87140-617-2 C1352

Printed and bound in Japan

Frank Lloyd Wright
Architecture

Edited and Photographed by Yukio Futagawa
Text by Bruce Brooks Pfeiffer

GA TRAVELER 007

38	**Administration Building for S. C. Johnson & Son Company** Racine, Wisconsin, 1936
94	**Research Laboratory for S. C. Johnson & Son Company** Racine, Wisconsin, 1944
102	**Florida Southern College** Lakeland, Florida, 1938
142	**Solomon R. Guggenheim Museum** New York, New York, 1943-59
160	**Tower for H. C. Price Company** Bartlesville, Oklahoma, 1952
184	**Marin County Government Center** San Rafael, California, 1957

Frank Lloyd Wright
Archi

228	**Unity Temple** Oak Park, Illinois, 1905	
250	**Anne Merner Pfeiffer Chapel,** **Florida Southern College** Lakeland, Florida, 1938	
268	**William H. Danforth Chapel,** **Florida Southern College** Lakeland, Florida, 1953	
276	**Unitarian Meeting House** Shorewood Hills, Wisconsin, 1947	
292	**Beth Sholom Synagogue** Elkins Park, Pennsylvania, 1954	
300	**Annunciation Greek Orthodox Church** Wauwatosa, Wisconsin, 1956	

Cover: Solomon R. Guggenheim Museum

tecture

Public Buildings

by Bruce Brooks Pfeiffer

Foreword

The public buildings presented here include the S. C. Johnson & Son Company administration building and research tower, Florida Southern College campus, the Solomon R. Guggenheim Museum, the H. C. Price Company office and apartment tower, and the Marin County Civic Center. Frank Lloyd Wright designed many other public buildings, but for various reasons they were never built. These range from an amusement park in 1895 for Wolf Lake, Illinois to the famous 1956 Mile High skyscraper for Chicago.

When Wright undertook a public commission, he always sought the design solution that would provide a comfortable and inspiring environment for both employees and visitors. Unlike so many other public buildings, monumentality never had a place in Wright's architecture. He believed that monumentality overwhelmed the human soul and that a good building must serve humanity:

"A good building is the greatest of poems when it is organic architecture. The fact that the building faces and is reality and serves while it releases life, makes daily life better worth living and makes all the necessities happier because of useful living in it, makes the building none the less poetry, but more truly so. Every great architect is—necessarily—a great poet. He must be a great original interpreter of his time, his day, his age."[1]

Administration Building for S. C. Johnson & Son Company, Racine, Wisconsin, 1936

Herbert F. Johnson (Hib), president of the S. C. Johnson & Son Company, went to Taliesin in the summer of 1936 to discuss with Frank Lloyd Wright the possibility of his designing their company's new administration building. Johnson had already employed an architect for the work but neither he nor his officers were satisfied with the design.[2] Wright, desperately in need of work, proposed a building of unusual beauty as well as practicality, a building "as inspiring a place to work in as any cathedral ever was in which to worship."[3] Returning to Racine, Johnson sent Wright a letter formally giving him the commission.

はじめに

この巻に掲載した公共建築は，S・C・ジョンソン&サン社管理棟及び研究実験棟，フロリダ・サザン・カレッジ・キャンパス，ソロモン・R・グッゲンハイム美術館，H・C・プライス社オフィス&アパートメント・タワー，マリン郡市庁舎である。フランク・ロイド・ライトはこれ以外にも数多くの公共建築を設計したが，様々な理由から実施には至らなかった。そこには，1895年のイリノイ州ウォルフ・レイクのアミューズメント・パークから，1956年のシカゴに計画された有名なマイル・ハイ・スカイスクレイパーまで多岐に渡る作品が含まれている。

　公共建築の依頼を受けると，ライトは常に，そこに働く人と訪れる人，その両者が快適に感じ，精神の高揚を感じられる環境をつくりだすようなデザインを探した。公共建築の多くとは違って，ライトの建築ではモニュメンタリティの占める場所はない。モニュメンタリティは人の心を圧倒してしまう。よい建物は人間性に仕えなければならないとライトは信じていた。

　「よい建物は，それが有機的建築(オーガニック・アーキテクチャー)であるとき，素晴らしい一遍の詩なのである。建物が現実に直面する，生活を解放する一方で生活に仕えるという事実は，日々の生活をより価値あるものにし，有益な生活のためのあらゆる日常の必要をより満足のいくものとなし，それでいながら詩である以上に詩そのものである建物をつくりあげる。偉大な建築家は皆――必然的に――偉大な詩人である。彼は，その時，その日，その時代の偉大なる独創的表現者であらねばならない。」[1]

S・C・ジョンソン&サン社管理棟，1936年

S・C・ジョンソン&サン社の社長ハーバート・F・ジョンソン（Hib）は，1936年の夏，新しい管理棟の設計を依頼できるかどうかフランク・ロイド・ライトと話し合うためにタリアセンを訪れた。ジョンソンは既に設計を他の建築家に頼んでいたが，自身も，社の役員もその案に満足していなかった。[2] ライトは仕事がどうしても欲しいという想いを賭けて，実用に適うと同時に，並はずれた美しさを備えた，「あらゆるカテドラルが，人の心に神への祈りを誘発したように，人を生き生きと働く気持ちにさせる場所となる」[3] 建物を提案した。ラシーンに戻ると，ジ

"Next day came a note from Hib enclosing a retainer (one thousand dollars) testifying to his appreciation of what he saw on that occasion ...What a release of pent-up creative energy—the making of those plans! Ideas came tumbling up and out onto paper to be thrown back in heaps—for careful scrutiny and selection. But, at once, I knew the scheme I wanted to try. I had it in mind when I drew the newspaper plant at Salem, Oregon, for Editor George Putnam, which he had been unable to build. A great simplicity."[4]

Wright was referring to the Capitol Journal building that he had designed in 1931 with a large workroom whose ceiling was supported by dendriform columns—slender at the base and spreading at the top like mushrooms or lily pads. For the Johnson building, he developed the columns further by making them both taller and more graceful. The site for the building was an urban location with views onto city streets. As with the Larkin building, Wright chose to seal the building off from its environment and let light pour down into the general workroom from the spaces between the column pads above.

The entrance to the building is in the center of the complex, a carport/garage on one side, and the foyer on the other. This provides a sheltered entry from the extremes of the Wisconsin climate. The foyer is open to the third level and the columns here rise dramatically to the skylights above. Directly beyond the foyer is the Great Workroom, a two-story space with mezzanine balconies on three sides and a bridge over the reception desk in the lobby on the fourth side connecting them. On the mezzanine level, over the entrance, there is a theater with seating for 250 for daytime lectures or films. Along with this lecture hall / theatre are a projection booth, kitchenette, and dishwashing area. The third and uppermost level is a penthouse that provides the private offices for the officials of the company. Originally, Wright intended the offices to have partitions of brick, but later he changed to partitions of glass tubes and wood. A balcony on this penthouse level looks down into the lobby and the Great Workroom, as well. This creates a connection between officials and employees, working as one "family", a solution that proved most successful in the Larkin Building. A partial basement below provides for storage, rest rooms, employees lounges, and other functions. The basement is accessible via spiral stairs placed in the Great Workroom at convenient intervals. Heating is provided by means of gravity heat, iron pipes under the floor that circulate hot water, the same solution he was using in the Usonian houses. Above the roof rise two brick "nostrils", as they are called, that bring air into building for air-conditioning.

"Weight herein this building by way of a natural use of steel in tension, appears to lift and float in light and air: 'miraculous' light dendriforms standing up against the sky take on integral character as plastic units of a plastic building construction entire, *emphasizing* space instead of standing up in the way as mere inserts for support.

ョンソンはライトに，正式に設計を依頼する旨の手紙を送った。

「翌日，Hibから，昨日彼が見たものに対する賛辞の証となる手付け金（千ドル）を同封した短い手紙が来た。閉じこめられていた創造的エネルギーの——これらのプランをつくるという——なんという解放だろうか！ アイディアが奔出し，紙の上に描かれ，投げ出されて山のように積み上げられた——慎重に吟味し選ぶためである。しかし，すぐに，私が試したいと思うスキームが分かった。オレゴン州セーラムに編集主幹のジョージ・パットナムの依頼で新聞社の工場の図面を描いたときに考えたものであったが，結局，彼はその建物を建てることが出来なかったのである。その素晴らしい単純性。」[4]

ライトは1931年に設計した，広いワークルームの天井が，樹形状の柱——基部がほっそりとして，頂部がキノコや睡蓮の葉のように広がっている——に支えられたキャピトル・ジャーナルの建物に目を向けたのである。ジョンソン・ビルディングでは，彼は柱をより高く，より優美なものにして，それをさらに発展させた。建物の敷地は街路に面した都市の一角であった。ラーキン・ビルディングと同じように，ライトはその周辺環境から建物を封じ込めることを選び，広がった柱頭の間に生まれる透き間からオフィス全体に天空光が降り注ぐようにしたのである。

建物のエントランスはコンプレックスの中央にあり，片側にカーポート／ガレージ，片側にホワイエがある。この構成によって，エントリーはウィスコンシンの非常に厳しい気候から守られる。ホワイエは3階まで吹抜け，その柱は頭上のスカイライトに向かってドラマティックに立ち上がっている。ホワイエの正面前方にグレート・ワークルームがある。2層吹抜けの空間で，メザニン・バルコニーが三方を囲み，残る一面に置かれたロビーのレセプション・デスクの上を架け渡すブリッジがバルコニーを結んでいる。エントランスの上にくるメザニン・バルコニーには，昼間，講演や映写会が開かれる250席のシアターがある。このレクチャー・ホール／シアターに沿って，映写ブース，キチネット，洗い場が続く。3階にあたる一番上のレベルはペントハウスで，社の重役用個室オフィスが並んでいる。最初，ライトはこれらのオフィスに煉瓦の仕切壁を考えていたが，後になって，チューブ状ガラスと木の組み合わせに変更した。このペントハウスのバルコニーからは，ロビーとグレート・ワークルームを見下ろせる。これによって役員と社員の間に，一つの"家族"のように働くというつながりが生まれた。それはラーキン・ビルディングで最も成功を収めた点である。1階下の一部を占める地階には倉庫，洗面所，社員ラウンジ，その他の機能空間がある。地階へはグレート・ワークルーム内に，利用しやすい間隔で配置された螺旋階段から出られる。暖房は床下に通した鉄パイプに温水を循環させ，重力による暖気の上昇を利用する方法が採用されているが，同じ方法をライトはユーソニアン・ハウスで用いている。屋根の上には煉瓦でつくられた2本の"鼻孔"が立ち上がっている。空調のために空気を建物内に送り込むことからその名がつけられた。

「スティールの緊張材を自然に使うことで，建物のこの場所の重さは

The main clerical work force was all correlated in one vast room, 228 by 228 feet. This great room, air-conditioned, besides the top lighting and rift for light at the cornice level, is daylit also by rifts in the brick walls. And the heating system of the main floor of the building is entirely beneath the floor slab. The structure is hermetically sealed and air-conditioned with this gravity heat."[5]

The brickwork throughout is of exceptional workmanship, and the brick walls and parapets are capped with fine Kasota sandstone. The white concrete columns, with light pouring down from above, produce the effect that has been likened to a forest of birch trees. Where the ceiling of the mezzanine meets the exterior brick walls, the pads of the columns stop short of the walls and the corner is taken up with a glass skylight.

As construction began on the building, the Wisconsin Building Commission voiced concern about the ability of the dendriform columns to support the twelve tons calculated for each column. To demonstrate the soundness of the columns, Wright had a sample column poured and propped up on the building site. A steam shovel then began piling weighed gravel and cement bags on the pad of the column. No cracks appeared until the load had reached sixty tons. The column had proved itself and construction then went on.

The "windows" throughout the building are actually glass tubes (Pyrex) wired to aluminum racks, yielding a delicate crystalline light. Several interior partitions are also made up of these glass tubes. An enclosed bridge lit overhead by glass tubes connects the penthouse level with a squash court above the garage below. This serves as an employee recreation deck. Walking through this glass and brick bridge produces the sensation of entering a "space ship" bound for another planet.

Wright also designed the innovative office furniture, the desks and chairs here called "Work Stations". As it was in the Larkin building thirty years earlier, the design for the furnishings is as important a detail as the design of the building itself. In this way a continuity and completeness is achieved.

The building opened on April 21, 1939. On the weekend of its opening, twenty-six thousand people toured the building including the press. Widely published, it quickly became an icon of modern public building design.

Research Laboratory for S. C. Johnson & Son Co., Racine, Wisconsin, 1944

In 1943, the Johnson Company decided to expand their product line beyond wax and consequently needed also to increase their laboratory research facilities. Johnson explained to Wright the type of building he wanted, "It is a plain factory kind of job that should be built by an engineer or contractor like our other factory buildings.

光と空気のなかに引き上げられ，浮遊しているように見える。空に向かって立ち上がる"奇跡のように"軽い樹形状の柱が，全体が彫塑的に構築された建物の彫塑的ユニットの一部となり，単なる支柱として立ち上がるのではなく，空間を〈強調する〉のである。中心的な事務の仕事についている従業員全員は，228フィート×228フィートの，この巨大な一室空間のなかに互いに連係して働くことになる。この空調された大空間へは，トップライトとコーニス・レベルの切り込みの他に，煉瓦壁の切り込みからも外光が差し込む。建物主階の暖房システムは，床下全体に設置されている。建物は密閉され，この重力熱によって空調される。」[5]

全体の煉瓦積みは素晴らしい出来映えで，煉瓦壁とパラペットはきめの細かいカソタ砂岩で頂部が覆われている。上方から外光が降り注ぐ白いコンクリートの柱は，白樺の林に似た効果をつくりだす。メザニン・バルコニーの天井が外壁と出会うところで，柱頂部の広がりは，壁にまで達せず，コーナーをガラスのスカイライトが埋めている。

建物の工事が始まると，ウィスコンシン州建築委員会は，計算上，それぞれの柱にかかる12トンの荷重を樹形状の柱が支えることができるかどうか懸念を表明した。この柱の強度を示すために，ライトは建物の敷地にテスト用の柱を立ち上げた。次に，柄付きのスコップが，柱の睡蓮の葉のような頂部に重りの砂利とセメント袋を積み上げ始めた。荷重が60トンになるまで，亀裂は入らなかった。柱は強度を証明し，工事は進められた。

建物全体を通して"窓"は，実際には，アルミ・ラックに針金で取り付けたチューブ状ガラス（パイレックス）で構成され，繊細で澄んだ光を浸透させている。ガラスのチューブを透過して上から光が差し込む囲まれたブリッジが，ペントハウス階と，下のガレージの上にあるスカッシュ・コートを結んでいる。ここは社員のレクリエーション・デッキとしての役割を果たす。このガラスと煉瓦のブリッジを渡って行くと，別な惑星へ出発する"宇宙船"に乗り込む気持ちになる。

ライトはまた，机や椅子など独創的なオフィス家具をデザインし，それはここでは"ワーク・ステーション"と呼ばれた。30年前のラーキン・ビルディングがそうであったように，家具のデザインは，建物そのもののデザインと同様に重要であった。これによって，全体が連続性をもち，完璧なものが生まれるからである。

建物は1939年4月21日に一般公開された。その週末には，報道関係者を含め2万6千人が建物を見学した。広く報道され，建物は瞬く間に，近代的な公共建築のイコンとなった。

S・C・ジョンソン＆サン社研究実験棟，1944年

1943年，ジョンソン社は，製品ラインをワックス以外にも広げることを決定し，その結果，研究実験施設を拡張することが必要になった。ジョンソンは彼が望む建物のタイプをライトに説明した。「それは，私たちが持っている他の工場の建物のように，技術者や建設業者が建てるよう

Yet because of its proximity to your masterpiece, it should have a relationship thereto and we feel it would be unfair to you and mistake on our part if we didn't ask how you think you would want to fit into such a picture."[6]

Wright had always been enamored with the *Thousand and One Nights* and this accounts for this most remarkable letter he wrote to Johnson about the type of building he envisioned.

"December 14, 1943

And thou sayest, and thou be not sleepy, tell us more of thy pleasant tales. Whereupon Shaharazad replied "with love and good will." It hath reached me, O King of the Age, that Aladdin said to the Sultan ....

Dear Hibbard:

Why build a heavy building sodden upon the ground—facing awkwardly upon unsightly streets when by creating a charming interior court space for parking the lighting would come from above or from the court. A gallery would follow above and around that court space, O master. And bridge-tunnels would be seen connecting this space and the administration building itself to the research laboratory, which is as a tall—shaft would rise from the center of the court, etc. My Lord, etc. ... What a miracle of beautiful planning will be there to instruct thy foes, delight thy friends and convince thy subjects of the illustrious character of thy reign, O my Caliph?"[7]

Johnson was obviously won over by this poetic and romantic appeal. Wright called the design "Helio-Laboratory", remarking that all the floors in the tower would have the benefit of ample daylight, and by December of the same year, he wrote Johnson "I have a good scheme ready for you to see ... I think you'll get a thrill out of the drawings."[8]

In Wright's original proposal, each floor projected slightly out from the one beneath it, in the same manner as St. Mark's Tower and the Rogers Lacy Hotel. However, this was abandoned because it would necessitate making new formwork for each level thus incurring a substantial increase in the construction costs. The tower, in its final version, is fourteen stories tall, twelve of the stories alternating between a square plan and a circular mezzanine. The mezzanine provides space for recording data research in conjunction with the work going on down below. As the circular floor does not touch the outer wall, it allows the added height any apparatus or equipment might need on the floor below.

As the section of the tower reveals, all floors are cantilevered out from a central core. This core rises the full height of the tower, and on each level there is a toilet, stairway, and elevator. Within this core are also the vents and utility shafts required for heating, cooling, and the removal of fumes from the use of chemicals. The core rises out of what Wright called a "tap root" foundation: a central shaft forty-four feet deep. A reinforced concrete flange, like the handle of a sword,

なプレーンな工場です。しかし，それがあなたの傑作の傍らに建つがゆえに，それとの関係を持たせるべきであり，もし私たちが，そうした状況に相応しいものとして，どのようなものを望ましいと思われるかをお訊ねしないとしたら，それはあなたに対し不公平となり，私たちにとっての誤りとなるであろうと感じております。」[6]

ライトはかねて，『アラビアンナイト』に魅了されており，そしてそのことは，ライトがジョンソンに彼が思い描く建物について書いた，次の驚くような手紙を説明している。

「1943年12月14日
　汝は申した。眠くはないと。面白き物語のつづきを語り聞かせよ。シェヘラザードは『敬愛と忠誠の心をもちまして』と答えた。何なりと御用をお申しつけ下さい，おお我らが国王よ，アラジンはスルタンに言いました……

親愛なるヒッバード：
　駐車のための魅力的な中庭をつくることによって，光が上方からあるいは中庭から入ってくるのに，始末に困る見苦しい道路に面したこの土地を覆い尽くす重々しい建物をなぜ建てることがあるでしょうか。おおご主人さま，その中庭の上を，中庭の周りを，ギャラリーが周り巡るでしょう。そして，ブリッジ・トンネルが，この空間と管理棟を，丈高いシャフトのように中庭の中央から立ち上がるタワーに結んでいるのを見ることになるでありましょう。……陛下……この美しい計画案のなんという奇跡が，あなたさまの敵に知らしめ，友を喜ばせ，あなたさまの王国の輝かしい特質について，あなたさまが抱いておられる主題を得心させるべくそこに存在することになるでありましょうか，おお我がカリフよ？」[7]

ジョンソンは明らかに，この詩的でとっぴな懇願に説き伏せられた。ライトはこのデザインを，タワーのすべての階が豊かな光の恩恵に浴することに注目して"ヘリオ（太陽）ラボラトリー"と呼び，同じ年の12月，ジョンソンにこう書いた。「ごらんに入れるばかりになった素晴らしいスキームがあります……ドローイングからは震えるような感動を覚えられることと存じます。」[8]

ライトの最初の案では，セント・マークス・タワーやロジャース・レイシー・ホテルと同じ方法で，各階は順にその下の階よりわずかに突き出していた。しかし，この案は放棄された。各階ごとに別な型枠を必要とするため，建設コストの大幅な上昇を招くからである。タワーの最終案は，14階建て，そのうち12階分は，四角形プランと円形のメザニンが交互に積層して行く。メザニンはその下の階で進行中の仕事に連係して実験データを記録するスペースを提供する。円形の床は外壁に接触しないために，下の階にどのような装置や設備も必要とせずに，高さを加えることができる。

断面で分かるように，各階は中央コアからキャンティ・レバーで外に突き出している。コアはタワーの高さいっぱいに立ち上がり，各階に洗面所，階段，エレベータがある。コア内にはまた，暖冷房，化学品の使

attached to the taproot and sunk underground, assures stability. The outer shell of the tower is sheathed in glass tubes with a low brick wall on each of the square levels. The glass tubes were intended, as with the main administration building, to provide defused daylight all around and on all levels.

The Tower is placed in the center of a large open court surrounded by parking. The tower is entered from the same covered central area as the administration building. The ground level of the tower contains the reception area while the remainder of this level is reserved for the existing carports. On the second level, the plan takes the shape of a large T, the central part connecting the administration building to the tower. The entrance on the second floor is used mainly by the staff. In one wing, there are also library, lounge, and dining area, all grouped around a masonry mass that provides a fireplace for each area, along with a workspace adjacent to the dining room. An outdoor roof garden with pool is featured close to the lounge. The second level also provides for a photographic studio, film processing and finishing, conference rooms, and offices, connected directly to the library on the second level of the tower. The third level of this expanded office extension is given over to the advertising department and connects to the main administration building by means of the existing brick and glass bridge. On this level, which occupies only a portion of the T-plan, there are additional offices with a reception area under a dome of glass tubes.

A basement level, eleven feet below ground level, extends out from the tower in three directions. Here are testing laboratories, storage rooms for chemicals, special climate controlled rooms, as well as locker rooms for the employees. This basement area is a vast and complex arrangement. The largest room is the pilot laboratory, a two-story space beneath the west wing of the courtyard. Equipped with a ceiling hoist and a network of pipes, it reaches twenty feet above the floor, with a mezzanine. Machinery throughout provides air filtering and exhaust systems to remove any poisonous or toxic gases that might result in the process of experimentation. Four tall, elegant dendriform columns support the ceiling, similar to the ones in the administration building, and give both beauty and drama to an otherwise purely industrial and utilitarian space.

Florida Southern College, Lakeland, Florida, 1938

"When Dr. Ludd M. Spivey, the presidential good-genius of Florida Southern College, flew north to Taliesin, he came with the express and avowed purpose of giving the US at least one example of a college wherein modern life was to have the advantages of modern science and art in actual building construction. He said he wanted me as much for my Philosophy as for my Architecture. I assured him they were inseparable.

用から発生するガスの排気の必要に対応した通気孔とユーティリティ・シャフトが設置されている。コアは，ライトが，"主根"基礎と呼んだ，44フィートの深さに達する中央シャフトから立ち上がっている。刀の柄のような鉄筋コンクリートのフランジが"主根"に装着され，地下に沈められて安定性を確かなものとした。タワーの外殻はチューブ状ガラスで包まれ，四角形平面の階に面しては低い煉瓦壁が回されている。チューブ状ガラスは，主屋の管理棟と同様に，各階で周囲から拡散する昼光を差し入れることを意図したものである。

タワーはパーキングが取り囲む広いオープン・コートの中央にある。建物内へは管理棟と同じ，屋根で覆われた中央エリアから入る。1階はレセプションがある他は既存のカーポートのために残されている。2階は大きなT形平面を形成し，その中央部分は管理棟とタワーを結んでいる。2階のエントランスは主にスタッフが使用する。ウィングの一つにはまた，ライブラリー，ラウンジ，ダイニング・エリアがあり，そのすべてが，ダイニング・エリアに隣接するワーク・スペースと共に，各エリアに暖炉を提供している組積造のマッスの周りに集められている。プール付きの屋上庭園がラウンジの近くにある。2階にはまた，写真スタジオ，フィルムの現像引き延ばし室，会議室，オフィスがあり，タワー2階のライブラリーと直接つながっている。2階オフィスの上に拡がる3階は，広告部門にあてられ，煉瓦とガラスの既存ブリッジで主屋である管理棟とつながれている。T形プランの一部を占めるだけのこの階には，チューブ状ガラスのドームの下に，レセプション・エリアの付いたサブ・オフィスがある。

地盤面より11フィート下にある地下階は，タワーから三方向に広がっている。ここには，試験用実験室，化学品の貯蔵室，特別に温度が調節された部屋，従業員用ロッカー・ルームがある。この地下階は広大で，複雑な配置構成になっている。最も大きな部屋はコートヤードの西ウィングの下にある2層の高さの空間で，パイロット・ラボラトリーである。天井に設置された巻き上げ装置と配管網によって，床上20フィートに達する中2階を構成できる。実験の過程で発生する可能性のある有毒ガスを取り去り，空気を濾過し，排気する機械システムが全体に配置されている。管理棟にあるのと同様な，背が高く優美な樹形状の柱4本が天井を支え，さもなければ純粋に工業的で実用的な空間に，美しく劇的な性格を与えている。

フロリダ・サザン・カレッジ，1938年

「フロリダ・サザン・カレッジの総長にふさわしい天分を備えた，尊敬すべきラッド・M・スパイヴィー博士が，タリアセンに向かって北に飛んだとき，彼は，近代科学や近代芸術を十分に活用した建物のなかで近代的な生活が営まれるカレッジを少なくとも一つ，アメリカにつくろうという明白で公然とした目的を抱いていた。彼は私の建築と同じ重さをもって私の哲学を望んでいた。私は彼に，2つは切り離せないものです

And ever since, owing to Dr. Spivey's unremitting efforts, this collection of college buildings has been in a continuous state of growth. Their outdoor-garden character is intended to be an expression of Florida at its floral best.

Study these buildings from the inside out if you would know something about the kind of building we call Organic Architecture... The path we call Organic Architecture is along the center-line of an indigenous culture for these states in which we live, because there can be no great life for our people without the integral culture of an Architecture of our own ....

All we know about great civilizations is what we learn of them from what remains of their Architecture ....

So, as for these buildings in which a true portion of America moves, studies, works and has its being, if you would honestly try to understand these Florida Southern College buildings and would really know what they are all about (whether you like them or not), something important to our country's future as a democratic nation will transpire. Because not only do buildings last long but in these buildings here and now you may see something of your own tomorrow that is yours today.[9]

Three Seminar Buildings, 1940

The three seminar buildings are identical in plan and connected as one structure. At the entrance, there are faculty offices, followed by a workspace for secretaries, and a large lecture room at the other end. Originally used for seminars, they were later converted into additional administrative offices. Construction conforms to the general character of the Frank Lloyd Wright campus, concrete blocks in some instances plastered, in others instances specially designed blocks.

Roux Library, 1941

The library was designed in 1941, but construction was delayed until the end of the Second World War in 1945. Wright has taken the plan for the Barnsdall Little Dipper kindergarten (Hollywood, California, 1923) and cleverly adapted it on an expanded scale to become the plan for this library. He converted what was the Barnsdall outdoor bowl into the main reading room, while the original school portion has been converted into a space for the stacks. Where the circular reading room meets the angular area for the stacks there are two entrances, one on each side. The entrances gain a foyer, with a centrally placed fireplace. Stairs behind the fireplace ascend to the mezzanine level as well as descend to the lower level. A projected area opposite the fireplace provides the station for the librarian in the reading room, visible from all the desks. The desks are arranged on three

と断言した。

それ以来，スパイヴィー博士の不断の努力によって，カレッジの建物のコレクションは増え続けていった。その野外庭園のような性格は，フロリダの花々が最も美しいときを表現しようとしたものである。

我々が有機的建築(オーガニック・アーキテクチャー)と呼んでいる建物について何かを知りたいならば，これらの建物を内から外へと学んで行くことである。有機的建築と我々が呼ぶものの道筋は，我々がその内で生きる固有の文化のセンターラインに沿って伸びている。なぜなら，建築という総合的な文化を自ら所有することなしに，我々人民の偉大なる生活はあり得ないだろうからである……

偉大なる文明について我々が知るすべては，残された建築から学んだものにほかならない……

それゆえに，アメリカの真の一部である人々が，行き交い，学び，働き，存在するこれらの建物，つまりフロリダ・サザン・カレッジの建築群を誠実に理解しようと試み，それらのすべてがいかなるものであるか真に知るならば（好むと好まざるとにかかわらず），民主主義国家としての我々の国の未来にとって重要な何かが明らかになるだろう。建物は長く残るばかりでなく，そうした建物のなかにあって，直ちに，今日のあなたのものにほかならぬ，あなた自身の未来について何かを知り得るかもしれないのだから。」[9]

3つのセミナー棟，1940年

3つのセミナー棟は，平面構成は全く同じで，互いにつながって一つの構造体を形成する。エントランスには，秘書たちのワークスペースに続いて教職員室があり，反対側の端に大教室がある。これらの棟は，本来はセミナーに使われていたが，後に改造されて，管理事務室を補足することになった。建物はフランク・ロイド・ライトが設計したキャンパス各棟の全体的な性格に従い，ある場合はコンクリート・ブロックにプラスター塗り，ある場合には特別にデザインしたブロックを使用している。

ルー図書館，1941年

ルー図書館は1941年に設計されたものだが，工事は第二次大戦の終わる1945年まで延期された。ライトはその平面構成をバーンズドール・リトル・ディッパー幼稚園（ハリウッド，カリフォルニア，1923年）から取り，そのスケールを拡張して巧みに適合させ，図書館のプランに変えている。バーンズドール幼稚園では野外の円形運動場であった所を主閲覧室に，校舎であった所を書架スペースに転換している。円形の閲覧室が書架の並ぶ角張ったエリアと接するところに，各側に一つずつ，計2つのエントランスがある。エントランスを入ると，中央に暖炉のあるホワイエがくる。暖炉の背後にある階段は，下の階に降りると同時にメザニン・レベルに上っている。暖炉の反対側に突き出したエリアには，閲覧

"Study Terraces", each one two steps up from the one below. High windows on the exterior wall as well as circular clerestories admit natural light. The stacks for the books are located on the main level, a lower level, and a mezzanine. Light wells in between the stacks receive natural light from skylights in the "Lantern Roof" above. The seven skylights, equipped with louvers, line up with the light wells below to assure the stacks of sufficient daylight. On the main floor, the librarian's office is located near the stacks and close to one of the entrances. On the opposite side, there is an open well to a Chapel on the lower level. The specially designed concrete blocks are typical of those at the college and the roof is sheathed in copper. The esplanade connects the library with the rest of the campus.

After Wright's death the college required more library space and another, larger, building was constructed. The Roux library, now known as the Thad Buckner Building, was refitted to accommodate more administrative offices and an assembly room.

Industrial Arts Building, 1942

The preliminary drawings for the Industrial Arts Building were produced in 1942, but due to the restriction of building materials during World War II and the constant struggle Dr. Spivey faced to raise funds—especially for a building of this size—construction was delayed until 1952. The original program was ambitious and called for space for a refectory, recreational pavilion, entertainment amphitheater, domestic sciences, drafting room, weaving pavilion, and lecture amphitheater in addition to the usual provisions for the industrial arts. The general plan is a large "U" with a central wing extending from the refectory on the right and ending in an amphitheater, open on both sides to garden courts. The other sections of the building provide for wood and metal workshops and an art department. The roof structure is similar to that of the drafting room at Taliesin West, although reinforced concrete is used here for the sloped beams instead of wood.

Administration Building, 1945

The Administration Building of 1945 is at the main entrance to the campus. One side of the building is adjacent to the public parking lot while the opposite side faces the large circular fountain pool that Wright intended to be a "Water Dome". A double esplanade passes between the building dividing it into two separate structures. The larger of the two contains the offices of the president, the dean, and other administrative personnel, and a directors' room. The building is U-shaped and wraps around a pool, while the president's office opens onto an outdoor walled terrace. The four offices at the corners of the building have no outside windows, but skylights on the mezza-

室の司書のステーションが置かれ，すべての読書机から見える。読書机は，3つの"スタディ・テラス"に配置されている。スタディ・テラスはそれぞれその下のテラスから2段ずつ高くなっている。円形の高窓と同時に，外壁にとられたハイ・ウインドウから自然光が差し込む。書架は，主階，下の階，メザニンにそれぞれ置かれている。書架の間の光井は，上の"越し屋根"に取り付けられたスカイライトから落ちてくる自然光を受け止める。ルーバーの付いた7つのスカイライトは，下の光井と列を成し，書架に十分な昼の光が確実に入るようになっている。主階では，司書のオフィスは書架の近く，エントランスの一つに近い位置にある。その反対側は，下の階の礼拝堂に向かって吹抜けている。特別にデザインされたコンクリート・ブロックは構内の他の建物に共通してよく使われているものであり，屋根は銅葺きである。遊歩道が図書館と他の建物を結んでいる。

　ライトの死後，大学側は図書館の拡張を望み，別にさらに大きな建物が建設された。ルー図書館は管理事務室と会議室1室に改装され，現在，サッド・バックナー・ビルディングと呼ばれている。

インダストリアル・アーツ棟，1942年

インダストリアル・アーツ棟のプレリミナリー・ドローイングは1942年には描き上げられていたが，第二次大戦中の建設材料の制約と，基金を集めるに際しスパイヴィー博士が常に直面した困難（この規模の建物になると特に難しかった）ゆえに，着工は1952年まで延期された。最初の計画案は野心的なもので，インダストリアル・アーツに必要な通常の設備に加え，食堂，レクリエーション・パビリオン，エンタテイメント・アンフィシアター，家政学室，製図室，織物館，レクチャー・アンフィシアターが要求されていた。全体プランは大きな"U形"で，右手の食堂から中央ウィングが伸び，両側面がガーデン・コートに開いたアンフィシアターで終わっている。建物の他の部分は，木工と金工のワークショップ，美術学部のためのスペースにあてられている。屋根構造は，タリアセン・ウェストの製図室と同様なものだが，ここでは，傾斜する梁には木材ではなく鉄筋コンクリートが使われている。

管理事務棟，1945年

1945年につくられた管理事務棟はキャンパスへの正面入り口にある。建物の片側は公共の駐車場に隣接し，反対側は，ライトが"ウォーター・ドーム"とすることを意図していた大きな円形の噴水池に面している。建物の間を通る2路線の遊歩道が，建物を2つの分離した棟へと分割している。大きな方の棟には総長，学部長，その他の管理職のオフィス，指導教官室がある。建物はU形で，プールの周りを包む一方，総長のオフィスは壁で囲まれた戸外テラスに開いている。建物のコーナーにある4つのオフィスは，外に面して窓はないが，メザニン・レベルの上のス

nine above provide natural lighting to these areas. The second floor is open above the president's office and the directors' room while also providing additional offices. The smaller building contains a spacious lobby on the ground floor, with an office for the registrar and a room for consultation. It is primarily a square structure, with an extension on the left for the bursar's office, rest rooms, and stairs to the second floor. A diagonal line on the second floor separates the area that is open to the first floor from further office space on the mezzanine that overlooks the lobby below. The double esplanade engages both buildings with openings in the roof over planting areas flush with the walkway. This lavishly landscaped concourse runs from the Administration Building to the library.

Science and Cosmography Building, 1953

In 1941, Wright was asked to make some tentative plans for a Science and Cosmography Building, but these were temporarily abandoned in favor of buildings considered more important at that time. In 1953, this project was revived as a two story L-shaped building with a basement. The elongated part of the plan is pierced on the ground floor with three openings to divide the building into four areas: the physics department, biology and botany departments, earth and life sciences department with lecture room, and finally the orrery. Rotating 90 degrees from the physics department is a one-story structure, likewise separated by an opening, devoted to citrus studies (as one would expect in a college in Florida.) Over the physics department on the second floor is the mathematics department, then the chemistry studies and lecture rooms. The earth science area is open to the second level. Above the orrery is the observatory. The portion of the building that contains the orrery and observatory differs the most from the other FSC designs: a hemisphere rises out of a square base. The basement beneath the orrery contains more laboratories and biochemical research. The exterior of the square section has an interesting treatment of plaster walls with geometric bands running along the edges on four sides. In this part of the building, the composition of square and circular forms, special concrete blocks, and large square perforated concrete blocks with glass reveals an artful combination of design elements.

Solomon R. Guggenheim Museum, New York, New York, 1943-59

The Solomon R. Guggenheim Museum with its dramatic spiral design is the most innovative and, arguably, the most remarkable of Frank Lloyd Wright's constructed public buildings. Wright first introduced the spiral ramp in the unbuilt Gordon Strong Automobile Objective of 1925, for Sugarloaf Mountain, Maryland. Here he em-

カイライトから自然光が入る。2階は，総長オフィスと指導教官室の上が吹抜けとなっている一方で補足のオフィスも配されている。小さな方の棟には，1階に広いロビー，教務係のオフィス，学生相談室がある。これは，ほぼ正方形の建物で，会計係のオフィス，洗面所，2階への階段が左手に延びている。2階では，対角方向に延びる線が，1階に吹抜けたエリアを，下のロビーを見下ろすメザニン・レベルの追加的なオフィス・スペースから分けている。2路線の遊歩道が，歩道と高さを揃えた植栽エリアの上に開口をとった屋根で2つの棟を結んでいる。この植物が豊かに植えられた遊歩道は管理事務棟から図書館まで続いている。

科学・天文学棟，1953年

1941年，ライトは，科学・天文学棟のために試験的にいくつかのプランをつくるように依頼されたが，これらのプランは，当時，より重要と考えられた建物のために一時的に放棄されていた。1953年，このプロジェクトは地下室の付いた，2階建てのL形の建物として復活した。プランの細長い部分は，建物を4つのエリアに分けるために3つの開口が1階に穿たれている。4つのエリアは物理学，生物植物学，地球生命科学（レクチャー・ルーム付き），オーラリ（惑星・衛星などの運動や位置を説明するための一種の太陽系儀）にそれぞれあてられている。物理学科から90度振った位置に，同様に開口で分離された1階建ての構造体があり，柑橘類の研究施設にあてられている（フロリダの大学に期待されるものとして）。物理学科の上，2階は数学科，化学研究室，レクチャー・ルームがある。地球科学エリアは2階まで吹抜けている。オーラリの上には天文台がある。建物の，オーラリと天文台を納めた部分は，構内の他のデザインから最もかけはなれていて，四角形の基部から球形が立ち上がっている。オーラリの下の地下室には，さらにいくつかの実験室と生化学研究室がある。四角形部分の外観は，プラスター壁の四周に，エッジに沿って幾何学模様の帯を回し，面白く扱っている。建物のこの部分は，四角形と円形，特別なデザインのコンクリート・ブロック，ガラスをはめた四角形の大きな有孔コンクリート・ブロックで構成され，デザイン・エレメントの巧みな組合せを見せている。

ソロモン・R・グッゲンハイム美術館，1943-59年

劇的な螺旋状のデザインを持つソロモン・R・グッゲンハイム美術館は，実際に建てられたフランク・ロイド・ライトの公共建築のなかで，最も独創的で，ほぼ間違いなく，最も優れたものである。ライトが螺旋状のスロープを初めて使ったのは，実現しなかったが，1925年にデザインされた，メリーランド州シュガーローフ・マウンテンのゴードン・ストロング・オートモビル・オブジェクティヴスであった。ここで彼は，屋外スロープを，自動車のために1つ，2つ目を歩行者のために採用し，両方とも上に行くに従って狭めている。ライトはグッゲンハイム美術館

ployed one exterior ramp for automobiles and a second for pedestrians, both of which narrowed as they rose. Wright reverses this in the Guggenheim Museum where the spiral widens as it rises and becomes the building itself, not simply the means of moving through it.

On June 1, 1943, Wright received a letter from the Baroness Hilla Rebay, the curator of Guggenheim's collection of modern art asking for his help in creating a home for these works of art. By June 29, a contract had been signed. Guggenheim wanted a building unlike any other and Wright was anxious to begin work on a design, but a suitable site proved elusive. As the year drew to a close, Wright wrote to Rebay, "... I am so full of ideas for our museum that I am likely to blow up or commit suicide unless I can let them out on paper."[10]

Originally, Guggenheim was looking for a site near Riverdale, which would have dictated a horizontal design. But when he began looking for sites in downtown Manhattan, Wright telegraphed Rebay "Believe that by changing our idea of a building from horizontal to perpendicular we can go where we please. Would like to present the implications of this change to Mr. Guggenheim for sanction."[11] Wright prepared six different watercolor perspectives.[12] One, rendered in turquoise and white, was a structure of six stories connected by ramps. On the sketch plan for this proposal, he has inscribed "Constant ramp" and indicated a small circular structure.[13] At this point, a continuous spiral ramp became central to the scheme and was employed in all but one of the other perspectives. He wrote, "A museum should be one extended expansive well proportioned floor space from bottom to top—a wheel chair going around and up and down, *throughout*."[14]

Plans and elevations indicate that Wright selected the rising spiral perspective rendered in white and showed it to Guggenheim who responded, "This is it. I knew you would do it."[15] The following month property was acquired on Fifth Avenue and Wright was pleased to note that the actual lot dimensions closely corresponded to his preliminary studies. The general scheme placed the ramp as a continuous exhibition space, open to a court below that was lit by a domed skylight overhead. Along the ramp was a continuous clerestory window on the exterior wall providing daylight for the paintings placed against the wall. Artificial light would be available as needed. The wall rose at a slight slant to the clerestory, much as the painter's easel might be angled. The scheme envisioned that visitors would take an elevator to the top of the ramp and slowly descend to the ground floor.

The design further provided two auditoriums and a luxurious two-level apartment for Rebay as well as offices and workrooms for the museum's staff in a separate wing. On the backside of the lot, a four-story structure followed the lot line and connected this wing to the main gallery. Another connection from the office wing extended over to the gallery on the Fifth Avenue side and provided a sheltered en-

ではこれを逆転して，上に行くほど広げ，単なる動線ではなく建物そのものとして構成した。

1943年6月1日，ライトはグッゲンハイムの近代美術コレクションのキュレーター，ヒーラ・リーベイ男爵夫人から，これらの芸術作品を収蔵する場所をつくることに手を貸してほしいという手紙を受け取った。6月29日，契約書が交わされた。グッゲンハイムは，他のどの建物とも違うものを望み，ライトはデザインに着手することを切望したが，適切な敷地の決定はなかなかに困難であった。その年が終わりに近づき，ライトはリーベイに手紙を書いた。「……美術館のためのアイディアがあふれかえって，紙の上にはきだすことが出来ないと，はちきれるか，自殺してしまいそうです。」[10]

最初，グッゲンハイムは，リヴァーデイルに近い敷地を探していた。その土地であれば水平に伸びるデザインが主体になっただろう。しかし彼がマンハッタンのダウンタウンに敷地を探し始めると，ライトはリーベイに電報を送った。「建物を水平に伸ばすアイディアを垂直なものに変えることで，満足されるものになることを信じて下さい。許可を頂くために，この変更が意味するものをグッゲンハイム氏にお見せしたいと思います。」[11] ライトは水彩で描かれた，6種類の透視図を用意した。[12] 碧青色と白で描いた1枚は，スロープでつなげられた6層の建物だった。この案のスケッチ・プランにライトは"連続するスロープ"と書き込み，小さな円形の構造物を示している。[13] この時点で，螺旋状に連続するスロープは，スキームの中心的な存在となり，他の透視図のうち1枚を除くすべてに採用された。彼は書いている。「美術館は下から上まで，よく均整をとって伸び広がる一つの空間としなければならない――車椅子が，上へ下へと，〈全体を〉動き回る。」[14]

平面と立面は，白で描かれた，螺旋が登って行く透視図をライトが選び，次のように答えたグッゲンハイムに見せたことをうかがわせる。「まさにこれだ。君がそうするだろうとわかっていたよ。」[15] 翌月，フィフス・アヴェニューの敷地が購入され，ライトは，現実になった敷地が，彼のプレリミナリー・スタディにぴったりと対応していることを喜んで記している。全体計画では，スロープは連続する展示空間を構成し，頭上を覆うドームの形をしたスカイライトからの光で明るい下のコートに開放されている。スロープに沿って外壁に高窓が連続して取られ，スロープの壁にかけられている絵画に昼光を届ける。必要な場合は人工照明も使える。壁は，画家のイーゼルと同じくらいの角度をとって，高窓に向かってわずかに傾斜している。このスキームは，来館者がエレベータでスロープの頂部まで上がり，ゆっくりと1階に向かって降りてくることを想定していた。

デザインにはさらに，2つのオーディトリアムと別なウィングに美術館スタッフのオフィスとワークルームと同時に，リーベイのための2層で構成された贅沢なアパートメントが加わっている。敷地の背面側には，4層の建物が境界線に沿って，このウィングをメイン・ギャラリーへ結んでいる。オフィス・ウィングからのもう一つの連結部がフィフス・ア

trance to the museum and the workspaces.

Construction was held up while Guggenheim waited for building costs to go down, which did not, and he died in November 1949 without seeing even ground broken for the museum. His nephew, Harry F. Guggenheim, became president of the foundation and the final piece of property on the corner of Fifth Avenue and 88th Street was acquired in 1951. This gave the museum full frontage from 88th Street to 89th Street and required an entirely new set of plans. Wright now switched the Rotunda from the north back to the south as it was originally placed in 1943-44 and broadened the Fifth Avenue elevation with an expanded horizontal band reaching across the entire building. Also added was a high-rise building to serve as a backdrop for the Rotunda and Monitor. This would have provided a bookstore, historical galleries, and eleven floors of studio apartments, the rental of which would add to the museum's revenues. In a 1955 revision, Wright added a space on the first level of the Rotunda to provide a visitor's waiting room and architectural archives. This new space interrupts the horizontal line and projects out towards Fifth Avenue, and then swings back in to engage the wall of the Grand Gallery on 88th Street. The Grand Gallery is a triangular two-story space lit from skylights above, and intended for the display of objects larger than the spaces on the ramp.

With the appointment of James Johnson Sweeney as the new director, additional changes were made. Finally, after what seemed like an interminable series of delays and postponements, ground was broken on August 16, 1956. By 1958, its form was clearly visible as the great spiral ramp rose to the fifth and final level.

The building as constructed is considerably simpler than the one proposed in 1945. This simplicity came as the result of the need to economize and to eliminate unnecessary elements as the program itself became less complex over the years. The result is a far better building than the one proposed in 1945, less complicated and possessing a great sense of repose.

The commission spanned sixteen years, and was the most contentious, difficult, time-consuming, expensive, and exhausting commission of Wright's career. As the building neared completion, doubts arose from artists, from the museum's director, and from the trustees about the appropriateness of the museum for the exhibition of paintings. They doubted the sloped surface of the wall as the proper way to exhibit paintings; they doubted the narrow clerestory skylights above as the way to light the paintings. For the color of the building itself, the director favored dead white, which Wright steadfastly opposed on the grounds that it would be too blinding and obliterate the paintings on the walls. Wright specified a soft eggshell color instead. Seeing the strength of this opposition, Wright appealed to Harry Guggenheim to intercede for him and not compromise the idea behind this new type of museum:

ヴェニュー側に面したギャラリーまで延び，美術館とワークスペースに覆われたエントランスを構成する。

　建設は，工費が下がるのをグッゲンハイムが待つあいだ中止され，そして工費が下がらないうちに，彼は1949年11月，美術館の起工式さえ見ることなく世を去った。彼の甥，ハリー・F・グッゲンハイムが財団の理事長となり，1951年，フィフス・アヴェニューと88番ストリートの角に面した部分が，最後に購入された。これによって，美術館は88番から89番ストリートまで通してフィフス・アヴェニューに面することになり，全面的に新しいプラン一式が必要となった。ライトはそこで，ロトンダを北側から，1943年から44年の段階ではもともとそこにあった南側に戻し，フィフス・アヴェニュー側の立面は，建物の端から端まで横断する幅広の帯で広げた。また，ロトンダとモニターの背景の役割を果たす高層の建物も加えられた。ここにはブックストア，歴史ギャラリー，11階分を占めるスタジオ・アパートメントが入る。アパートはレンタルされ美術館の収入源に加わるだろう。1955年の修正で，ライトはロトンダの1階に，来館者の待合室と建築アーカイヴとするスペースを加えた。この新しいスペースは，水平な線に割って入り，フィフス・アヴェニューに向かって突き出してから，後ろに向きを変えて88番ストリートに面したグランド・ギャラリーの壁と結合する。グランド・ギャラリーは三角形をした2層の空間で頭上のスカイライトから照らされ，スロープに沿った壁に飾るには大きすぎる作品の展示空間として用意された。新しい館長にジェイムズ・ジョンソン・スィーニーが任命されたことにより，さらに変更が加えられた。いつ果てるとも知れないように見えた遅延や延期の後，1956年8月16日，ようやく工事が始まった。1958年には，巨大なスロープが5階から最上階まで立ち上がるにつれて，その形が姿をあらわした。

　建設された建物は，1945年に提示された案よりも，かなりシンプルなものになっている。この簡潔性は，工費を節減する必要と，何年もの間にプログラムそのものが複雑さを減じるに従って，不必要な要素を取り去った結果，生まれたものであった。それは，余計な複雑さが消え，落ち着いた静けさを獲得して，1945年に提示された案よりはるかに優れたものとなっている。

　この仕事は16年の歳月に渡り，ライトのキャリアのなかで，最も，闘争的で，困難であり，時間を費やし，高価につき，消耗した仕事であった。建物が完成に近づくにつれ，アーティスト，美術館のディレクター，評議員から，絵画の展示に対する美術館の適切性について疑問が持ち出された。彼らは傾斜する壁が，絵画の展示に相応しいか，壁の上の細い高窓からの採光が絵画を照らす方法として適切であるかに疑問を抱いたのである。建物そのものの色彩についても，ディレクターはつや消しの白を好んだが，ライトは，それはあまりに際立ちすぎ，壁の絵画を抹殺してしまうだろうと，その場で断固として反対した。ライトはその代わりに，落ち着いた淡黄色を指定した。こうしたことに対する反対の強さを見て，ライトはハリー・グッゲンハイムに，この新しいタイプの美

"I am fully aware that but for you the Museum would never have been built. It is because of that that I plead with you now not to fail me in completing this work as it was originally conceived. I know that you are my friend but, believe me, Harry, I have lived many years longer and have practiced the art of architecture not to satisfy merely my own self, but to benefit my fellow men as well. I deeply wish that you stand by me at this most crucial moment of a perfect expression of a museum to present the paintings in the most perfect way possible.... I have not been too well, as you probably have heard and part of my distress is due to the struggle over the Museum. I wished we could have gotten together when Olgivanna and I were in New York. I could then have assured you of my appreciation and deep gratitude for what you have done to contribute the Museum to the world." [16]

Wright died six months before the completed building opened to the public in October 1959, when thousands flocked to see this most remarkable, if controversial, New York monument.

Tower for H. C. Price Company, Bartlesville, Oklahoma, 1952

"This skyscraper, planned to stand free in an open park and thus be more fit for human occupancy, is as nearly organic as steel in tension and concrete in compression can make it; here doing for the tall building what Lidgerwood made steel do for the long ship. The ship had its steel keel: this concrete building has its steel core. A composite shaft of concrete rises through the floors, each slab engaging the floors at nineteen levels. Each floor proceeds outward from the shaft as a cantilever slab extended from the shaft, similar to the branch of a tree from its trunk. The slab, thick at the shaft, grows thinner as it goes outward in an overlapping scale pattern in concrete until at the final outer leap to the screen wall it is no more than 3 inches thick. The outer enclosing screens of glass and copper are pendant from the edge of these cantilever slabs. The inner partitions rest upon the slabs." [17]

The construction of the Price Tower was the realization of an idea for an American skyscraper, which Frank Lloyd Wright had originally proposed in 1929. The plan of the Price Tower corresponds closely to the 1929 St. Mark's project except that only one of the four quadrants is allocated for duplex apartments, the other three being rental offices.

"In plan, a 1-2 triangle is here employed, because it allows flexibility of arrangement for human movement not afforded by the rectangle. The apparent irregular shapes of the various rooms would not appear irregular in reality; all would have great repose because all are not only properly in proportion to the human figure but to the figure made by the whole building." [18]

The lobby is two stories high with three elevators servicing the

術館の背後にあるアイディアを危うくすることのないよう仲裁に入ってくれることを嘆願した。

「あなたのお力がなければ，この美術館が建てられてこなかったであろうことを，私は十分に承知しております。それゆえに，今，私は，最初に考えた案のようにこの作品を失敗することなく完成できますようにとあなたに嘆願するのです。あなたが私の友人であることを私は存じておりますが，私を信頼して下さい，ハリー。私はあなたより遥かに多くの年月を生き，建築芸術を仕事にしてまいりました。それは単に私の満足のためではなく，我が同胞を益するためなのです。可能な中で最も完璧な方法で絵画を展示するために，美術館を完璧な形で表現するこの最も重大な瞬間において，私の側に立って下さることを心の底から切望しております……。たぶんお聞き及びのように，私はあまり元気といえる状態ではありません。私の心痛の一部は，美術館を巡る争いによるものです。オルジヴァンナと私がニューヨークに滞在する際，お目にかかることができたらと願っております。そのときに，あなたが世界にこの美術館を捧げるためになされたことに対する，私の感謝と深い尊敬を確信していただけることと存じます。」[16]

完成した建物は1959年10月に公開されたが，その6ヶ月前，ライトは世を去った。異論の余地があるにせよ，最も素晴らしいニューヨークのモニュメントとなったこの建物を見ようと，公開時には数千の人が押し寄せた。

プライス・タワー，1952年

「開放的な公園のなかに一人立つものとして計画され，それゆえに，人がその内を占めるのにより相応しいものとなるだろうこのスカイスクレイパーは，スティールを緊張材に，コンクリートを圧縮材に用いて，出来る限り有機的につくられている。ここでは，リッジャーウッドが長い船をつくるためにスティールで行ったことを高層の建物で行うのである。その船は竜骨を備えていた。このコンクリートの建物はスティール・コアを備える。コンポジット式のコンクリート・シャフトが各階の床を貫いて立ち上がり，各スラブは19層の床を固定する。各床はシャフトから延び出るキャンティレバー・スラブとして，幹から差し出る枝のように，シャフトから外に差し出される。シャフトのところからコンクリートの折り重なるパターンを描いて外に行くに従って薄くなり，スクリーン・ウォールへと最後の一飛びの部分では3インチ以上の厚さはない。ガラスと銅で構成された外側を覆うスクリーンは，これらのキャンティレバー・スラブの端から吊られている。内部の間仕切りはスラブの上に乗っている。」[17]

プライス・タワーの建設は，もともとは，フランク・ロイド・ライトが1929年に提案したアメリカのスカイスクレイパーのためのアイディアを現実のものとするものであった。プライス・タワーのプランは，1929年のサント・マークス・プロジェクトによく似ているが，円を分割した

rental offices. A private lobby serves the apartment residents. The offices of the Price Company, which built oil pipelines all over North and South America, occupied the top floors, the sixteenth floor being a buffet and kitchen with an outdoor dining terrace. The nineteenth floor was the private office for Mr. Price, located in three quadrants to provide the reception area, a lavatory, and the office. The fourth quadrant is a roof garden adjacent to the office.

The eight duplex apartments are similar in plan to the St. Mark's scheme. On the main level, there is the entry, lavatory, kitchen, and living room. This section of the plan rotates 45 degrees from the rest of the plan to provide a two-story space adjacent to the two window walls of the living room. Two bedrooms and a bathroom are located on the mezzanine above. Shutters in both bedrooms close off the rooms from the living room below when desired. The master bedroom enjoys a small outdoor planted balcony. The other three quadrants for the offices are planned with provisions for a reception area, lavatory, and three private offices or examination rooms. In some instances the offices are varied in the number of rooms, with partitions of glass set into metal frames, or plywood where privacy is required. All offices and apartments have access to an outside concrete stairway, which also serves as a fire escape. The windows for the offices have horizontal copper fins while the apartments have vertical fins. The tower is so positioned on the site that these vertical louvers protect the glass from direct sun during the summer months. The structure is all reinforced concrete with copper louvers and copper panels on alternating exterior wall surfaces, presenting a pleasant blend of verdigris in the copper and off-white in the concrete. The aluminum furniture throughout the structure is also of the architect's design.

On the ground floor, the tower connects to a two-story structure housing both a retail store and the Public Service Company of Oklahoma. On the second floor, adjacent to the mezzanine of the tower there is additional retail space and offices for the company below. Covered parking is provided on both the north and south sides of the building. Rooftop planting over the parking garages at the base of the tower and the landscaped gardens give the building a park-like setting.

When asked about the building Harold Price responded:

"We wanted a building of our own. We agreed to build a three-story building with another company taking the entire first floor. My two sons, Harold and Joe, recently graduated from the University of Oklahoma, suggested we get Frank Lloyd Wright to design the building. They argued that it would cost no more to get a building with a beautiful, outstanding design than it would to get the usual box-type design. We all appreciated the benefits we had received from living in our community, a community that had been very helpful to a young man with no material assets. Therefore, we decided to build a structure, which would be a credit to our city for years to come.

4象限の内一つだけが，デュプレックス・アパートメントにあてられ，他の3つがレンタル・オフィスであることだけが違う。

「プランには，三角形をここでは採用しているが，人の動きに対し，四角形では得られない，柔軟な配置を許してくれるからである。様々な部屋の明らかに不規則な形は，実際の場においては不規則には感じられないだろう。すべてが素晴らしい落ち着きを見せるだろう。なぜなら，すべてが，人の体にばかりでなく，建物全体によってつくられた形にふさわしい均整を備えているからである。」[18]

ロビーは2階まで吹抜けで，エレベータ3基がレンタル・オフィスへ通じている。アパートメントの住民には専用ロビーが用意されている。南北両アメリカ全域で石油パイプラインに関わっていたプライス社のオフィスは，最上階を占め，16階には戸外にダイニング・テラスの付いた，ビュッフェとキッチンがあった。19階は，四分円の3つにレセプション，洗面所，オフィスが置かれたプライス氏専用のオフィスだった。4つめはオフィスに隣接する屋上庭園である。

8つのデュプレックス・アパートメントは，そのプランにおいて，セント・マークス計画のものに似ている。メイン・レベルには玄関，洗面所，キッチン，リビングルームがある。プランのなかでこの部分は，残る平面から45度振られ，リビングルームの2枚のウインドウ・ウォールの隣に2層吹き抜けたスペースをつくりだしている。寝室2つと浴室がメザニン・レベルにある。両方の寝室にはシャッターが付き，必要なときは，下のリビングルームから部屋を閉めきることができる。主寝室は，植え込みのある小さなバルコニーを楽しめる。オフィス用につくられている他の3つの四分円には，レセプション・エリア，洗面所，3つの個室オフィスあるいは調査室にあてられる設備が用意されている。いくつかの場合，オフィスは，金属枠にガラス，またはプライバシーが必要な場合は合板をはめた間仕切りによって部屋数を変えられる。すべてのオフィスとアパートメントからコンクリートの外階段へ出られ，ここは火災の場合の避難階段としても使われる。銅製の薄板が，オフィスの窓には水平方向に，アパートメントの窓には垂直方向に取り付けられている。タワーは，これらの垂直のルーバーが夏のあいだ直射日光をガラス面から守るような方向に，敷地に配置されている。鉄筋コンクリート造に銅のルーバーとパネルが交互に表面を構成し，銅の緑青とコンクリートのオフホワイトが混合して感じの良い色調を見せている。建物全体に使われているアルミ家具もライトのデザインである。

1階でタワーは2階建ての建物と連結し，ここには，小売店とオクラホマの公共サービス会社が入っている。タワーのメザニン・レベルに隣接するその2階は，もう一つ小売店舗と下の会社のオフィスがある。建物の北と南の両側に，屋根付きのパーキングがある。タワーの基部にあるパーキング・ガレージの屋上の植え込みと造園された庭が建物に公園のような背景を与えている。

この建物について聞かれたとき，ハロルド・プライスはこう答えた。

「私たちは自社ビルを建てようと思っていました。1階全部を別な会

However, I did not believe that Mr. Wright would be interested in such a small building. My sons telephoned him and made an appointment. We went to Taliesin. I told him I wanted a three-story building with about 25,000 square feet of floor space. He said immediately that three floors was most inefficient and suggested ten floors of 2,500 square feet each. We finally compromised on nineteen floors, and included apartments with the offices." [19]

Marin County Government Center, San Rafael, California, 1957

Following a visit to the site for the proposed Marin County Government Center, Frank Lloyd Wright conceived a solution that would link together four isolated hill crowns by way of one horizontal building-line, spanning the valleys in between with graceful arches. These arches fulfill their purpose as foundation supports and covered entrance drives. Rising from these arches the various levels of the building appears to float from hill to hill. From within there is an unimpeded view of the surrounding park, lagoon, and countryside; from without the building forms a tranquil line in harmony with the environment. Parking areas, arranged to conform to the contours of the hill slopes, are directly adjacent and accessible to the main building.

Known as the Marin County Civic Center, it is actually a government center and is labeled as such on Wright's preliminary drawings. The building is in two main sections, the smaller one for the county Administration Building, and the larger one for the Hall of Justice. The Center is an elongated plan that changes direction at the central hill in order to bridge over to the next hills. A central mall, with light wells and covered by a plastic skylight extending the full length of the building, affords natural light into what ordinarily would be dark interior corridors. In this manner, each office has at least one source of natural light. While the arches that span the valleys between the hills support the structure, the arches of the upper levels, whose light steel frames are embedded in metal lath and cement plaster, are hung from the edges of the floor slabs on the outdoor balconies to form sunshades for the windows. These exterior balconies provide further ease of access between the different departments of the county government. In both the Administration Building and the Hall of Justice there is an entrance level, with three levels above. The entrance level provides access to the floors above by means of escalators, elevators, and stairs. Also located on the entrance level are provisions for maintenance, mechanical, and storage. Where the Hall of Justice meets the Administration Building there is a circular form. The uppermost level contains a library on the first level there is a cafeteria which opens onto a triangular prow in which there is a paved terrace for outdoor dining, a garden, and a pool. A watercourse from the pool spills through the wall to a half-circular catch pool below. At one

社が使う，3階建ての建物を建てることに考えがまとまりました。オクラホマ大学を卒業したばかりの二人の息子，ハロルドとジョーが，建物の設計をフランク・ロイド・ライトに頼もうと提案したのです。二人は普通のハコ型の建物を手に入れるにも，美しく，優れたデザインを手に入れるにも同じようにお金がかかるだろう，と主張しました。私たちはこの土地での生活から受けてきた恩恵に感謝していました。地元の人たちは，物質的な財産を持たぬ若者をよく助けてきてくれました。ですから，私たちは，いつまでもこの街を訪れるに価させるような建物をつくることに決めたのです。しかし，ライトさんが，こんな小さな建物に関心を持ってくれるだろうとは思っていませんでした。息子が電話し，面会の約束をとりました。タリアセンに行き，25,000平方フィートほどの床面積を持つ，3階建ての建物にしたいと話すと，ライトさんはすぐに3階建てというのは最も効率が悪いのですと言い，各階が2,500平方フィートの10階建てにしたらと提案してきたのです。結局，19階建てにして，オフィス付きのアパートメントを含めることに落ち着きました。」[19]

マリン郡政庁舎，1957年

提示されたマリン郡庁舎の敷地を訪れたあと，フランク・ロイド・ライトは，離れた4つの丘の頂を，優美なアーチを描いてその間に横たわる谷間を架け渡して行く，水平に延びる建物で一つに結ぶ案を考えた。アーチは支持基盤となりエントランス・ドライヴの屋根となる。アーチから，建物の様々なレベルが丘から丘へと浮かぶように立ち上がる。内部からは，周囲の公園，沼地，田園風景が一望に見晴らせる。外側から見ると，建物は周囲の環境と調和しながら静かな一本の線を描いている。丘の斜面の等高線に合わせて配置されたパーキング・エリアは，中心となる建物に隣接し，車を降りてすぐに建物へ入れる。

　マリン郡市庁舎として知られるこの建物は，実際は政庁舎で，ライトのプレリミナリー・ドローイングにはそのように記されている。建物には大きく2つの部分があり，小さい方が郡の庁舎，大きな方が裁判所である。建物は長く引き伸ばされたプランで，次の丘に架け渡すために，中心にある丘のところで方向転換している。光井がつき，建物全長を伸びるプラスティックのスカイライトで覆われた中央モールは，通常は薄暗い内部廊下に自然光を降り注ぐ。これによって，各オフィスは，最低でも一箇所からは外光が差し込むことになる。谷間を架け渡すアーチが建物を支持する一方で，軽量のスティール・フレームがメタルラスとセメント・プラスターに埋め込まれた上階のアーチは，屋外バルコニーの上に床スラブの端から吊られて窓の日除けを構成する。屋外バルコニーは郡政府の様々な部局の間の行き来をさらに容易にしてくれる。事務棟と裁判所棟のどちらにもエントランス・レベルがあり，その上に3つの階が重なっている。上階へはエスカレータ，エレベータ，階段が通じている。エントランス・レベルにはメンテナンス，機械室，収納の各設備も配置されている。裁判所と事務部門が接する部分は円形である。最上

edge of this garden terrace there rises a tall spire of reinforced concrete, steel, and gold anodized aluminum, which is the stack for the boiler room on the level below.

In the Administration Building, office partitions, assembled in channels fastened on ceiling and floor, can be relocated to meet changing spatial requirements. Doors in the glazed exterior walls can also be repositioned to correspond with office relocations. Electrical, telephone, and heating-ventilating outlets are spaced on a unit system of 2'8" x 5'4" to provide an extremely high flexibility of office arrangement. The roof is a thin concrete shell with blue sprayed-plastic membrane and a gold anodized aluminum facia.

An important consideration in planning the building are the long roof edges, both inside at the mall and on the outside. The length is so extreme that it would be practically impossible to guarantee a perfectly straight-line edge. To prevent this from happening, circular globes are attached, in the manner of dentils, to the roof edges on both sides resulting in geometric pattern that cleverly disguise any deviation from a perfectly straight line. Another important feature is the gold-anodized aluminum balcony railing on the third level which casts ever-changing shadow patterns on the balcony. Patterns of this nature, caused by architectural features, Wright often called "eye music."

Wright did not live to see the completion of the working drawings, but Taliesin Associated Architects working in collaboration with former apprentice Aaron G. Green, a San Francisco architect, carried the project through. A fair pavilion, amphitheater, and children's park also designed for the center were not built, although a post office, Wright's only design for the Federal Government, was. The plan is two graceful arcs forming an expanded elliptical space. A third arc gracefully becomes the roof over the front entrance. In the center of the glass exterior wall of the lobby is a globe, with the flagpole rising out of it and penetrating through the overhanging roof. Outside, reaching out from the building on both sides are low circular planting boxes.

When Frank Lloyd Wright presented his design for the Marin County Civic Center, he addressed the citizens of Marin:

"Beauty is the moving cause of nearly every issue worth the civilization we have, and civilization without a culture is like a man without a soul. Culture consists of the expression by the human spirit of the love of beauty .... In Marin County you have one of the most beautiful landscapes I have seen, and I am proud to make the buildings of this County characteristic of the beauty of the County."[20]

Conclusion

The public buildings described above serve divergent needs. Each has a unique architectural form, but all are examples of "organic architecture."

階には図書室がある。1階にはカフェテリアがあり，戸外食堂・庭園・プールが配された石敷きのテラスが広がる三角形の舳先に面している。プールから続く水路は，壁伝いに水を下のキャッチ・プールへこぼし落とす。

　事務棟では，天井と床の溝にはめて固定するオフィスの間仕切りは，空間構成を変更する必要に応じて位置を変えられる。ガラス張りの外壁にとられたドアも，オフィスの位置変更に合わせて移動できる。電気，電話，暖房や通気のためのアウトレットは，2フィート8インチ×5フィート4インチ間隔のユニット・システムにのって配置されているので，オフィスは非常に柔軟に編成できる。屋根は薄いコンクリート・シェルに青い色を吹き付けたプラスチックの薄膜で覆われ，金色に酸化被膜処理したアルミの鼻隠しが付いている。

　建物を計画するうえで重要な考慮の対象になったのは，モールのある内側，外側共に，長い屋根のエッジであった。非常な長さがあったので，エッジを完璧にまっすぐな線で構成することを保証するのは現実的には不可能であるように思われた。そうした場合を想定して，軒蛇腹のように円形の球体を屋根の両側のエッジに付けたので，たとえ完璧な直線から外れていても，巧みに偽装してしまう幾何学パターンが生まれた。また別の重要な特徴は3階のバルコニーの金色に酸化被膜処理したアルミの手摺で，それはバルコニーに絶え間なく変化する影を落としている。建築的特徴から生まれたこうしたパターンを，ライトはよく"アイ・ミュージック"と呼んでいた。

　ライトは実施図面の完成を見ることなく世を去ったが，タリアセン・アソシエイテッド・アーキテクツが，以前の見習い生でサンフランシスコの建築家アアロン・G・グリーンと協力してプロジェクトを最後までやり遂げた。展示パビリオン，円形劇場，子供公園もデザインされていたが実際には建てられなかった。だが，ライトの唯一の連邦政府からの依頼による作品である郵便局は建設された。そのプランは優美な2本の弧が膨らんだ楕円形のスペースを形づくっている。3番目の優美な弧が正面エントランスを覆う屋根になる。ロビーのガラス張りの外壁の中央に地球儀があり，そこから旗竿が上に伸びて屋根を貫いている。外部には，建物の両側から，低い円形のプランターが伸び出している。

　フランク・ロイド・ライトがマリン郡市庁舎のデザインを発表したとき，彼はマリン郡の市民にこう述べた。

　「美は，私たちの文明のほとんどすべての問題を価値あるものとしている感動をもたらす源泉なのです。そして文化のない文明は，魂のない人間のようなものです。文化は，美を愛する人間の精神によって表現されたもので構成されています……マリン郡には，私の知る最も美しい風景の一つがあり，その美しさに特徴づけられたこの郡に建物を建てることを誇りに思います。」[20]

結び

ここに紹介してきた公共建築は様々なニーズに応えたものである。それ

Wright defined "organic architecture" many different ways over the course of his life. Perhaps the clearest definition he gave described it as appropriate to Time, to Place, and to Man. "I have always wanted to build for the man of today, build his tomorrow in, organic to his own Time and his Place as modern Man."[21] By "Time" he means a building that belongs to the time in which it is built, not an aggregation of historic styles and applied tastes. By "Place" he means the natural environment and the building's harmonious relationship to it. And by "Man" he means the building must serve mankind, sheltering, embracing, inspiring, and liberating.

The vast majority of his work was residential and he applied the principles of organic architecture to every home he designed. He placed just as much emphasis on these qualities in his public work. Where the conditions of the building site were not conducive to integration with the surrounding landscape, such as the Johnson Wax buildings, he turned the buildings inward and endowed the interior with a sense of beauty and repose lit from above. When he had an especially beautiful site, such as Marin County or Lakeland, Florida, he placed the buildings lovingly within their natural settings, making them inspirational to the occupants. The Price Tower, "the tree that escaped the crowded forest", stands within its own park on a full city block more residential than urban in feeling.

These public buildings represent only a fraction of the public buildings Wright designed but never saw realized. Three others were tragically demolished: the Midway Gardens (Chicago, 1913-1929), the Larkin Building (Buffalo, 1903-1950), and the Imperial Hotel (Tokyo, 1916-1968). They live on in photographs and the collective architectural memory as important landmarks of twentieth century architecture.

Bruce Brooks Pfeiffer

Taliesin West April 16, 2003

それは固有の建築形態を備えているが，そのすべてが"有機的建築"の例証となっている。

　ライトは，生涯にわたって，"有機的建築"を様々に定義してきた。最も明快な定義は，おそらく，時と，場所と，人に，相応しいものと，説明したものだろう。「私はいつも，今に生きる人のために，その明日のために，近代人としての，その人自身の時と場所のために建てたいと望んできた」[21]「時」という言葉は，歴史様式の集合や実際的なテイストではなく，その時代に所属する建物を意味し，「場所」という言葉は自然環境と建物の調和のとれた関係を意味し，「人」という言葉は，建物は人類に仕えなければならないこと，人を守り，抱きとめ，元気づけ，自由にしなければならないことを意味したのである。

　ライトの作品の大半は住宅であり，彼は有機的建築という原則を，彼がデザインしたすべての住宅に適用した。彼はそれらの特質を公共建築においても同じように強調した。周囲の風景を取り込むには適さない敷地の場合には，ジョンソン・ワックス社のように，建物を内に向けて構成し，上方から光が差し込む，安らぎのある落ち着きと美しさを内部空間に与えた。マリン郡やフロリダのレイクランドでは，その自然背景のなかに丁寧に建物を配置し，そこを訪れる人たちに生き生きとした感動を与えるものとしてつくりあげた。プライス・タワーは，"混み合う森を逃れてきた樹木"のように，都市的というより住宅のような趣で一街区を占め，自らが公園のように緑をまとって立っている。

　この巻にとりあげた公共建築は，ライトがデザインしたが実現することのなかった公共建築を含めると，その一部を代表するにすぎない。実際に建てられたもののなかで，他の3つの建物は，非常に悲しいことだが取り壊された。ミッドウェイ・ガーデンズ（シカゴ，1913-1929），ラーキン・ビルディング（バッファロー，1903-1950），帝国ホテル（東京，1916-1968）。これらは，写真のなかに，そして20世紀建築の重要なランドマークとして集積された建築の記憶のなかに生きている。

ブルース・ブルックス・ファイファー
　　　　　　　　　　　タリアセン・ウェストにて　2003年4月16日

1: *Frank Lloyd Wright Collected Writings Volume 3*, B. B. Pfeiffer ed. (New York: Rizzoli, 1993), p.310

2: Jonathan Lipman, *Frank Lloyd Wright and the Johnson Wax Buildings* (New York: Rizzoli, 1986), p.3

3: Frank Lloyd Wright, *An Autobiography* (New York: Barnes & Noble Books, 1998), p.472

4: ibid., pp.468-469

5: ibid., p.473

6: Johnson to Wright, October 4, 1943. Reprinted in *Letters to Clients—Frank Lloyd Wright*, B. B. Pfeiffer, ed. (Fresno, California: The Press at California State University, 1986), p.232

7: Wright to Johnson, December 14, 1943. ibid., p.234

8: Wright to Johnson, December 6, 1943. ibid., p.234

9: Frank Lloyd Wright, *Architectural Forum*, September 1952

10: Wright to Rebay, December 18, 1943. *Frank Lloyd Wright the Guggenheim Correspondence*, B. B. Pfeiffer, ed. (Fresno, California: The Press at California State University, 1986), p.22

11: ibid., p.25

12: drawings #4305.008, 745, 746, 747, 748, 749

13: drawing # 4305.091

14: *Guggenheim Correspondence*, p.40

15: Frank Lloyd Wright Archives, #2401.364, p.1

16: Wright to Guggenheim, November 28, 1958, in *The Guggenheim Correspondence*, p.275

17: Frank Lloyd Wright, *The Story of the Tower* (New York: Horizon Press, 1956), pp.15-16

18: ibid., p.17

19: ibid., pp.8–9

20: Frank Lloyd Wright Archives, #1001.084

21: *Collected Writings Volume 5*, p.190

註：
1：Frank Lloyd Wright, "Collected Writings", Volume 3, B. B. Pfeiffer ed.(New York: Rizzoli, 1993), p.310
2：Jonathan Lipman, "Frank Lloyd Wright and the Johnson Wax Buildings"(New York: Rizzoli, 1986), p.3
3：Frank Lloyd Wright, "An Autobiography"(New York: Barnes & Noble Books, 1998), p.472
4：前掲書, pp.468-469
5：前掲書, p.473
6：ジョンソンからライトへ。1943年10月4日。"Letters to Clients—Frank Lloyd Wright", B. B. Pfeiffer ed.(Fresno, California: The Press at California State University, 1986), p.232
7：ライトからジョンソンへ。1943年12月14日。前掲書, p.234
8：ライトからジョンソンへ。1943年12月6日。前掲書, p.234
9：Frank Lloyd Wright, "Architectural Forum", 1952年9月号
10：ライトからリーベイへ。1943年12月18日。"Frank Lloyd Wright The Guggenheim Correspondence", B. B. Pfeiffer ed.(Fresno, California: The Press at California State University, 1986), p.22
11：前掲書, p.25
12：図面 #4305. 008, 745, 746, 747, 748, 749
13：図面 #4305. 091
14："Guggenheim Correspondence", p.40
15：FLLW FDN Archive #2401.364, p.1
16：ライトからグッゲンハイムへ。1958年11月28日。"Guggenheim Correspondence", p.275
17：Frank Lloyd Wright, "The Story of the Tower"(New York: Horizon Press, 1956), pp.15-16
18：前掲書, p.17
19：前掲書, pp.8-9
20：FLLW FDN Archives #1001.084
21："Collected Writings", Volume 5, p.190

Administration Building for S. C. Johnson & Son Company
Racine, Wisconsin, 1936

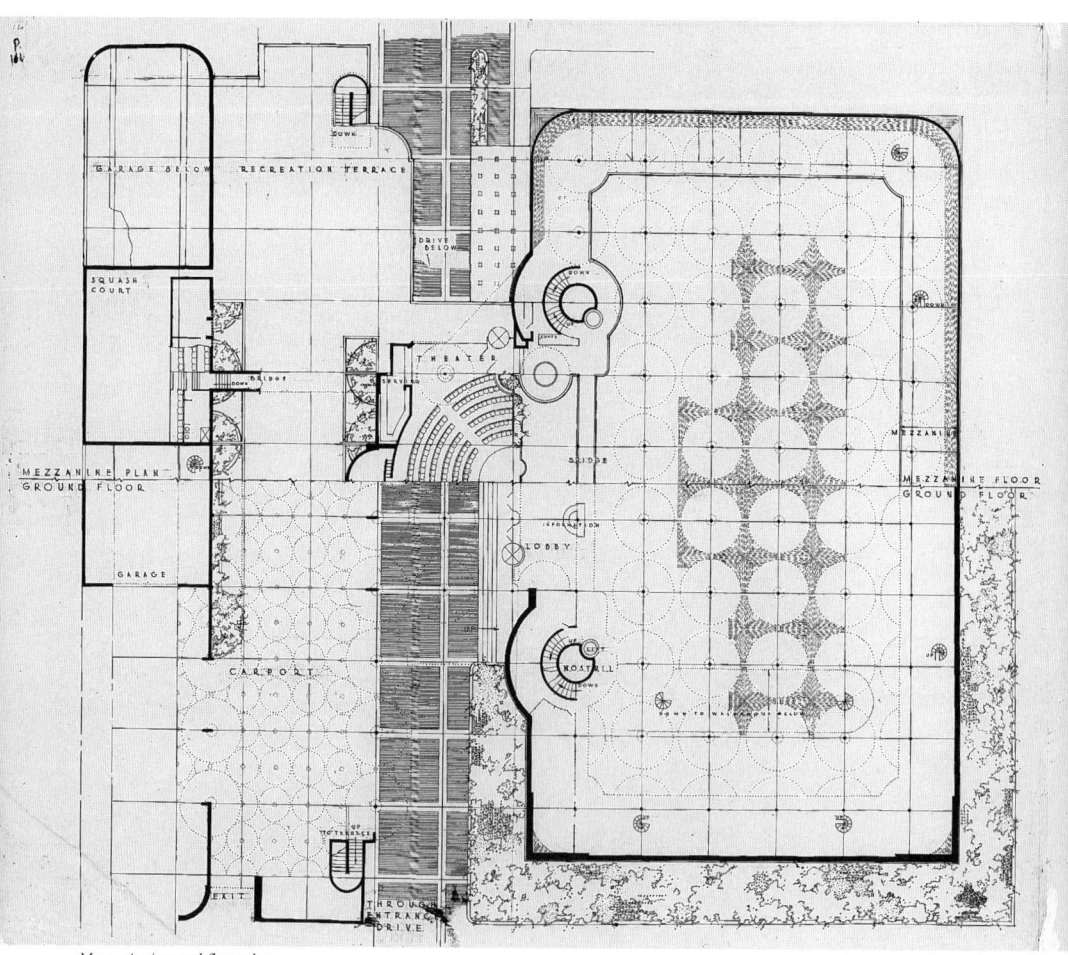

Mezzanine/ground floor plan

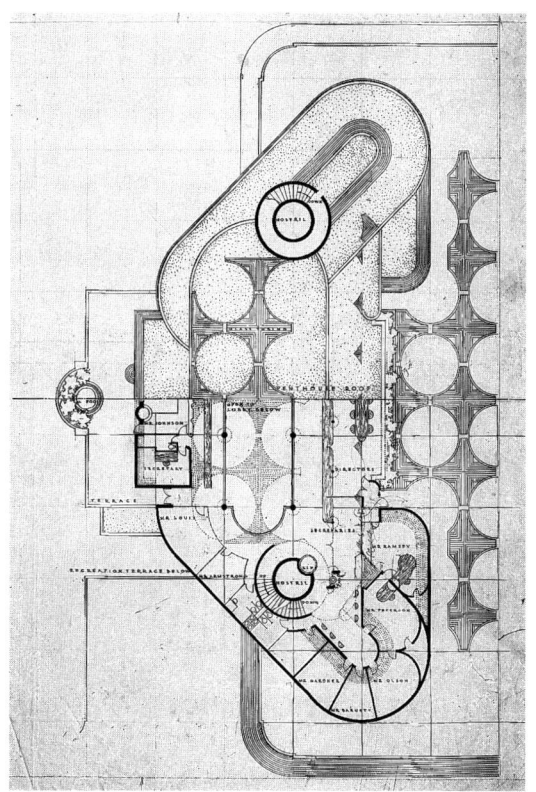

Penthouse plan

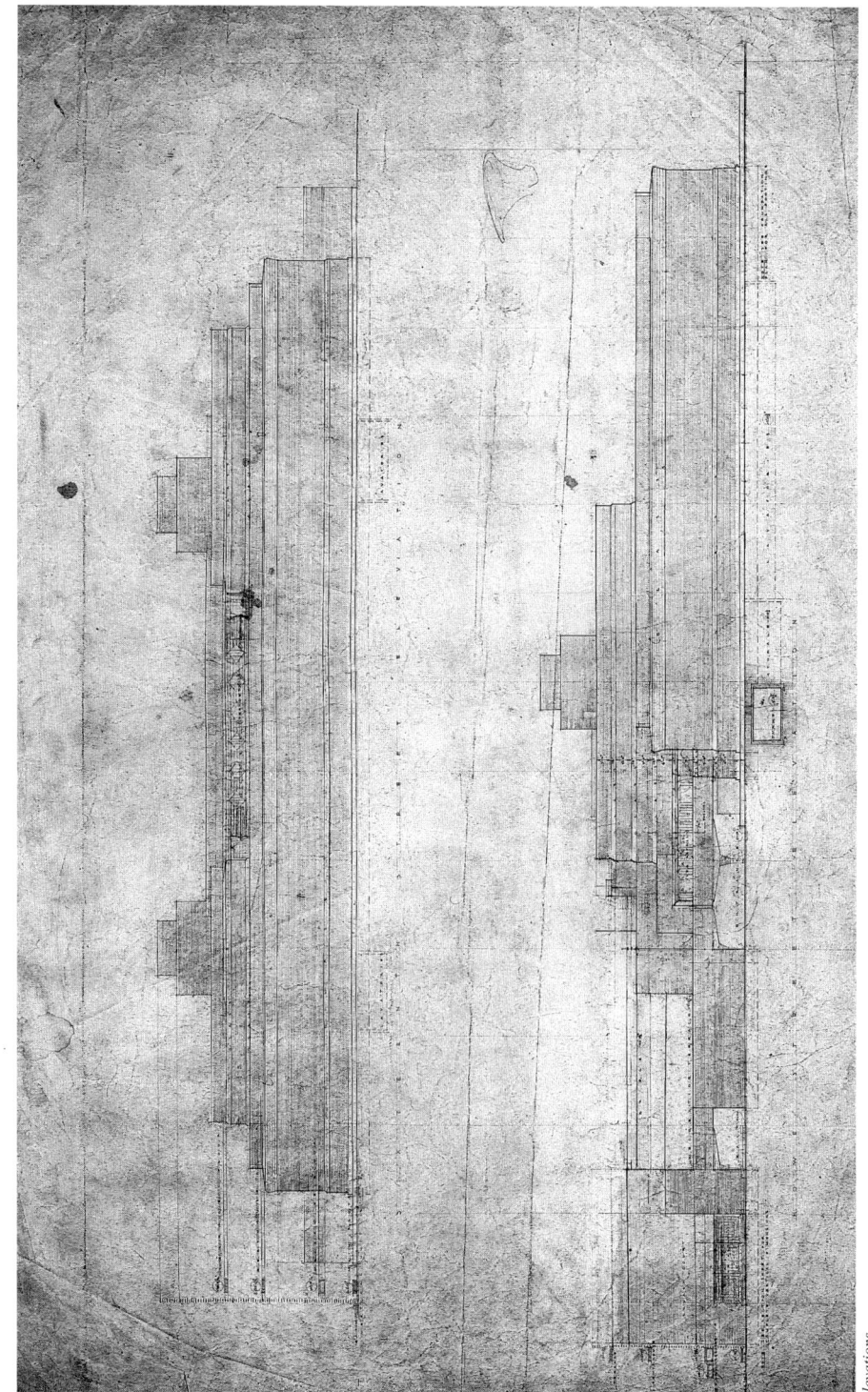

Elevations

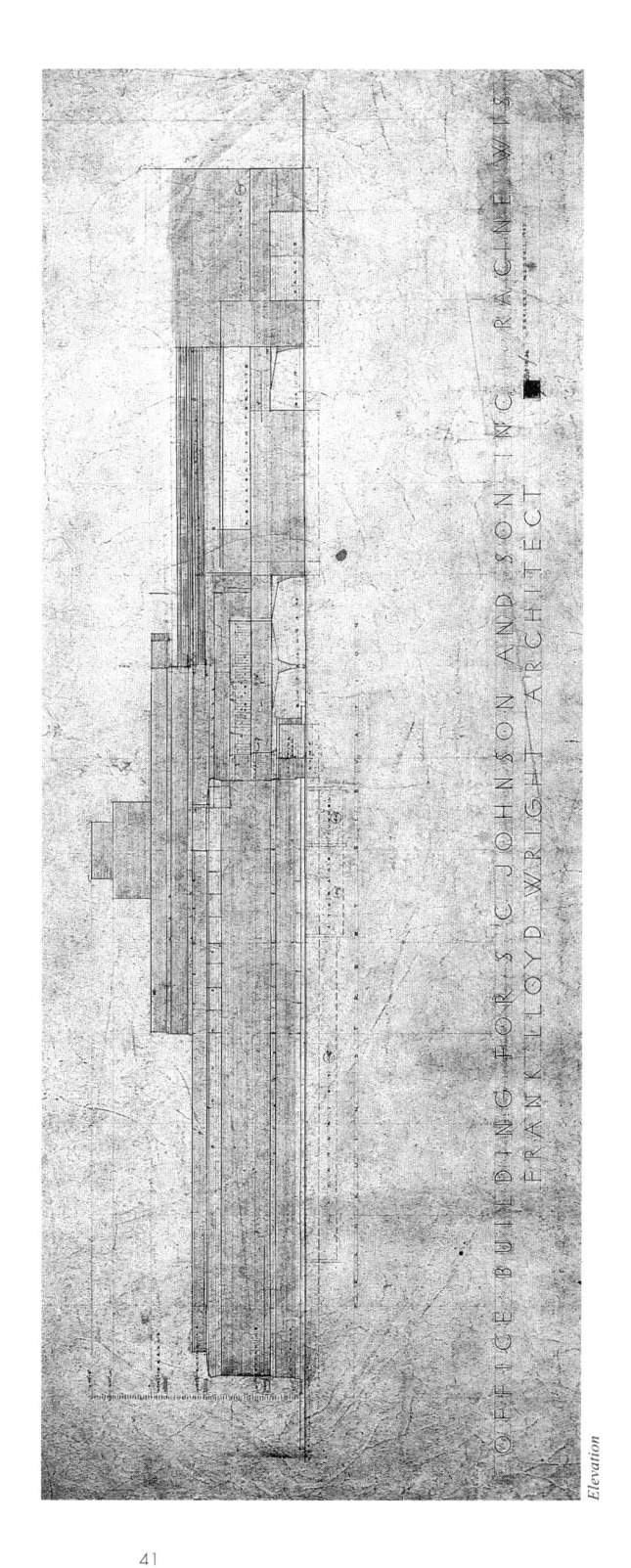

Elevation

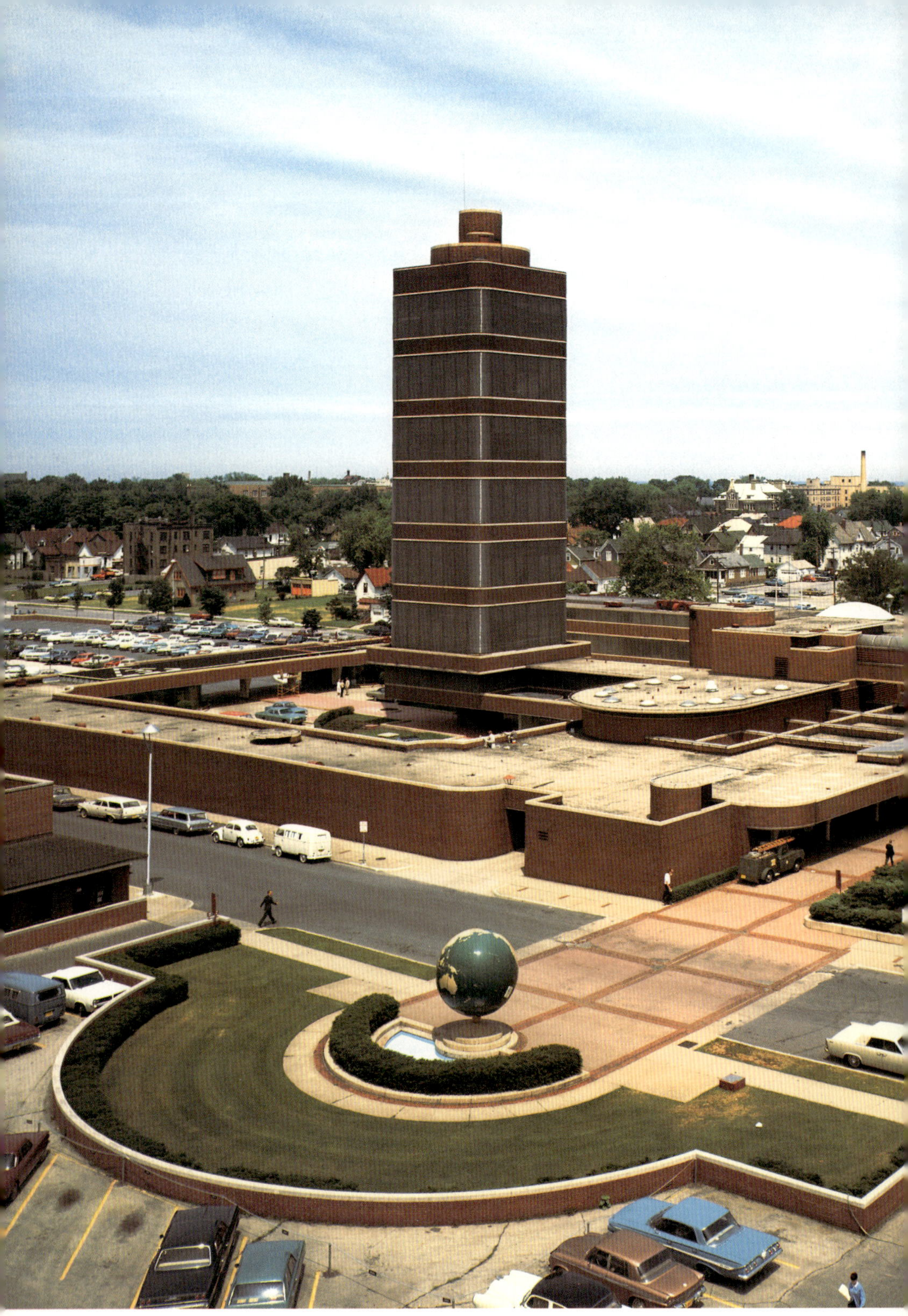

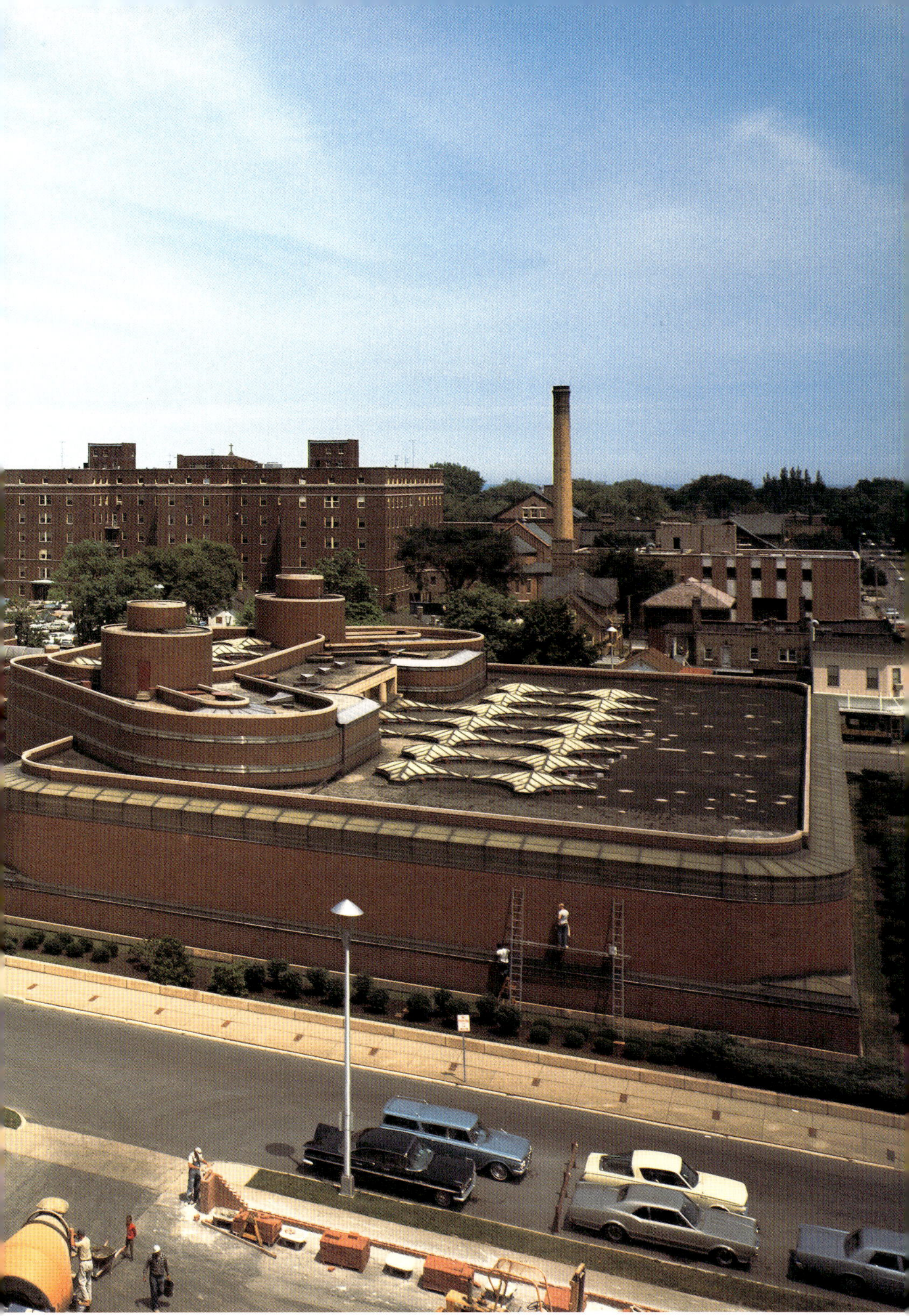

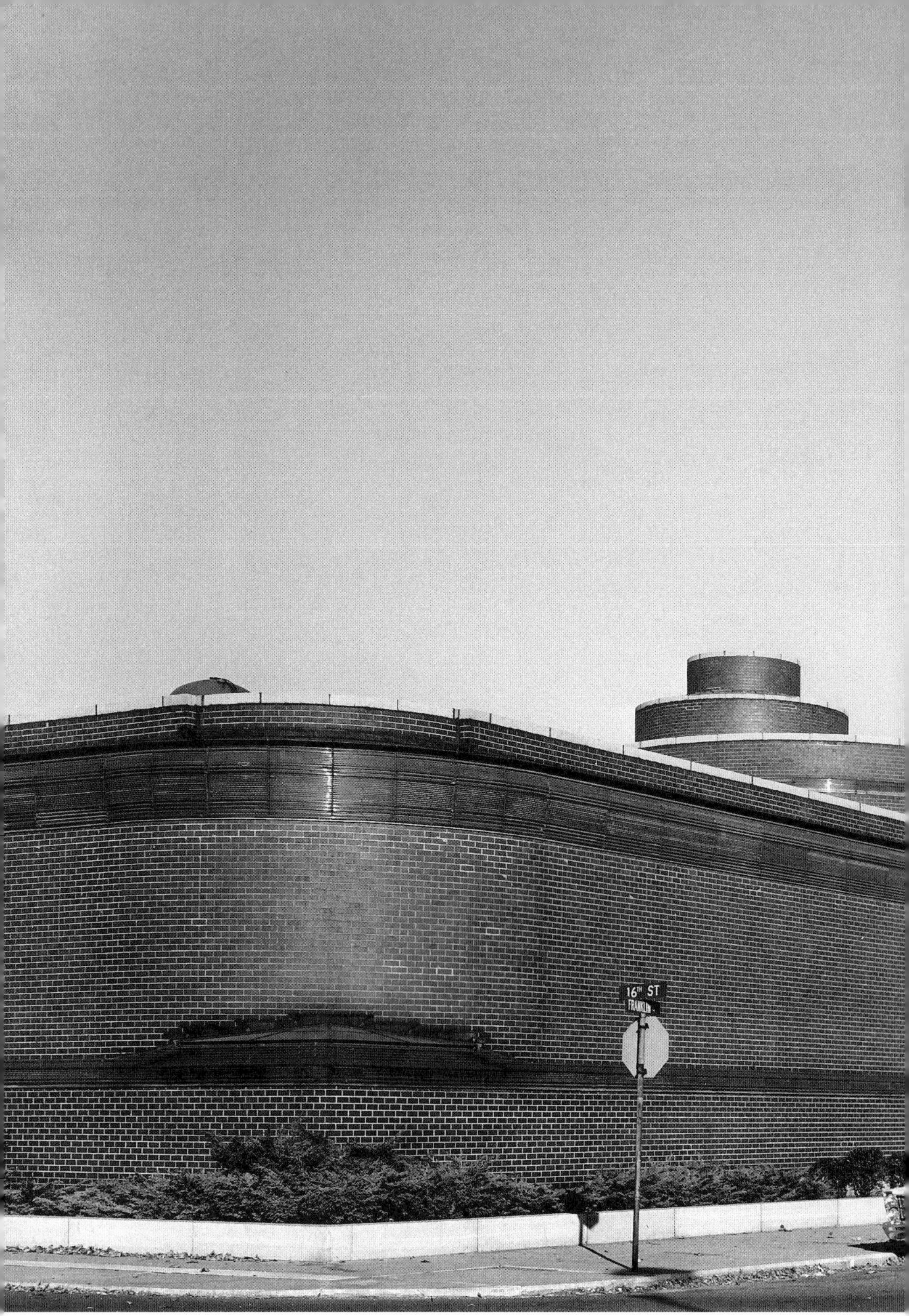
16TH ST

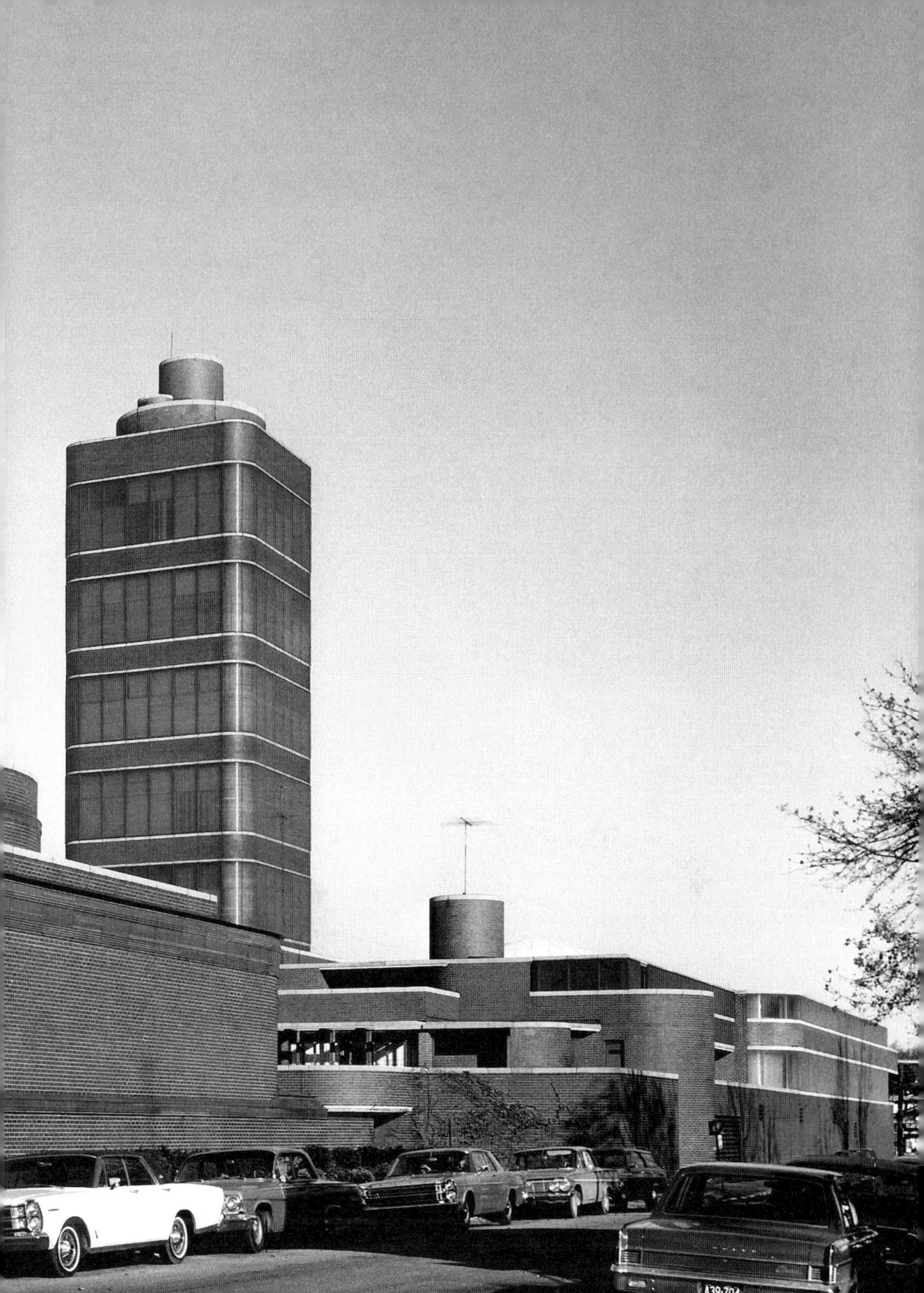
A39-704

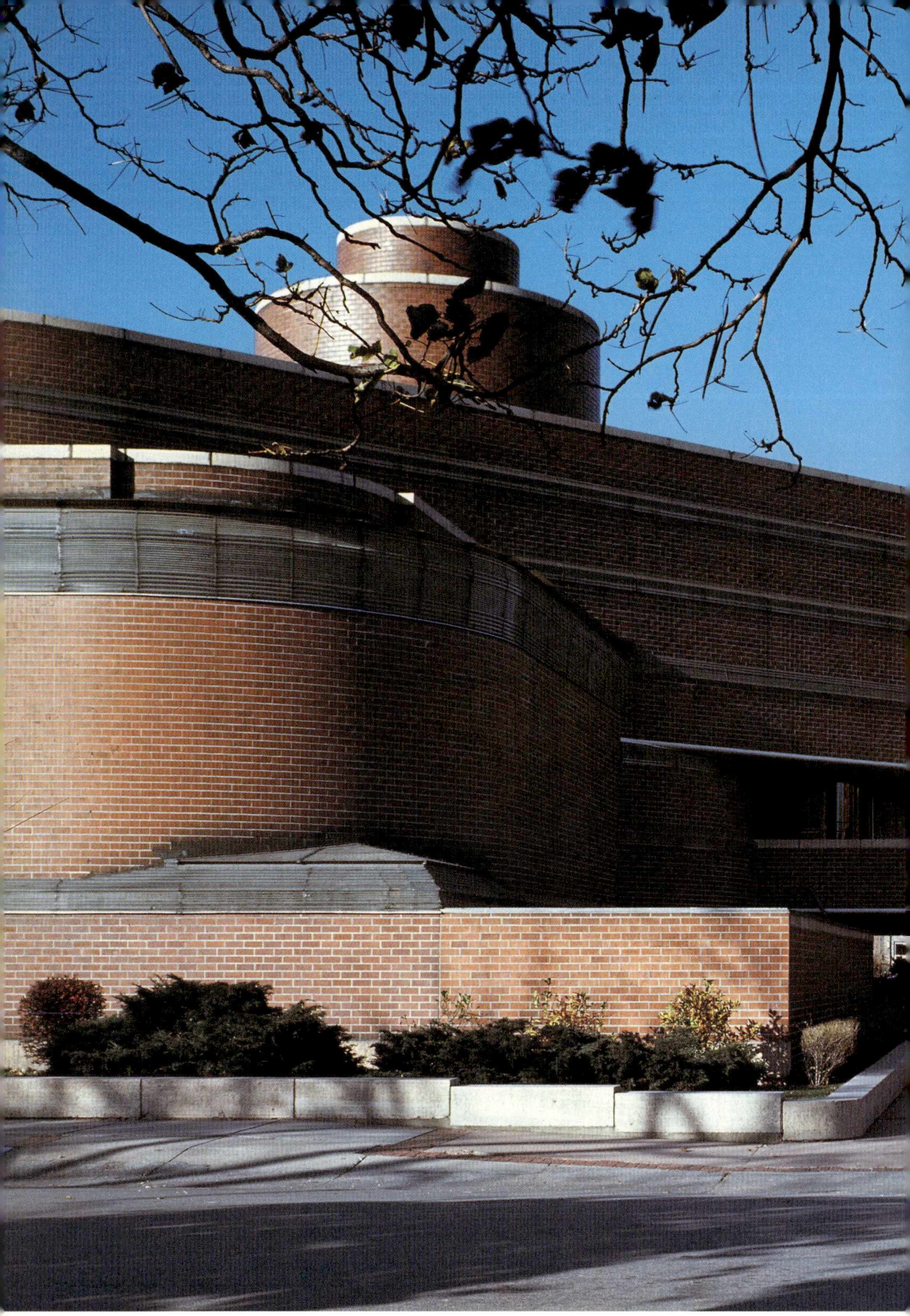

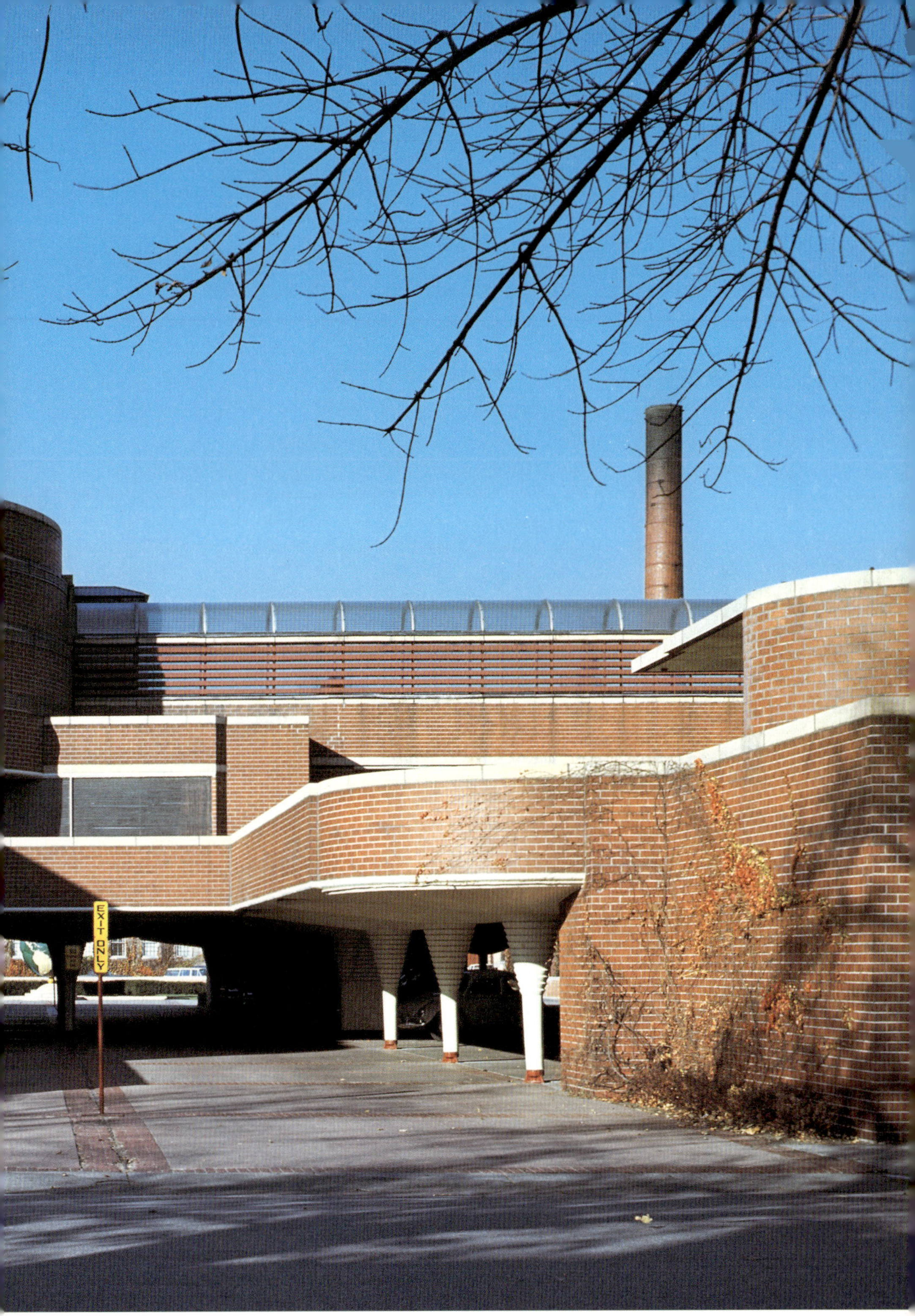
EXIT ONLY

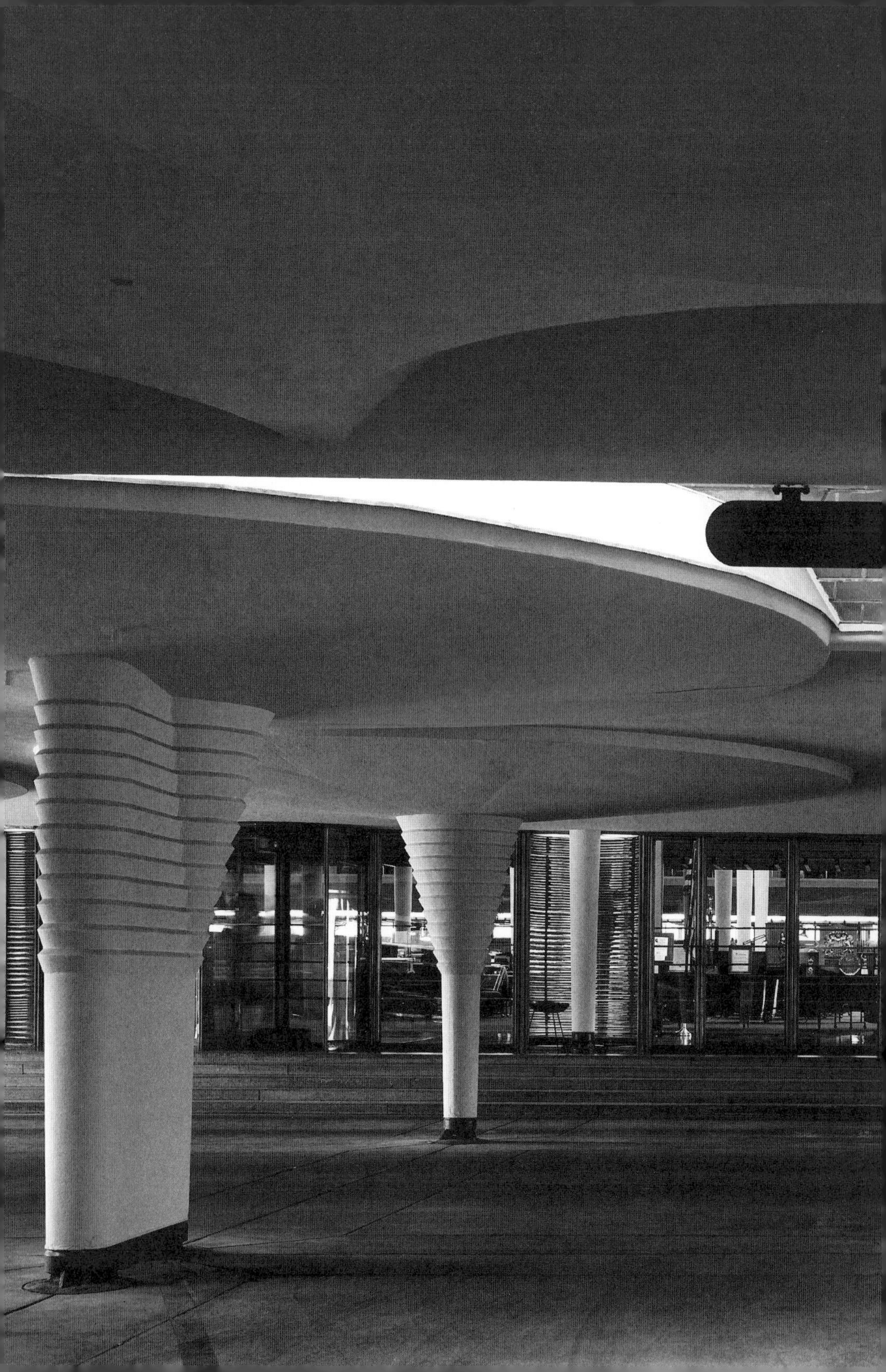

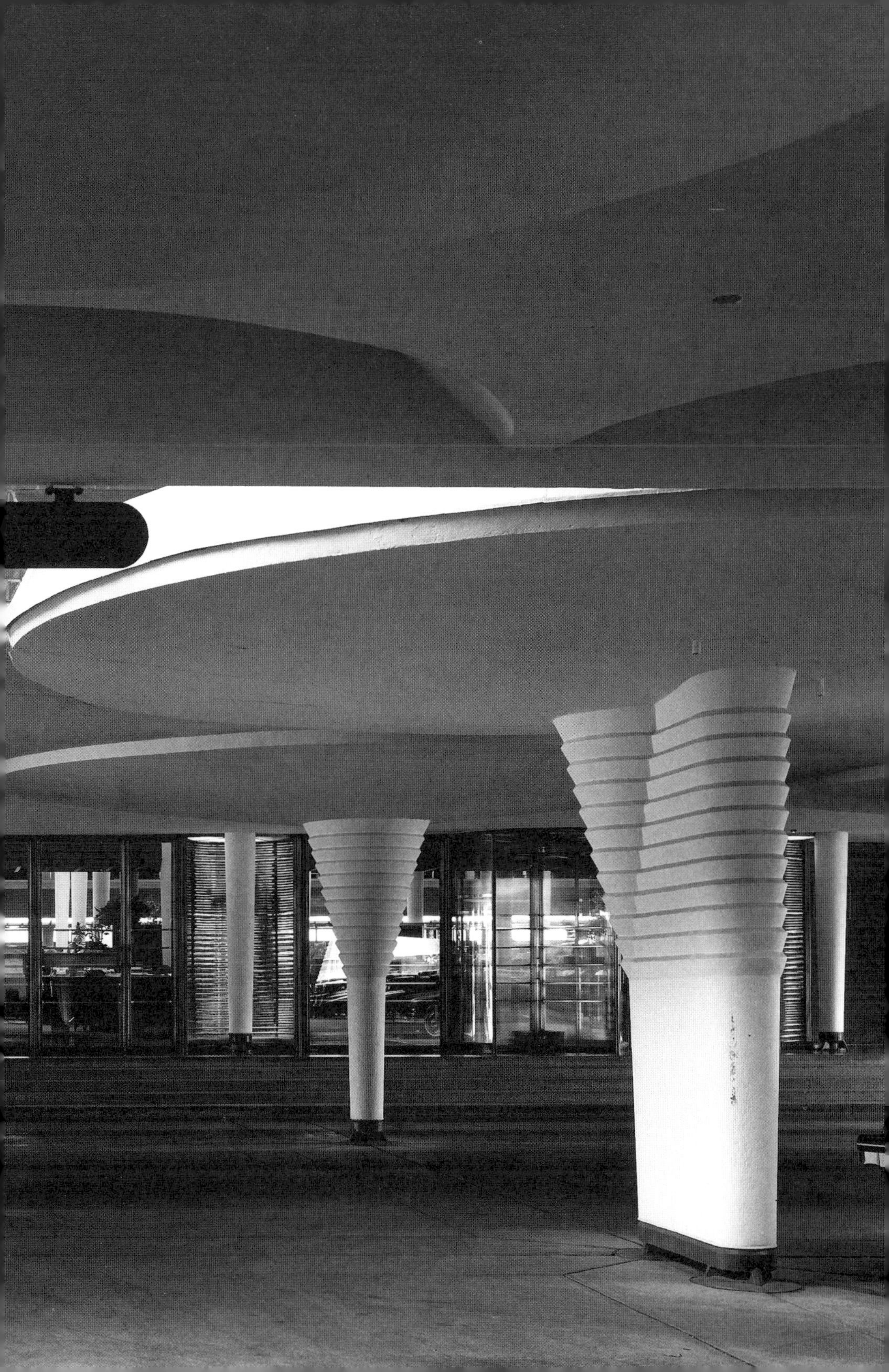

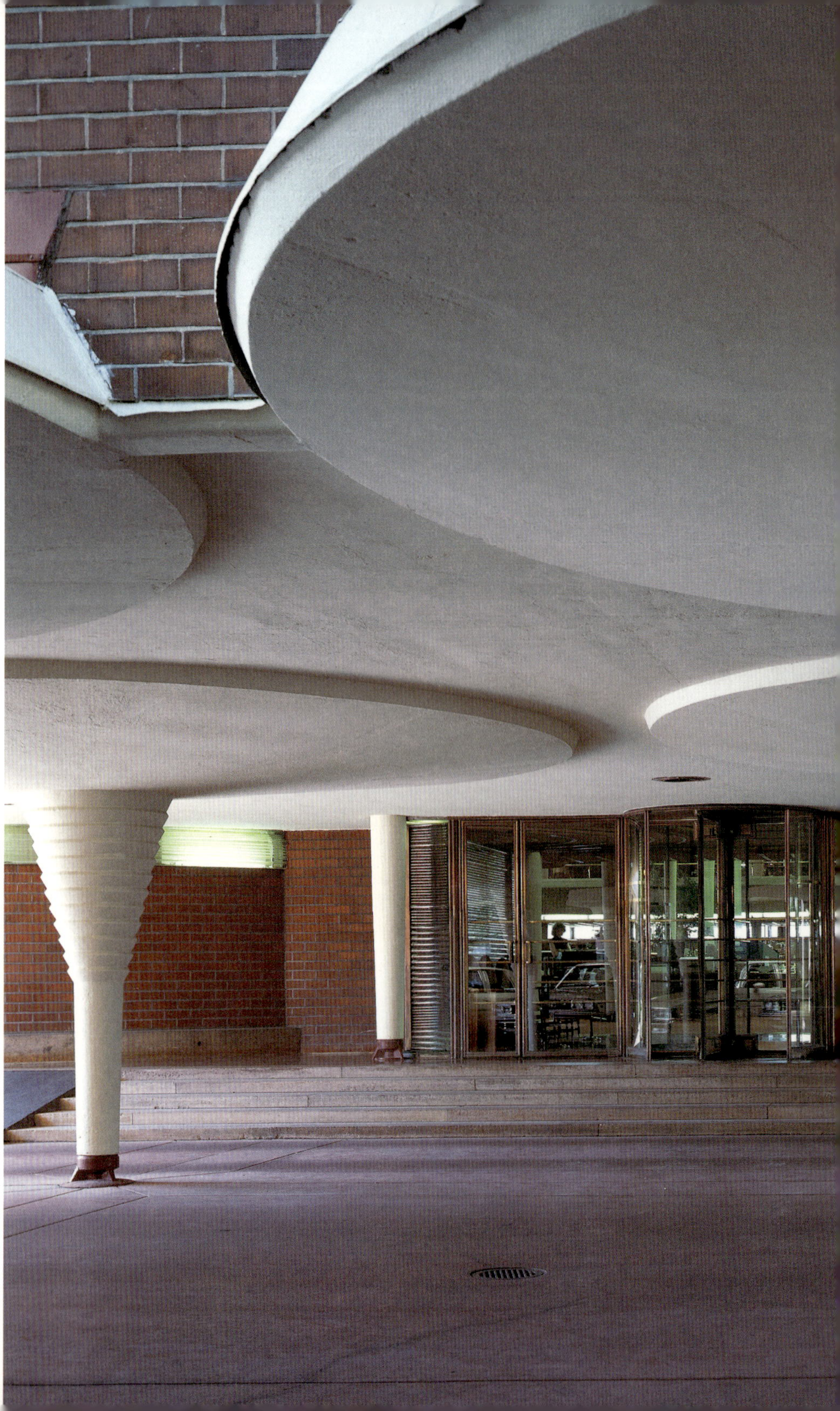

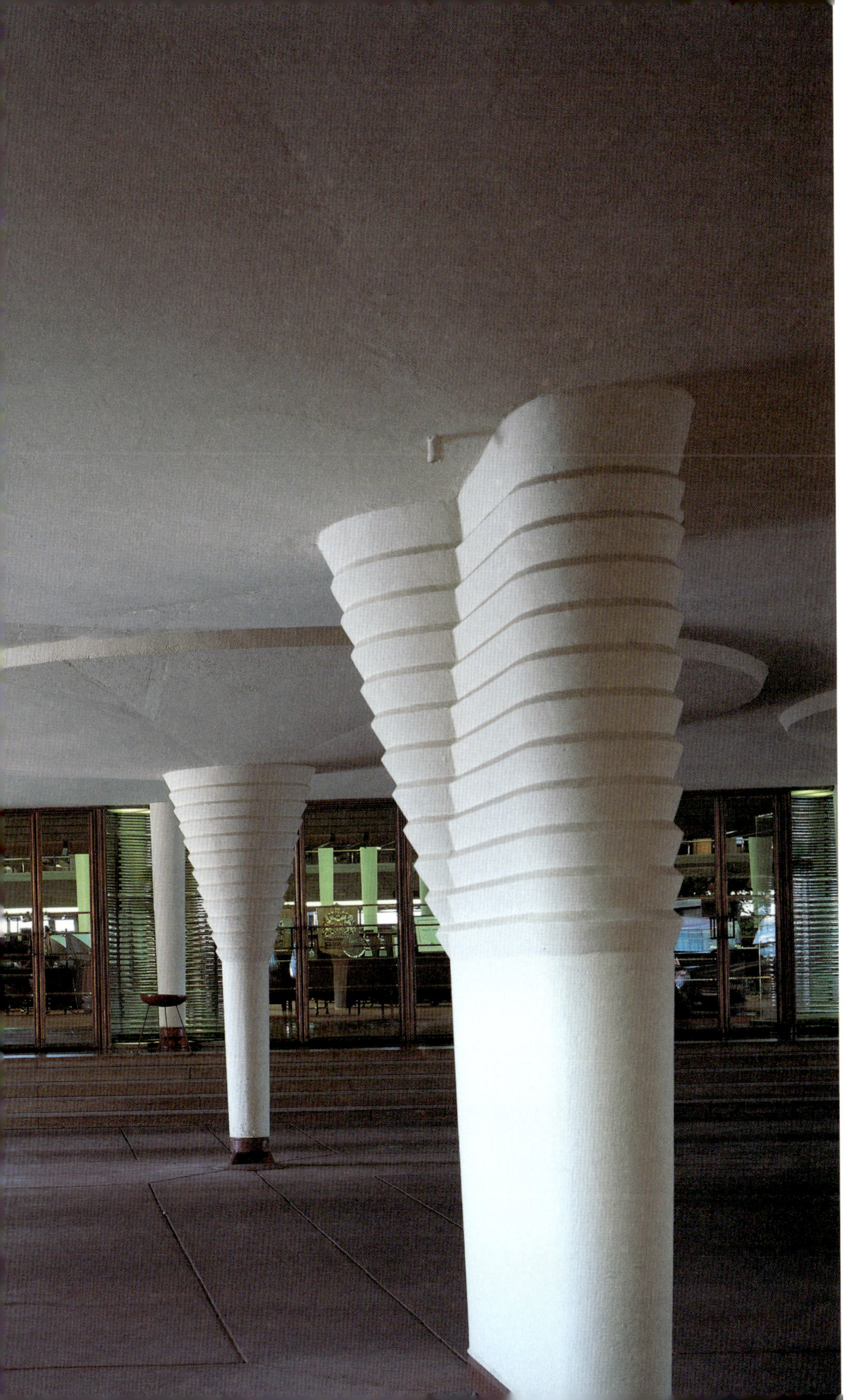

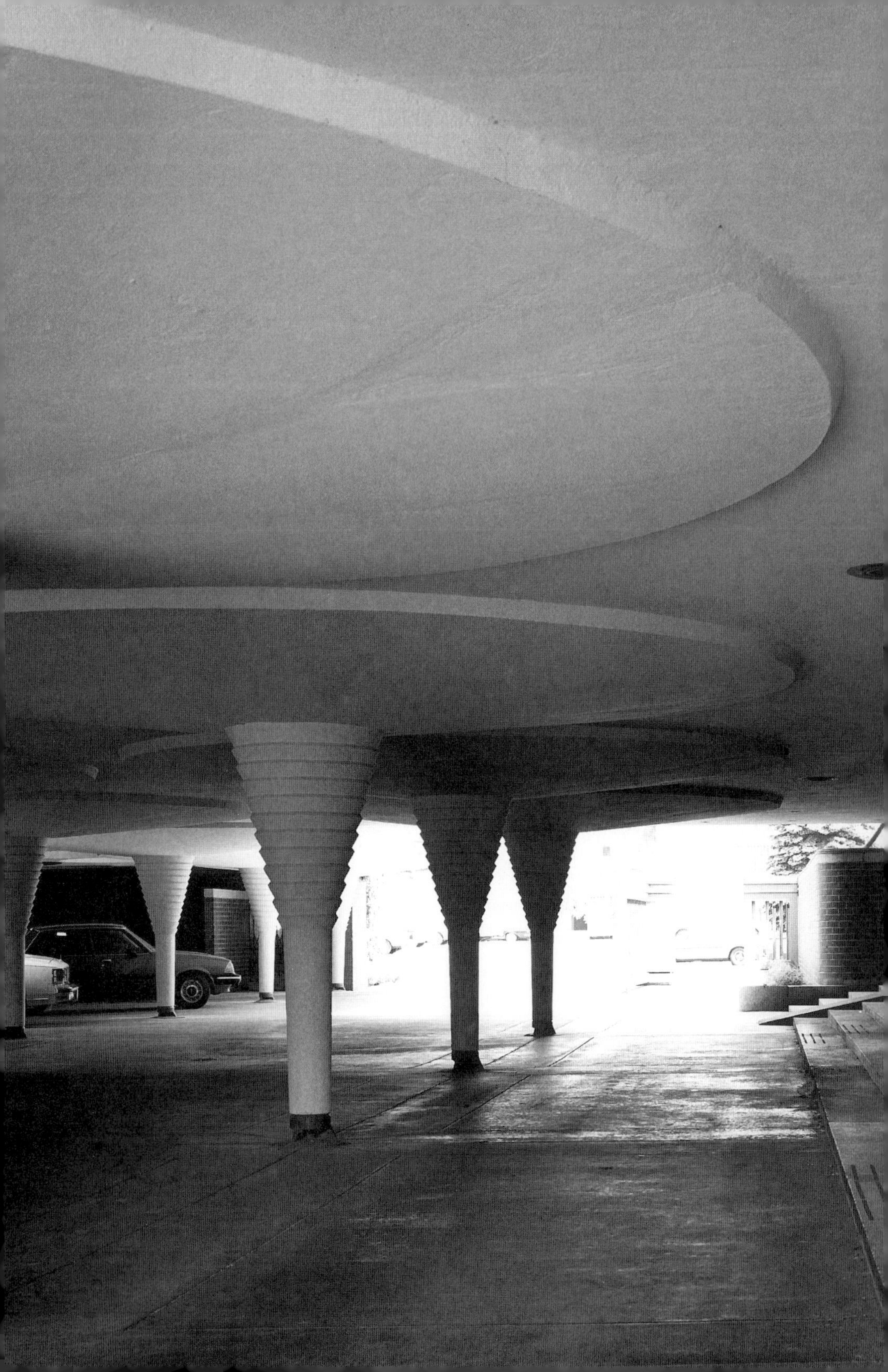

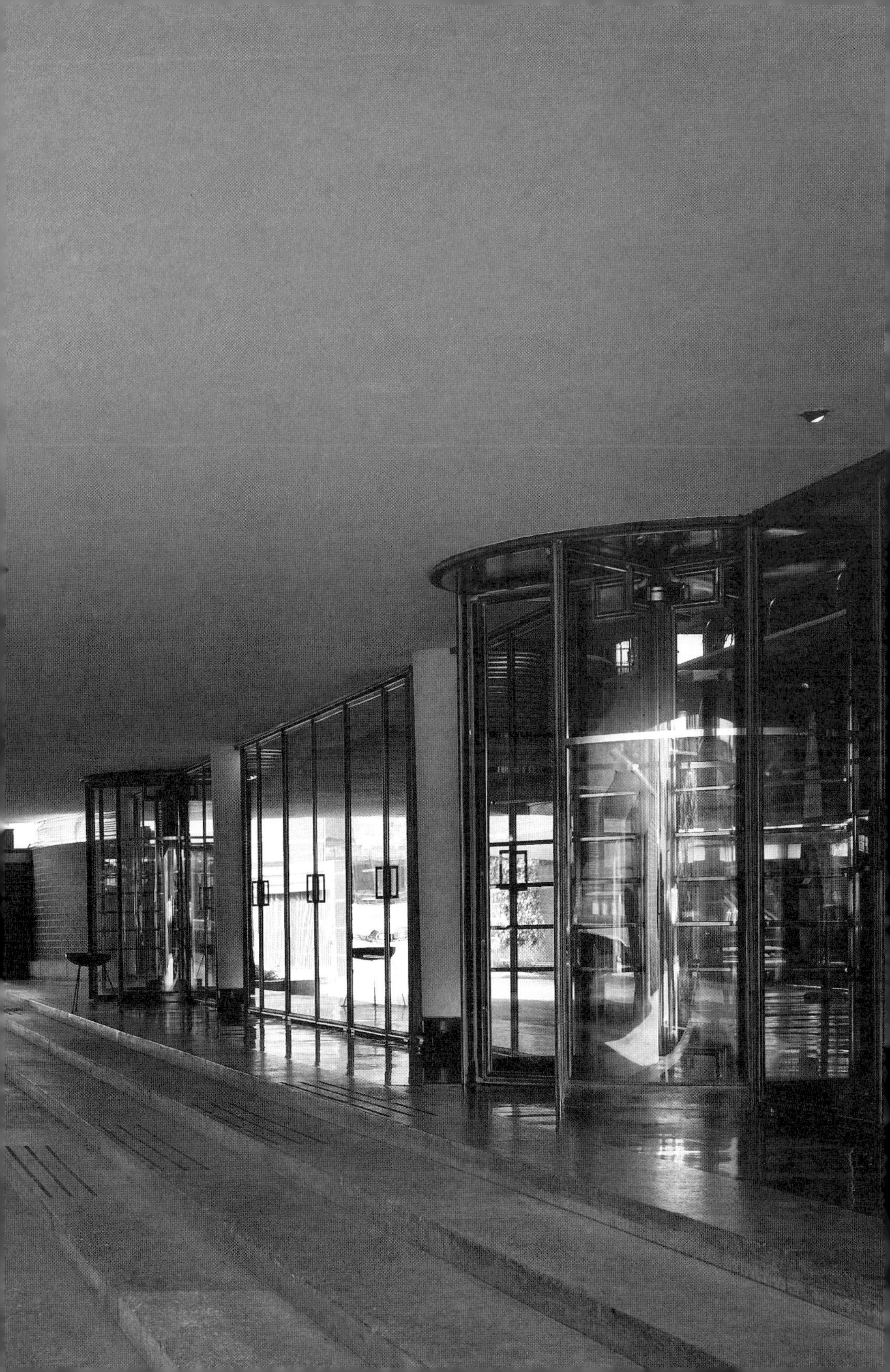

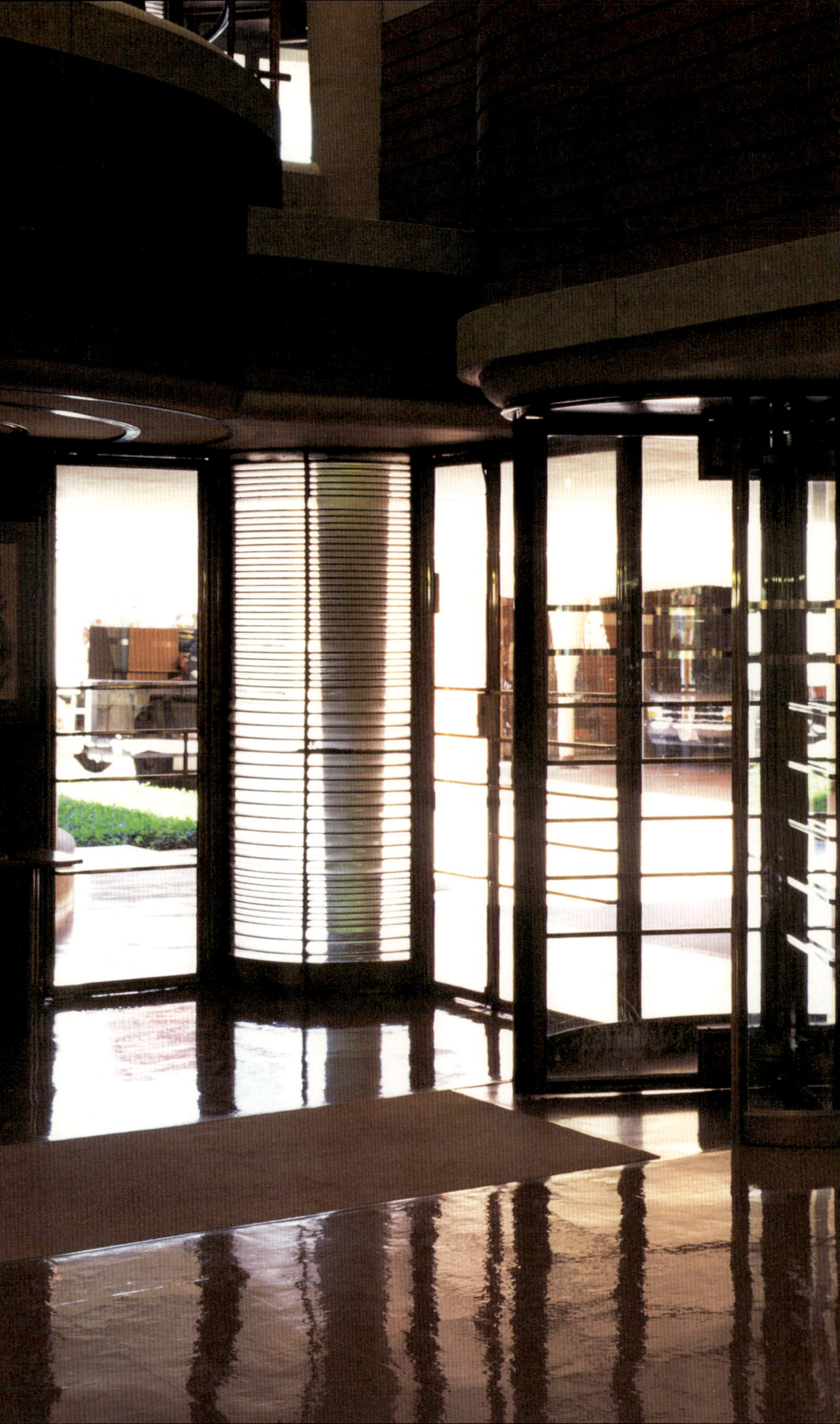

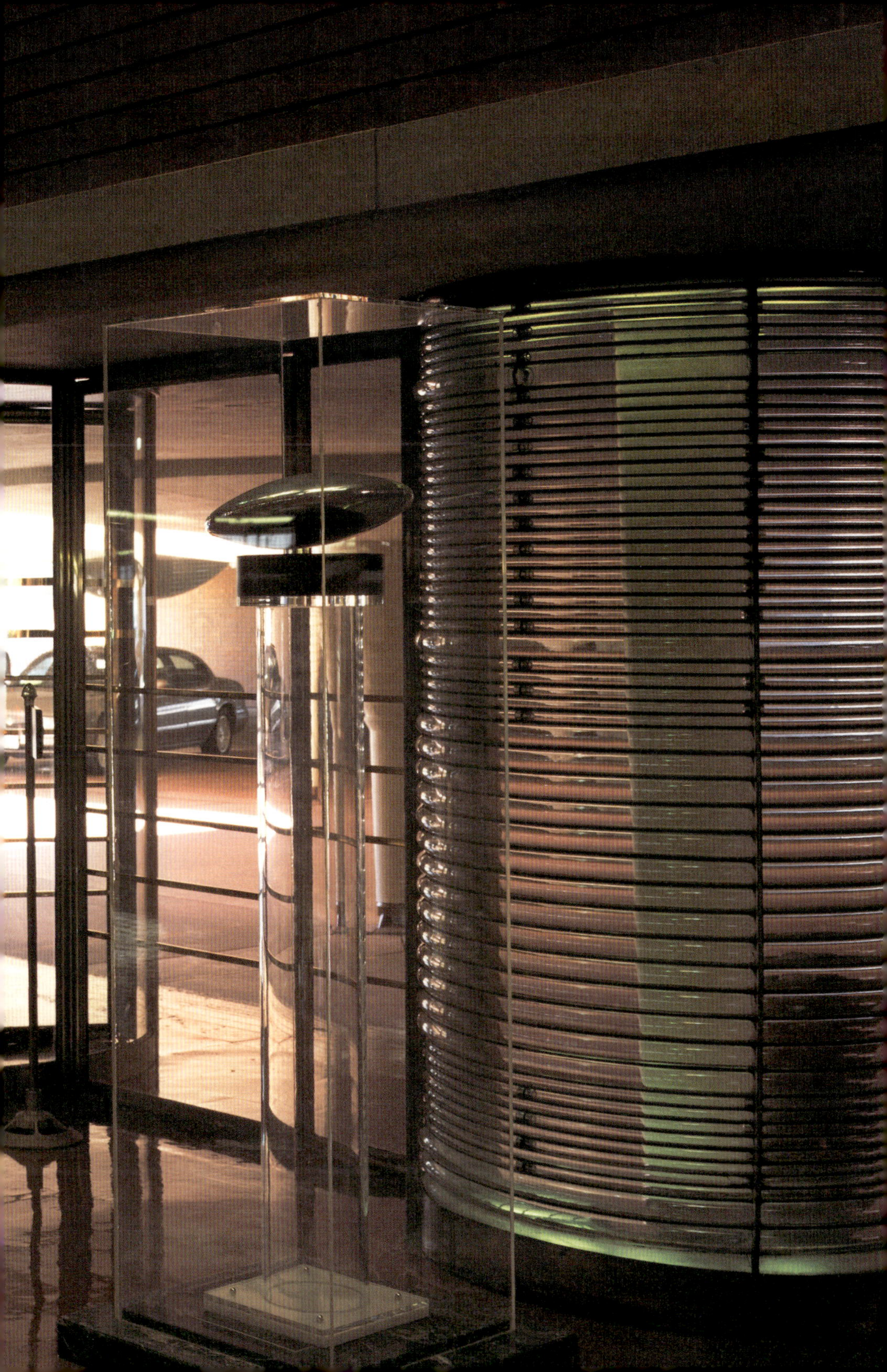

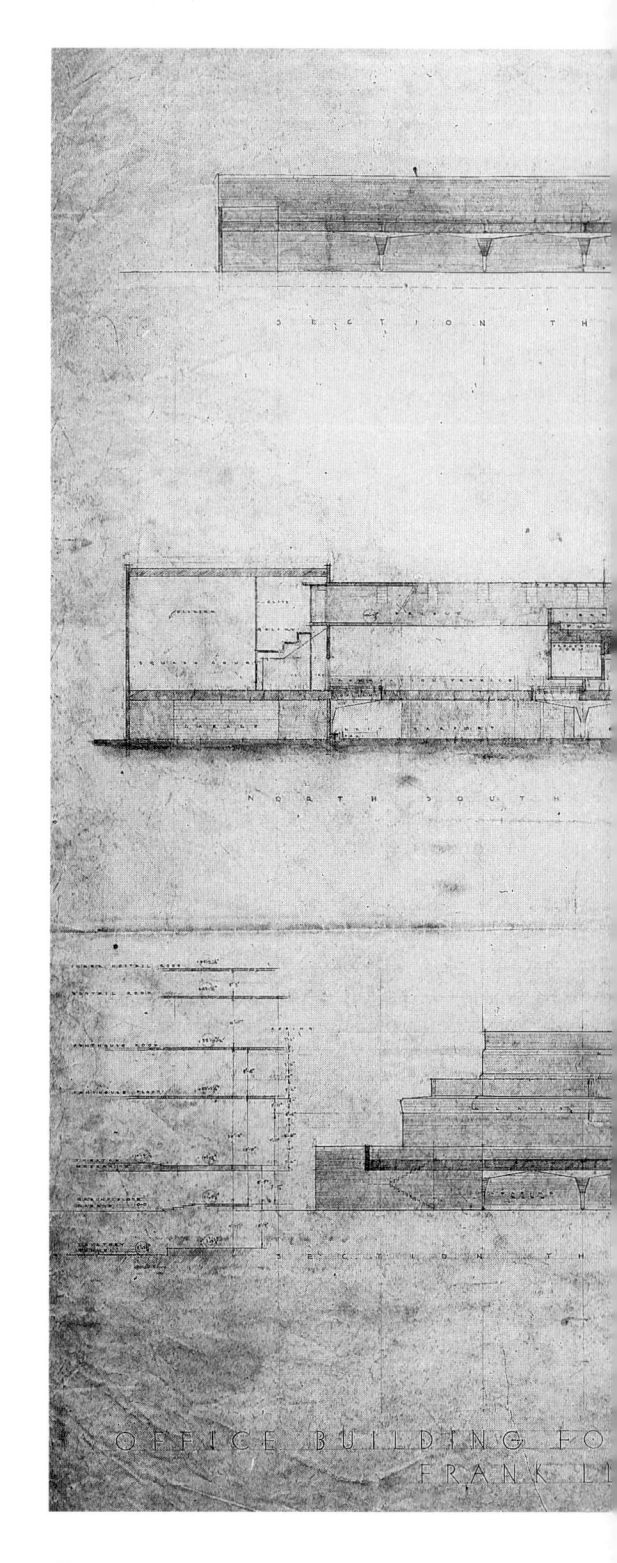

OFFICE BUILDING FO
FRANK LL

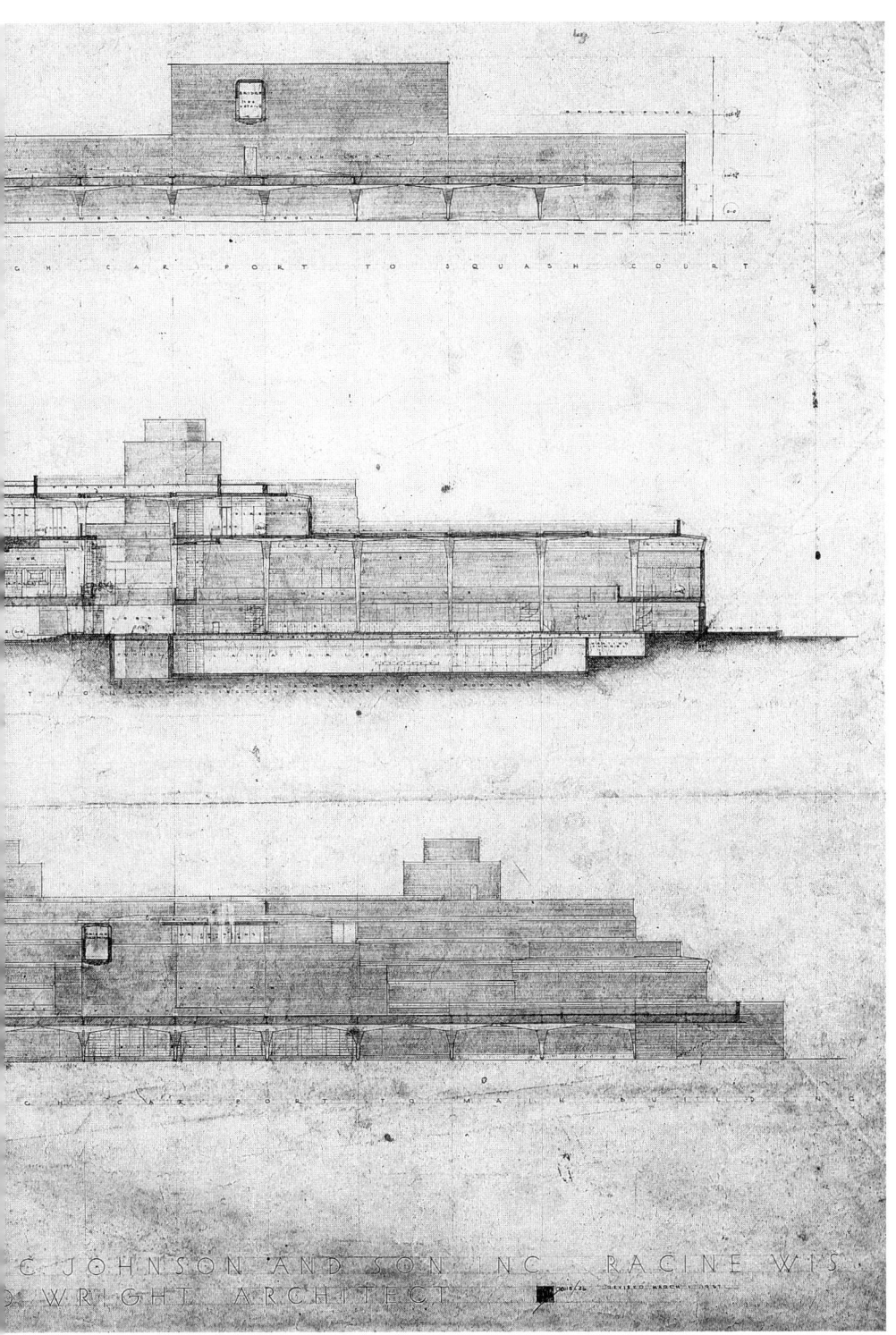

Sections

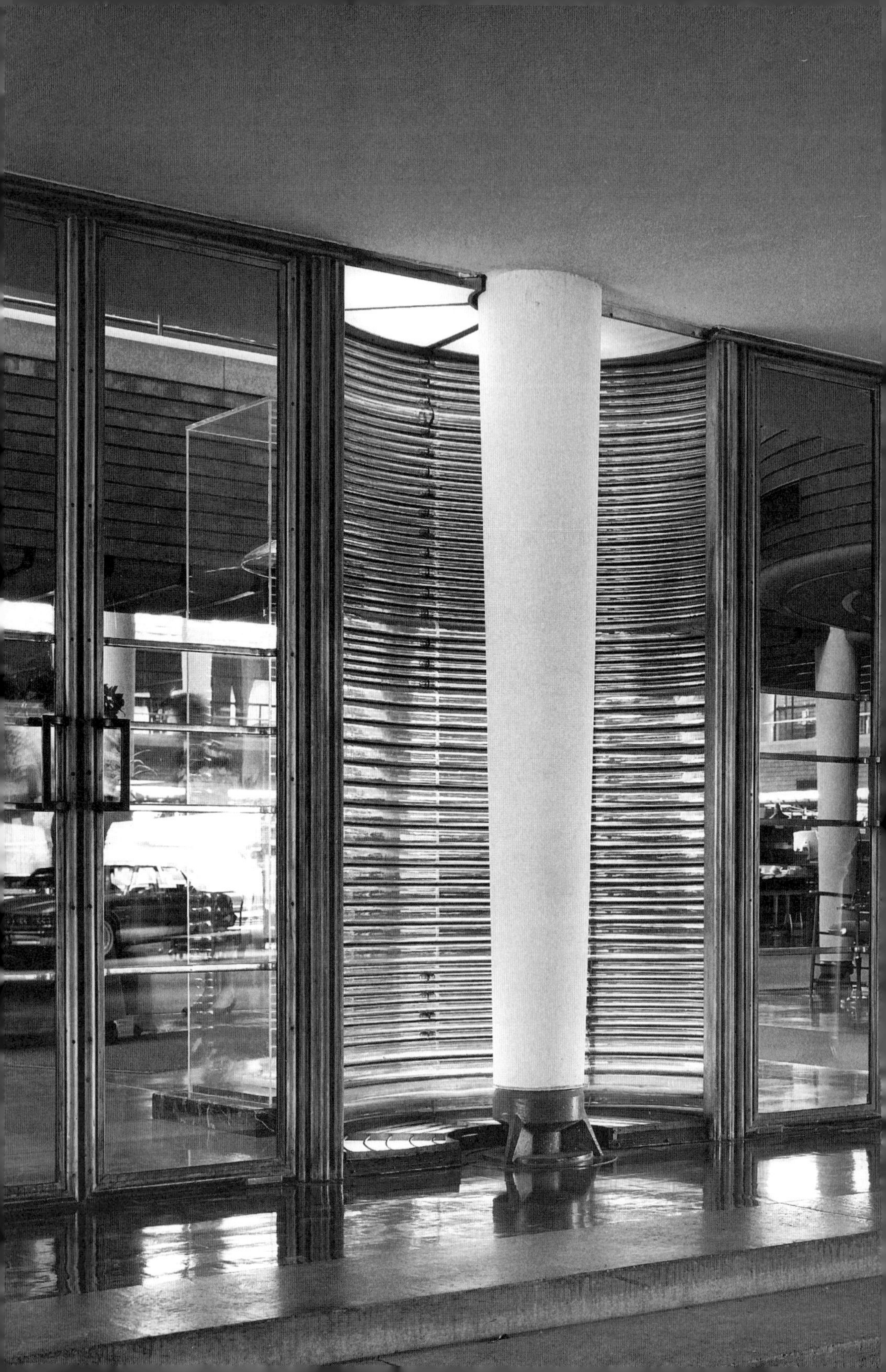

RONDELLE SCHEDULE
TOURS STARTING
FROM THE R NDELLE
1 BLOCK NORTH

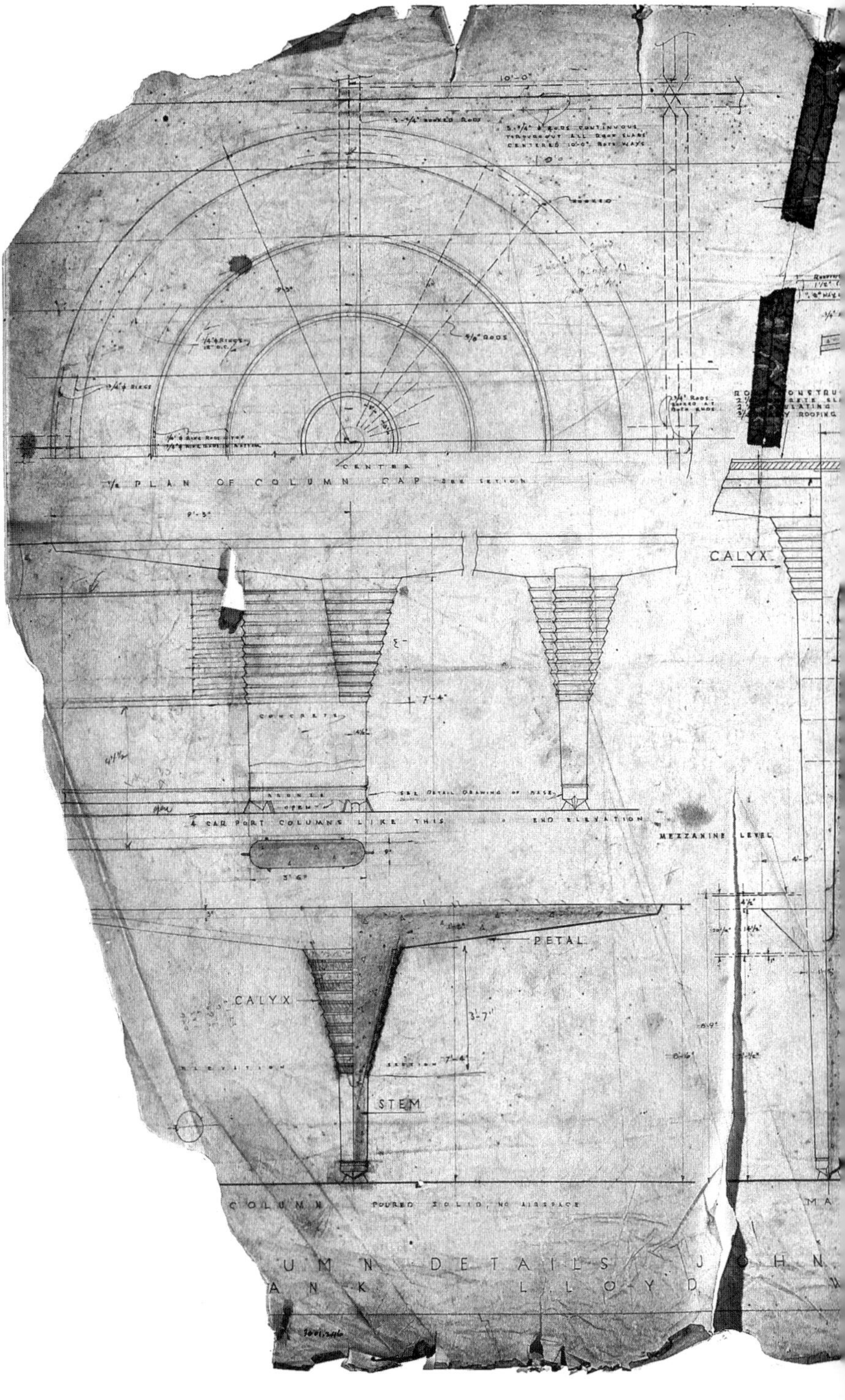
1/2 PLAN OF COLUMN CAP SEE SECTION
CENTER
CALYX
CONCRETE
4 CAR PORT COLUMNS LIKE THIS
END ELEVATION
MEZZANINE LEVEL
PETAL
CALYX
STEM
COLUMN POURED SOLID, NO AIRSPACE
UMN DETAILS JOHN
ANK LLOYD

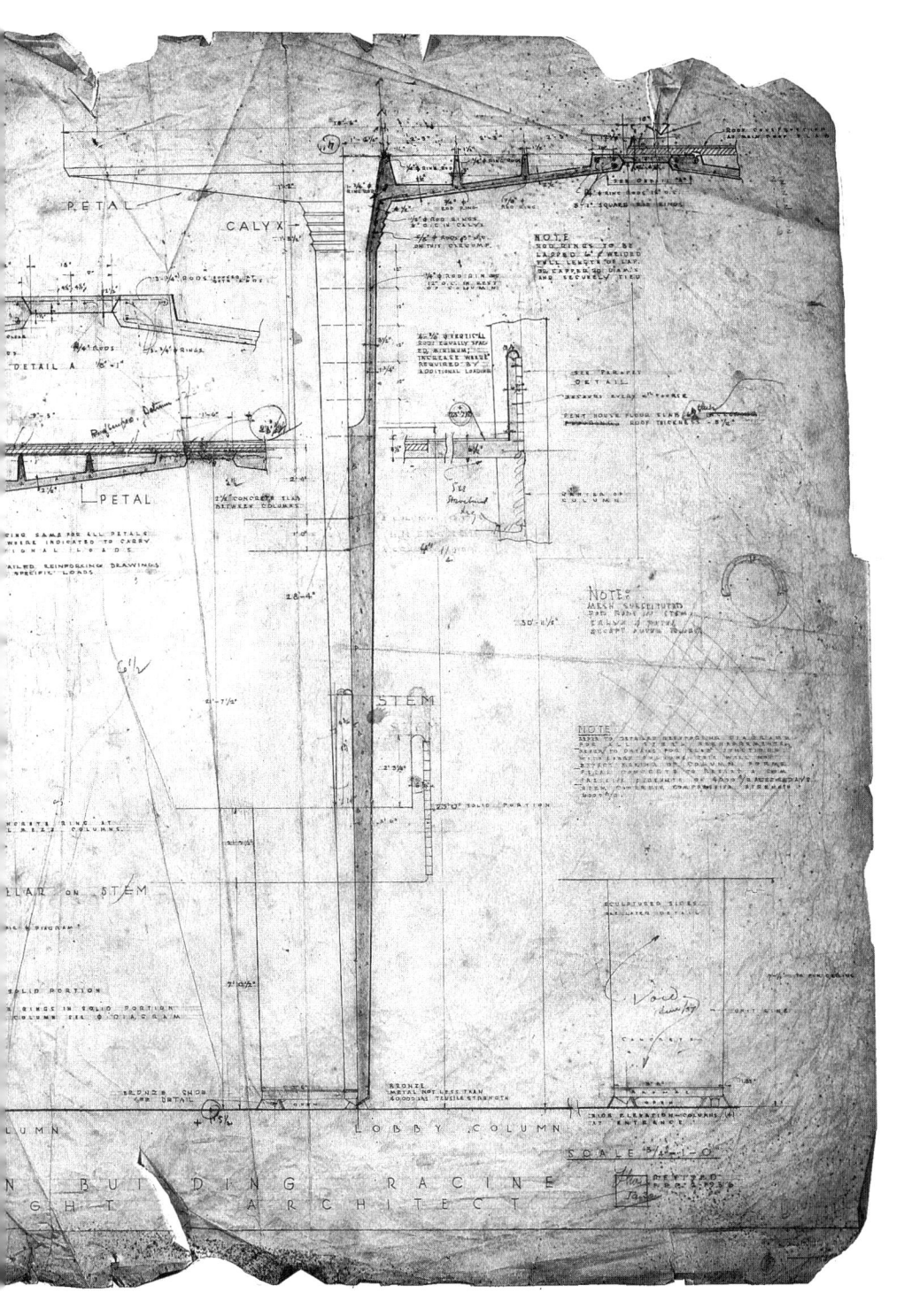

Column details

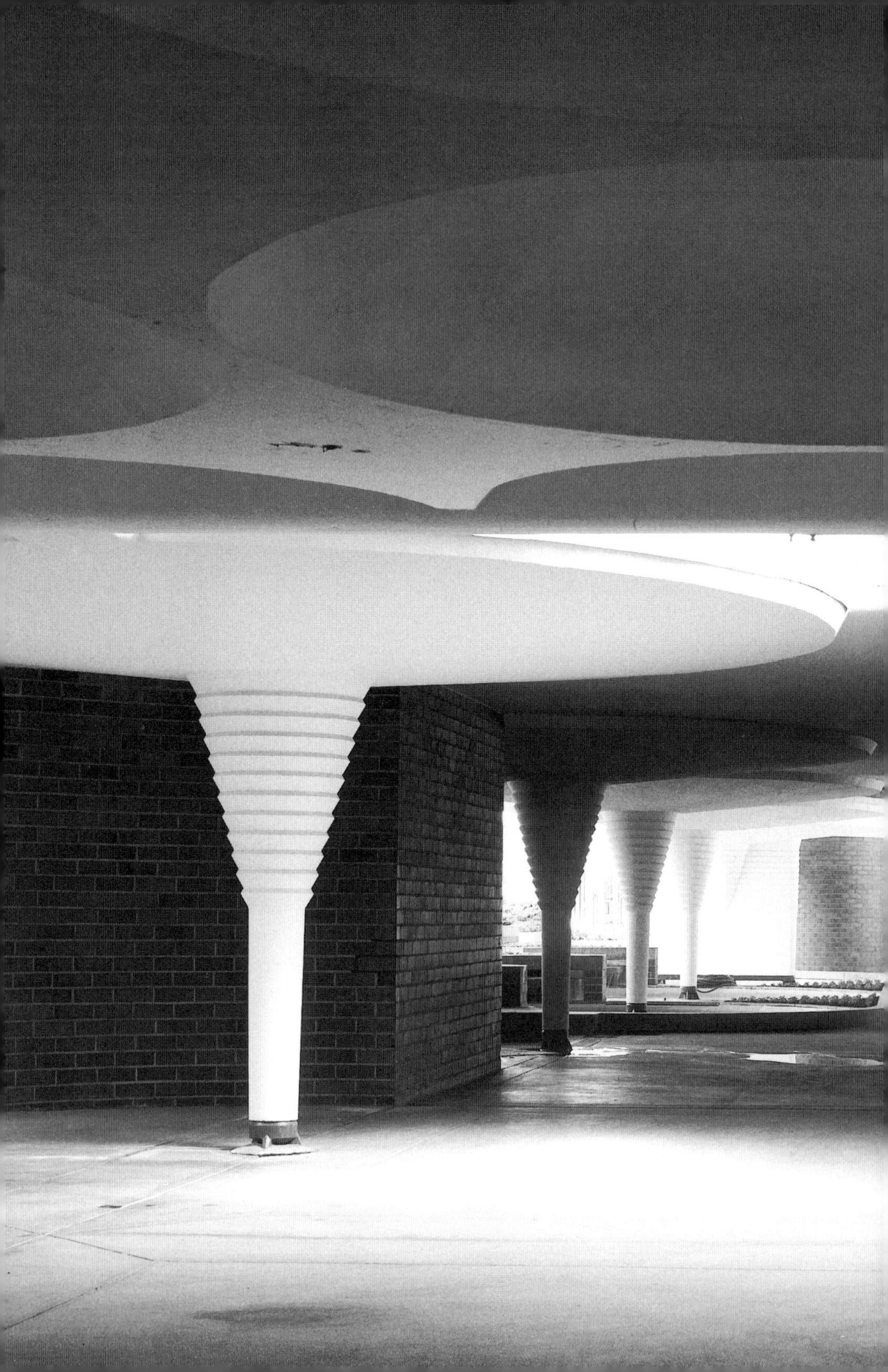

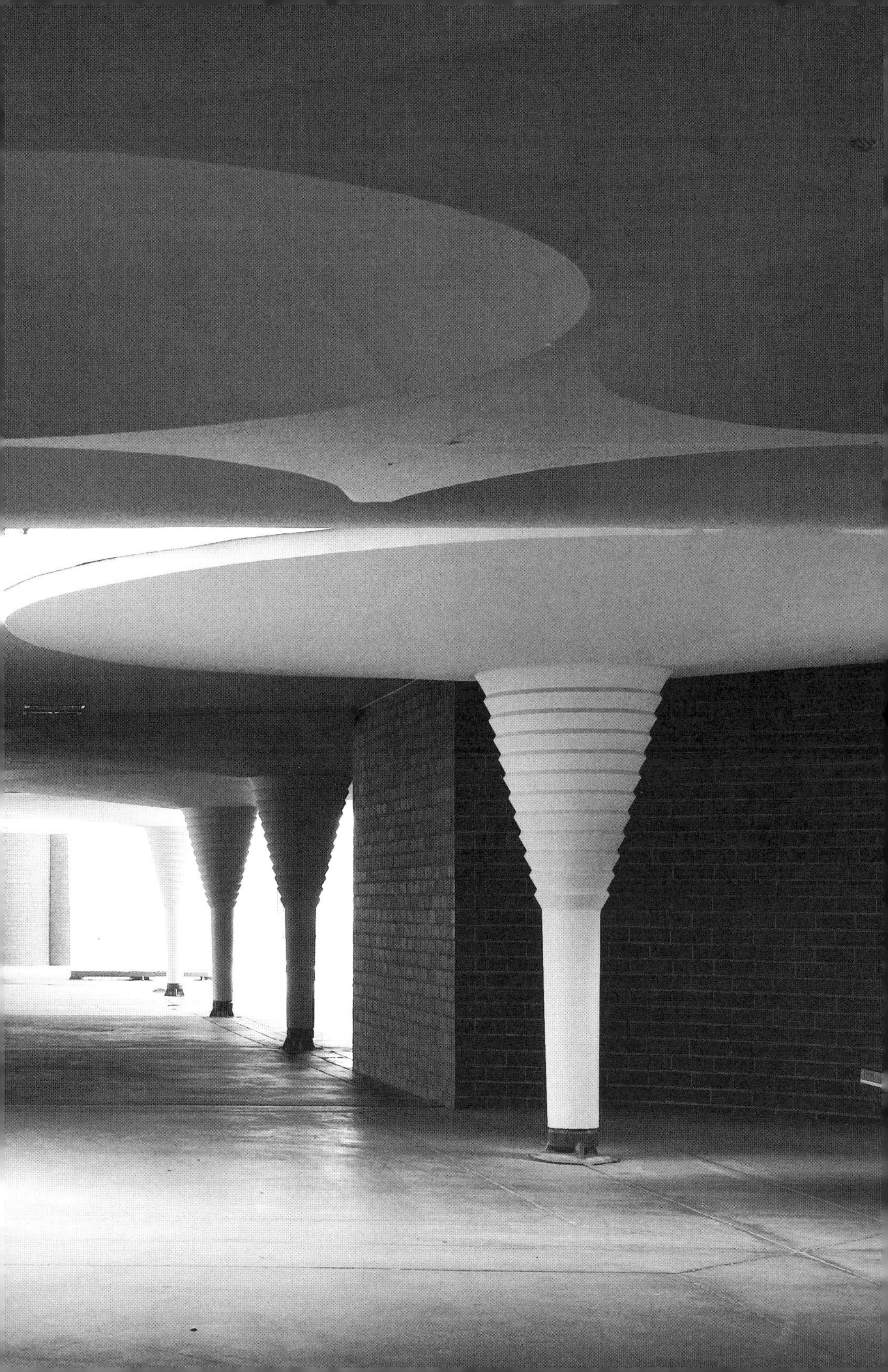

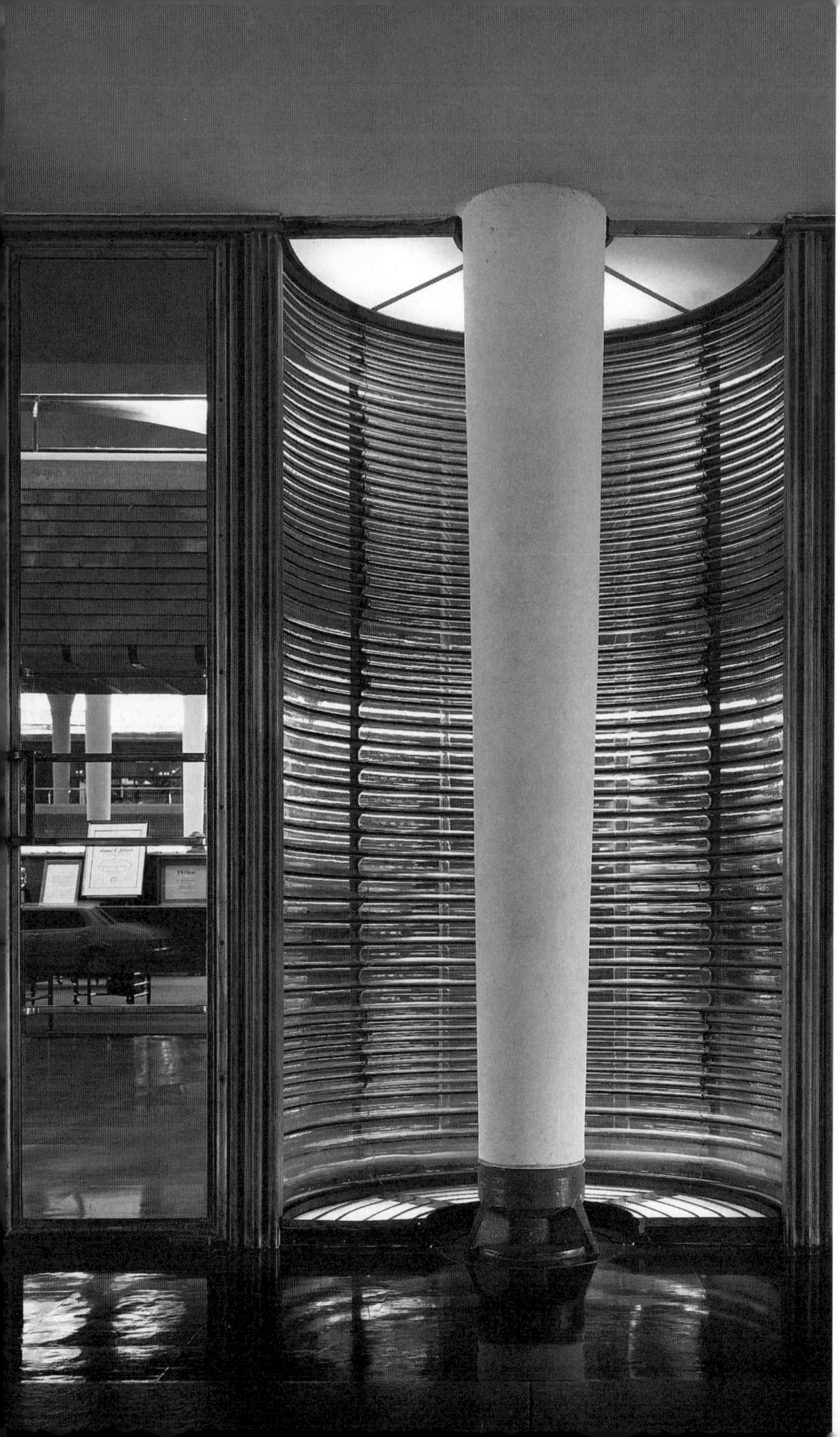

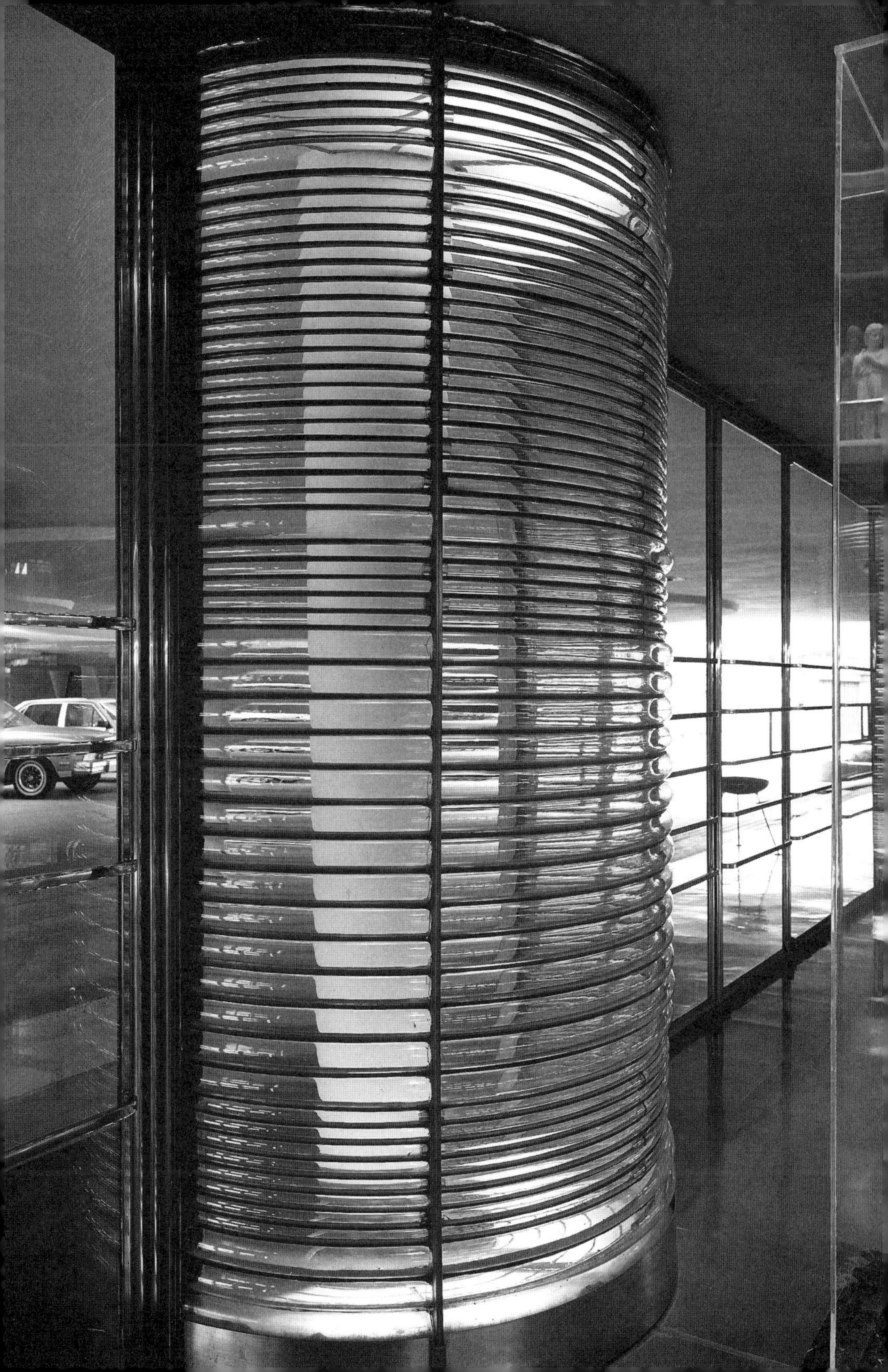

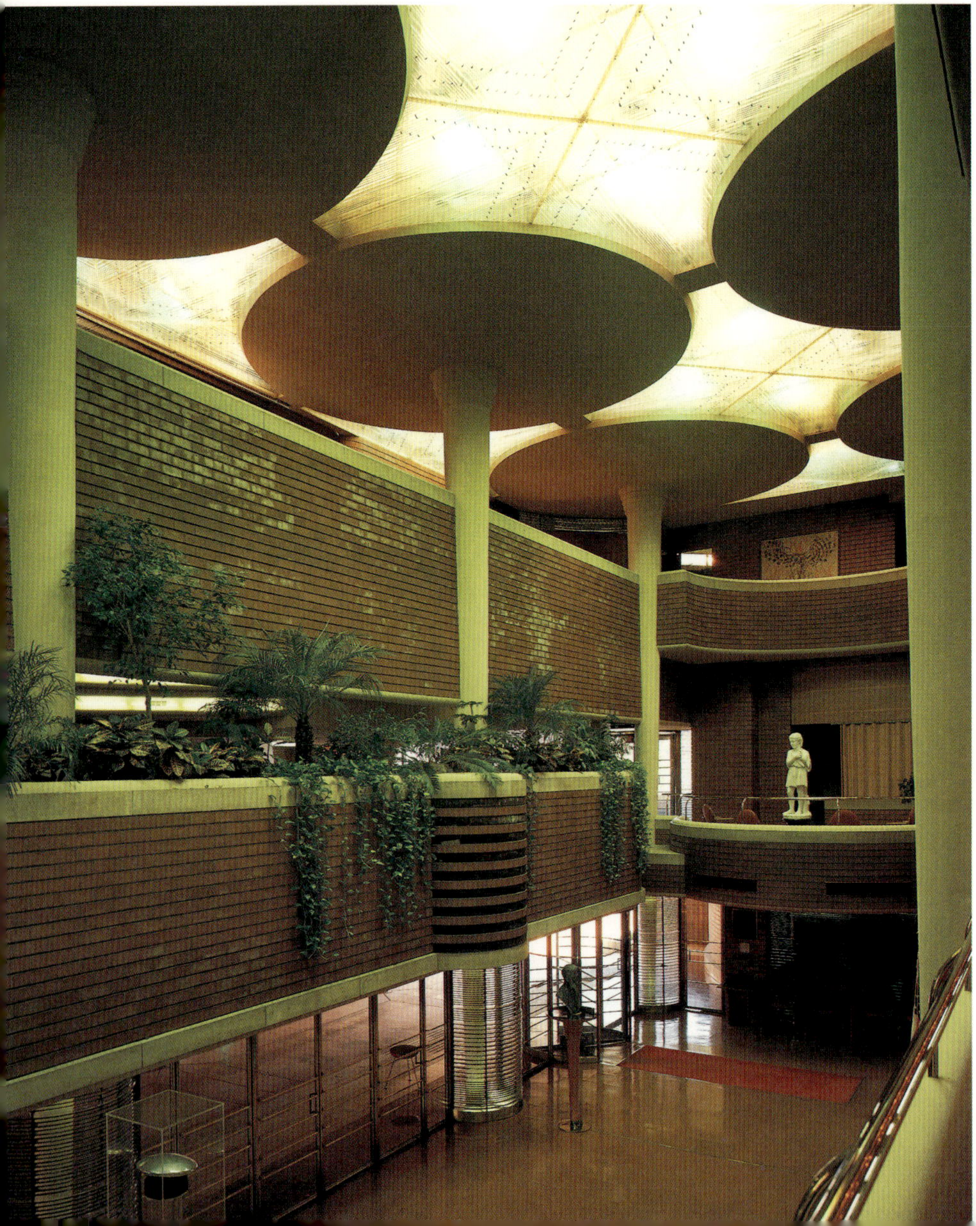

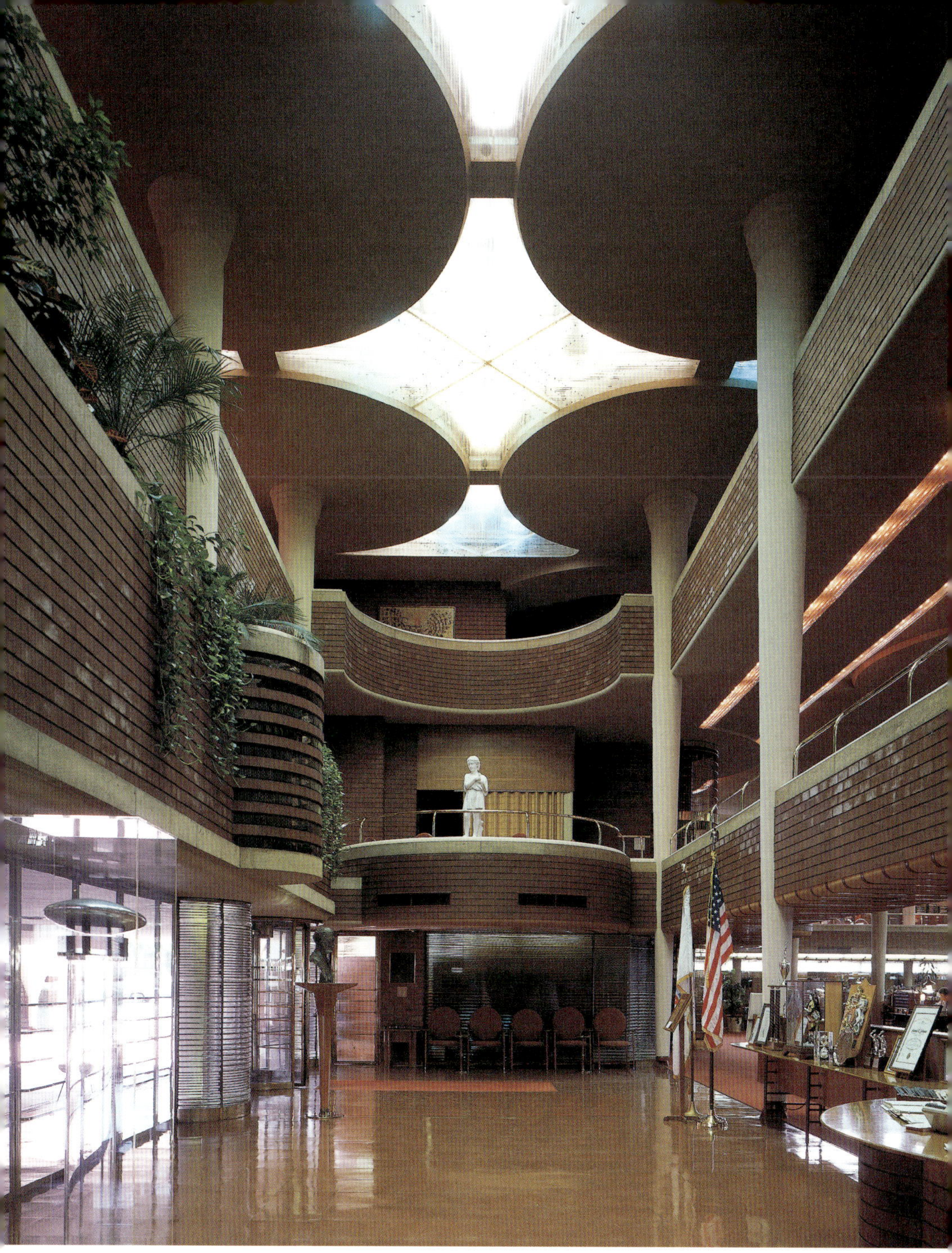

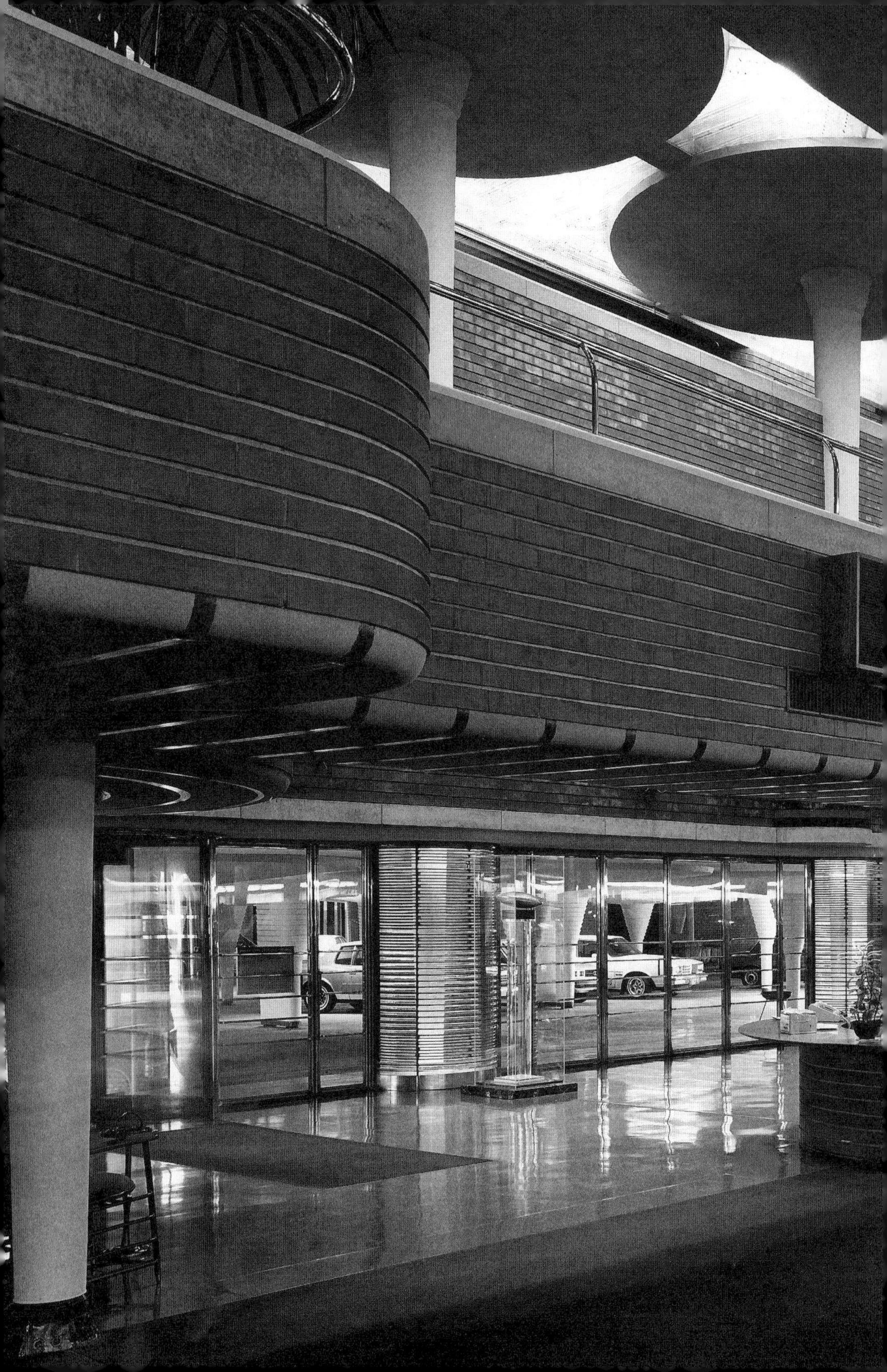

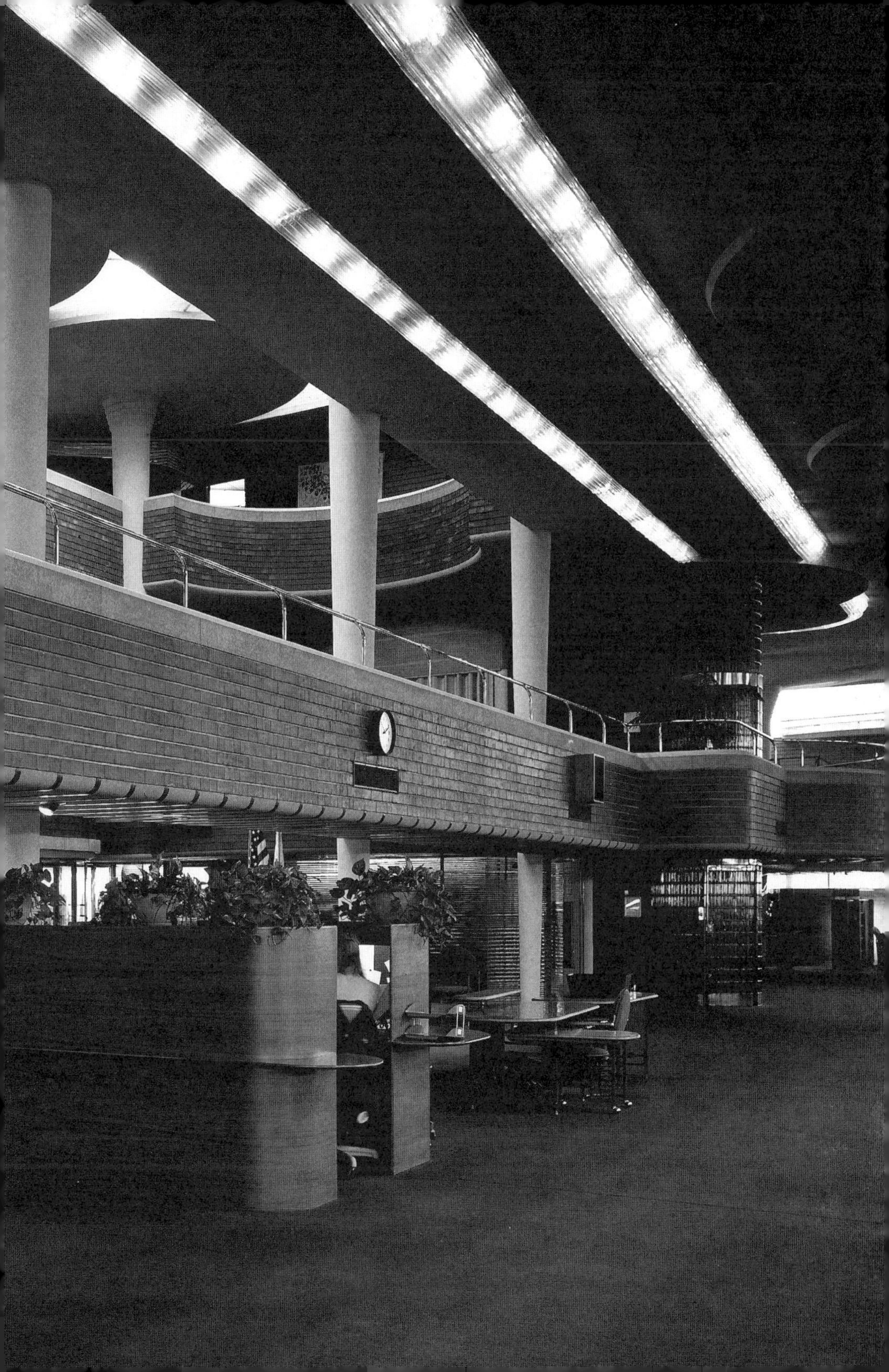

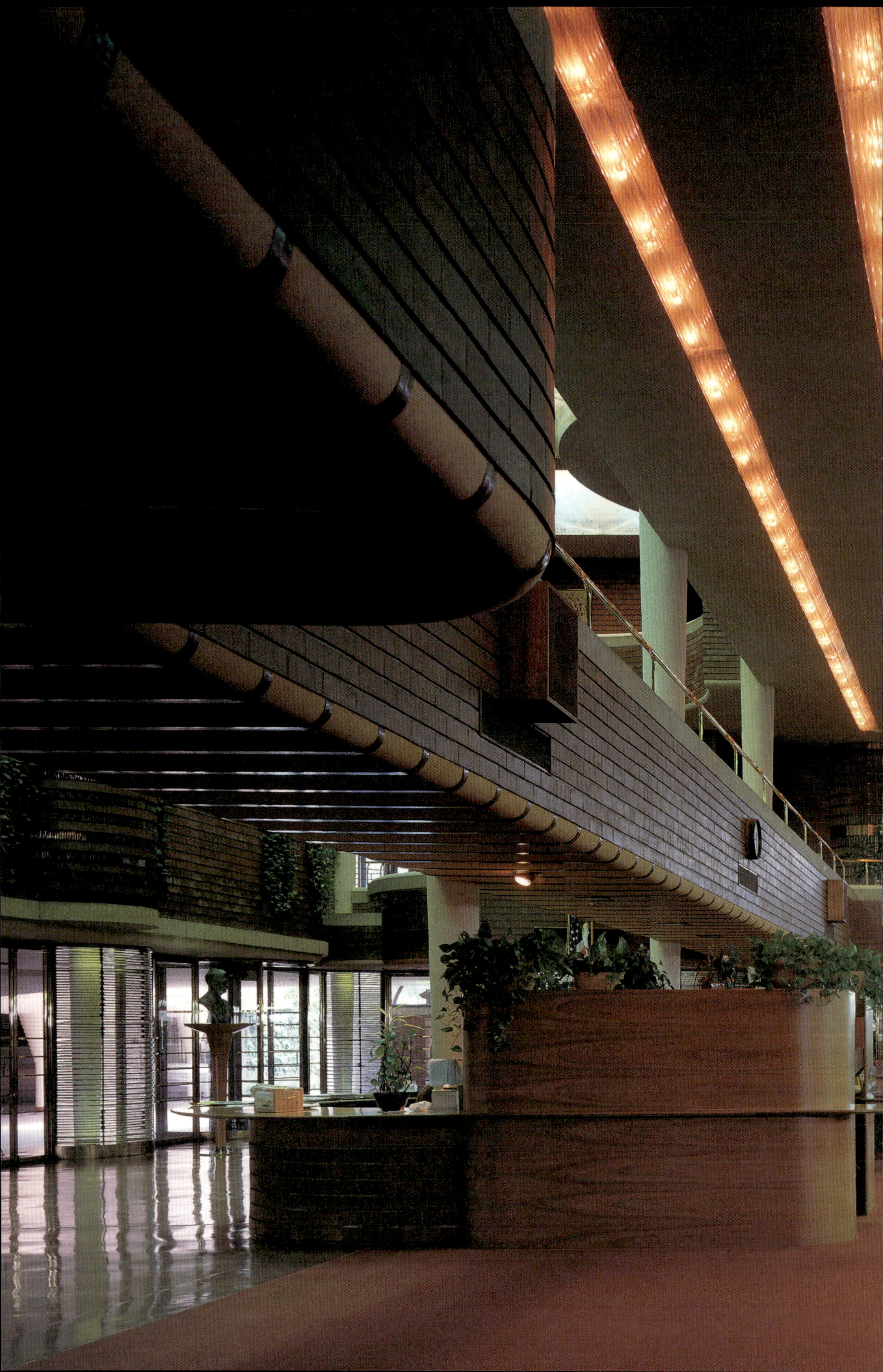

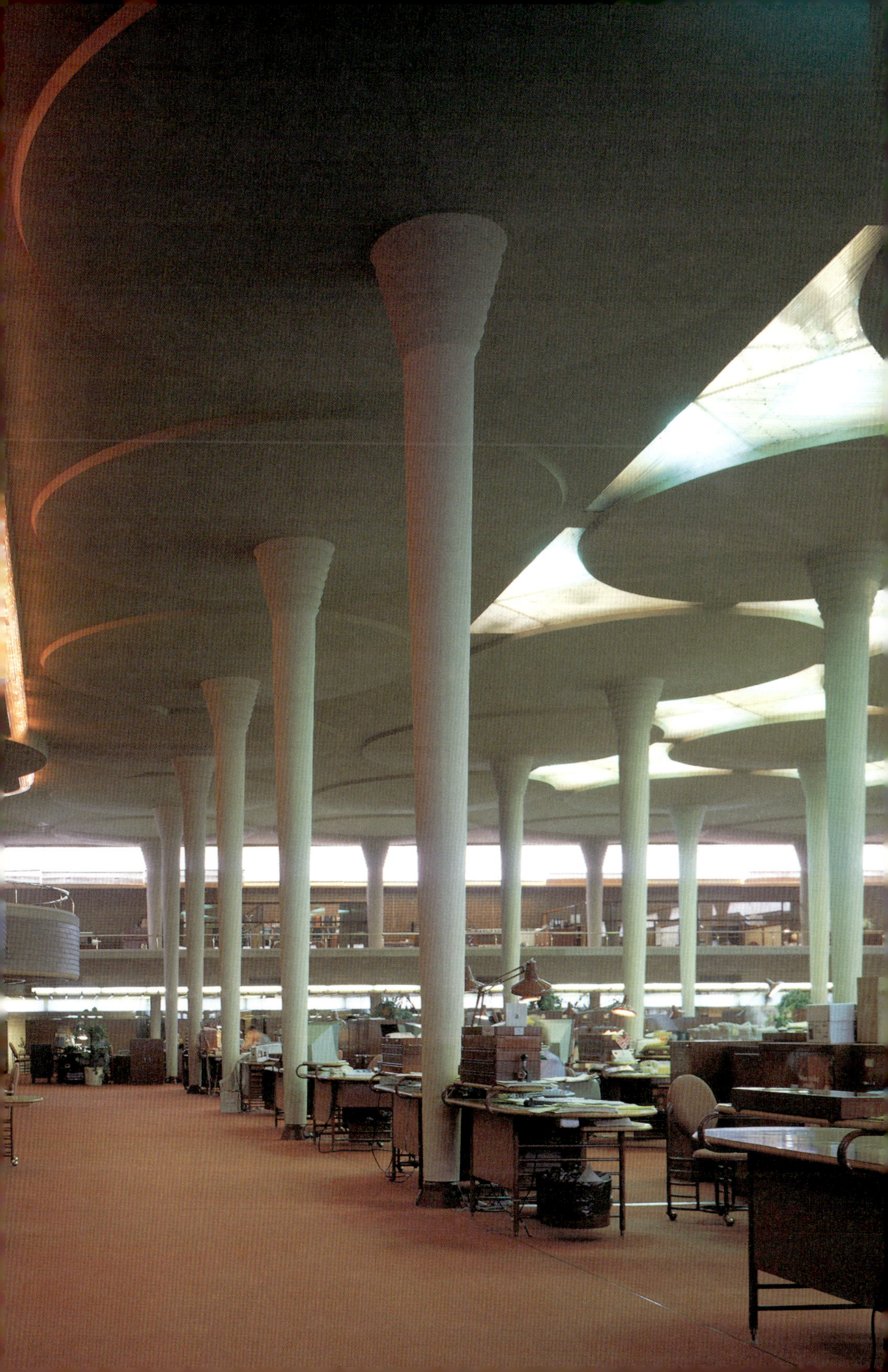

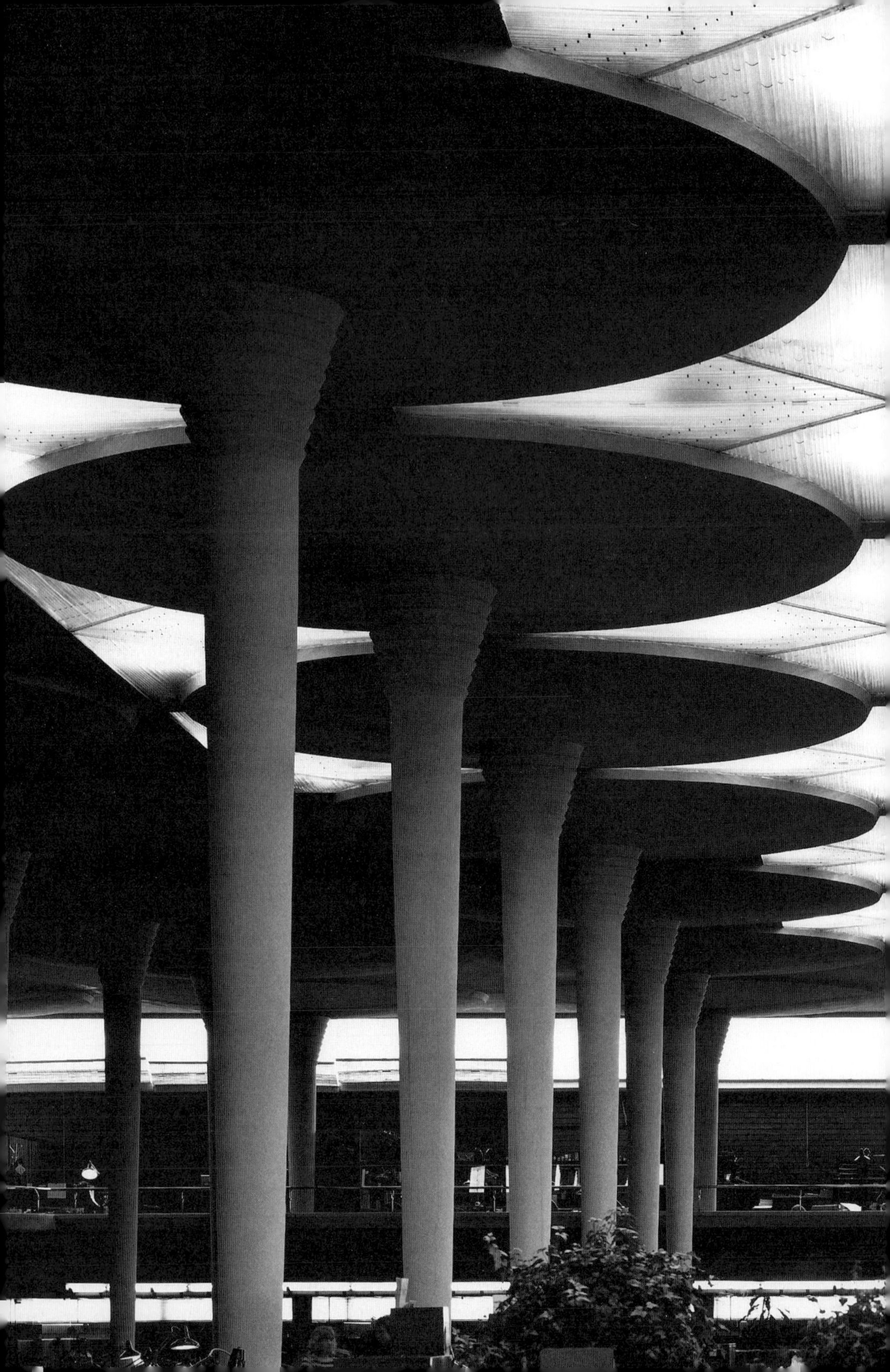

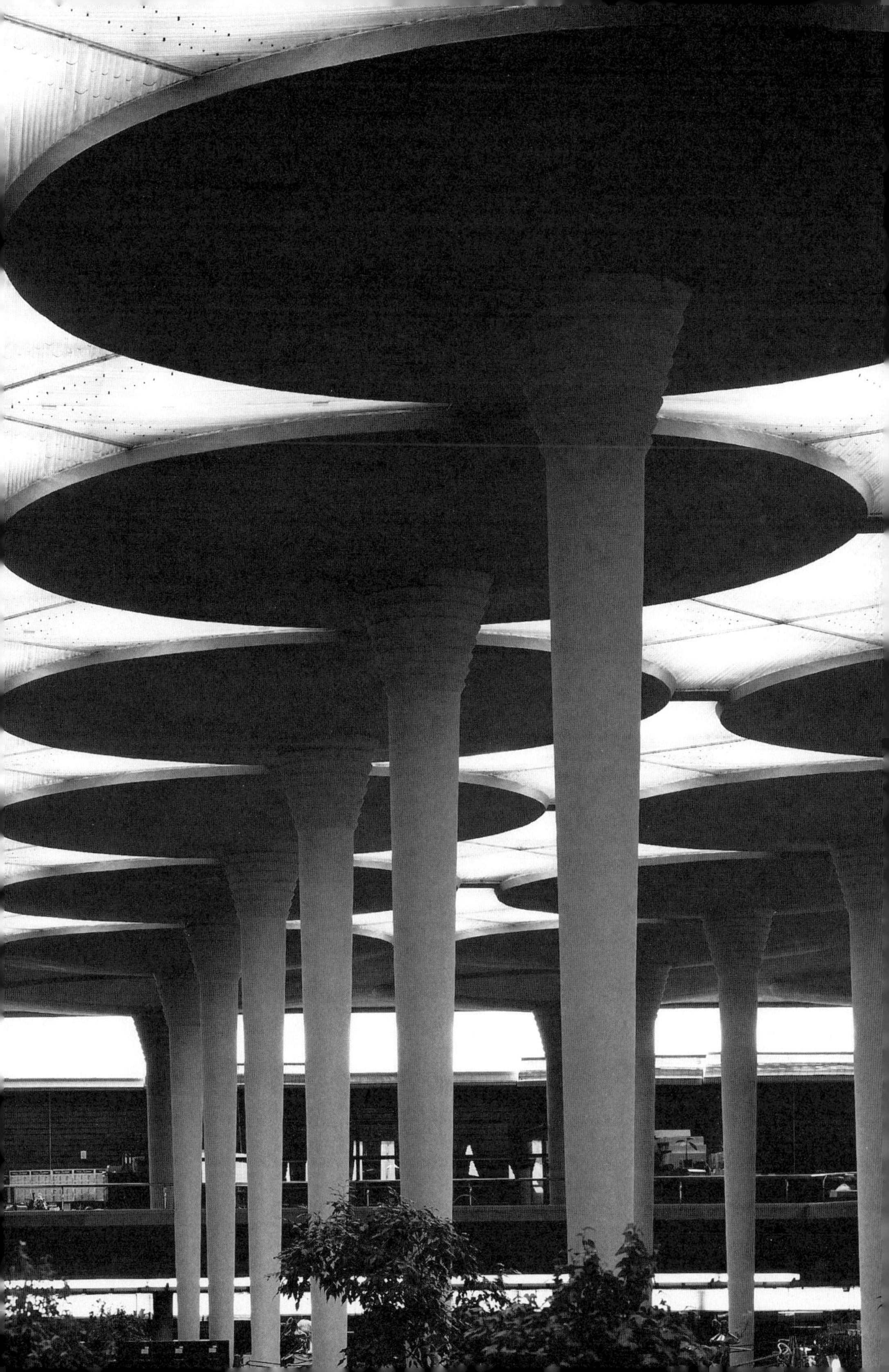

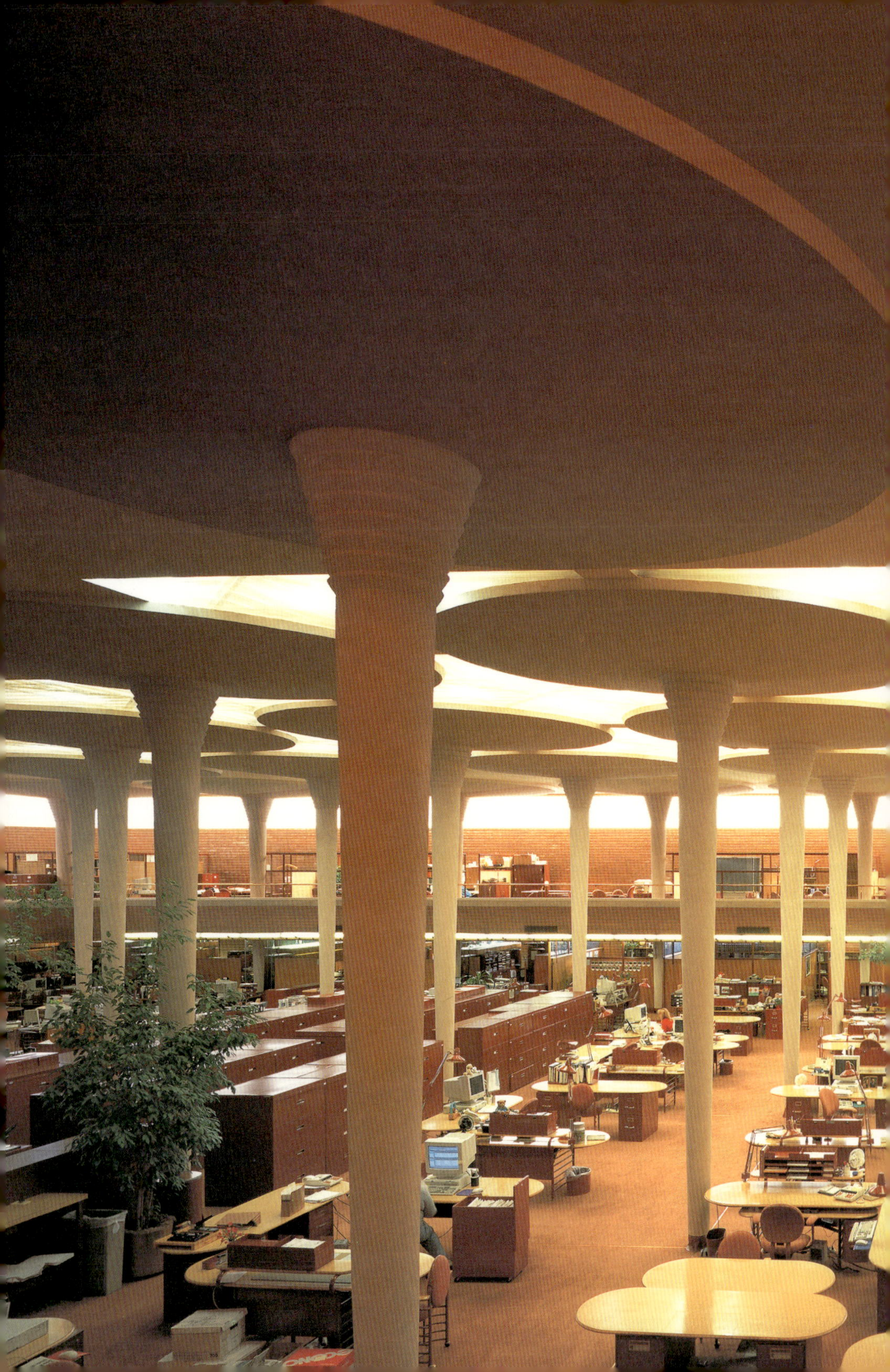

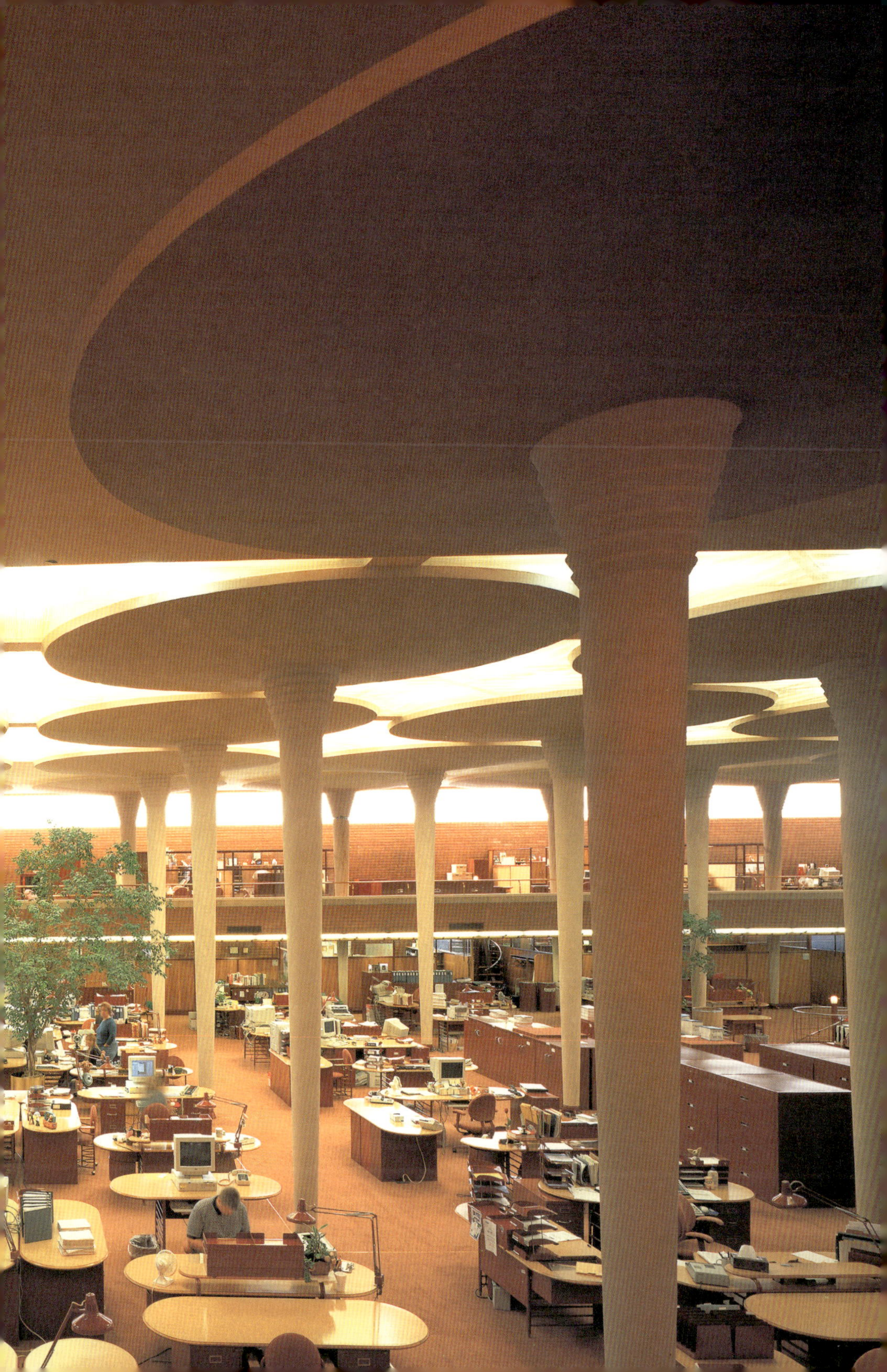

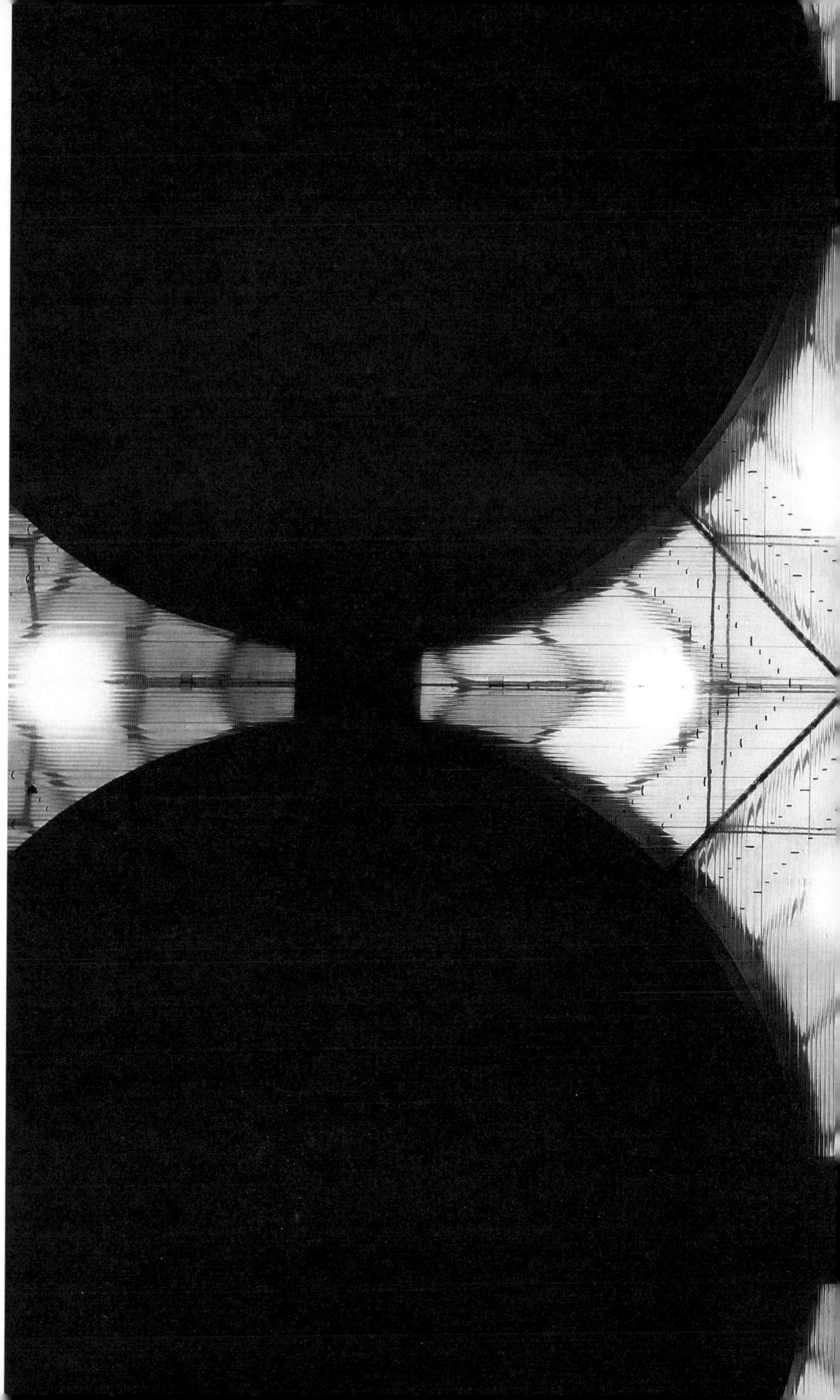

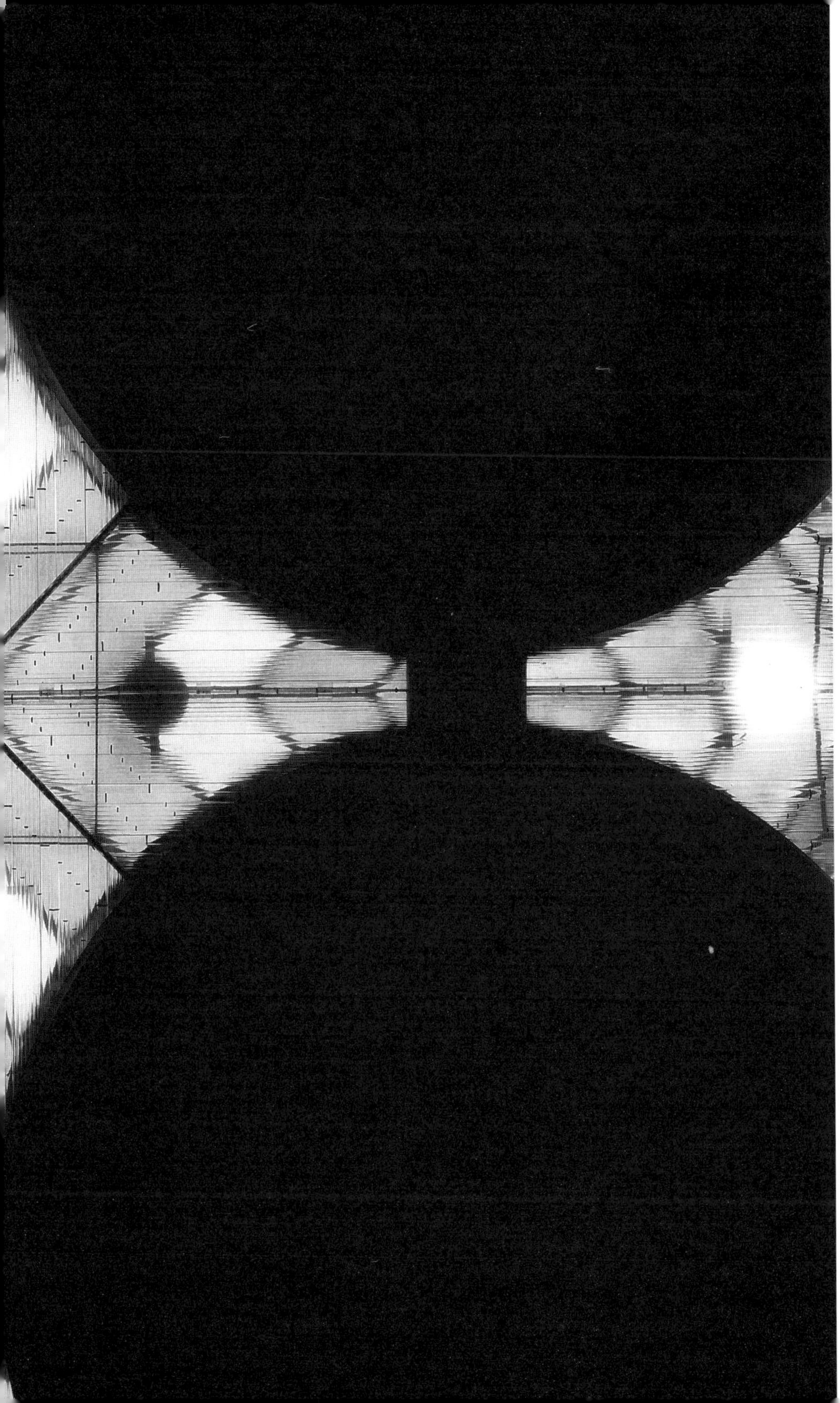

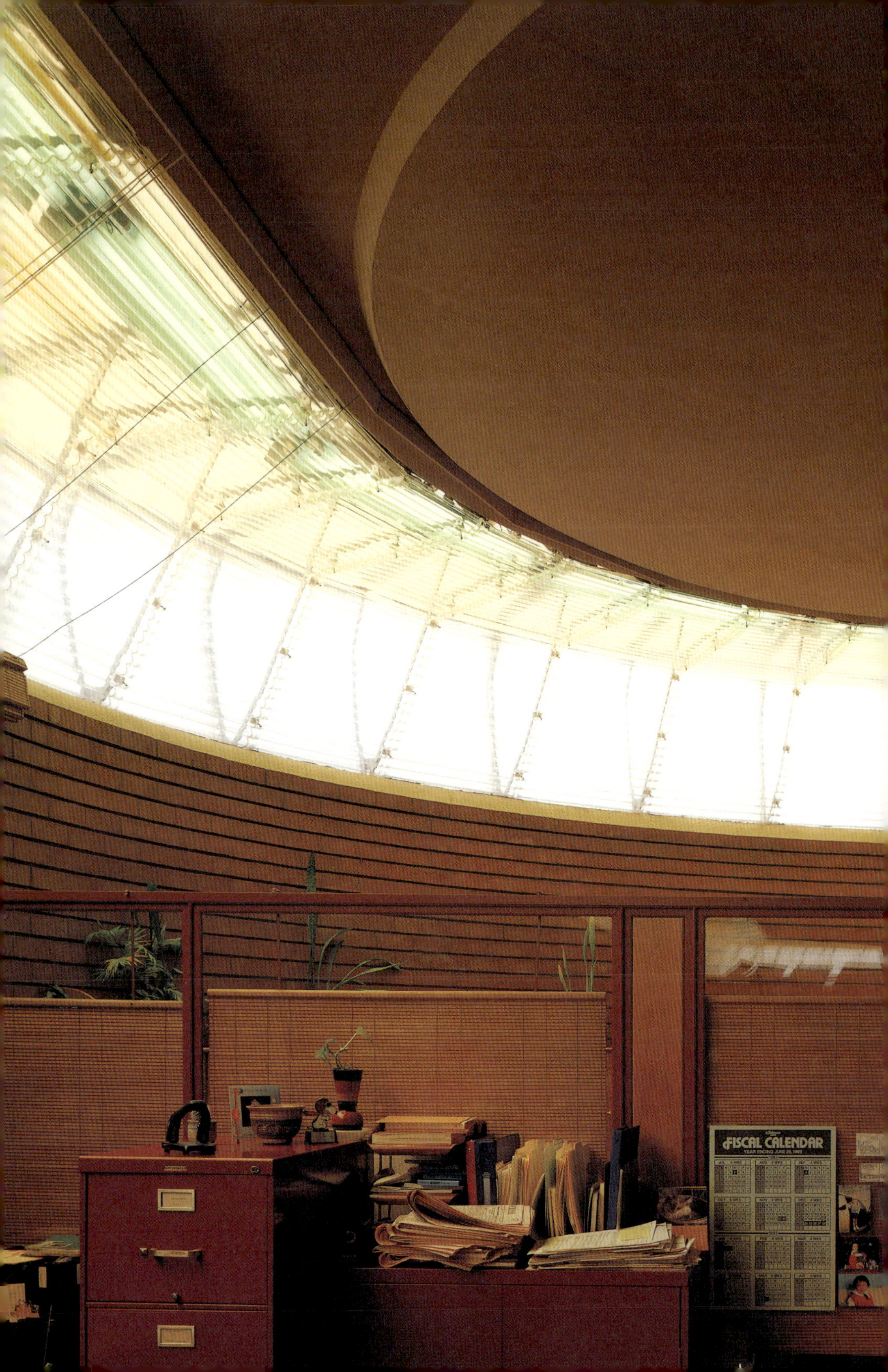
FISCAL CALENDAR

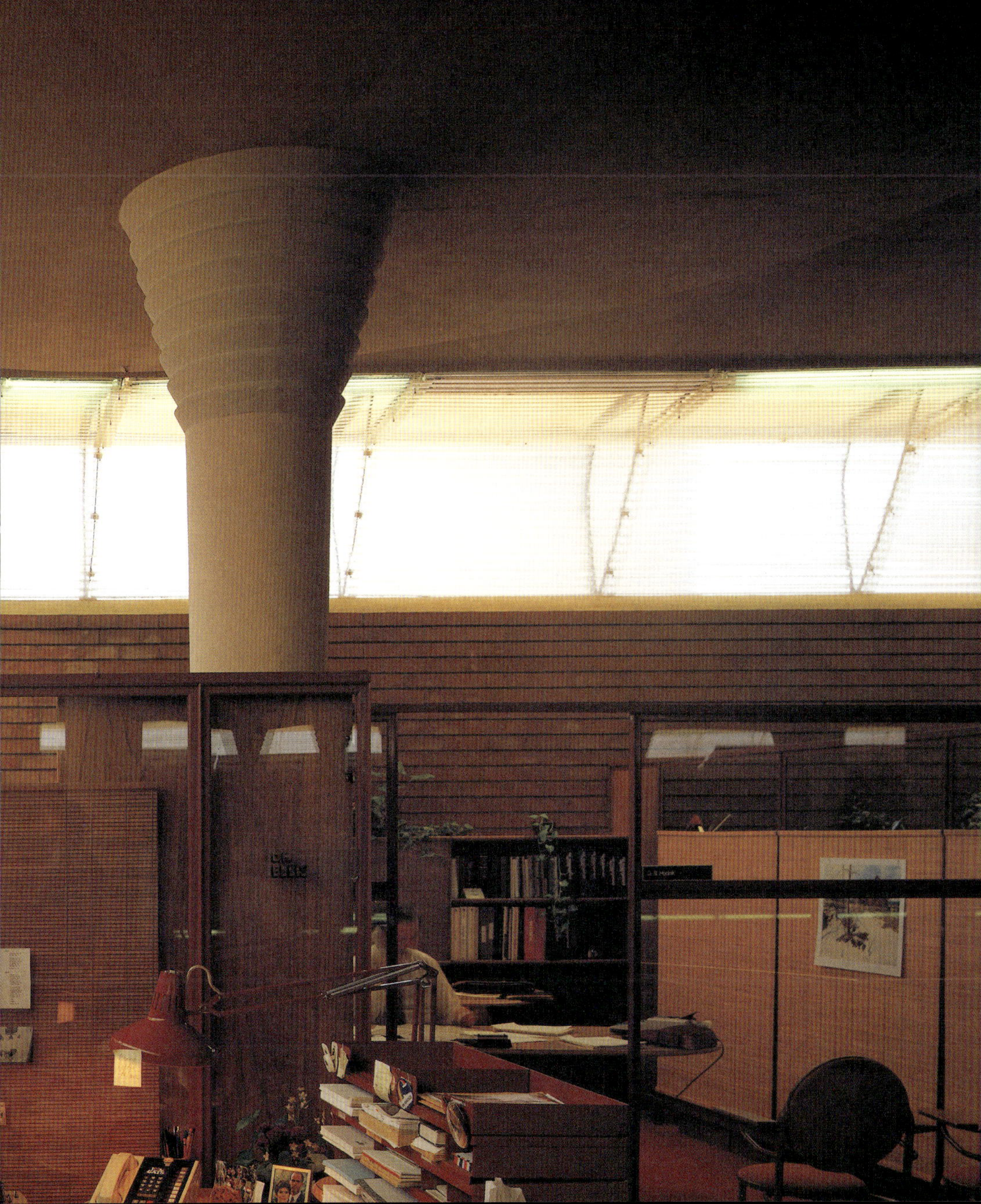

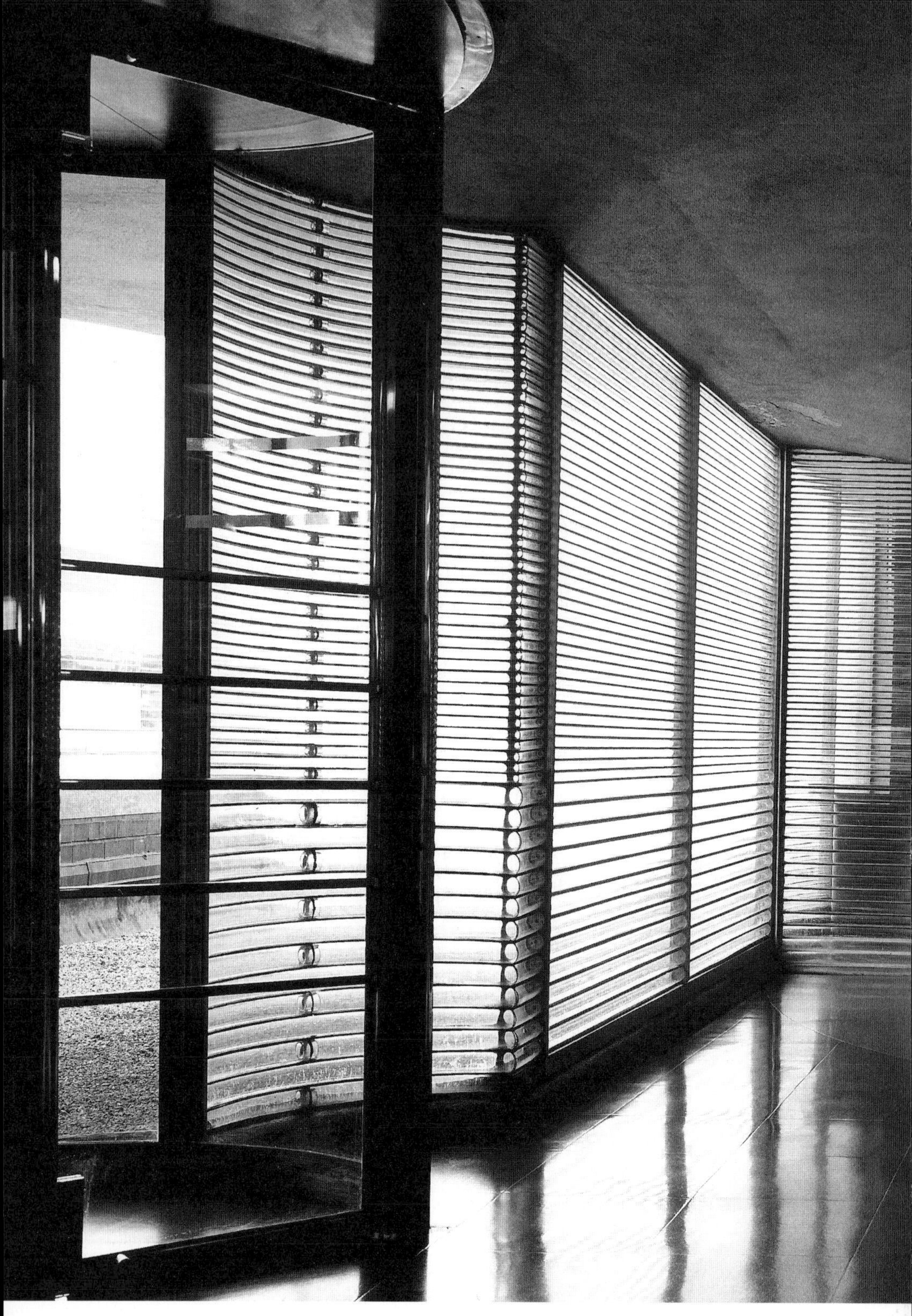

RECREATION
Invest in the future of America
WANTED Carpenter ANTS

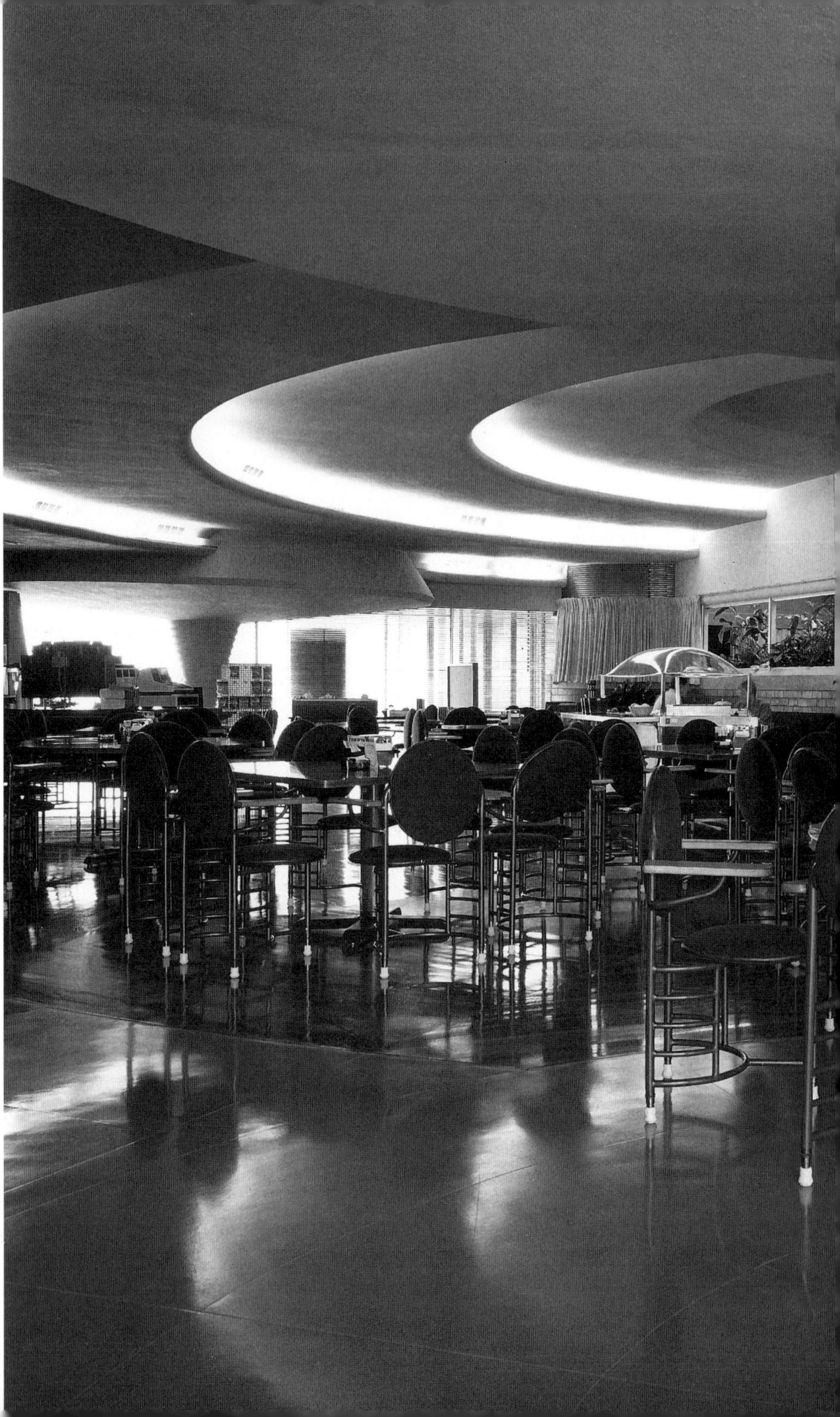

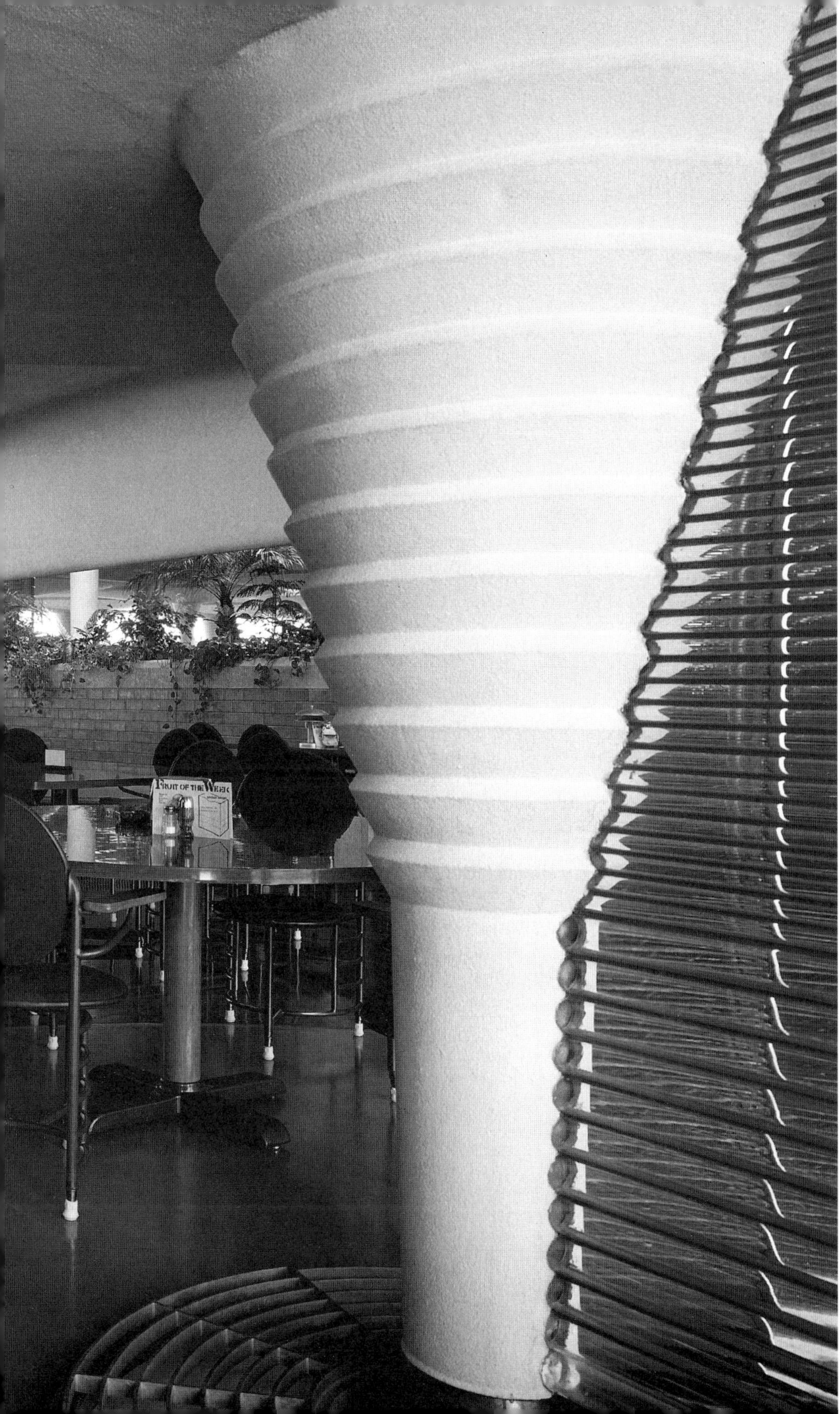
FRUIT OF THE WEEK

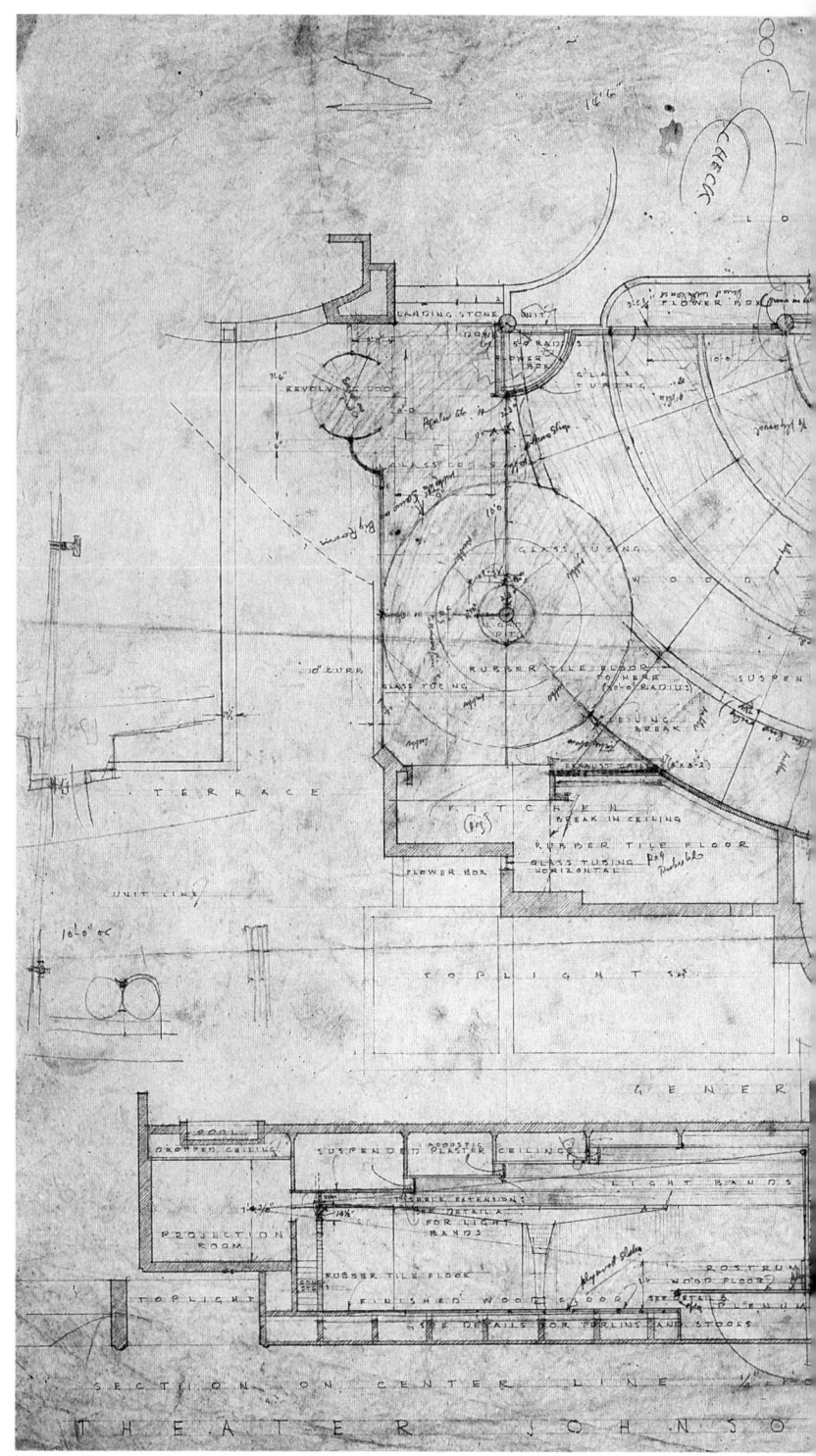

Theater: plan and sections

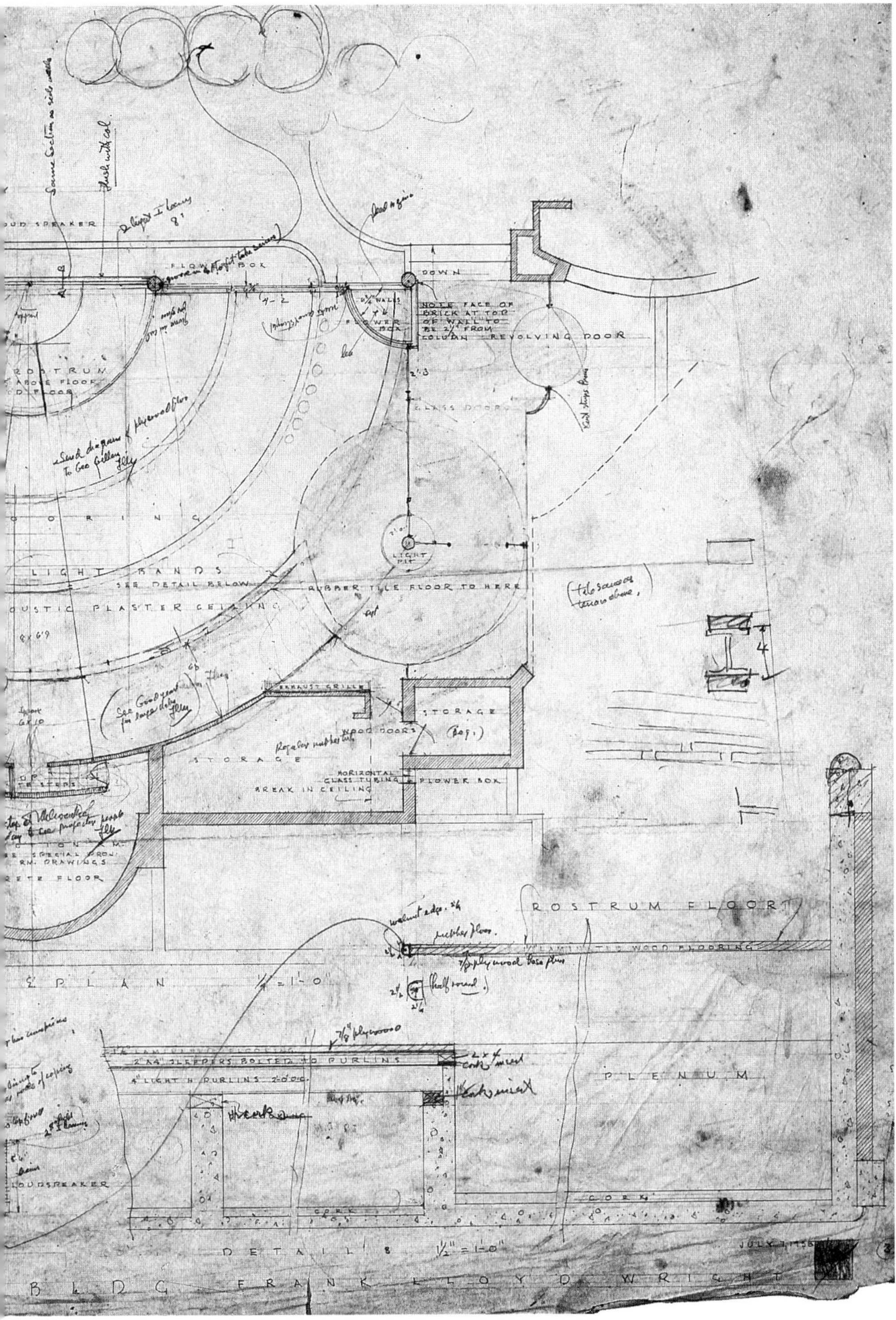

NOTE FACE OF BRICK AT TOP OF WALL TO BE 2¼" FROM COLUMN
DOWN
REVOLVING DOOR
GLASS DOORS
FLOWER BOX
LIGHT PIT
LIGHT BANDS
SEE DETAIL BELOW
RUBBER TILE FLOOR TO HERE
EXHAUST GRILLE
STORAGE
WOOD DOORS
HORIZONTAL GLASS TUBING
FLOWER BOX
BREAK IN CEILING
ROSTRUM FLOOR
LAMINATED WOOD FLOORING
PLAN 1/4" = 1'-0"
2" X 4" SLEEPERS BOLTED TO PURLINS
PLENUM
CORK
LOUDSPEAKER
DETAIL 8 1½" = 1'-0"
FRANK LLOYD WRIGHT

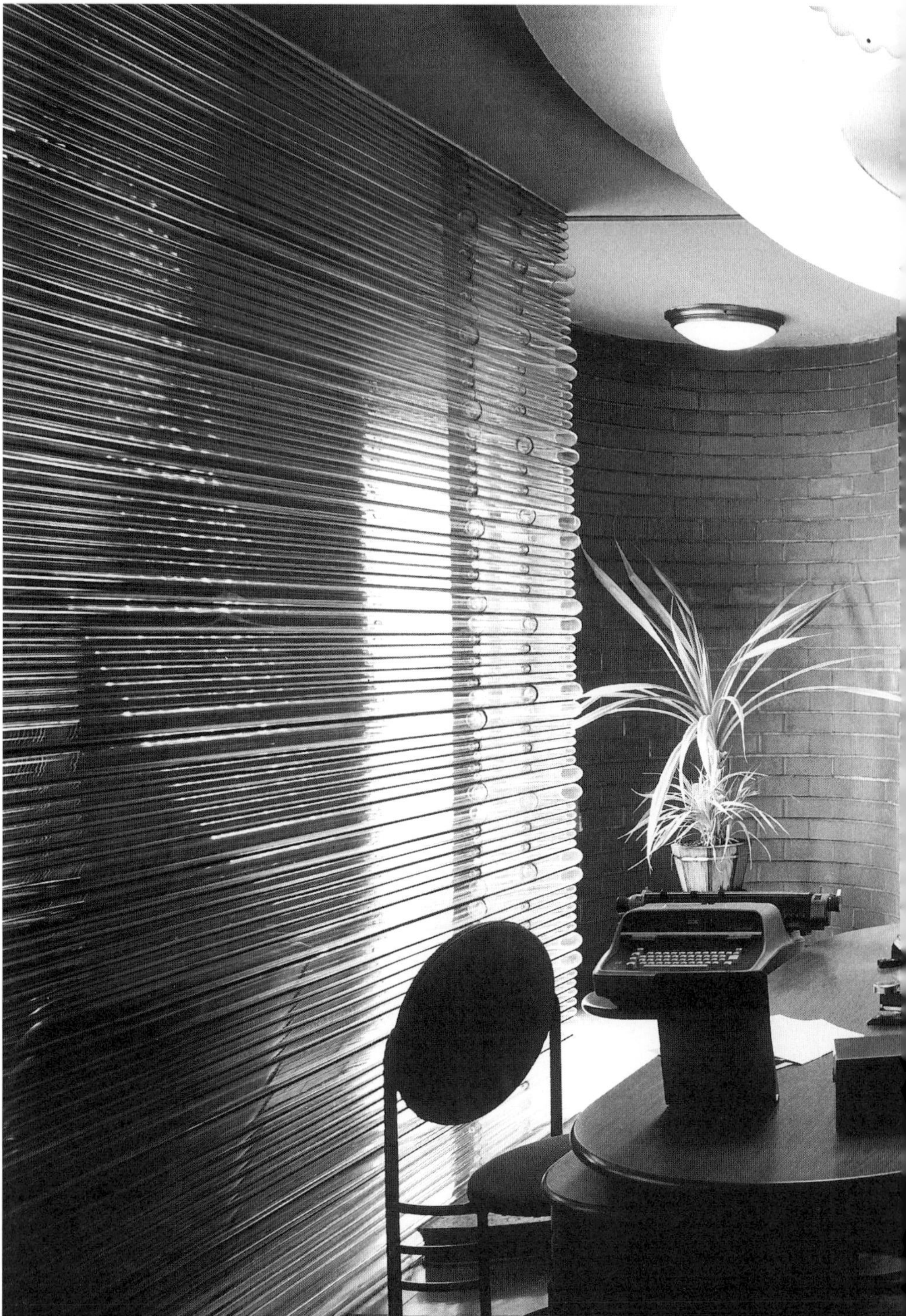

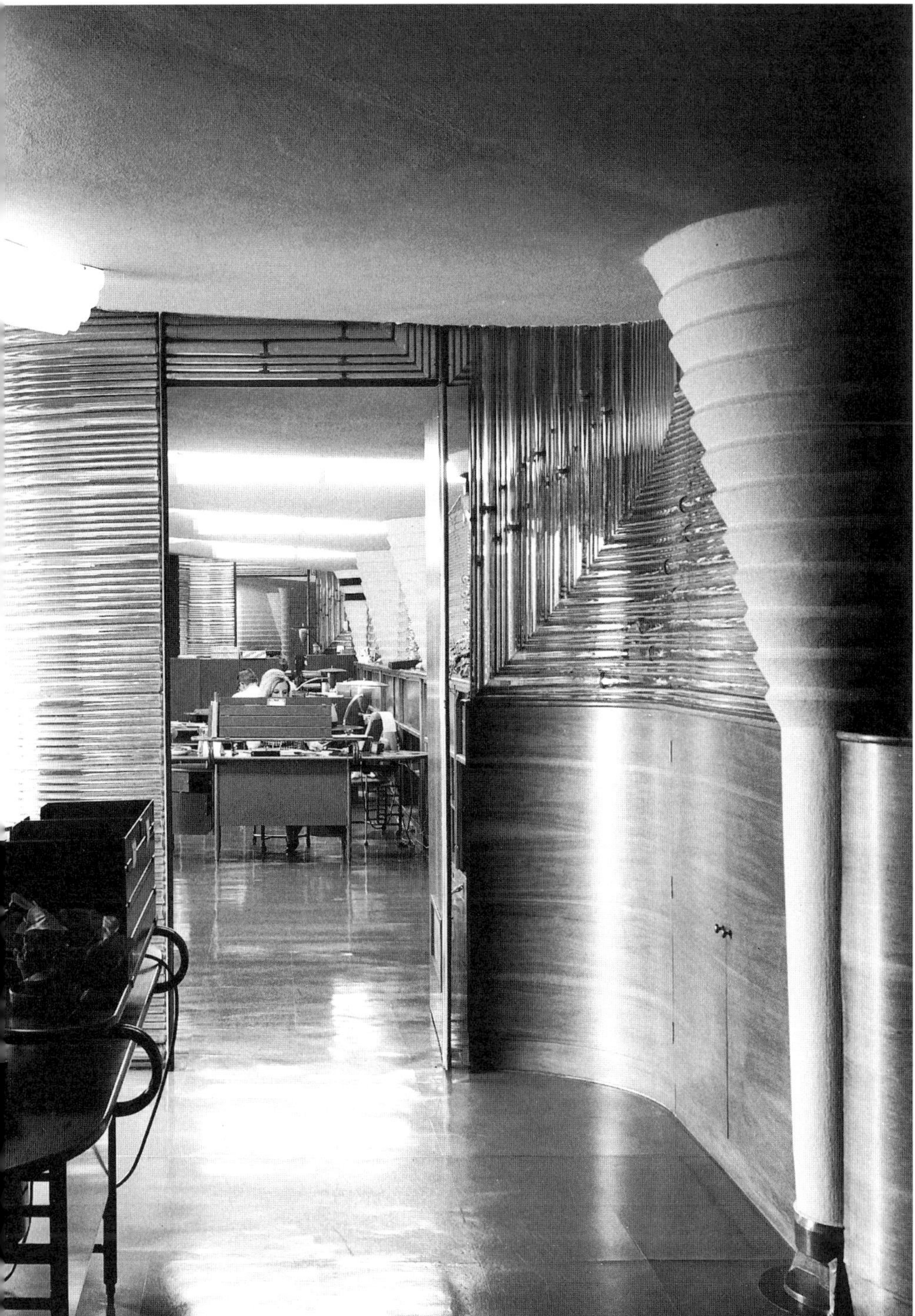

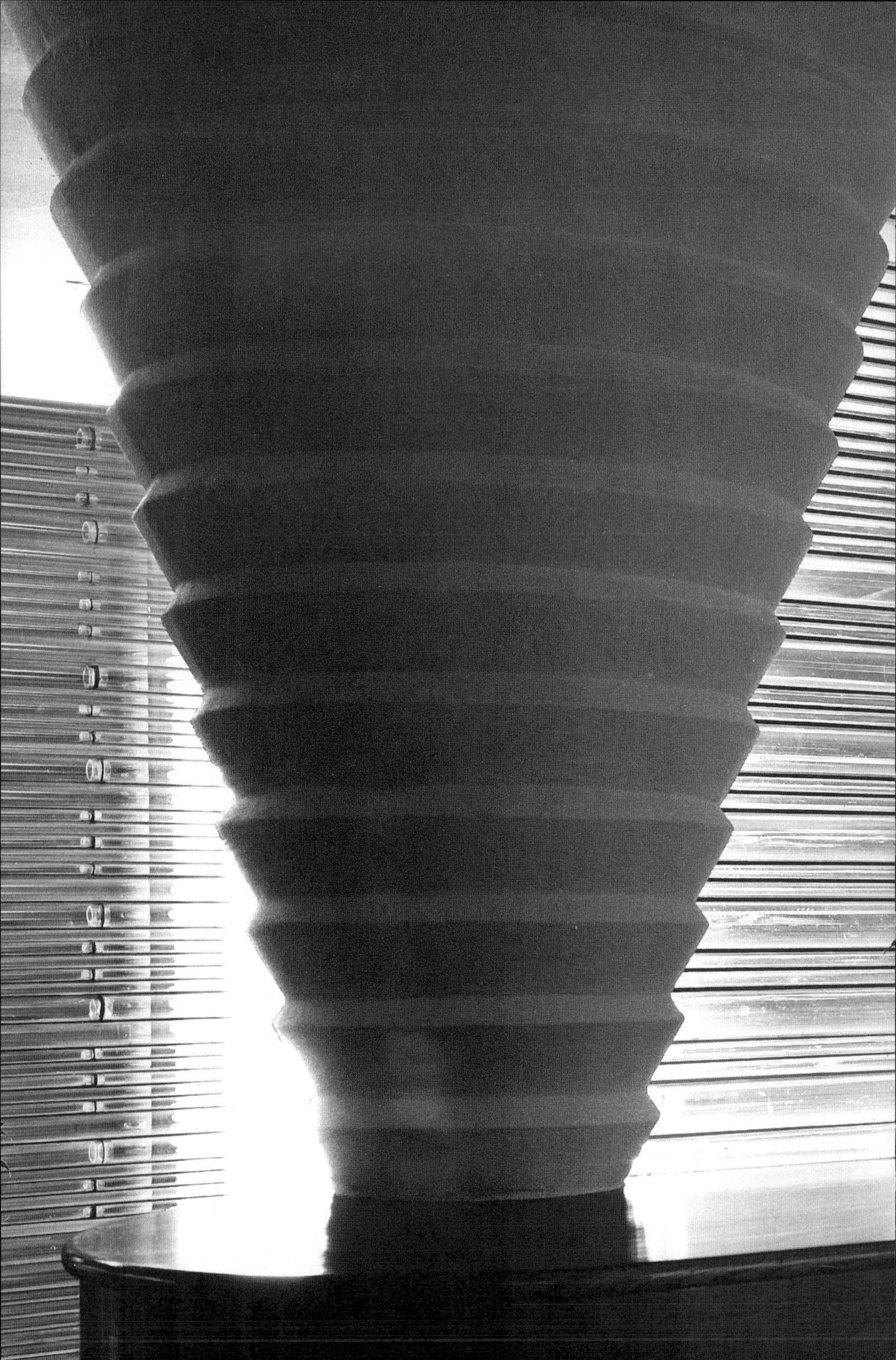

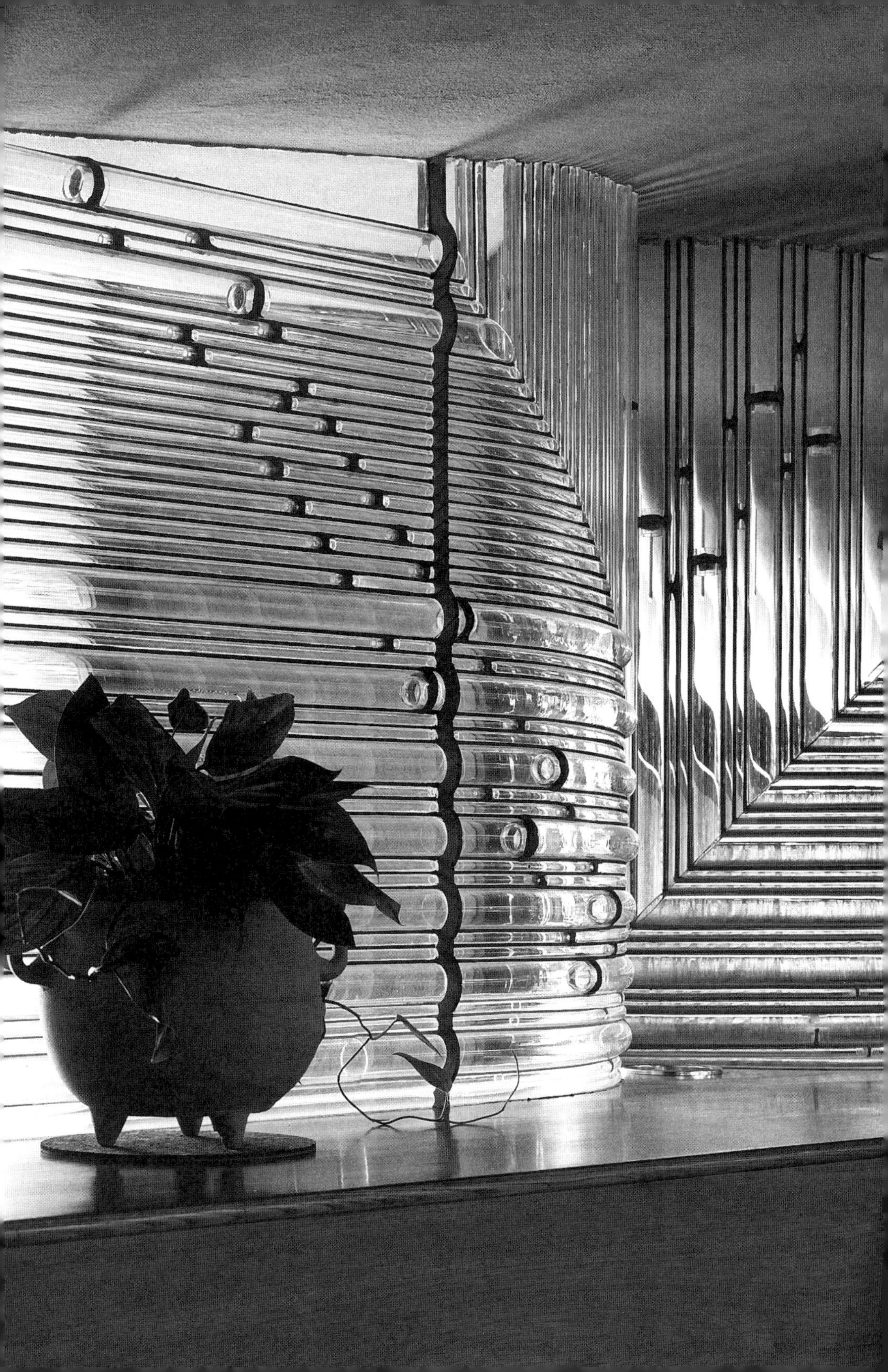

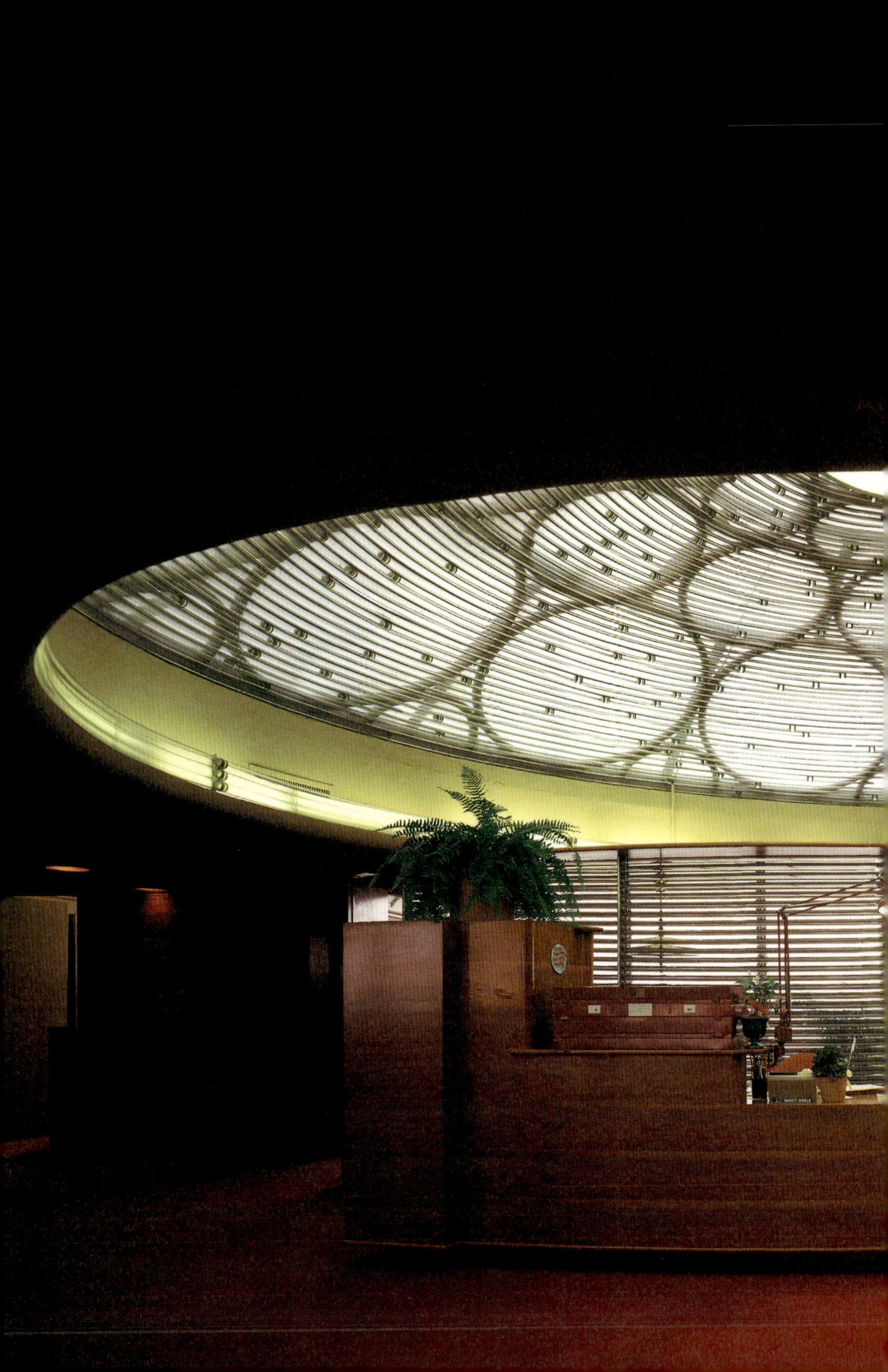

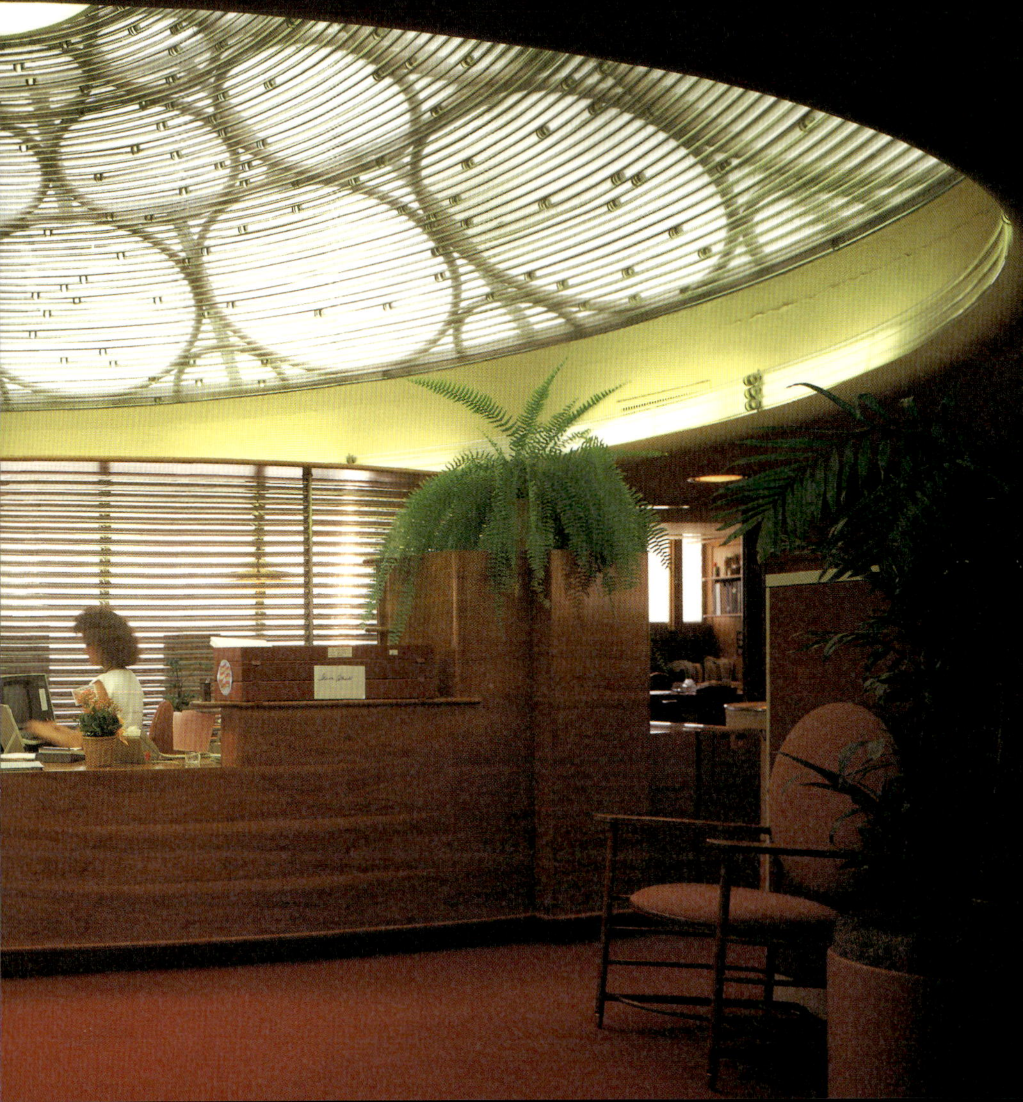

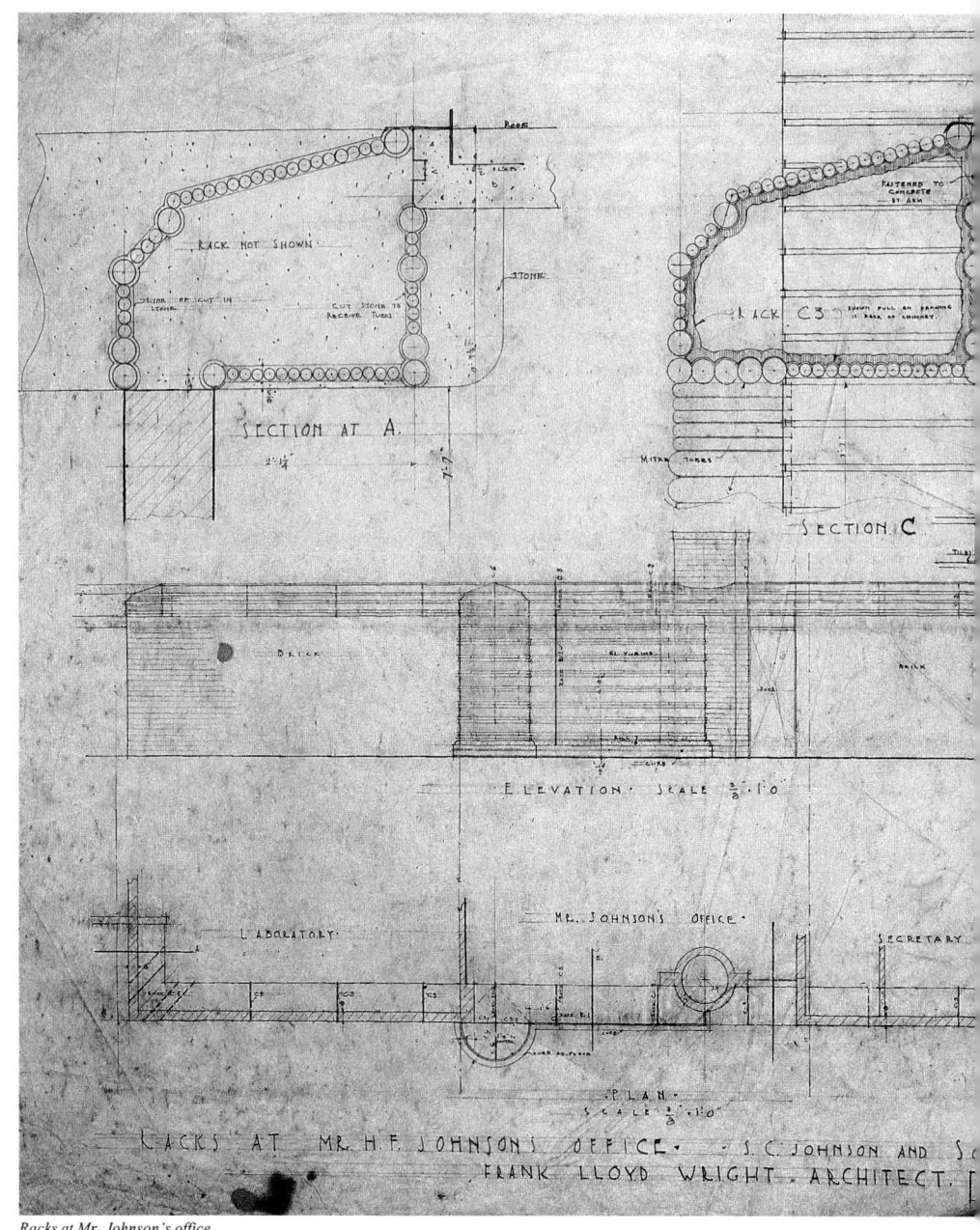

Racks at Mr. Johnson's office

SECTION B

SECTION D.

SCALE OF LARGE SECTION
3" = 1'-0"

OFFICE BUILDING · RACINE WISCONSIN.
OCT. 6· 1936

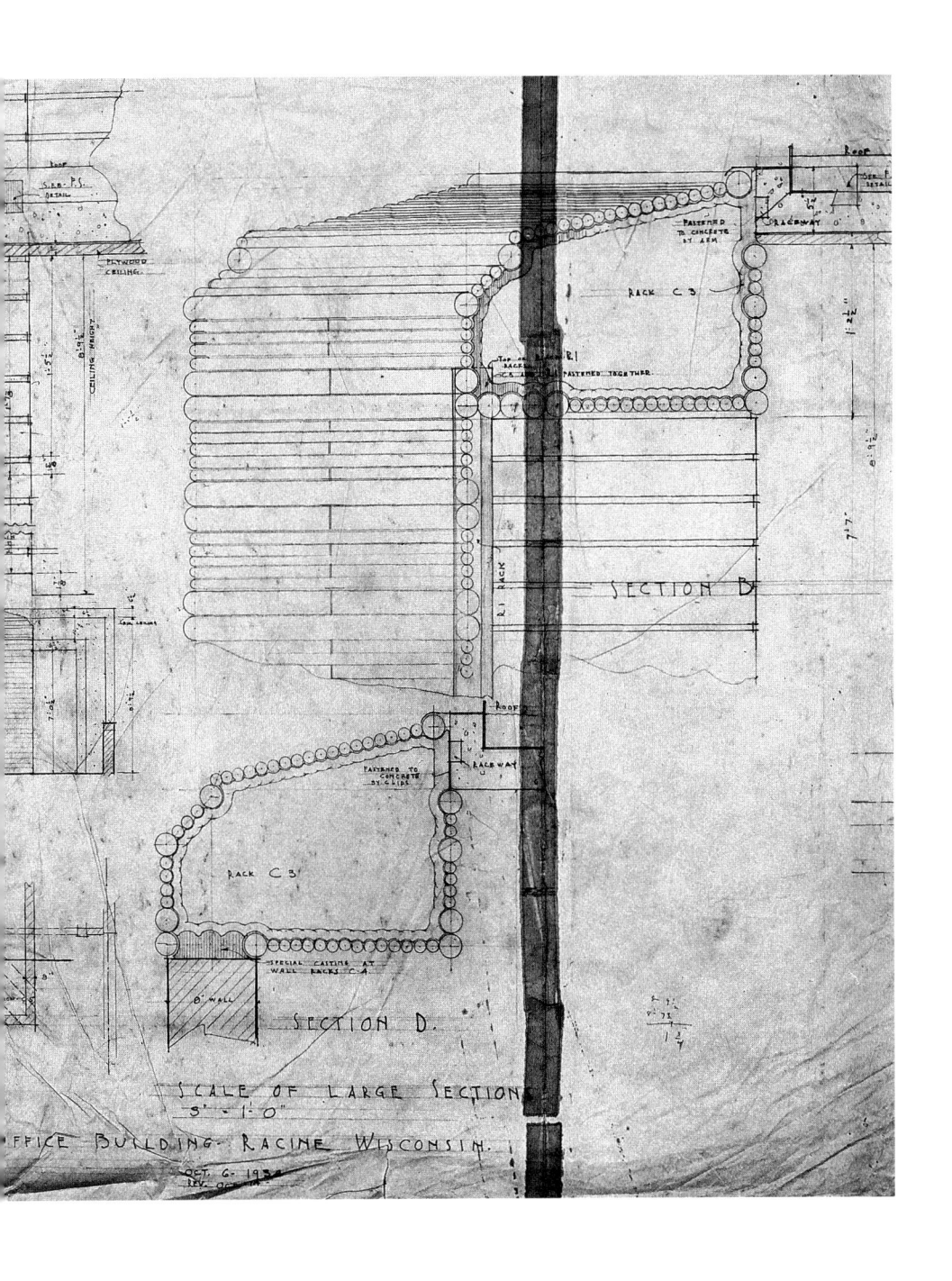

Research Laboratory
for S. C. Johnson & Son Company
Racine, Wisconsin, 1944

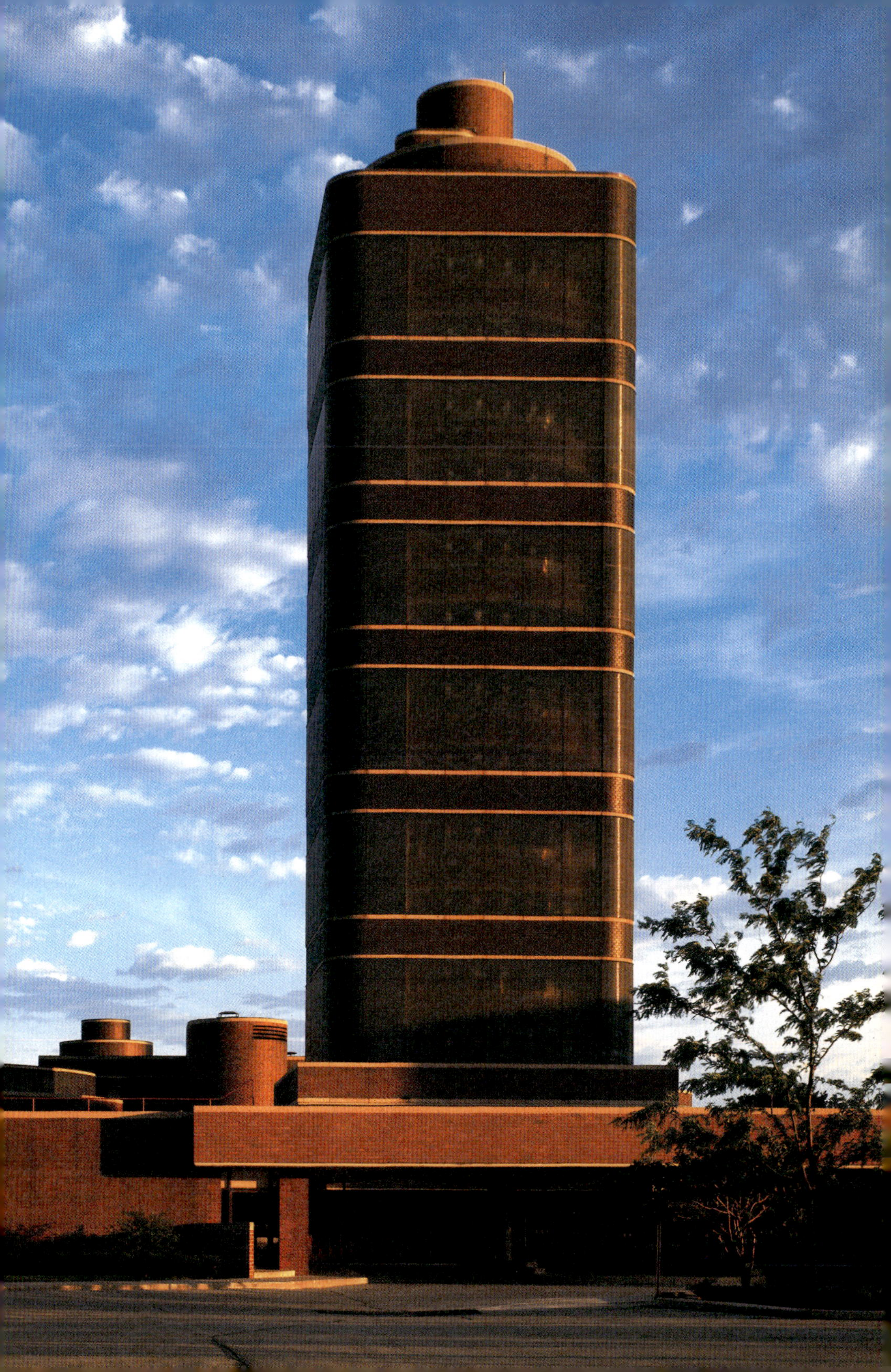

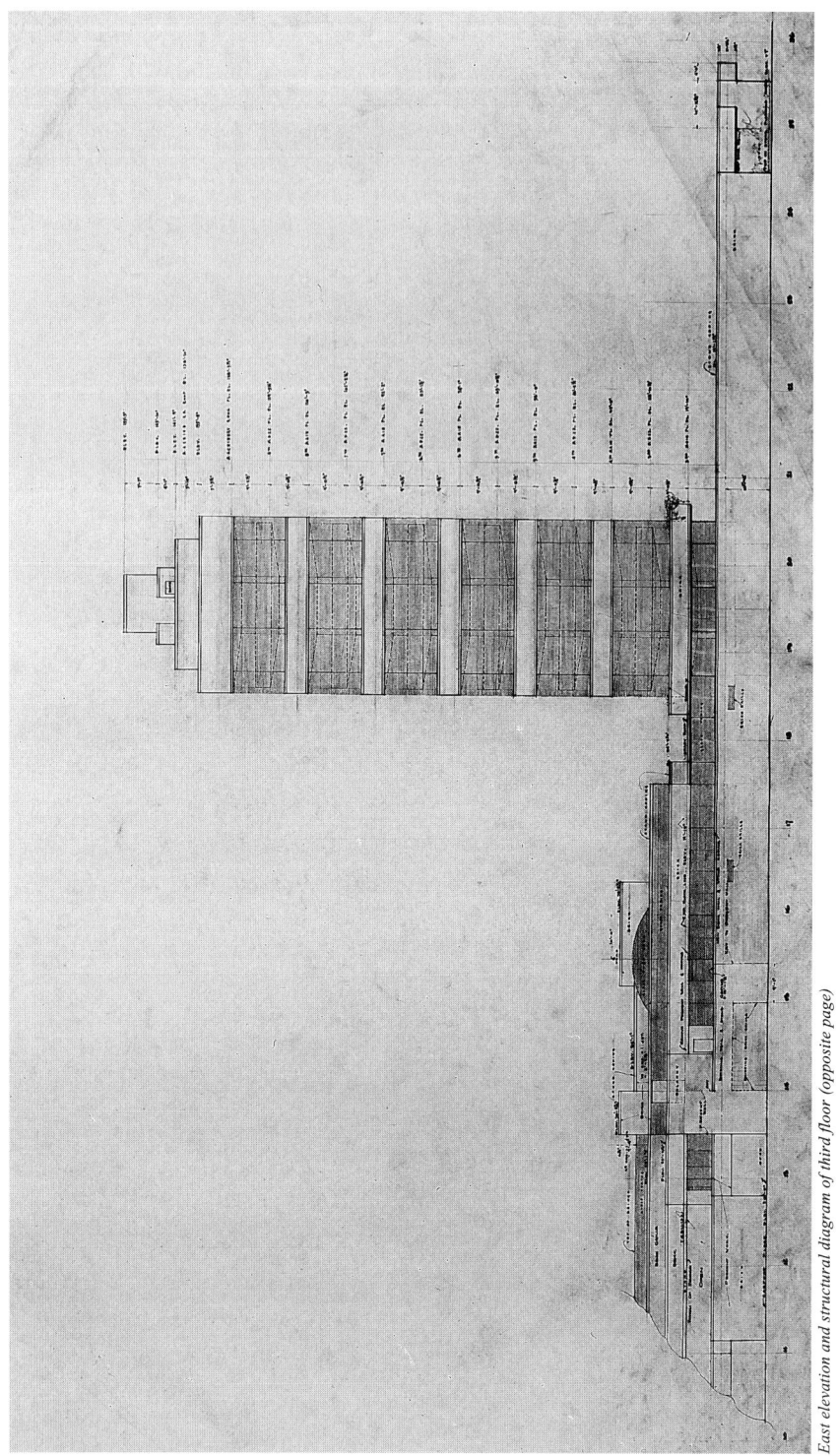

East elevation and structural diagram of third floor (opposite page)

97

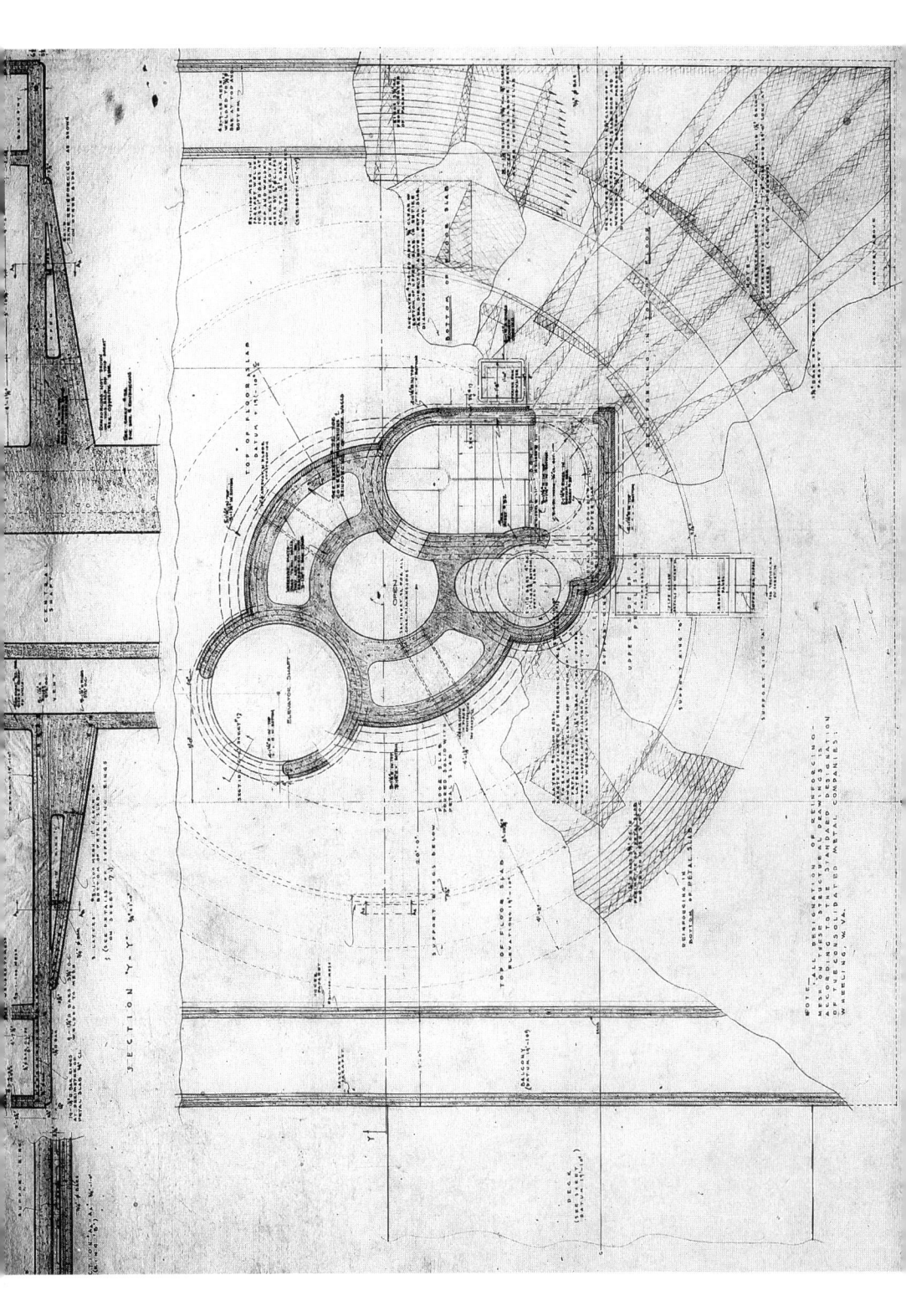

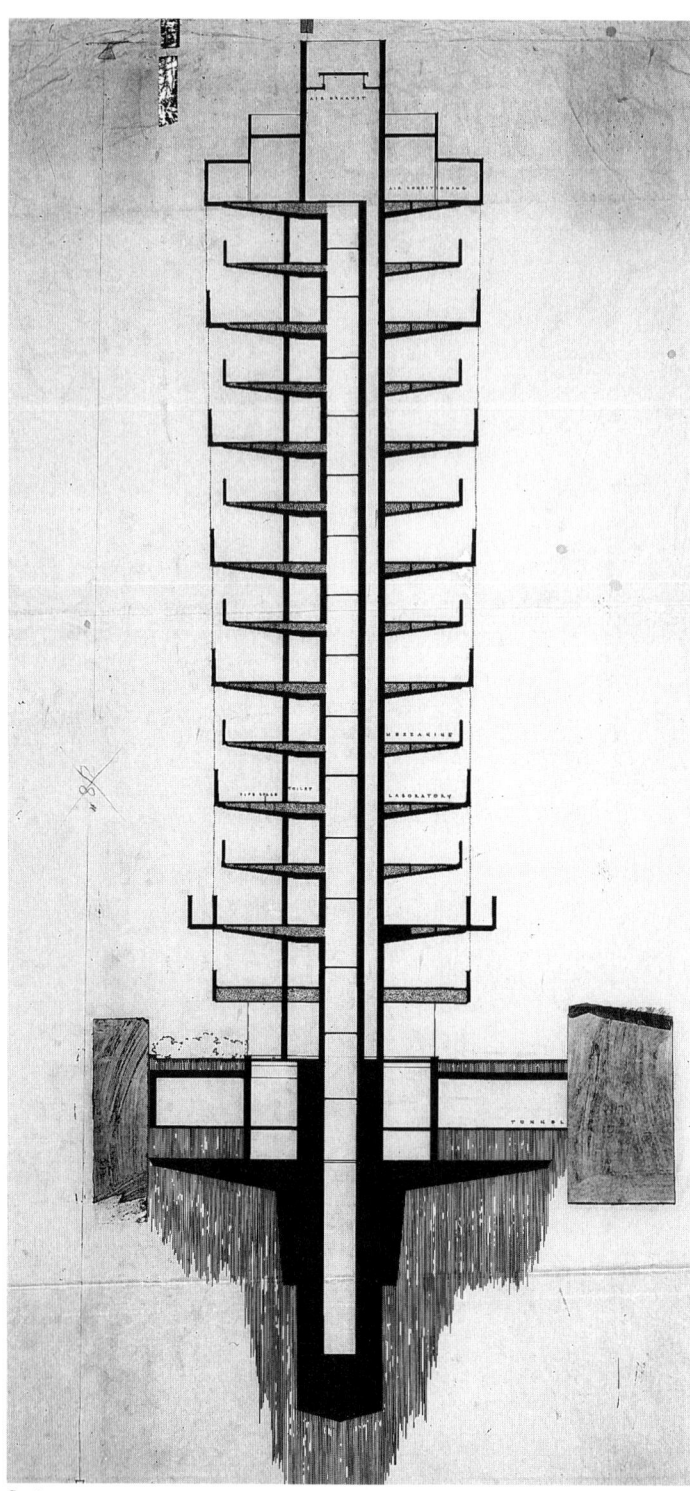

Section

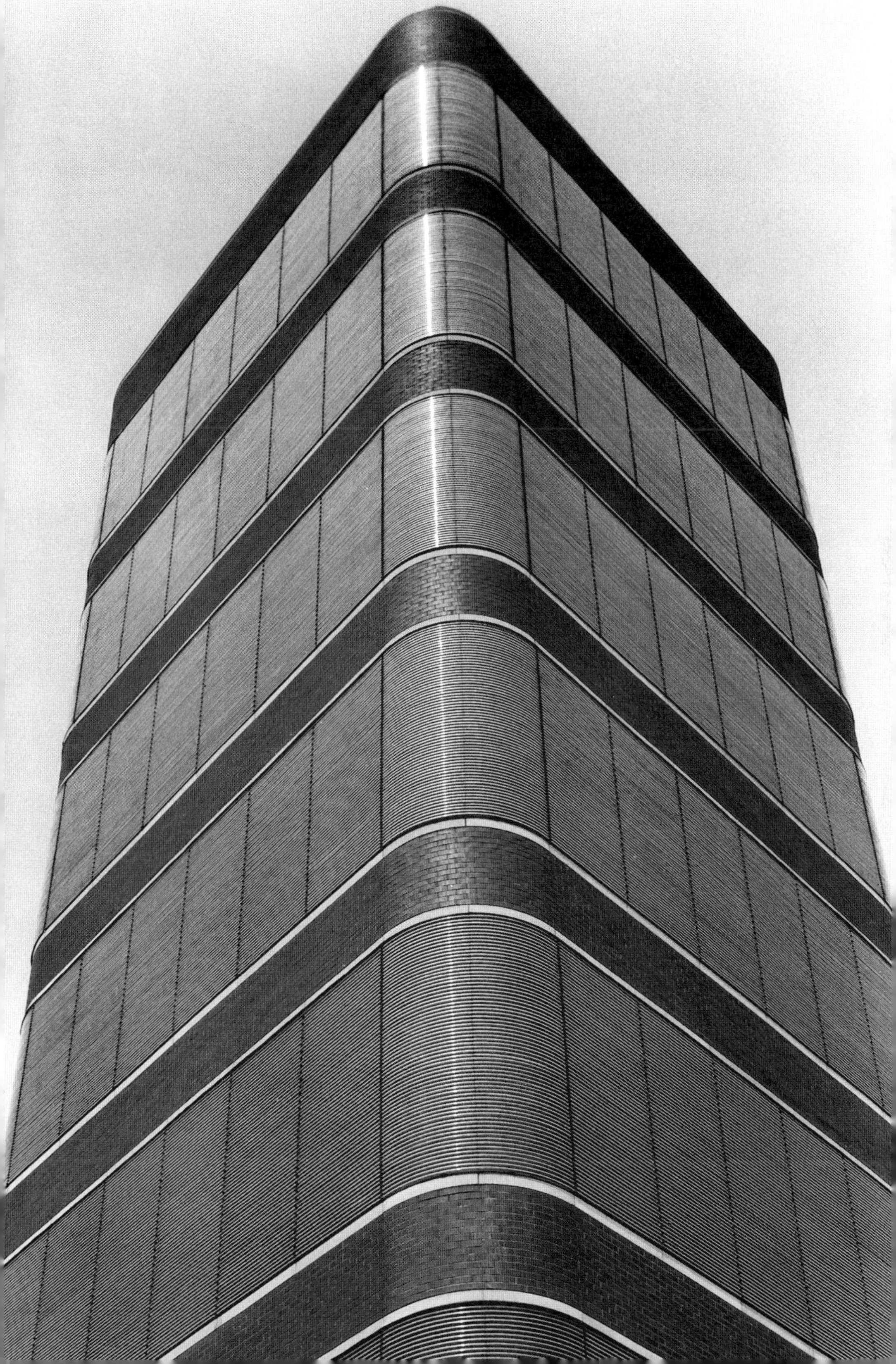

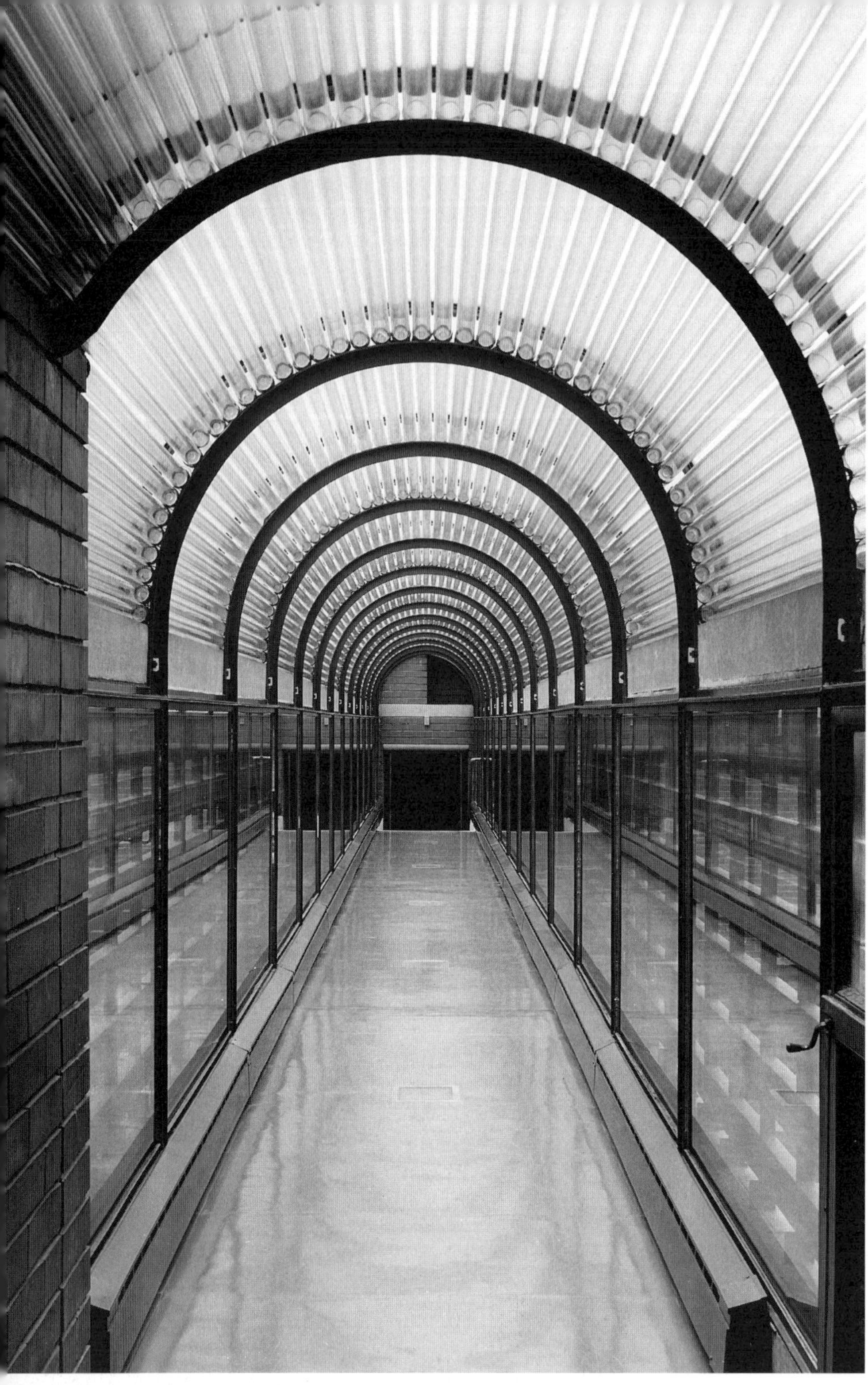

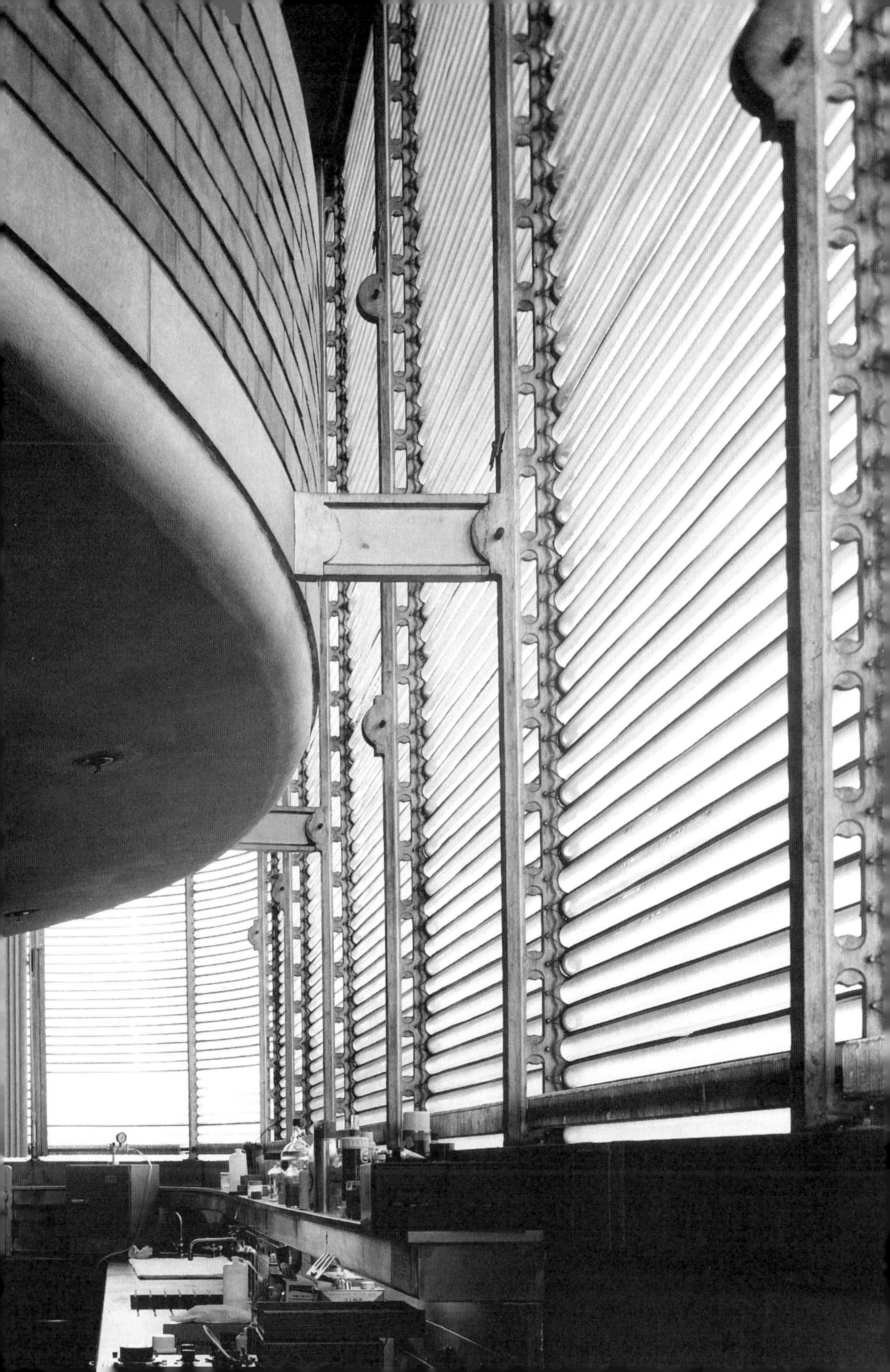

Florida Southern College
Lakeland, Florida, 1938

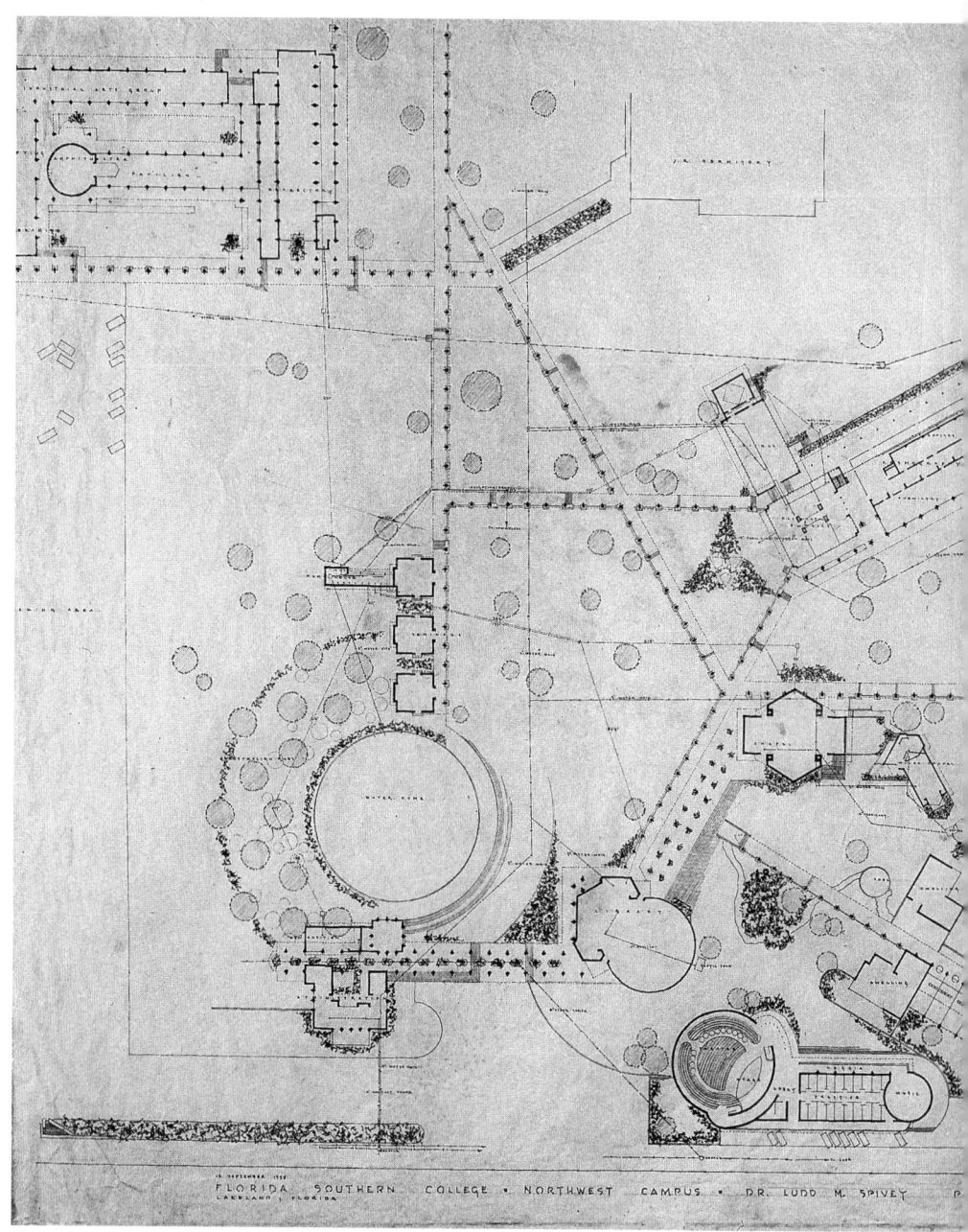

Master plan

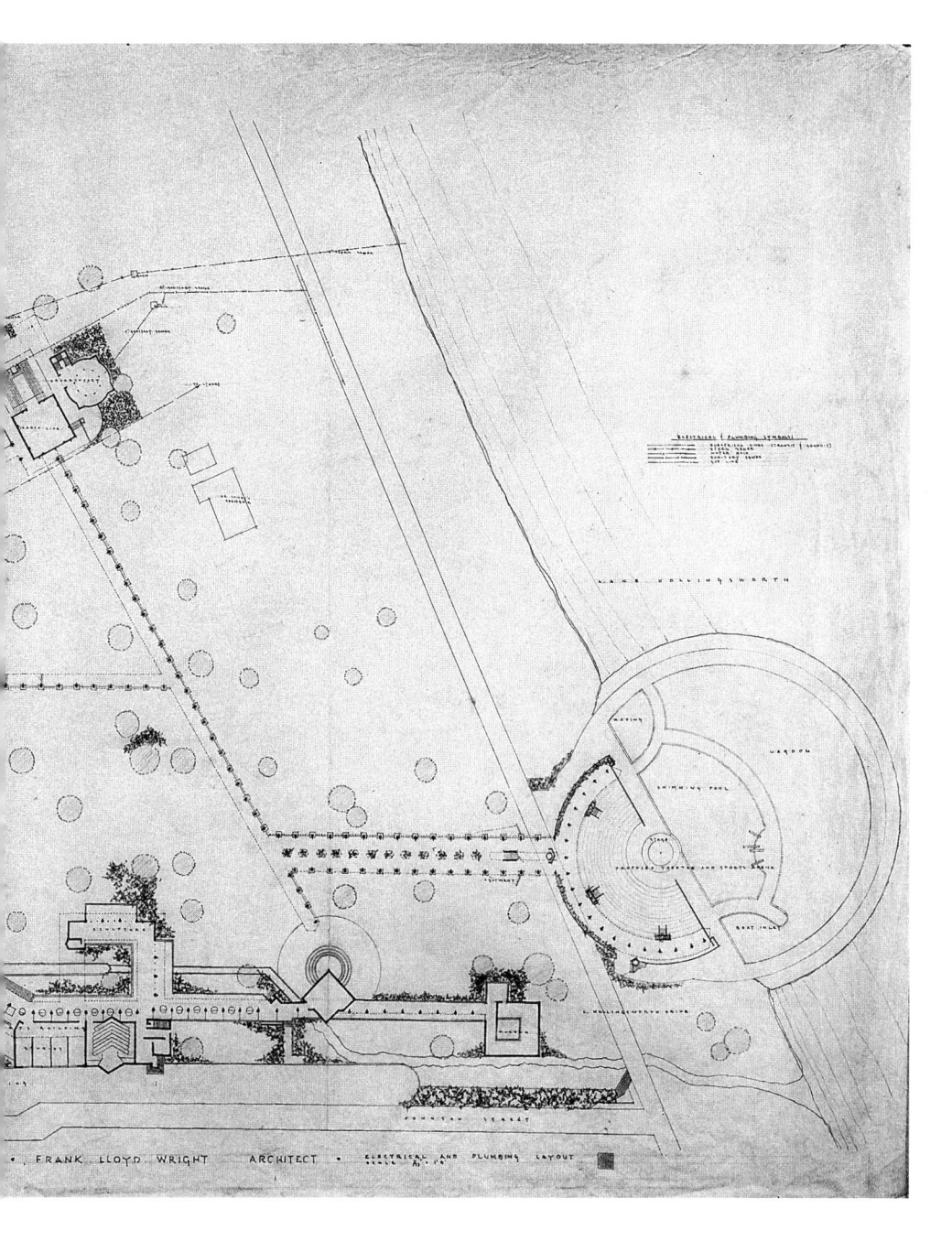

FRANK LLOYD WRIGHT ARCHITECT · ELECTRICAL AND PLUMBING LAYOUT

Three Seminar Buildings,
Florida Southern College, Lakeland, Florida, 1940

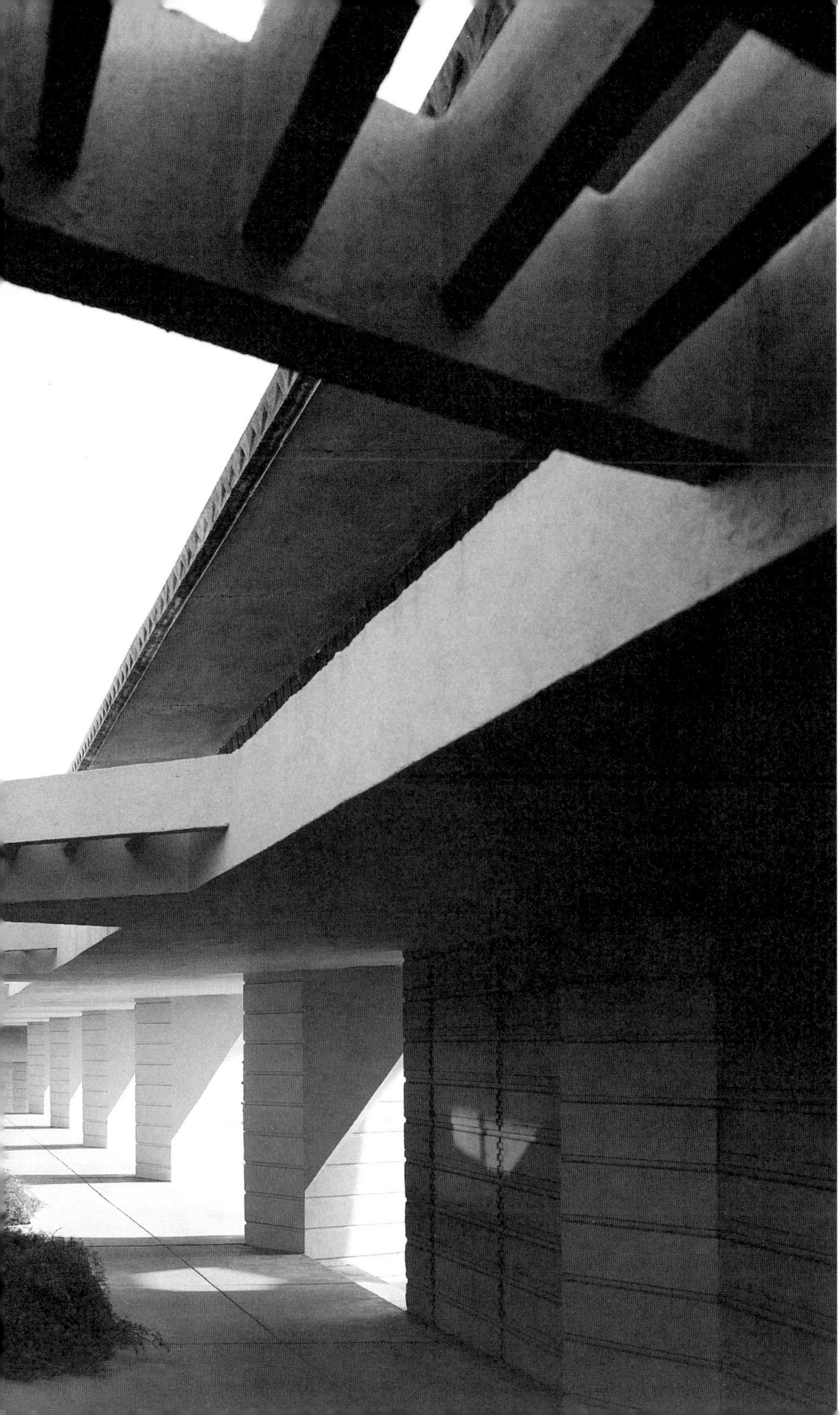

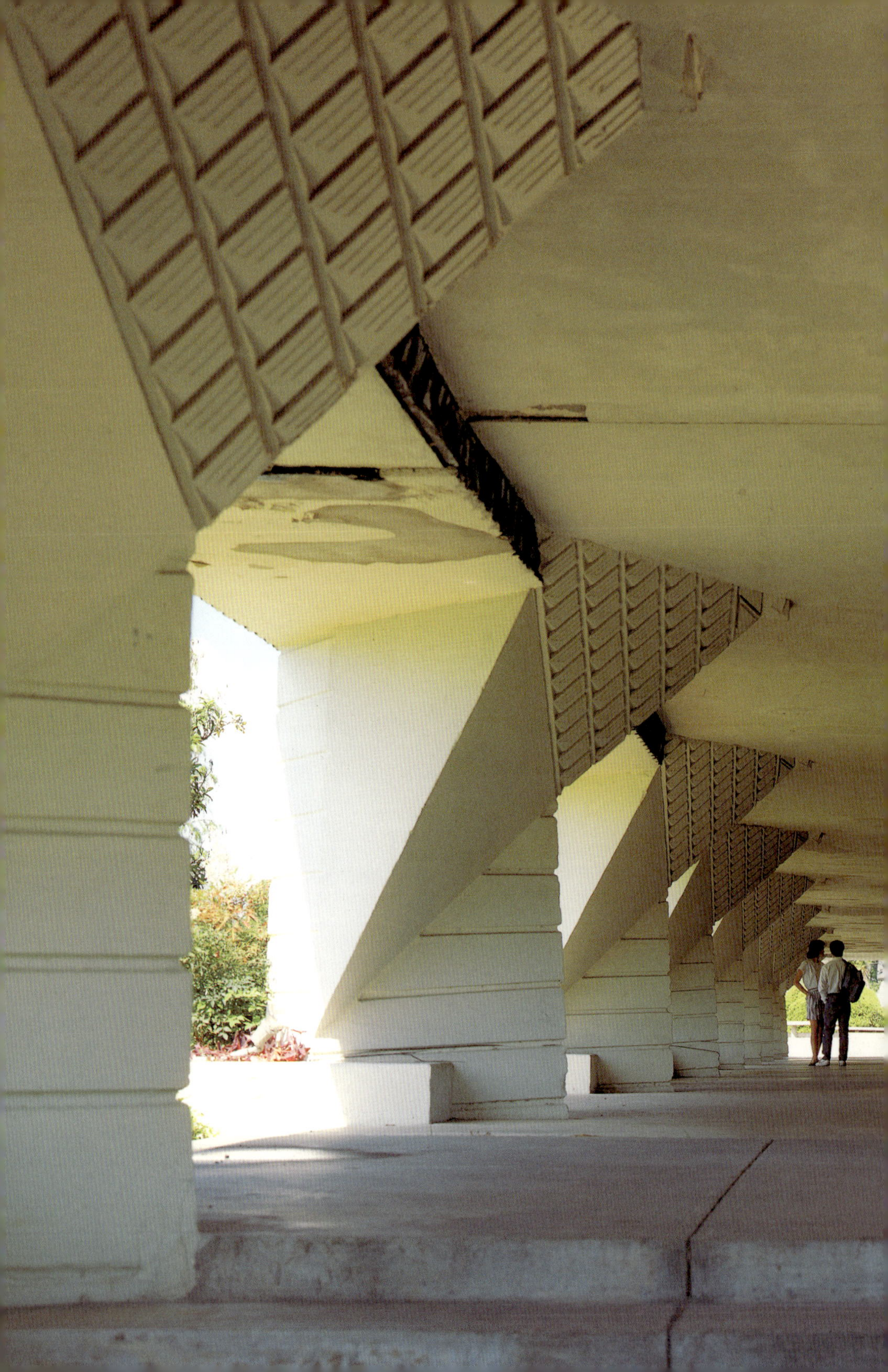

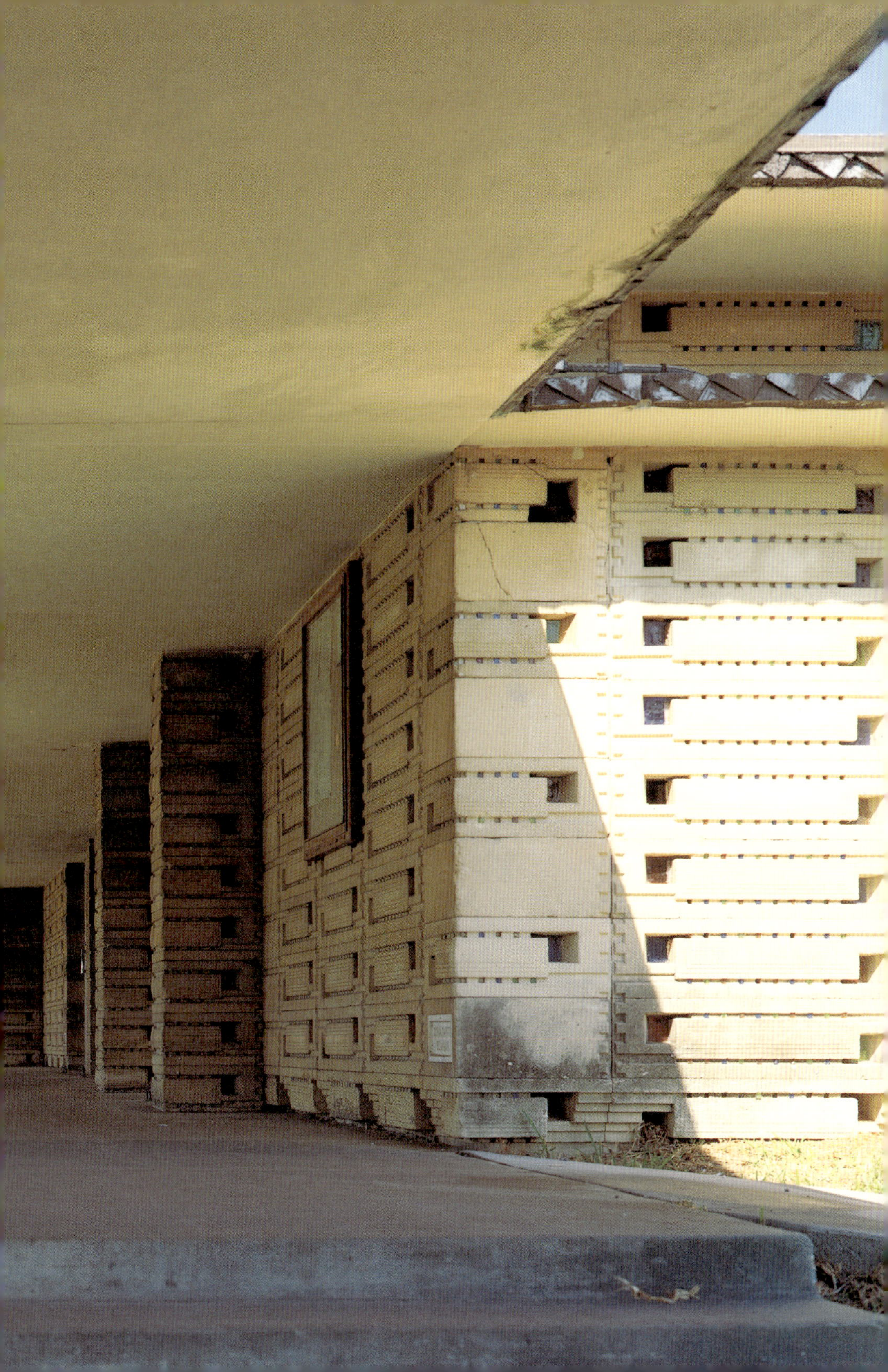

West elevation

Plan

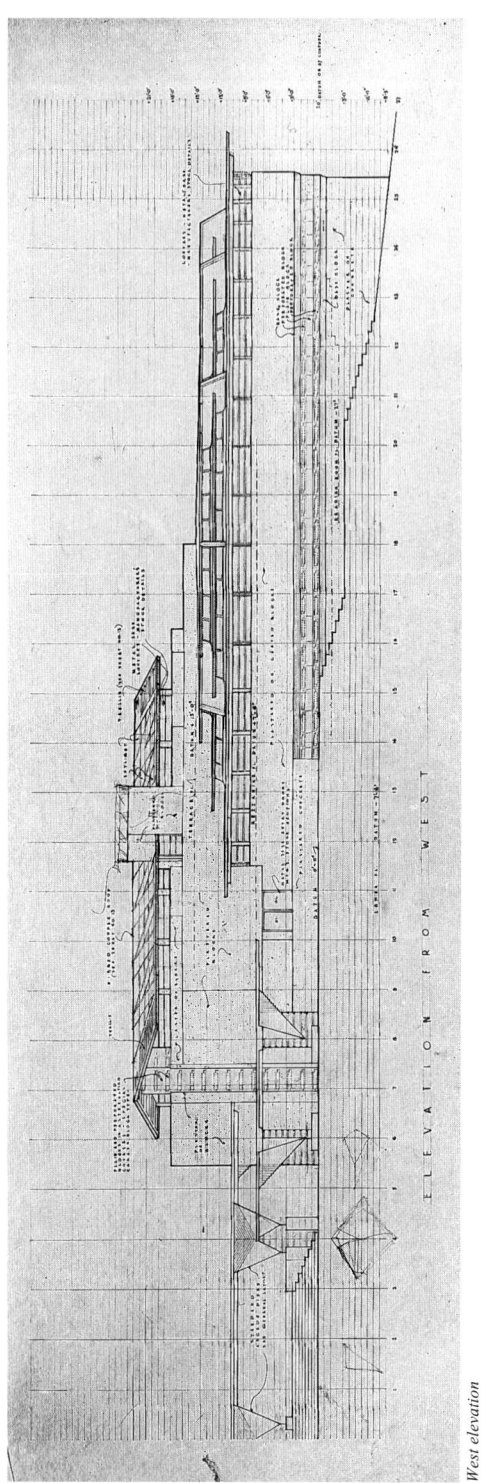

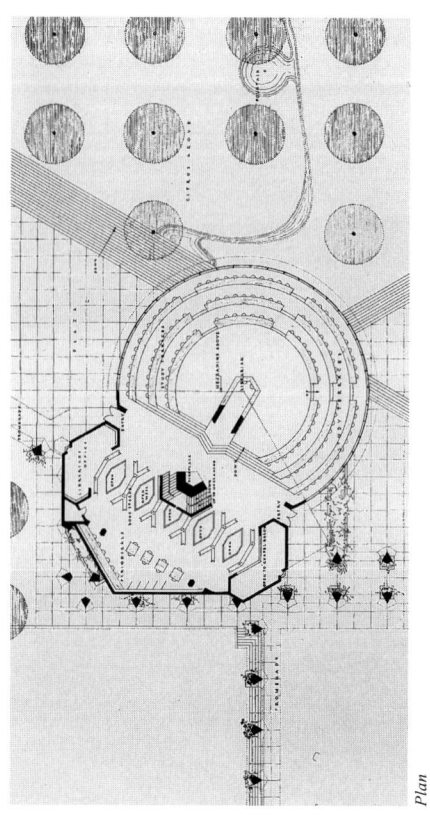

Roux Library,
Florida Southern College,
Lakeland, Florida, 1941

East elevation

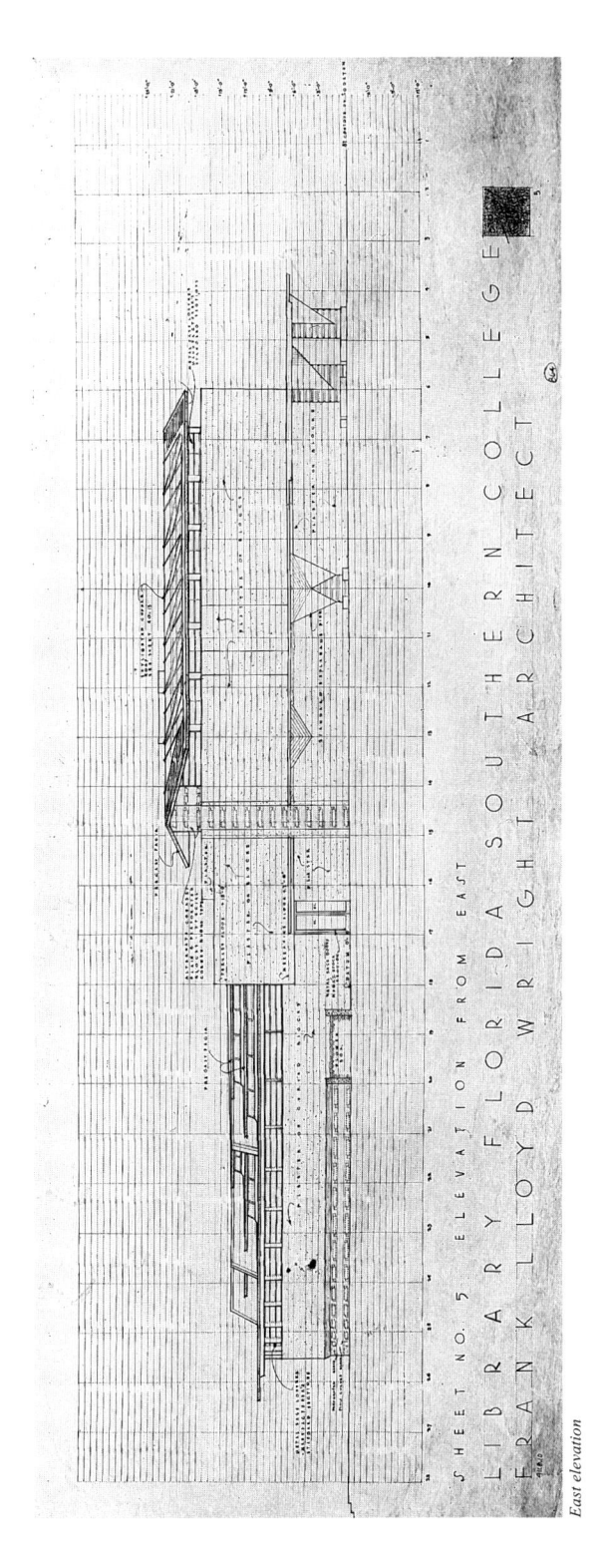

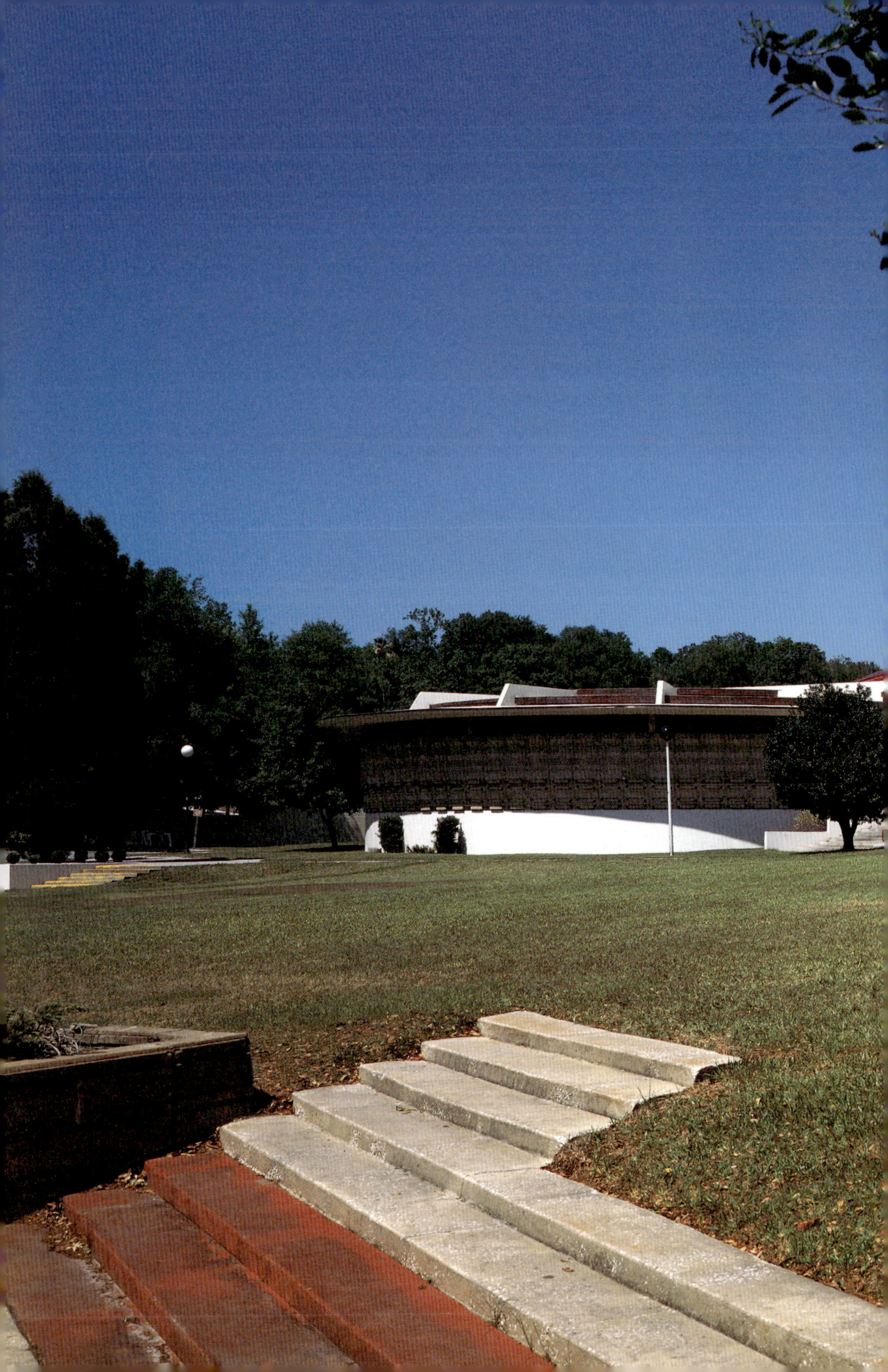

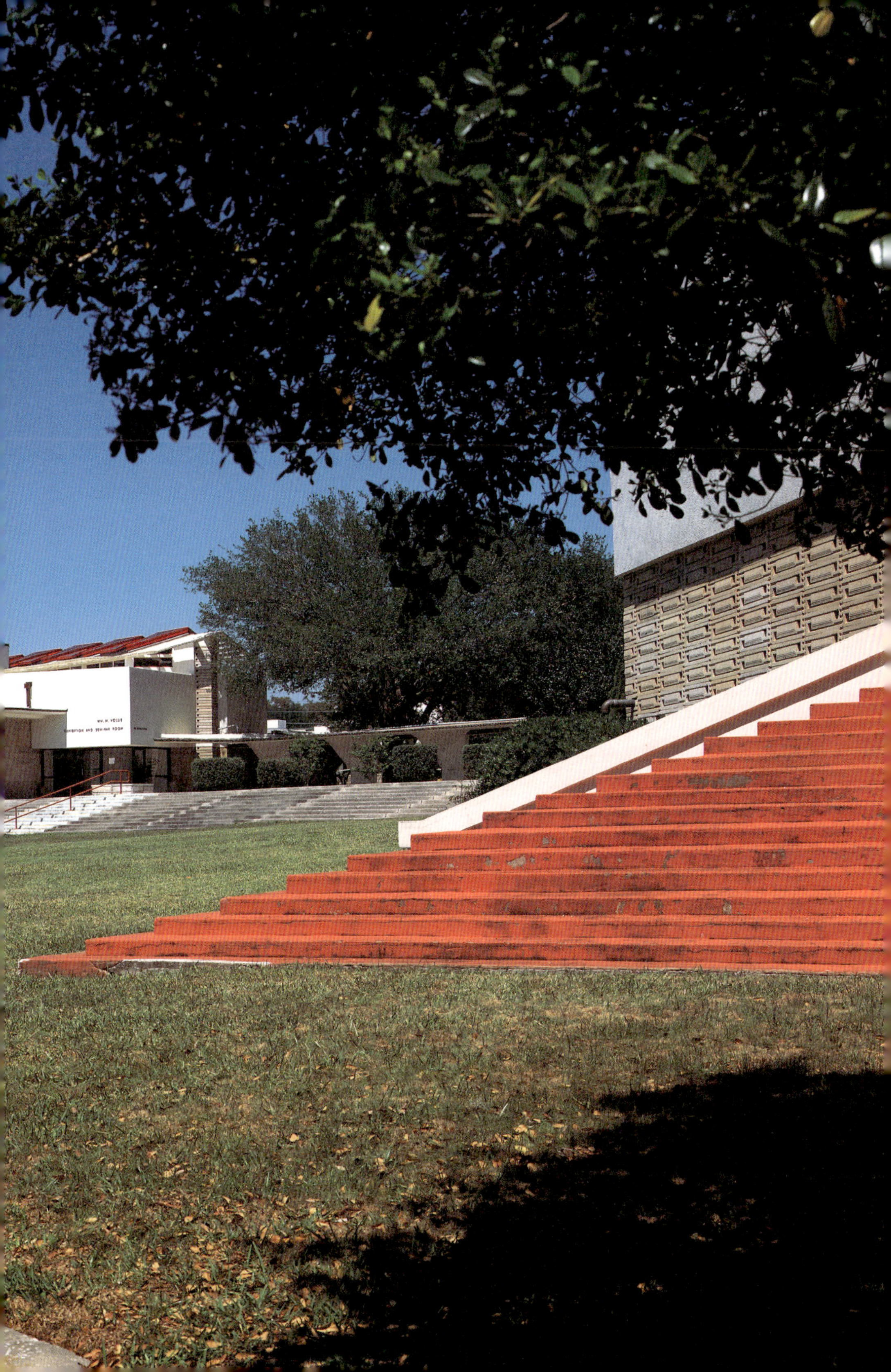
EXHIBITION AND SEMINAR ROOM

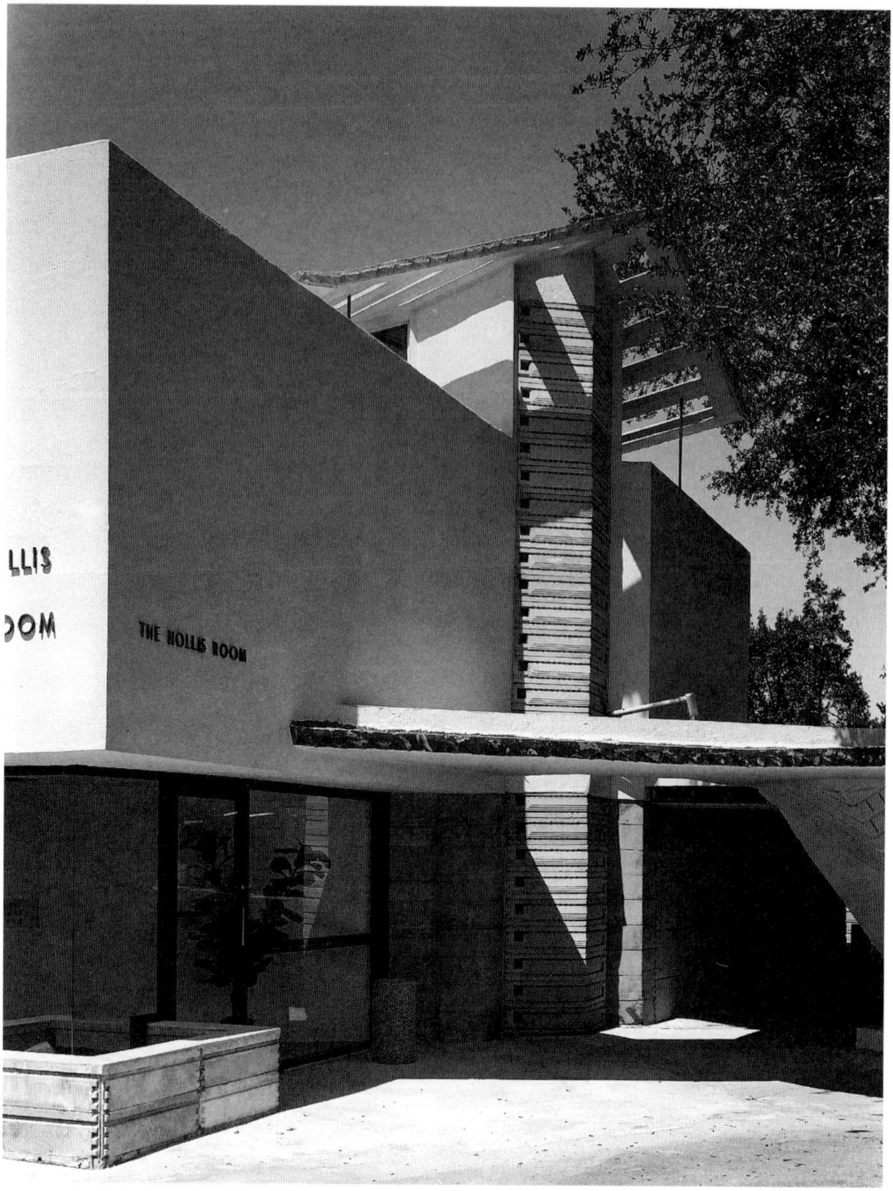
LLIS
OOM
THE HOLLIS ROOM

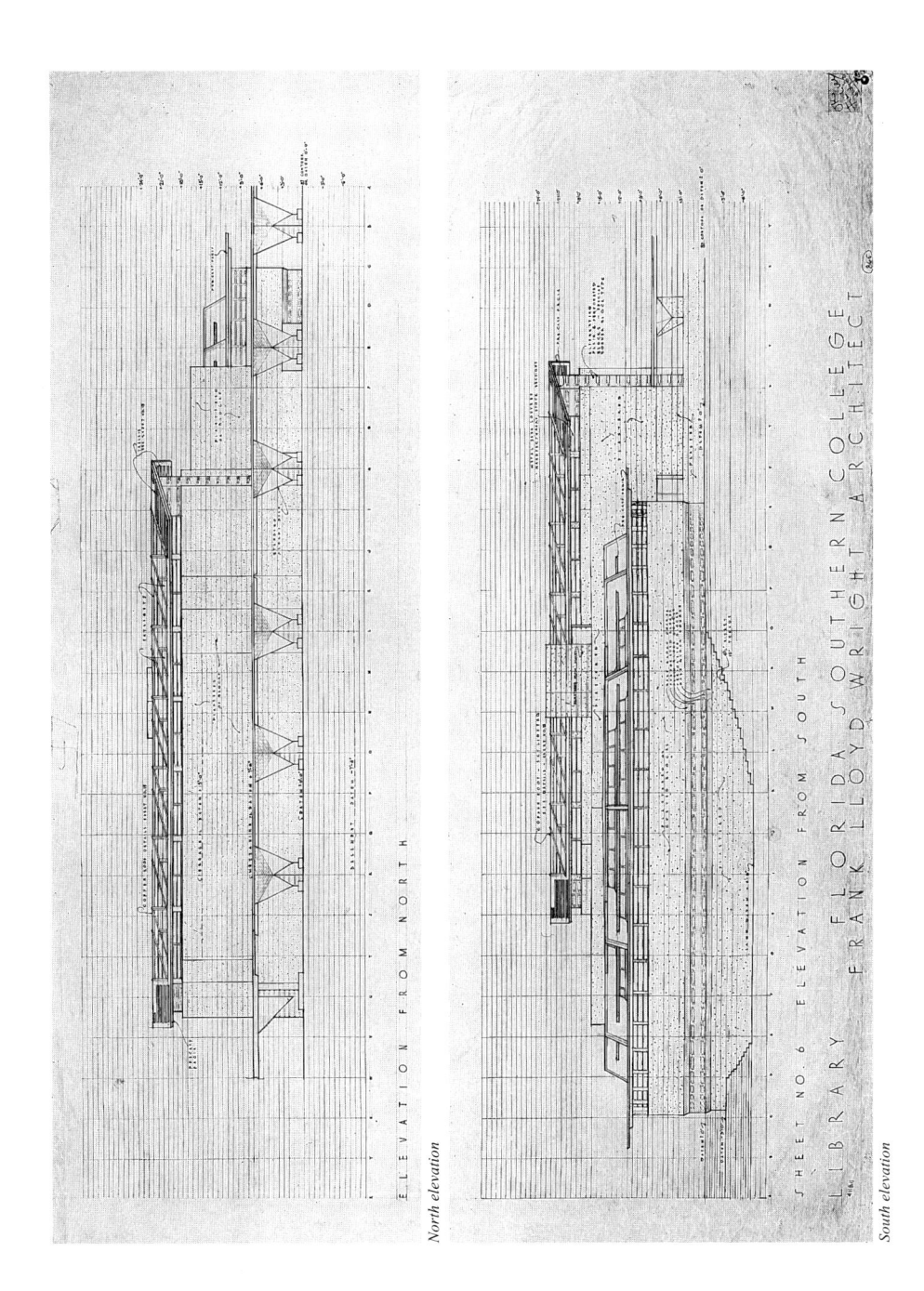

North elevation

South elevation

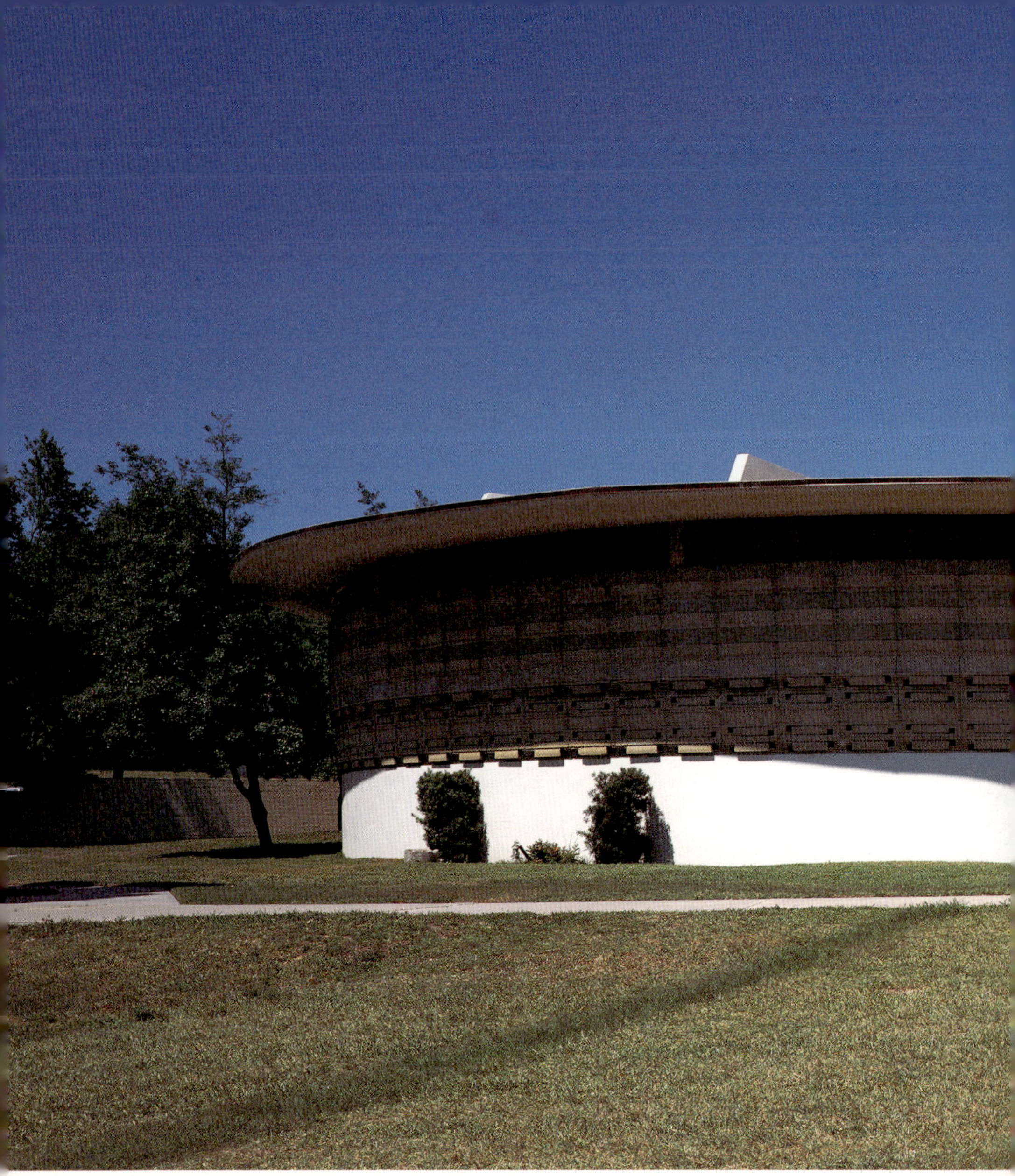

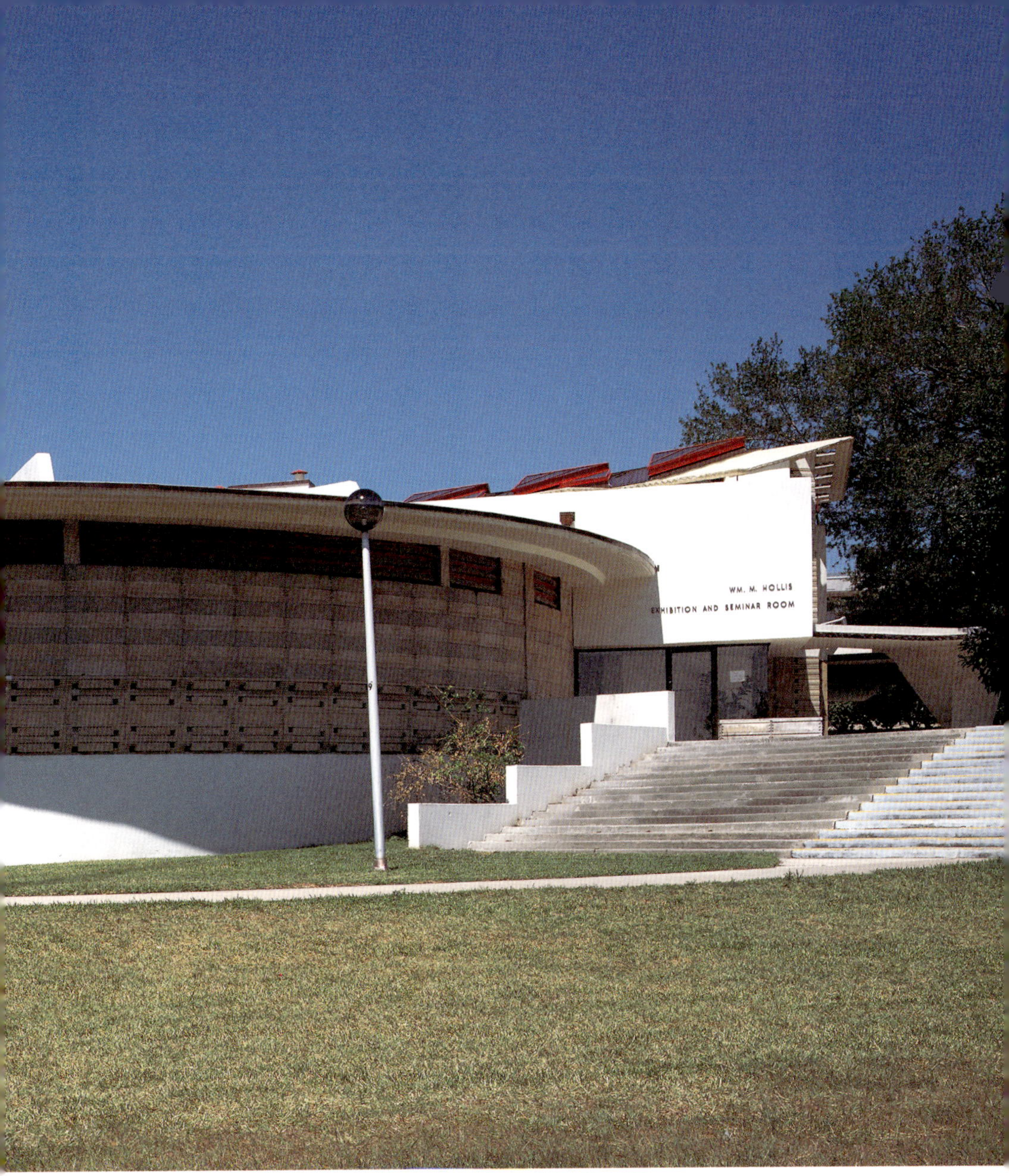
WM. M. HOLLIS
EXHIBITION AND SEMINAR ROOM

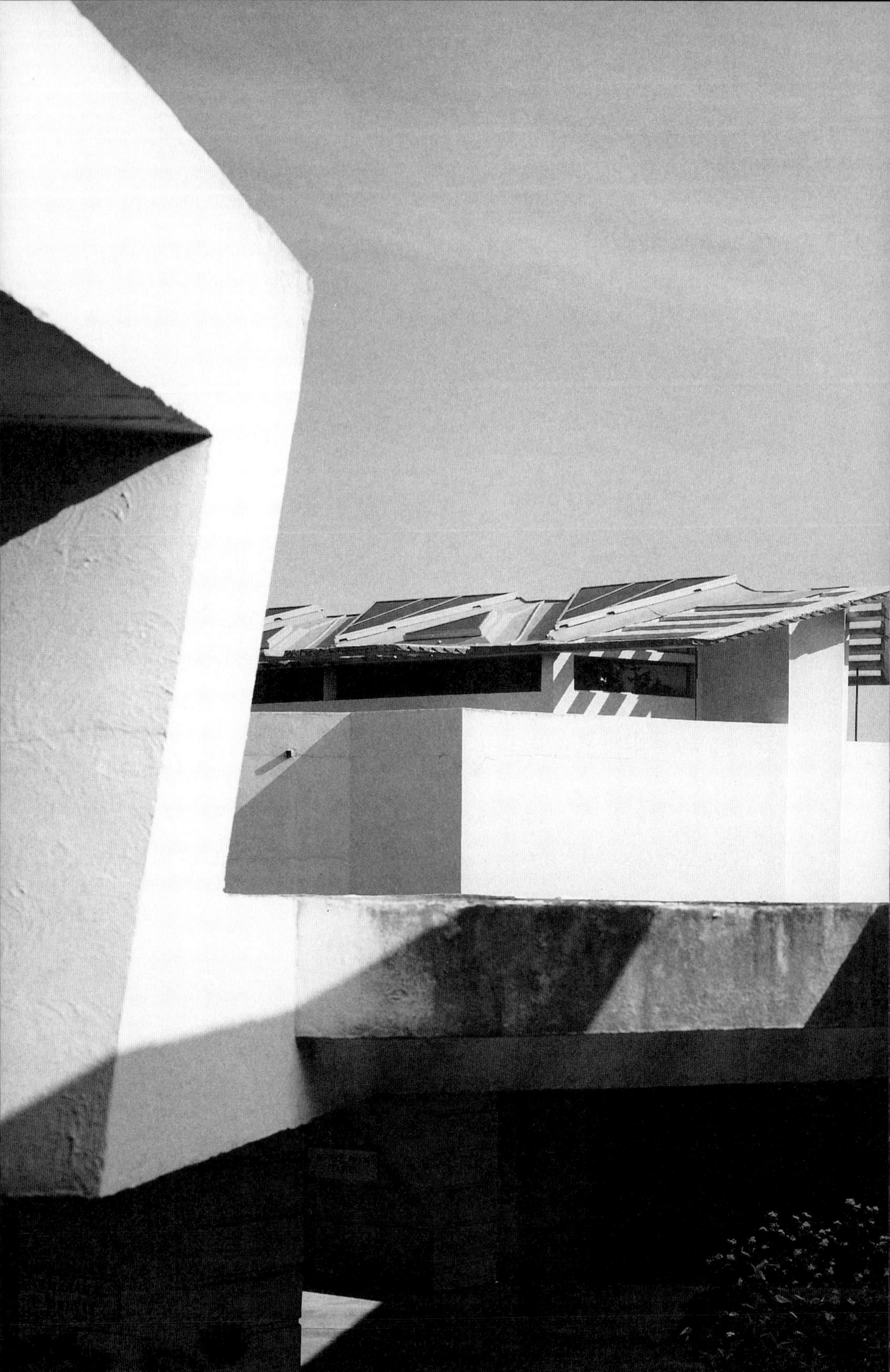

MAX AND
LOTTY SELIG

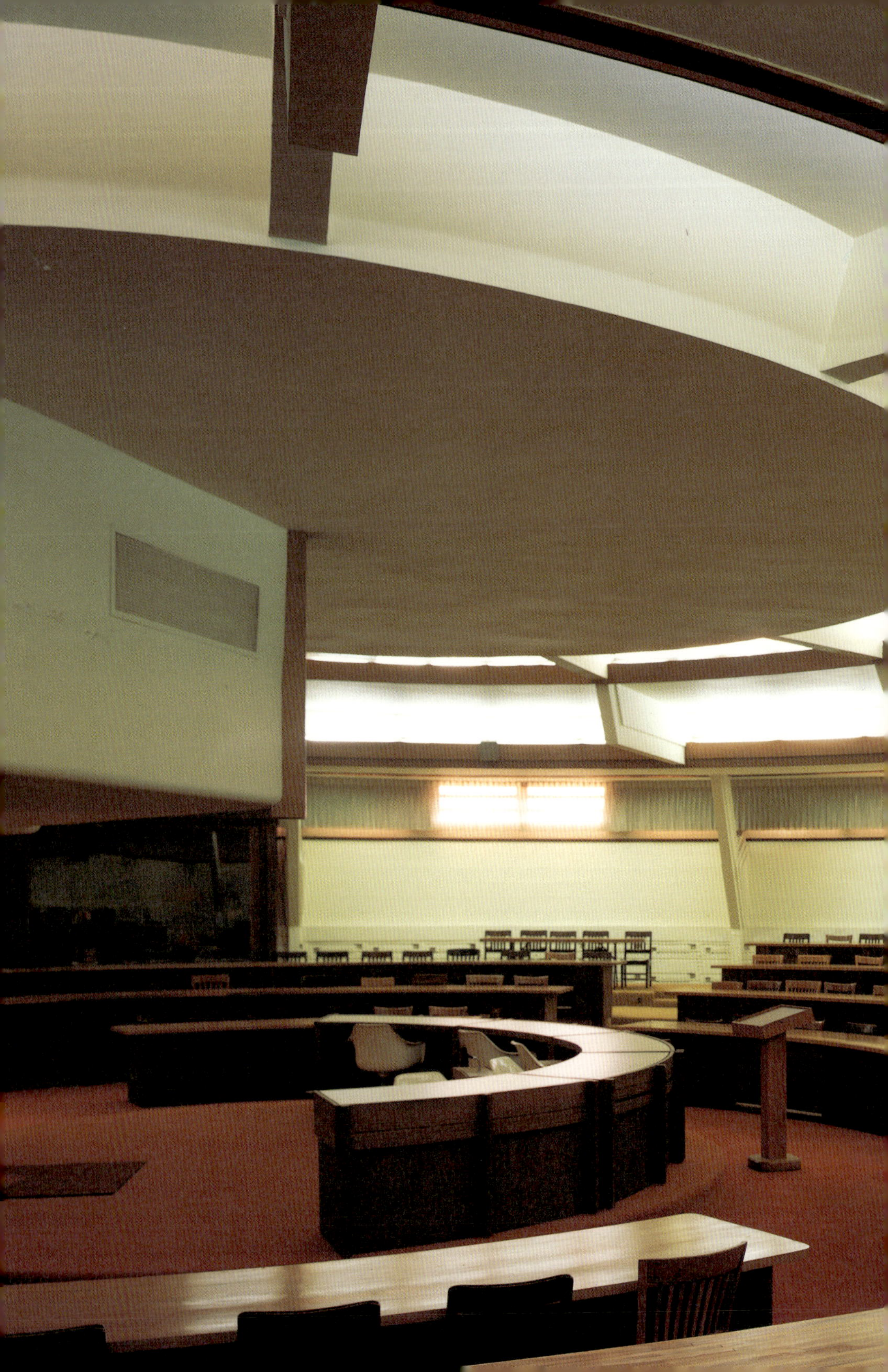

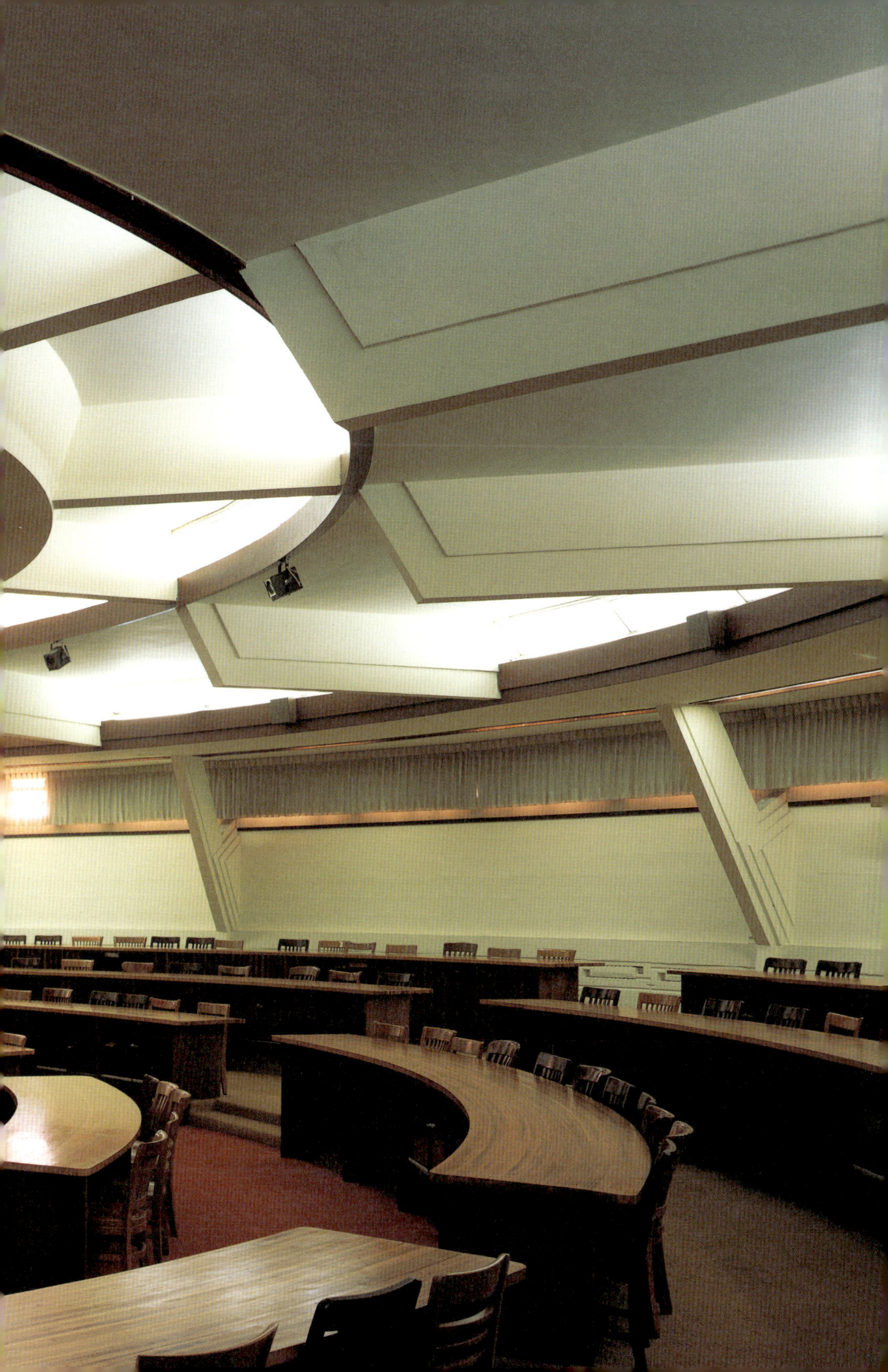

Industrial Arts Building, Florida Southern College, Lakeland, Florida, 1942

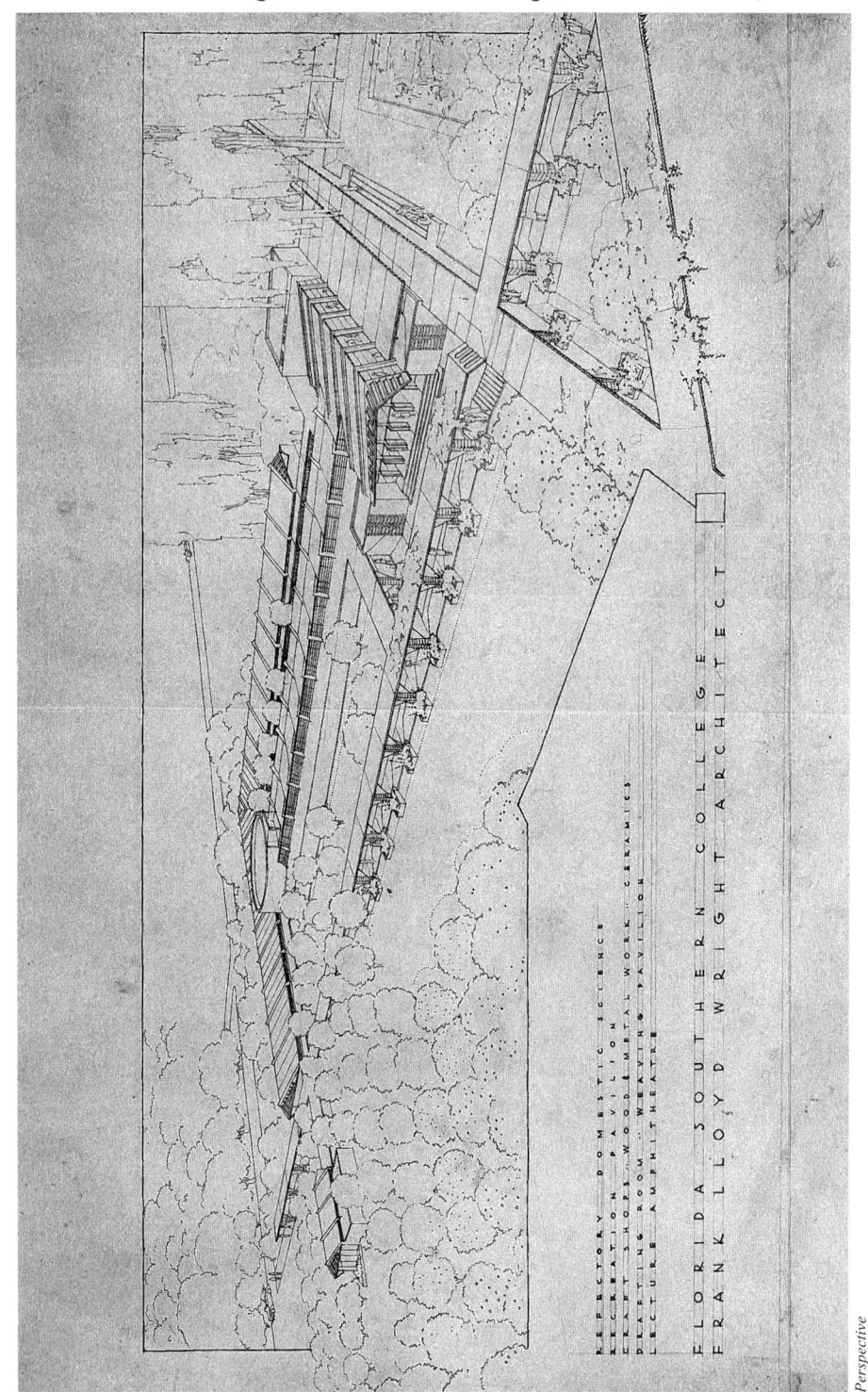

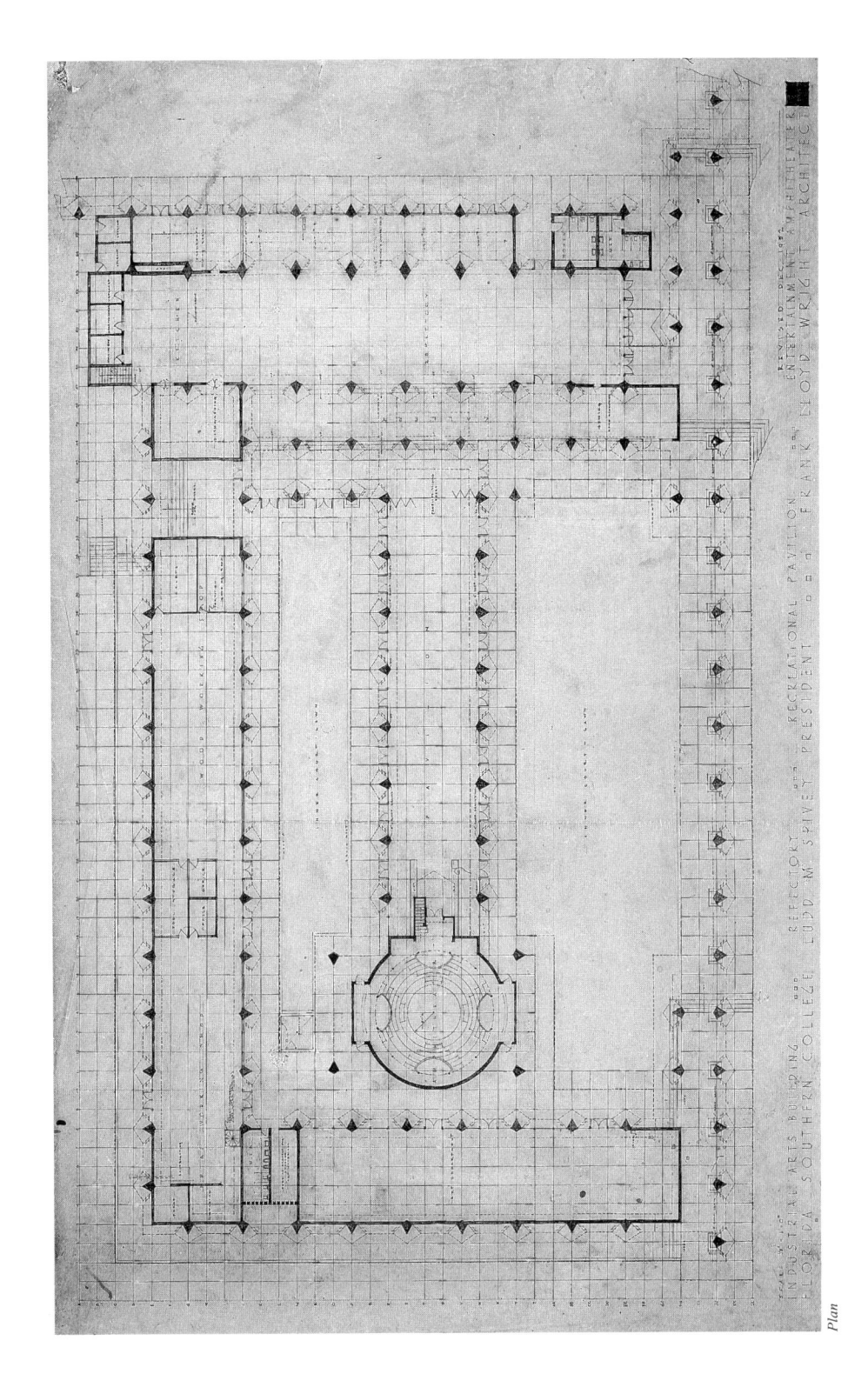

Plan

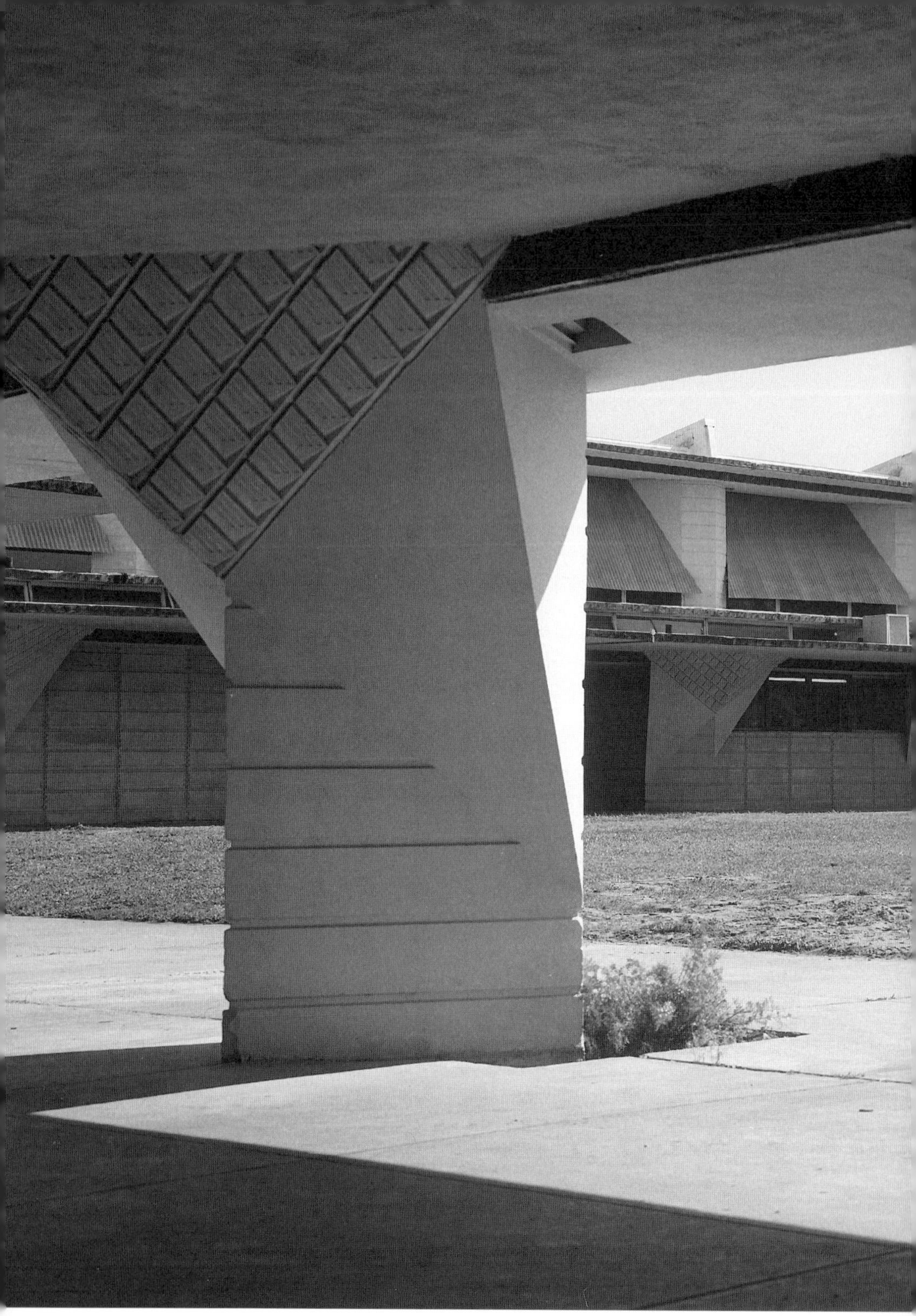

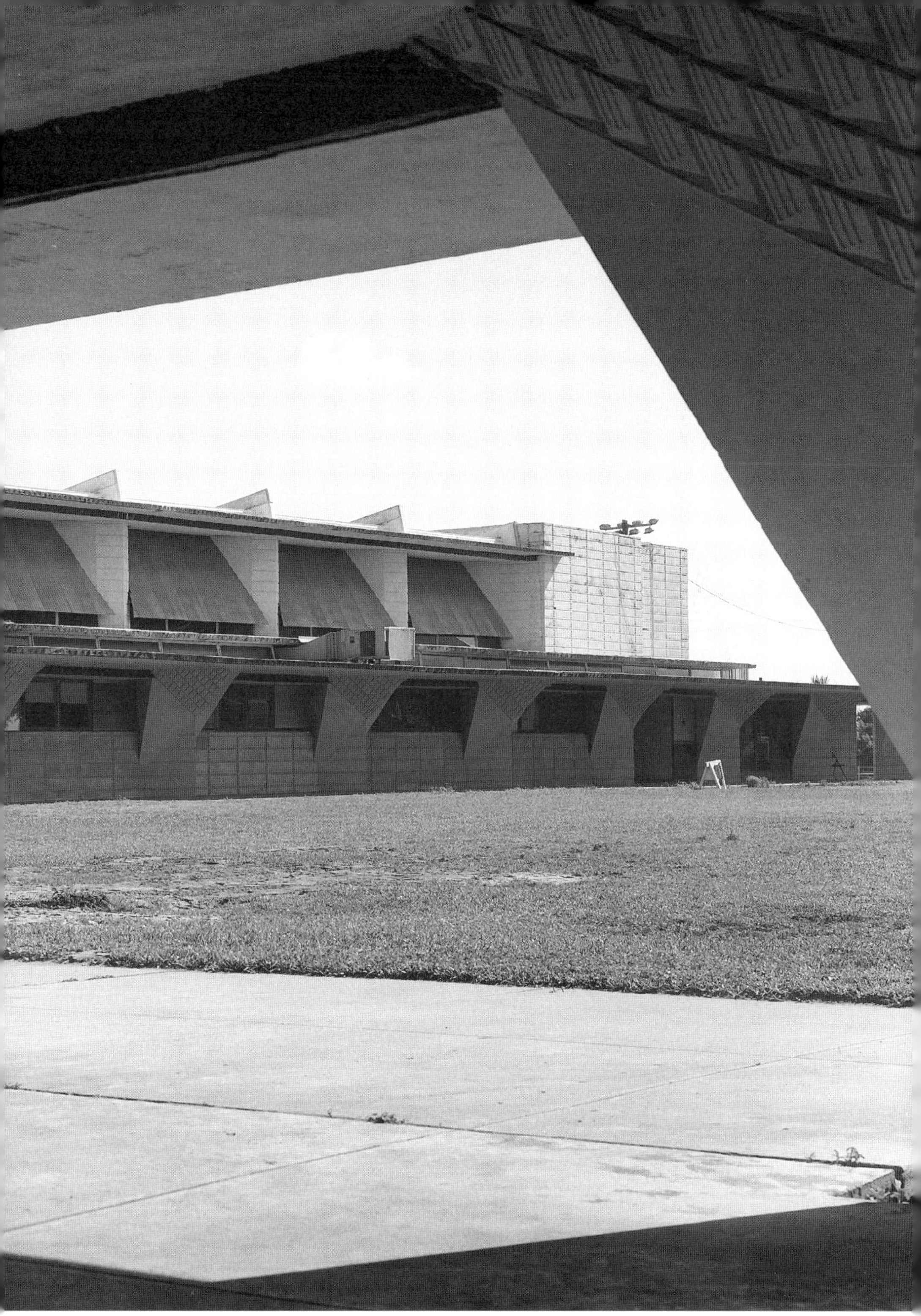

Administration Building, Florida Southern College, Lakeland, Florida, 1945

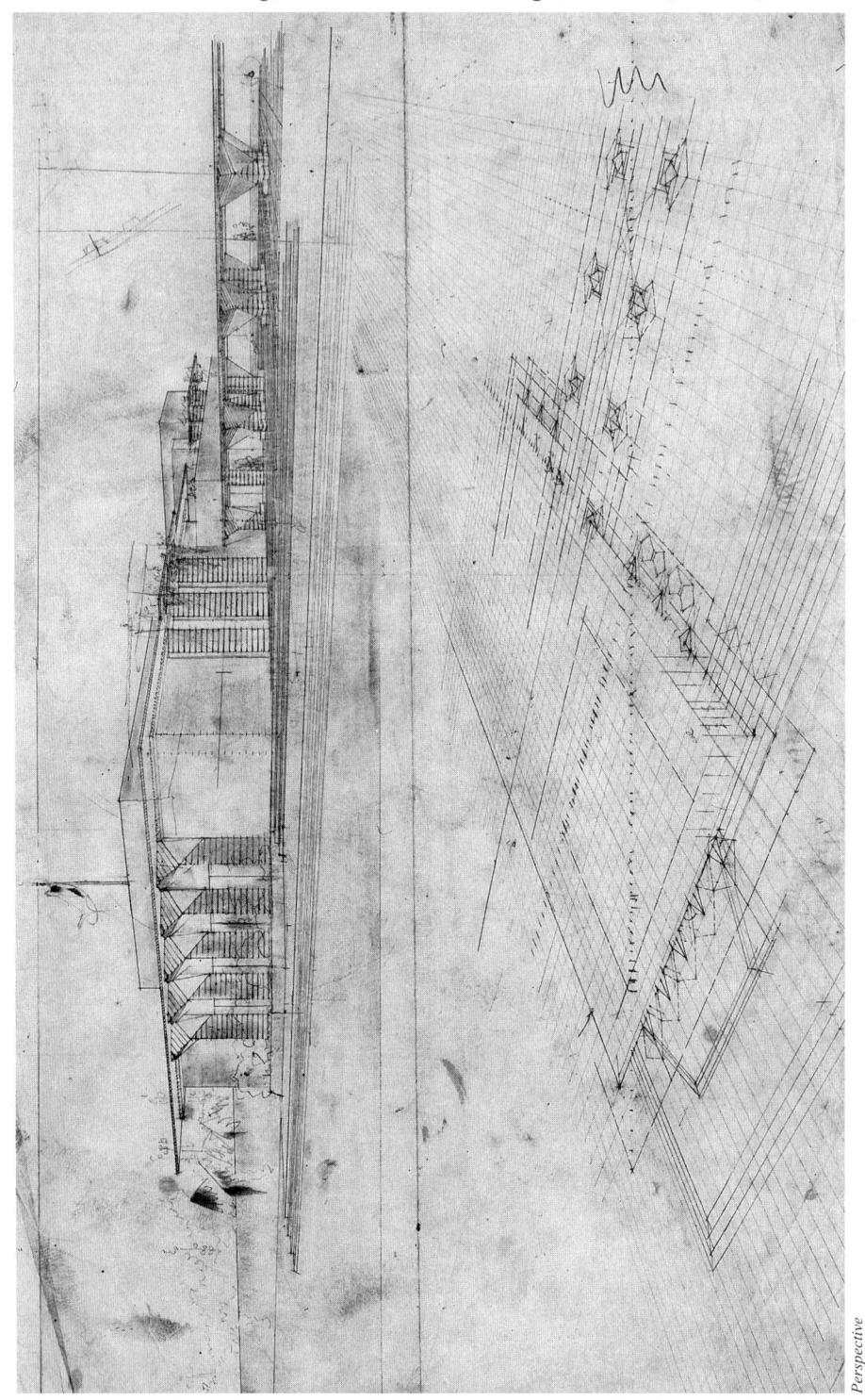

Perspective

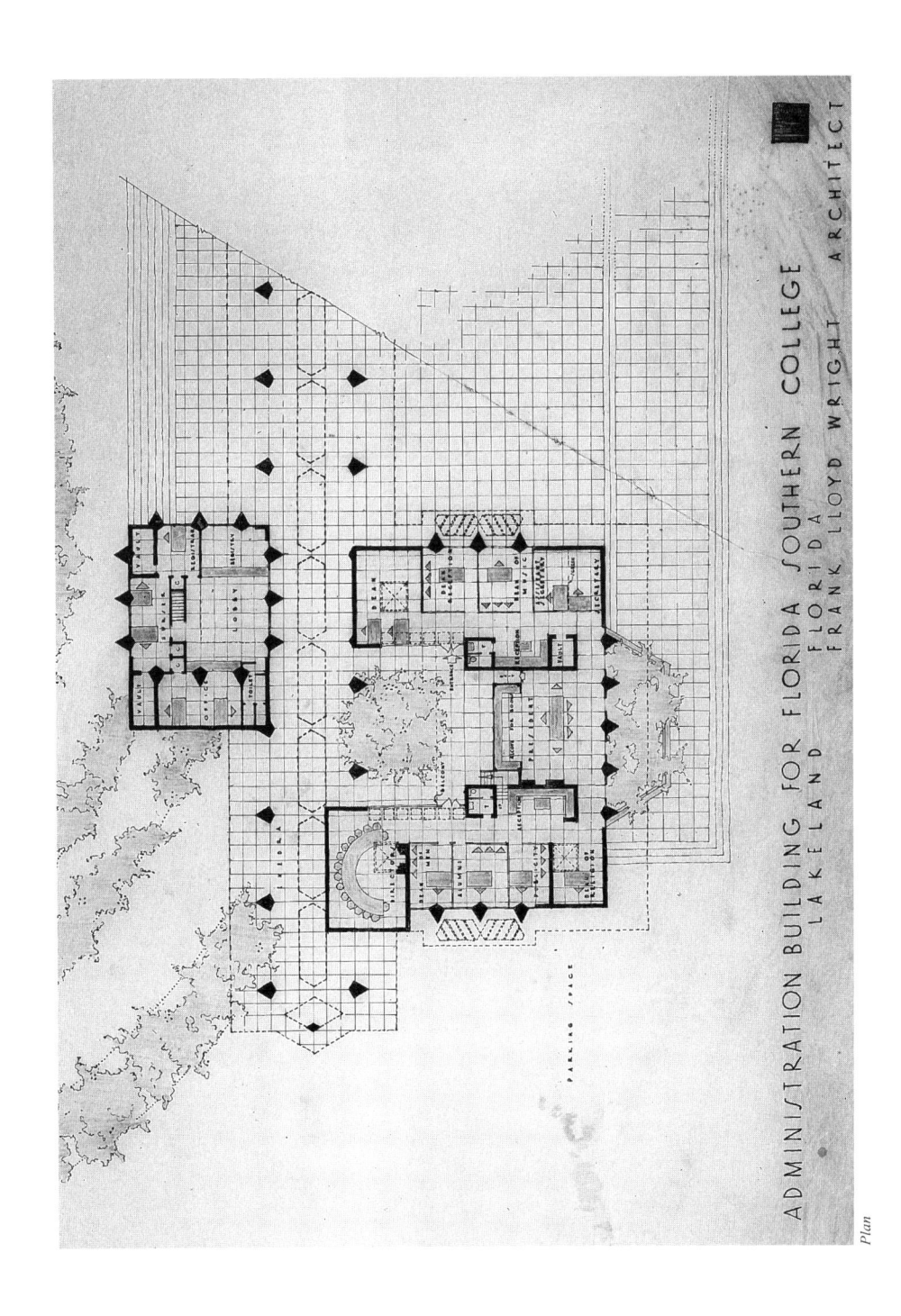

Plan

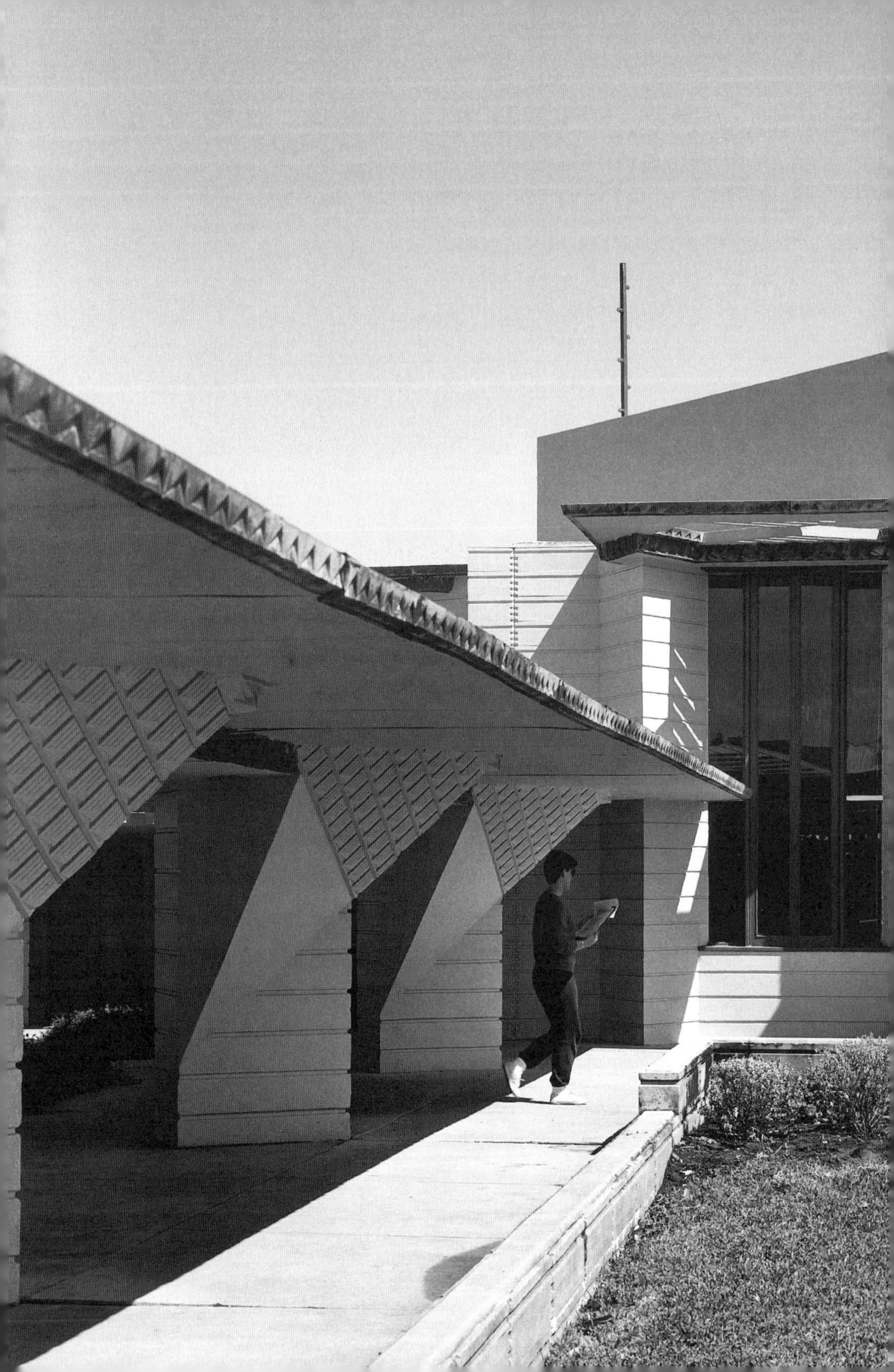

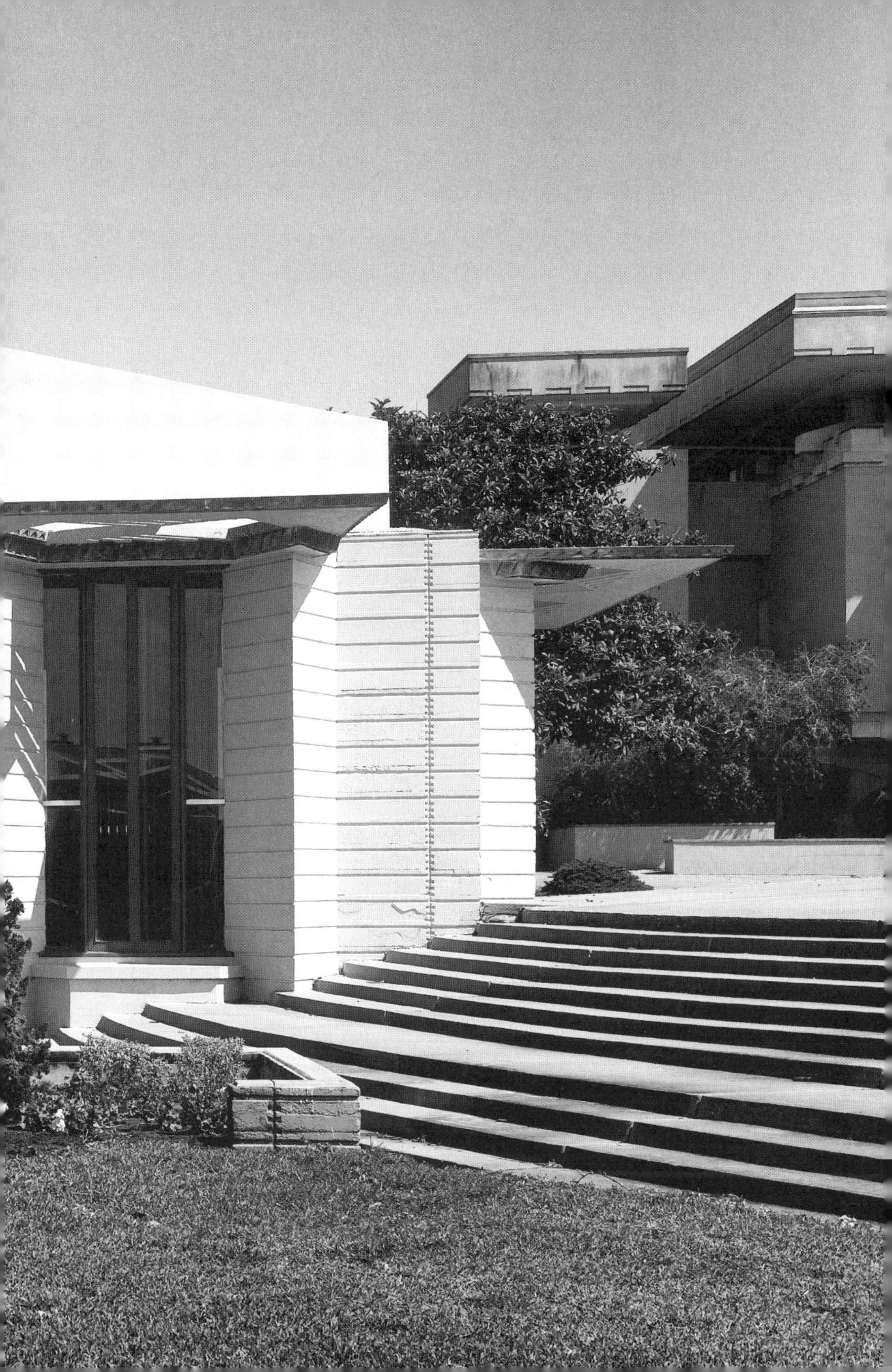

Science and Cosmography Building,
Florida Southern College, Lakeland, Florida, 1953

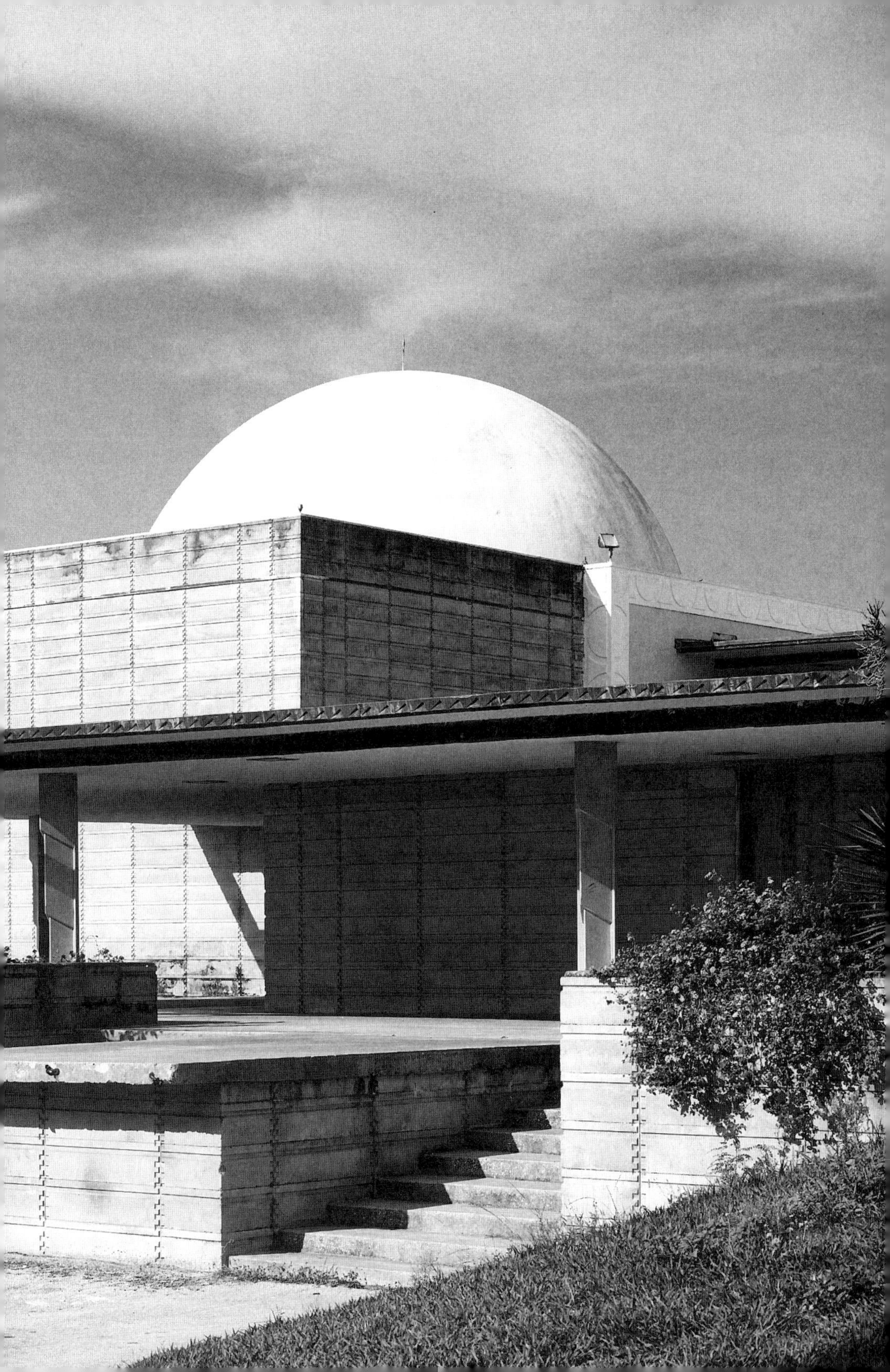

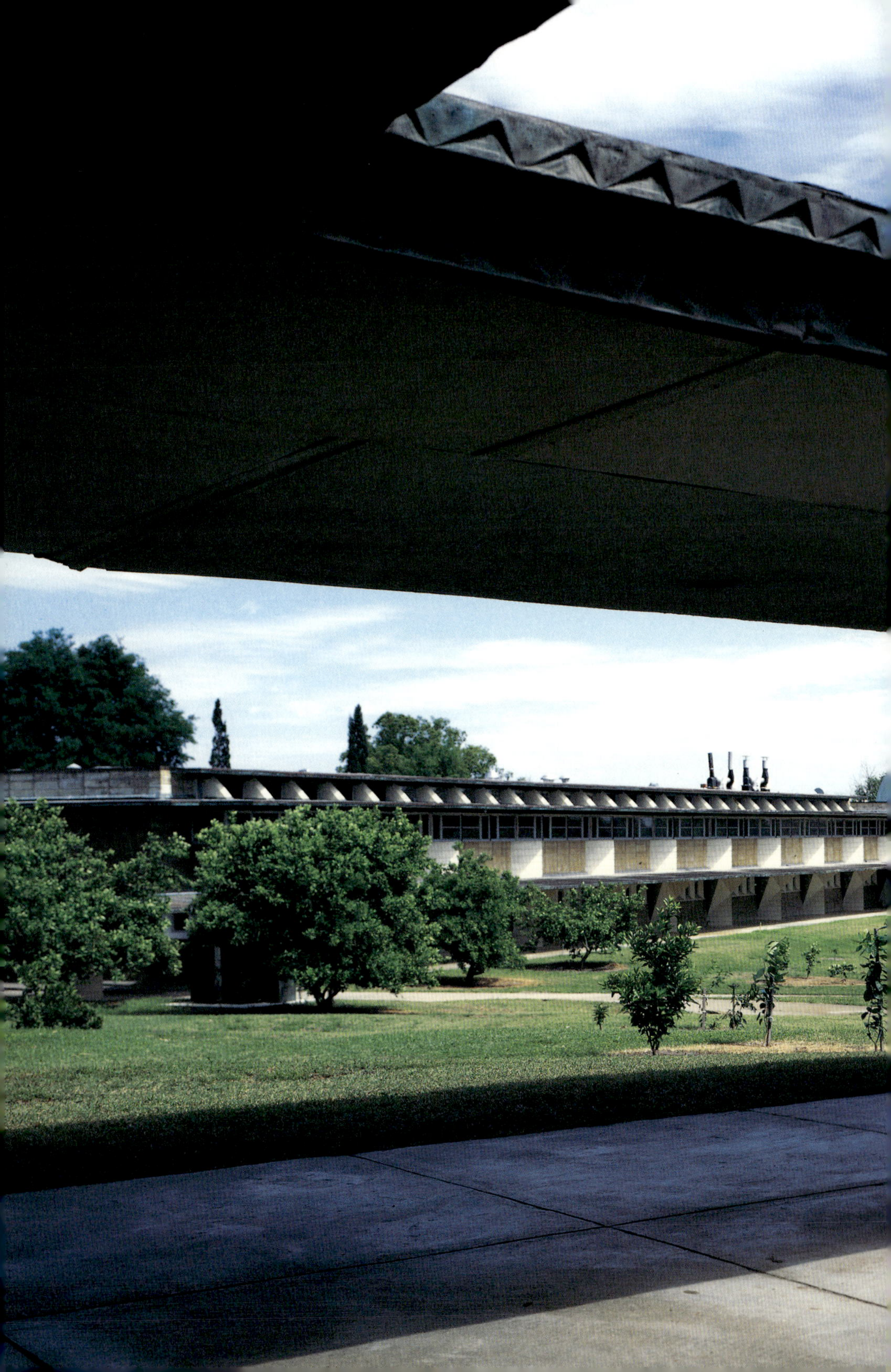

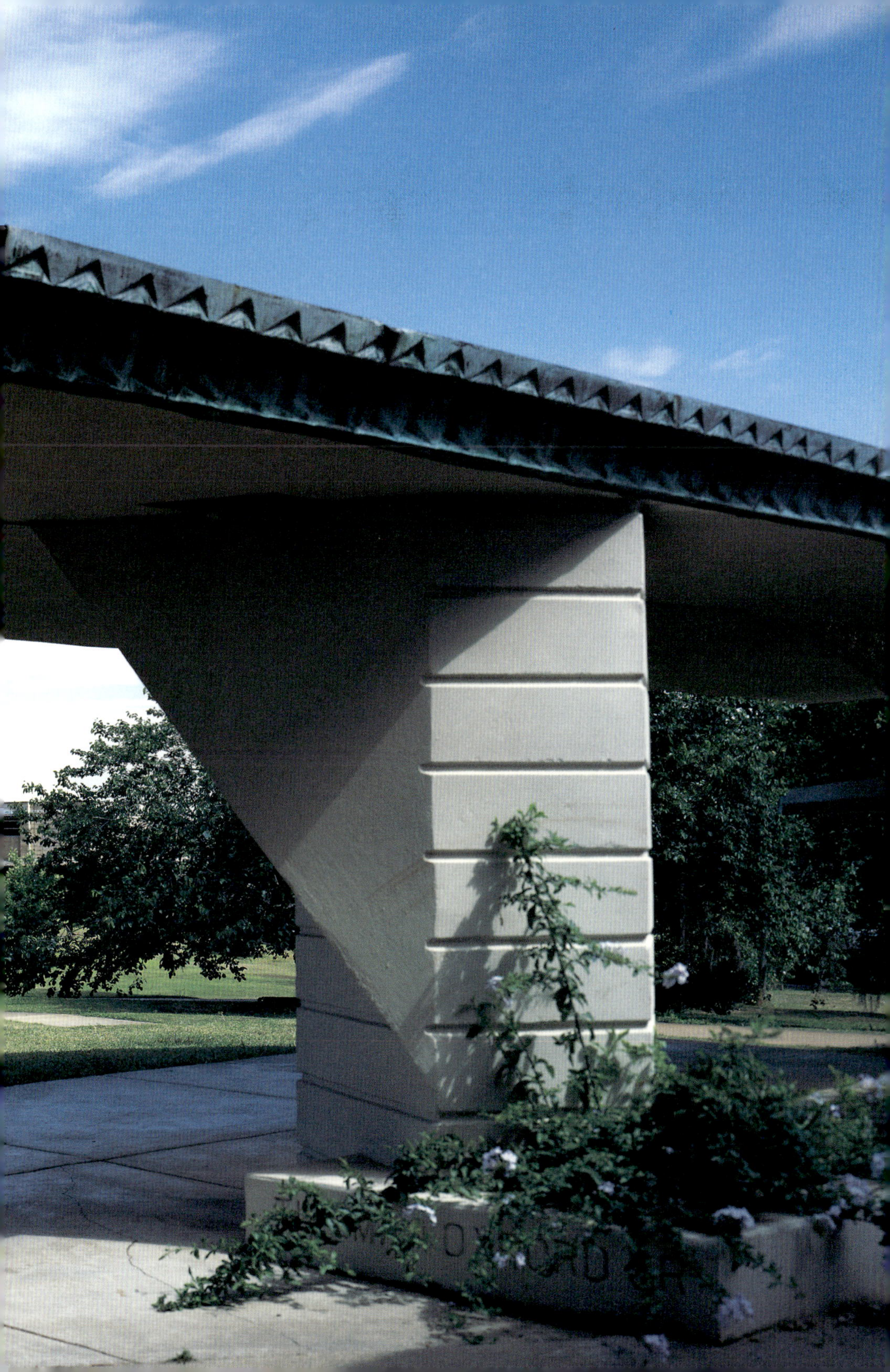

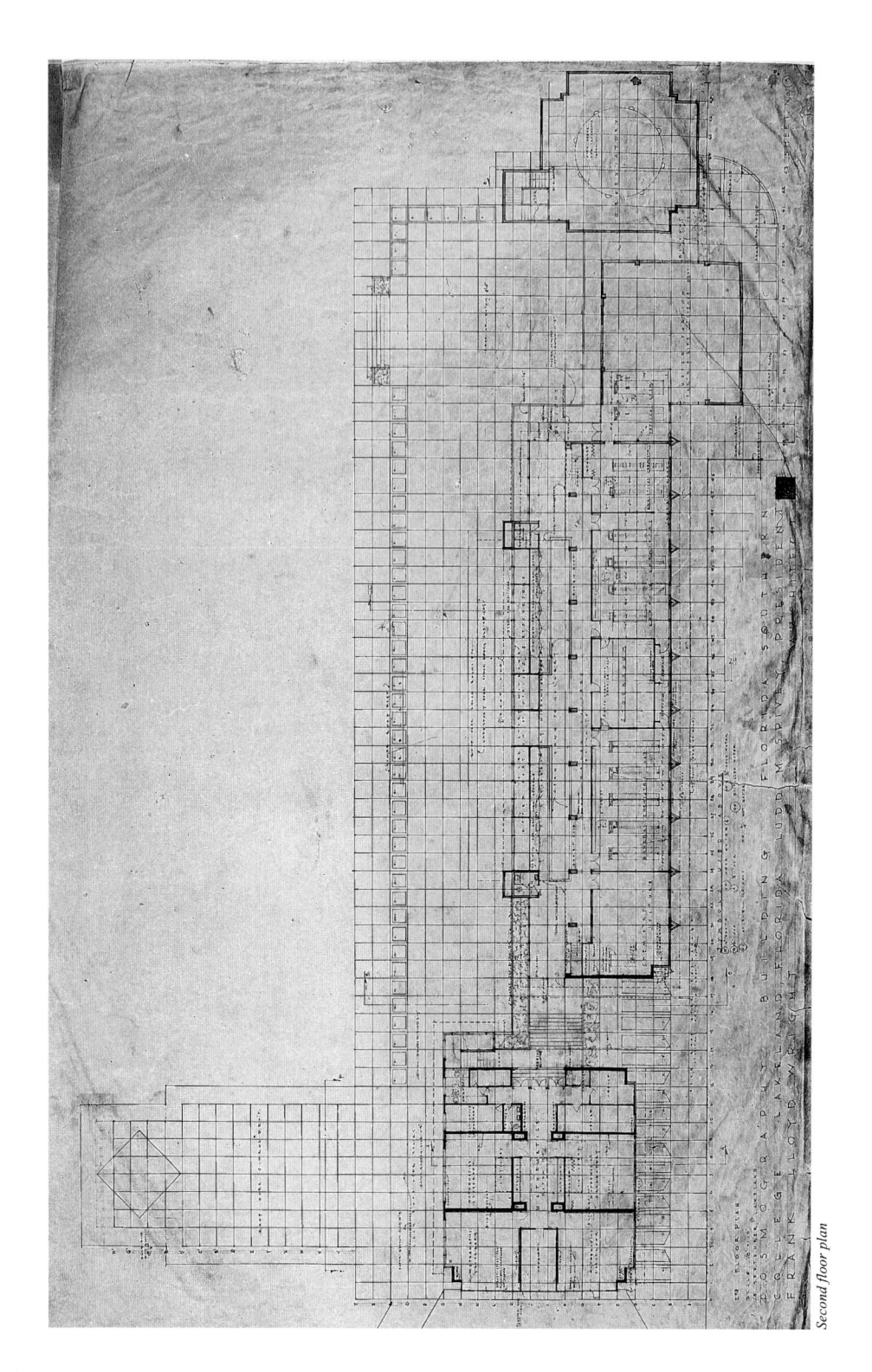

Second floor plan

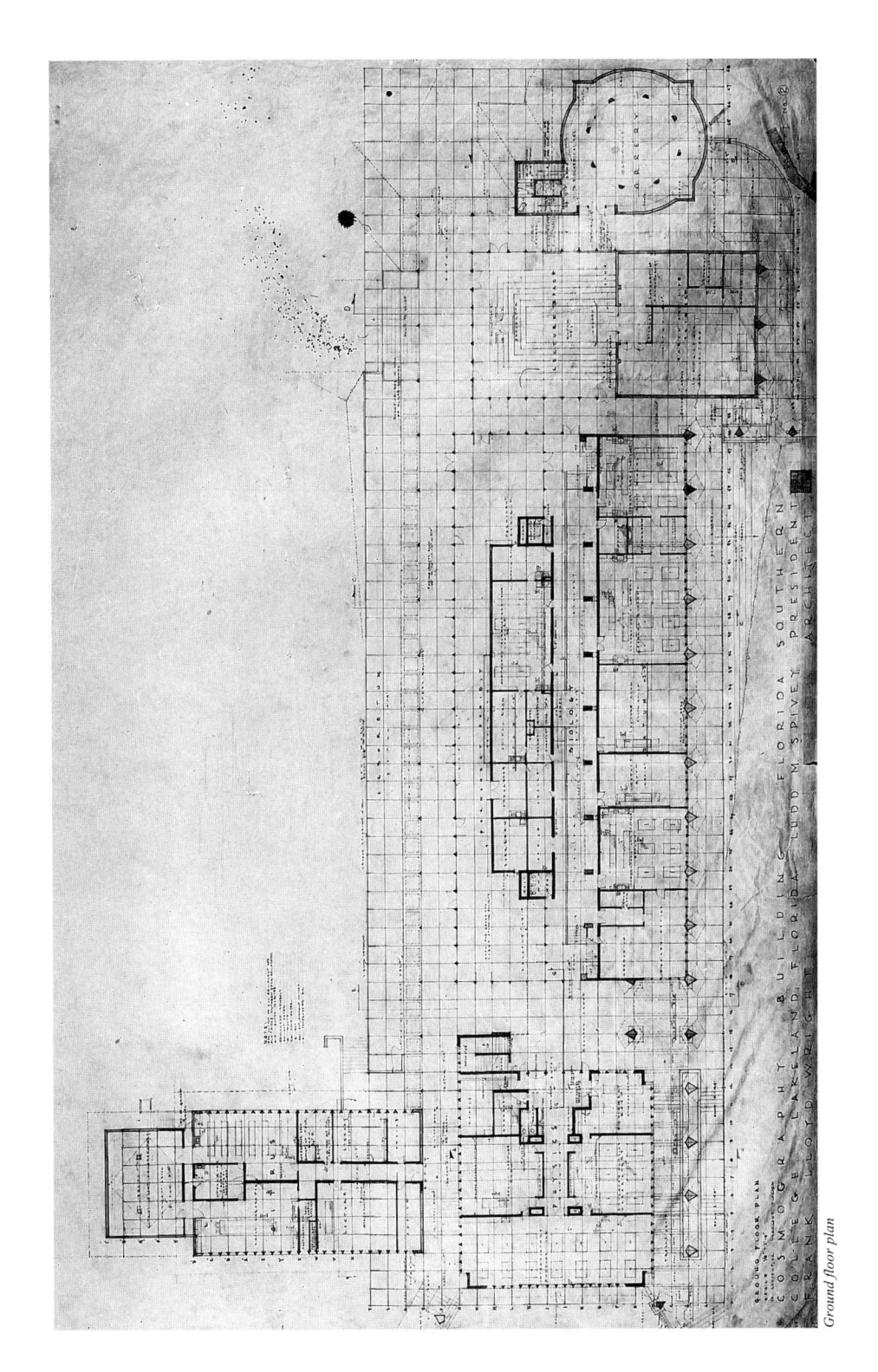

Ground floor plan

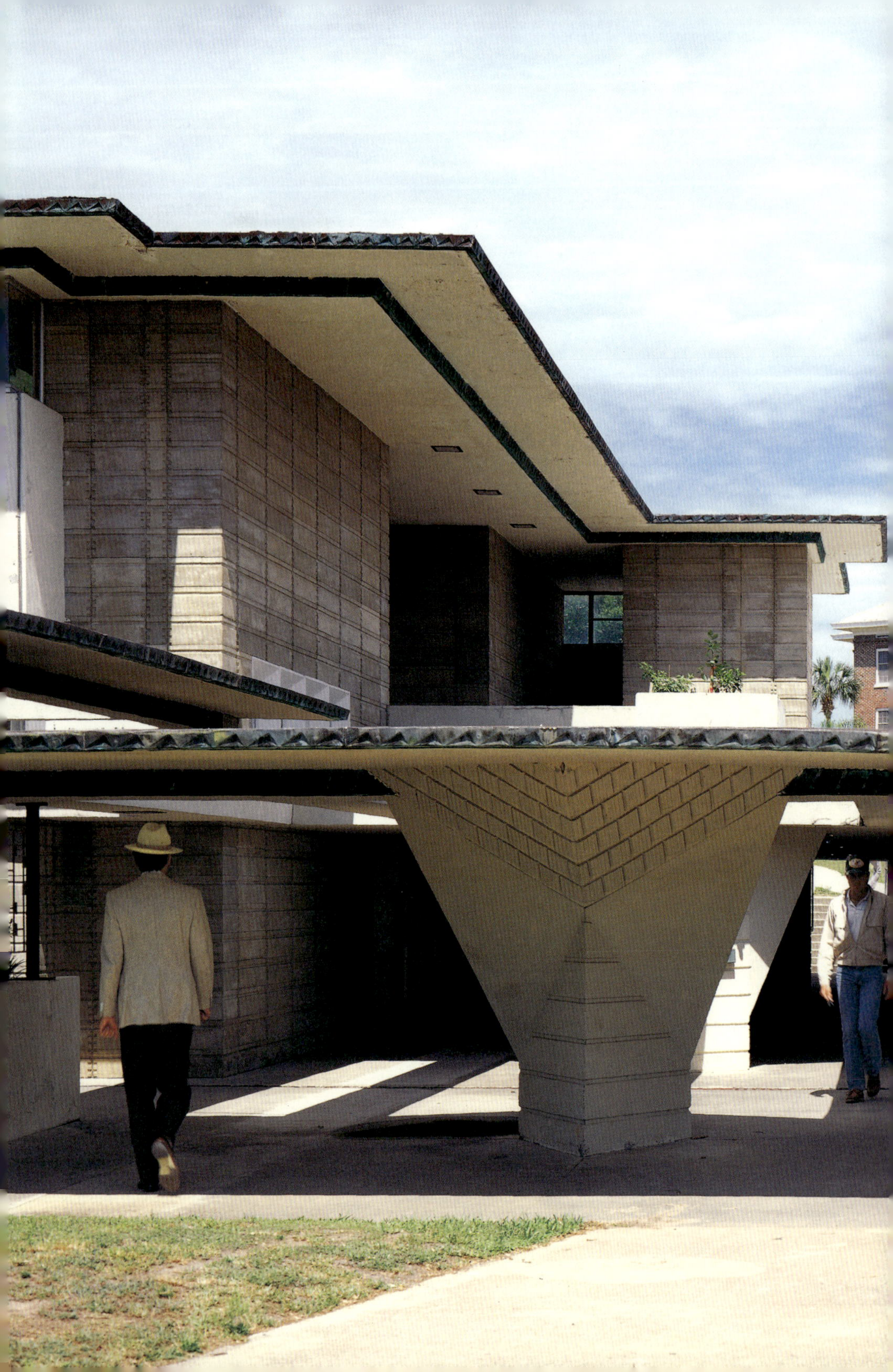

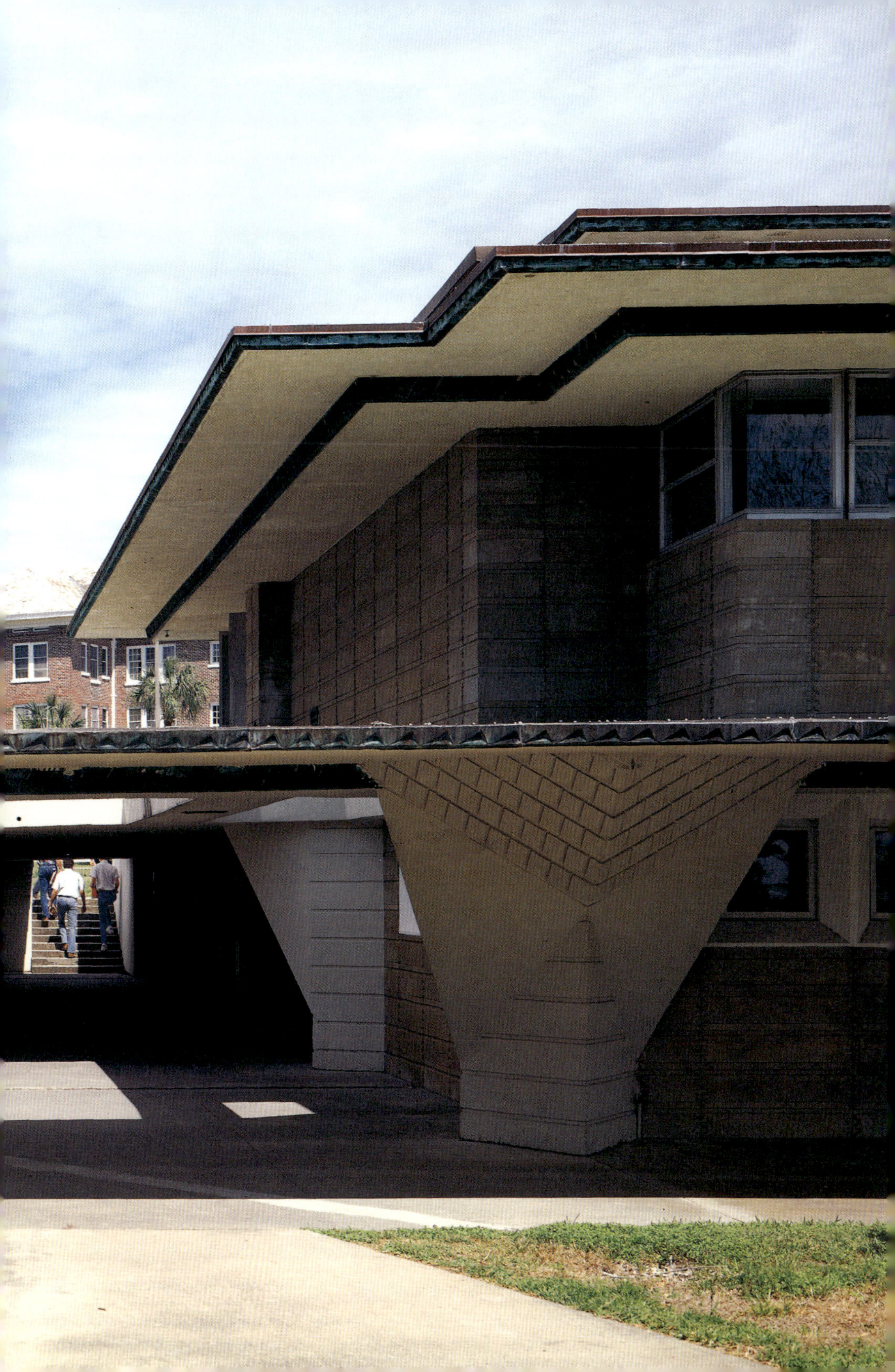

S. W. WALKER R. H. ALDERMAN LUDD M. SPIVEY

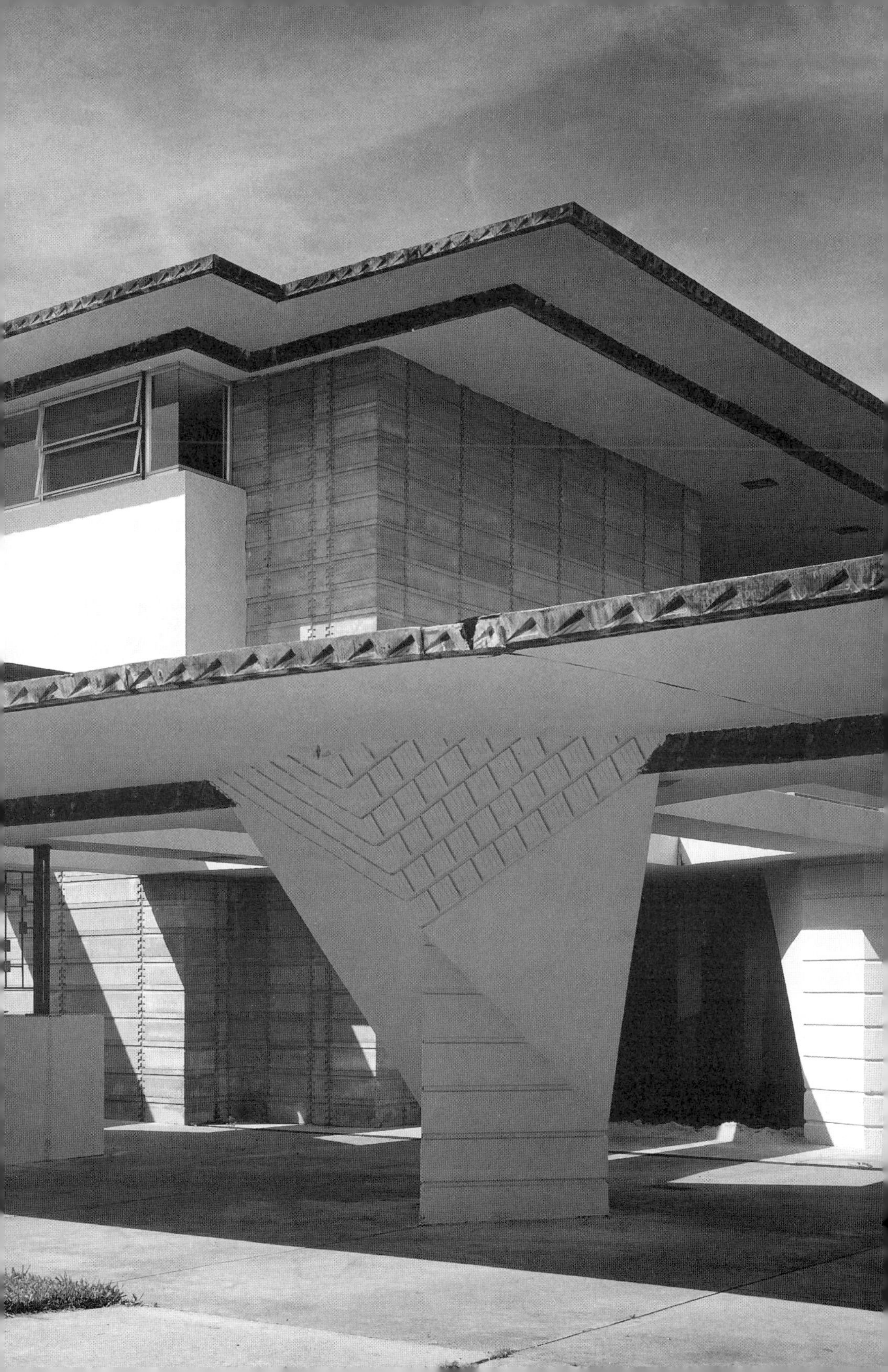

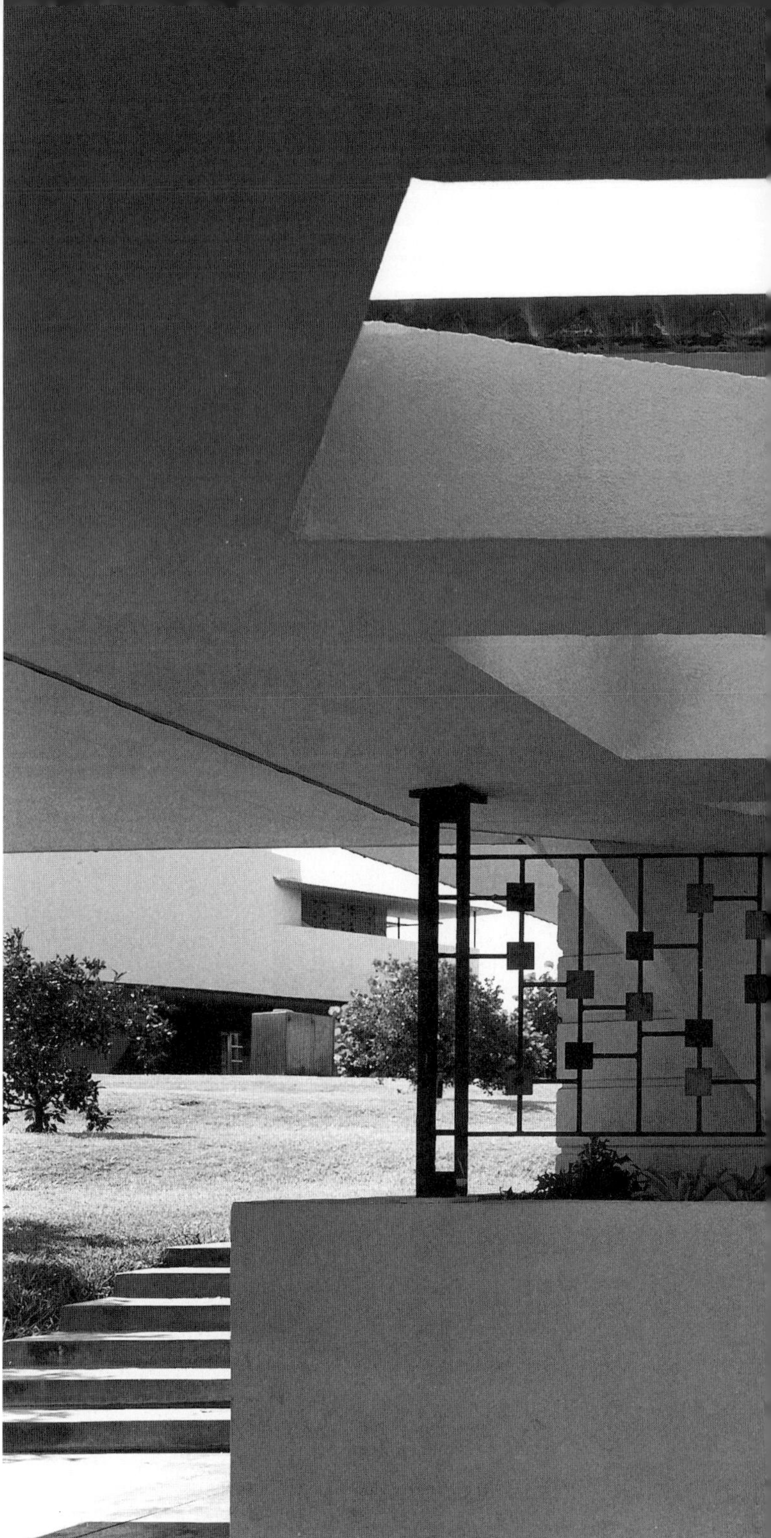

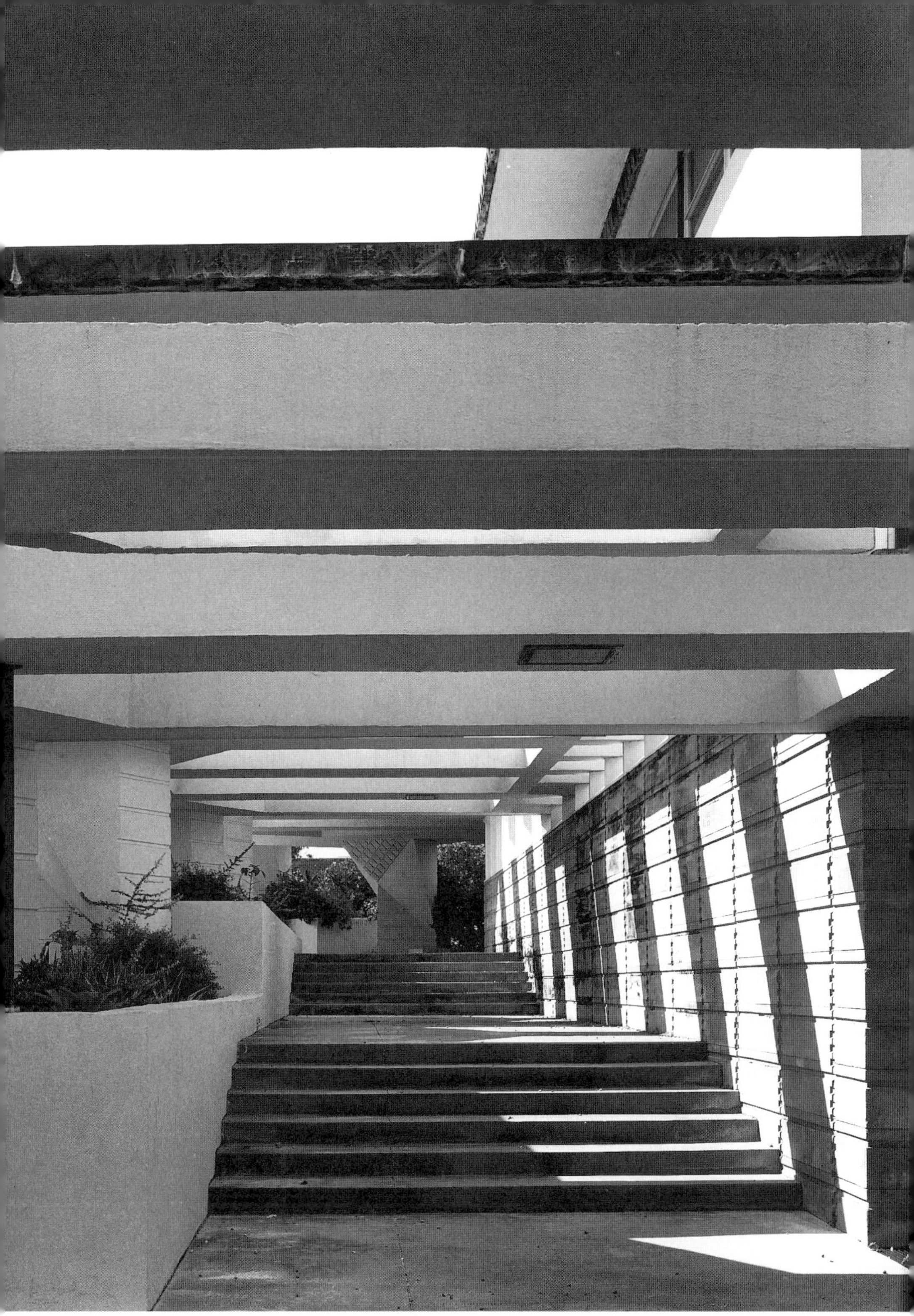

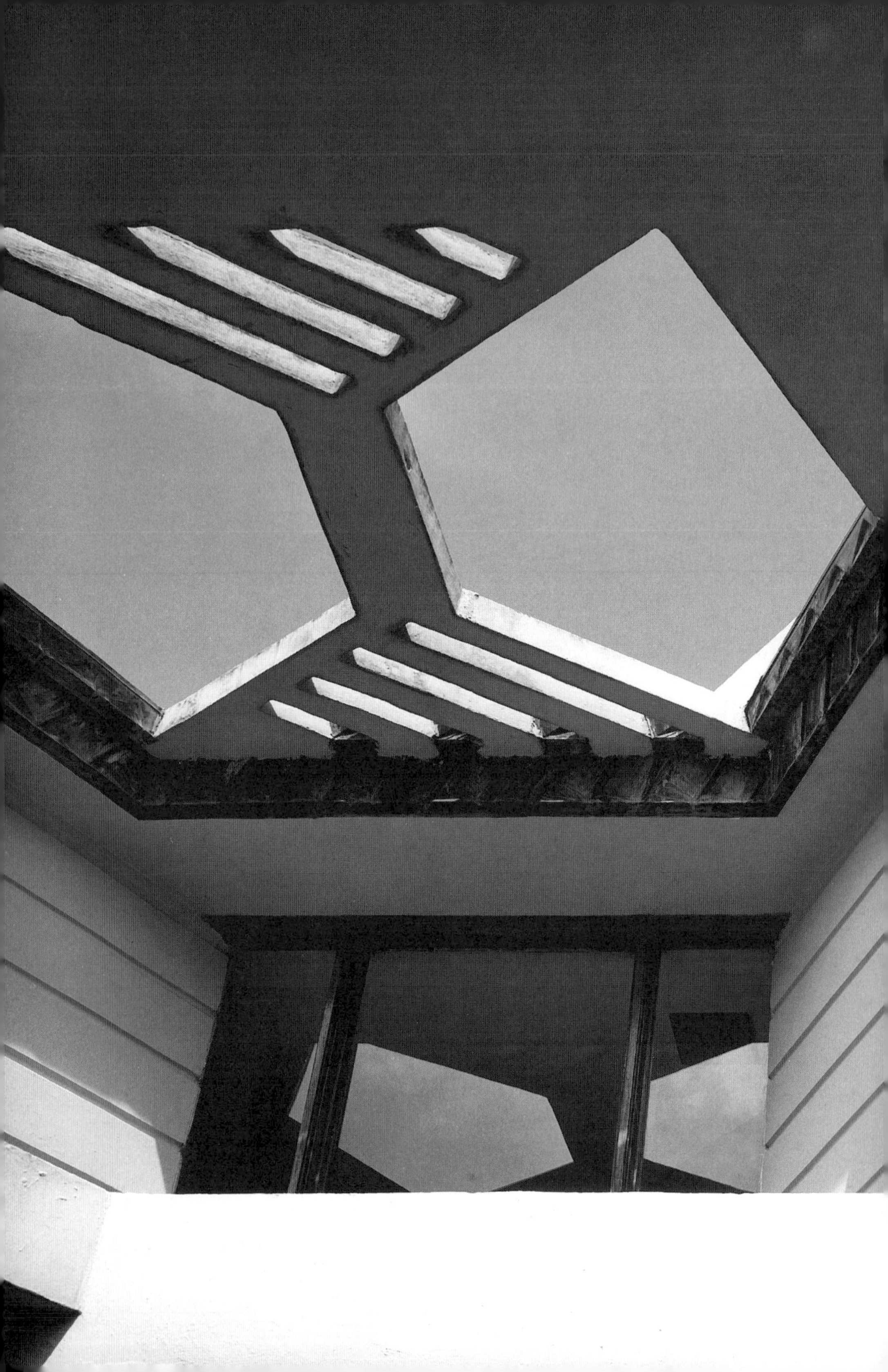

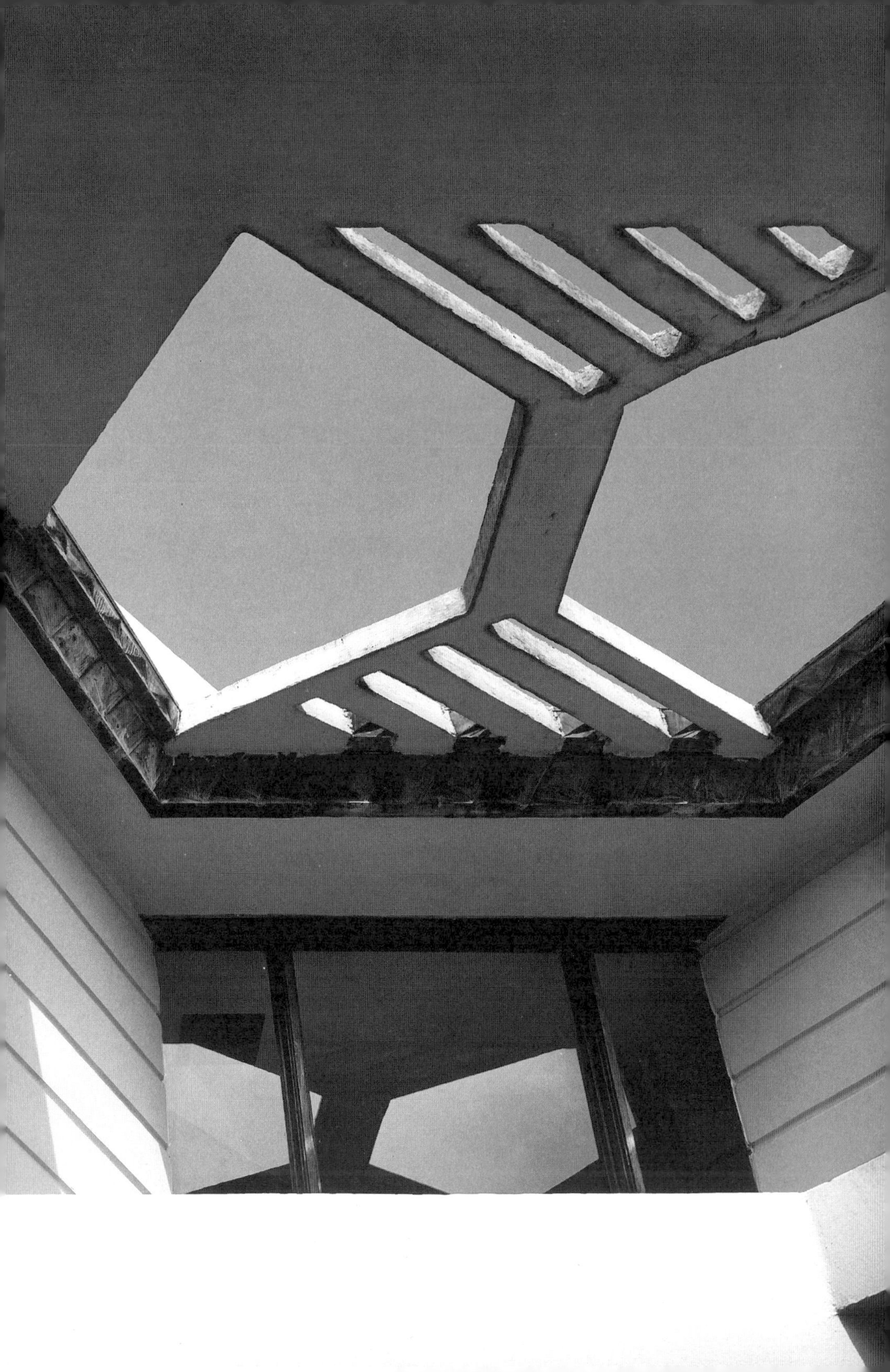

THE SOLOMON

Solomon R. Guggenheim Museum
New York, New York, 1943-59

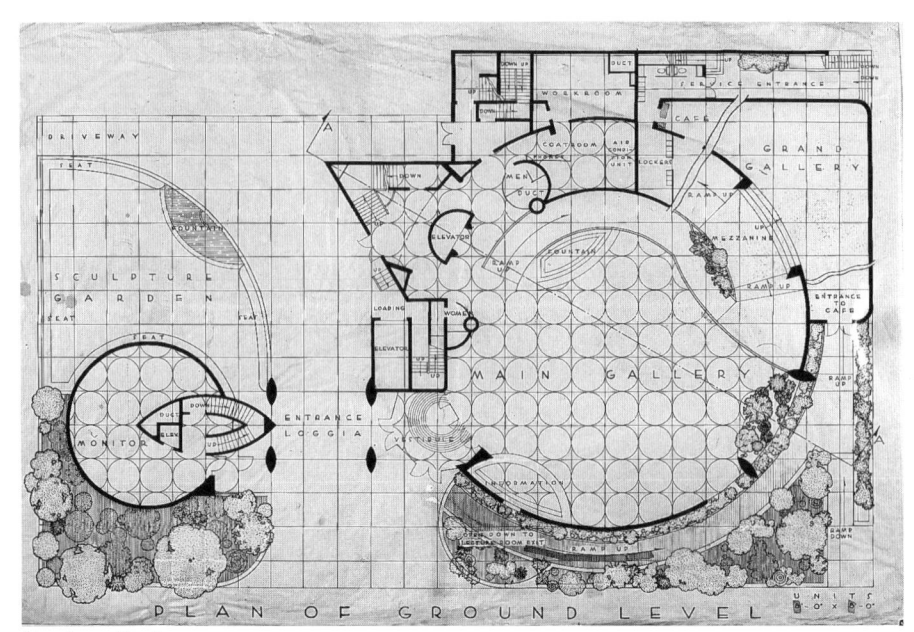

Plan of ground level

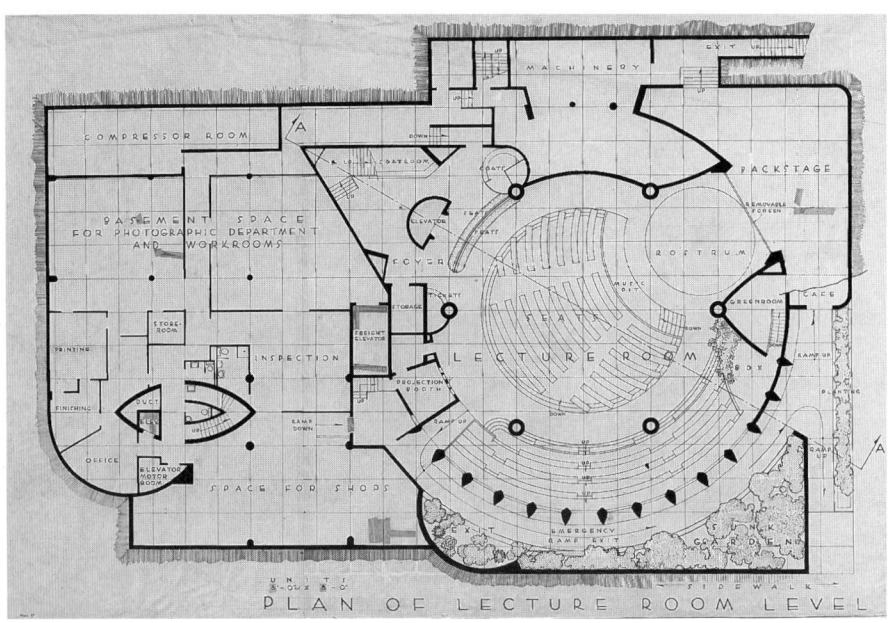

Plan of lecture room level

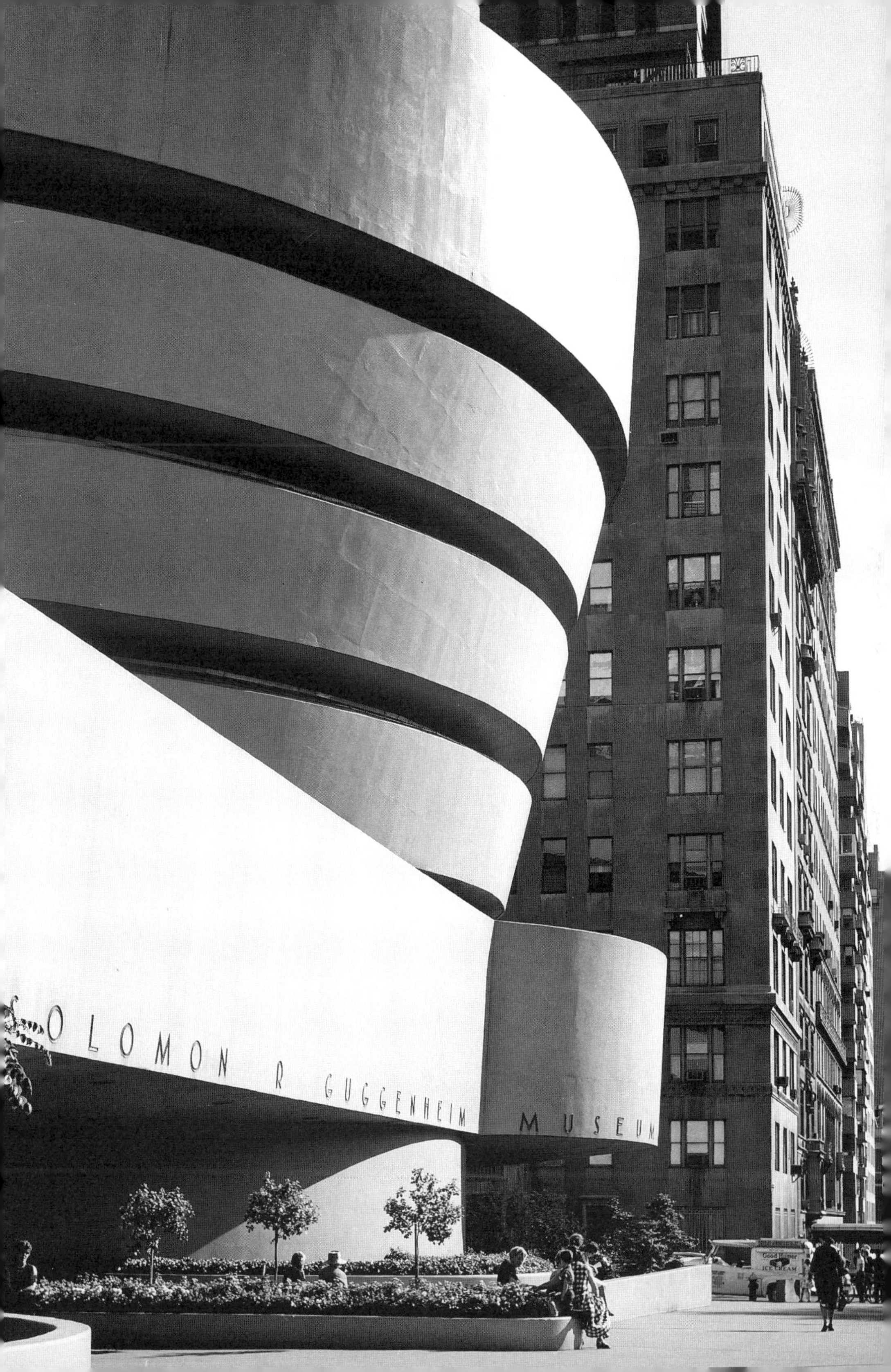
OLOMON R GUGGENHEIM MUSEUM
Good Humor
ICE CREAM

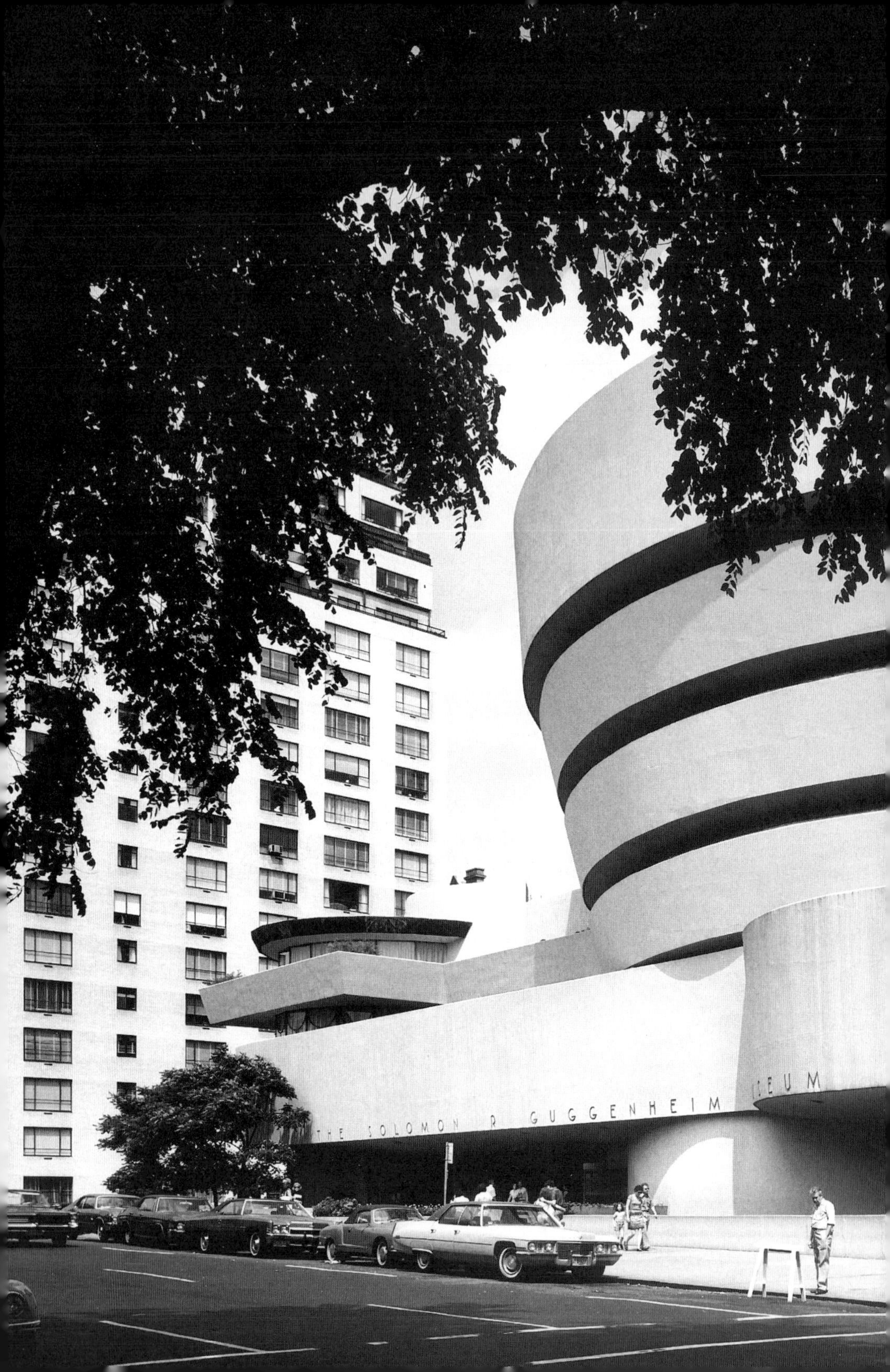
THE SOLOMON R GUGGENHEIM

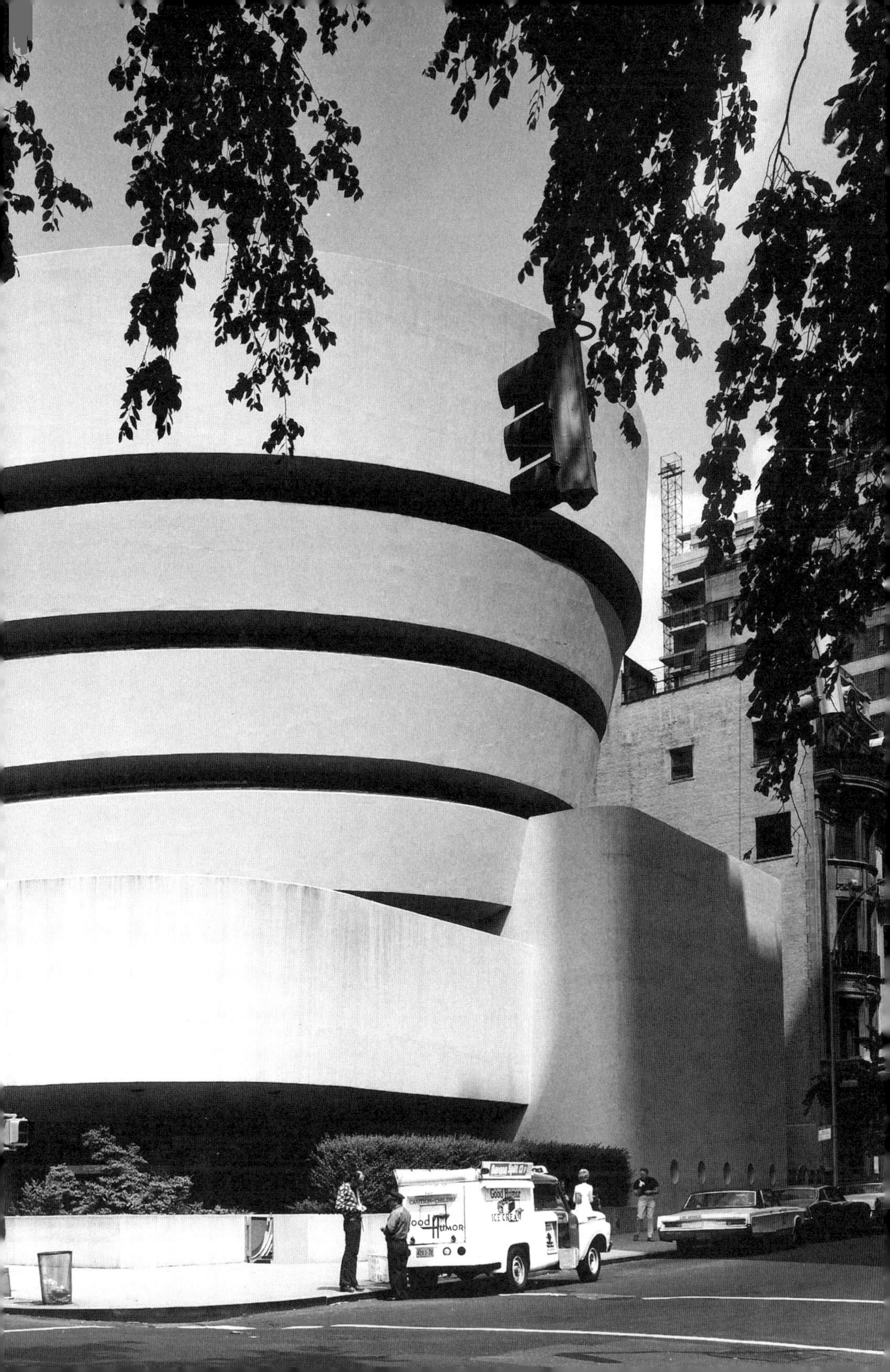
Good Humor

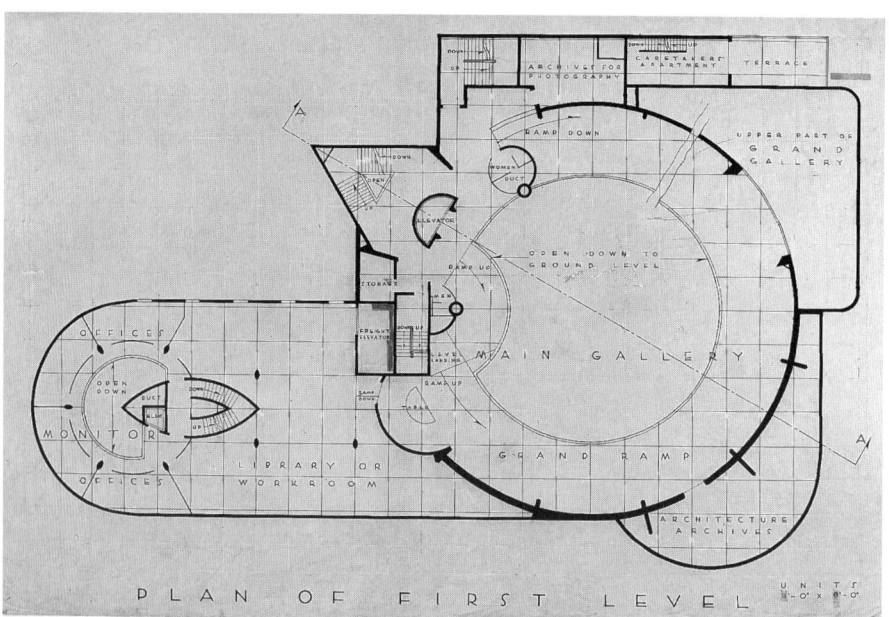

Plan of first level

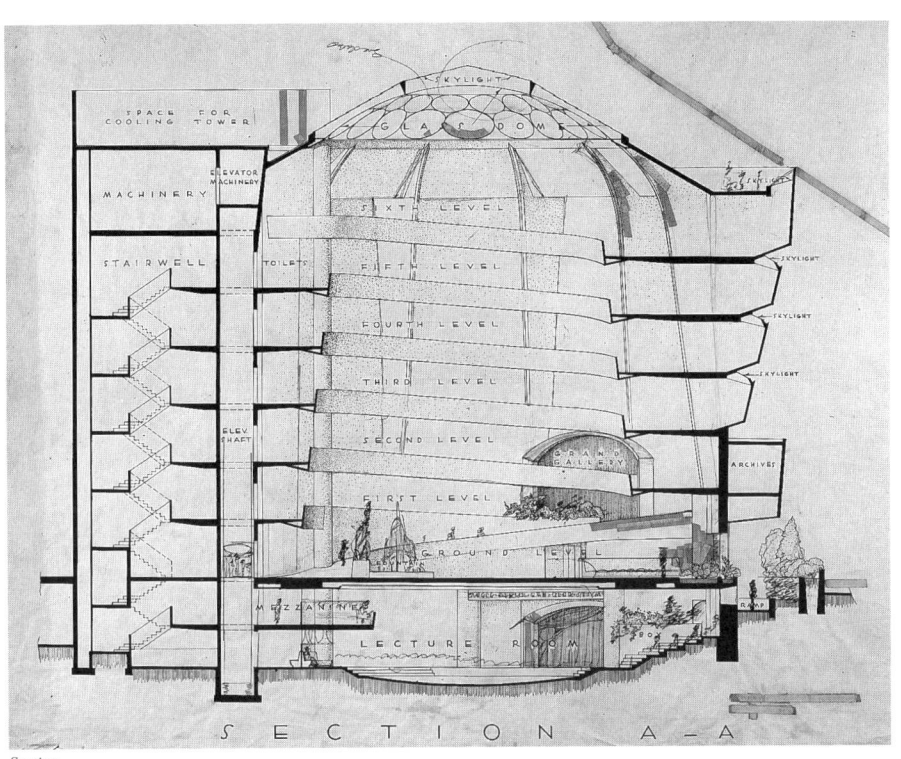

Section

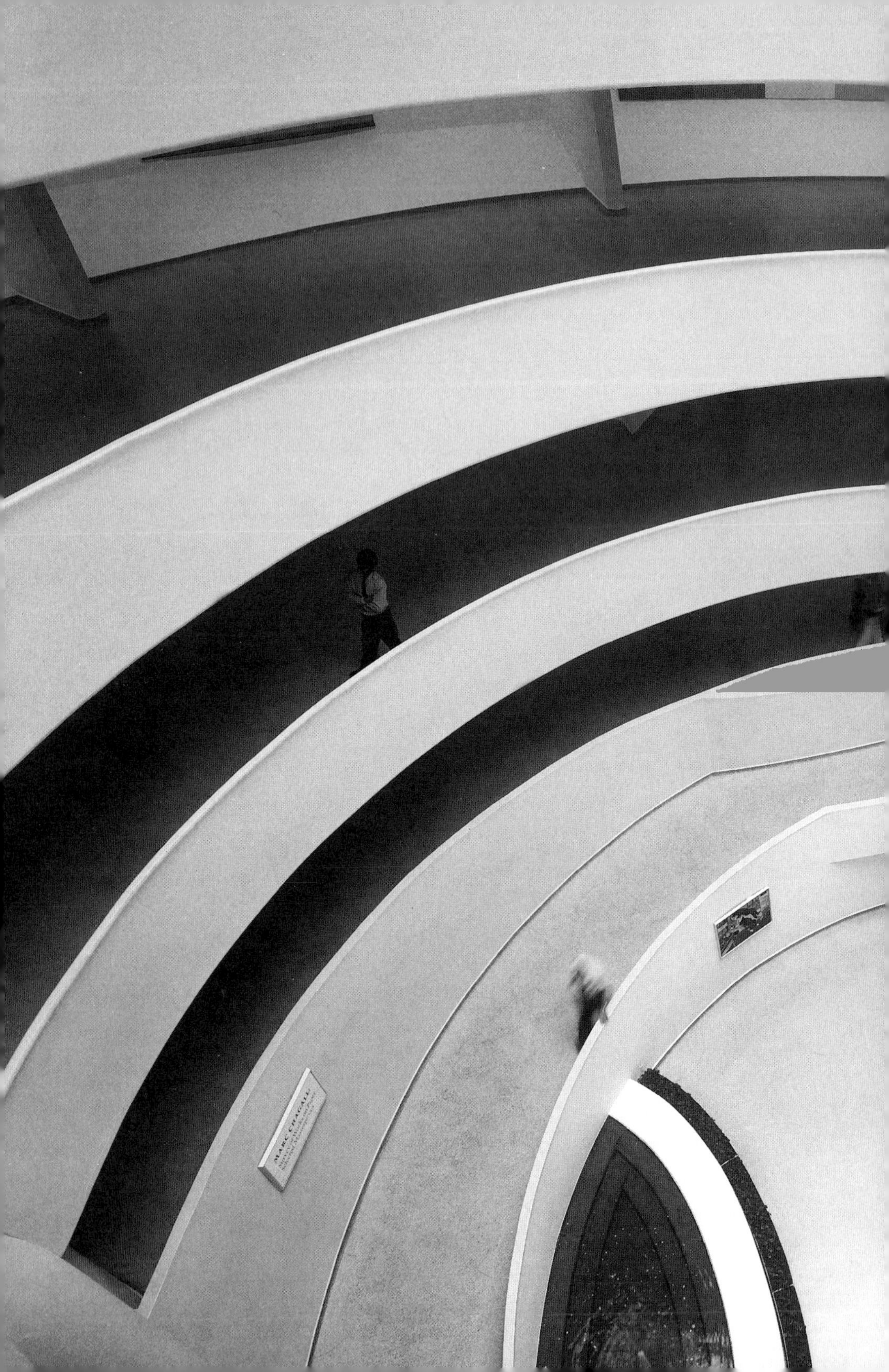
MARC CHAGALL

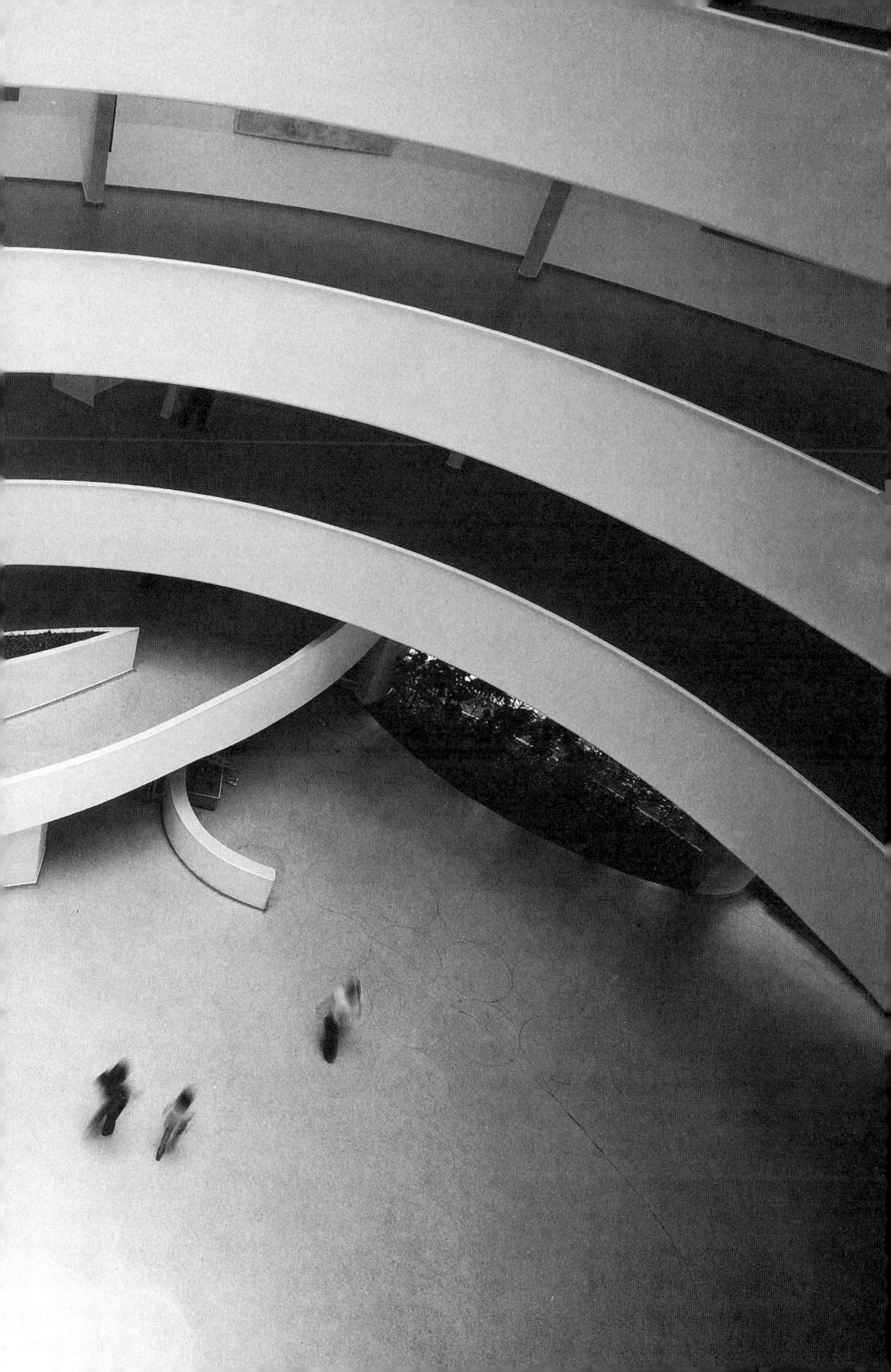

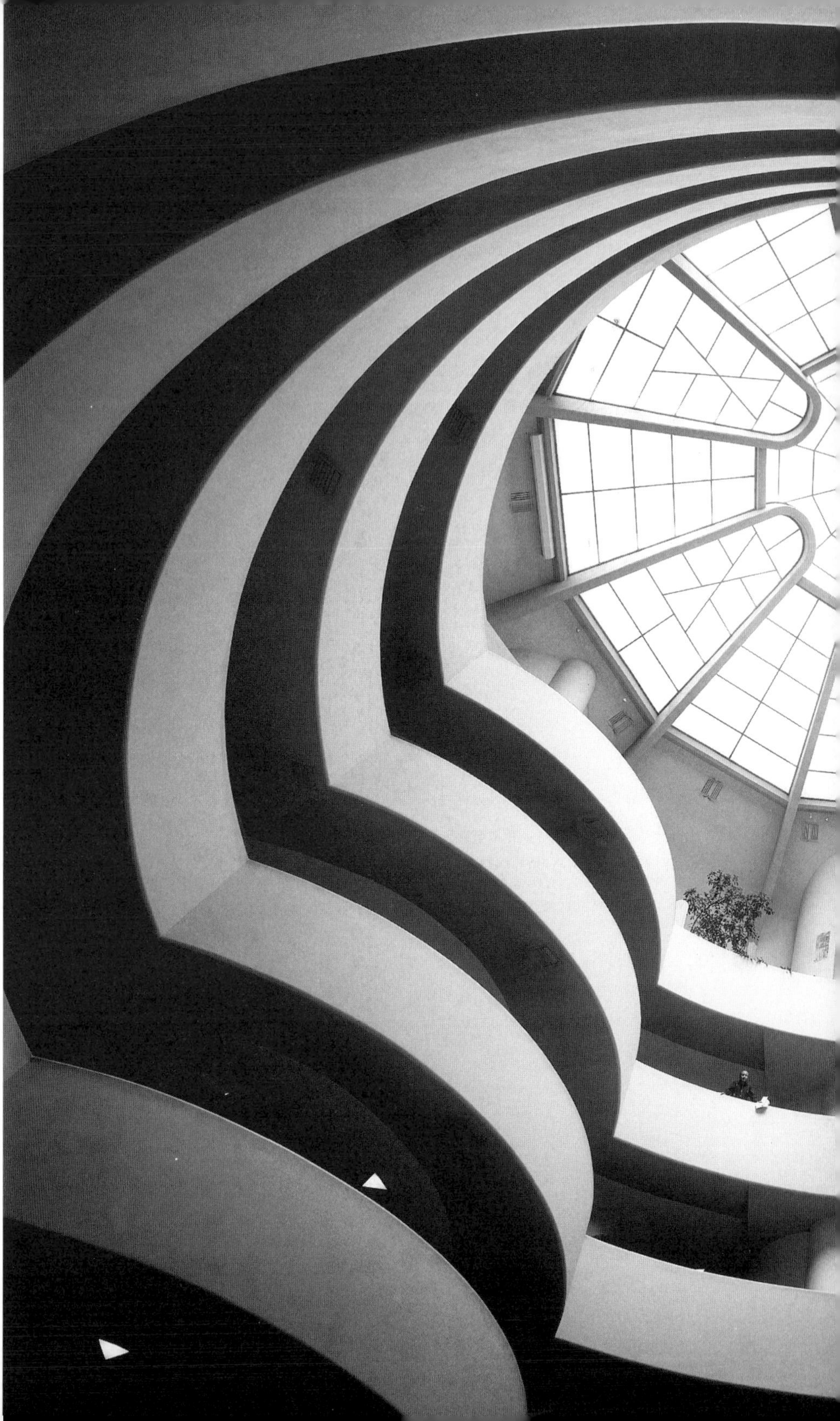

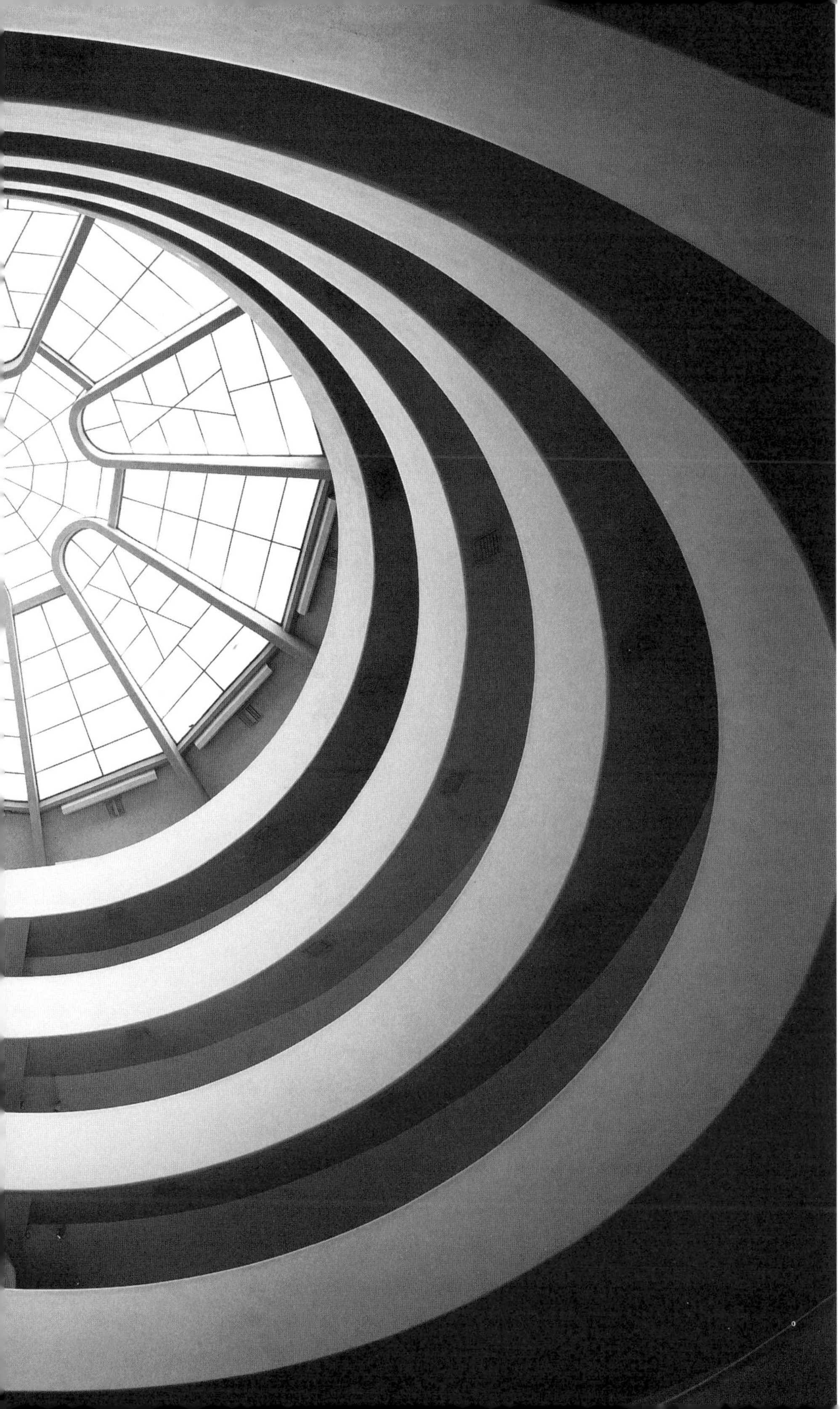

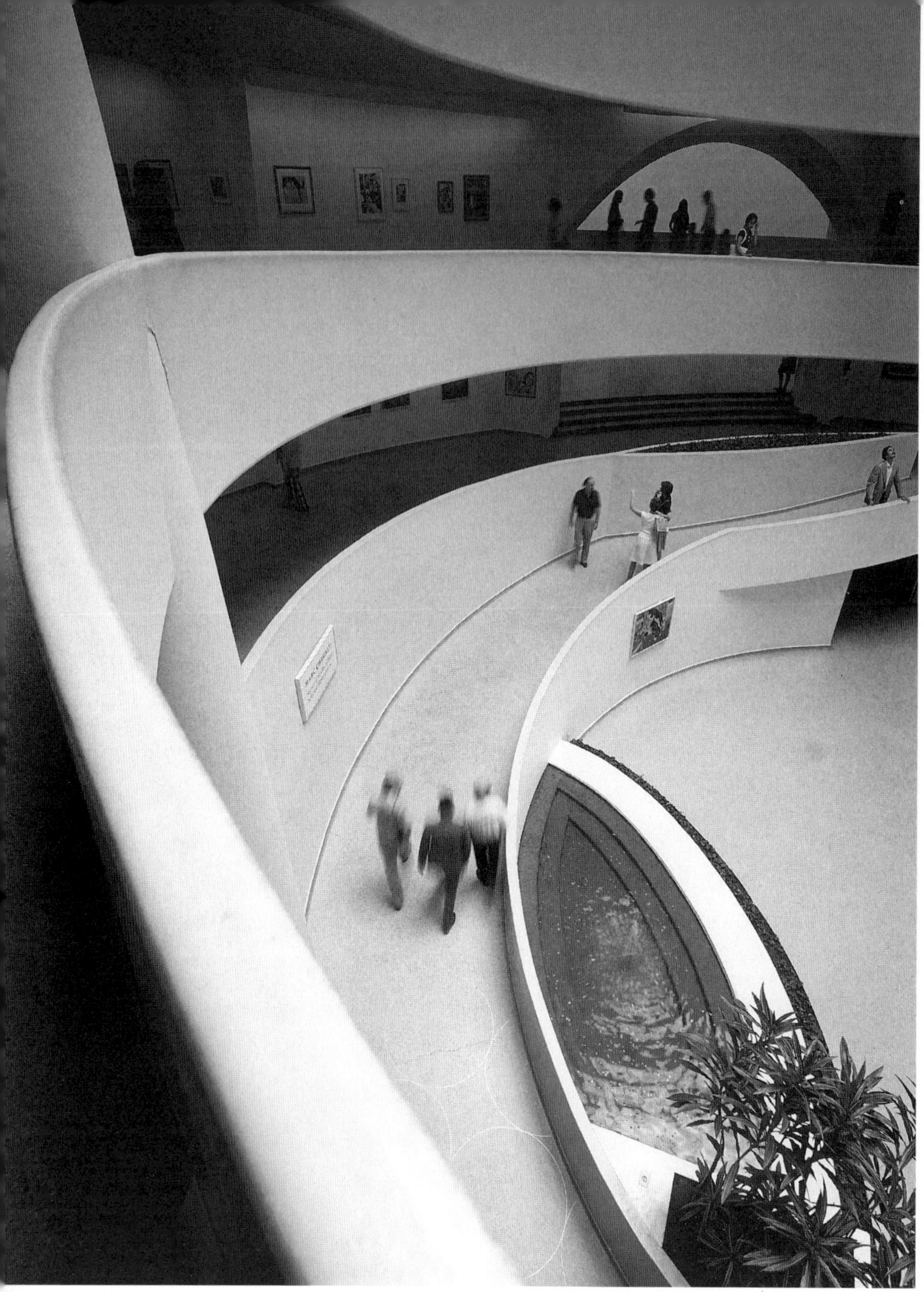

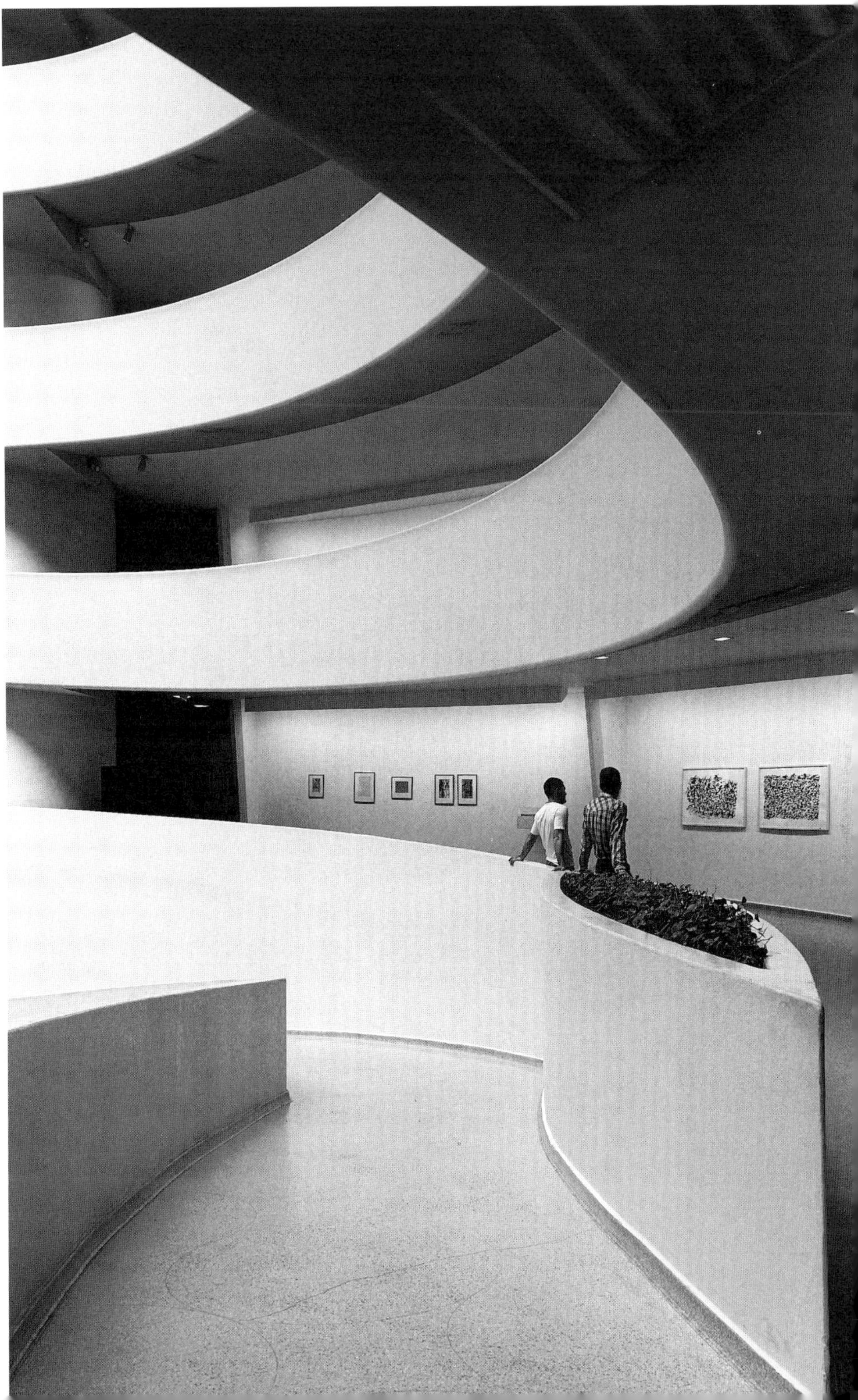

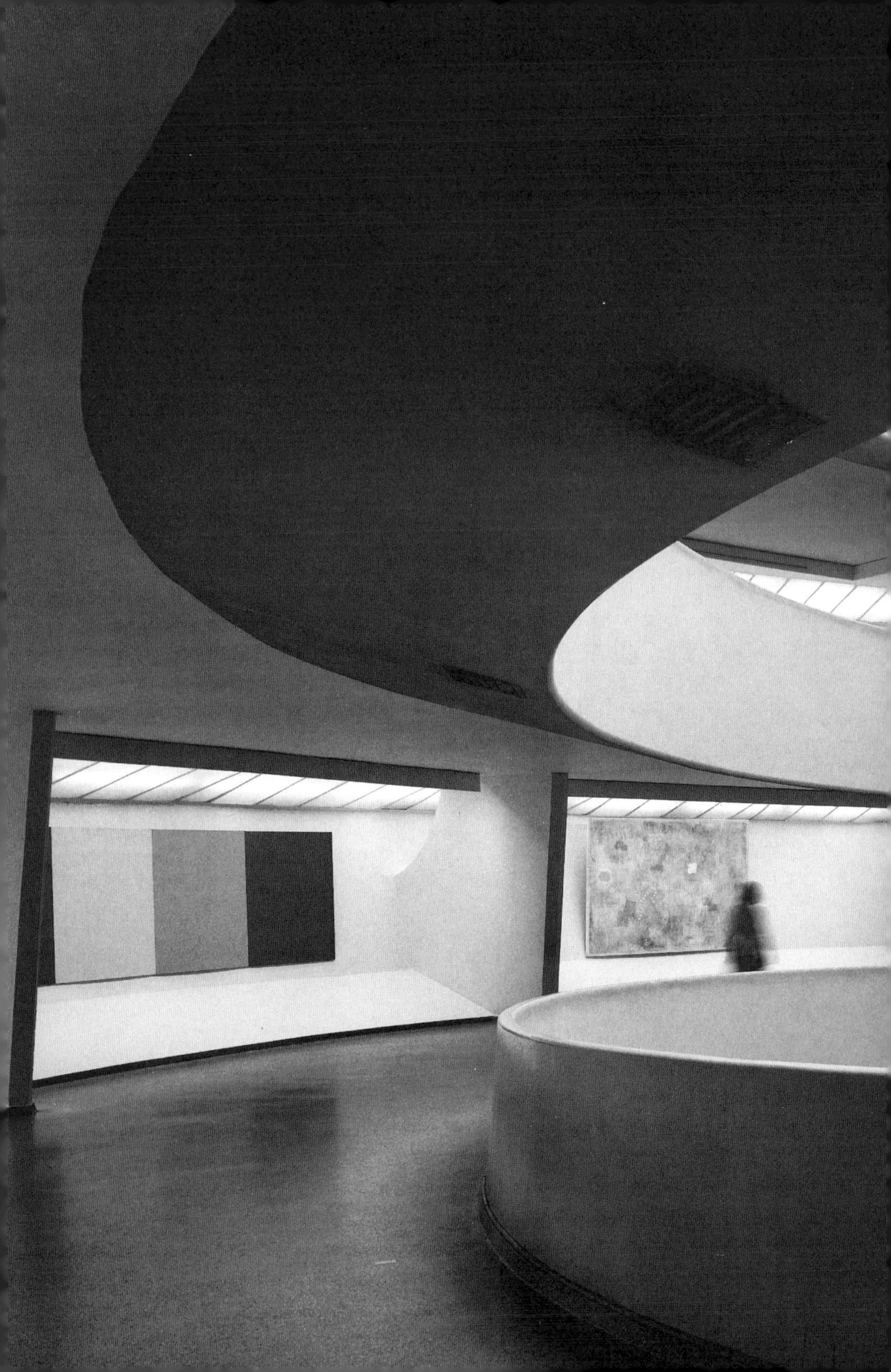

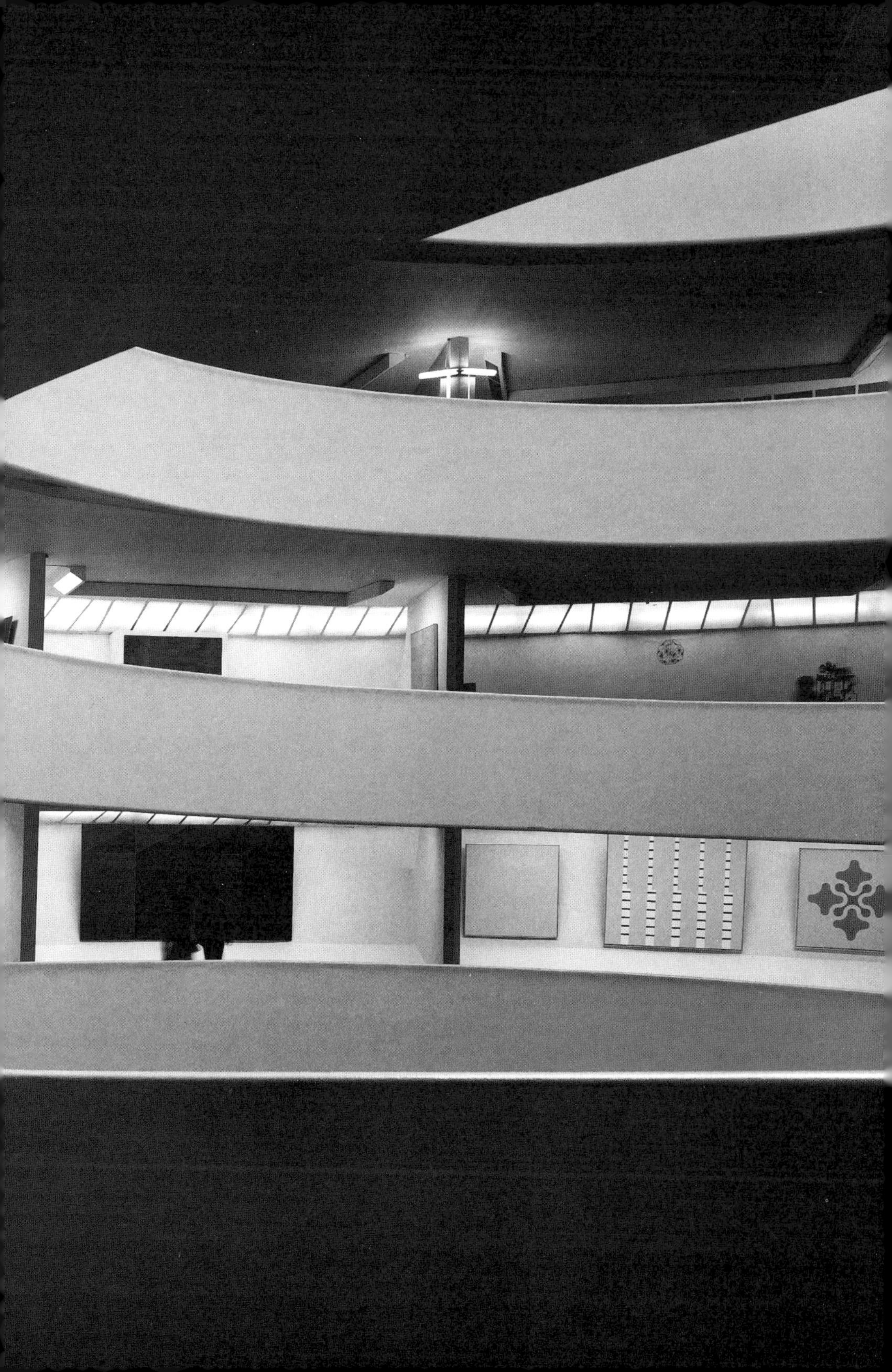

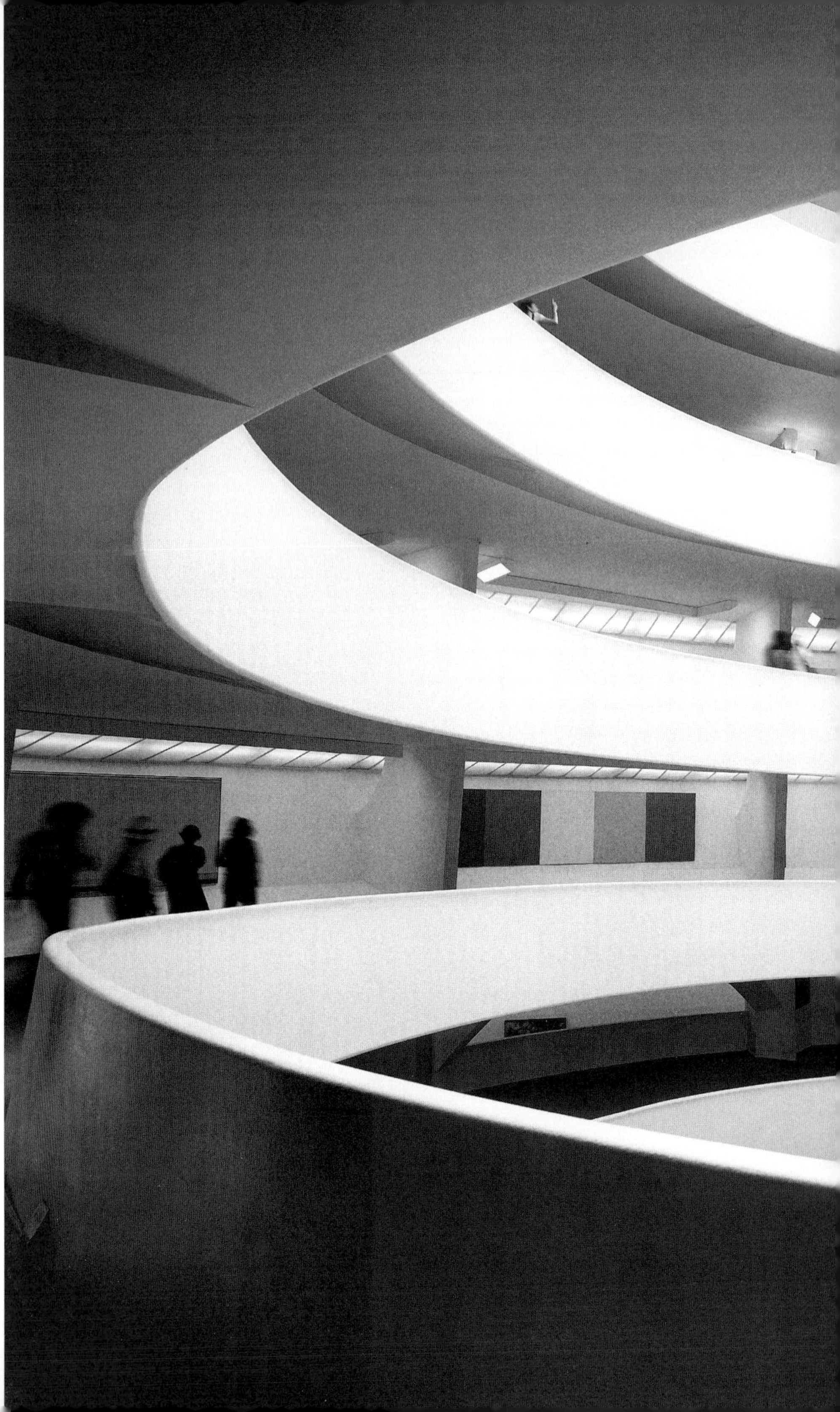

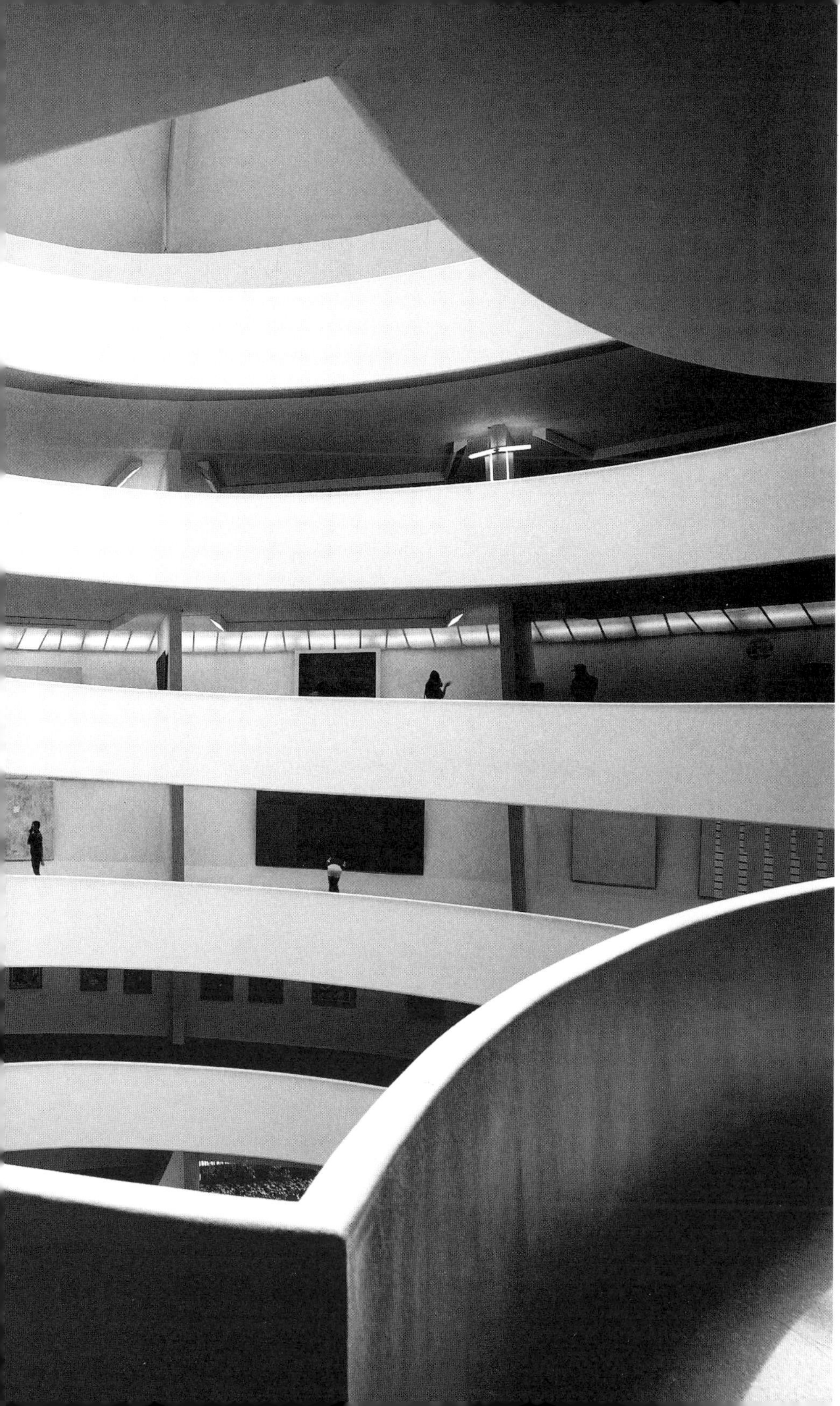

Tower for H. C. Price Company
Bartlesville, Oklahoma, 1952

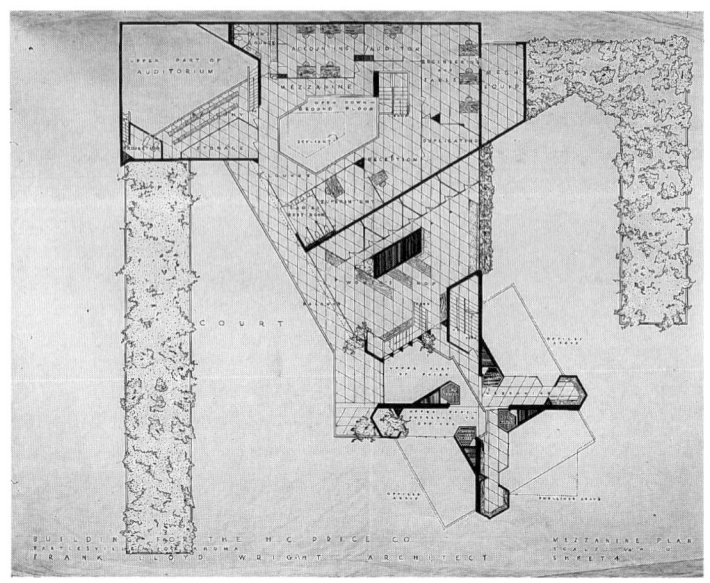

Mezzanine plan

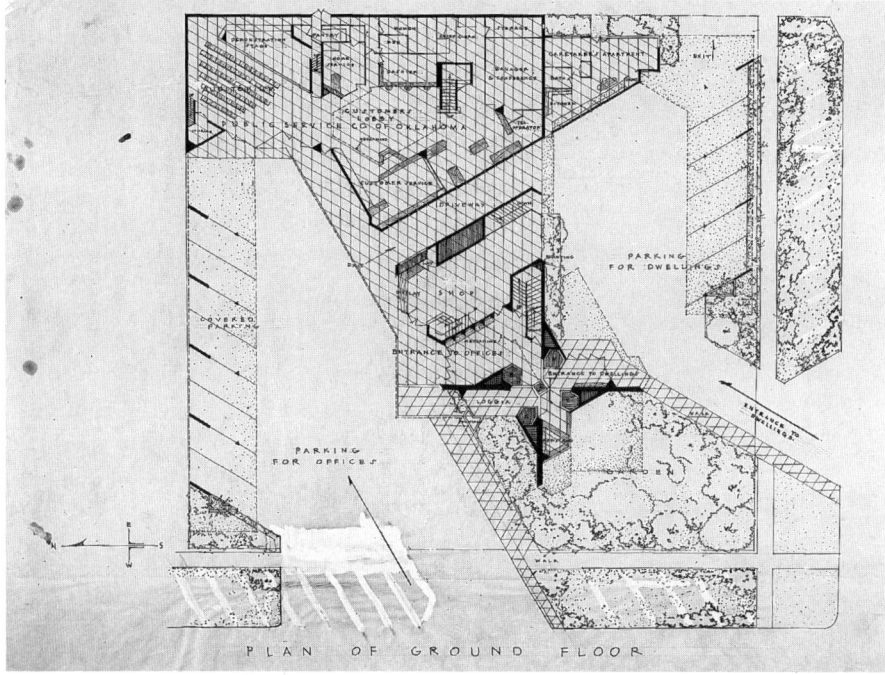

Ground floor plan

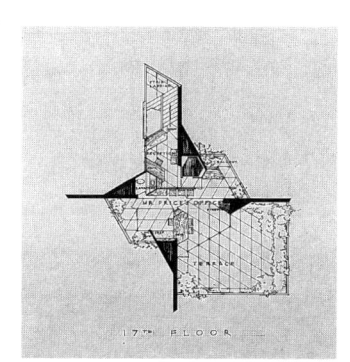

17th floor plan

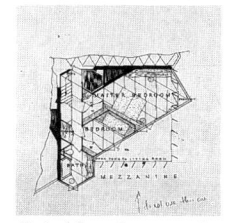

Typical floor plan: mezzanine

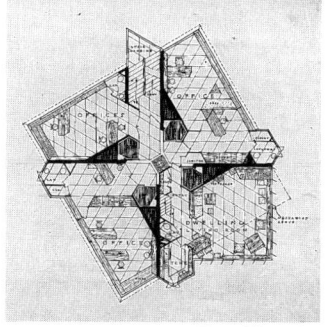

Typical floor plan

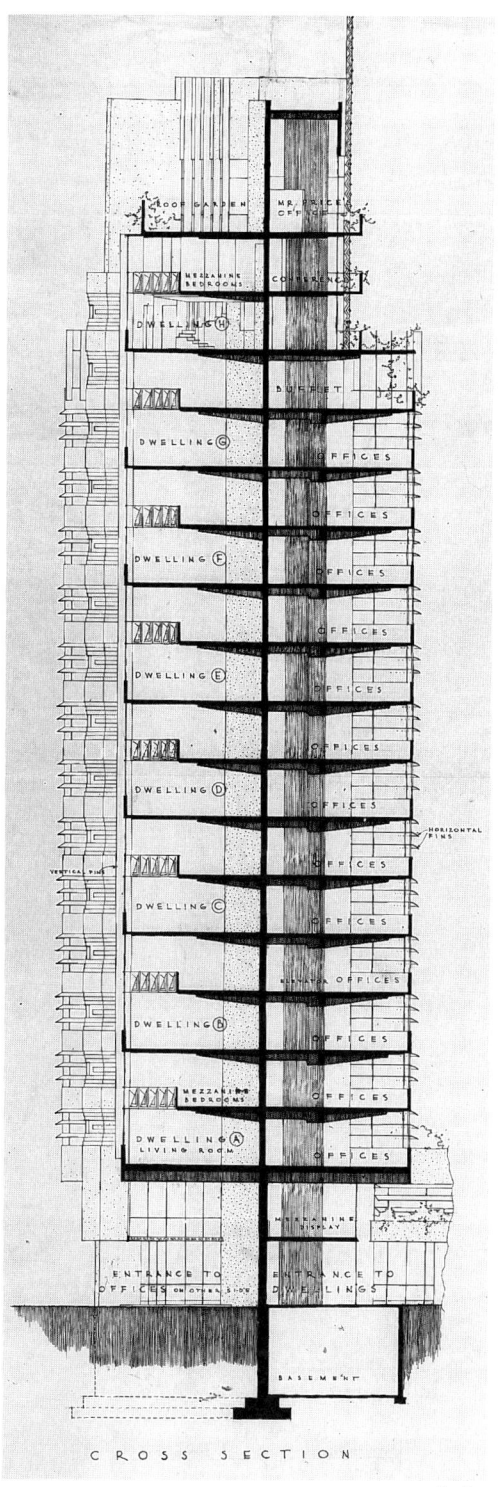

Section

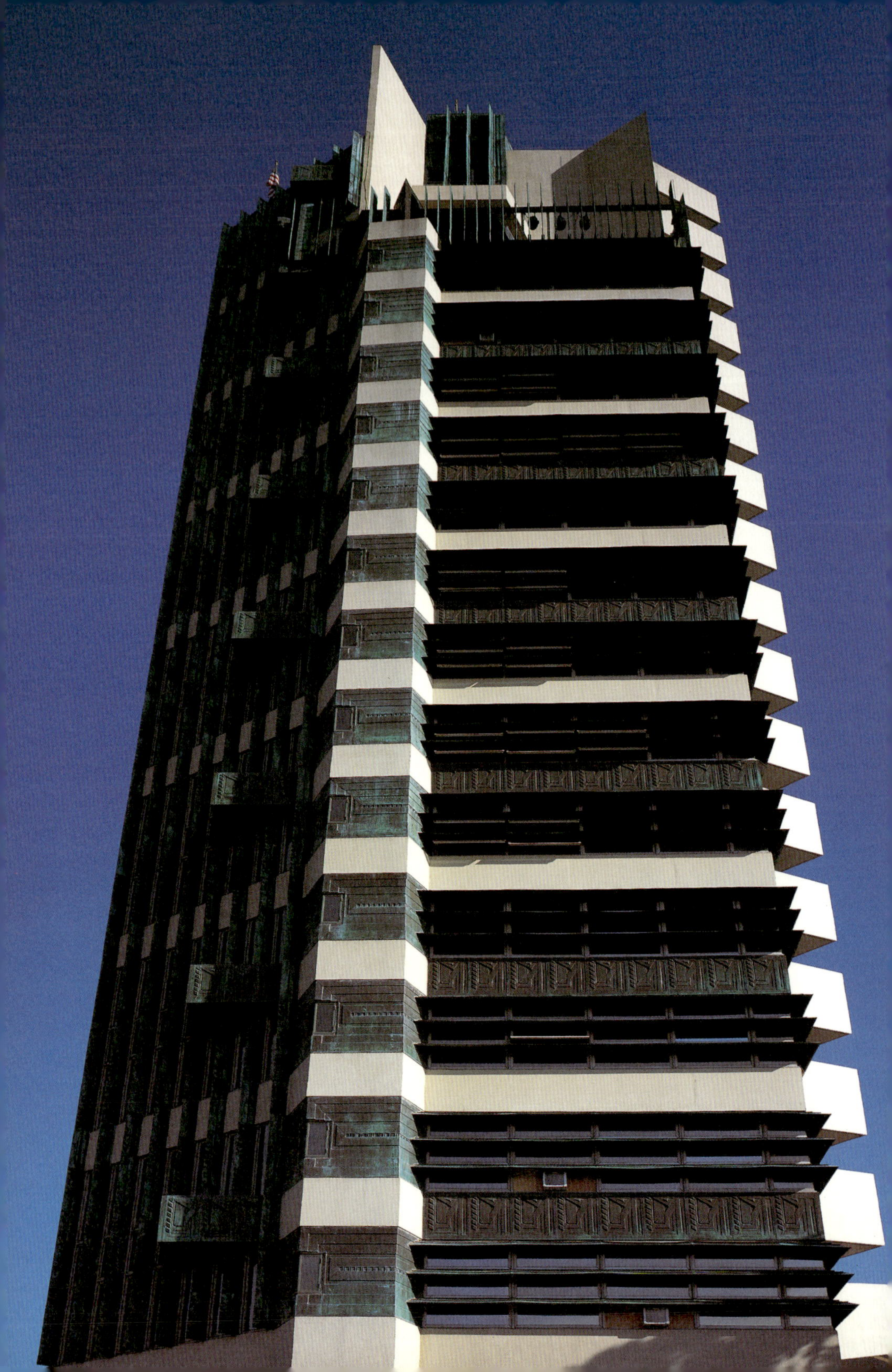

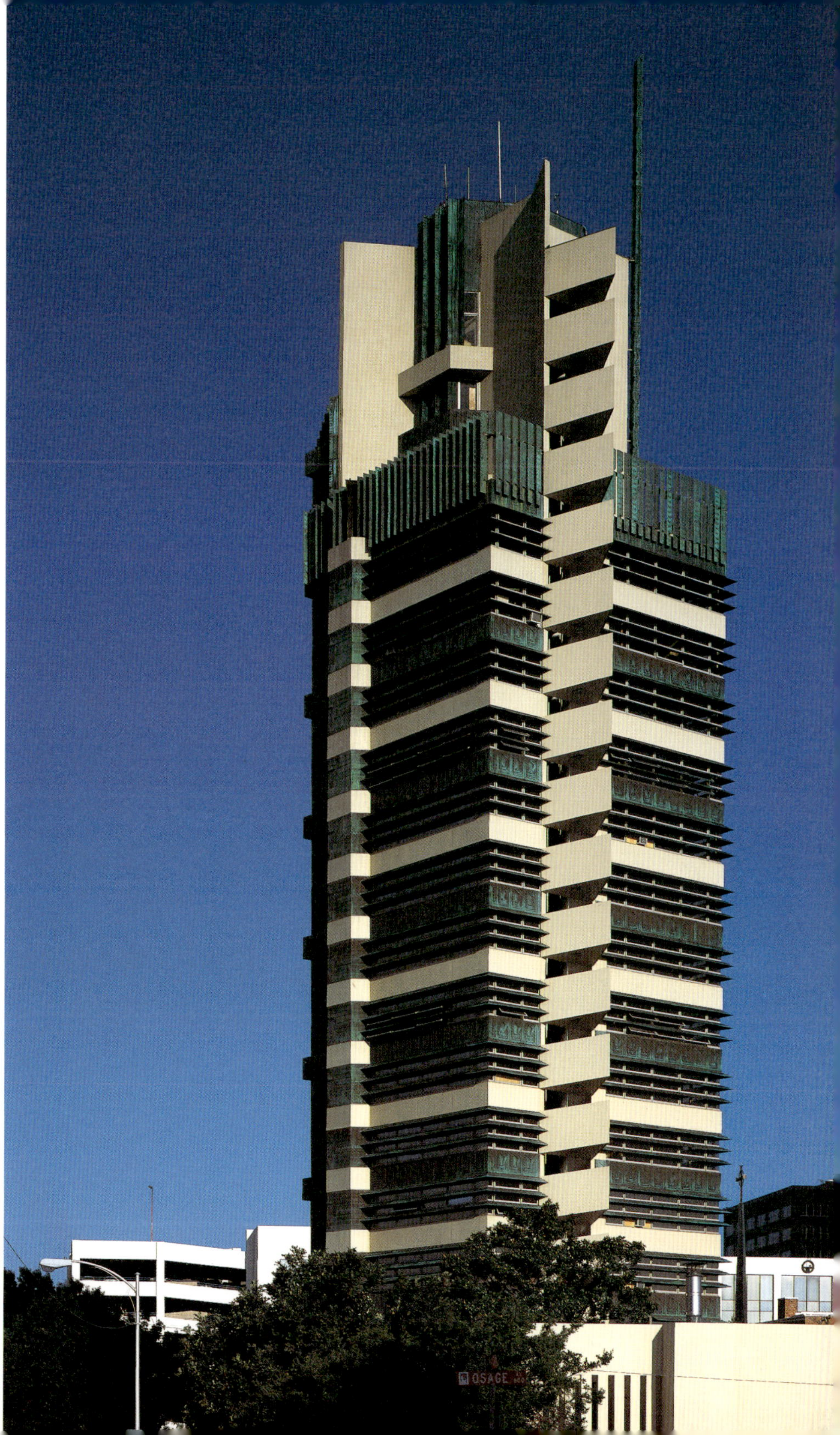
OSAGE

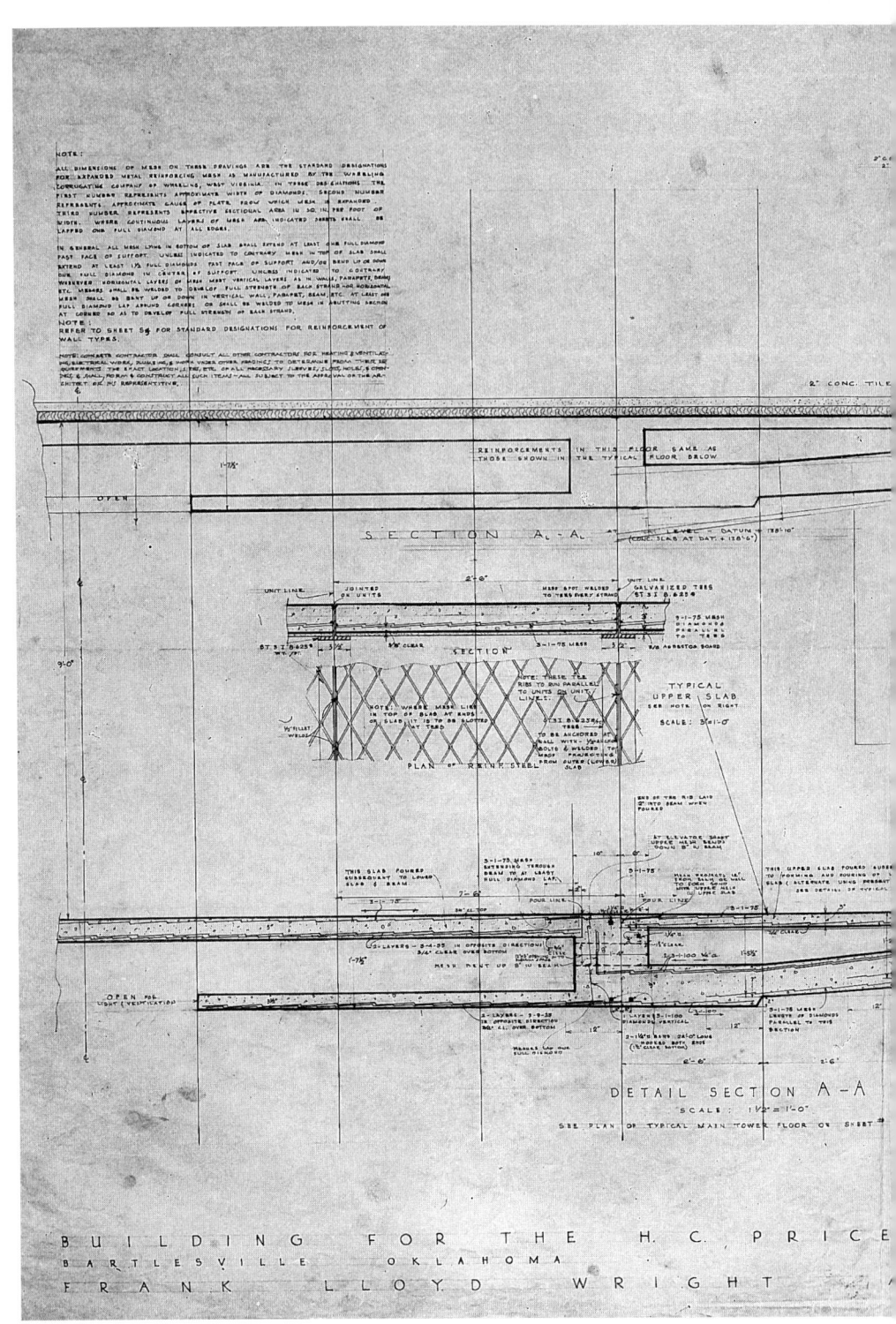

Structural details

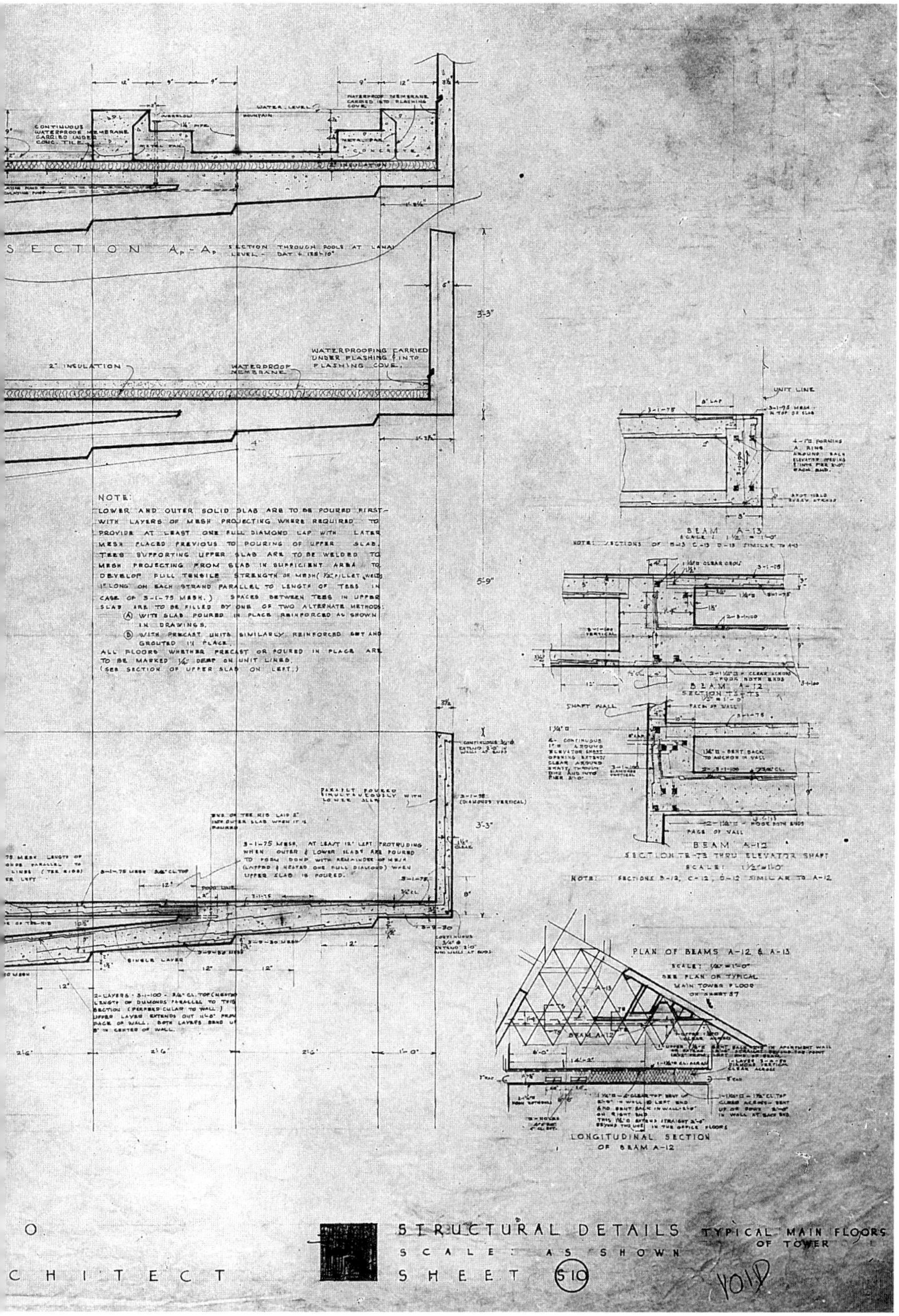
SECTION A_p-A_p SECTION THROUGH POOLS AT LANAI LEVEL - DAT. + 135'-10"
CONTINUOUS WATERPROOF MEMBRANE CARRIED UNDER CONC. TILE
WATER LEVEL
WATERPROOF MEMBRANE CARRIED INTO FLASHING COVE.
CONCRETE
INSULATION
2" INSULATION
WATERPROOF MEMBRANE
WATERPROOFING CARRIED UNDER FLASHING & INTO FLASHING COVE.
NOTE:
LOWER AND OUTER SOLID SLAB ARE TO BE POURED FIRST WITH LAYERS OF MESH PROJECTING WHERE REQUIRED TO PROVIDE AT LEAST ONE FULL DIAMOND LAP WITH LATER MESH PLACED PREVIOUS TO POURING OF UPPER SLAB. TEES SUPPORTING UPPER SLAB ARE TO BE WELDED TO MESH PROJECTING FROM SLAB IN SUFFICIENT AREA TO DEVELOP FULL TENSILE STRENGTH OF MESH (1/2" FILLET WELDS 1" LONG ON EACH STRAND PARALLEL TO LENGTH OF TEES IN CASE OF 3-1-75 MESH.) SPACES BETWEEN TEES IN UPPER SLAB ARE TO BE FILLED BY ONE OF TWO ALTERNATE METHODS:
(A) WITH SLAB POURED IN PLACE REINFORCED AS SHOWN IN DRAWINGS.
(B) WITH PRECAST UNITS SIMILARLY REINFORCED SET AND GROUTED IN PLACE.
ALL FLOORS WHETHER PRECAST OR POURED IN PLACE ARE TO BE MARKED 1/8" DEEP ON UNIT LINES.
(SEE SECTION OF UPPER SLAB ON LEFT.)
PARAPET POURED SIMULTANEOUSLY WITH LOWER SLAB
3-1-75 MESH, AT LEAST 12" LEFT PROTRUDING WHEN OUTER & LOWER SLABS ARE POURED TO FORM BOND WITH REMAINDER OF MESH (LAPPED & NESTED ONE FULL DIAMOND) WHEN UPPER SLAB IS POURED.
SINGLE LAYER
2-LAYERS - 3-1-100
UNIT LINE
BEAM A-13
SCALE: 1 1/2" = 1'-0"
NOTE: SECTIONS OF B-13 C-13 D-13 SIMILAR TO A-13
BEAM A-12
SHAFT WALL
FACE OF WALL
BEAM A-12
SECTION TB-TB THRU ELEVATOR SHAFT
SCALE: 1 1/2" = 1'-0"
NOTE: SECTIONS B-12, C-12, D-12 SIMILAR TO A-12
PLAN OF BEAMS A-12 & A-13
SCALE: 1/8" = 1'-0"
SEE PLAN OF TYPICAL MAIN TOWER FLOOR ON SHEET 57
LONGITUDINAL SECTION OF BEAM A-12
STRUCTURAL DETAILS TYPICAL MAIN FLOORS OF TOWER
SCALE: AS SHOWN
SHEET 510
VOID

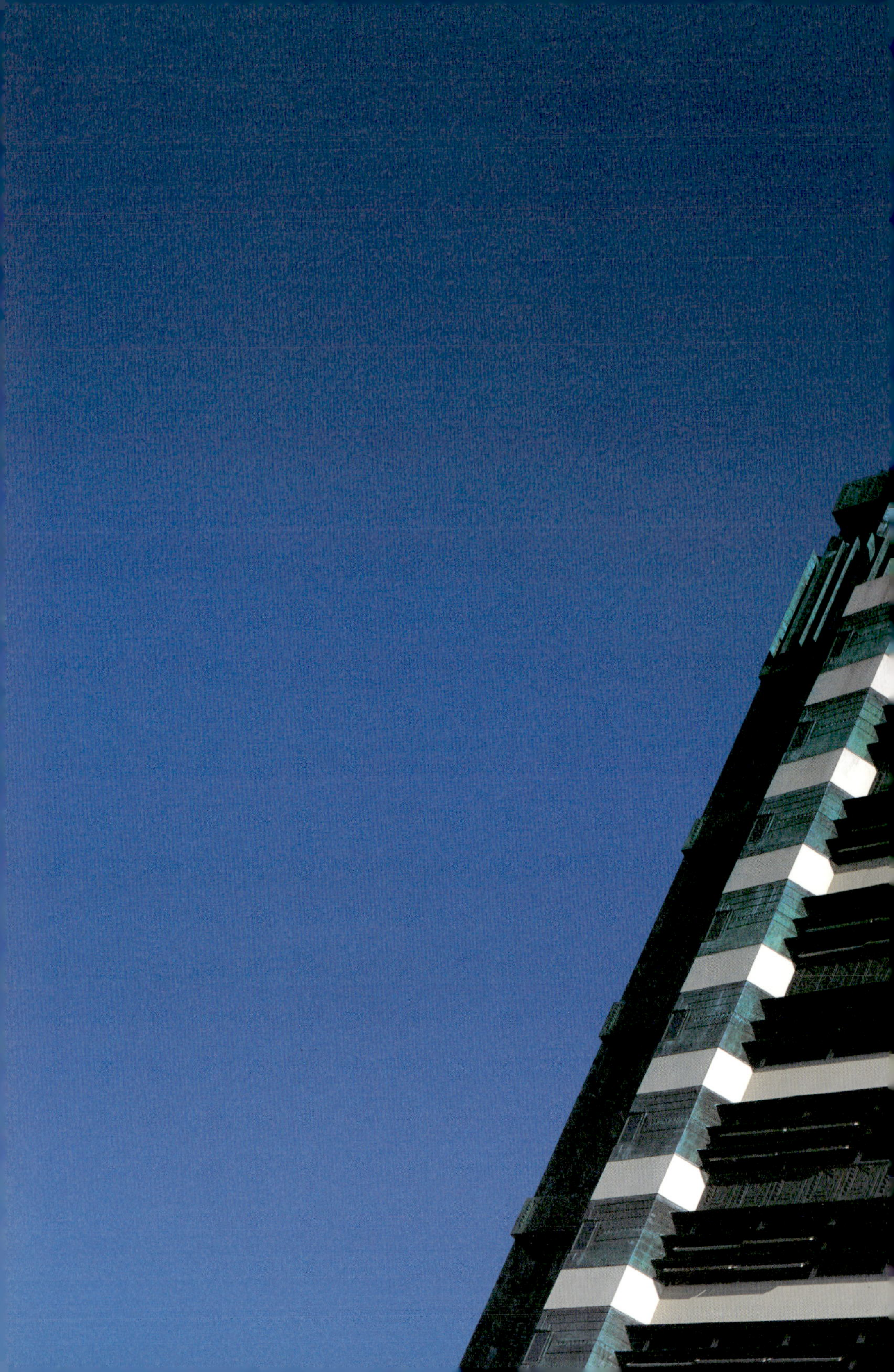

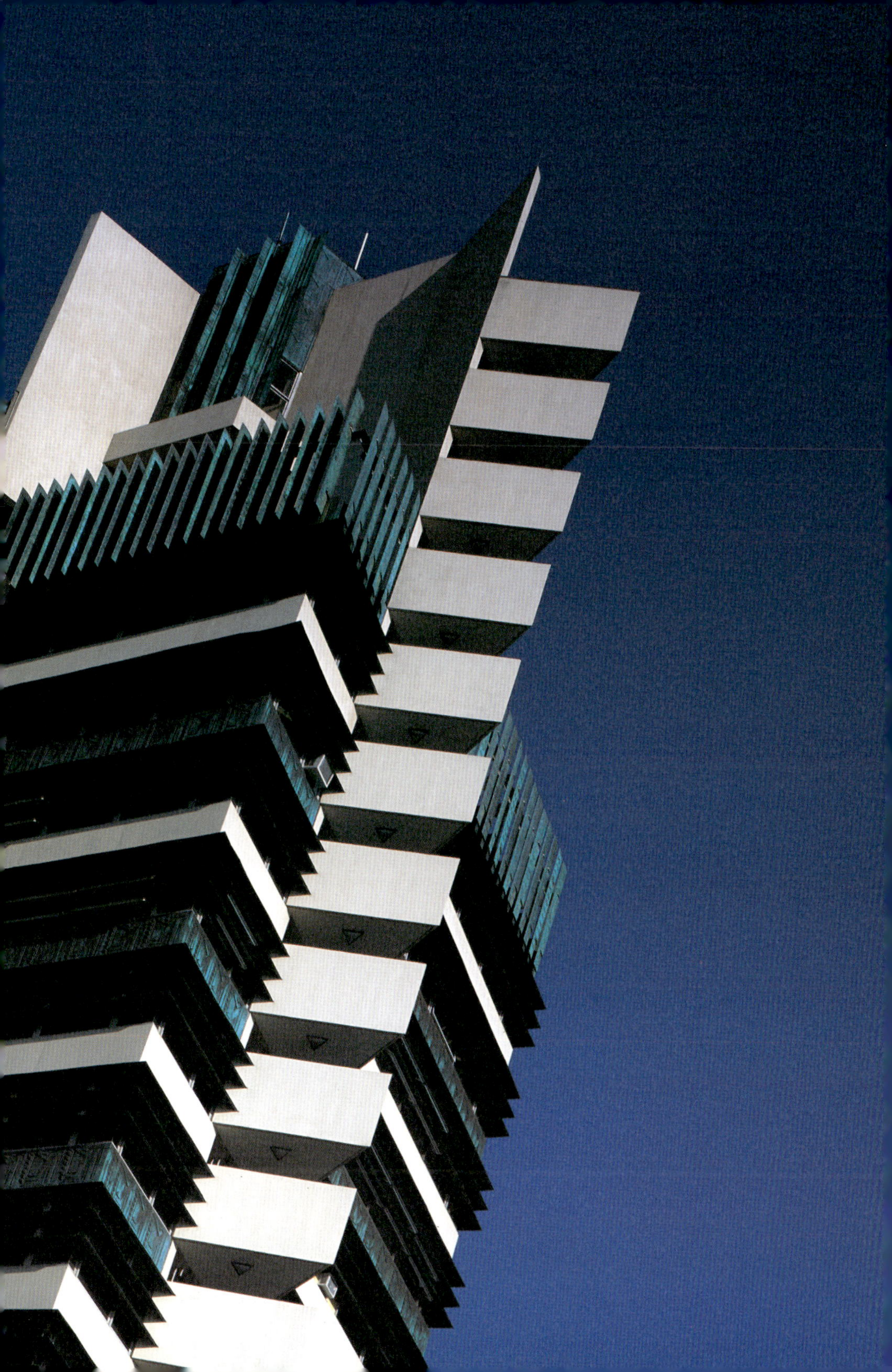

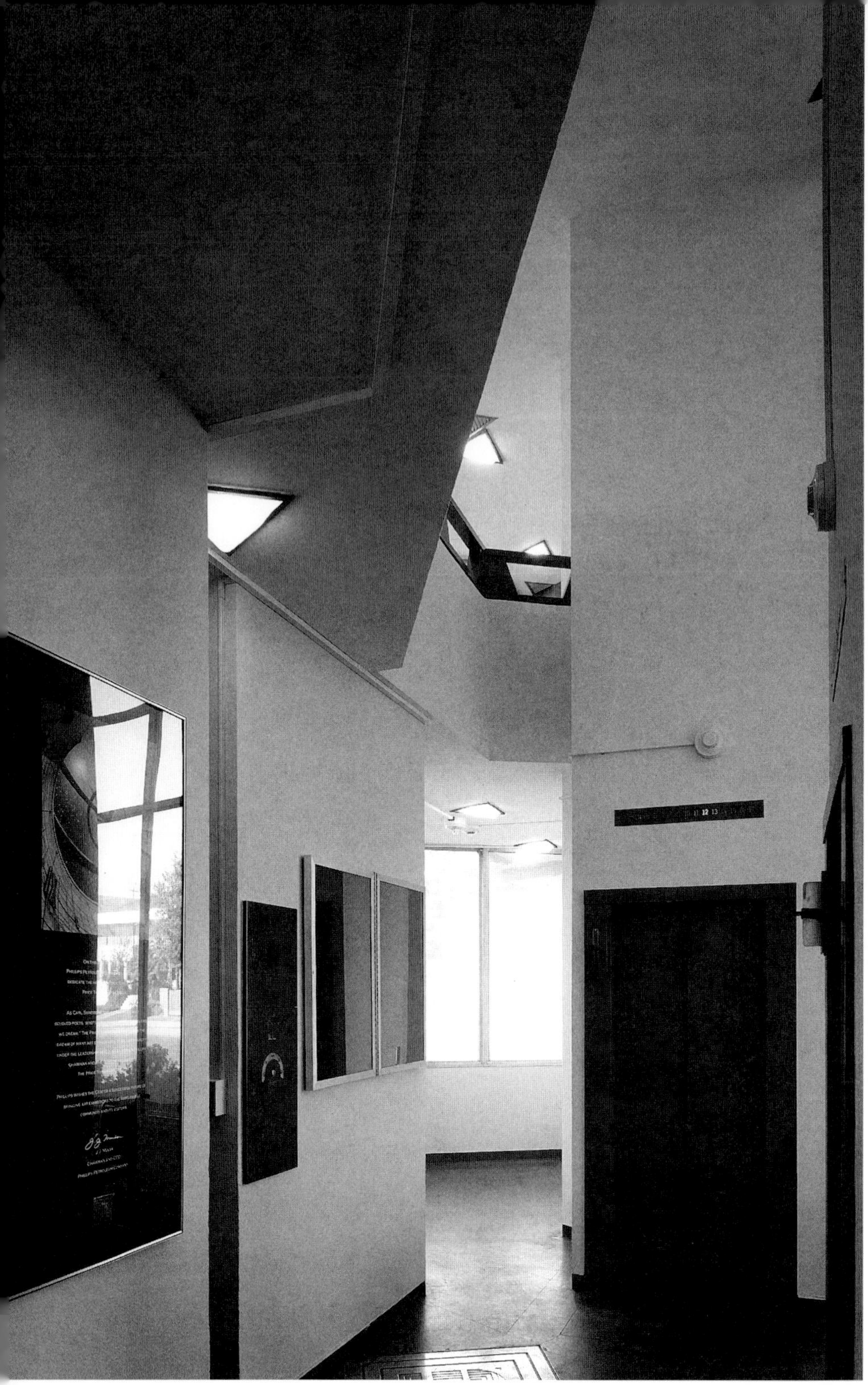

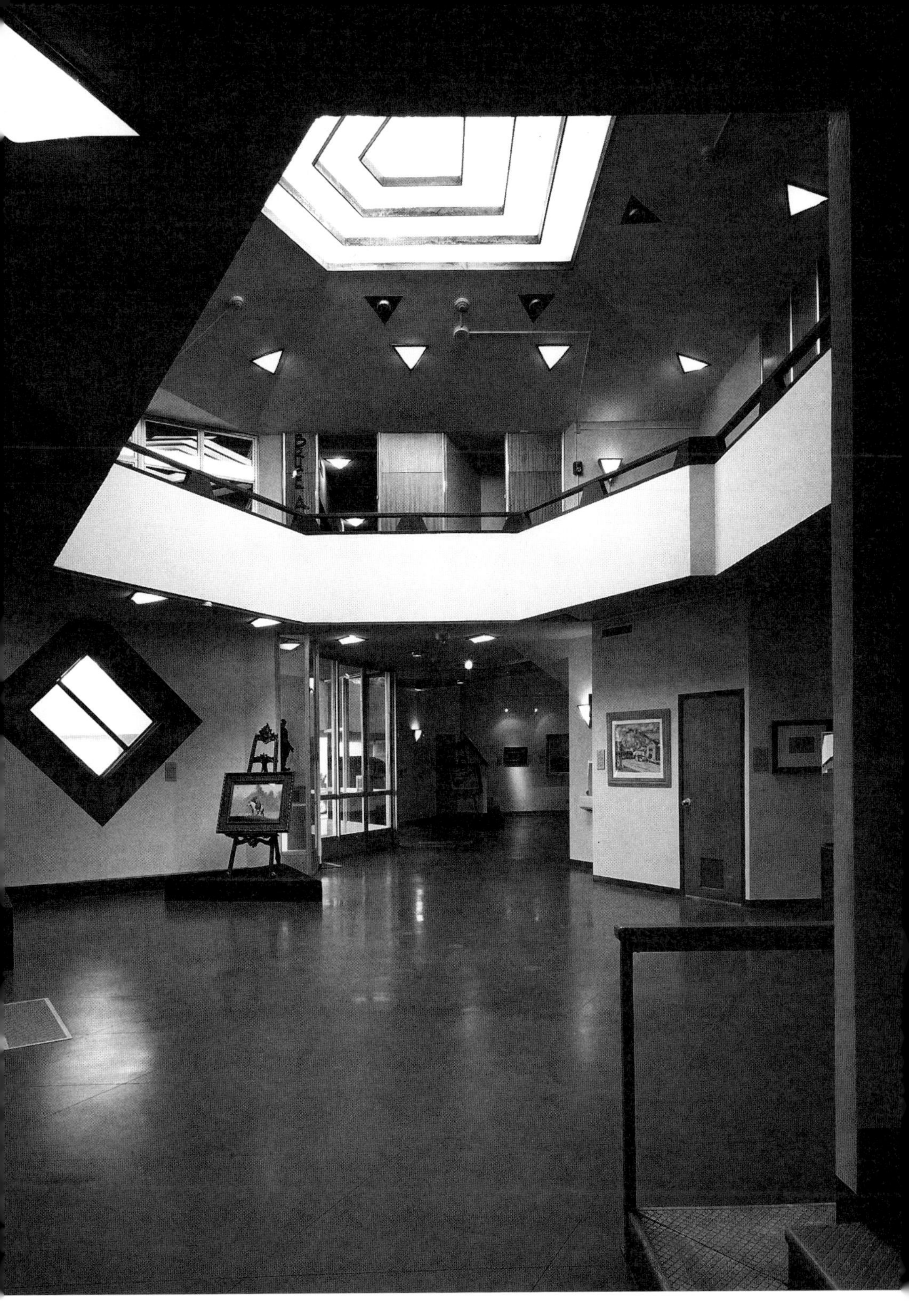

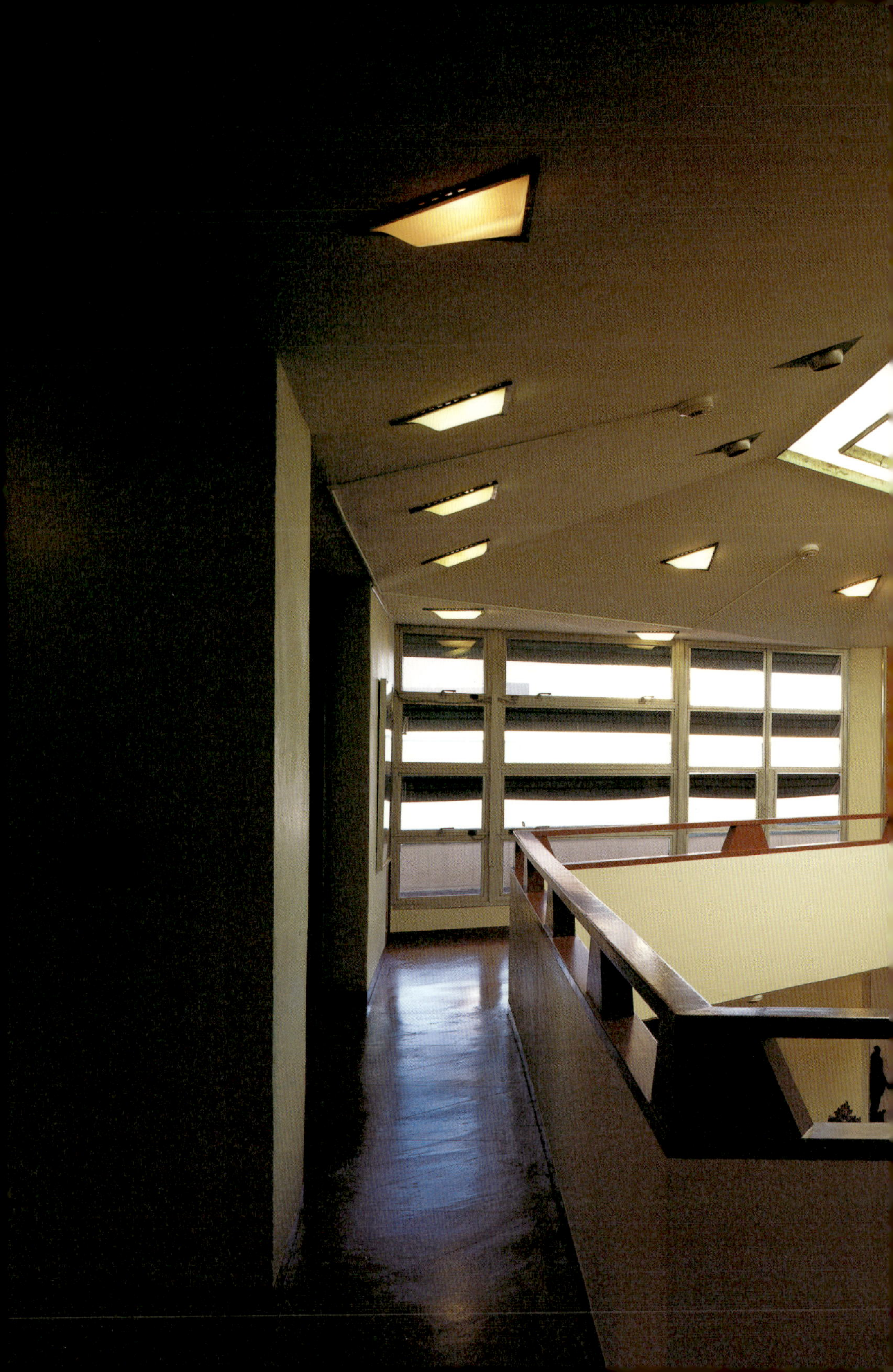

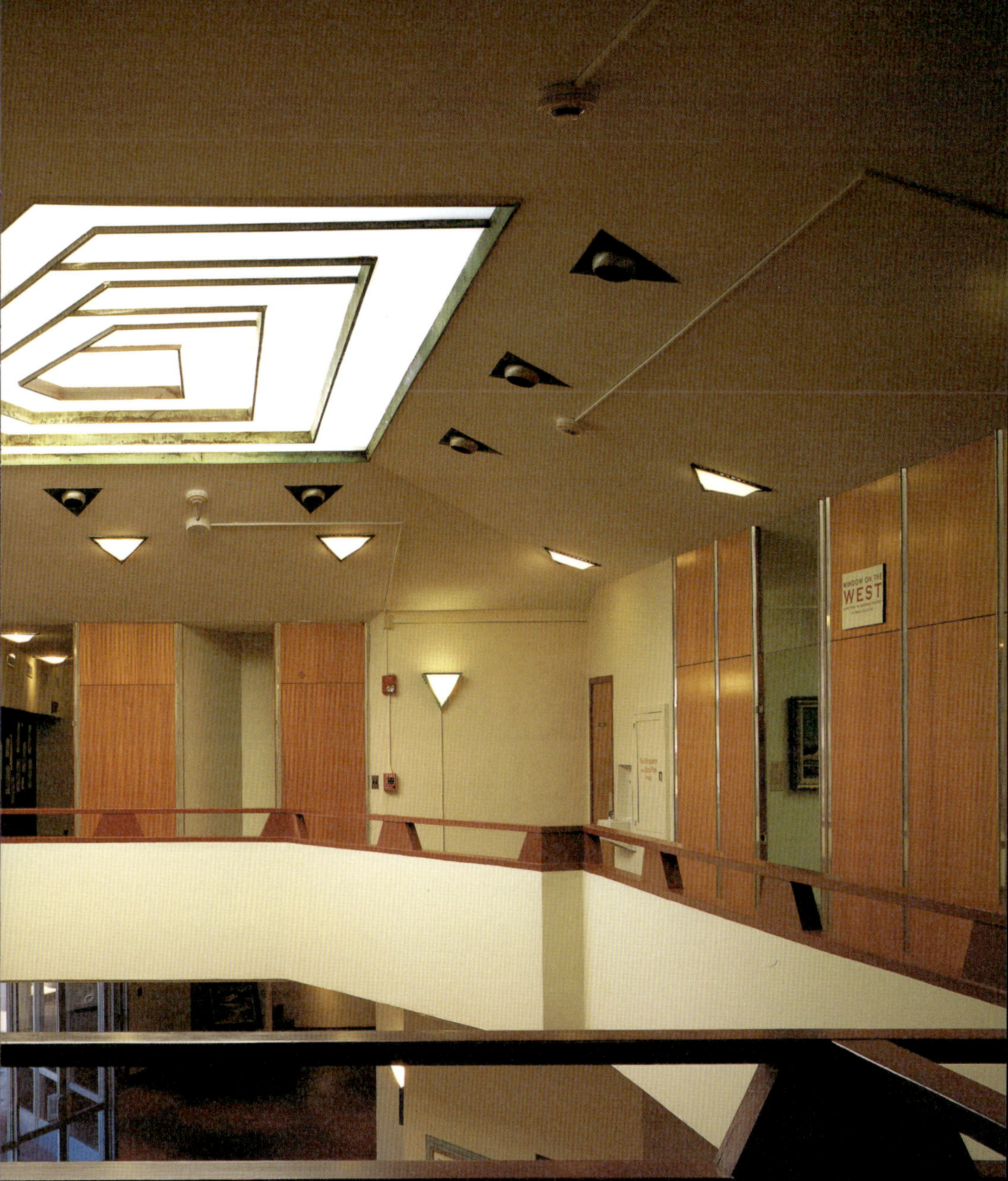
WINDOW ON THE
WEST

Interior perspective of living room

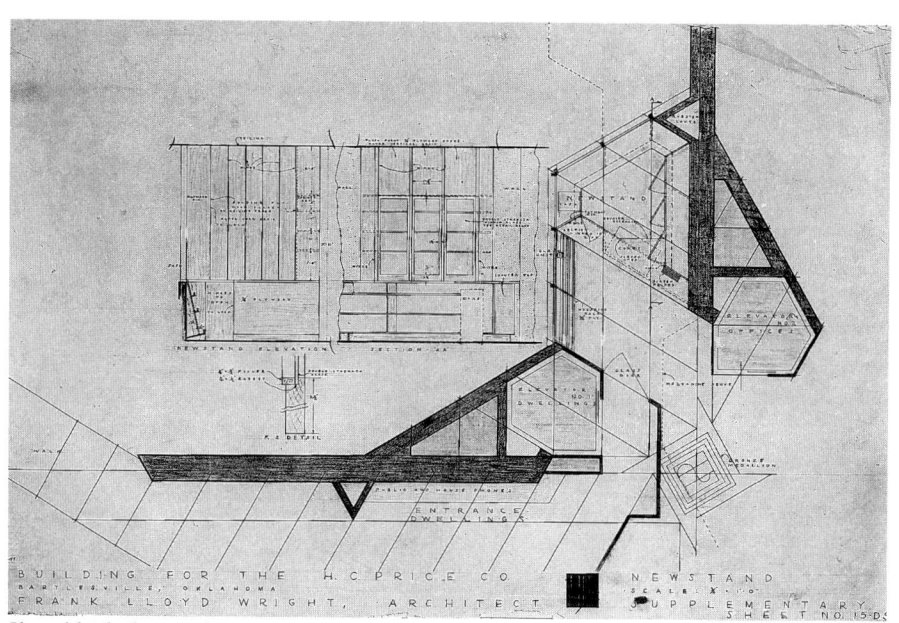

Plan and details of newsstand

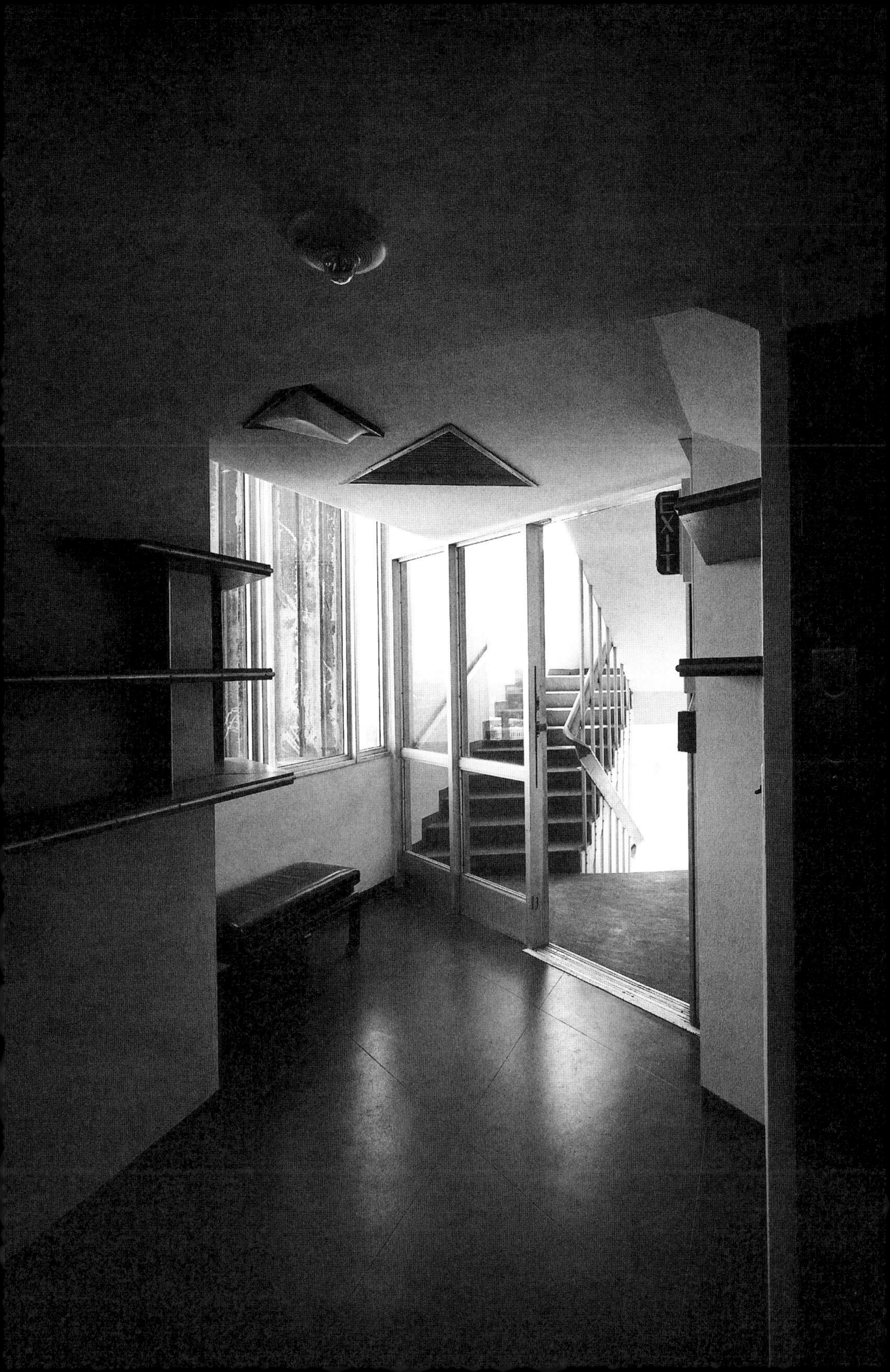
EXIT

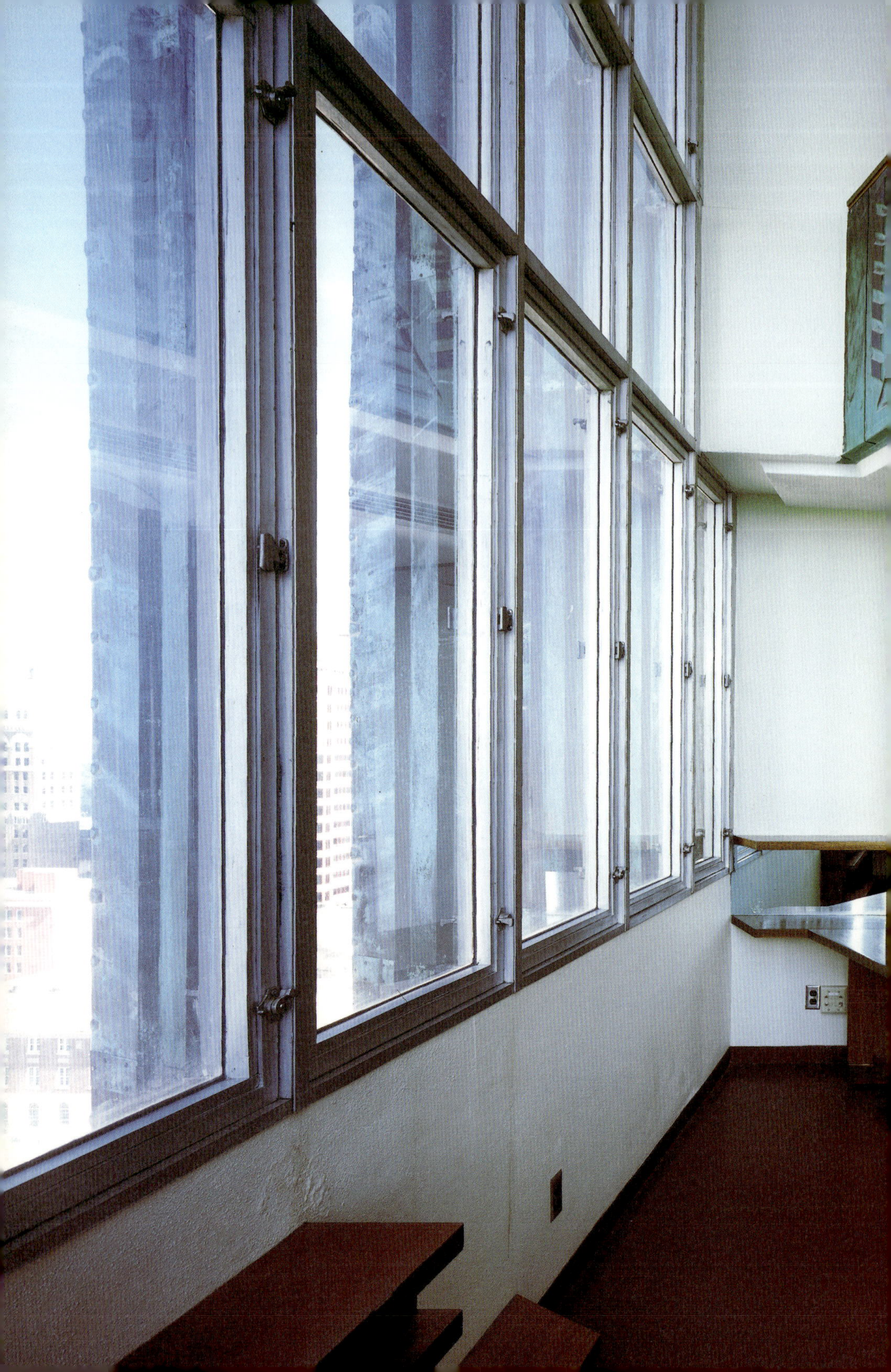

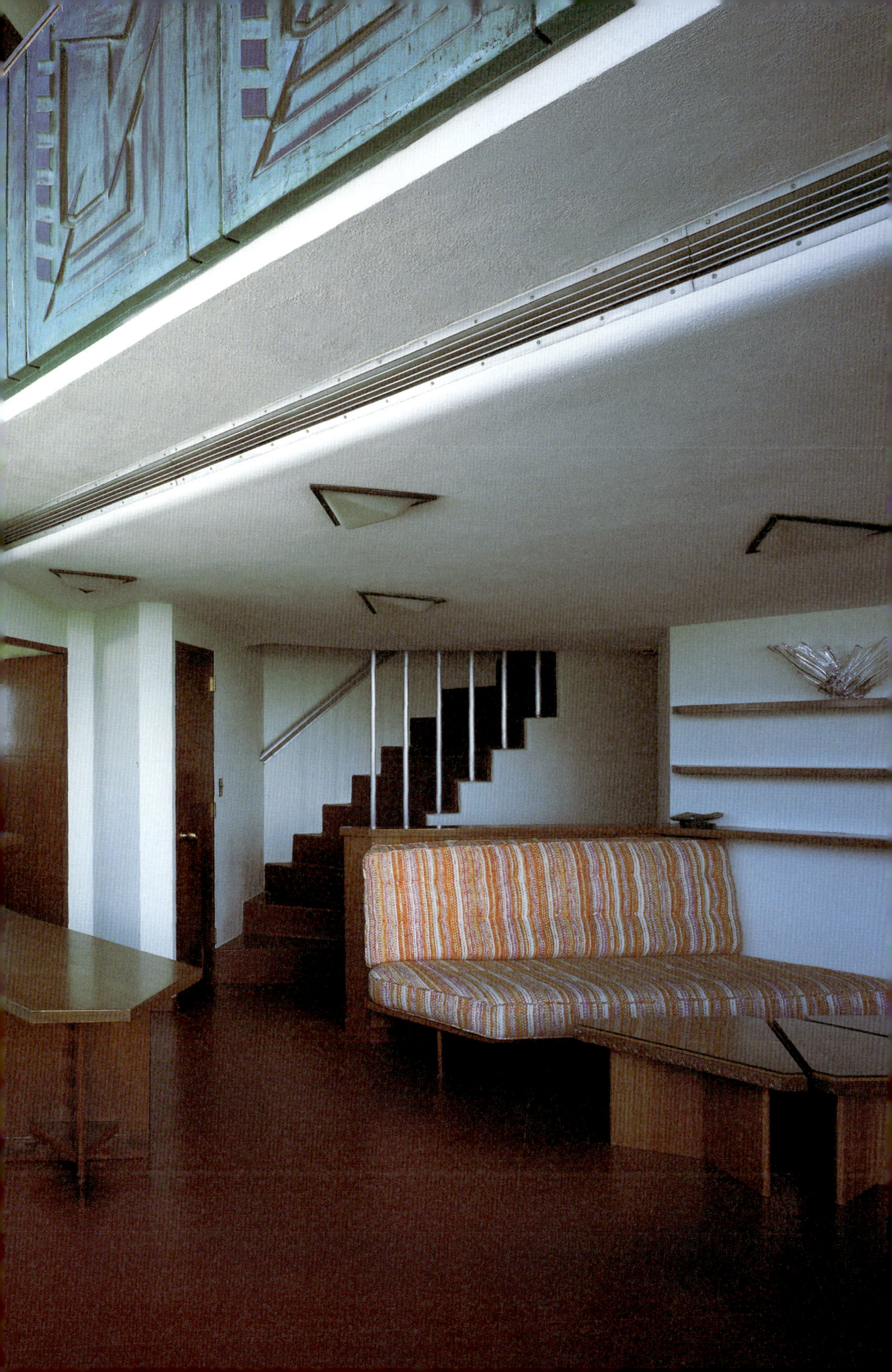

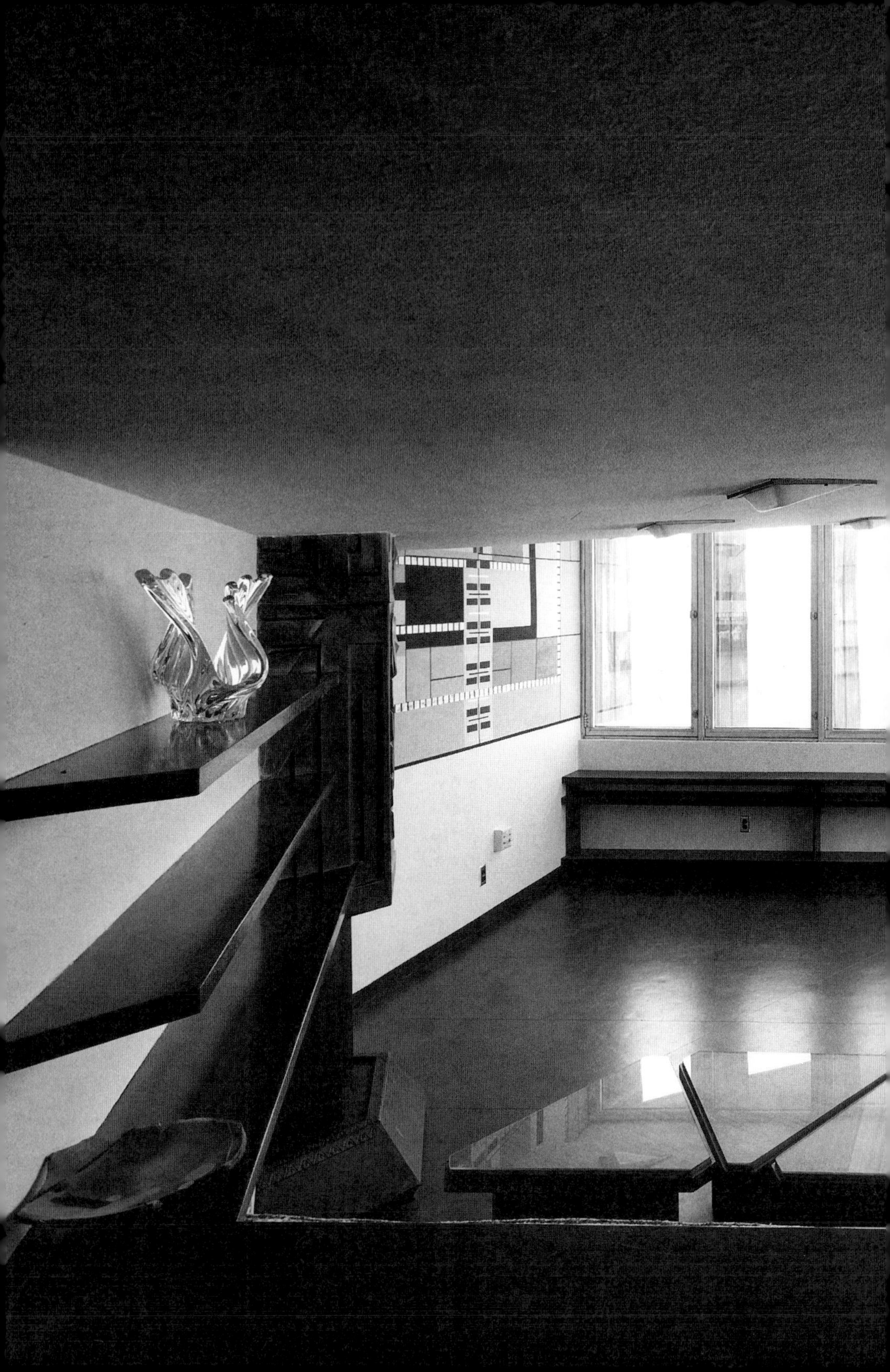

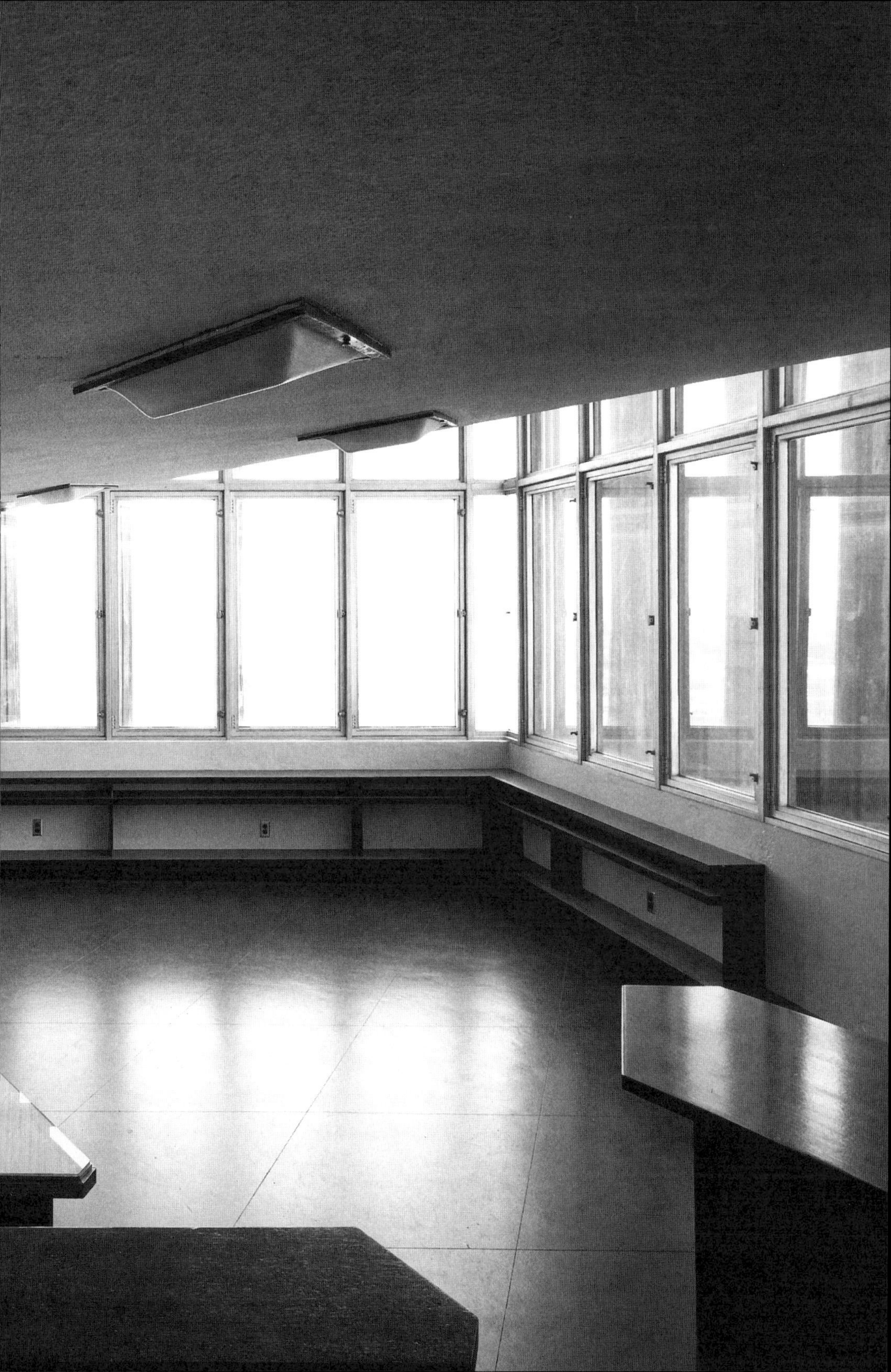

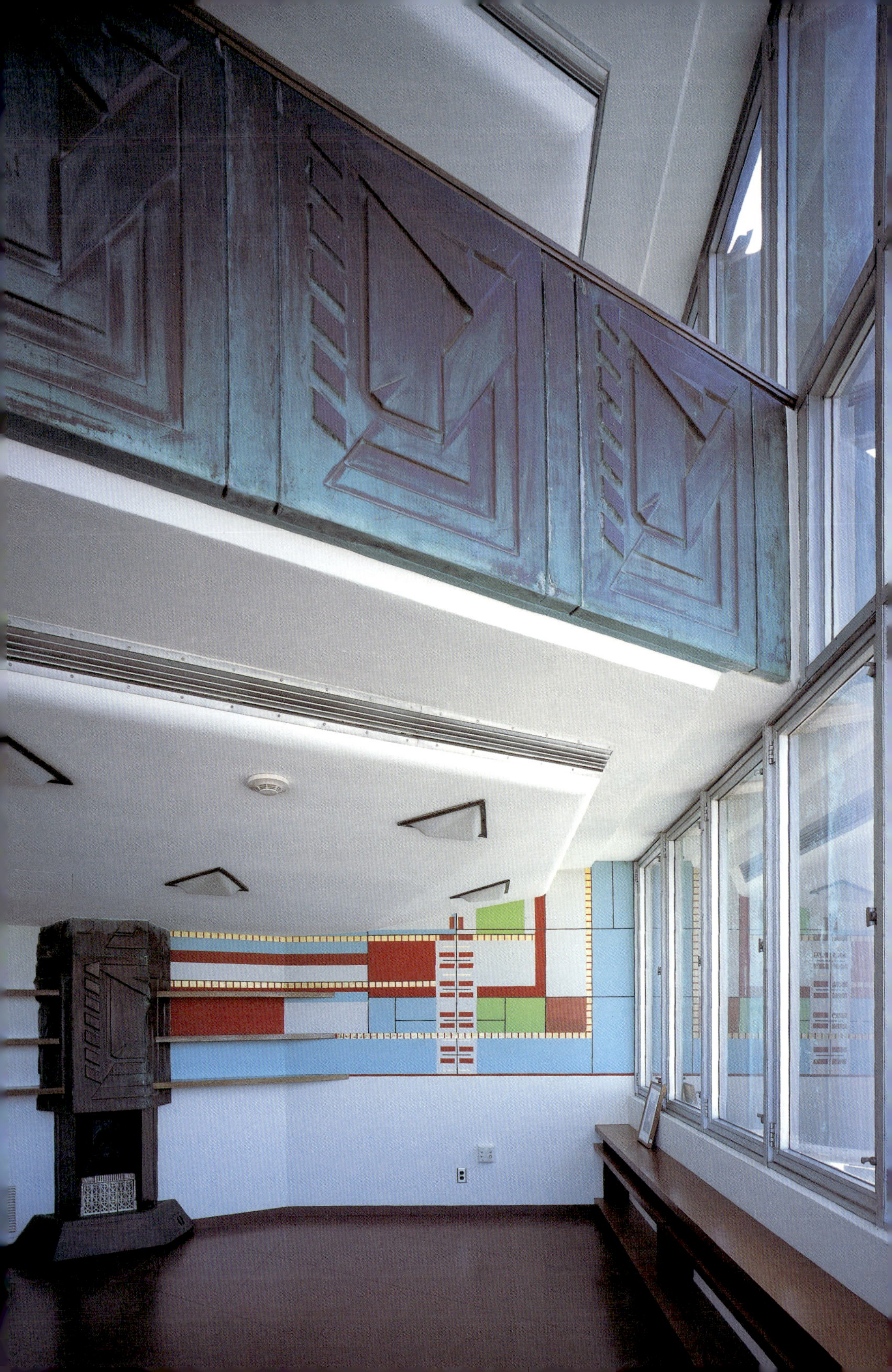

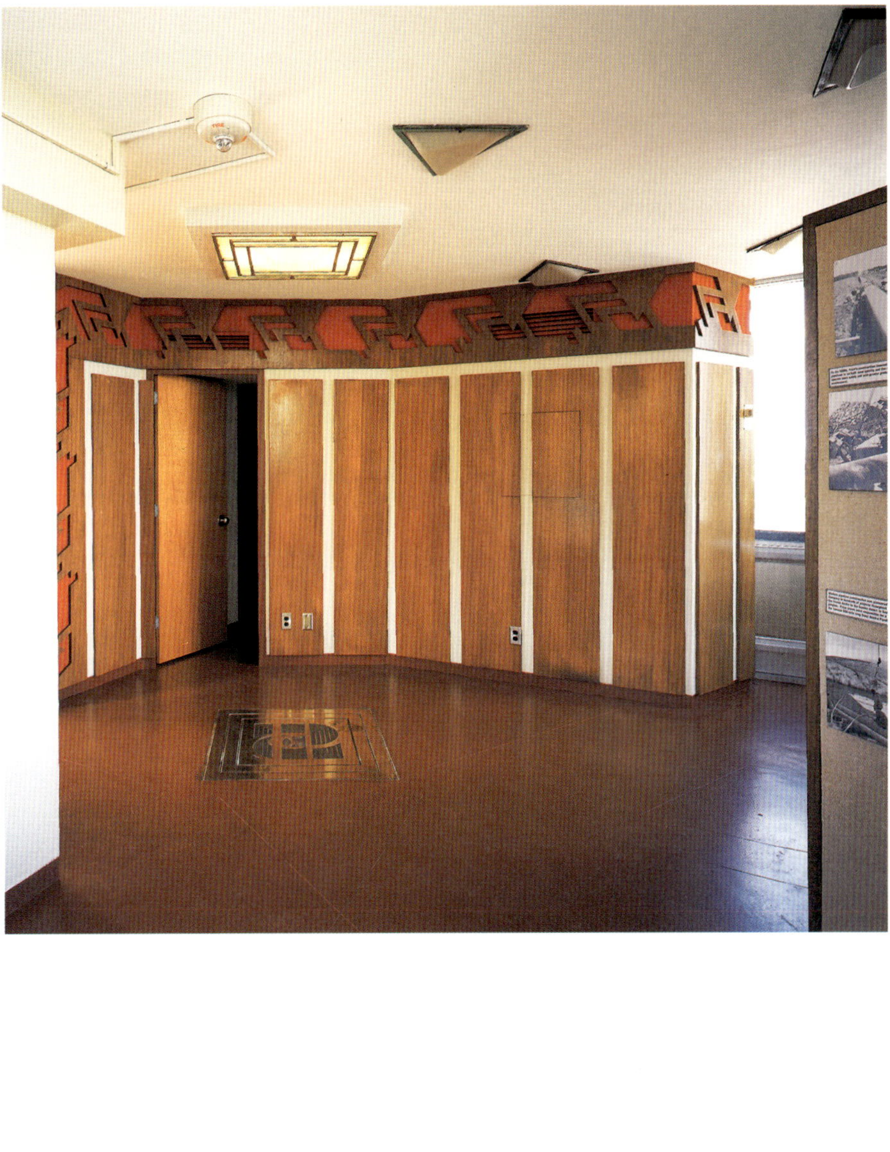

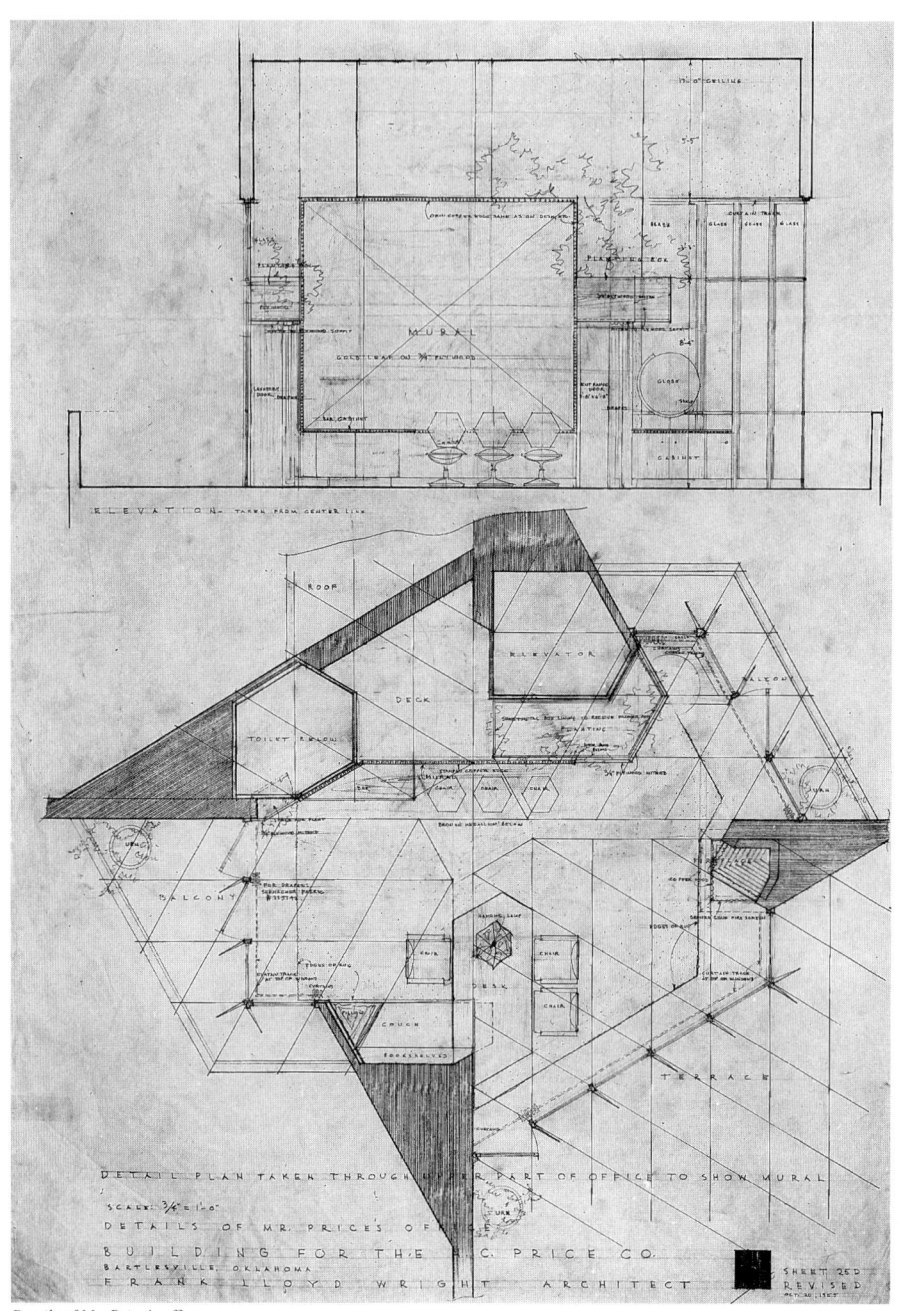

Details of Mr. Price's office

Interior perspective of Mr. Price's office

Interior perspective of typical residence

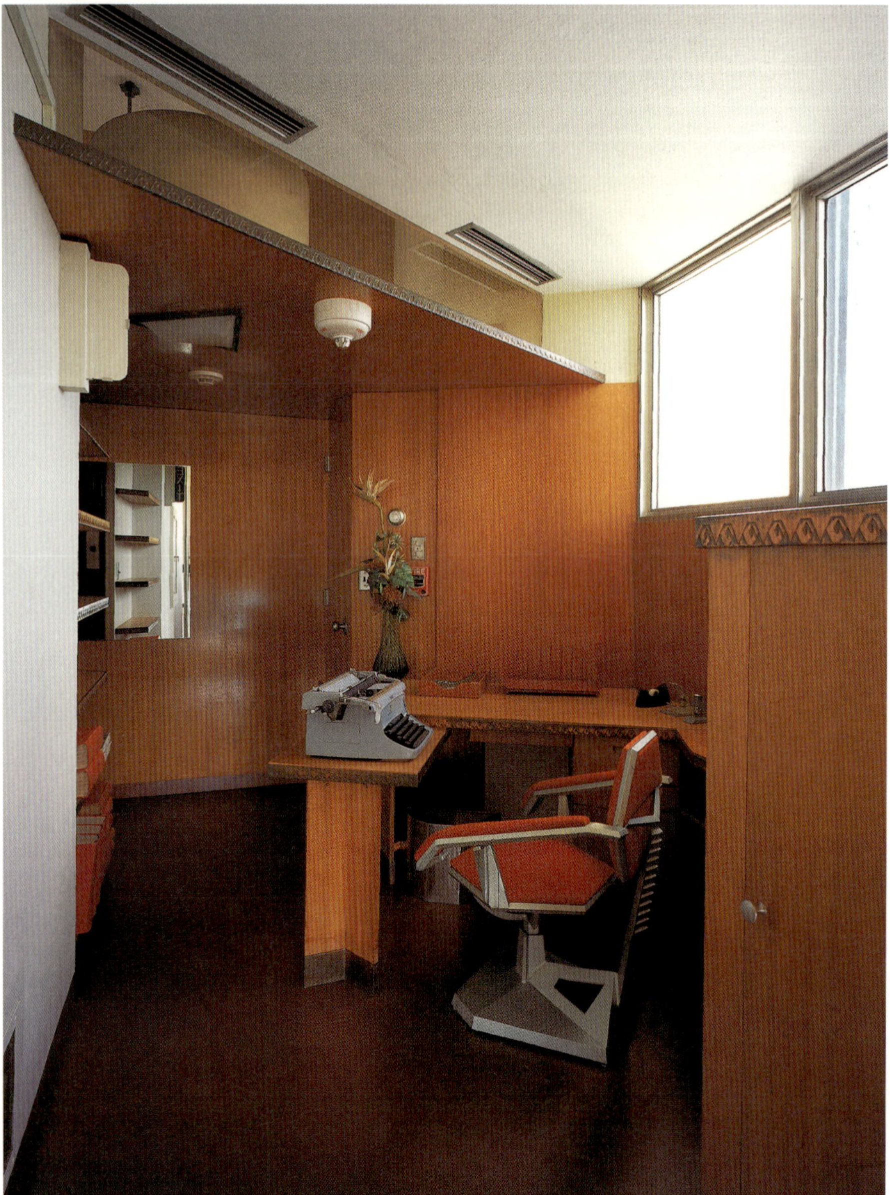

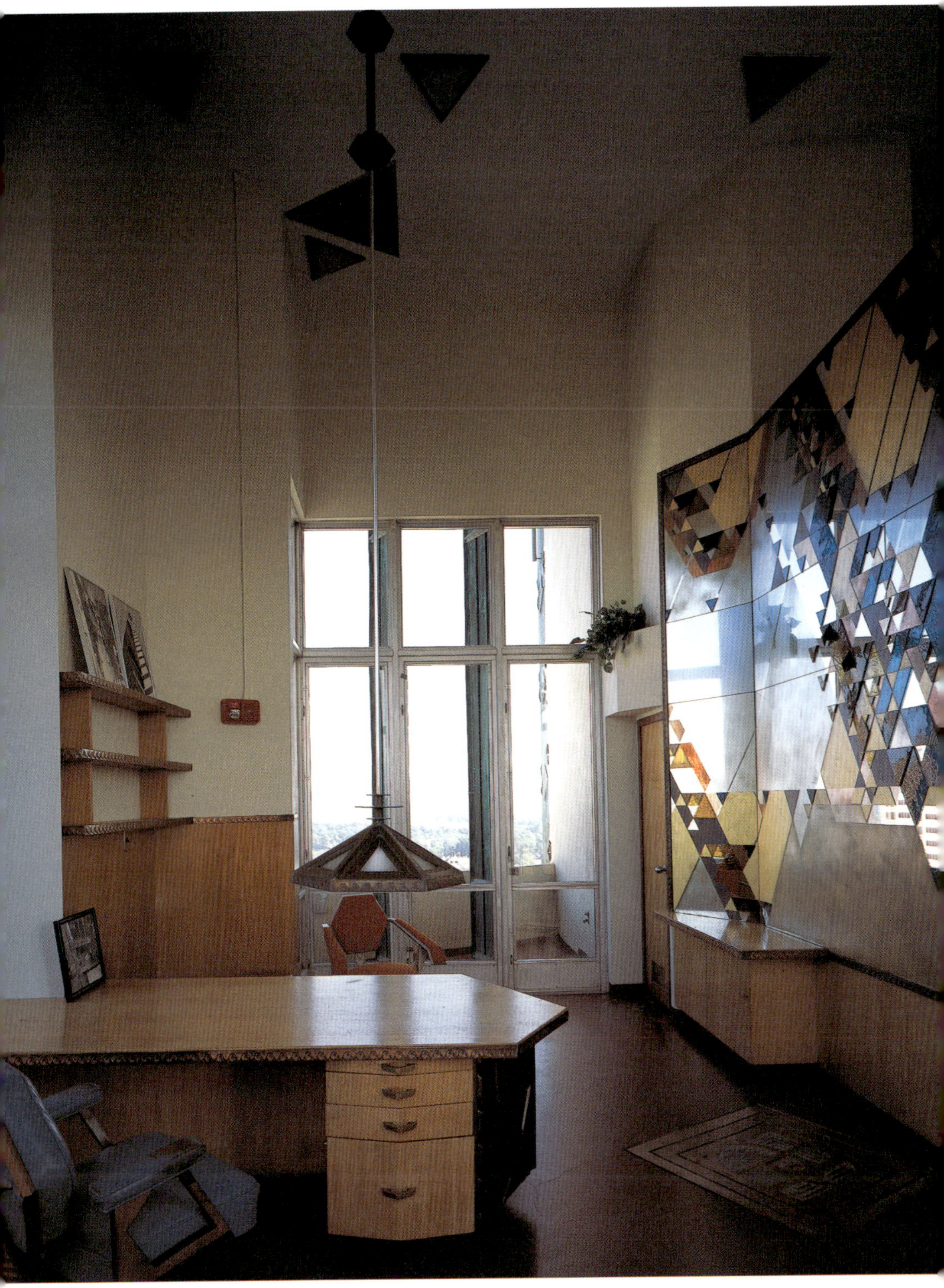

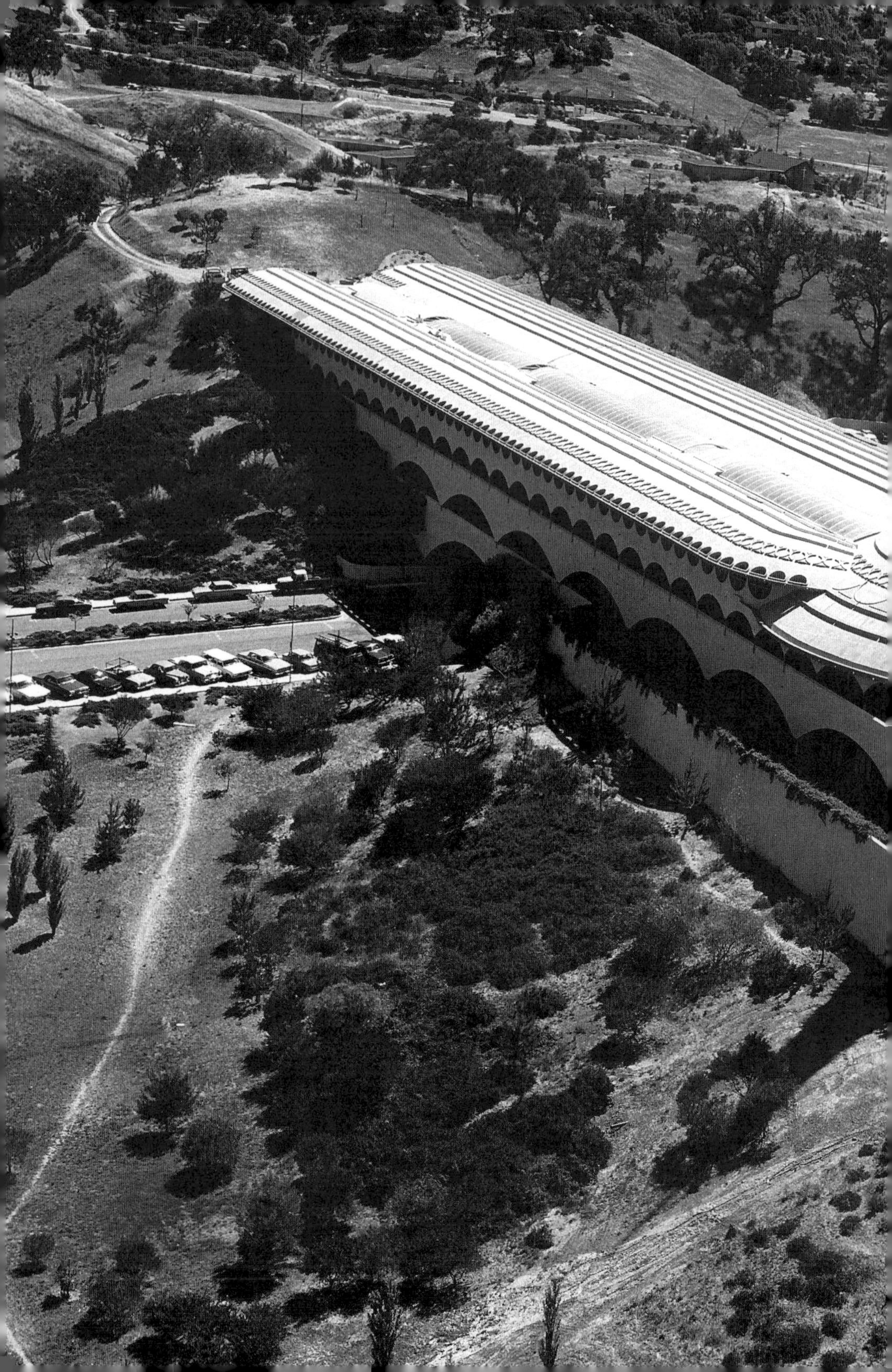

Marin County Goverment Center
San Rafael, California, 1957

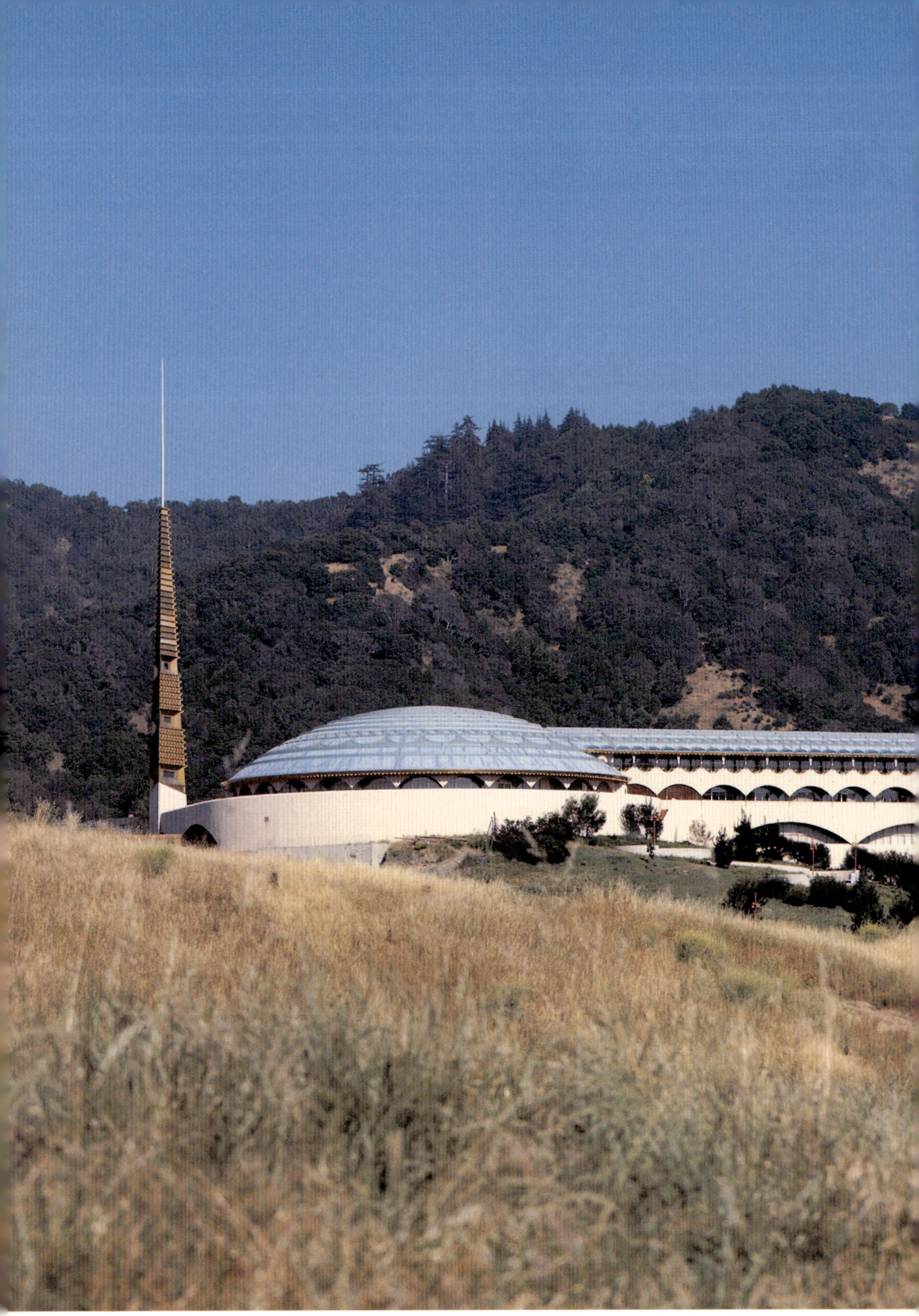

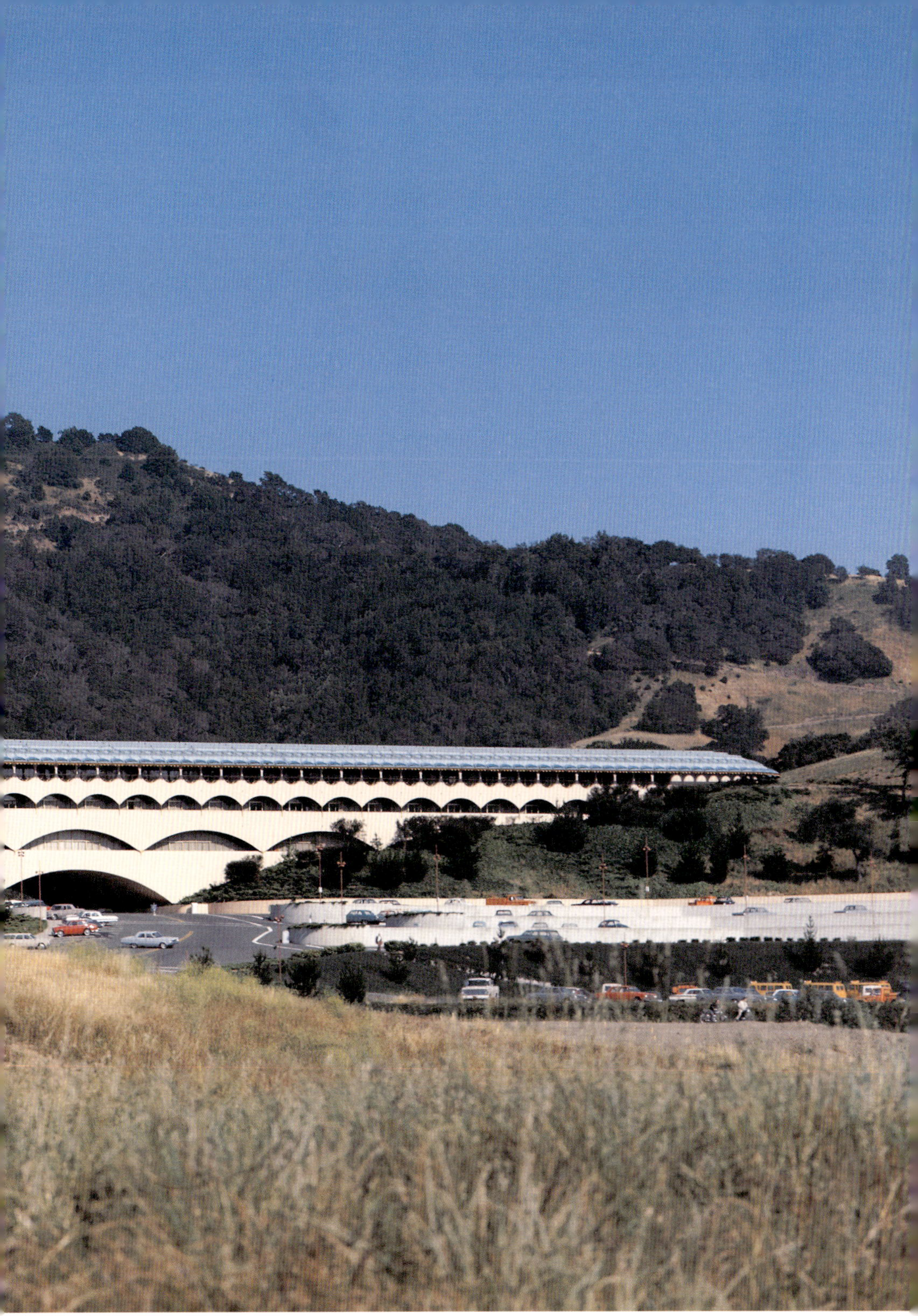

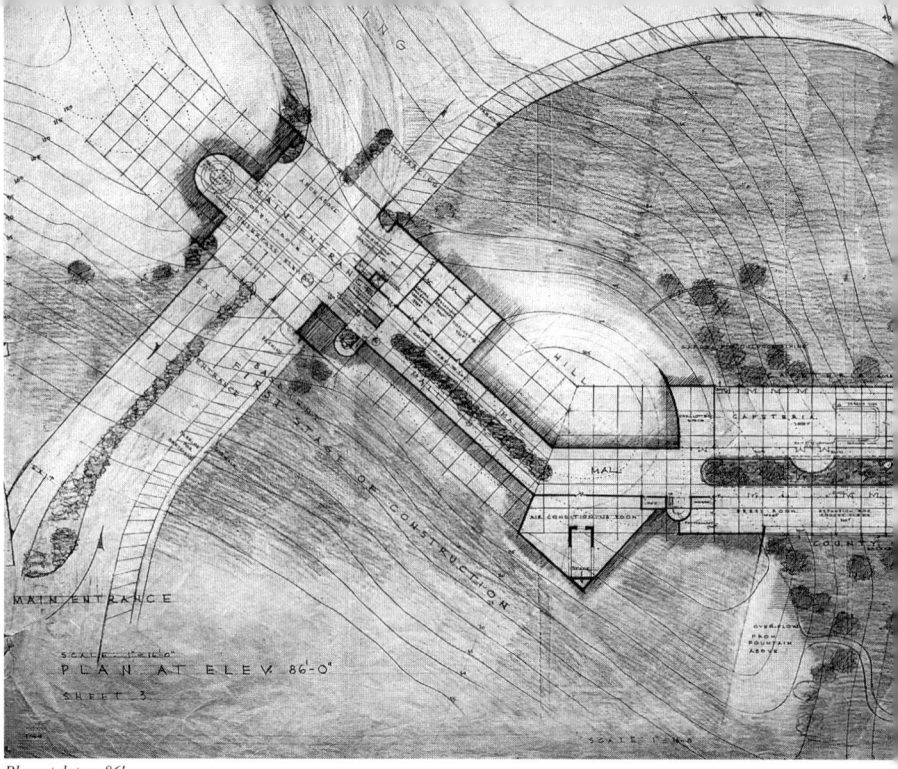

Plan at datum 86'

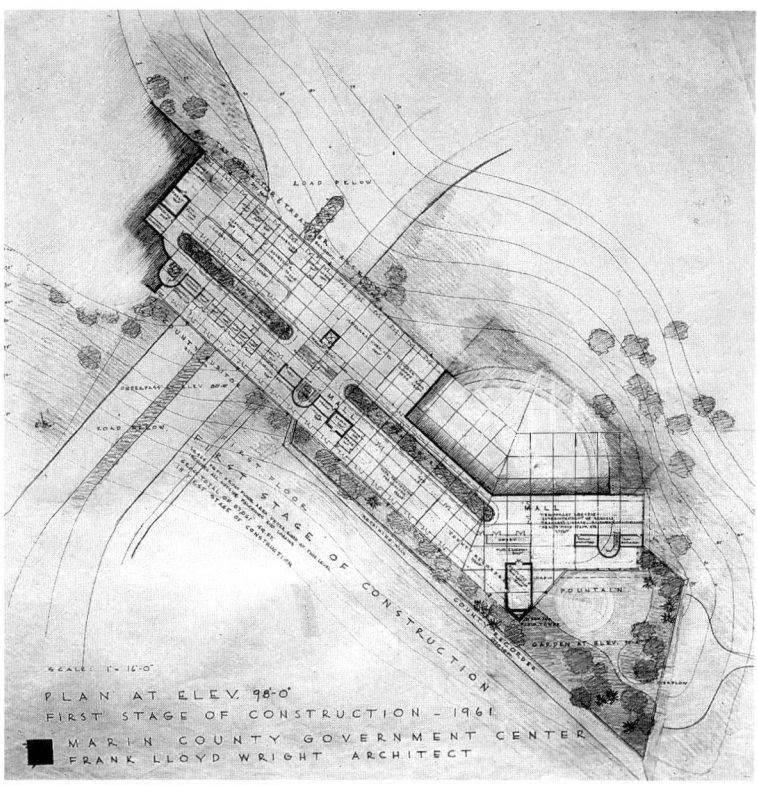

Plan at datum 98', Administration Building

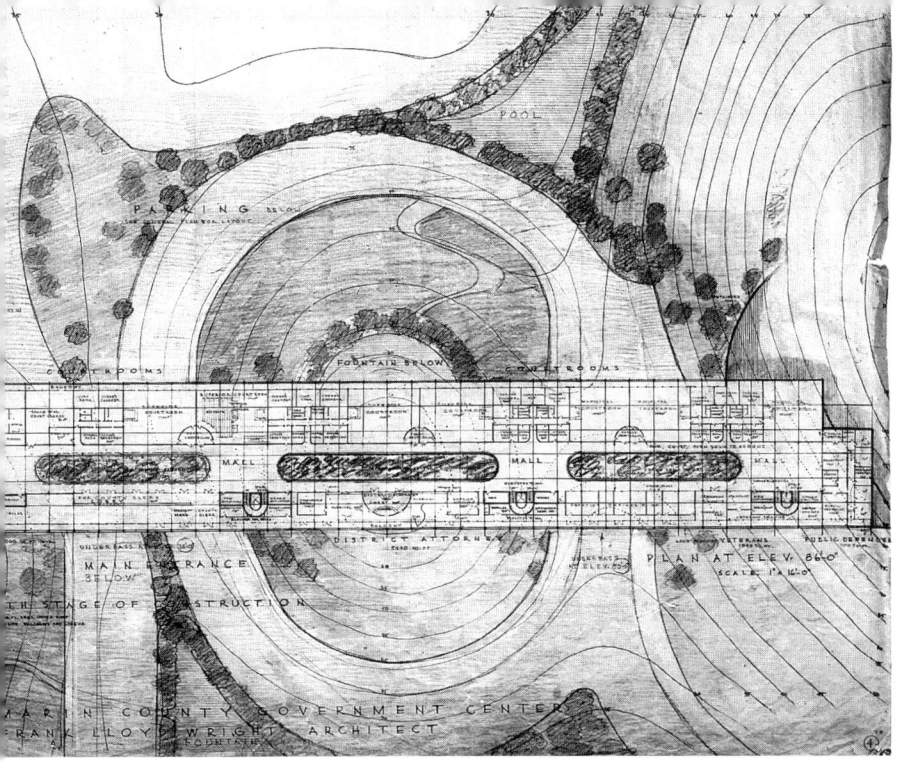

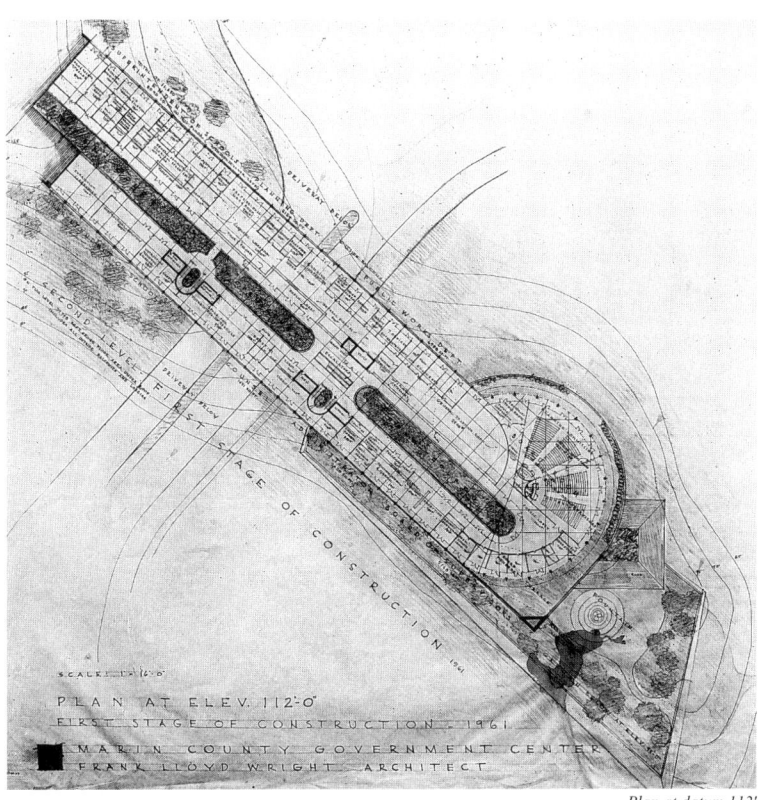

Plan at datum 112'

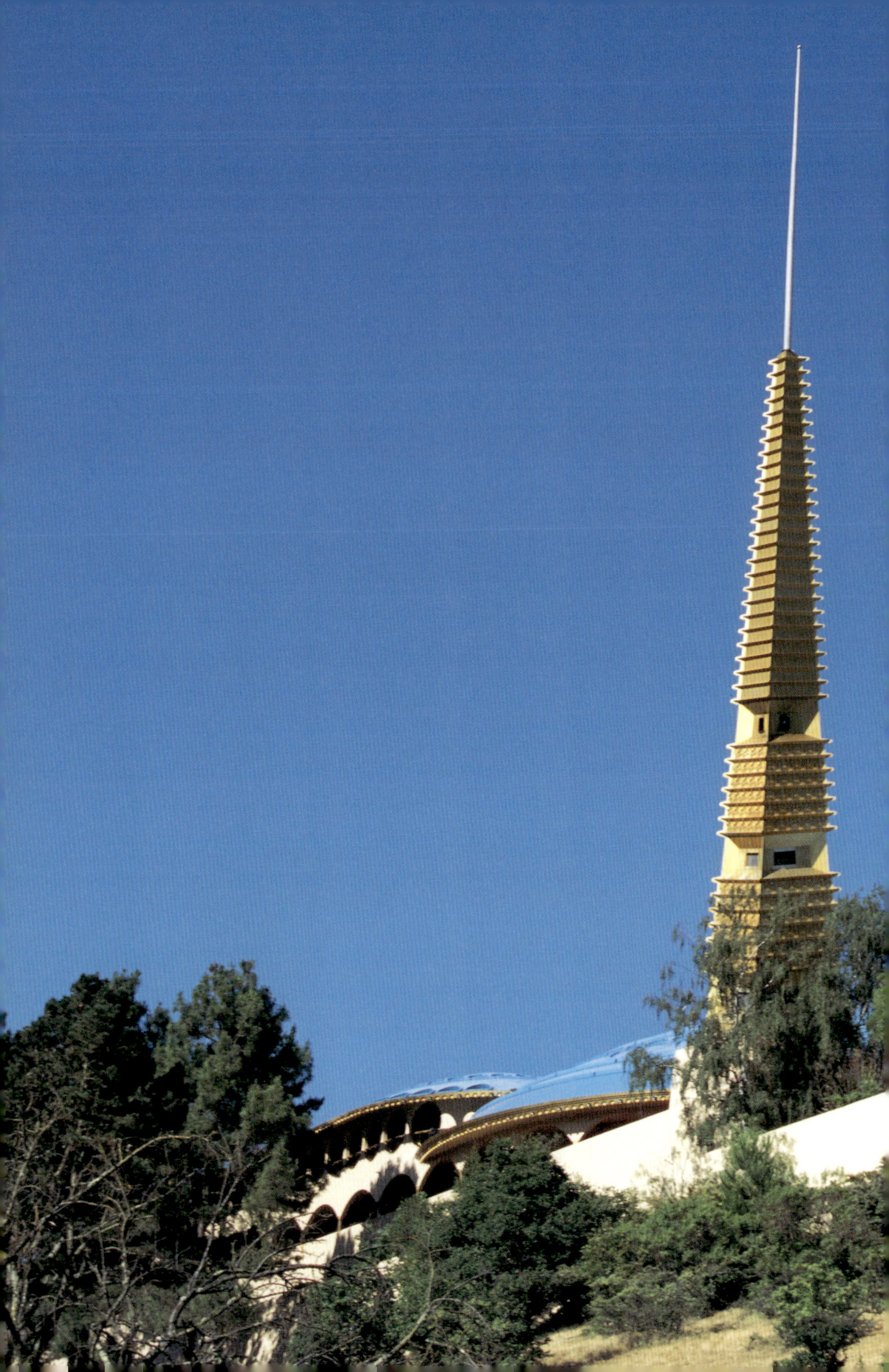

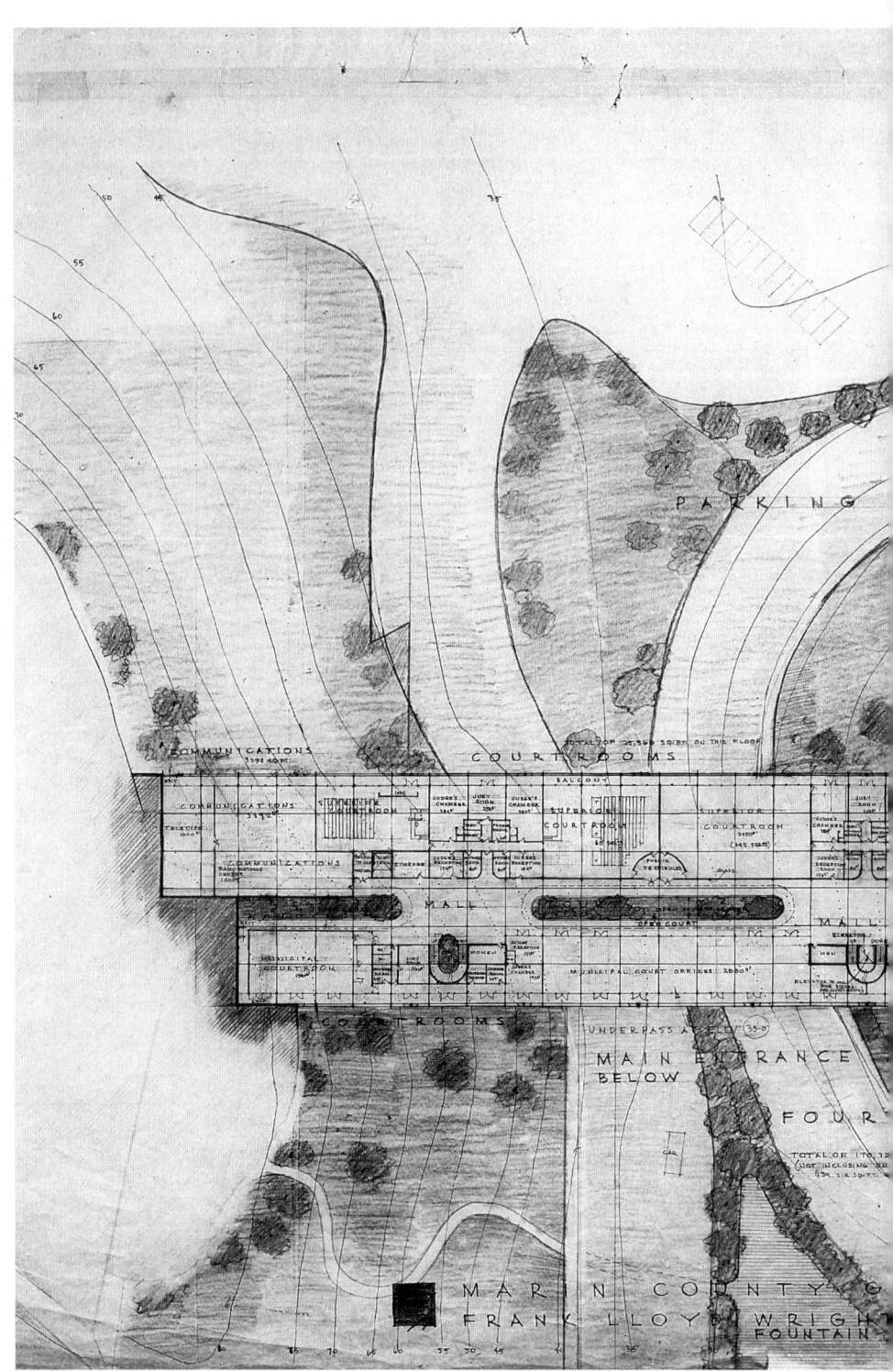

Plan at datum 74'

POOL

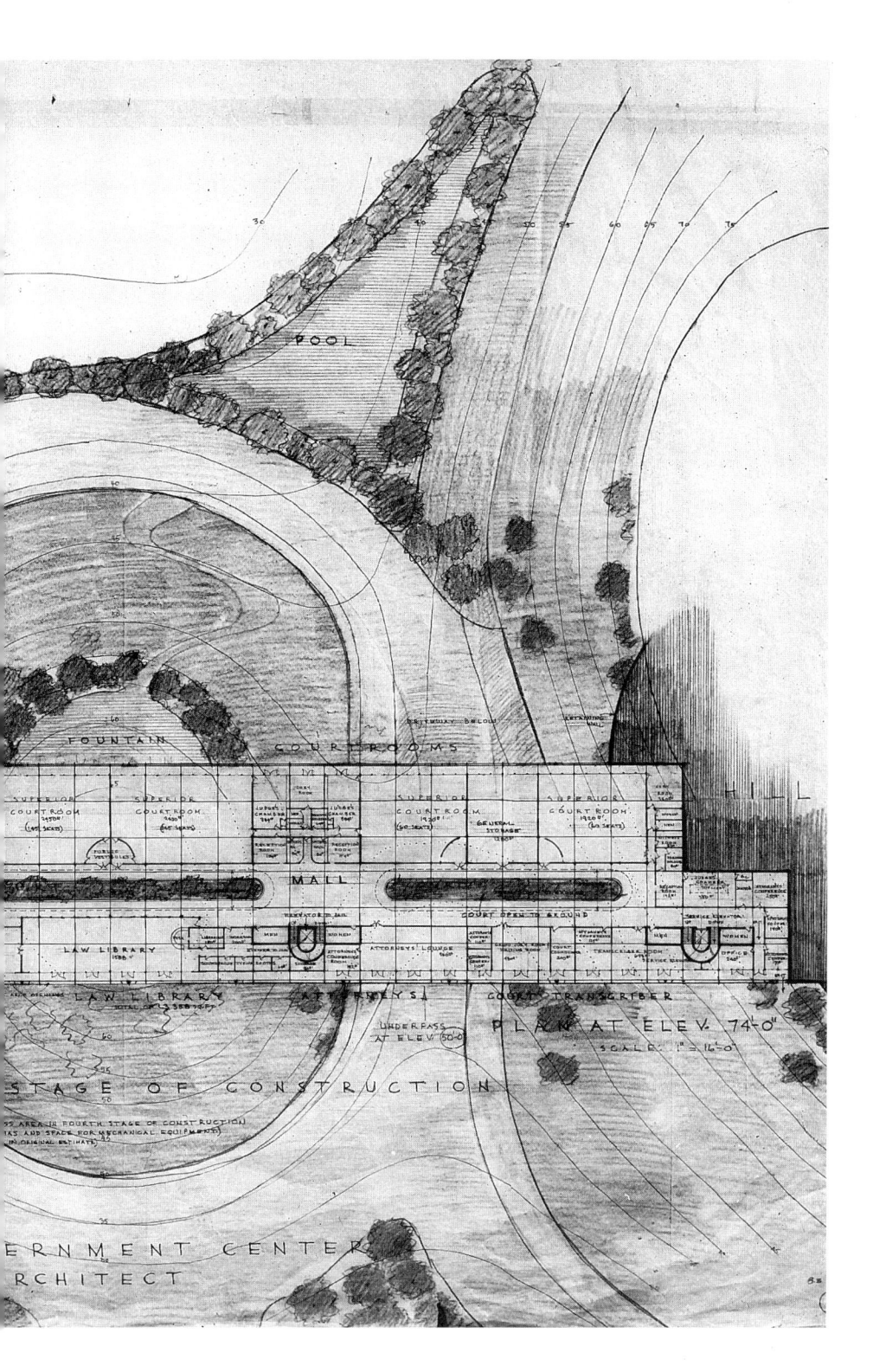

FOUNTAIN COURTROOMS HILL

SUPERIOR COURTROOM	SUPERIOR COURTROOM	JUDGES CHAMBER	JUDGES CHAMBER	SUPERIOR COURTROOM	GENERAL STORAGE	SUPERIOR COURTROOM	

MALL

LAW LIBRARY | ATTORNEYS LOUNGE

LAW LIBRARY | ATTORNEYS | COURT TRANSCRIBER

UNDERPASS AT ELEV. 50'0"

PLAN AT ELEV. 74'-0"
SCALE 1" = 16'-0"

...STAGE OF CONSTRUCTION

...ERNMENT CENTER
...RCHITECT

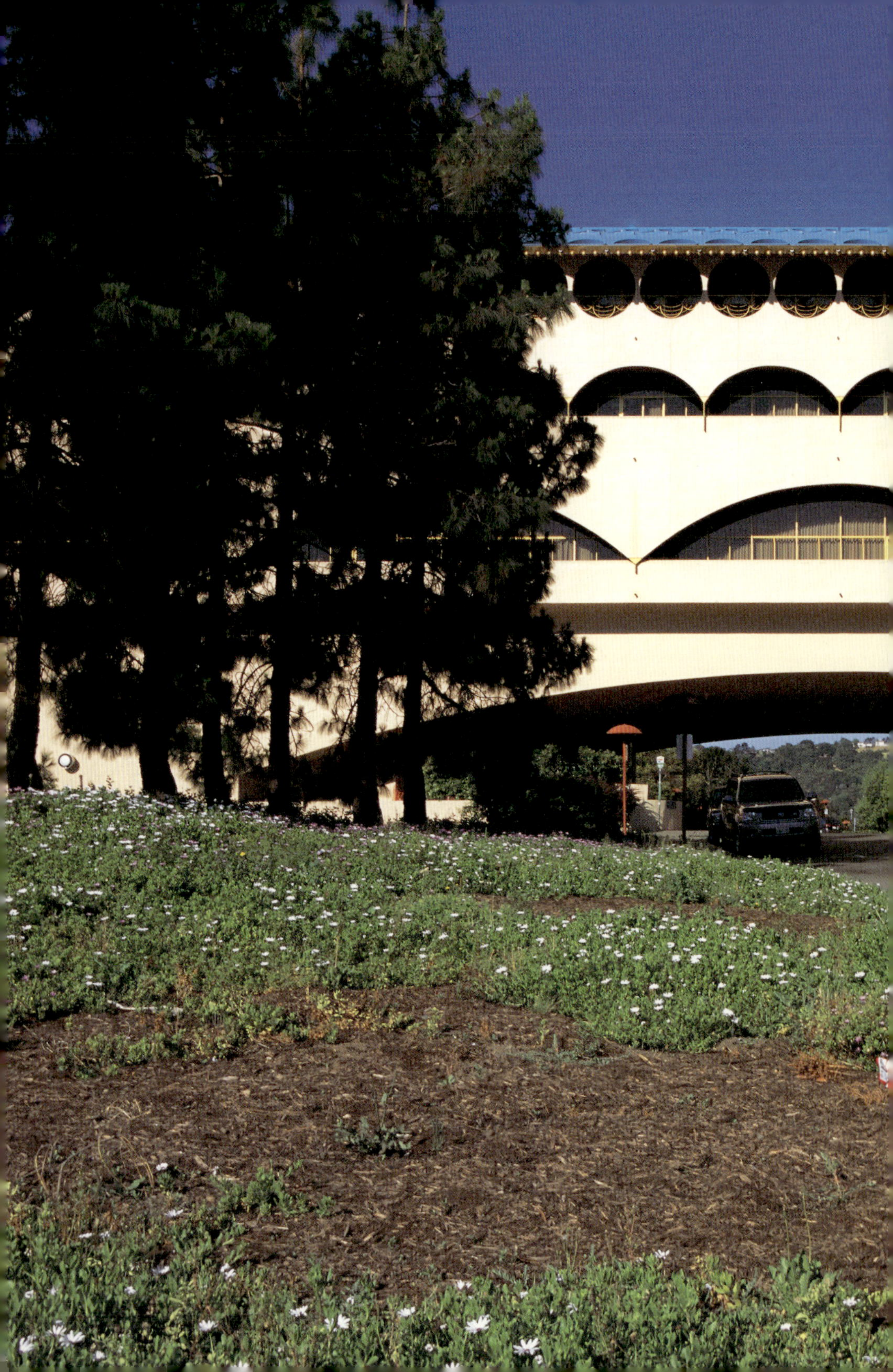

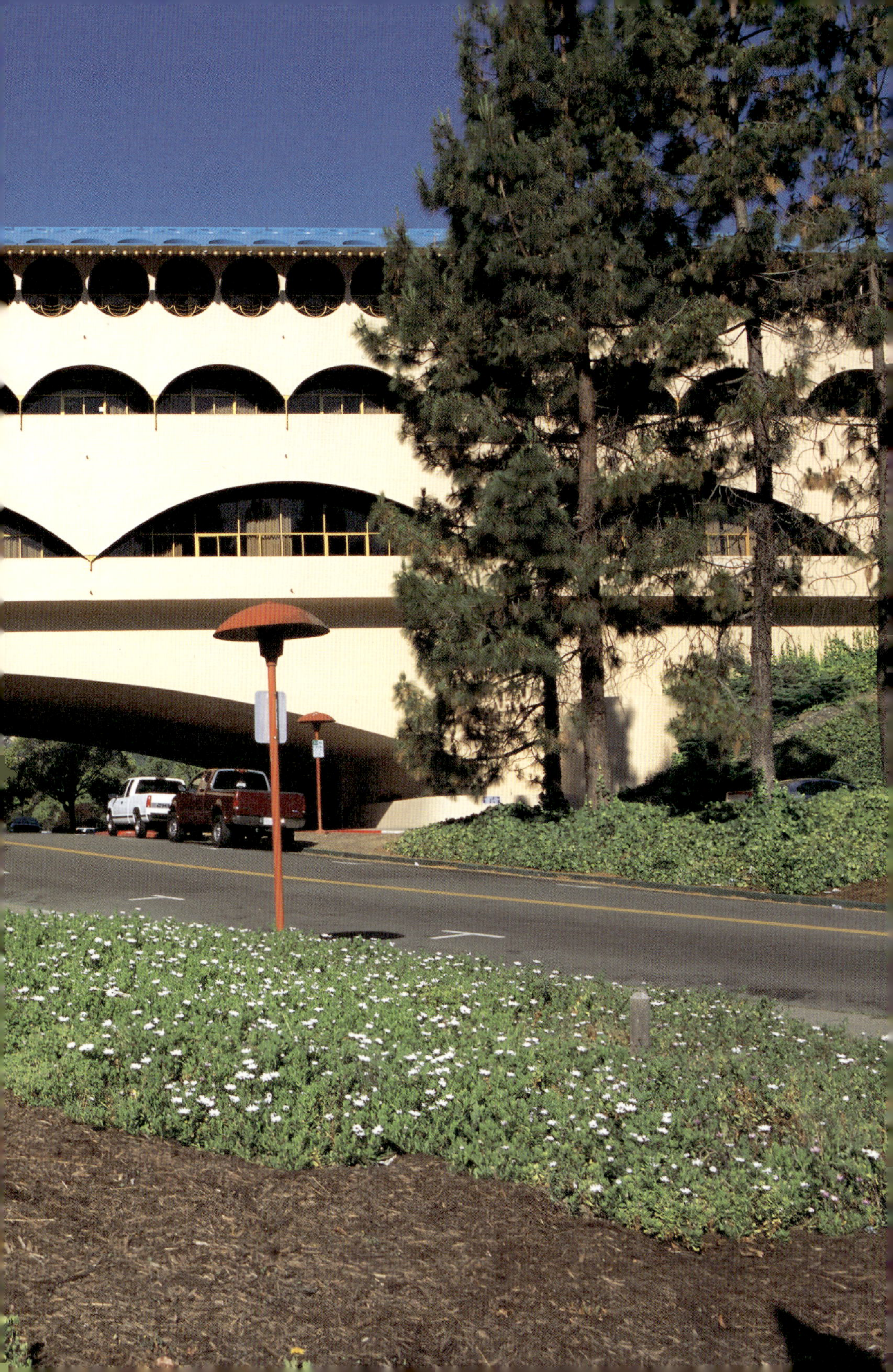

NO SMOKING

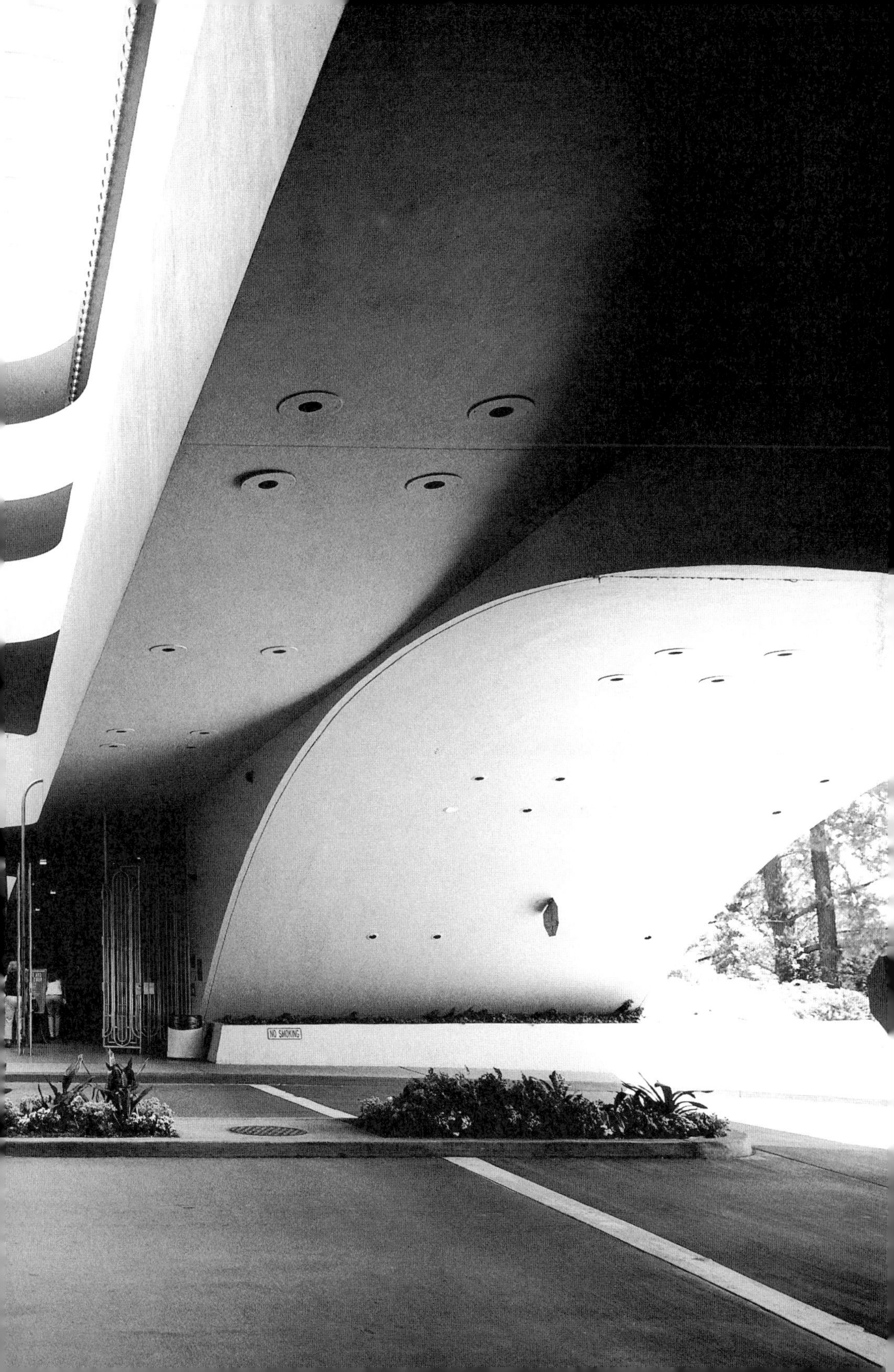
NO SMOKING

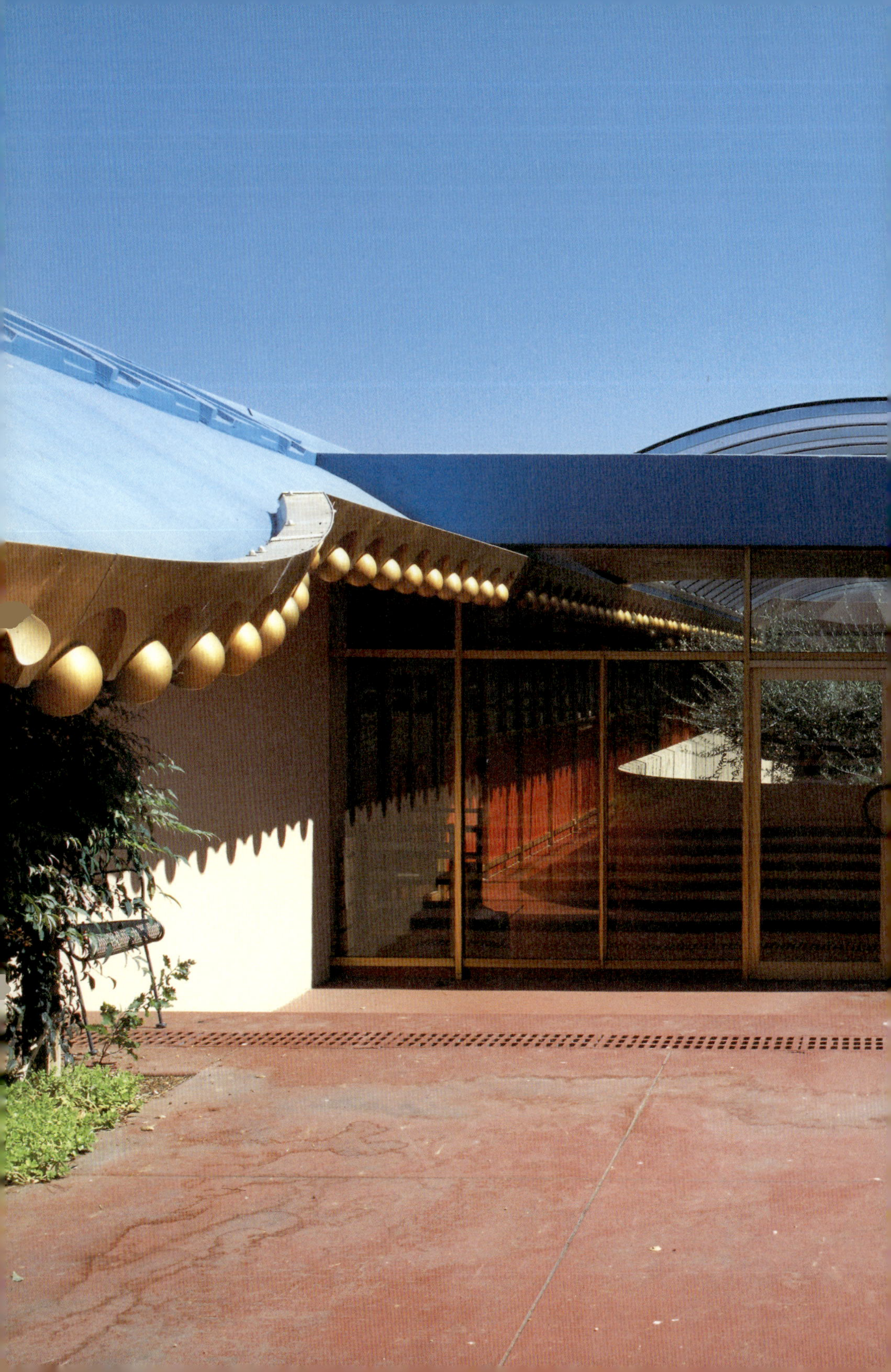

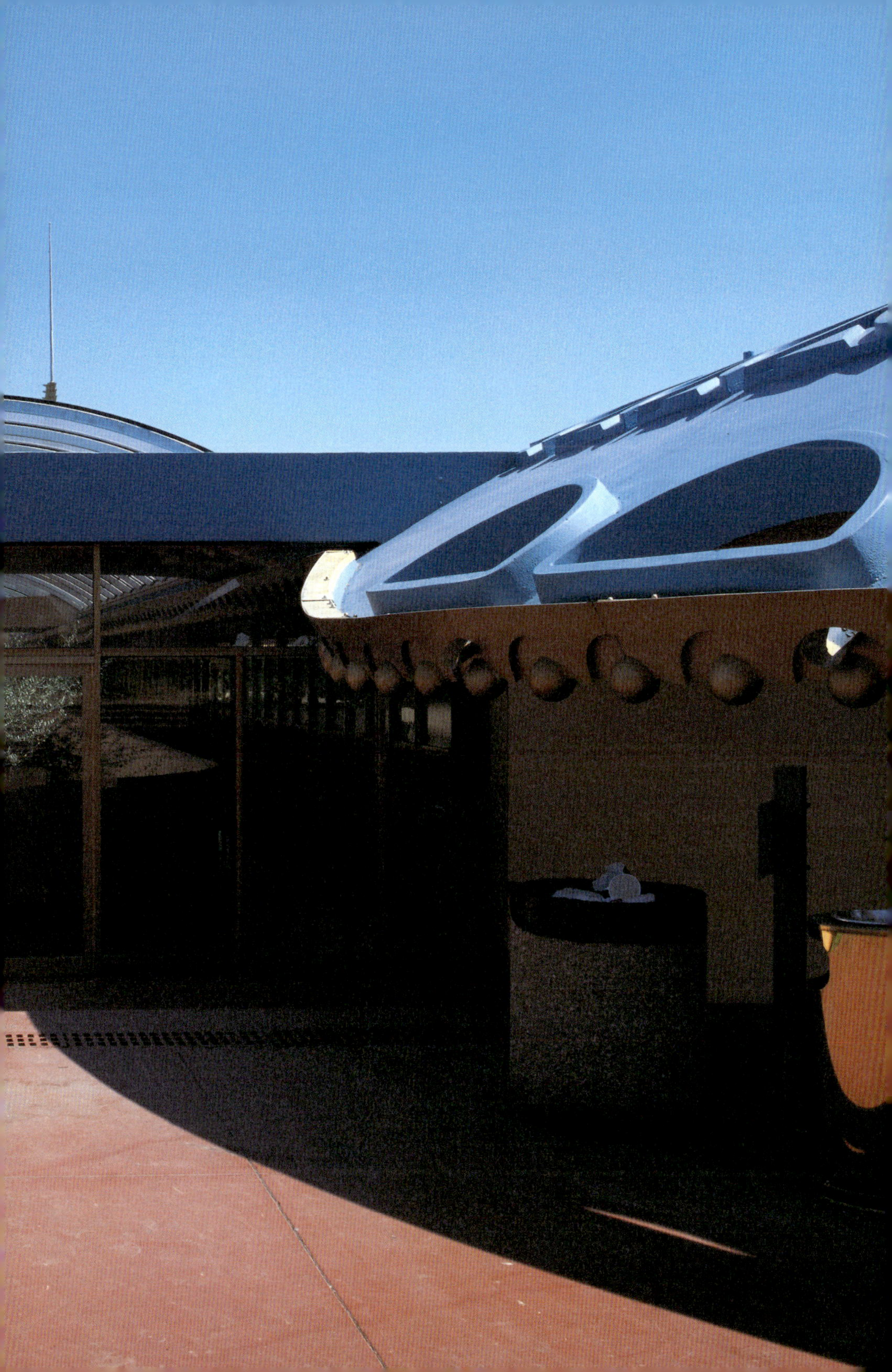

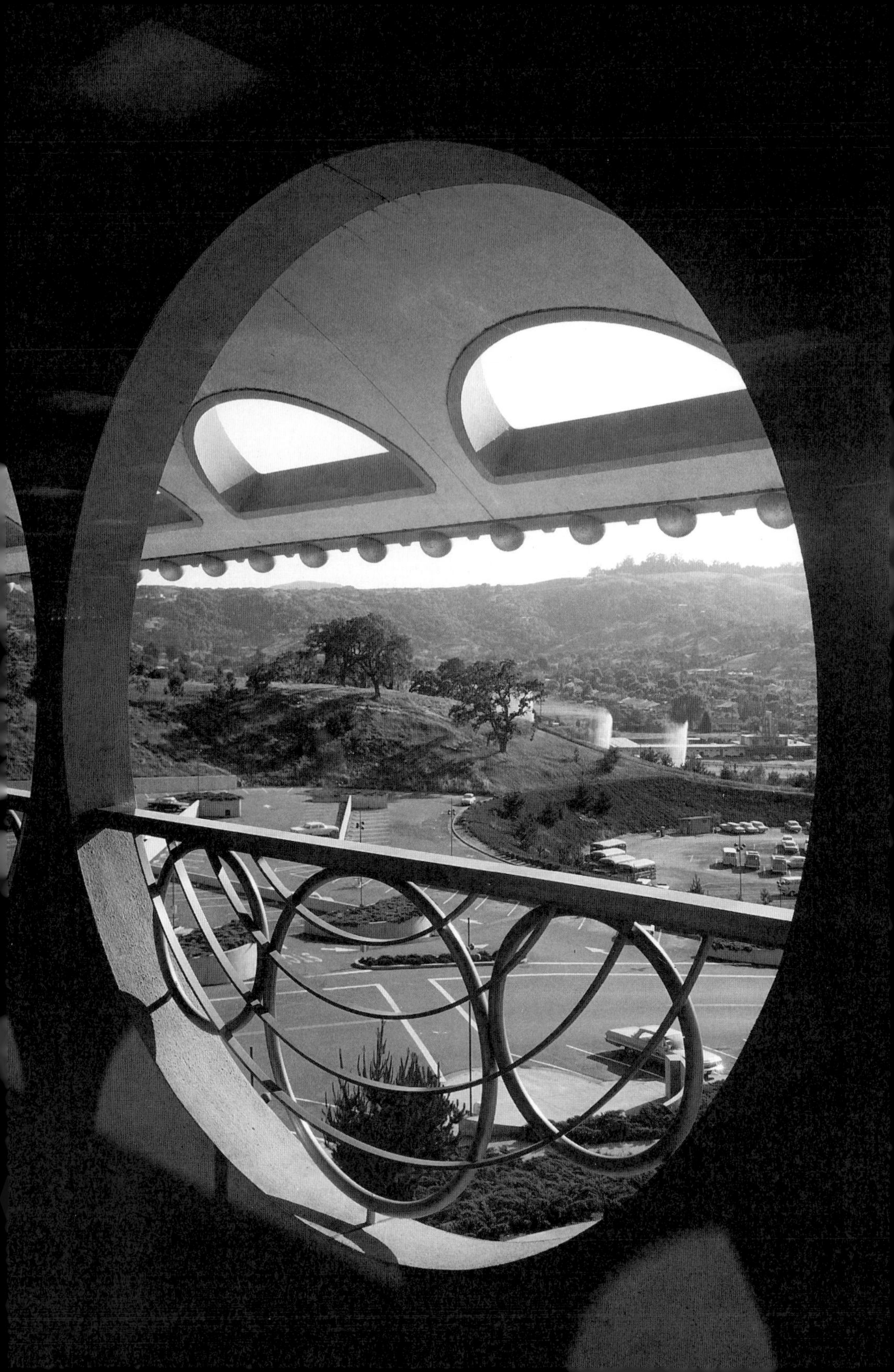

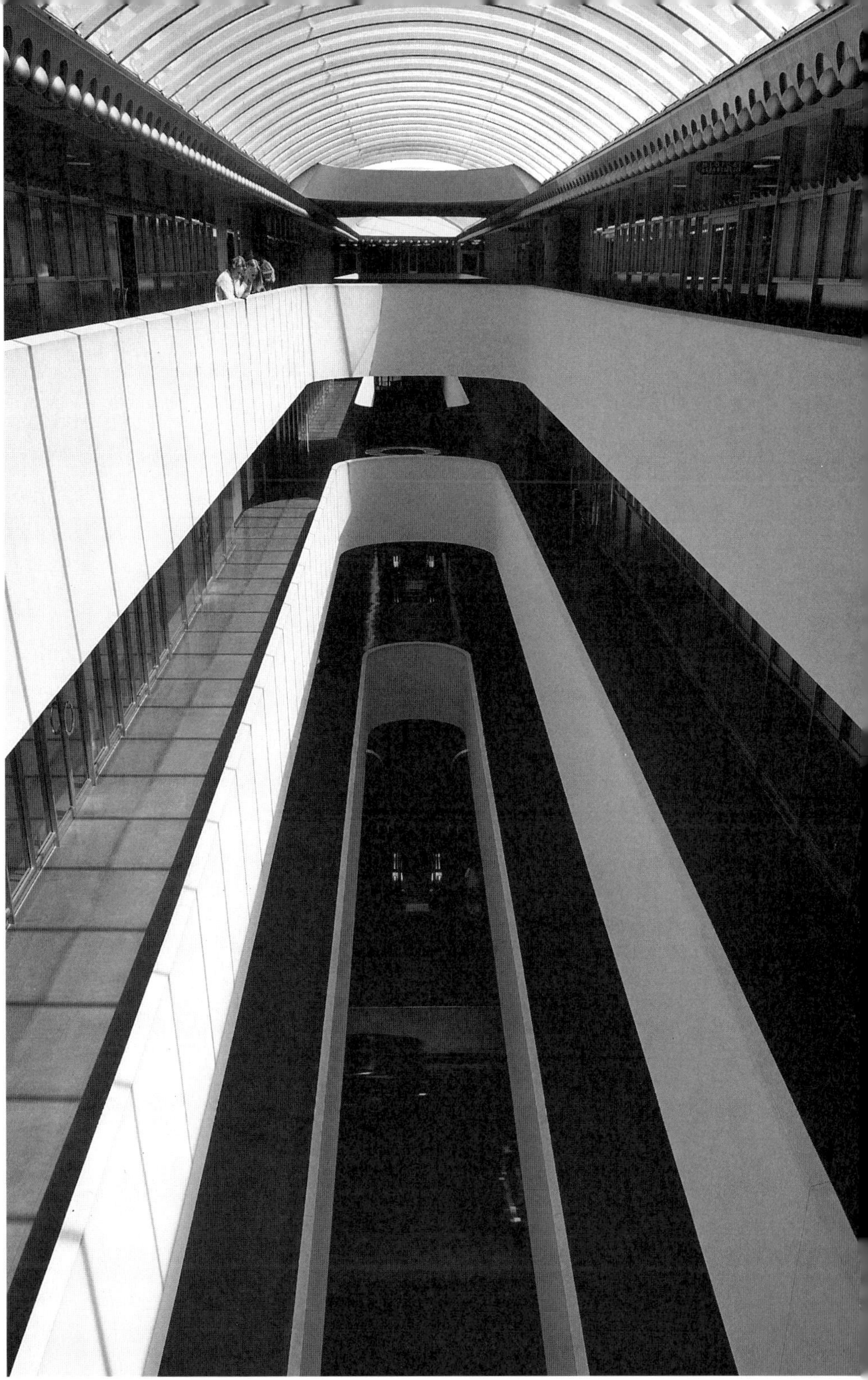

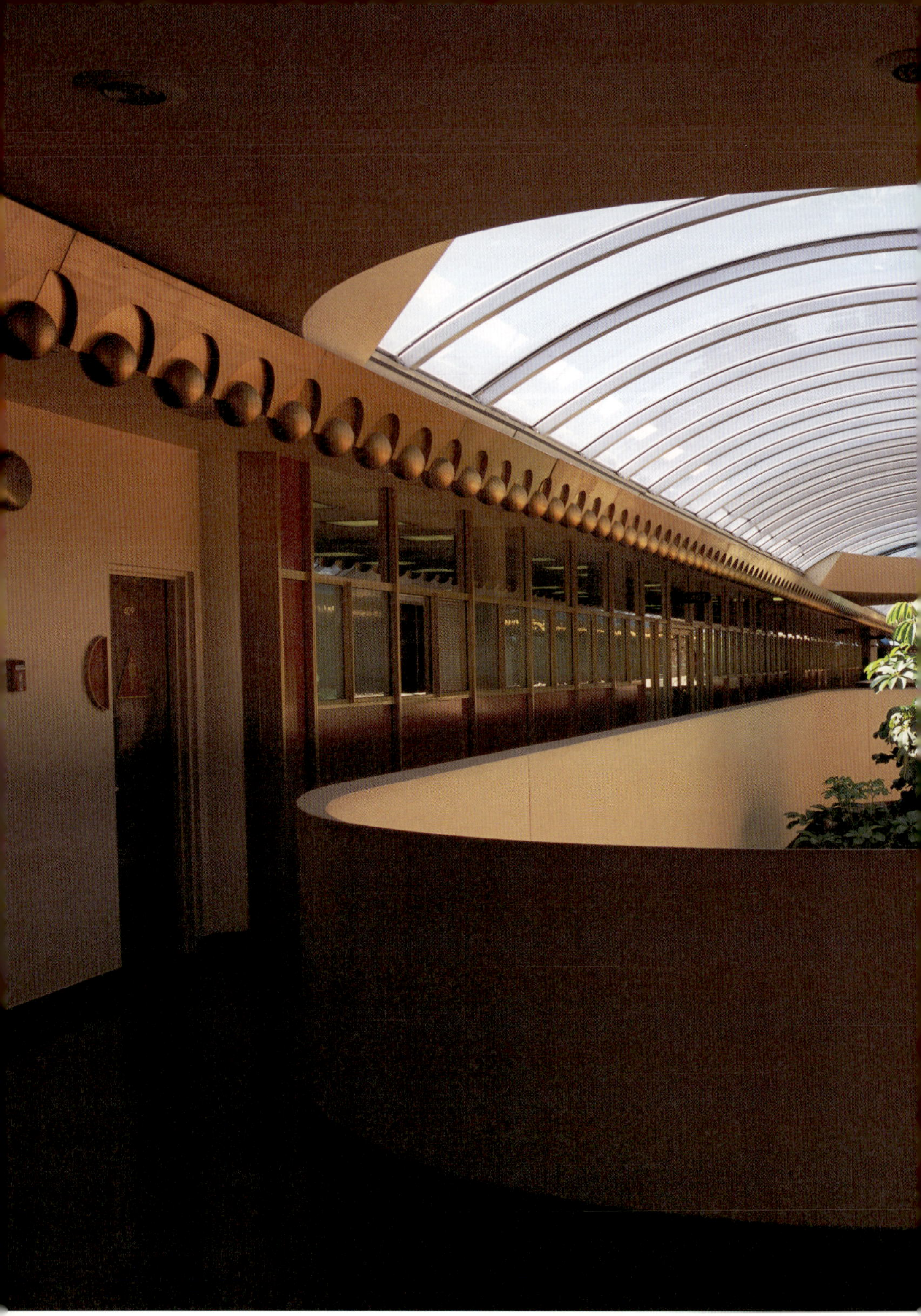

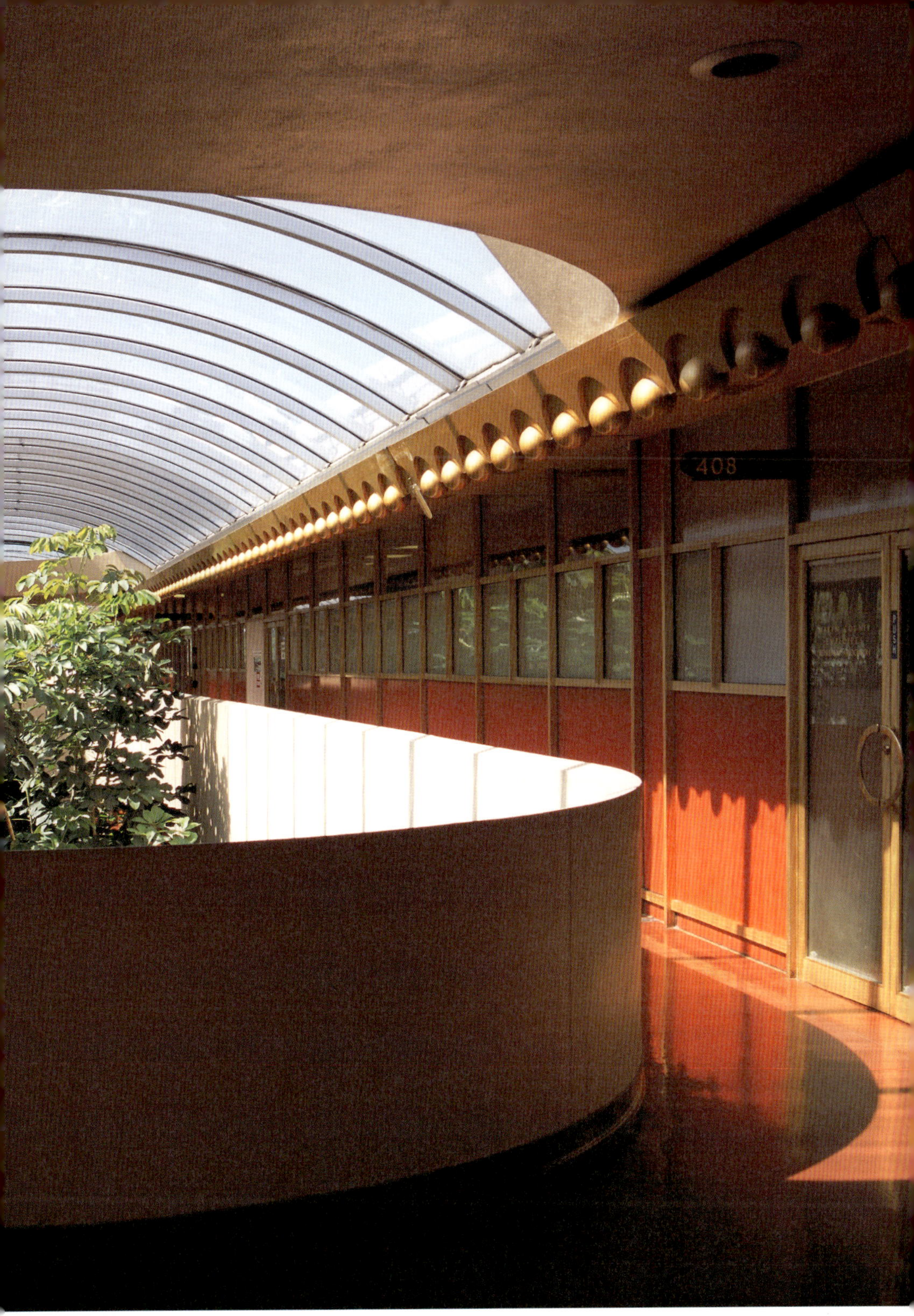
408

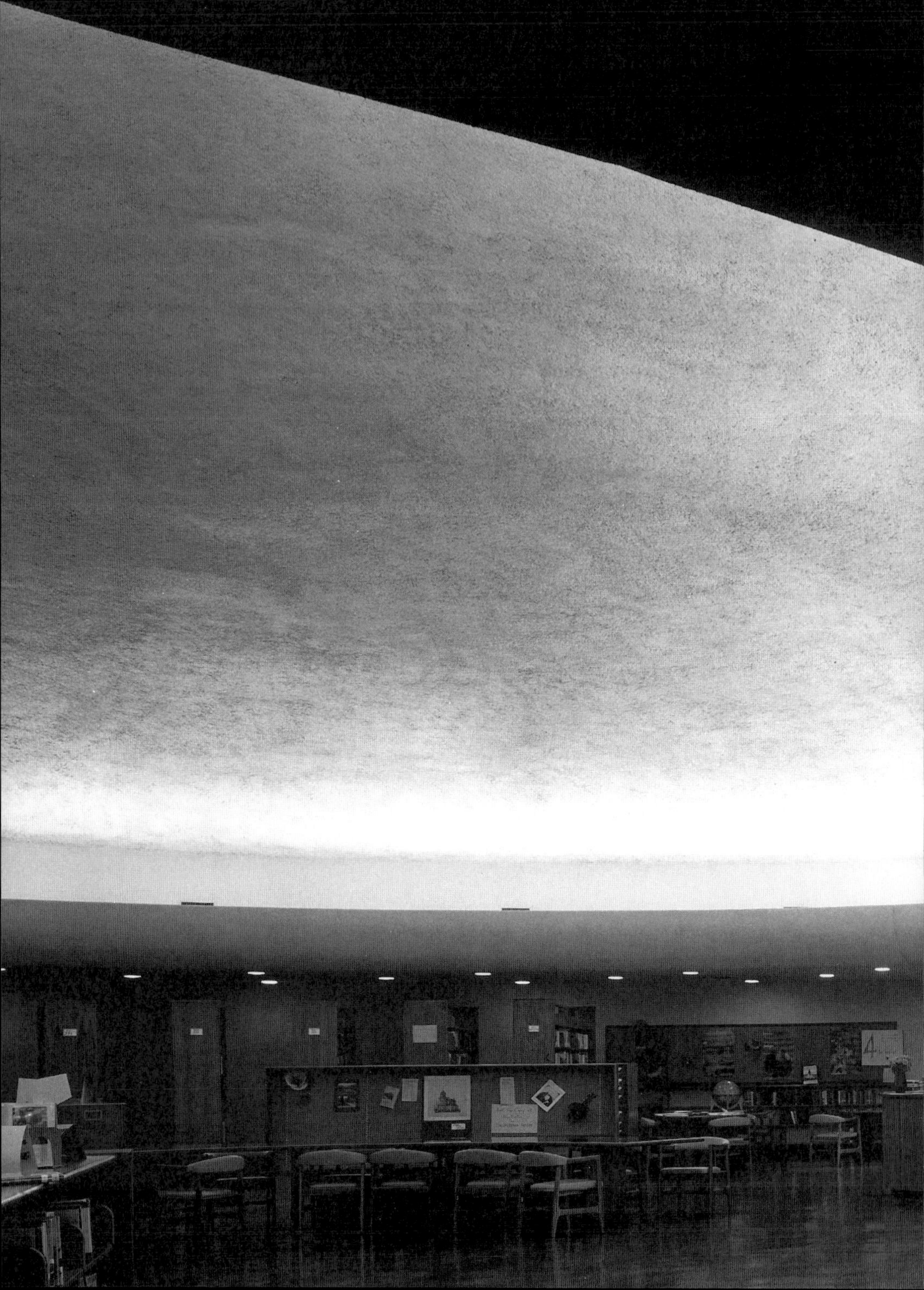

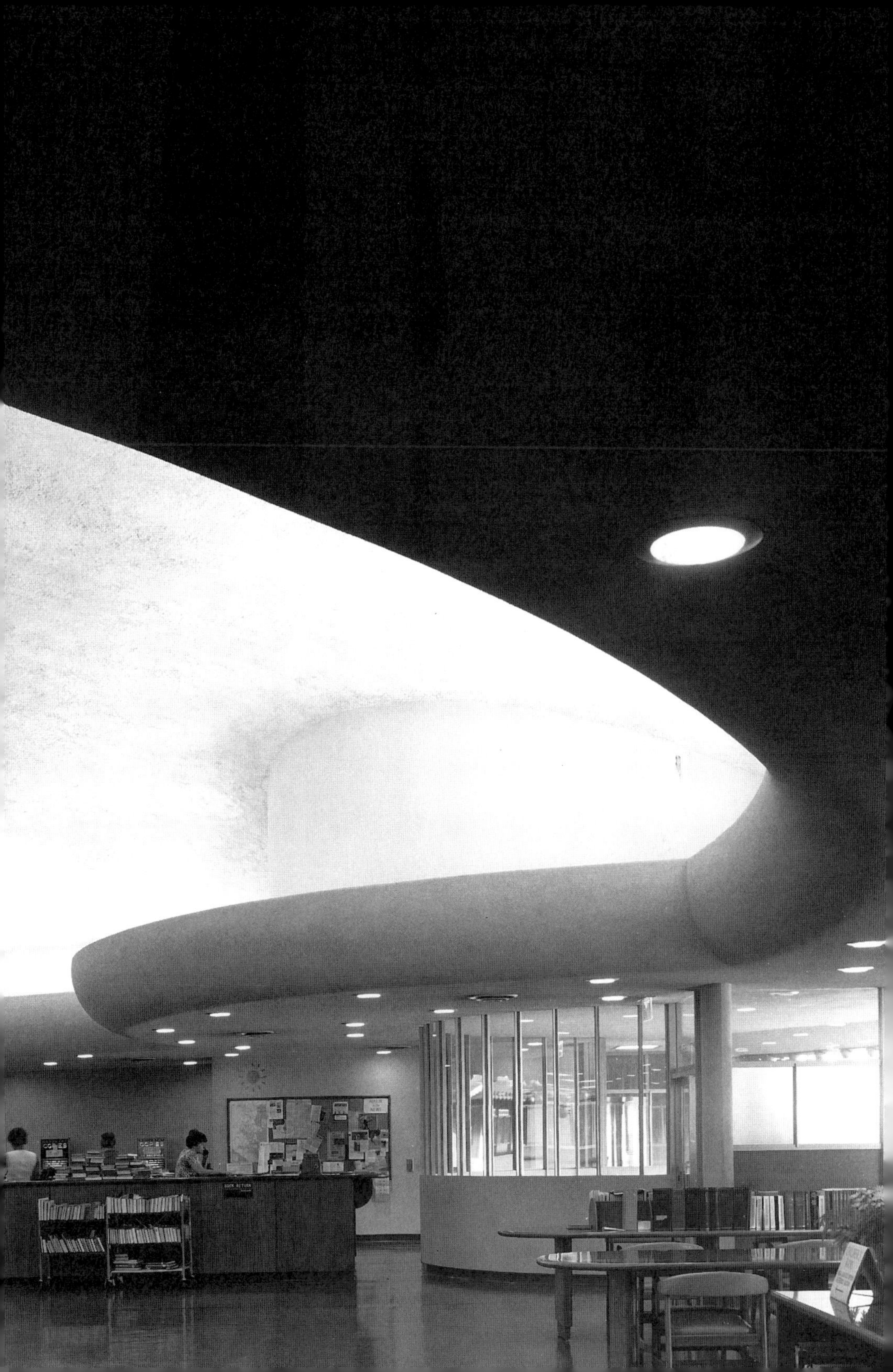

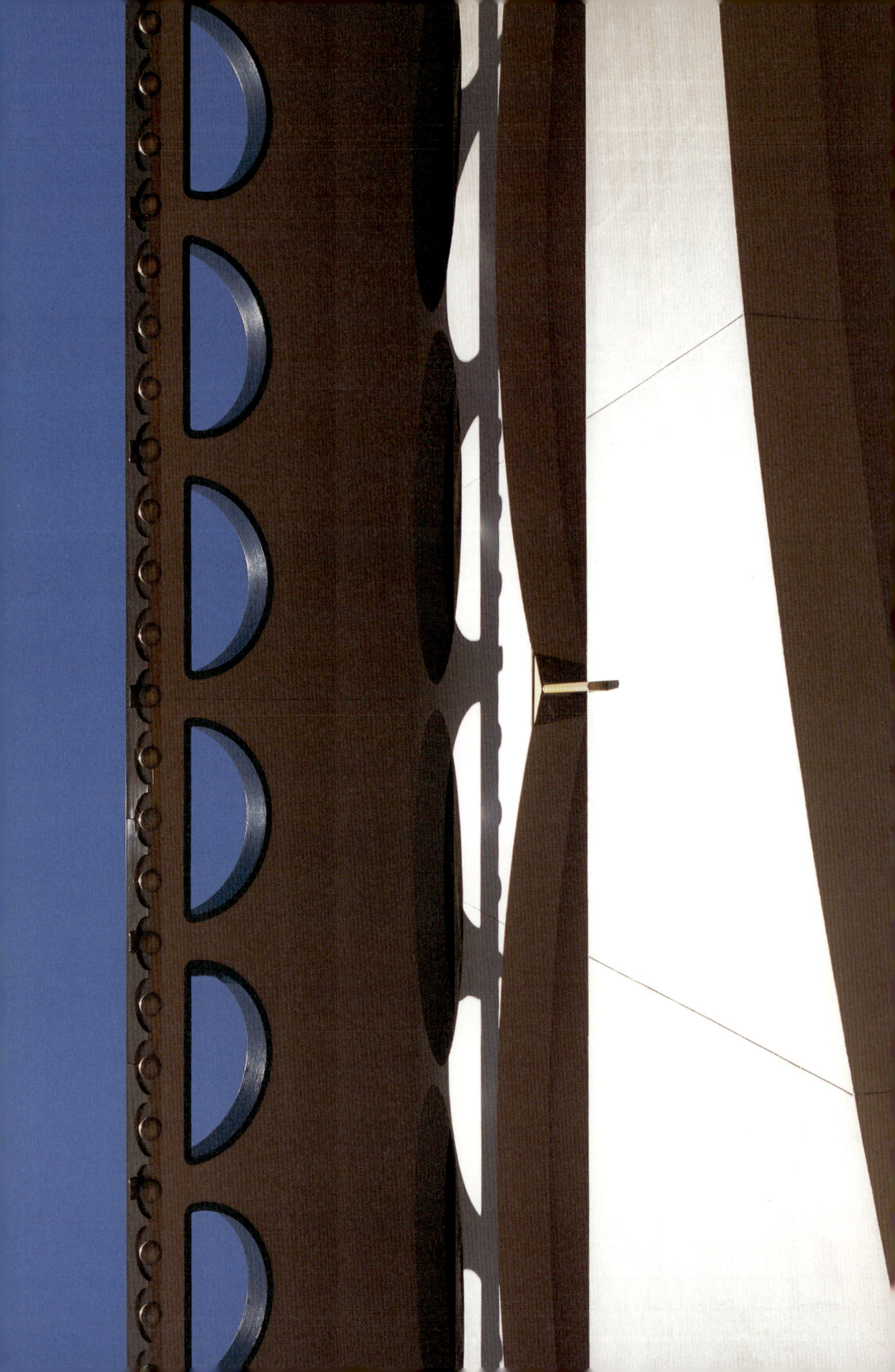

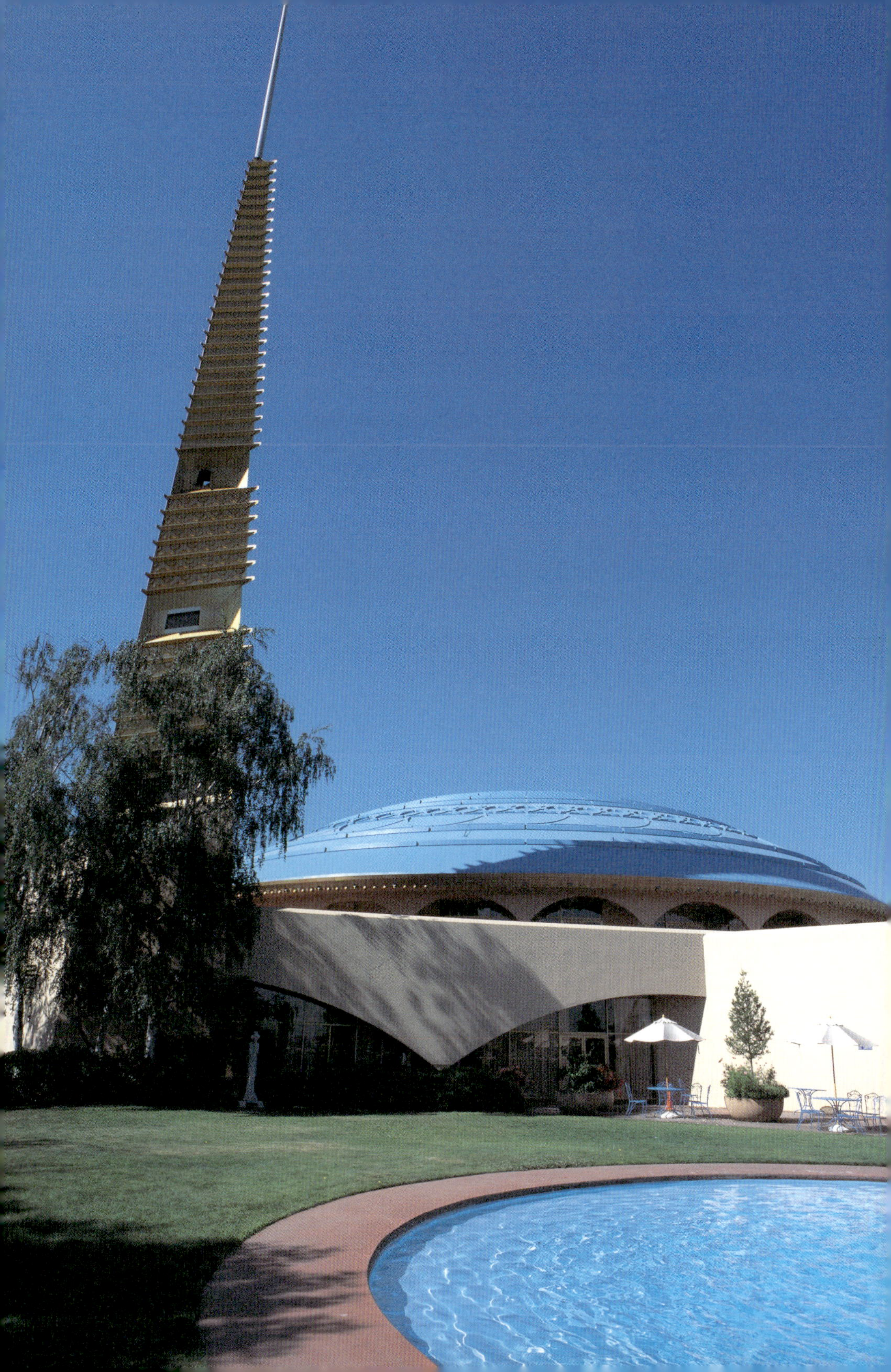

Religious Buildings
by Bruce Brooks Pfeiffer

Foreword
Both of Frank Lloyd Wright's parents came from long lines of preachers, Baptist on his father's side, Unitarian on his mother's. It, therefore, seems only natural for Wright to show a special interest in religious buildings. In fact, his very first design was for a chapel for the Lloyd-Jones family graveyard near Spring Green, Wisconsin, in the valley to which Wright's grandfather immigrated in the mid nineteenth century. In 1885, when the commission arose, Wright wrote to his uncle, Jenkin Lloyd-Jones, with some sketches for the building. "I have forwarded to you today my preliminary sketches for 'Unity Chapel', I have simply made them in pencil on a piece of old paper but the idea is my own and I have copied from nothing. Any changes which you may think proper or anything to be taken off if you will let me know I will make it satisfy you. If however you think the designs not worthy of consideration please return them as I should like to keep them ...."[1]

The commission ultimately went to Chicago architect Joseph Lyman Silsbee, for whom Wright would soon work, and if Wright's drawings were returned to him, they have not survived. He maintained, however, that his first "job" was the design for the dropped ceiling of this family chapel. In describing the chapel when it was christened in 1886, the Reverend William C. Gannett wrote of the interior "Both [rooms] are wood-ceiled with pine in its own color; one is calcimined in terracotta, one in olive green. A boy architect belonging to the family looked after this interior ...."[2]

Wright would move far beyond this humble beginning and religious buildings would play an important, ongoing role in his work. From 1886 to 1959, he created designs for twenty-four different commissions, including chapels, mortuary chapels, churches of various denominations, and a synagogue.

Unity Temple, Oak Park, Illinois, 1905

"The first idea was to keep a noble room for worship in mind, and let that sense of the great room shape the whole edifice. Let the room inside be the architecture outside."[3]

はじめに

フランク・ロイド・ライトの両親は，父方はバプティスト，母方はユニテリアンと，共に何世代も続いた牧師の家系の出身であった。従って，ライトにとって，宗教建築に特別な関心を持つことはごく自然なことだった。事実，彼がまさに最初に設計したのが，ライトの祖父が19世紀半ばに移住してきたウィスコンシン州スプリング・グリーンに近い谷間にある，ロイド＝ジョーンズ家の墓地に建てる礼拝堂だったのである。1885年，この仕事が持ち上がったとき，ライトは建物の何枚かのスケッチと共に，叔父のジェンキン・ロイド＝ジョーンズにこう書き送っている。「今日，"ユニティ・チャペル"のプレリミナリー・スケッチをお送り致しました。一枚の古い紙に鉛筆で描いただけのものですが，アイディアは僕自身のもので，他から借用したところは何もありません。変えた方がよい，取り去った方がよいと思われる点は，どんなことでもお知らせ下さい。ご満足いただけるように致します。けれど，もし，このデザインが検討に値しないものであるとお思いになりましたら，スケッチをお返し下さいますようお願い致します。僕はそのスケッチをとっておきたいと思っておりますので……」[1]

この仕事は，結局，シカゴの建築家ジョセフ・ライマン＝シルスビーのものになったが，シルスビーはライトがほどなく働くことになる建築家で，もしライトの図面が彼の手元に返されていたら，図面が生かされることはなかっただろう。しかしライトはその建物を続けることになった。彼の最初の"仕事"はこの礼拝堂の天井のデザインだったのである。1886年，命名の際に記された説明文のなかで，ウィリアム・C・ガネット師は，その内部についてこう書いている。「両方［の部屋］は別々の色に塗られた松材で天井が張られている。一方は濃い茶色で，一方はオリーブ・グリーンに，カルシミンで上塗りされている。一族の少年建築家がこの内装を監督した……」[2]

ライトはこのささやかな一歩から，遥か遠くまで進み，宗教建築は彼の作品のなかで，終始，重要な役割を演じることになる。1886年から1959年のあいだに，ライトは，礼拝堂，斎場の礼拝堂，様々な宗派の教会，シナゴーグなど24にのぼる，性格を異にする宗教建築の依頼を受け，それぞれに創意に満ちたデザインをつくりあげたのである。

ユニティ教会，1905年

「最初の考えは，礼拝に相応しい，気品のある空間を心に留めおくこと，その崇高な空間の感覚が行き渡るように建物全体をかたちづくることだった。内部空間をして建築の外観となさしめよ。」[3]

1905年6月4日の夜，激しい雷雨のあいだに，雷が，オークパークのユニテリアン・ユニバーサリスト・ユニティ教会の高い尖塔に落ち，その結果起きた火災により建物は崩壊した。いくつかの点でそれは天恵ともいえるものだった。古い木造の建物は補修を必要としており，牧師であるロドニー・ジョンノット師は，ユニテリアンの思想をよりよく表現

On the night of June 4, 1905, during a severe thunderstorm, lightening struck the tall spire of the Unitarian-Universalist Unity Church of Oak Park and the resulting fire demolished the building. In some respects, this was providential. The old wooden building had been in need of repair and the pastor, Reverend Rodney Johonnot, had expressed a desire to construct a new church more expressive of Unitarian concepts. He envisioned a building less in keeping with traditional church architecture, even calling such a new structure a "Temple", It was also providential that Charles E. Roberts, a long-time friend and client of Frank Lloyd Wright's, was a prominent member of the building committee established to select an architect and find a new site.

Wright's first concern in his design for the new Unity Temple was to eliminate the traditional church steeple. He saw the steeple as a finger pointing upward to Heaven while he preferred Jesus' saying "The kingdom of Heaven is within you."

"First came the philosophy of the building in my own mind. I said, 'Let us abolish, in the art and craft of architecture, literature in any symbolic form whatsoever. The sense of inner rhythm deep planted in human sensibility lives far above all other considerations in art. Then why the steeple of the little white church. Why point to heaven .... Why not, then, build a temple, not to God in that way—more sentimental than sense—but build a temple to man, appropriate to his uses as a meeting place, in which to study man himself for his God's sake? A modern meeting-house and a good-time place.'

The pastor was a liberal. His liberality was thus challenged, his reason was piqued and the curiosity of all was aroused, What would such a building look like? They said they could imagine no such thing. 'That's what you came to me for,' I ventured. 'I can imagine it and I will help you create it.'"

For material, he chose concrete, because it was the cheapest available, and for the general form of the structure, he chose the square, because the wooden forms could be used for all four sides. The roof would be a reinforced concrete slab. The exterior concrete would be left natural:

"Then the Temple itself—still in my mind—began to take shape. The site was noisy, by the Lake Street car-tracks. Therefore it seemed best to keep the building closed on the three front sides and enter it from a court to the rear at the center of the lot. Unity Temple itself with the thoughts in mind I have just expressed, arrived easily enough, but there was a secular side to the Universalist church activities—entertainment often, Sunday school, feasts, and so on.

To embody these with the temple would spoil the simplicity of the room—the noble Room in the service of man for the worship of God. So I finally put the secular space designated as 'Unity House', a long, free space to the rear of the lot, as a separate building to be subdivided by movable screens for Sunday school or on occasion. It

した新しい教会の建設を以前から表明していたからである。彼は，そうした新しい建物を"テンプル"と呼びさえするほど，伝統的な教会建築とはかなり趣を異にする建物を思い描いていたのである。フランク・ロイド・ライトの以前からの後援者でありクライアントであるチャールズ・E・ロバーツが，建築家を選び，新しい敷地を見つけるために設立された建設委員会の有力なメンバーであったことも幸いした。

　新しいユニティ教会(テンプル)のデザインに対しライトが最初に考えたのは，伝統的な教会にはつきものの尖塔を取り去ることだった。彼は，イエスの言葉，「天の王国はあなたの心の内にある」に惹かれる一方，尖塔を天を指すものと見ていたからである。

　「私の心に最初に浮かんだのは，建物についての哲学であった。私はこう自分に語りかけた。『建築をめぐる芸術や工芸において，それが何であれ，どのような象徴的な形においても学識なるものを捨て去ろうではないか。人の感性のなかに深く植え付けられた内的な律動の感覚は，芸術に対するあらゆる思考のはるか上位に生きている。それでは，小さな白い教会の尖塔は何故存在するのか？　何故天を指しているのか……そして何故，尖塔とは異なる方法で神に向き合う教会(テンプル)を建てないのか——感覚よりももっと心情的で——集いの場所として使うに相応しい，人間のための，神のために自らを学ぶための教会(テンプル)を建てないのか？　現代的な集いの家，そして心安まる時をすごす場所を。』

　牧師は伝統的権威に囚われることのない人だった。彼の寛容さはこうして挑戦を受けとめ，彼の理性は刺激され，皆の好奇心が目覚めた。そのような建物はどんな風に見えるだろうか？　彼らはそうした建物を想像できないと言う。『それこそ，あなたが私のもとにいらした目的なのではないでしょうか』と私は思い切って言った。『私にはそれが想像できます。そしてあなたがそれを造られるのを手伝いましょう。』」

　材料については，ライトはコンクリートを選んだ。入手できる最も安価なものだったからである。建物の全体的な形については，四角形を選んだ。木製型枠は，4つの側面全部を利用できるだろうからである。屋根は鉄筋コンクリートスラブになるだろう。外壁のコンクリートは自然のままに残されるだろう。

　「そして，テンプルそのもの——いまだ私の心のなかにある——が形をとりはじめた。敷地は車の往来するレイク・ストリートの傍らにあり騒がしい。それゆえ，建物の三方を閉ざしたままにし，敷地中央，裏手に面した中庭から入るようにするのが最善であるように思われた。ユニティ教会(テンプル)そのものは，今説明したような，私の心にあった考えと共にごく自然に形をとったが，ユニバーサリストの教会活動には世俗的側面があった——頻繁に開かれる催し，日曜学校，祝祭などである。

　教会(テンプル)にこれらを統合すると部屋の単純性を損なうだろう——つまり神に祈る人間の儀式が行われる高貴な〈部屋〉の簡潔さが。そこで，結局，"ユニティ・ハウス"と呼ぶ世俗的な空間を配置した。それは敷地の背面に向いた，細長い自由な空間で，日曜学校や行事に合わせて可動の間仕切りによって分割できる別棟となっている。こうして，それは別な建

thus became a separate building but harmonious with the Temple—the entrance to both to be the connecting link between them."[4]

There is some serious speculation that this plan form of two connecting elements with the entrance placed in a smaller unit between them was the result of Wright's recent visit to Japan. In April 1905, he visited Nikko and presumably visited the Taiyu-in-byo. Here the worship hall and main sanctuary are two larger elements connected by a small one, a configuration similar to the plan of Unity Temple.[5] Nevertheless, there was another consideration in Wright's mind for placing the entrance as he did:

"And why not place the pulpit at the entrance side at the rear of the square Temple, and bring the congregation into the room at the sides on a lower level so those entering would be imperceptible to the audience? This would preserve quiet and the dignity of the room itself. Out of that thought came the depressed foyer or cloister corridor on either side, leading from the main lobby at the center to the stairs in the near and far corners of the room. Those entering the room this way could see into the big room but not be seen by those already seated within it.

And, important to the pastor, when the congregation rose to disperse, here was opportunity to move forward toward their pastor and by swinging wide doors open beside the pulpit allow the entire flock to pass out by him and find themselves directly in the entrance loggia from which they had first come in ....

The room itself—size determined by comfortable seats with leg-room for four hundred people—was built with four interior free standing posts to carry the overhead structure. These concrete posts were hollow and became free-standing ducts to insure economic and uniform distribution of heat. The large supporting posts were so set in plan as to form a double tier of alcoves on four sides of the room. I flooded these side-alcoves with light from above to get a sense of a happy cloudless day into the room. And with this feeling for light the center ceiling between the four great posts became skylight, daylight sifting through between the intersecting concrete beams, filtering through amber glass ceiling lights. Thus managed the light would, rain or shine, have the warmth of sunlight. Artificial lighting took place there at night as well. This scheme of lighting was integral, gave diffusion and kept the room-space clear."[6]

In another publication, Wright explained the location of the pastor within the great room: "The speaker is placed well out in the auditorium, his audience gathered about him in the fashion of a friendly gathering, rather than as fixed in deep ranks, when it was imperative that the priest make himself the cynosure of all eyes."[7]

Years later, Wright was speaking about some of his early buildings and the case of Unity Temple came up. He placed great significance in this work and explained why:

"When the Larking Building model first came, that stair tower at

物となったのだが，教会とよく調和している——両方の棟へサービスするエントランス〔テンプル〕は，2棟を結びつけることになるだろう。」[4]

　2棟に挟まれた小さなスペースに置かれたエントランスが，2つの棟を結ぶ構成は，ライトの日本訪問の結果ではないかという，ある重要な仮説が存在する。1905年4月，ライトは日光を訪れたが，おそらく大猷院廟にも立ち寄っている。その参拝場と中心となる神域は2つの大きな棟で構成され，両者を小さな棟がつないでおり，その配置はユニティ教会〔テンプル〕のプランに似ているのである。[5] しかしながら，ライトが決めたエントランスの配置については，彼の心には別な考えがあった。

　「そして，説教壇を，四角形の教会〔テンプル〕の後背部に位置するエントランス側に配置し，会衆を低いレベルに面した側から部屋のなかに入れるようにして，中にいる会衆にその動きがわからないようにしてはいけないだろうか？　これはその部屋の静けさと威厳を保つことだろう。この考えから，部屋の両側に，中央のロビーから部屋の四隅にある階段へ導く，低くなったホワイエ，つまり回廊が生まれた。部屋にこの道筋で入る人からはその広い空間を見ることができるだろうが，そのなかで既に席についている人には入って来る人は見えない。

　さらに，牧師にとって重要なことだが，会衆が散会しようと立ち上がったとき，ここは彼らを牧師の方に向かって前に進ませることになる。全信徒は牧師の傍らを過ぎて，説教壇のかたわらに開く，幅の広い両開き戸から，最初にこの部屋に入ってきたエントランス・ロッジアに直接出て行くからである。

　部屋そのものは——4人が脚を楽に投げ出せる余裕のある座り心地のよい椅子席によって大きさが決められた——上部の構造体を支えて空間内に離れて立つ4本の独立柱で組み立てられている。この4本のコンクリート柱は空洞にして，経済性を確保し，熱を均質に放射して部屋を暖めるダクトとなった。この大きな柱は，部屋の4側面に，2層に重なるアルコーブを形成するように配置された。私は晴れ渡る平穏な日の感じを部屋のなかに取り込むために，これらの側面にあるアルコーブを上方からの光で満たした。そしてこの光に対する思いと共に，4本の大柱に囲まれた中央の天井はスカイライトになった。交差する大梁の間を昼の光が木漏れ日のように落ちてきて，天井灯の琥珀色のガラスを通って濾過される。こうして操作された光は，雨の日も，晴れた日も，陽射しの暖かさを帯びるだろう。夜にはそこで，人工の光が同じようにその役割をつとめる。この照明についてのスキームは全体構成に不可欠な一部であり，光を乱反射させ，この部屋の空間を澄み渡ったものに保つことになる。」[6]

　別な出版物のなかで，ライトは会衆席のなかの牧師の位置を次のように説明している。「話し手が，会衆席のなかで十分に目立ち，牧師自らが威厳を持って衆目の的になるとき，会衆は列の奥深くにしばりつけられたままでいることなく，親しげな集いにおける流儀で彼のまわりに集まる。」[7]

　数年の後，ライトは自分の初期の建物について講演したが，そのなかでユニティ教会〔テンプル〕について触れている。彼はこの作品に非常に重要な位置を与え，その理由をこう説明している。

the corner was part of the mass, part of the building. I didn't know what was the matter. I was trying for something with some freedom that I had not got. Suddenly, the model was standing on the Studio table in the center, and I came in and saw what was the matter. I took those four corners and I pulled them out away from the building, made them individual features ... and there began the thing that I was trying to do .... I got features instead of walls. I followed that up with Unity Temple where there were no walls of any kind, only features; and the features were screens grouped about interior space. The thing that came to me by instinct in the Larkin Building, began to come consciously in Unity Temple. When I finished Unity Temple, I had it. I was conscious of the idea. I knew I had the beginning of a great thing, a great truth in architecture. And now architecture could be free."[8]

How Wright achieved this in Unity Temple is evident in the plan. The four concrete posts inside the building that also served as ducts for heating, rise to support the overhead reinforced concrete slab roof. The walls, therefore, do not serve as support for the roof, but as screens to prevent noise from the busy streets outside from coming into the room. As with the Larkin Building, he has pulled the four stair towers at the corners free from these screens by making an indentation at the place where the towers meet the wall-screens. The result is strong shadow lines, which break up the surface and visually separate towers from screens.

Anne Merner Pfeiffer Chapel, Florida Southern College, Lakeland, Florida, 1938

"The building as architecture is born out of the heart of man, permanent consort to the ground, comrade to the trees, true reflection of man in the realm of his own spirit. His building is therefore consecrated space wherein he seeks refuge, recreation, and repose for the body but especially for mind."[9]

The Pfeiffer Chapel was the first of the many Frank Lloyd Wright buildings designed for Florida Southern College. The walls of the lower, ground floor level are composed of patterned concrete blocks, while the walls of the upper sections are plastered concrete blocks, the smooth surfaces juxtaposed against the more decorative ones below. The plan of the chapel is an expanded hexagon, with two sides extending out. Four entrances to the chapel are placed at the four corners where these extensions meet the central space. Stairs on both sides ascend to the mezzanine. A raised platform, hexagonal in plan, holds the rostrum and seating for speakers. The rostrum is placed in full view of the congregation seated on the main level and the mezzanine. Behind this platform is an enclosed room for the convenience of the speakers. There is a choir on the upper level over this speaker area, with a dramatic perforated choir screen of cast

「ラーキン・ビルディングの模型が最初に出来上がったとき，コーナーにあるあの階段室はマッスの一部，建物の一部でした。私には何が問題なのか分かっていませんでした。そのときはまだ獲得していなかった，自由に関わる何かと取り組んでいました。スタジオ中央のテーブルの上に模型が置かれていたのですが，突然，何が問題であるかに気づいたのです。その4つのコーナーを取り上げ，建物から引き離して，個別の特徴的な要素にする……そして，私が試みようとしていたことがそこから始まったのです……私は壁の代わりに特徴的な要素を手に入れました。それは，いかなる種類の壁もなく，ただ特徴があるだけのユニティ教会(テンプル)をさらに徹底して追求したものなのです。特徴というのは，内部空間の周りに一団を構成する仕切り(スクリーン)のことです。ラーキン・ビルディングで直観的に浮かんだことは，ユニティ教会(テンプル)のなかで既に気づいていたことでした。ユニティ教会(テンプル)を終えたとき，私はそれを手にしていたのです。そのアイディアを意識していました。私はそれが偉大なること，建築における偉大なる真実の始まりであることを知っていました。そして今，建築は自由になるのではないでしょうか。」[8]

ライトがこのことをユニティ教会(テンプル)のなかで，どのように成し遂げたのかは，そのプランに明らかである。暖房用のダクトとしても働く，建物内部に置かれた4本のコンクリート柱が，頭上の鉄筋コンクリートの屋根スラブを支えるべく立ち上がっている。従って壁は屋根を支えてはいない。道路から部屋に入り込んでくる騒音を防ぐ仕切り(スクリーン)の役割を果たしている。ラーキン・ビルディングと同じように，彼は，仕切り壁と階段室が接する箇所をジグザグに押し出し，4つのコーナーにある4本の階段室(スクリーン)を，仕切り壁の拘束から解き放している。この結果，影が強い線を描いて立面を分断し，階段室を仕切り壁(スクリーン)から視覚的に切り離すのである。

フロリダ・サザン・カレッジ・アン・マーナー・ファイファー・チャペル，1938年

「建築と言い得る建物は，人の心から生まれ，大地の永遠の配偶者，樹木の仲間，精神王国の真の反映にほかならない。それゆえに，その建物は聖別された空間であり，その内に，人は，慰め，憩い，肉体の，特に心の安息を求める。」[9]

ファイファー・チャペルはフロリダ・サザン・カレッジにフランク・ロイド・ライトが設計した多くの建物のなかで最初のものであった。1階の壁の，低い部分は連続模様を描くコンクリート・ブロック，上の部分はプラスターで仕上げたコンクリート・ブロックで構成され，滑らかな表面が，下のより装飾的な壁面と対比的に並置されている。チャペルは，向き合う2側面が外に広がる六角形平面である。チャペルへの4つのエントランスは，これらの拡張部が四角形の中央空間と接する4つのコーナーに配置されている。両側に置かれた階段がメザニン・レベルへ上がって行く。高く持ち上げられた六角形平面を持つ台座が説教壇と聖職者席を支えている。説教壇は，主階とメザニンに座っている会衆をすべて見渡せる位

concrete. This screen stretches across the full width of the chapel. The great lantern tower that rises over the central section is the hallmark of the building. Here the traditional lantern tower of Europe's Romanesque and Gothic cathedrals is given new meaning with steel, reinforced concrete, and glass. On the two long sides, it is composed of plastered concrete blocks with geometric patterns. On the two short ends, the lantern is open, and large, cast-concrete planting boxes are supported by triangular elements extending from the sides. This lantern is one of the most intriguing and complex of Wright's designs. Inside, spectacular light is brought down into the chapel through the lantern, balanced by four flat skylights, while the area under the mezzanine is given a quieter, meditative atmosphere by the more subdued lighting produced by concrete blocks perforated with colored glass. In this building Wright has combined several architectural forms in concrete, steel, and glass to create a sense of transcendent serenity.

William H. Danforth Chapel, Florida Southern College, Lakeland, Florida, 1953

Although all of the drawings for this project are labeled "Minor Chapel", it is, in fact, known as The William H. Danforth Chapel in honor of its benefactor. Originally, Wright had sited the building parallel to the Pfeiffer Chapel, but later rotated it 30 degrees, repeating the angles of the larger chapel in both the front and the end walls. An extension from the long plan provides an anteroom, which opens on one end into a seminar room and, on the right, into the chapel along a side aisle. Here, there is a staircase to the mezzanine level. At the far end of the chapel, there is a jewel-like stained glass window set well under the gable roof. Directly outside this full-length window are two planting boxes that repeat the angle of the chapel's end wall. Overhead the roof is also prow-like. The mezzanine level provides balconies along each side above the aisles below. High windows on the balconies balance the light from the stained glass window at the prow. Over the anteroom and seminar room are two spaces labeled "Religion Dept", and "General Office", These spaces also serve for educational activities when needed. There is an outdoor balcony over the entrance. The plan of the building is reflected in the plan of the roof with its pointed prow and the horizontal projections of the roof over the side walls reflect the plan of the side aisles.

The chapel is used mainly for smaller religious services and weddings. The strong horizontality of the Danforth Chapel is further emphasized by its placement near the imposing verticality of the Pfeiffer Chapel.

置に置かれている。この台座の背後に講話者の控え室がある。その上のレベルに聖歌隊席があり，キャスト・コンクリートの印象的な有孔スクリーンが聖歌隊席に巡らされている。スクリーンはチャペルの幅いっぱいに延びている。中央に立ち上がる大きな頂塔は建物の特徴的な存在である。ここで，ヨーロッパのロマネスクやゴシック聖堂の伝統的な頂塔は，スティールと鉄筋コンクリートとガラスよって新しい意味を与えられた。2つの長手側はプラスター仕上げのコンクリート・ブロックが幾何学模様を描いている。2つの短い妻側は，頂塔は開いていて，キャスト・コンクリートの大きなプランターが両側から延びた三角形のエレメントによって支えられている。この頂塔はライトのデザインのなかで，最も興味をそそる複雑なものの一つである。内部では，4つの平坦なスカイライトと均衡をとりながら，壮麗な光が頂塔を通って堂内に降り注ぎ，その一方で，メザニンの下に広がるエリアは色ガラスをはめたコンクリートの有孔ブロックから生まれる和らげられた光によって，より静かで，瞑想的な雰囲気が与えられている。ライトは，この建物のなかに，日常性を超えた平安な静けさをつくりだすために，いくつかの建築形態をコンクリート，スティール，ガラスによって結びつけたのである。

フロリダ・サザン・カレッジ・ウィリアム・H・ダンフォース・チャペル，1953年

このプロジェクトのためのドローイングのすべてには"マイナー・チャペル"と名が付けられているのではあるが，実際は，その寄進者に敬意を表してウィリアム・H・ダンフォース・チャペルとして知られている。最初，ライトはこの建物をファイファー・チャペルに平行に配置したのだが，その後，30度振り，ファイファー・チャペルの角度をその正面壁と妻壁の両方に反復させた。細長い平面形からの延長部が控えの間を構成し，その一端はセミナールームに開き，右手は側廊に沿ってチャペルに開いている。ここにメザニン・レベルへ至る階段がある。チャペルの一番奥には切妻屋根の下に巧みに配置された宝石のようなステンドグラスの窓がある。建物の高さいっぱいに広がる窓のすぐ外には，チャペルの妻壁の角度を反復した形を持つプランターが2つ置かれている。その頭上の屋根もまた船の舳先に似ている。メザニンは，下の側廊の上，両側面に沿ってバルコニーを形成する。バルコニーの高窓は舳先にあるステンドグラスの窓からの光と均衡をとる。控えの間とセミナールームの上は，"宗務局"と"総長事務室"と名付けられた2つの空間である。これらのスペースも必要な場合は教室として使われる。エントランスの上ではバルコニーが屋外に突き出ている。建物のプランは，先端がとがった，舳先のような屋根のプランに投影され，側壁にかぶさる屋根の水平な張り出しは，側廊のプランを反映している。

　チャペルは主に，少人数の礼拝や結婚式に使われている。ダンフォース・チャペルの強い水平性は，垂直性の際立つファイファー・チャペルのそばにあることで，さらに強調される。

The Unitarian Meeting House, Shorewood Hills, Wisconsin, 1947

"ASPIRATION—Unity—the ideal of Unitarianism appears in Madison as a structure revealing what the congregation professes to believe—In significant form—the Unitarian Ideal."[10]

At Unity Temple in Oak Park, Wright employed the square, symbolically standing for unity and equality, as the predominant design form. In this design, he chose the triangle, the symbol of aspiration, as the dominant form.

"In Unity Church [Unitarian Meeting House] there you see the Unitarianism of my forefathers found expression in a building by one of the offspring. The idea, 'Unitarian', was unity. Unitarians believed in the unity of all things. Well, I tried to build a building here that expressed that over-all sense of unity. The plan you see is triangular. The roof is triangular and out of this triangulation—aspiration— you get this expression of reverence without recourse to the steeple. The building itself, covering all, all in all and each in all, sets forth—says what the steeple used to say, but says it with greater reverence, I think, in both form and structure."[11]

The larger triangle is the sanctuary or auditorium, while connected to it is a smaller triangle, the "Hearth Room", a social room so-called because of its great limestone fireplace. The Hearth Room has a low ceiling, whereas the ceiling of the Sanctuary begins at a low deck and then rises dramatically up to the triangular prow at the far end. Here, at the prow, is the rostrum and lectern raised a few steps above the auditorium floor, with a projecting balcony above for the chorus. The plaster ceiling is dotted with circular lights that appear as stars in the firmament. Tall windows on either side of the prow bring more light into the room. Wright's original plan showed the prow as a screen of concrete blocks perforated with stained glass insets, but when the church purchased a sloped site facing a grove of oak trees with Lake Mendota in the distance, Wright opened the prow with clear glass. The lofty and inspirational quality of the rising ceiling in the auditorium finds expression on the exterior, as though two hands were held together in the attitude of prayer, the reality of the space proceeding from within outward. On the edge of the deck where the ceiling begins to rise is lettered the parable, "Do you have a loaf of bread, break the bread in half and give half for some flowers of the Narcissus, for thy bread feeds the body indeed, but the flowers feed the soul."

Moveable benches provide the seating in the auditorium so that the room can be rearranged for concerts. The adjacent Hearth Room can accommodate additional seating when desired. While the auditorium provides a view onto a more distance landscape, the Hearth Room focuses its view on the evergreen garden directly outside. The entrance to the building is at one end, from a covered porch that gains the lobby, with office and kitchen nearby. Both the

ユニテリアン・ミーティング・ハウス，1947年

「[熱望(アスピレーション)]——ユニティ（単一性）——ユニテリアンの教義の理想は，マディソンでは，会衆が信仰を告白することを明かす建物として現れる——意味を示す形態——ユニテリアンの理想。」[10]

オークパークのユニティ教会(テンプル)で，ライトは全体を支配する形態として，ユニティ（単一性）と平等性を象徴的に意味する四角形を選んだ。ここでは，主要な形態として，熱望の象徴である三角形を選んでいる。

「ユニティ教会［ユニテリアン・ミーティング・ハウス］では，私の祖先のユニテリアン主義が，その子孫の一人による建物のなかに表現されているのを見ることになる。"ユニテリアン"の理想はユニティである。ユニテリアンはすべてのものの単一性を信じた。そこで，私はその全体的なユニティの感覚をここで表現する建物を建てようと試みた。プランはごらんのように三角形である。屋根は三角形で，そしてこの三角形分割——熱望——から，尖塔を頼みとすることなくこの関連する表現を得るのである。建物そのものは，すべてを覆い，すべてはすべてに，それぞれはすべてに，を宣言する——かつて尖塔が伝えてきたものを伝えるが，さらに大きな畏敬の念をもって伝えるのである。私は形態と構造の両方によって伝えたいと思っている。」[11]

大きな方の三角形は聖域，つまり会衆席で，一方，小さな方の三角形がそれにつながり，そこは，広いライムストーンの暖炉があるために"炉辺の部屋"と呼ばれる親睦のための部屋である。炉辺の部屋は天井が低いのに対し，聖域の天井は，低いデッキから始まり一番奥の三角形の舳先に向かって劇的に上昇している。この舳先のところに説教壇と聖書台が会衆席の床から数段上がって位置し，その上に聖歌隊のためのバルコニーが張り出している。プラスター仕上げの天井には，蒼空の星のように現れる円形の照明が点々と並んでいる。舳先の両側にとられた背の高い窓からさらに多くの光が差し込む。ライトの最初のプランでは，舳先はステンドグラスが填め込まれた有孔コンクリートブロックのスクリーンになっているが，教会が，遠くにメンドータ湖の見える樫の木立に面した斜面を敷地として購入したとき，ライトは舳先を開き，透明ガラスを填めたのである。上昇して行く会衆席の天井の，屹立し，人を鼓舞するような性格は，外部にその表現を見い出し，まるで祈る人が両手を組み合わせているように見え，空間の本質が内部から外に向かって進み出て行くかのようである。天井の上昇起点にあるデッキの端には比喩が刻まれている。「あなたがひと塊のパンを持っているならば，そのパンを半分に割り，その半分をナルキッソスの花々に与えなさい。なるほど，あなたのパンは身体を養いますが，花々は魂を養うのですから。」

会衆席のベンチは動かせるので，この部屋をコンサートのために再編することができる。必要なときは，隣の炉辺の部屋に補足的に座席を用意すればよい。会衆席からは遥か遠くの風景が望めるのに対し，炉辺の部屋は，すぐ外の常緑樹の茂る庭に焦点があてられている。建物のエントランスは片端にあり，ロビーのある屋根の付いたポーチからで，すぐ

auditorium and the Hearth Room can be entered from the lobby. On the opposite site is the Sunday school wing, with a loggia-gallery whose glass doors open onto an outdoor terrace, which overlooks lawn, gardens, and the oak grove on the hillside below. The original plan provided a parsonage at the far end of the Sunday school wing, but only the living room was constructed and labeled "West Living Room", with a fireplace and provisions for additional social events. The main building material is limestone, and the roofs are copper. In 1963, the Sunday school rooms were converted to offices and Taliesin Architects designed and built a new educational wing next to the area designated for the original parsonage.

Beth Sholom Synagogue, Elkins Park, Pennsylvania, 1954

"Mount Sinai—A Temple for Judaism in America—the Burning Bush and worshipers with a symbol of the Mount." [12]

In 1953, Rabbi Mortimer Cohen called upon Frank Lloyd Wright to ask if he would design a synagogue for the Beth Sholom Congregation in Elkins Park, near Philadelphia. When Wright accepted the commission, the Rabbi sent him voluminous material which he felt was pertinent to Judaism: documents, photographs, descriptions, suggestions, all intended to help illustrate the important symbols that should be considered in the design of a house of worship for Jews. Wright's final design, however, was not so much an outgrowth of study of that material as an expression of profound insight into the faith, a statement in architectural form to embody the Idea in its essence.

In 1928, Wright had designed an interdenominational cathedral to house chapels of various faiths within it, a shimmering structure of steel and glass in the form of a vast pyramid rising from concrete masses at the base to great heights above. This design became the progenitor for the synagogue now dedicated to the Jews of America. When the preliminary drawings were sent to Rabbi Cohen, the architect submitted a letter about the project.

"Dear Rabbi:

Herewith the promised 'hosanna'—a temple that is truly a religious tribute to the living God. Judaism needs one in America. To do it for you has pleased me. The scheme or plan is capable of infinite variation, and could be expanded or diminished and made into different shapes as might be desired.

The scheme is truly simple. Construction is modern as can be. Stamped copper shells erected for structural members are filled with concrete in which the necessary steel rods are embedded for stresses: the tops of the shells are removable for this purpose—thus no forming is necessary.

The building is set up on an interior temporary scaffold. The outer walls are double wired glass—a blue-tinted plastic inside—about an

そばにオフィスとキッチンがある。会衆席にも炉辺の部屋にもロビーから入ることができる。反対側には日曜学校のウィングがあり、ロッジア＝ギャラリーが付いていて、そのガラス戸は屋外のテラスに開き、そこからは芝生、庭、そして下の方、丘の斜面に広がる樫の木立が見渡せる。最初のプランでは、日曜学校のあるウィングの先端に牧師館が置かれていたが、リビングルームだけが建てられ"ウェスト・リビングルーム"と名付けられて、暖炉と補足的な親睦行事のための設備が付いている。主要な建築材料はライムストーン、屋根は銅である。1963年、日曜学校の部屋はオフィスに転換され、タリアセン・アーキテクツが、元は牧師館と示されていた土地の隣に新しい教育施設を建てた。

ベス・ショロム・シナゴーグ，1954年

「マウント・サイナイ（シナイ山）――アメリカに於けるユダヤ教の聖堂――"燃えているのに、燃え尽きない"柴（出エジプト記）とその山の象徴と共にある礼拝者。」[12]

1953年、ラビ・モーティマー・コーエンはライトに、フィラデルフィアに近いエルキンズ・パークのベス・ショロム信徒協会のためにシナゴーグを設計してほしいとフランク・ロイド・ライトに依頼した。ライトがこの依頼を引き受けると、ラビは、ユダヤ教に関係があると感じた膨大な資料を彼に送った。文書記録、写真、解説、提言、そのすべてが、ユダヤ人のための礼拝の家のデザインにおいて配慮すべき重要な象徴を具象化する助けとなるようにと考えてのことだった。しかし、ライトの最終案は、信仰〈への〉深い洞察を示す表現、その思想の精髄を形象化した建築的形態による表現として、それらの資料を勉強した自然の結果であるとまで言えるものではなかった。

1928年、ライトはその内部に様々な信仰の礼拝堂を納めた諸宗派共通のカテドラルを設計している。それは、基部のコンクリートのマッスから、スティールとガラスが非常な高さまで立ち上がって宏壮なピラミッドを形成し、光を受けて柔らかく煌いているものだった。このデザインは今、アメリカのユダヤ人のために捧げられたシナゴーグの原型となった。プレリミナリー・ドローイングがラビ・コーエンの元に送られたとき、ライトはその計画案について記した手紙を添えている。

「親愛なるラビ：

ここにお約束した"ホサンナ（神またはキリストを賛美する言葉）"を同封いたします――活ける神への真に宗教的な捧げものである礼拝堂。ユダヤ教はアメリカにその一つを必要としています。それをあなたのためになすことは私の喜びでありました。この計画案や平面構成は、無限の変奏が可能であり、広げることも縮めることもできますし、お望みであれば、異なった形にもできるでしょう。

この案はシンプルそのものです。工法はできる限り近代的なものになっています。構造材として立ち上げられた、打ち抜きの銅のシェルは、強化のために、必要な箇所には鉄筋コンクリートで充填されます。シェ

inch of air space between. Heat rises at the walls from the floor. The stained glass windows could be composed from scenes from the Bible?

Here you have a coherent statement of worship. I hope it pleases you and your people.

Faithfully, Frank Lloyd Wright   March 15, 1954"[13]

"You have taken the supreme moment of Jewish history and experience—the revelation of God to Israel through Moses at Mt. Sinai," replied the Rabbi, "and you have translated that moment with all it signifies into a design of beauty and reverence. In a word, your building is Mt. Sinai ...."[14]

Certain features pertinent to Judaism are made part of the design. The shape of the plan and the gently sloping facets of the main floor of the Temple itself were intended, as Wright stated, "... to create a kind of building that people, on entering it, will feel as if they were resting in the very hands of God." The large tripod beams from which are suspended the glass walls and roof (one and the same thing in this building) are marked with designs stamped in metal, which become large sculptured lamps running up the exterior of the beams to represent the Menorah—the Seven Branched Candles of Light. The Holy Ark, the Wings of the Seraphim, the Sacred Inscriptions are all there in the Synagogue as features of the architecture, parts of the building related to the structure as a whole—continuity of design wherein form proceeds from principle everywhere apparent. Mt. Sinai traditionally denotes revelation; revelation is synonymous with light; light is the essence of this edifice.

Over the entrance, at ground level, there is a projecting canopy to represent the hands of the Rabbi offering a benediction to his people as they enter the synagogue. Stairs on either side ascend to the main auditorium above. Placed as they are under a part of the roof that is not glazed, the effect is one of ascending by degrees from dimness below into the resplendent light of the auditorium itself. A choir screen behind the dais sets apart the raised area for the chorus. From the ground level entrance, stairs descend to a lobby, two lounges, one on each side, and the Sisterhood Chapel. In this lower portion of the synagogue all the walls are concrete, but a raised ceiling over the dais, which contains the Holy Ark and seats for the rabbi and cantor, is flooded with light.

Beth Sholom Synagogue is reinforced concrete, steel, glass, and plastic transmuted into an architectural expression of light as form. Indeed, there are no walls, as such, in the main auditorium: all is glass, silver toned in the morning sun, golden in the late afternoon. At night, the light from within creates a luminous Mt. Sinai—in the spirit of revelation.

ルの頂部はこの目的のために取り外しできるのです——この結果，型枠は必要ではなくなります。

　建物は内部に設置された仮設の足場の上に組み立てられます。外壁は網入りの二重ガラスで——内側は青い色に染められたプラスチックです——その間には1インチほどのエア・スペースがあります。暖気は床からこの壁の空隙を上がっていきます。ステンドグラスの窓は聖書から選んだ光景から構成することができるでしょうか？

　これは礼拝についての首尾一貫した表現なのです。それが，あなたとあなたの会衆を喜ばせることを願っております。

忠実なる　　フランク・ロイド・ライト　　　　　1954年3月15日」[13]

　「あなたは，ユダヤの歴史と体験の至高の瞬間を取り上げて下さいました——シナイ山でモーゼを通して神の啓示がイスラエルにもたらされた瞬間です」とラビは返事を出した。「そして，あなたはその瞬間を，その意味するすべてと共に，美しく敬虔なデザインへ翻案して下さいました。一言で言えば，あなたの建物はシナイ山です。」[14]

　ユダヤ教に関連するいくつかの特徴がデザインの一部をかたちづくっている。平面形と礼拝堂主階の緩やかに傾斜する小平面はライトがこう述べるように意図されている。「……人々が，その中に入ったときに，神の御手に憩っているのだと感じられるような種類の建物をつくること。」ガラス壁と屋根（この建物では同じ一つのものである）を支持する大きな三脚梁は，金属の型押し模様で特徴づけられ，外側では梁の上を頂部まで点々と飾る大きな彫刻的照明を構成し，メノラー——7枝の燭台——を象徴する。聖なる櫃（儀式用のトーラーの巻物を入れる箱），熾天使の羽，神聖な銘刻文，これらすべてが，建築的特色として，構造と関わり，建物全体をかたちづくる一部分として，すべてがこのシナゴーグのなかにある——あらゆるものが信条から生まれた形態であることが明白な，デザインの連続性。シナイ山は伝統的に啓示を意味する。啓示は光と同義である。光はこの建物の本質である。

　1階のエントランスの上には，信徒がシナゴーグに入って来る際に祝福を与えるラビの両手を象徴するようにキャノピーが張り出している。両側から階段が上のオーディトリアムに登っている。階段はガラスが填められていない屋根の部分の下に位置しているので，この結果，下のほの暗さから徐々に，会衆席そのもののまばゆい光のなかへ登って行くことになる。高座の背後の聖歌隊席の仕切壁は高くなったエリアを聖歌隊のために取り置いている。1階のエントランスから降りて行く階段は，ロビー，両サイドに一つずつあるラウンジ，修道尼のチャペルへ続いている。シナゴーグのこの部分の壁はすべてコンクリートだが，聖なる櫃，ラビと先唱者（典礼をつかさどり，祈祷文の独唱部分を歌い上げる役）の椅子が置かれた高座を覆う天井は光で満たされている。

　ベス・ショロム・シナゴーグは，鉄筋コンクリート，スティール，ガラス，プラスチックを，形態によって光の建築表現に変えたのである。確かに，中心にある会衆席には壁がない。すべてがガラスであり，朝の陽射しのなかでは銀色に，午後遅くには金色に彩られる。夜になると，

Annunciation Greek Orthodox Church, Wauwatosa, Wisconsin, 1956

"Worship a la Byzantium. The domed religion of antiquity at home in modern times—the Romance of its Past distinguished." [15]

The design for this remarkable building came from the brief response, "The dome and the cross" of Wright's wife Olgivanna, when asked about the predominant symbols of the Greek Orthodox Church, in which she was raised. Wright's original conceptual sketch (5611.001) shows the plan and elevation of the church and reveals how closely his initial thoughts on the design correspond to the final plan. The cross is immediately evident in the extremities of the plan from the basement to the main floor. The elevations reveal how the arms of the cross rise to support the balcony level, which is an inverted dome, a reflection of the dome above. Outside, steps rise up at the entry and a broad terrace accesses the narthex. From the narthex doors open directly into the auditorium. The lectern of the sanctuary is brought out into the center of the church, providing a clear view for all seating on the main level. Conforming to the tradition of the Greek Orthodox liturgy, behind the altar is the icon screen, with icons, in this case, originally executed by Wright's secretary and business manager, Eugene B. Masselink. Three spiral staircases ascend to the balcony above that runs the full periphery of the church. The part of the balcony over the sanctuary is reserved for the organ and choir. The spiral staircases are lit by tall poles with lights projecting out at right angles to the poles, the poles and lights extending up to become delicate shafts of light above the balcony. On the exterior, steps descend along the two sides of the church down to sunken gardens on each side. The lower area of the church itself is given over to a large banquet hall, with kitchen, rest rooms, choir robing, and mechanical. Extending out from this main part of the building and opening onto the sunken gardens are the Sunday school classrooms, offices, pastor's study, and finally a chapel at the end. The structure of the dome in the church is most innovative: it is a concrete shell that rests on a steel track containing thousands of ball bearings—to allow for contraction and expansion. The dome actually rotates slightly in response to temperature changes. The arches of reinforced concrete that form the semi-circular windows on the balcony level support the track. A concrete visor projects outside over these arches and windows. From inside, at the point where the dome meets the wall, a ring of cast glass spheres are set in between the reinforced concrete supports. As with the skylights in the Pfeiffer chapel, where one expects to find support, one finds light.

The circle symbolizes eternity. Here in this building, with the pastor and his congregation embraced within the circle, light pouring in from the arched windows above and the jewel-like glass spheres, there is a sense of oneness within Eternity.

内部から光輝くシナイ山をつくりだす——啓示の精神のなかに。

お告げの祝日ギリシャ正教会，1956年

「ビザンティウム風の礼拝。近代に場所を得た，丸天井の下での古代の宗教儀式——はるか昔の際立って高貴な存在の華やかな物語。」[15]

　この特異な建物のデザインは，ギリシャ正教会の主立った象徴について聞かれたとき，その世界で育ったライト夫人オルジヴァンナの，「丸天井と十字架」という簡潔な返事から生まれた。ライトの最初のコンセプト・スケッチ（5611.001）には教会の平面と立面が示され，彼の最初の考えが最終案に非常に近いものであったことがうかがえる。十字架は，地階から主階へ至るプランの先端に明白に現れている。立面を見ると，十字架の腕が，上を覆うドームを投影したような逆ドーム形のバルコニーを支えるため立ち上がっているのが分かる。外側では，階段がエントリーまで登り，幅の広いテラスが拝廊へ導く。拝廊の扉は，礼拝堂のなかへ直接開く。聖域の聖書台は教会の中央に運び出されているので，主階の座席のすべてからよく見える。ギリシャ正教の典礼の伝統に従って，祭壇の背後には，イコンの描かれた屏風があり，このイコンの原画は，ライトの秘書でビジネス・マネージャーであったユージン・B・マセリンクの手になるものである。3本の螺旋階段が，教会の周縁全長に延びている上のバルコニーまで登っている。聖域の上にくるバルコニーの部分は，オルガンと聖歌隊のために確保されている。螺旋階段は，背の高いポールから人々の方に真っ直ぐに突き出た照明で照らされ，このポールと照明は上昇して行き，バルコニーを照らす繊細な光の柱となる。外観では，階段は教会の両側に沿って，両側面に広がるサンクン・ガーデンに向かって降りて行く。教会の低層階には厨房の付いた広い宴会場，洗面所，聖歌隊の式服着替え室，機械室がある。建物のこの主要部から日曜学校の教室，オフィス，聖職者の書斎が延びてサンクン・ガーデンに直接面し，最後に突き当たりに小礼拝堂が位置する。教会のドーム構造は，非常に革新的なものである。コンクリートシェルは，収縮も拡張も可能とするために，数千個のボールベアリングの入ったスティール軌道に乗せられている。実際に，ドームは気温の変化に対応して周期的にわずかに変化する。バルコニー階に面した半円形の窓がかたちづくる鉄筋コンクリートのアーチが軌道を支える。コンクリートの眉庇がこれらのアーチと窓の外を覆って張り出す。内側から，ドームが壁と接する所で，キャストグラスの球が鉄筋コンクリートの支柱の間に設置されている。ファイファー・チャペルのスカイライトと同じように，支柱があるだろうと思う場所に，光を見つけるのである。

　円は永遠を象徴する。この建物でも，聖職者とその信徒は円のなかに抱かれ，光はアーチ型の窓，宝石のようなガラスの球から降り注ぎ，そこには〈永遠の存在〉のなかに一体感が生まれる。

Conclusion

"Concerning the traditional church as a modern building! Religion and art are forms of inner-experience—growing richer and deeper as the race grows older. We will never lose either. But I believe religious experience is outgrowing the church—not outgrowing religion but outgrowing the church as an institution just as architecture has outgrown the Renaissance and for reasons human, scientific and similar. I cannot see the ancient institutional form of any church building as anything but sentimental survival for burial. The Temple as a forum and a good-time place—beautiful and inspiring as such—yes. As a religious edifice raised in the sense of the old ritual? No. I cannot see it at all as living. It is no longer free." [16]

And so it was that Frank Lloyd Wright was able to interpret, in modern terms, construction methods, and materials, religious edifices for a variety of faiths because he understood the spirit underlying each without recourse to historical styles or forms. Church or synagogue—for him each was not only the house of God but also the house of man in search of God. Of whatever denomination, he honored and glorified its true Tradition in terms of architecture.

Bruce Brooks Pfeiffer

Taliesin West September 17, 2002

1: Frank Lloyd Wright to Jenkin Lloyd Jones, August 22, 1885
2: *Unity Magazine*, August 28, 1886. (AV#4115.067 Marlin Papers)
3: Frank Lloyd Wright, *An Autobiography* (New York: Barnes & Noble Books, 1998), p.154
4: ibid, pp.154-155
5: Masami Tanigawa, *Kanaya Hoteru Register Book ni Mirareru Wright no Toushuku Kiroku* (Architecture Institute of Japan Hokkaido Branch Research Bulletin, No.42, March 1987) pp.251-254
6: *An Autobiography*, pp.154-155
7: *Ausgeführte Bauten und Entwürfe von Frank Lloyd Wright* (Berlin: Wasmuth, 1910), plate LXIII
8: Frank Lloyd Wright to the Taliesin Fellowship, August 13, 1952. AV#1014.044, pp.16-17
9: *Frank Lloyd Wright Collected Writings Volume 2*, B. B. Pfeiffer ed. (New York: Rizzoli, 1992), p.97
10: Frank Lloyd Wright, Captions to his Buildings AV2401.367 Notes on the Hotel Sherman exhibit, October 1956
11: Frank Lloyd Wright, *The Future of Architecture* (New York: Horizon Press, 1953), p.23
12: Frank Lloyd Wright Captions to His Buildings, AV#2401.367 notes on the Hotel Sherman exhibit October, 1956
13: Wright to Cohen, March 15, 1954
14: Cohen to Wright, March 19, 1954
15: Frank Lloyd Wright Captions to his Buildings, AV #2401.367 notes on the Hotel Sherman exhibit, October 1956
16: *An Autobiography*, p.160

結び

「近代建築として伝統的な教会を考えること！ 宗教と芸術は内的体験がつくりだす形式であり——年を重ねるに従って豊かさと深さを増して行く。我々はその両方ともを決して失うことはないだろう。しかし、私は宗教体験は教会を超えて行くものだと——宗教を超えて行くのではなく、建築がルネサンス、人間の理性、科学、それに類したことを脱却して行くのと同じように機構としての教会を超えて行くのだと信じている。いかなる教会建築であっても、その古代の制度化された形態を、埋葬のための感傷的なサバイバル以上の何物であるとも私には見ることができない。フォーラムとしての、心安まる時を過ごす場所としての教会——美しく、人に希望を与えるようなものとしての——然り。古い典礼の感覚のなかに立ち上がる宗教建築(テンプル)として？ 否。私にはそれは生きたものとは全く見えない。それはもはや自由ではない。」[16]

それゆえに、その歴史的様式や形態を頼みとすることなしに、様々な宗教の根底に横たわる精神を理解したがゆえに、フランク・ロイド・ライトは、多様な信仰のための宗教建築を近代建築の用語、工法、材料に翻訳することができたのであった。教会あるいはシナゴーグは、彼にとって、神の家であるばかりでなく、神を探す人間の家でもあった。いずれの宗派であろうとも、彼は、建築の言葉によってその真の〈伝統〉を尊び、讃えたのである。

ブルース・ブルックス・ファイファー
タリアセン・ウェストにて 2002年9月17日

註：
1：フランク・ロイド・ライトからジェンキン・ロイド・ジョーンズへ。1885年8月22日
2："Unity Magazine" 1886年8月28日（AV#4115.067 Marlin Papers）
3：Frank Lloyd Wright, "An Autobiography"（New York：Barnes & Noble Books, 1998), p.154
4：前掲書, pp.154-155
5：谷川正己「金谷ホテル宿泊者名簿に見られるライトの投宿記録」（『日本建築家協会北海道支部紀要』42号、1987年3月）pp.251-254
6："An Autobiography", pp.154-155
7："Ausgeführte Bauten und Entwürfe von Frank Lloyd Wright"(Berlin: Wasmuth, 1910), Plate LXIII
8：フランク・ロイド・ライトよりタリアセン・フェローシップへ。1952年8月13日（AV#1014.044, pp.16-17）
9："Frank Lloyd Wright Collected Writings" Volume 2, B. B. Pfeiffer ed.(New York：Rizzoli, 1992), p.97
10：フランク・ロイド・ライトによる建物説明文（AV#2401.367）。1956年10月のホテル・シャーマンでの展覧会に際して書かれた。
11：Frank Lloyd Wright, "The Future of Architecture"（New York：Horizon Press, 1953), p.23
12：フランク・ロイド・ライトによる建物説明文（AV#2401.367）。1956年10月のホテル・シャーマンでの展覧会に際して書かれた。
13：ライトからコーエンへ。1954年3月15日
14：コーエンからライトへ。1954年3月19日
15：フランク・ロイド・ライトによる建物説明文（AV#2401.367）。1956年10月のホテル・シャーマンでの展覧会に際して書かれた。
16："An Autobiography", p.160

Unity Temple
Oak Park, Illinois, 1905

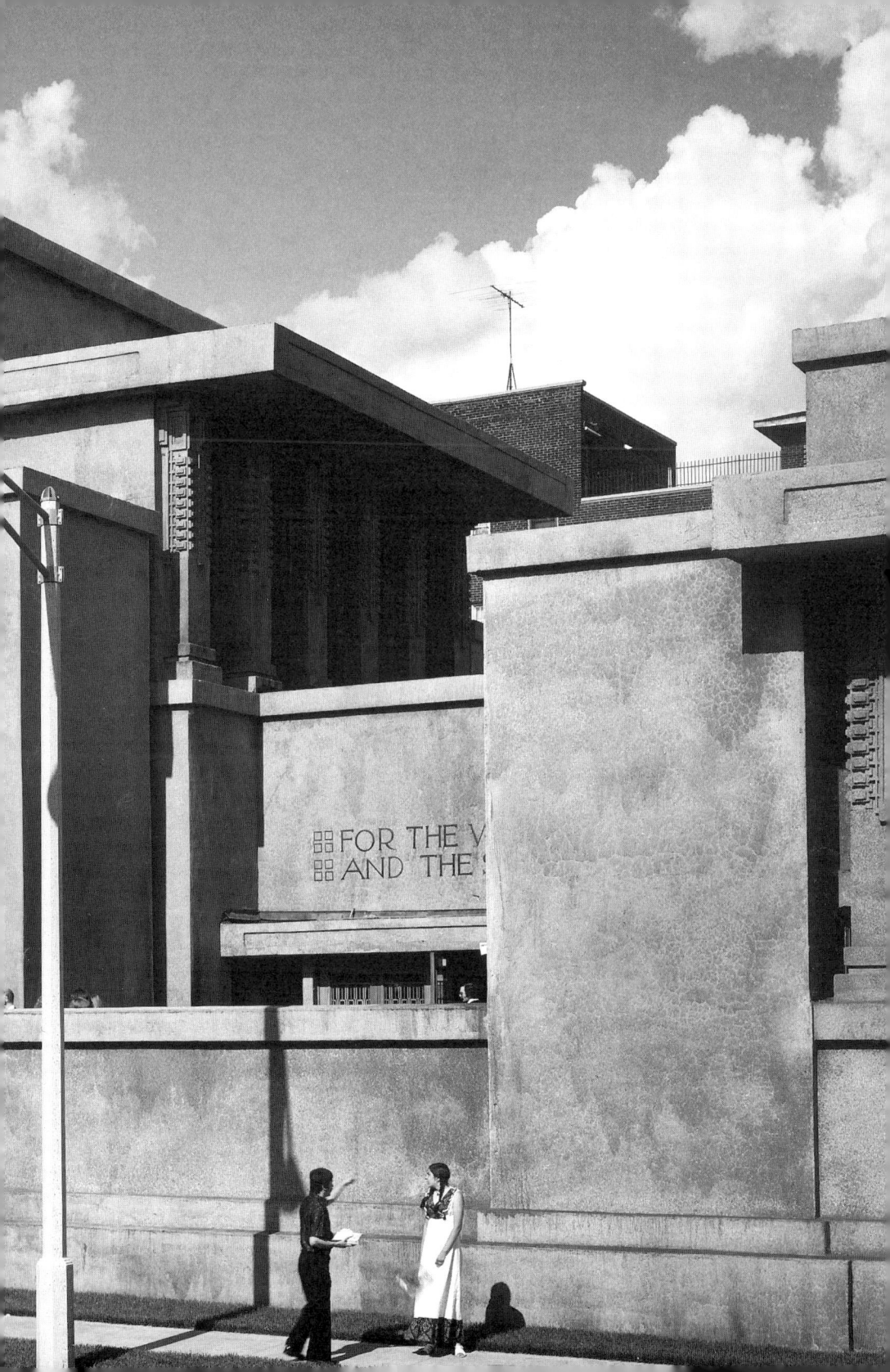

FOR THE W
AND THE S

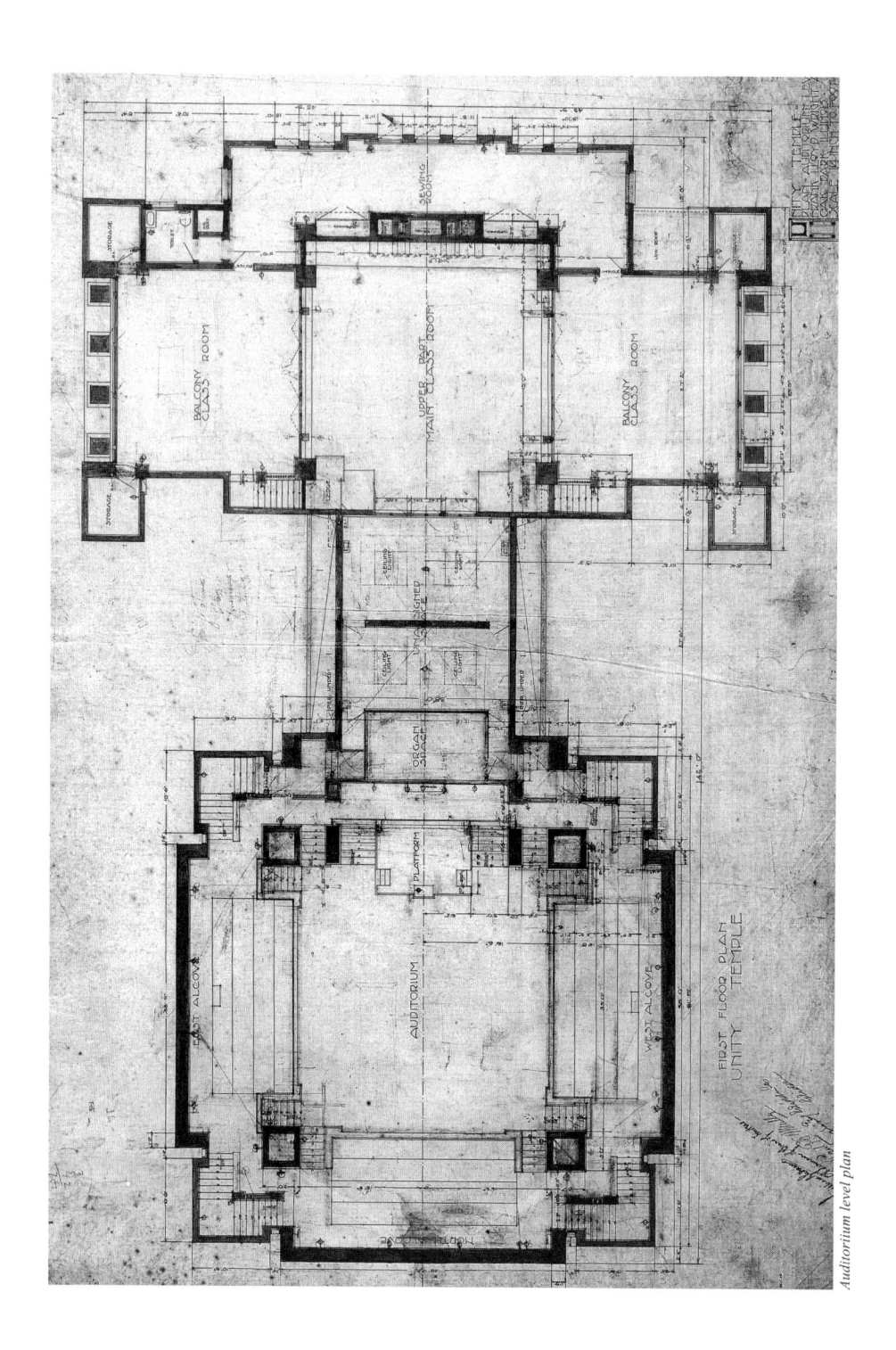

Auditorium level plan

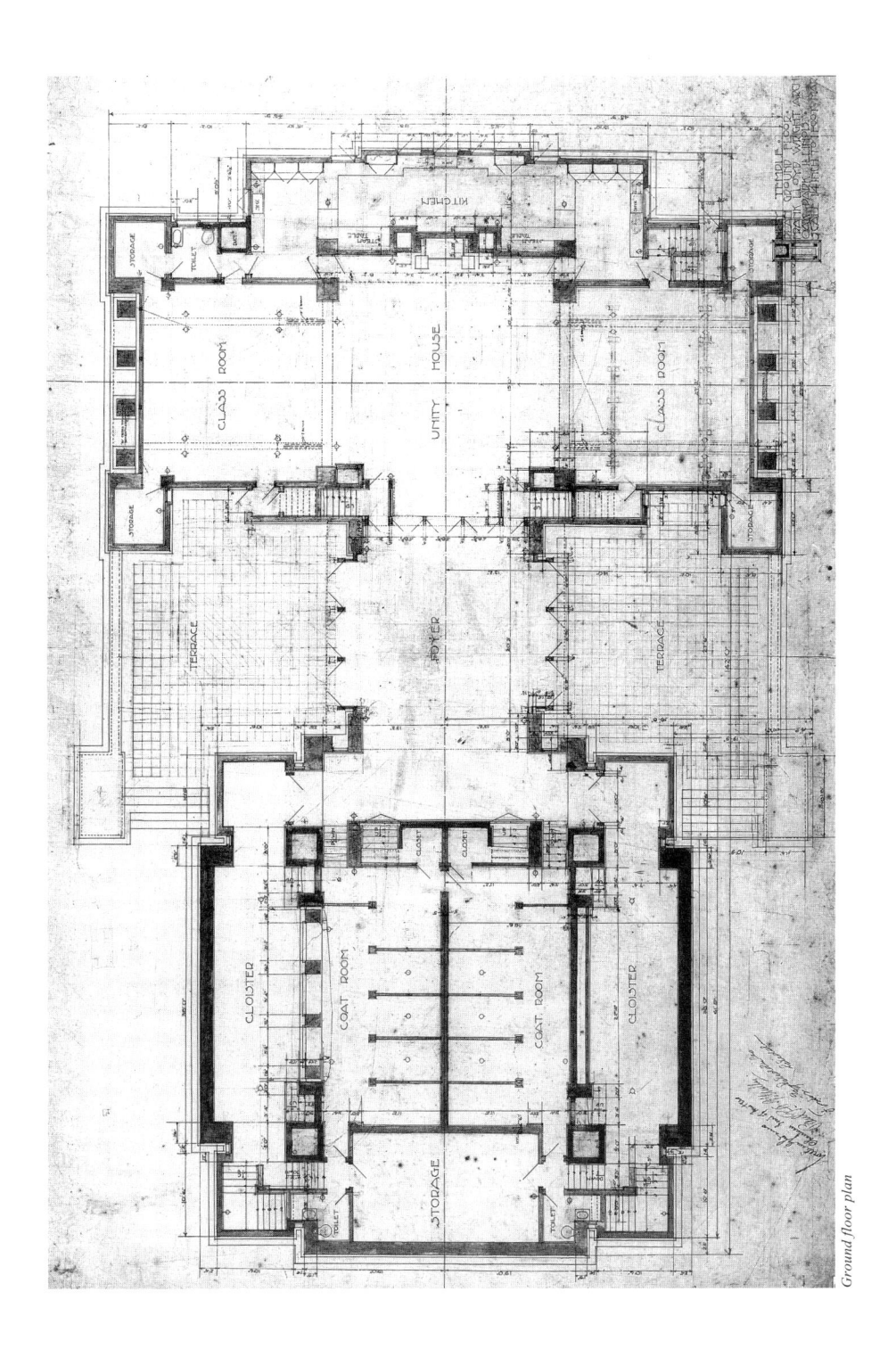

Ground floor plan

FOR THE Y
AND THE S

ORSHIP OF GOD
ERVICE OF MAN

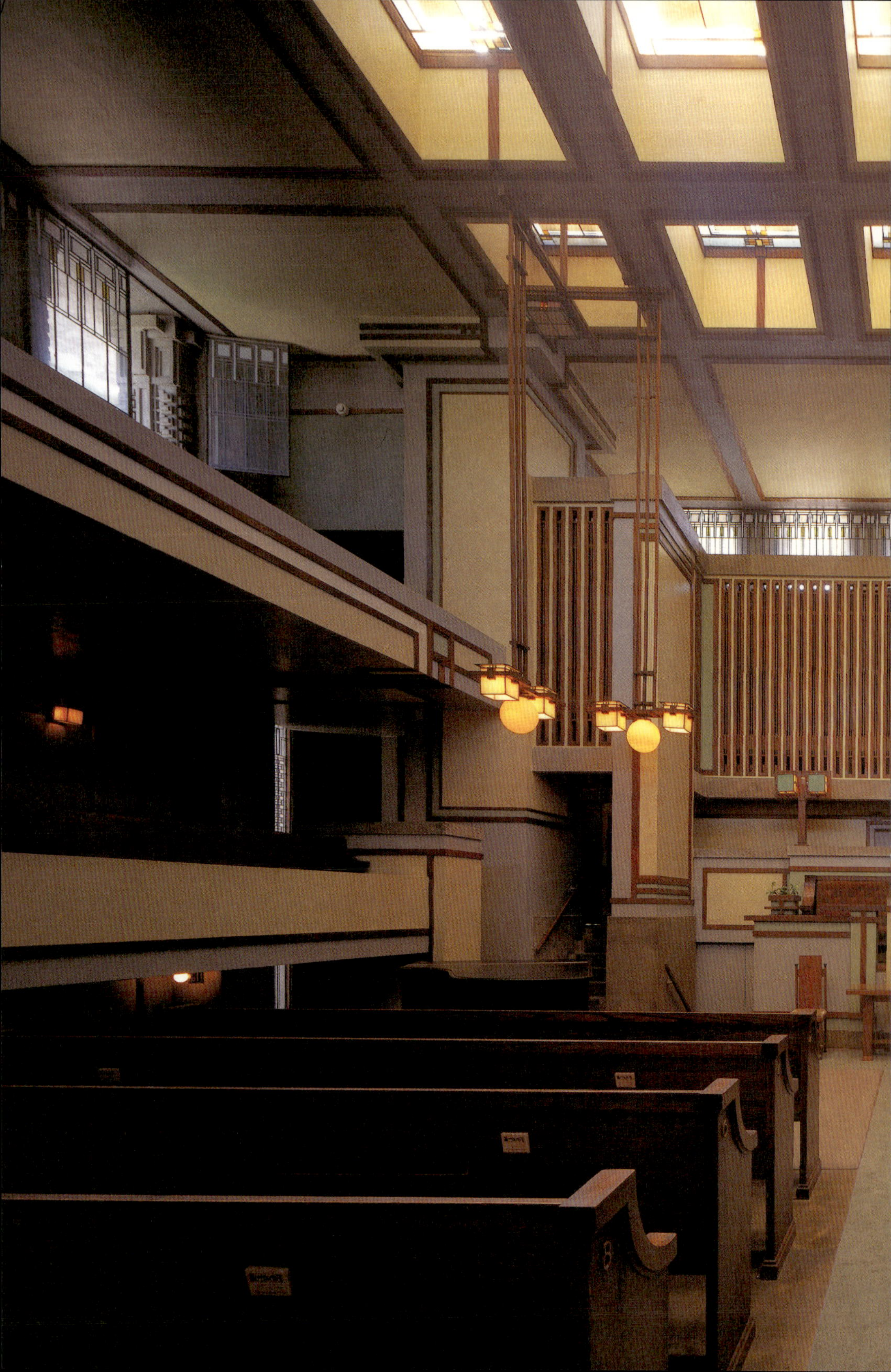

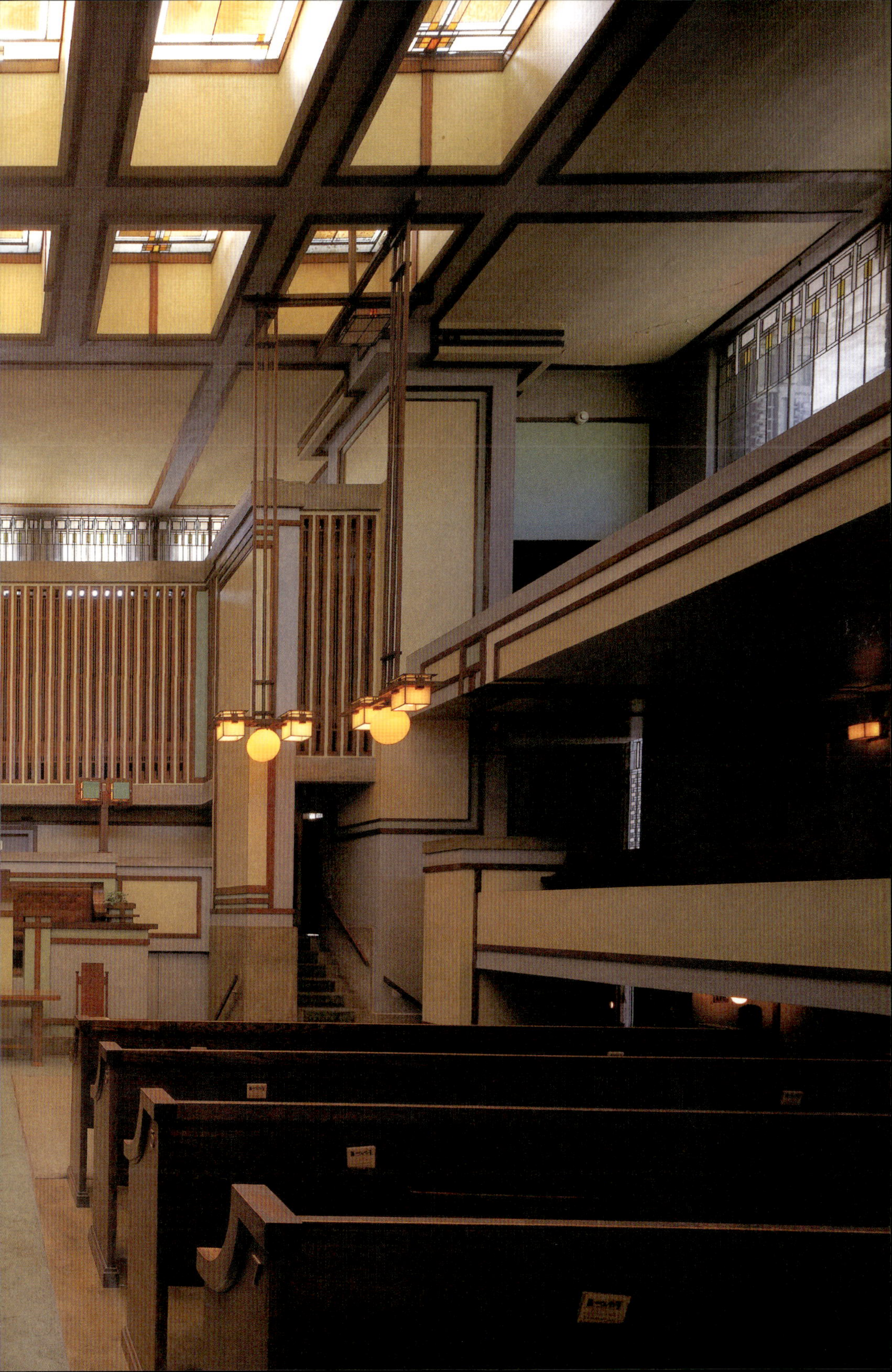

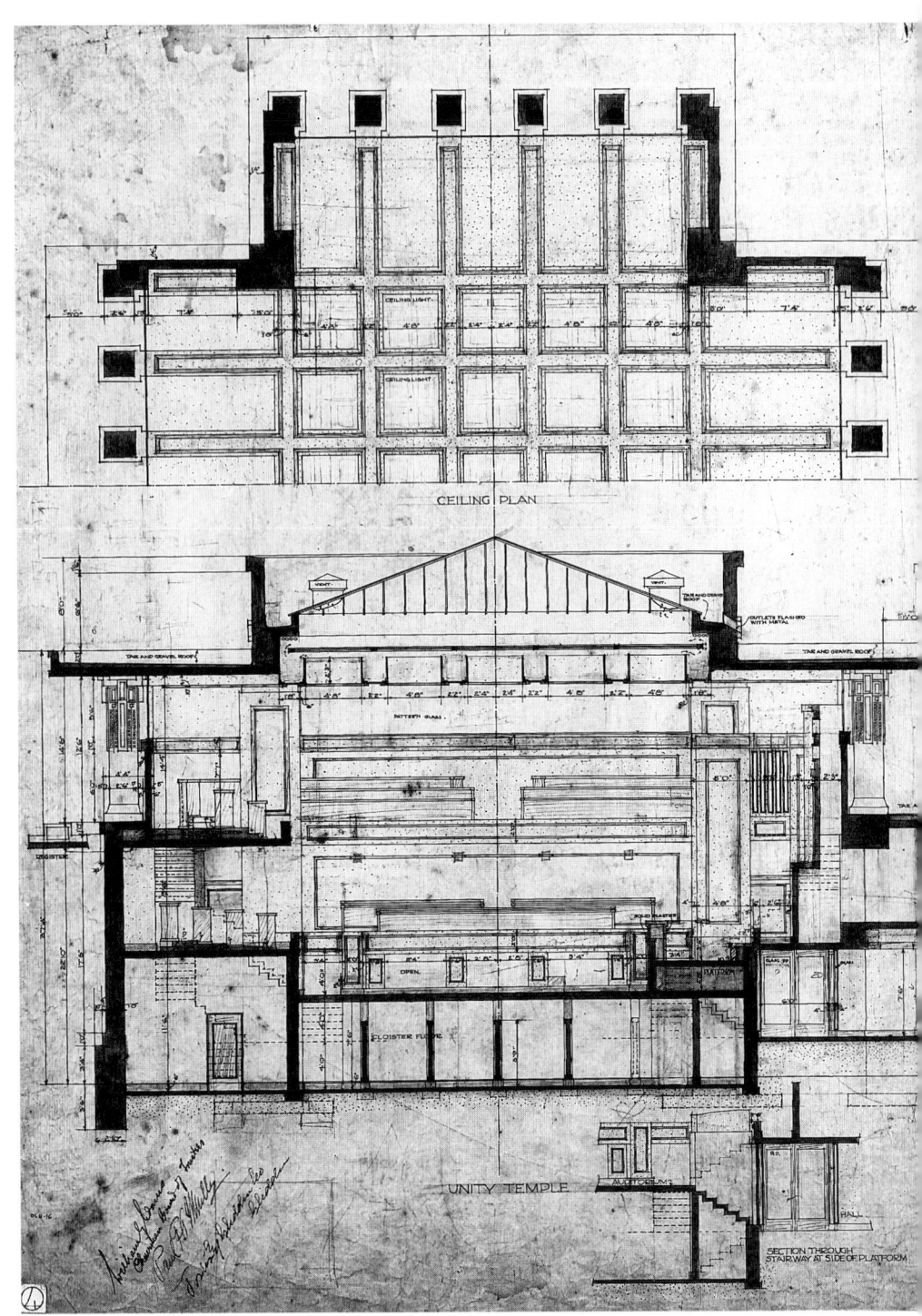

Ceiling plans and longitudinal section

CEILING PLAN

HALL   UNITY HOUSE

UNITY TEMPLE
LONGITUDINAL SECTION
FRANK LLOYD WRIGHT ARCHITECT
OAK PARK ILLINOIS
SCALE 1/4 INCH TO 1 FOOT MAR 1908

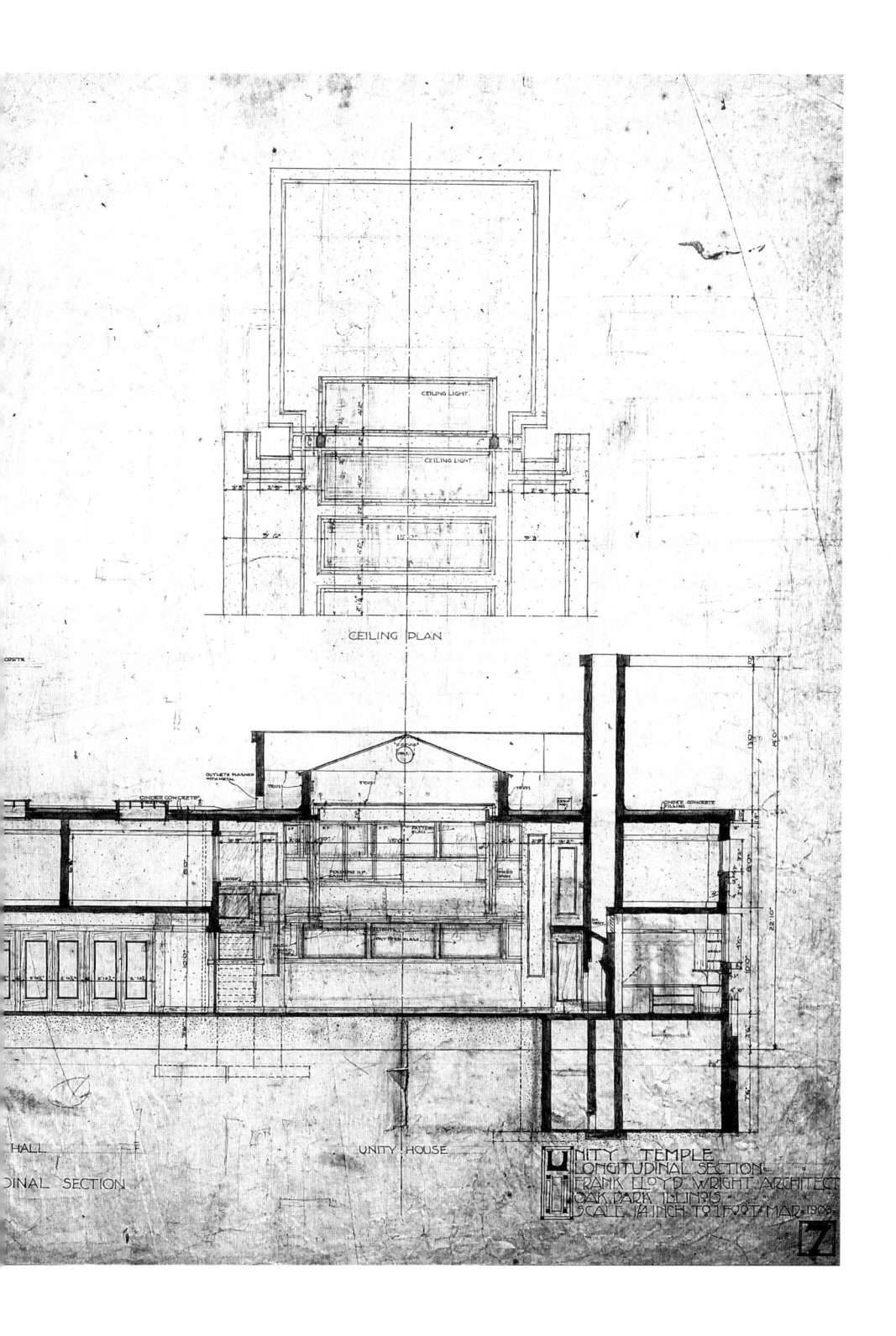

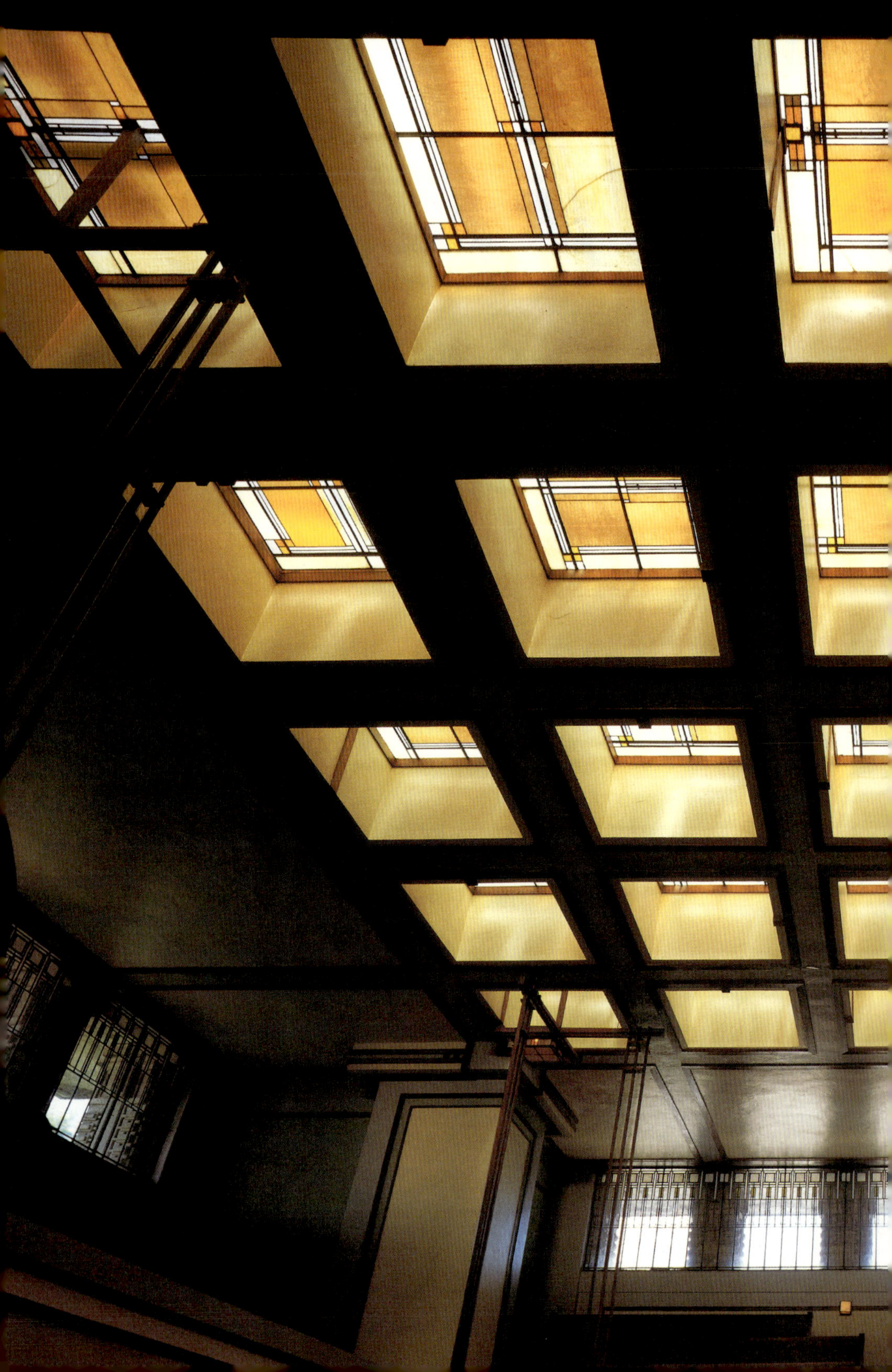

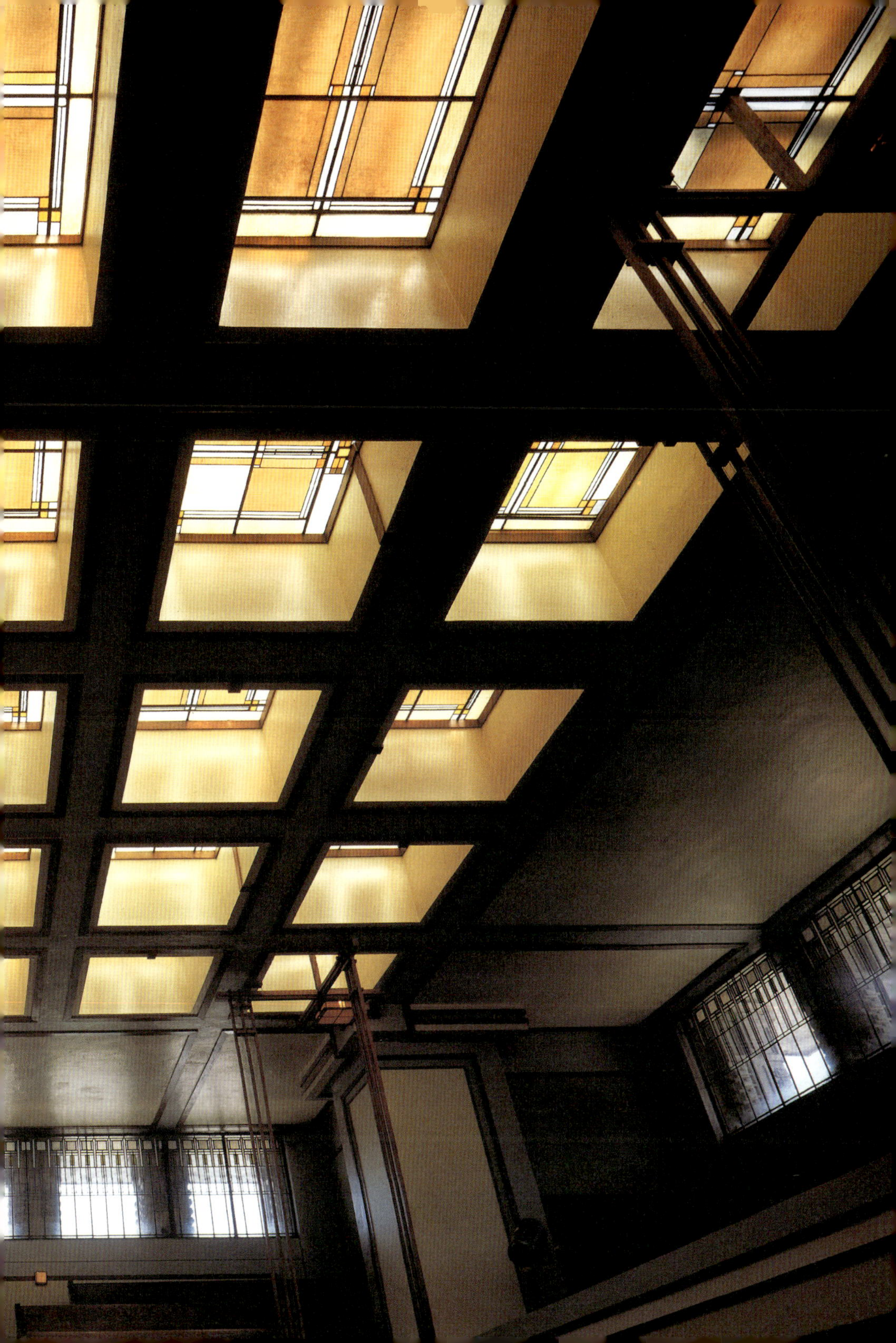

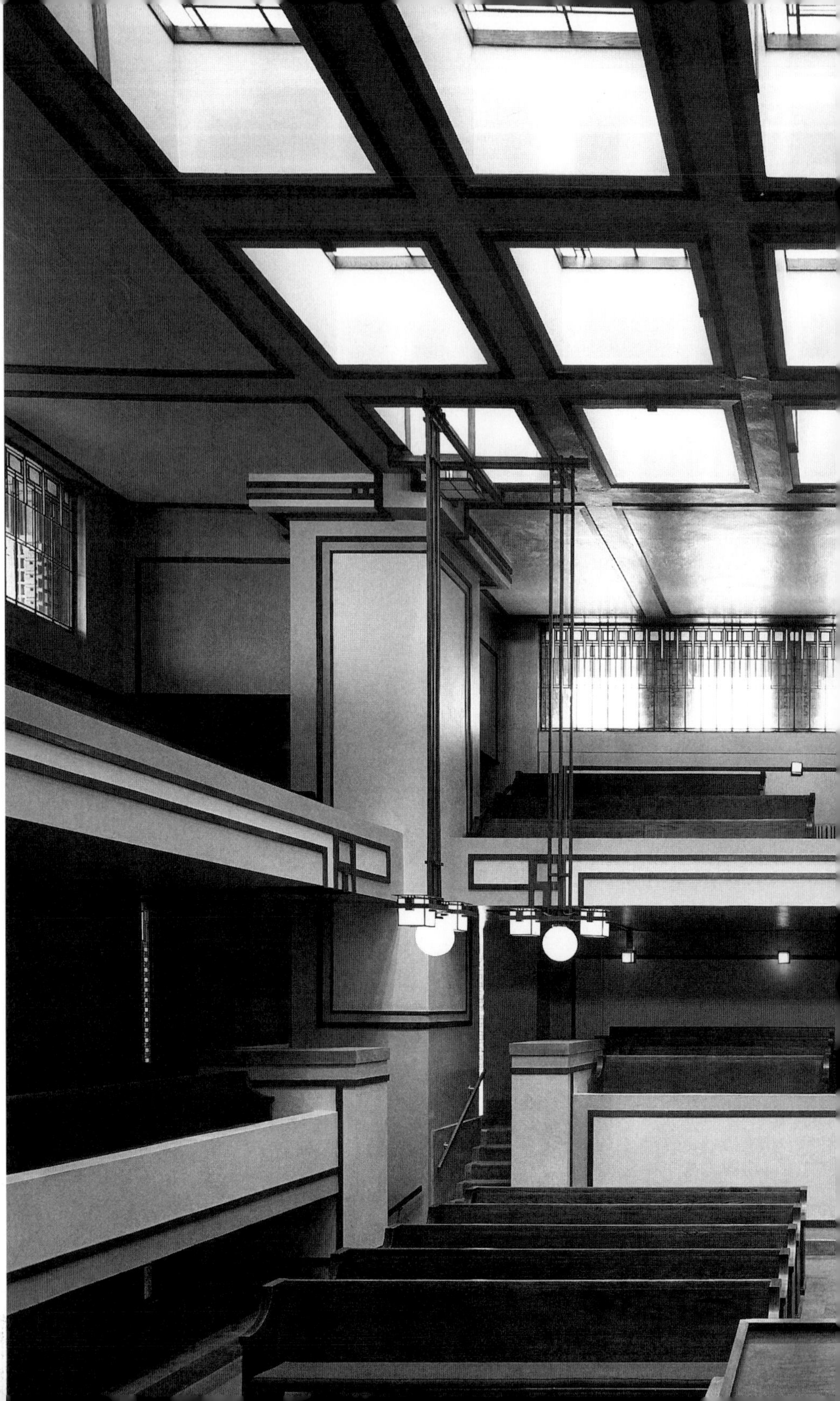

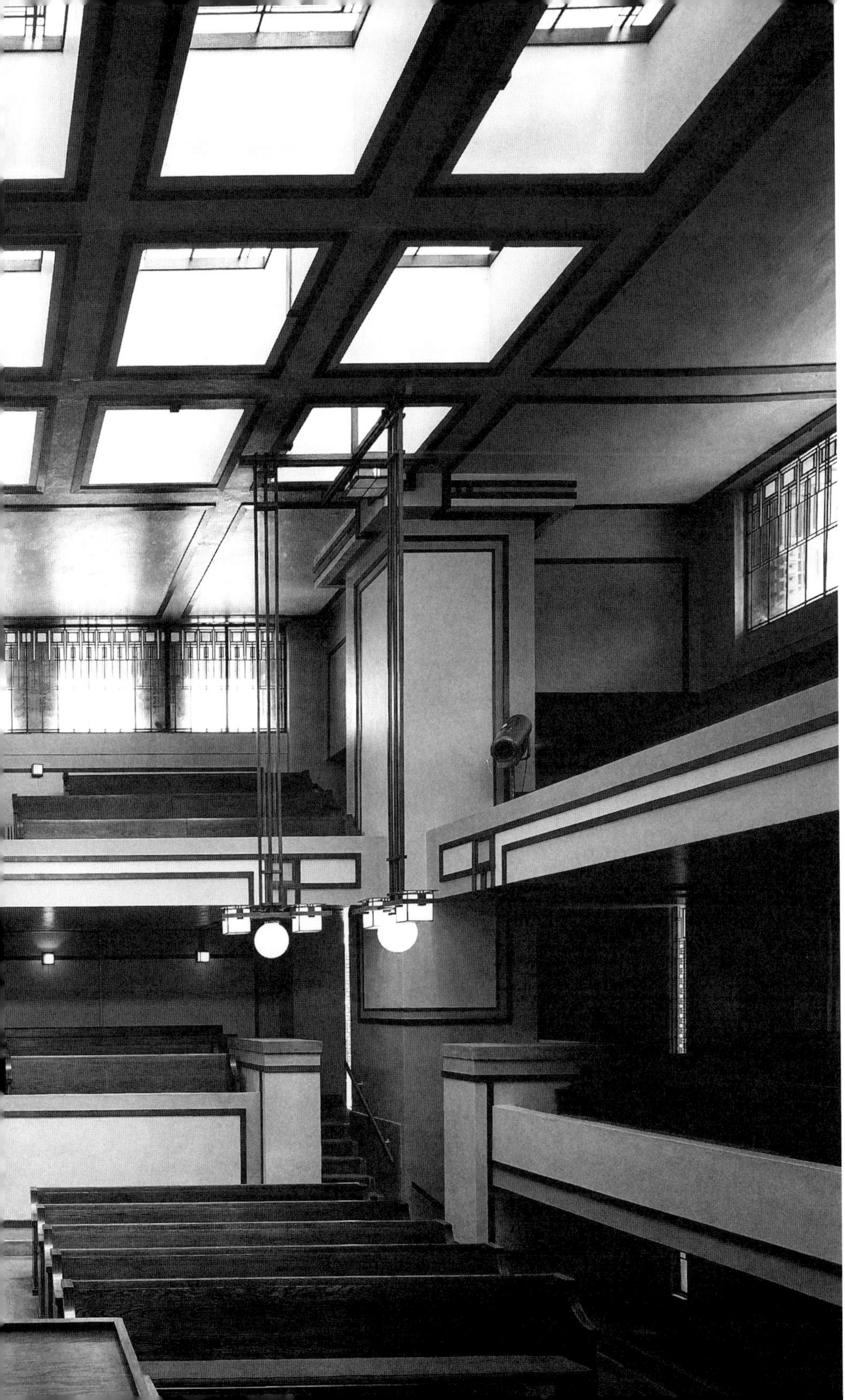

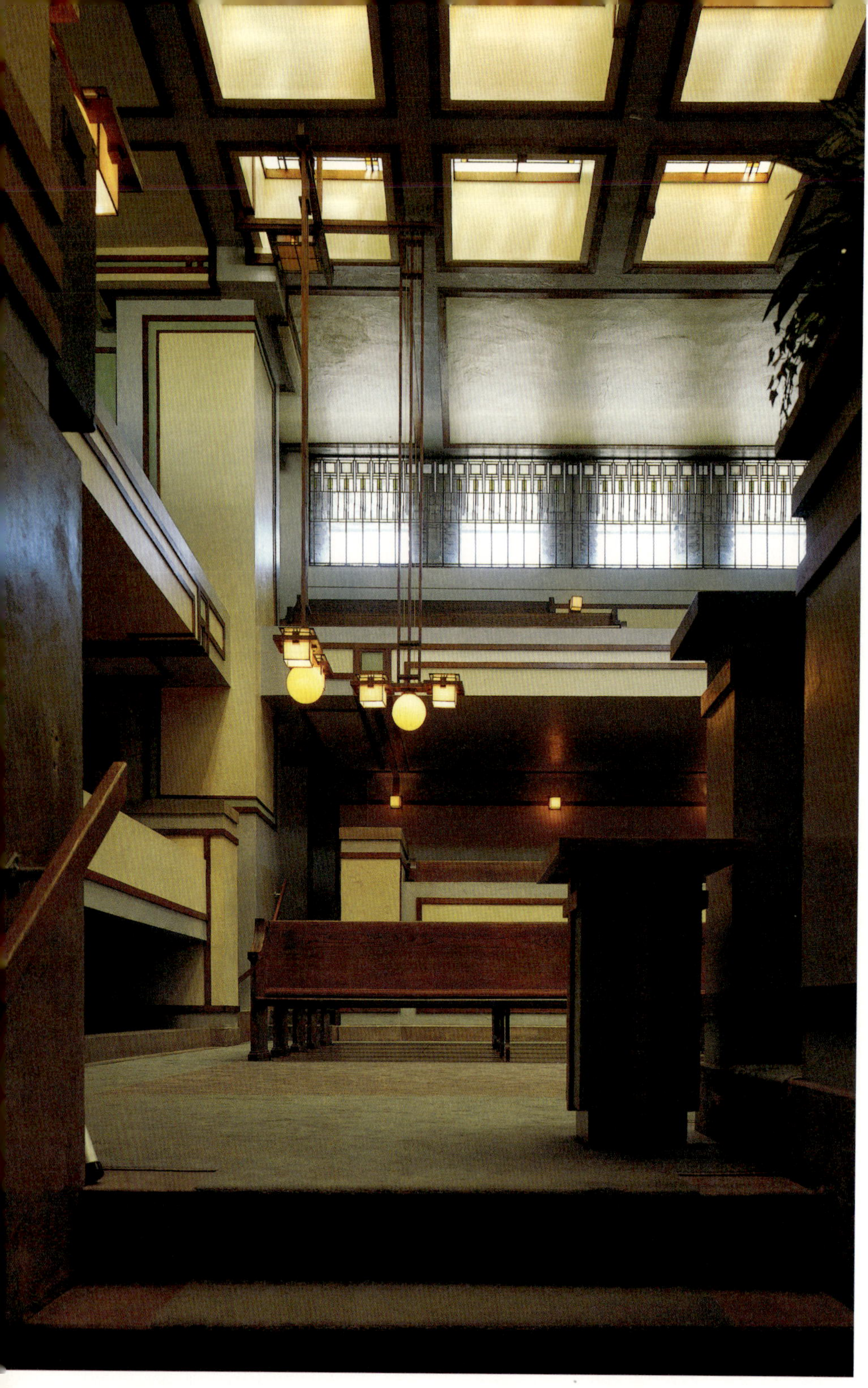

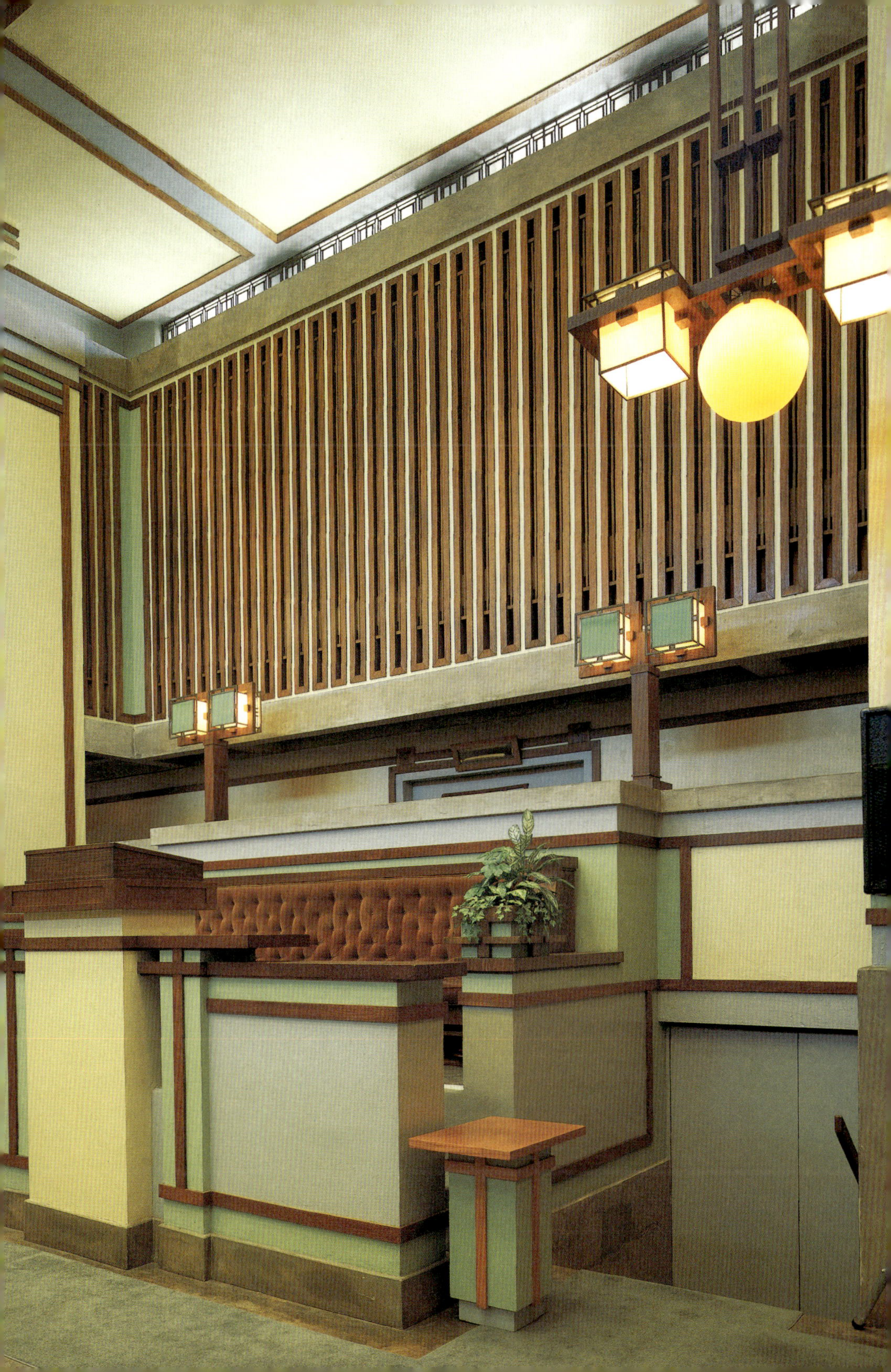

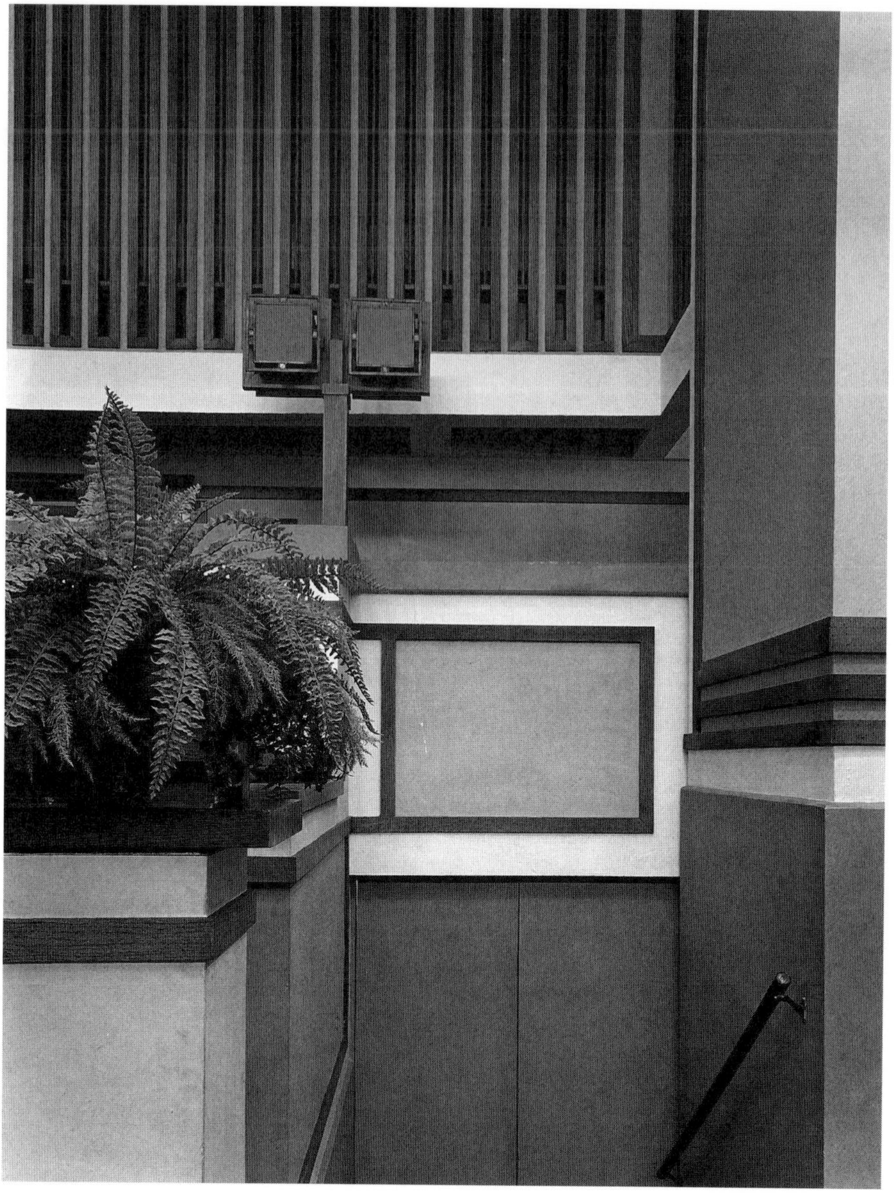

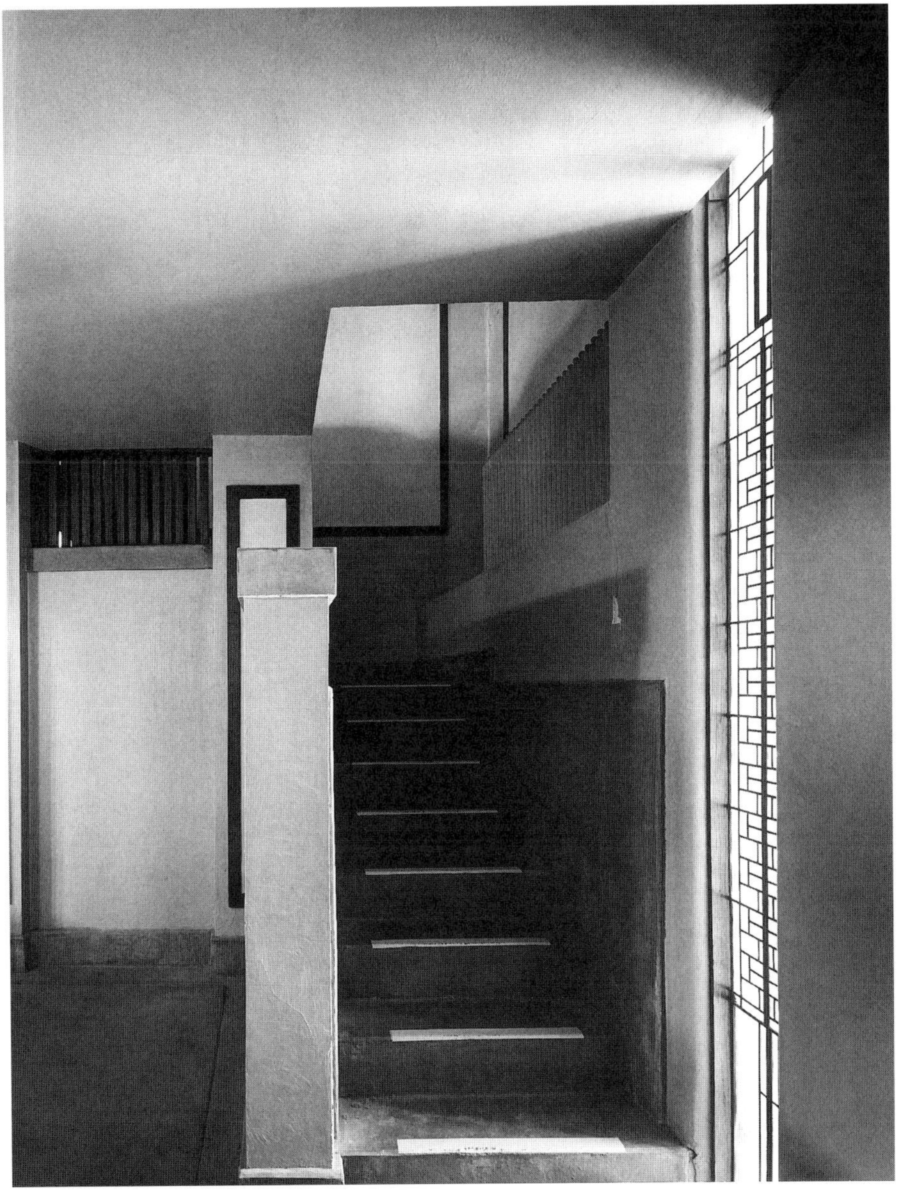

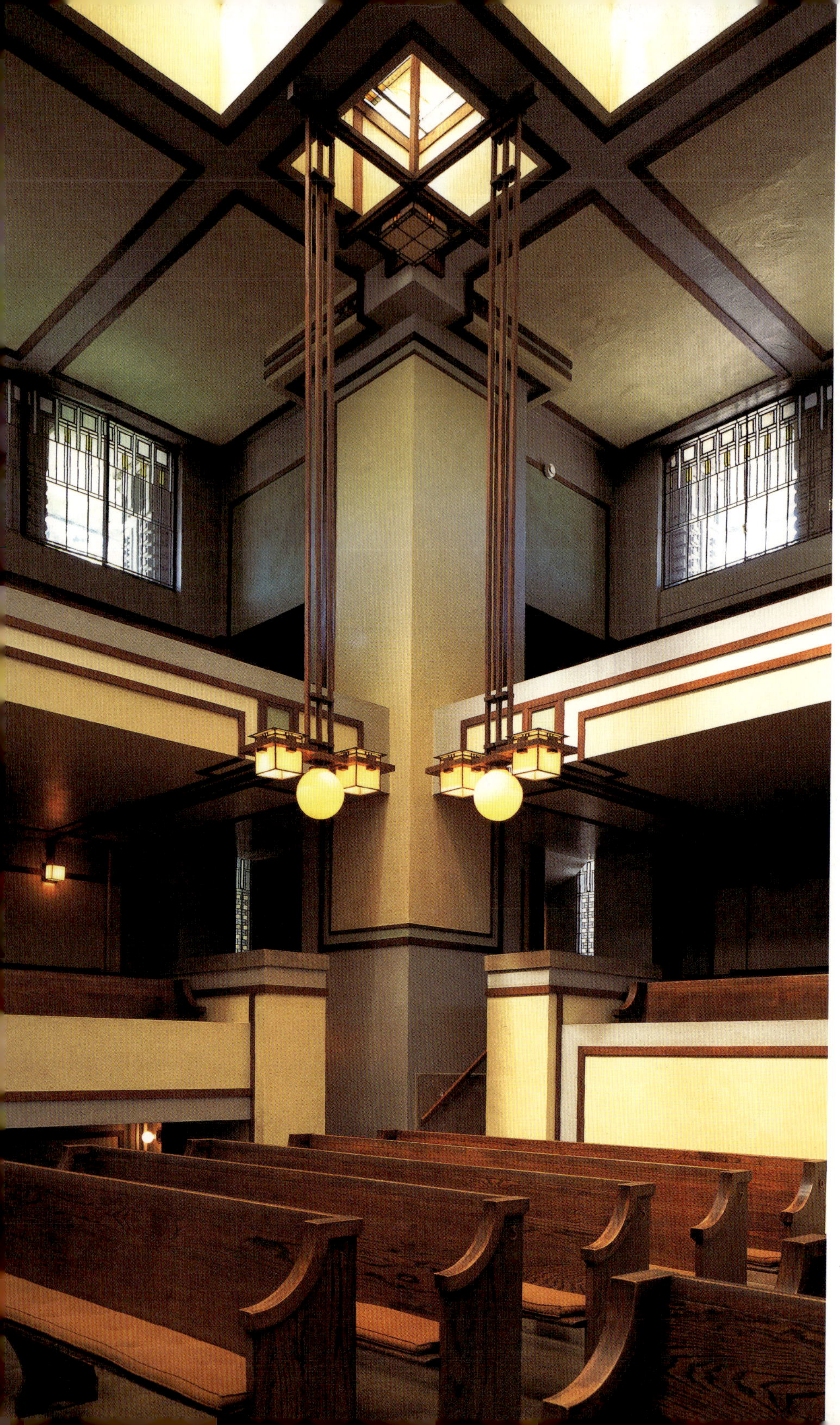

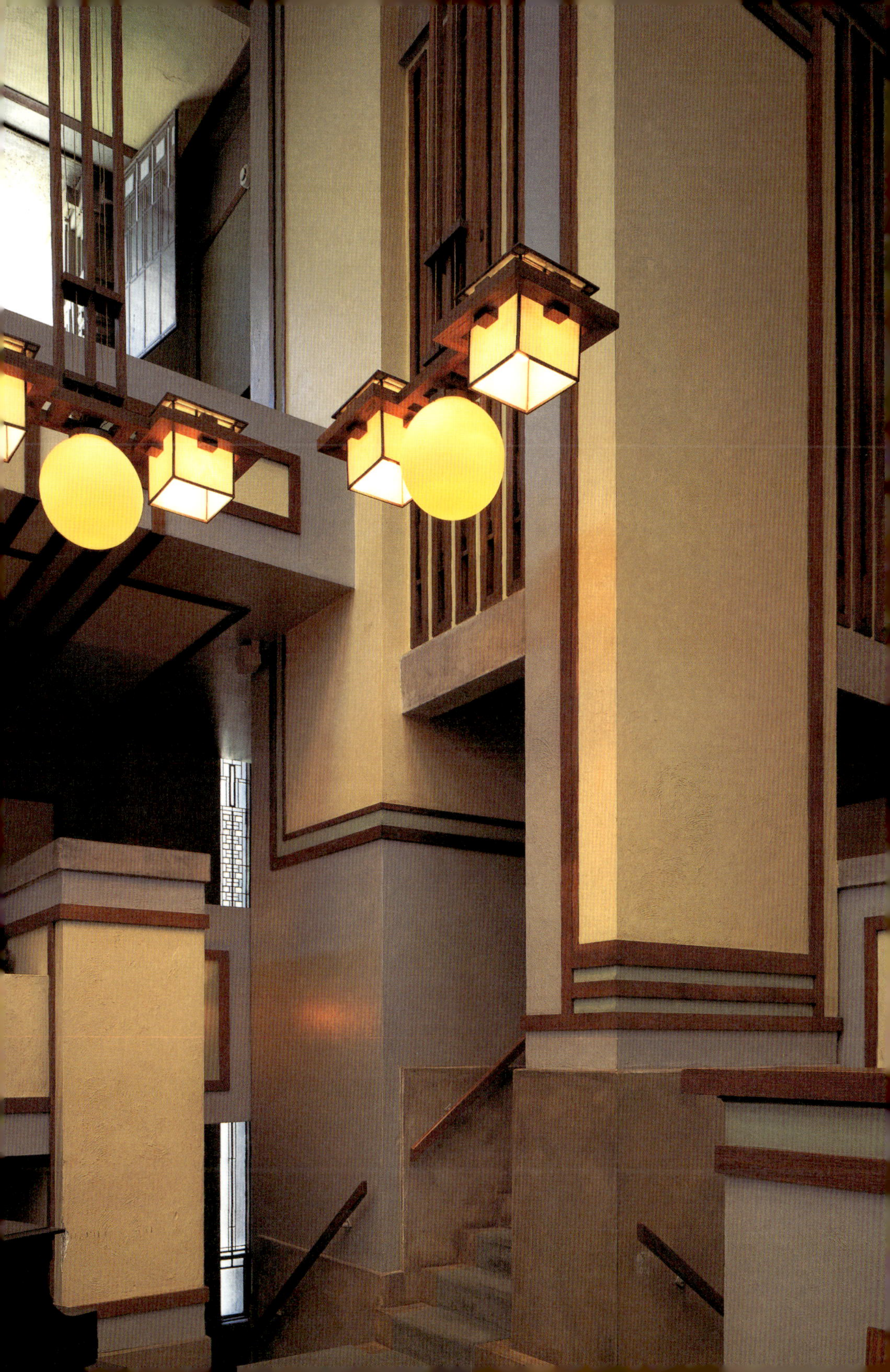

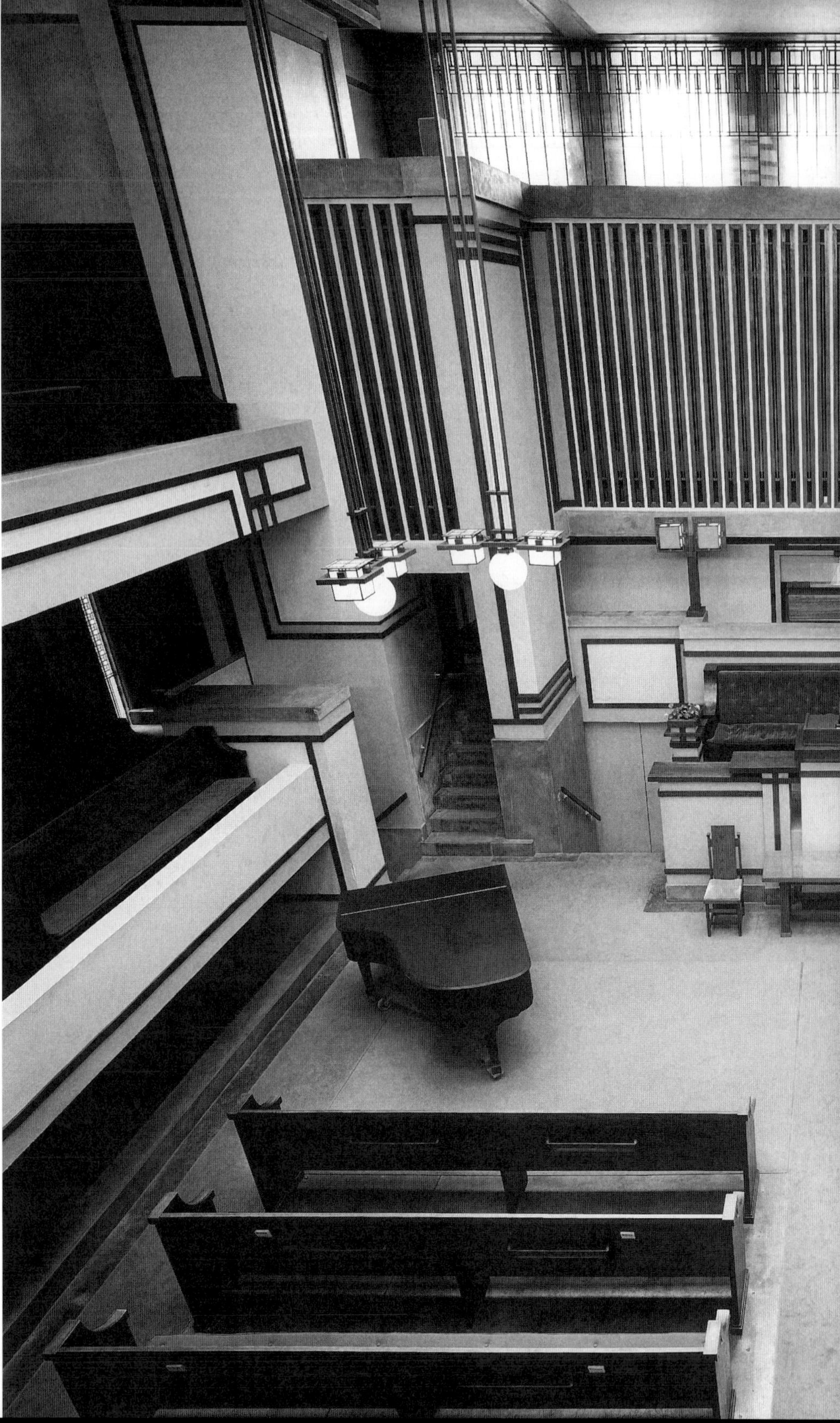

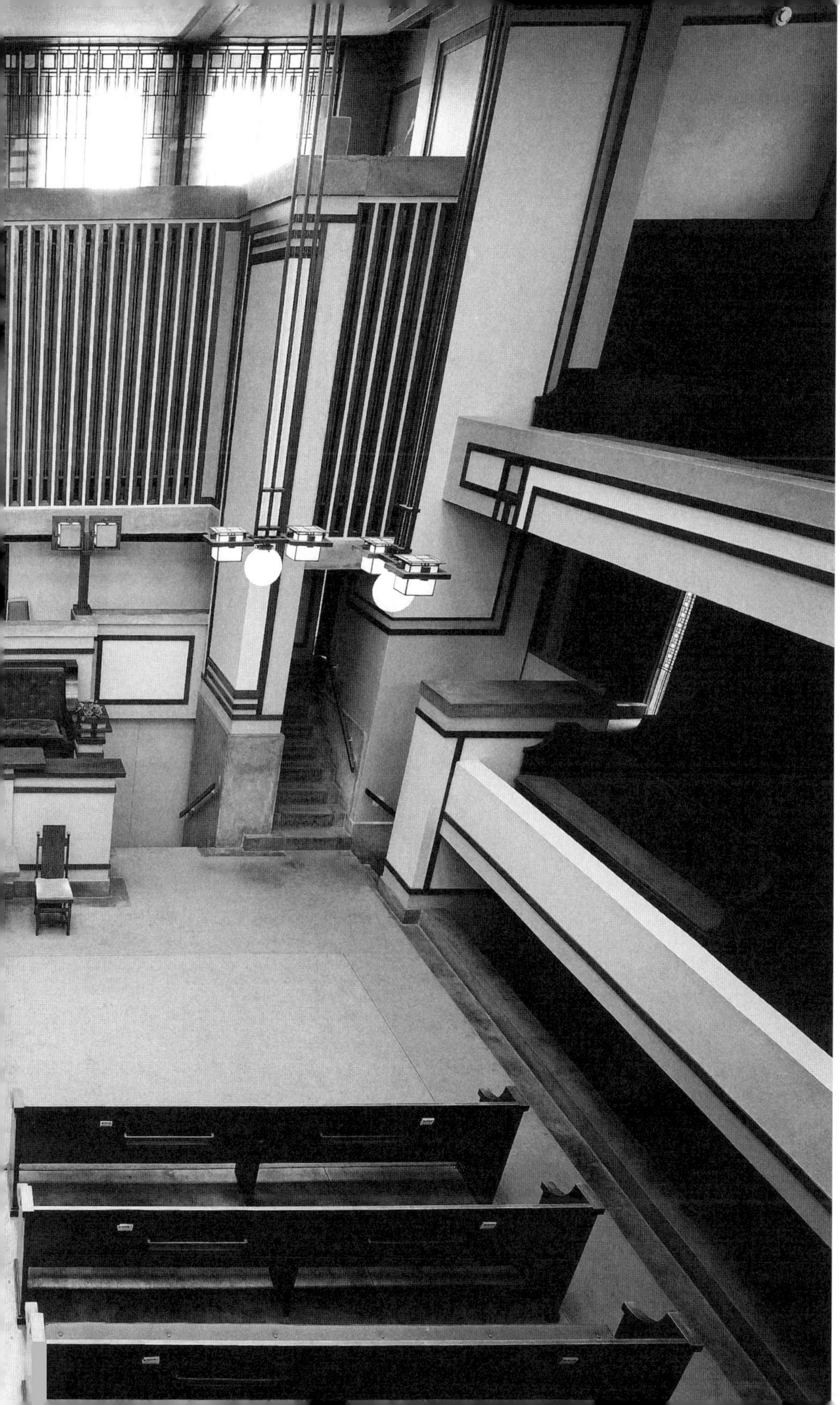

Anne Merner Pfeiffer Chapel
Florida Southern College, Lakeland, Florida, 1938

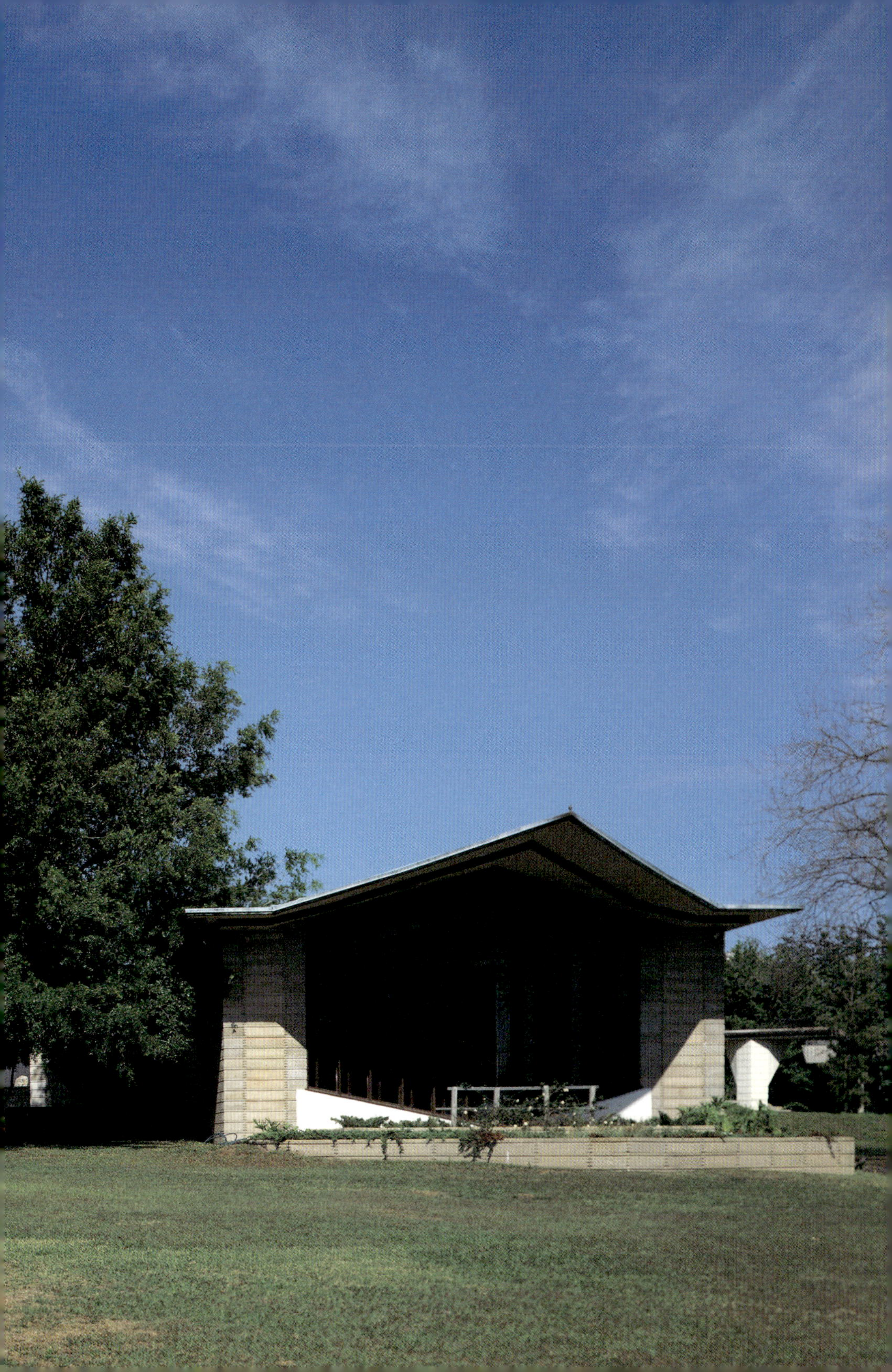

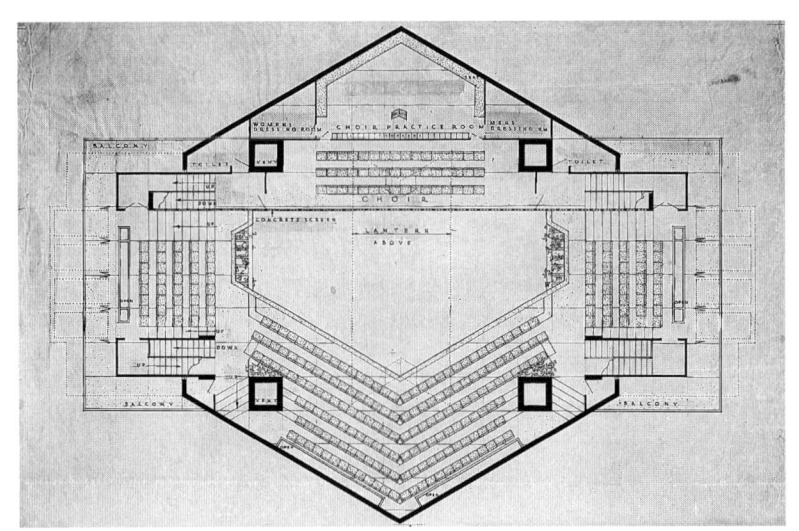

Balcony level plan

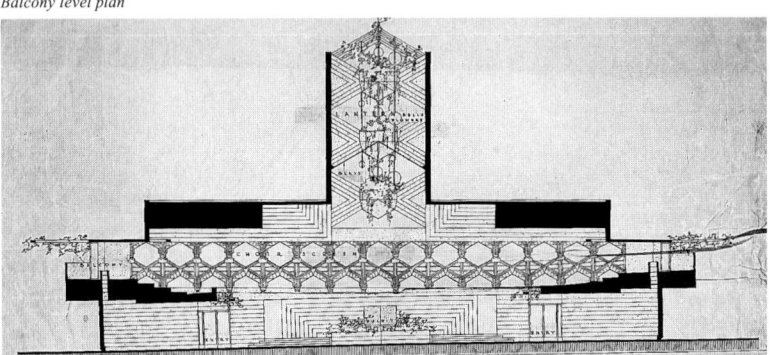

Section

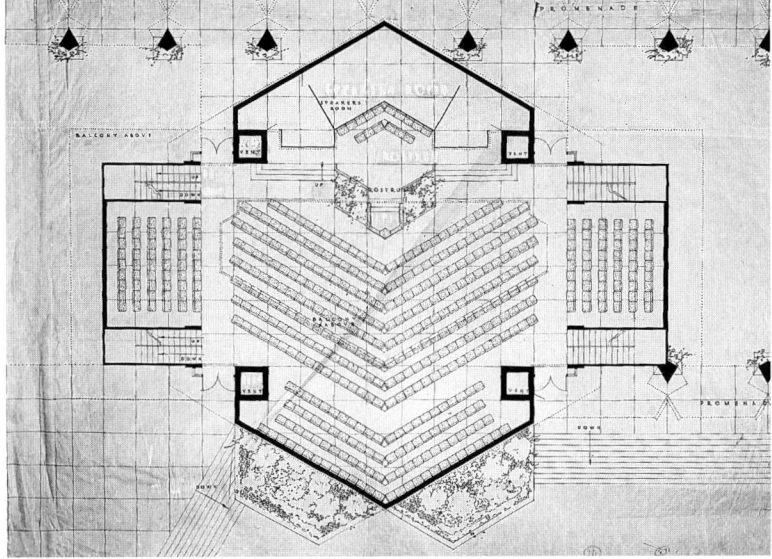

Ground level plan

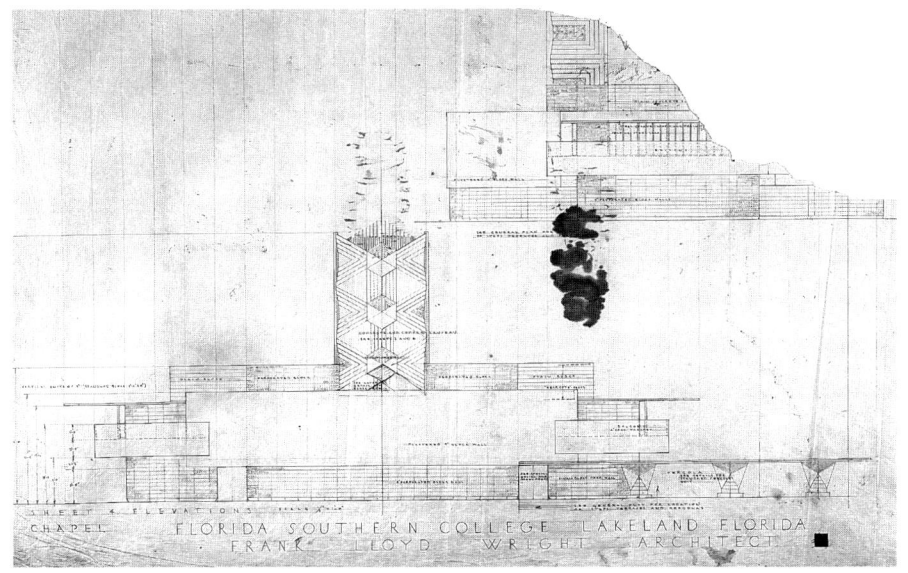

Elevations

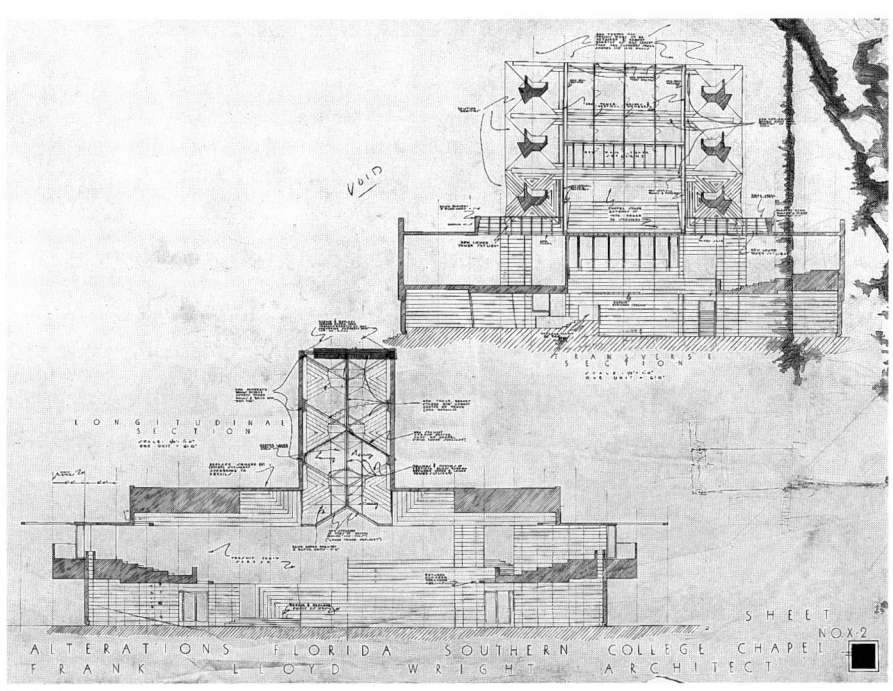

Sections

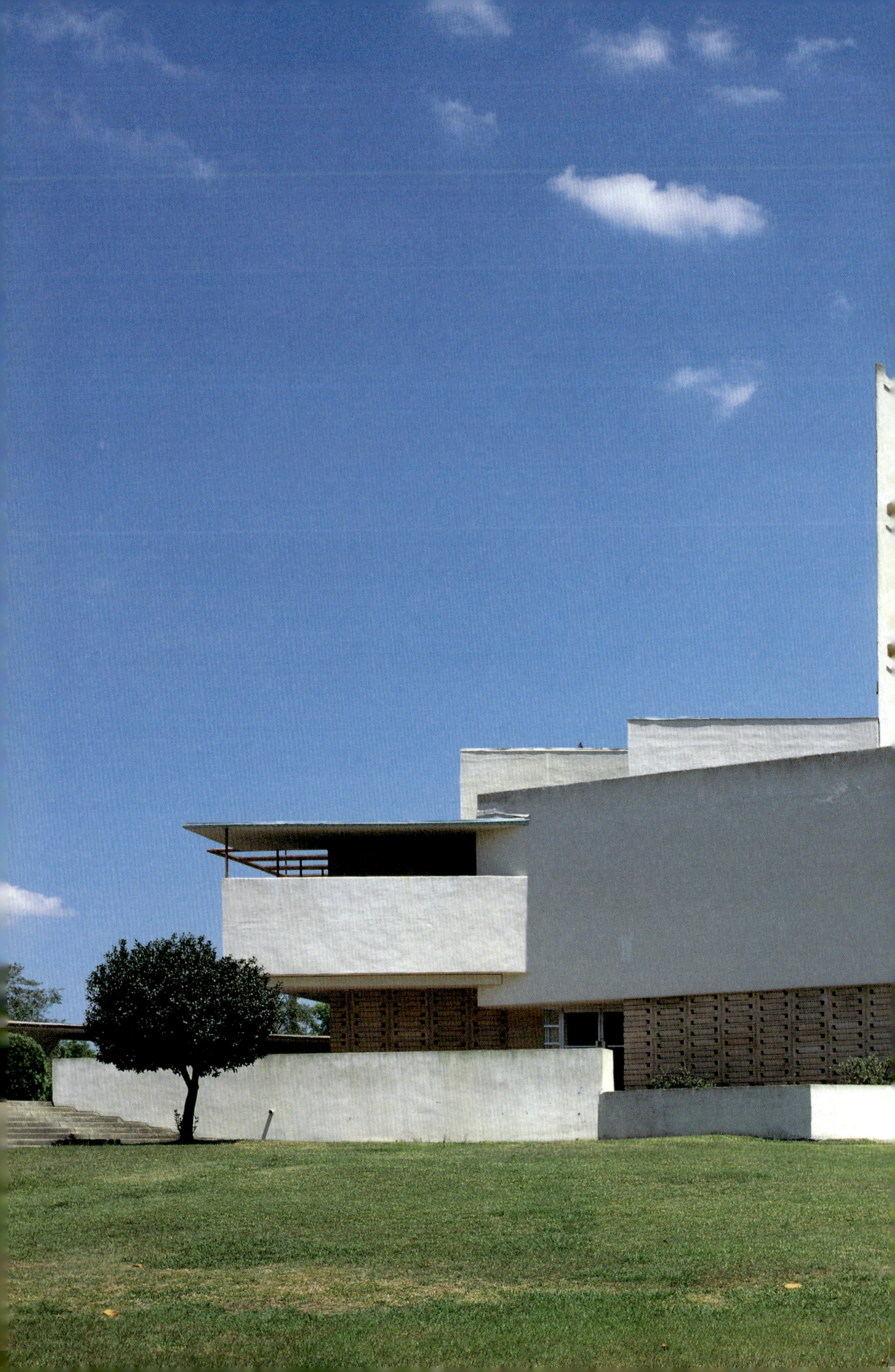

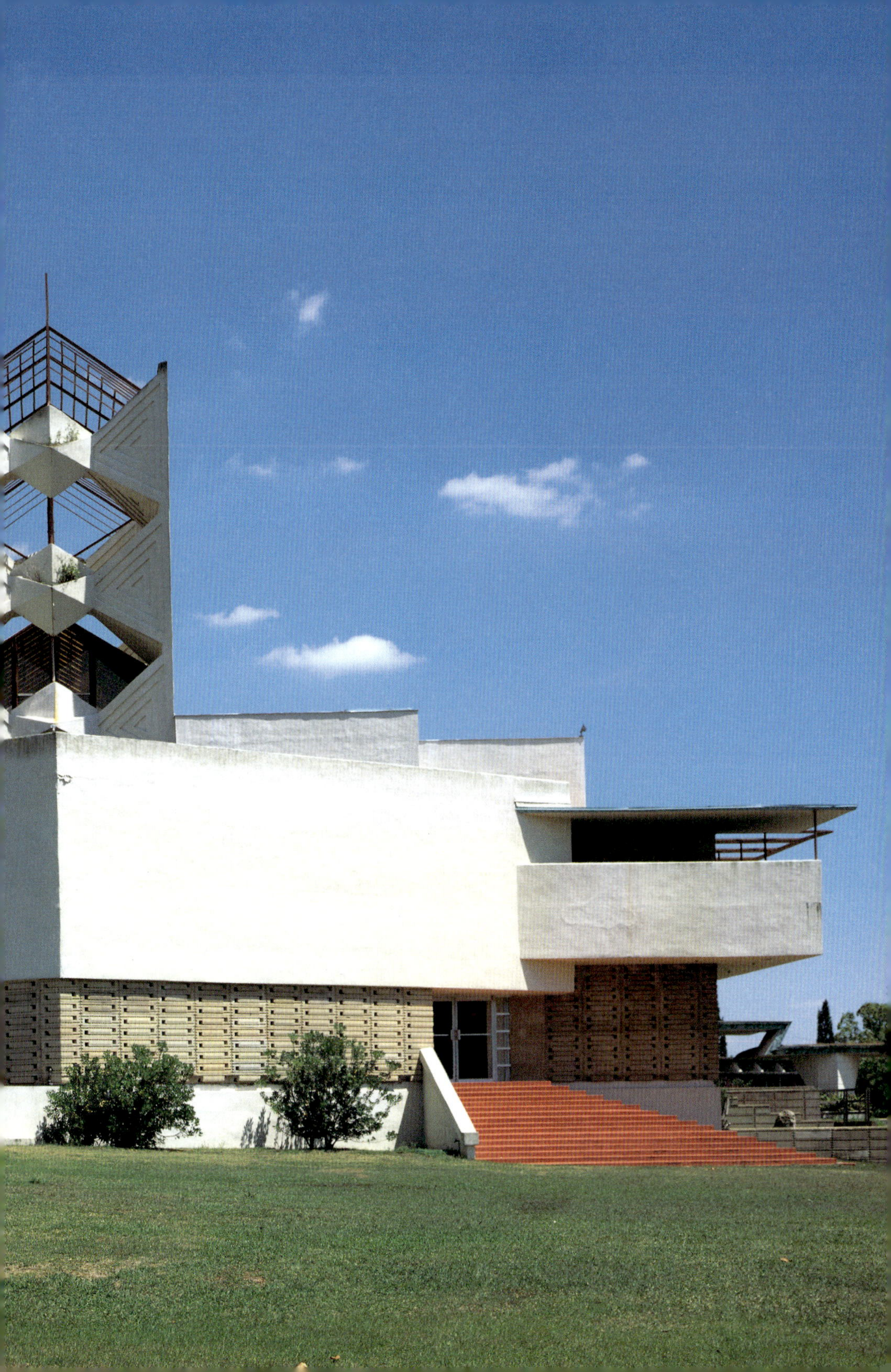

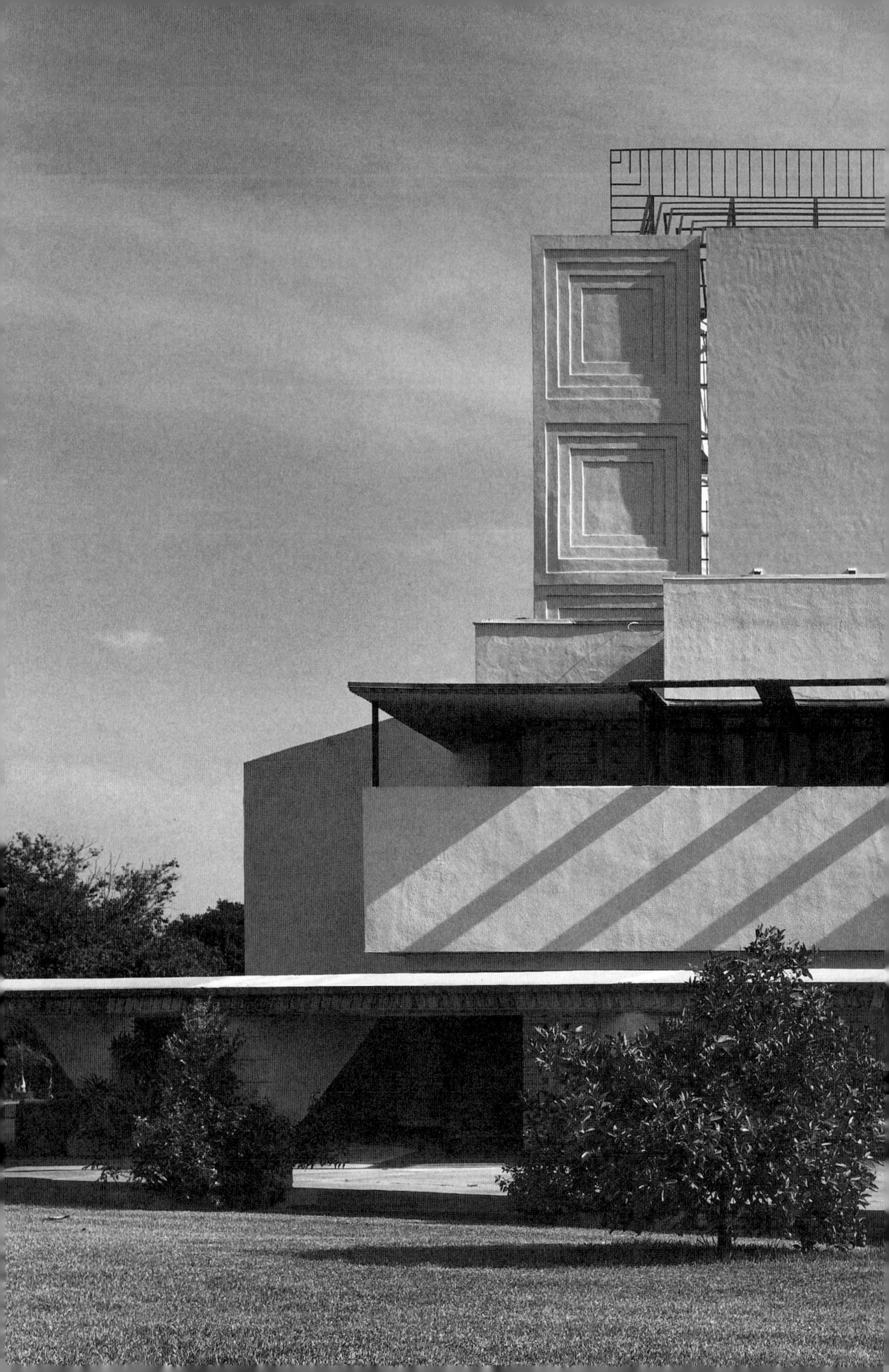

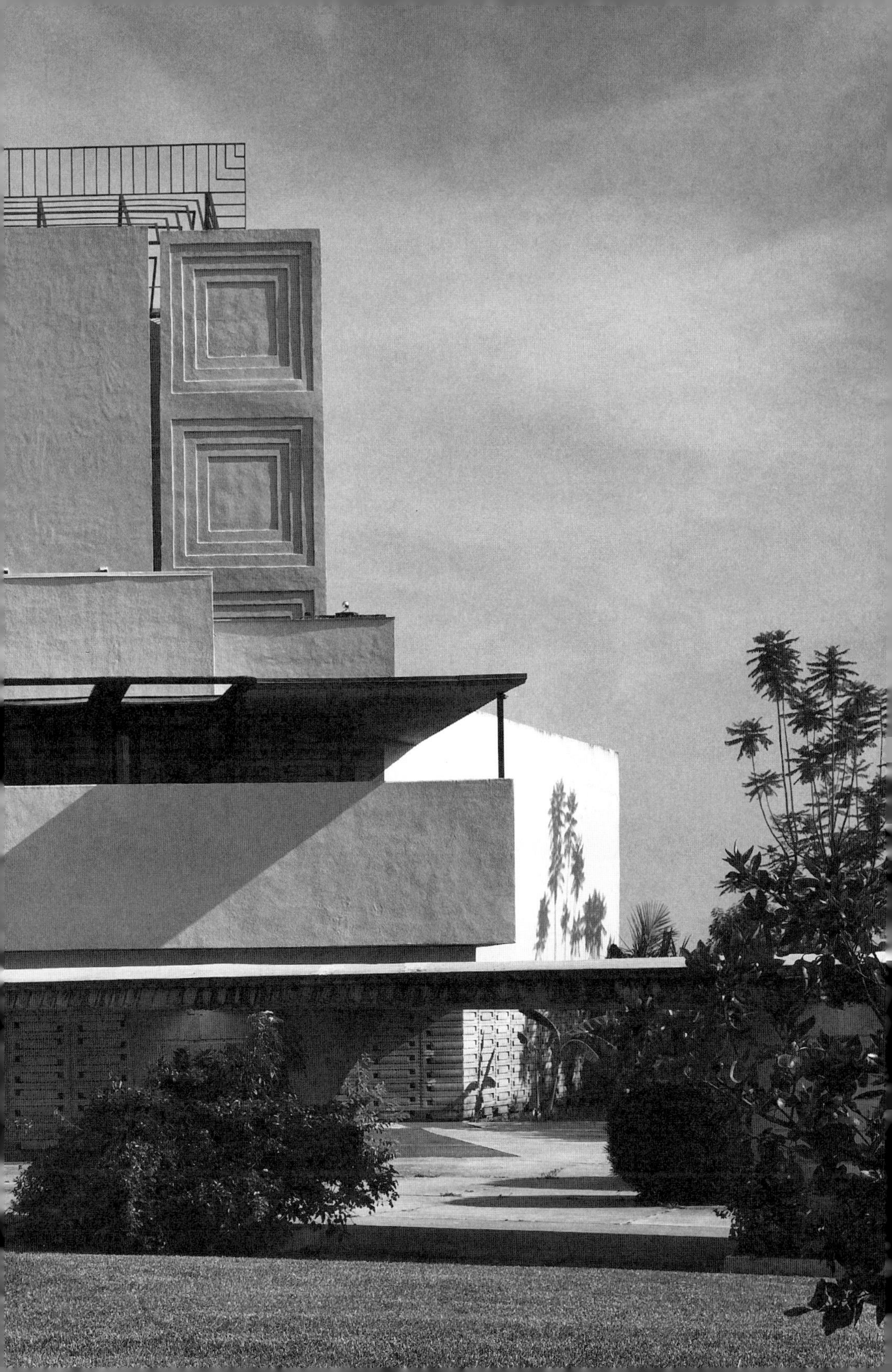

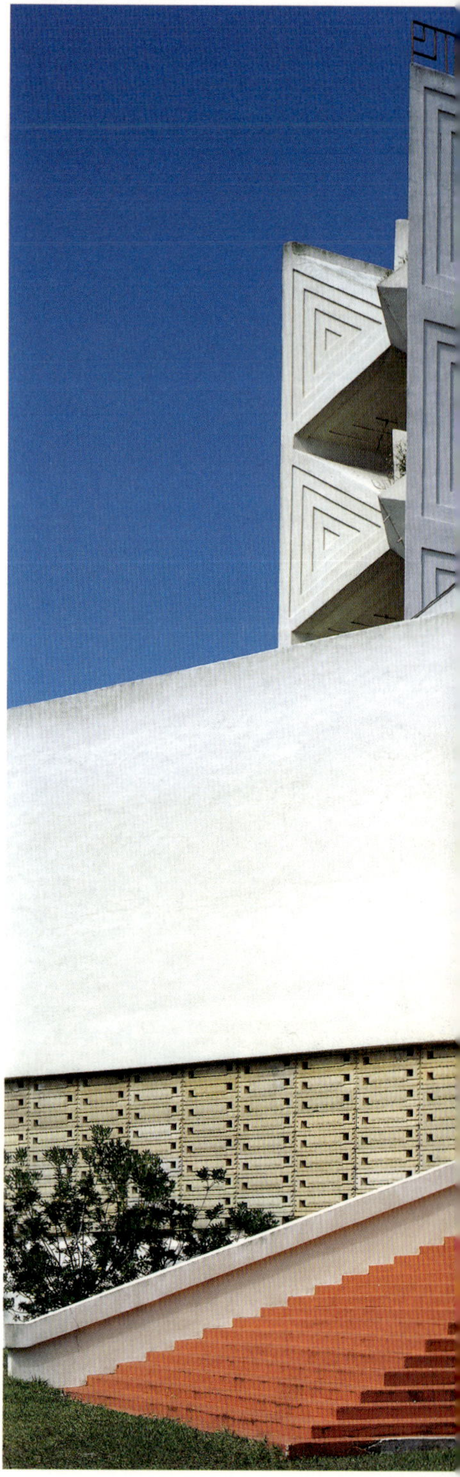

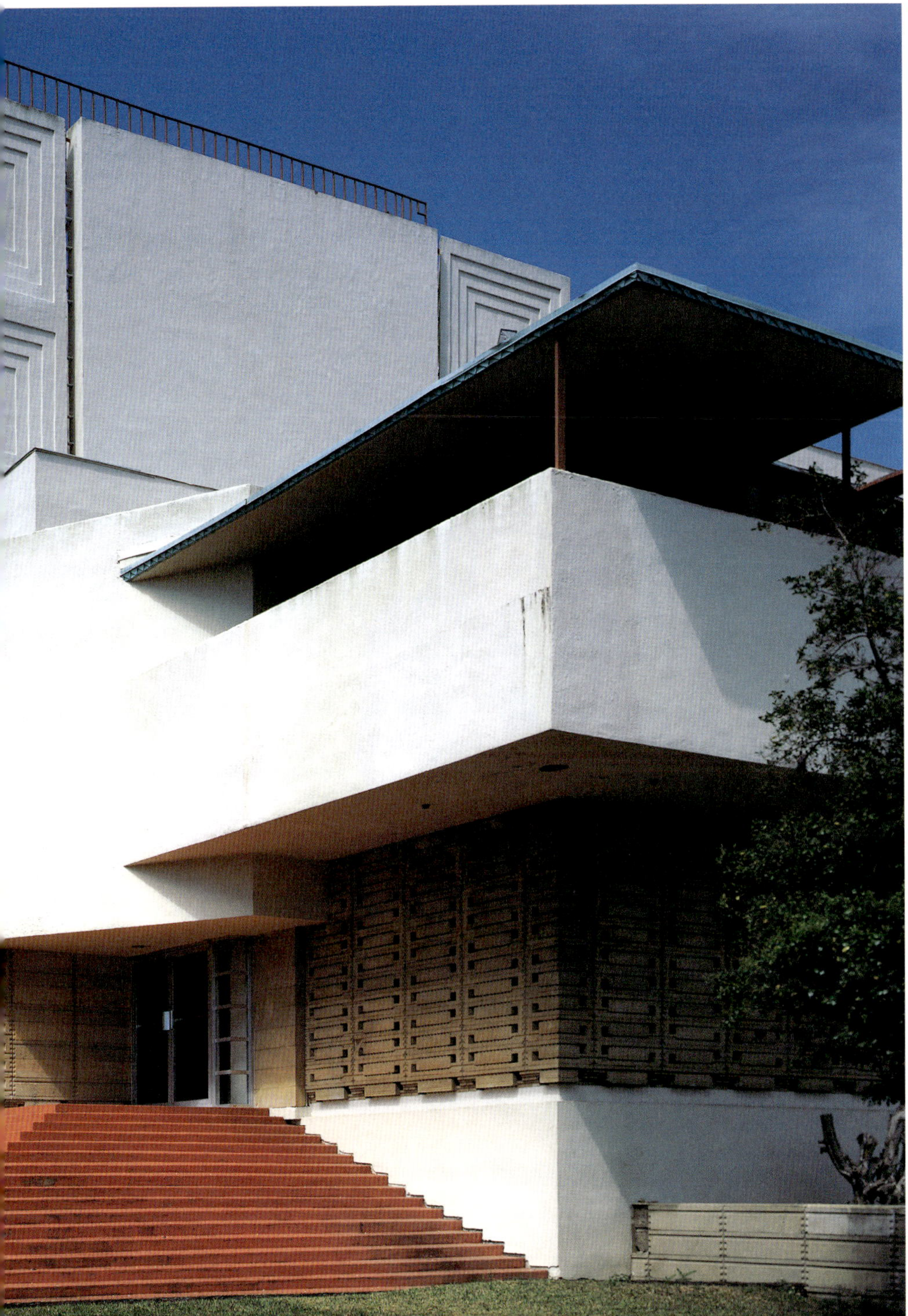

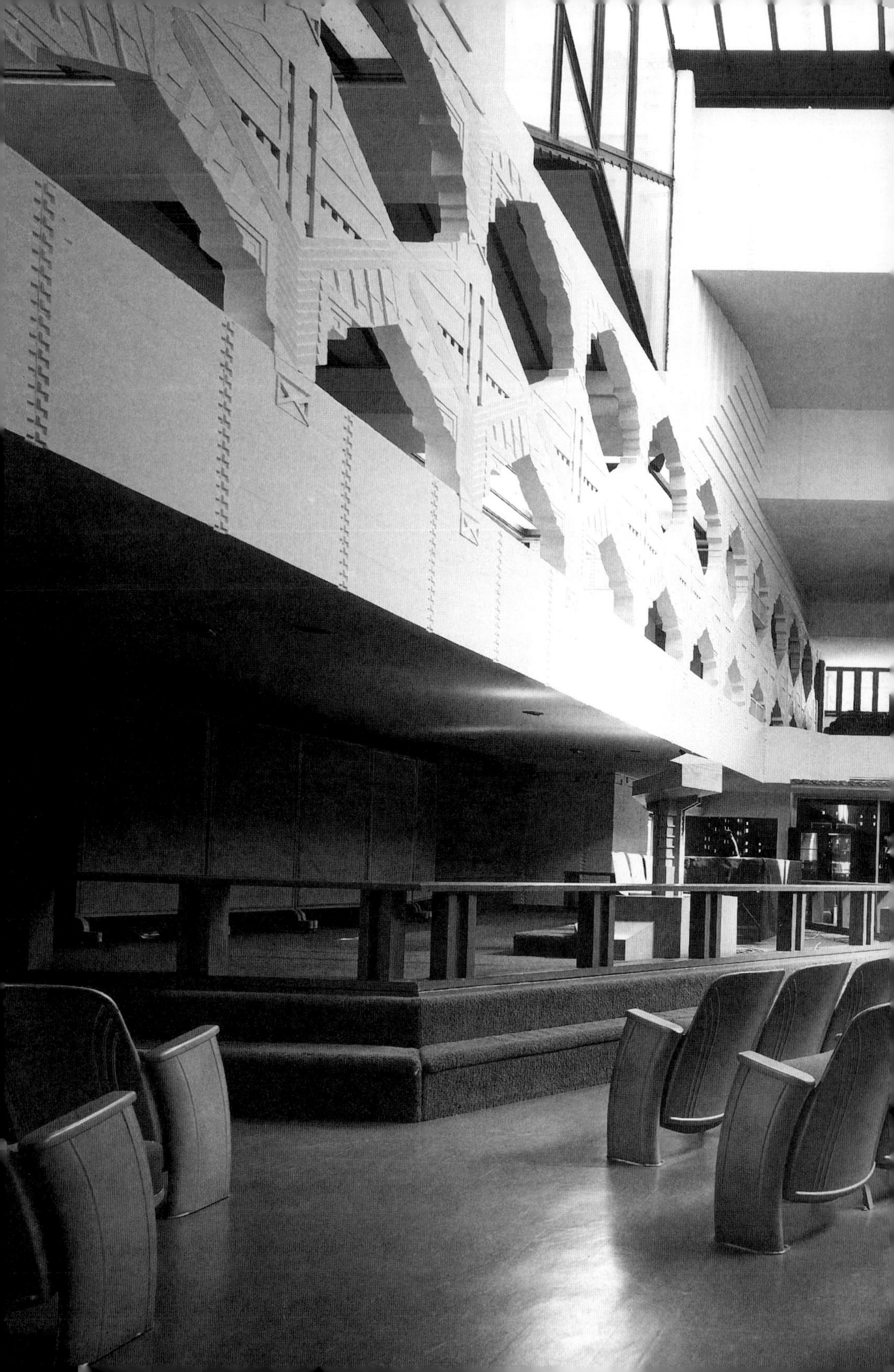

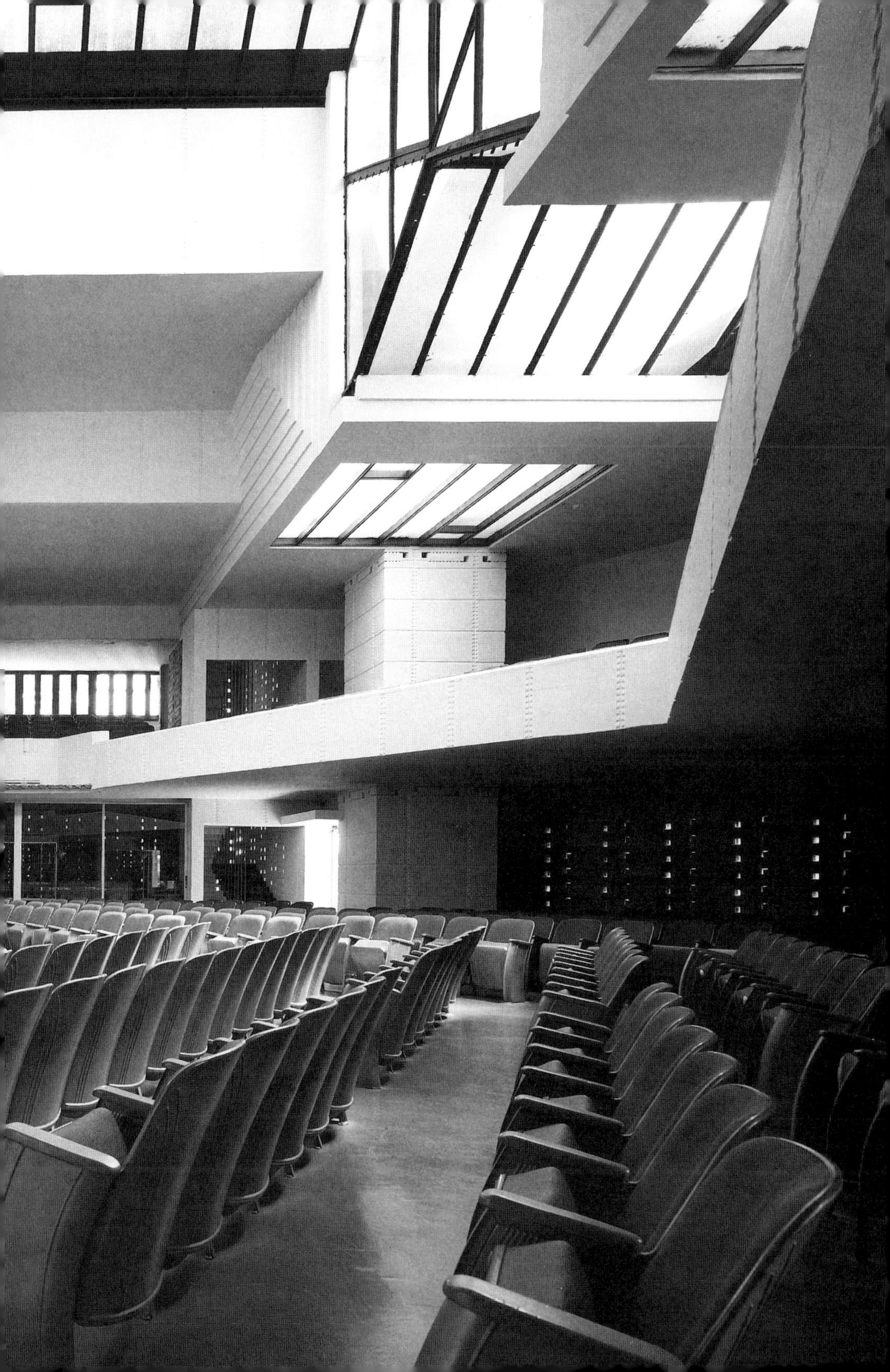

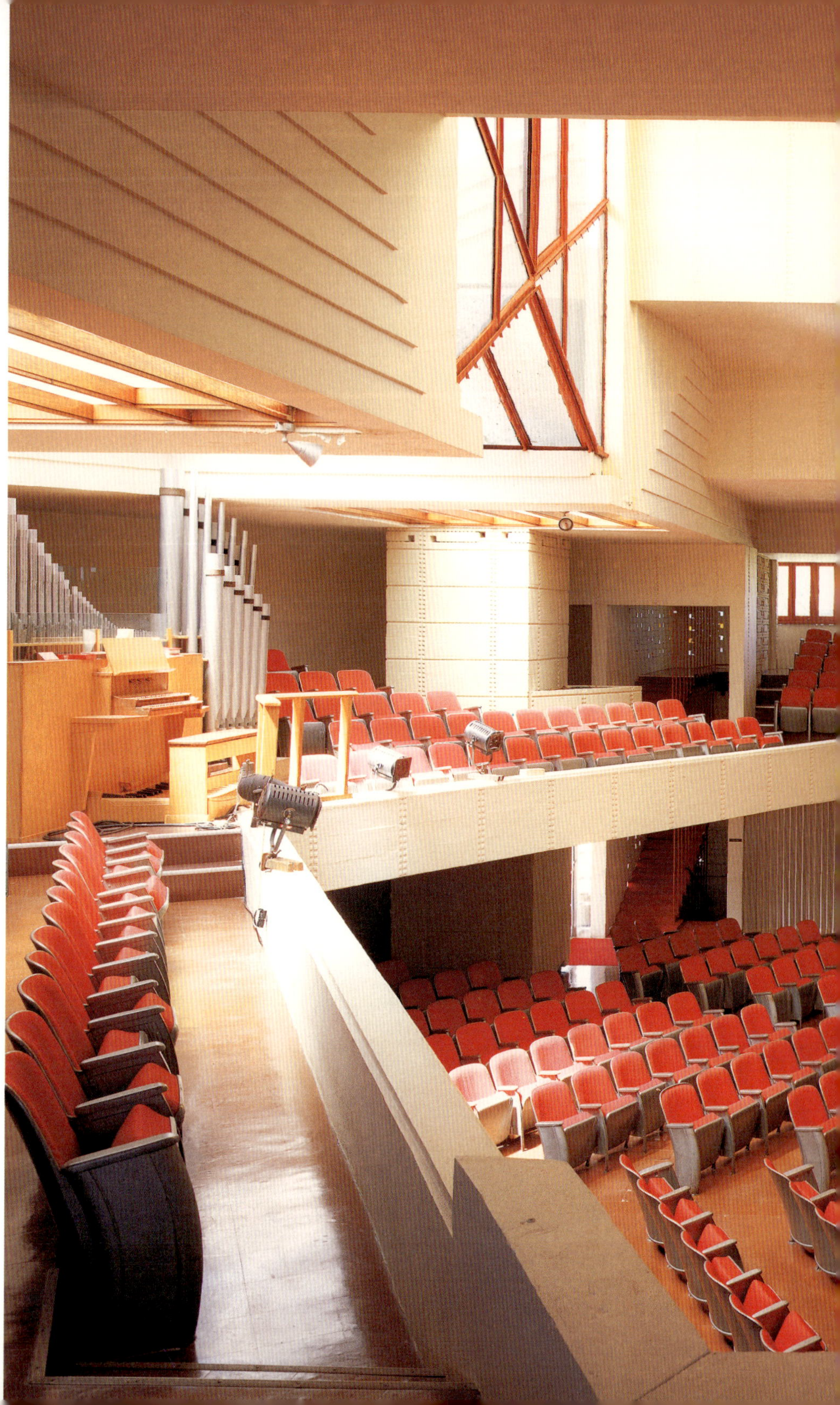

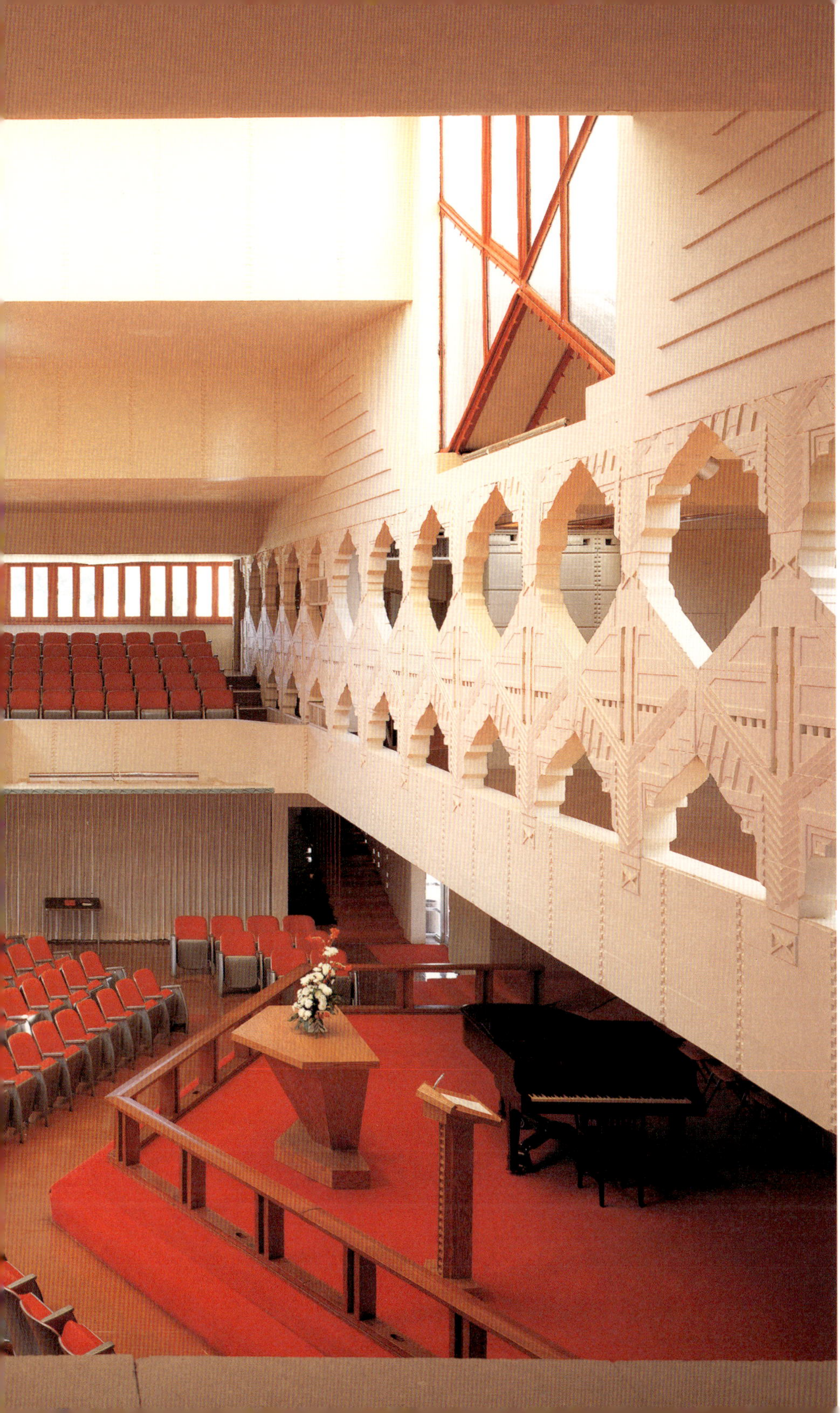

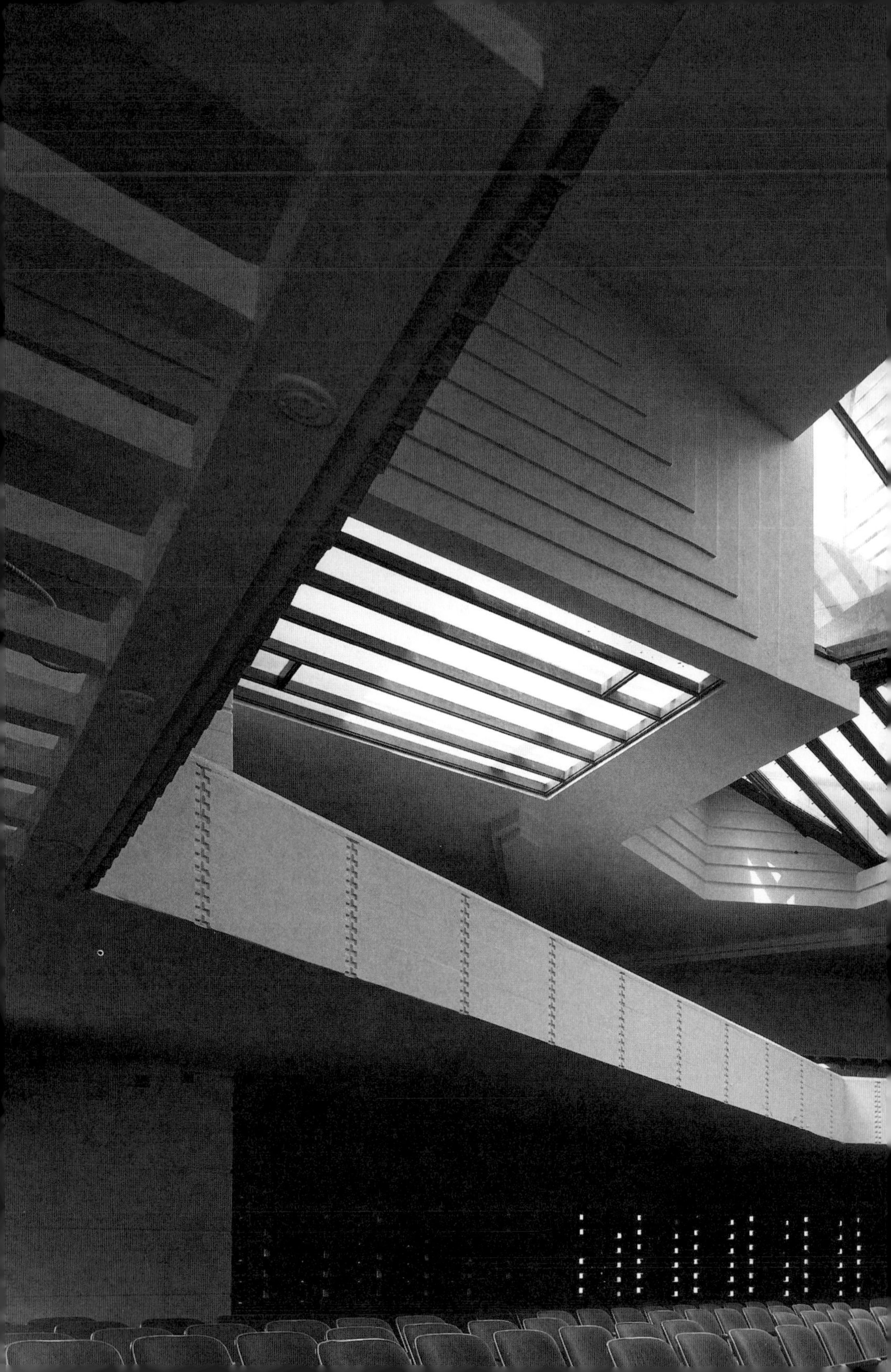

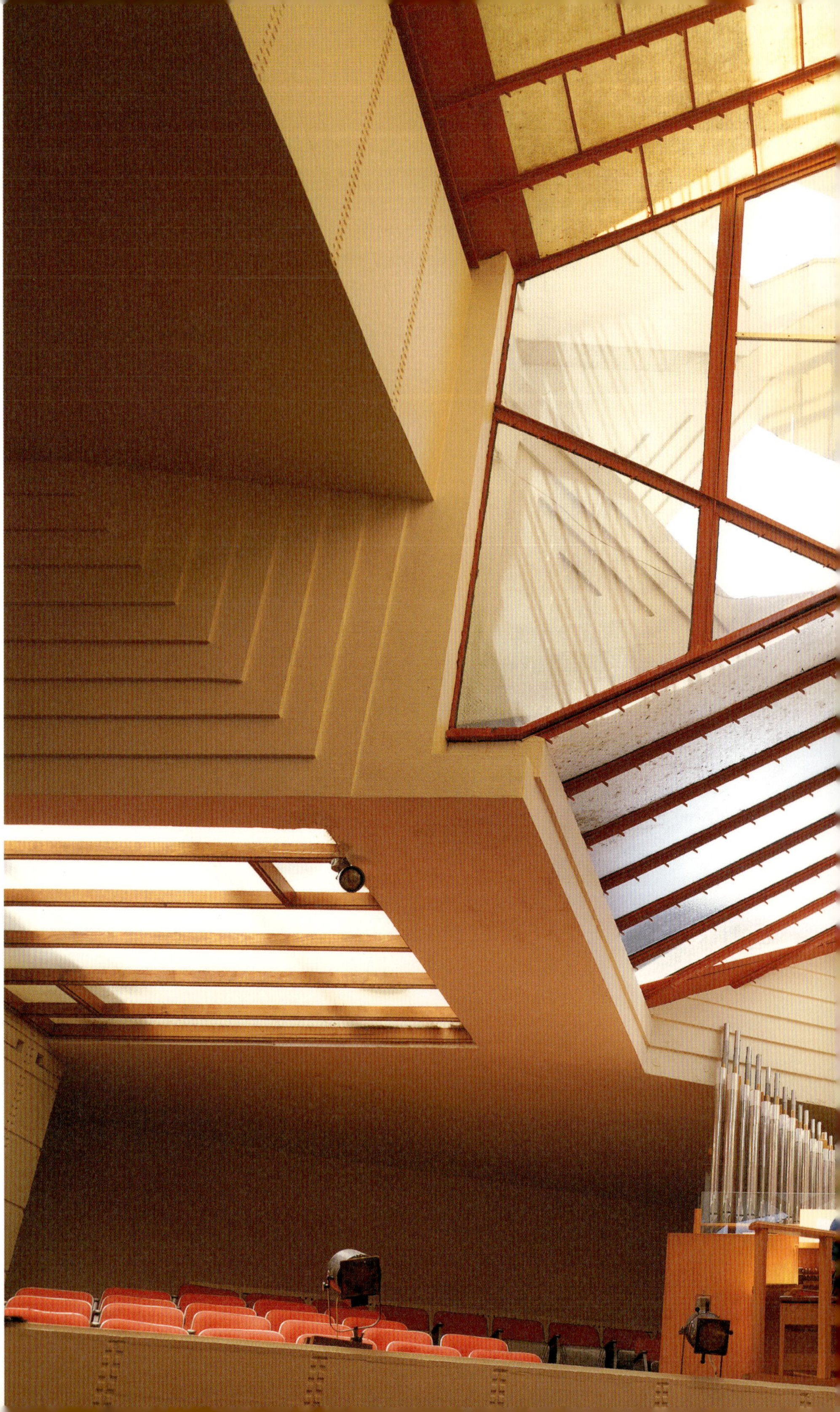

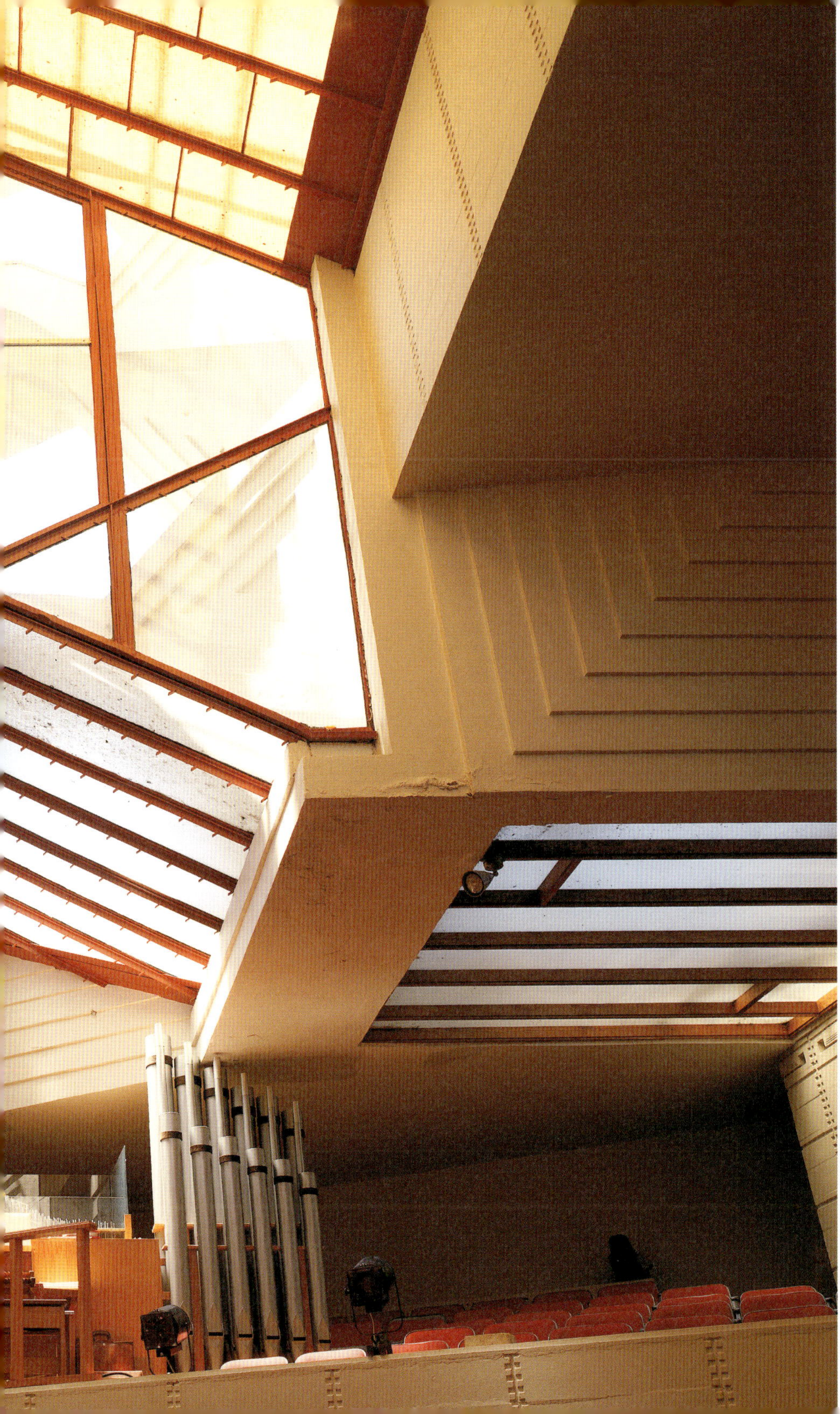

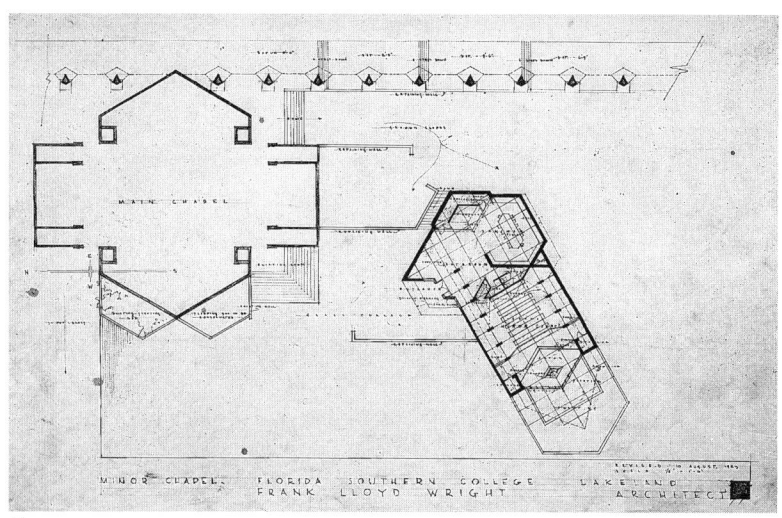

Plan

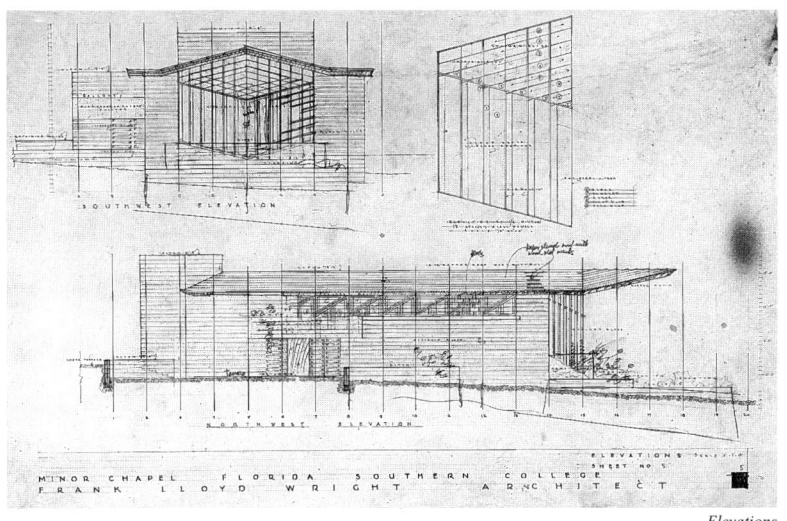

William H. Danforth Chapel
Florida Southern College, Lakeland, Florida, 1953

Elevations

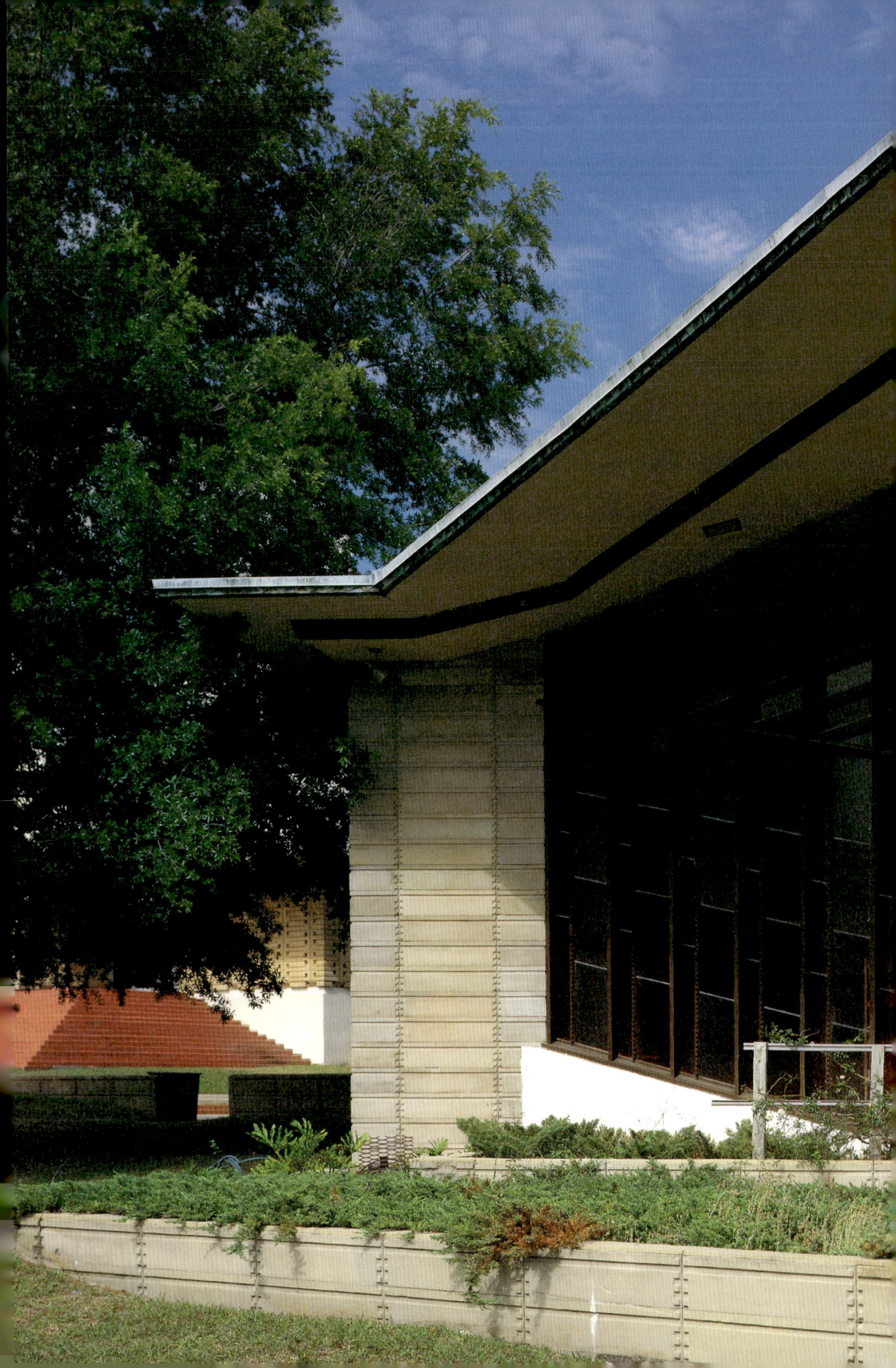

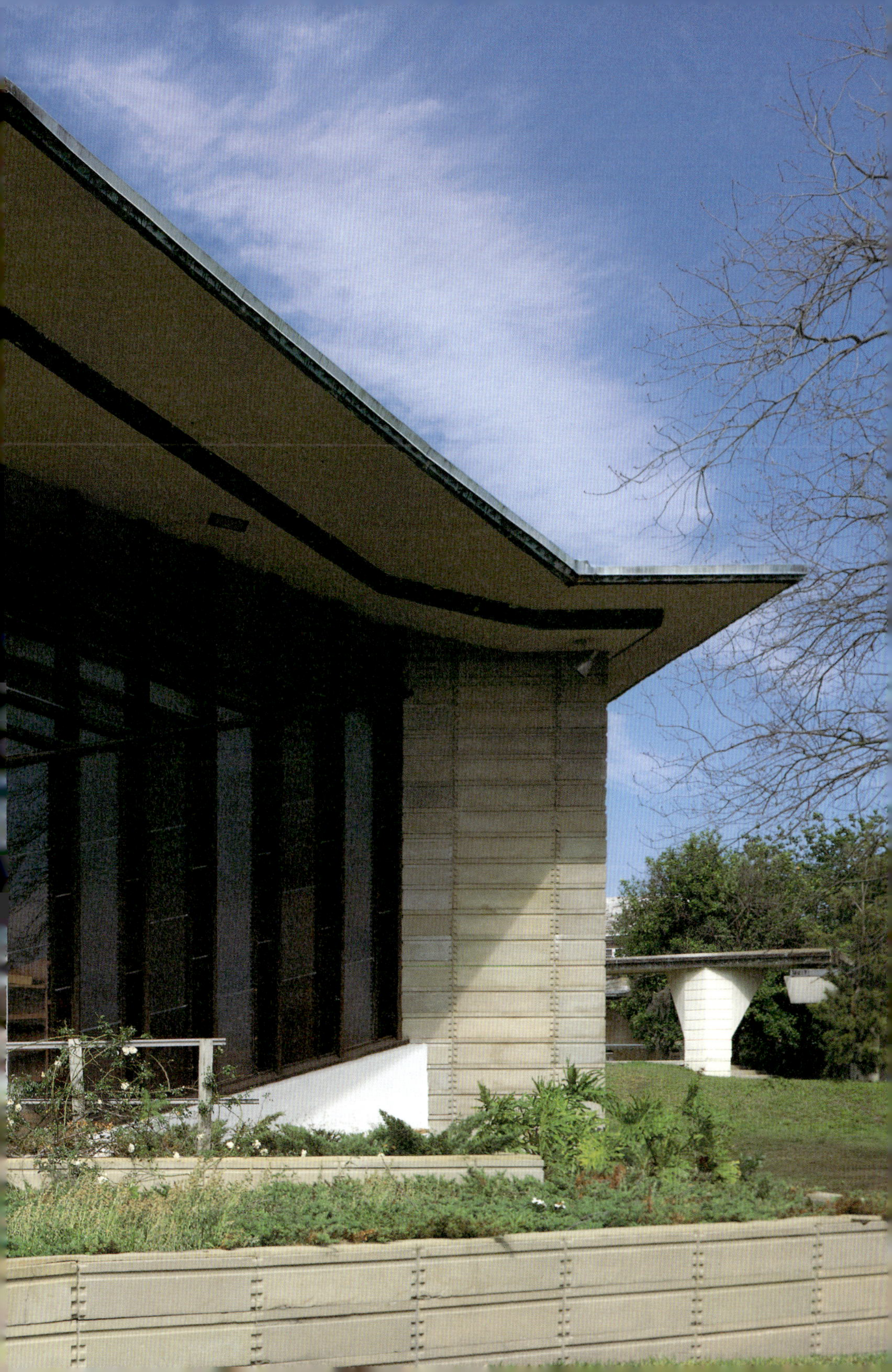

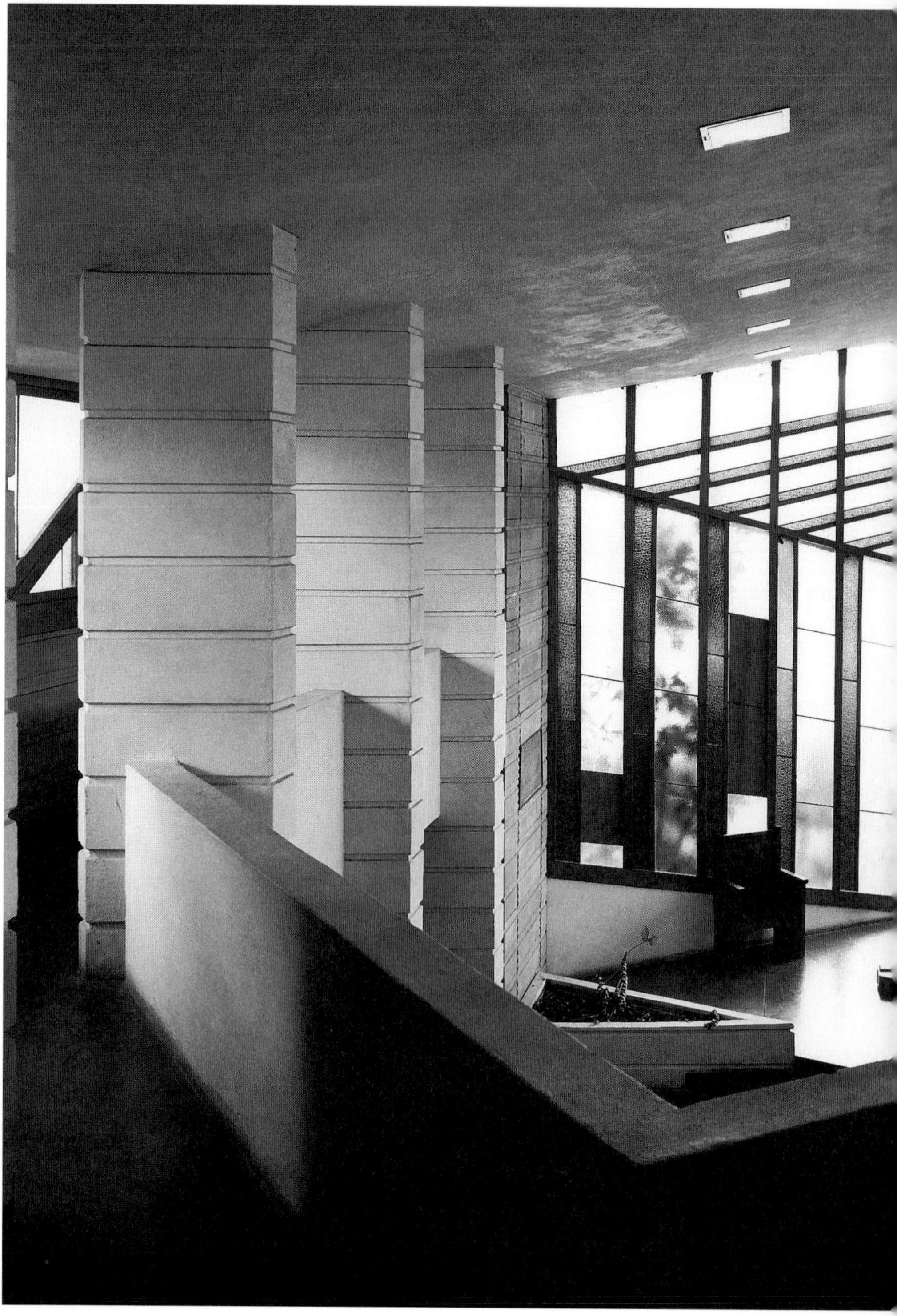

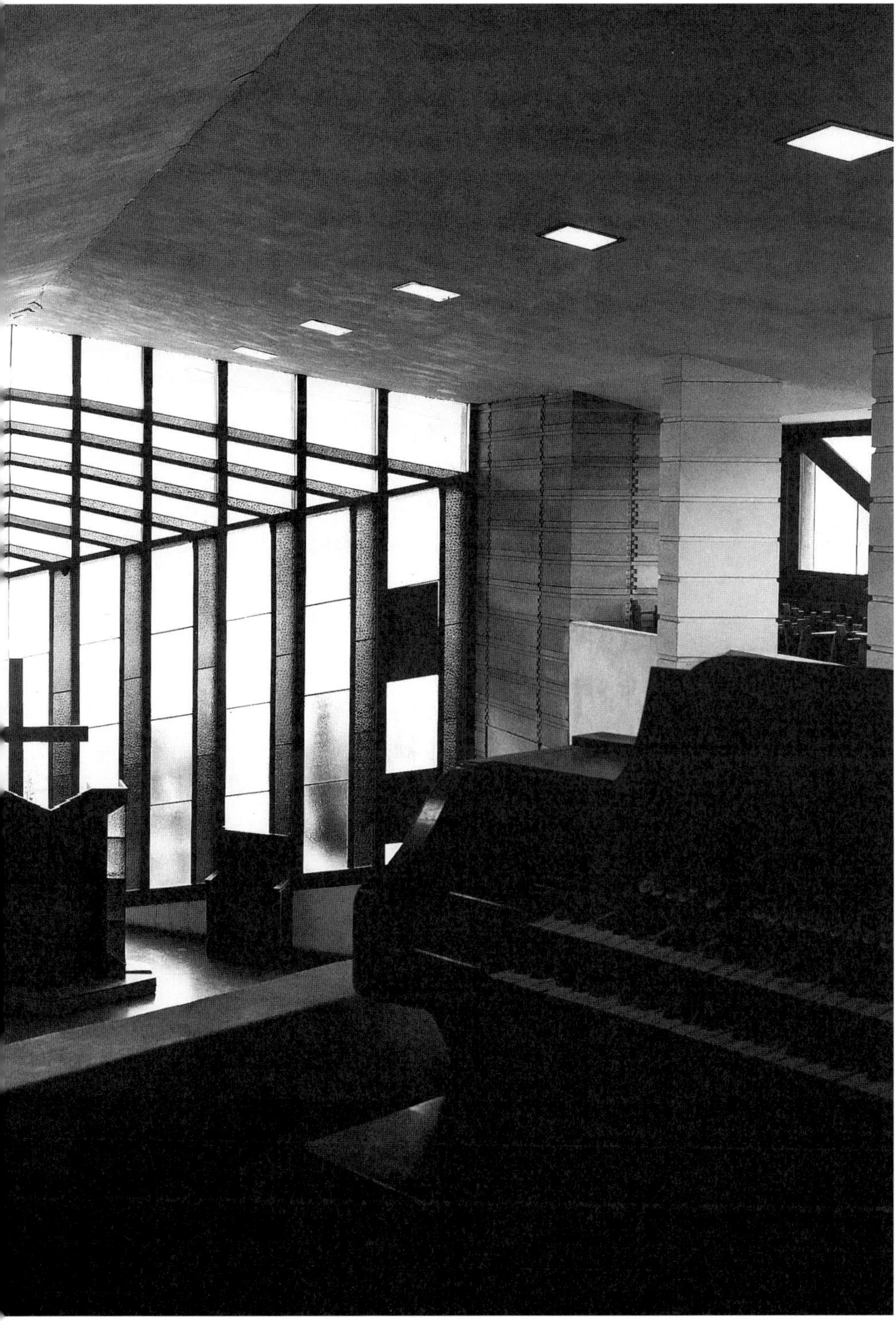

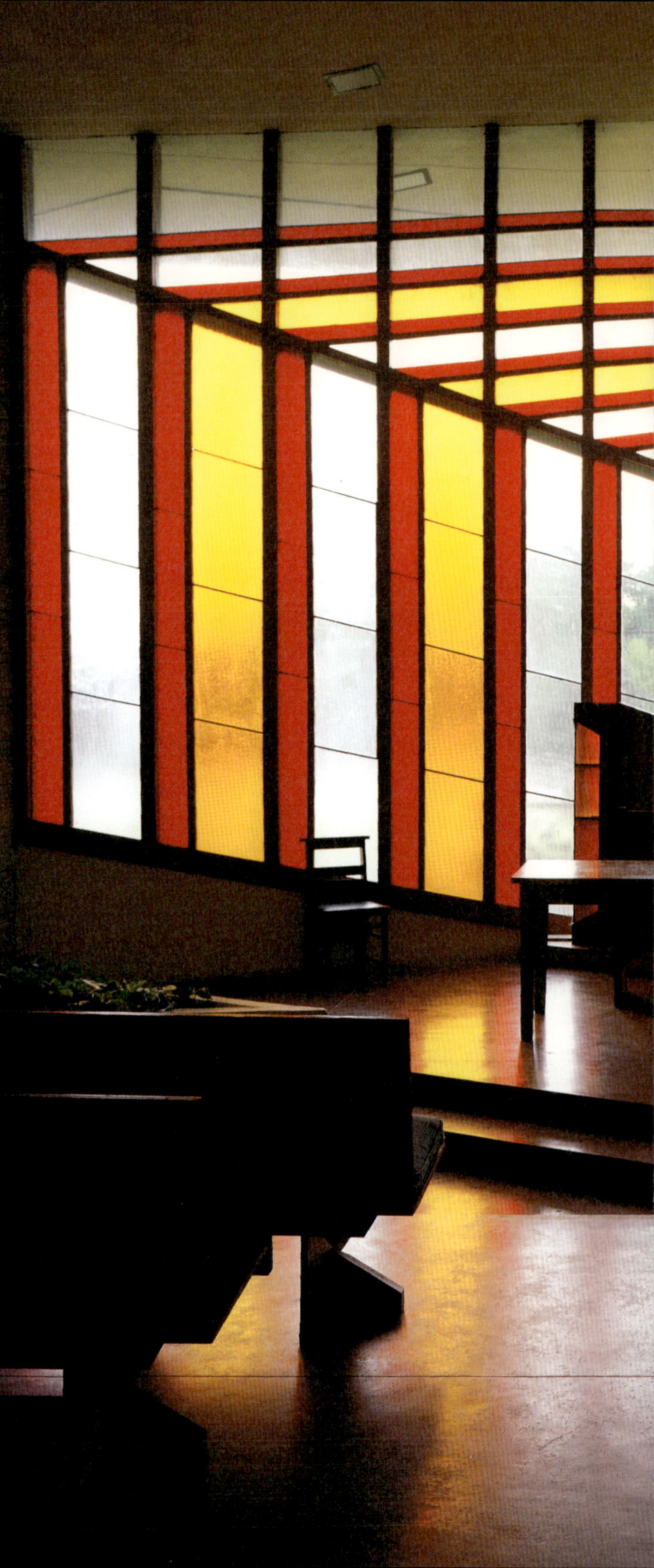

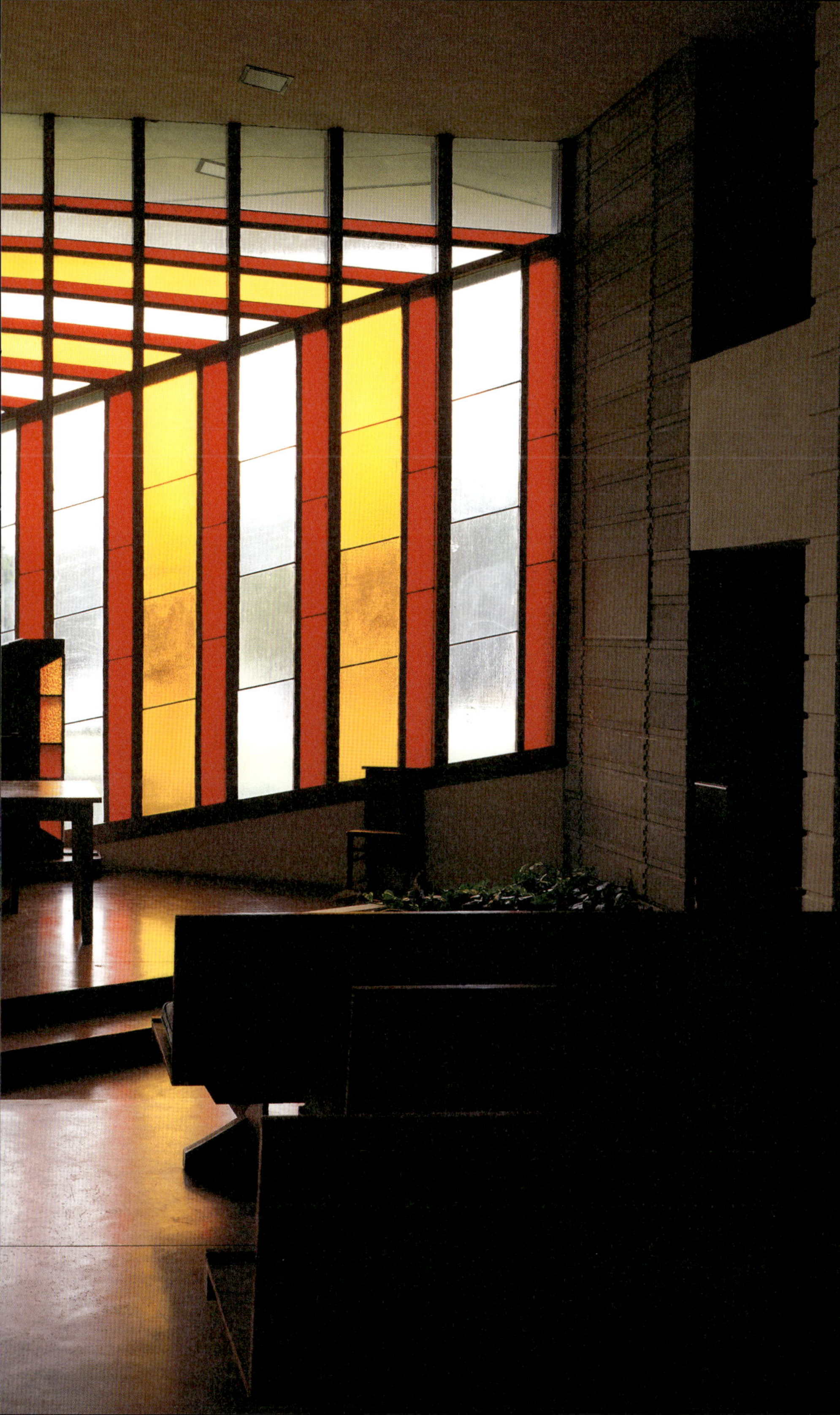

Unitarian Meeting House
Shorewood Hills, Wisconsin, 1947

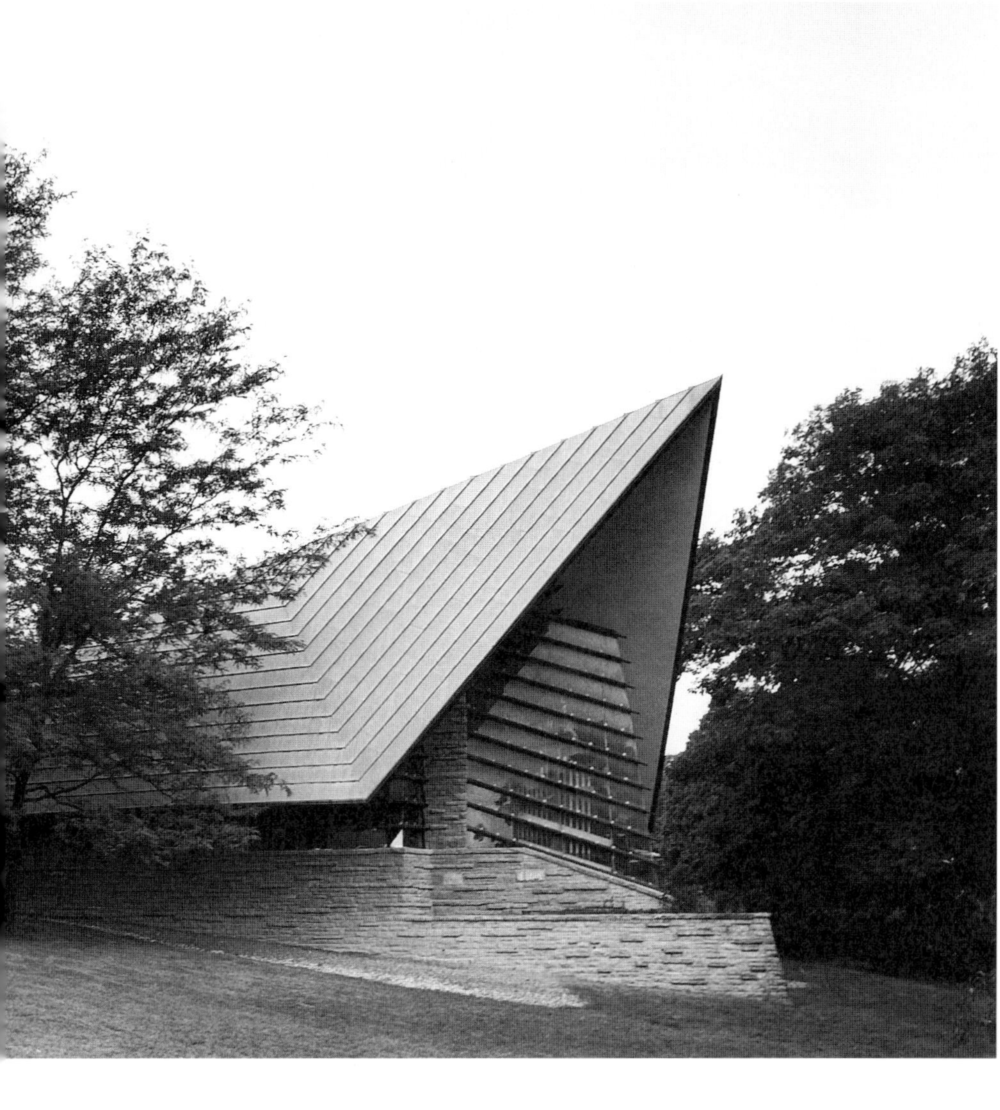

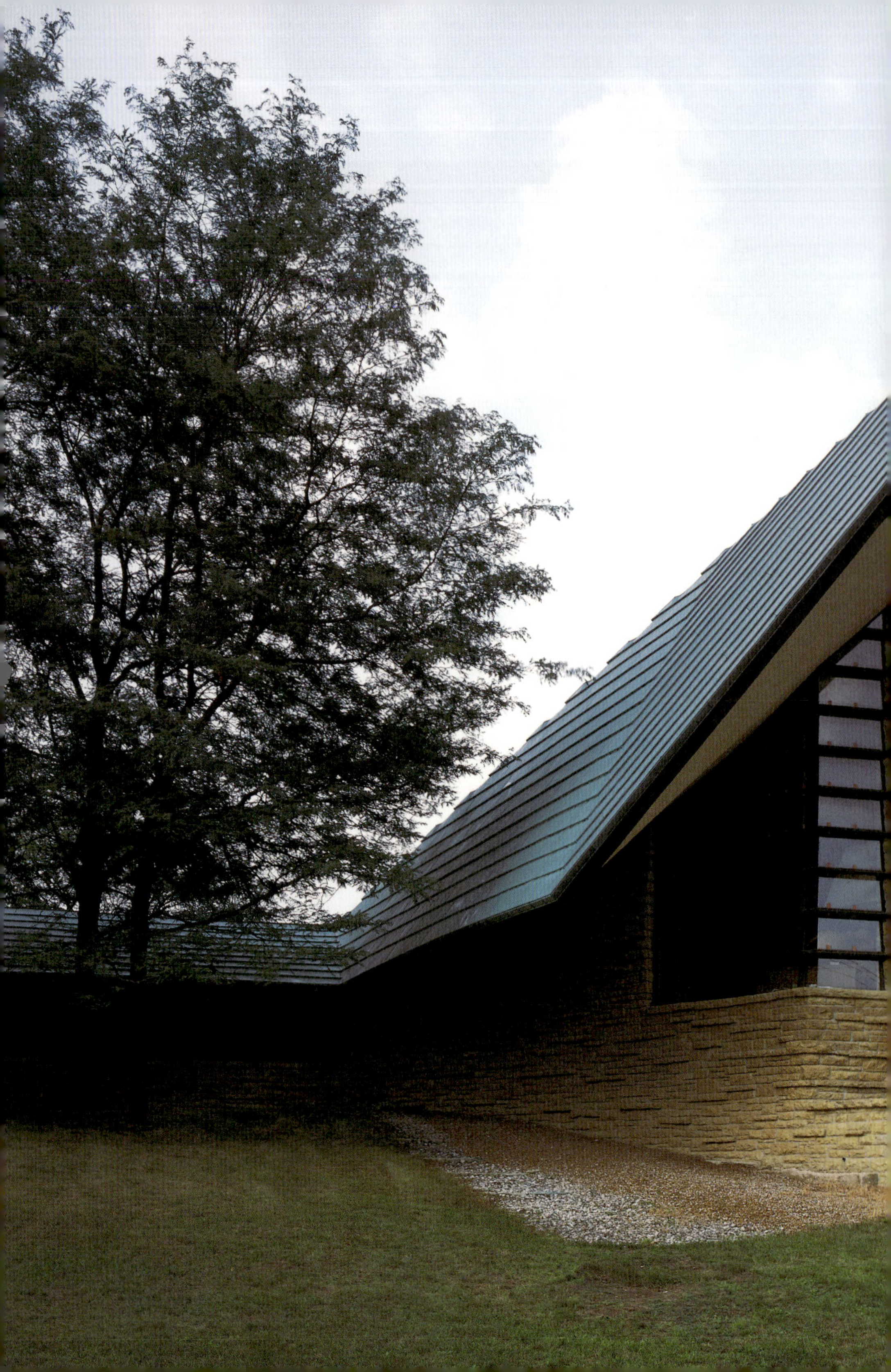

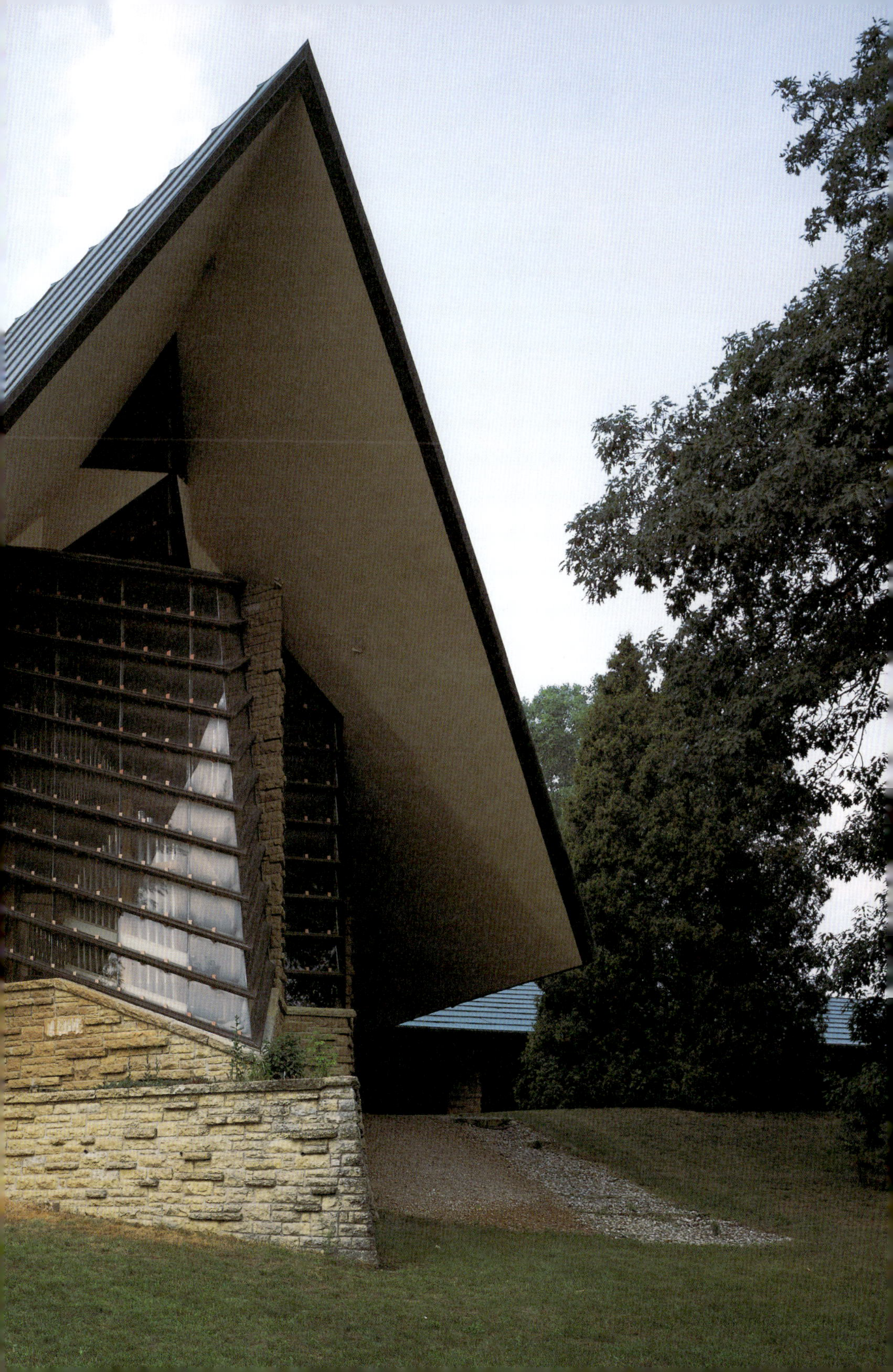

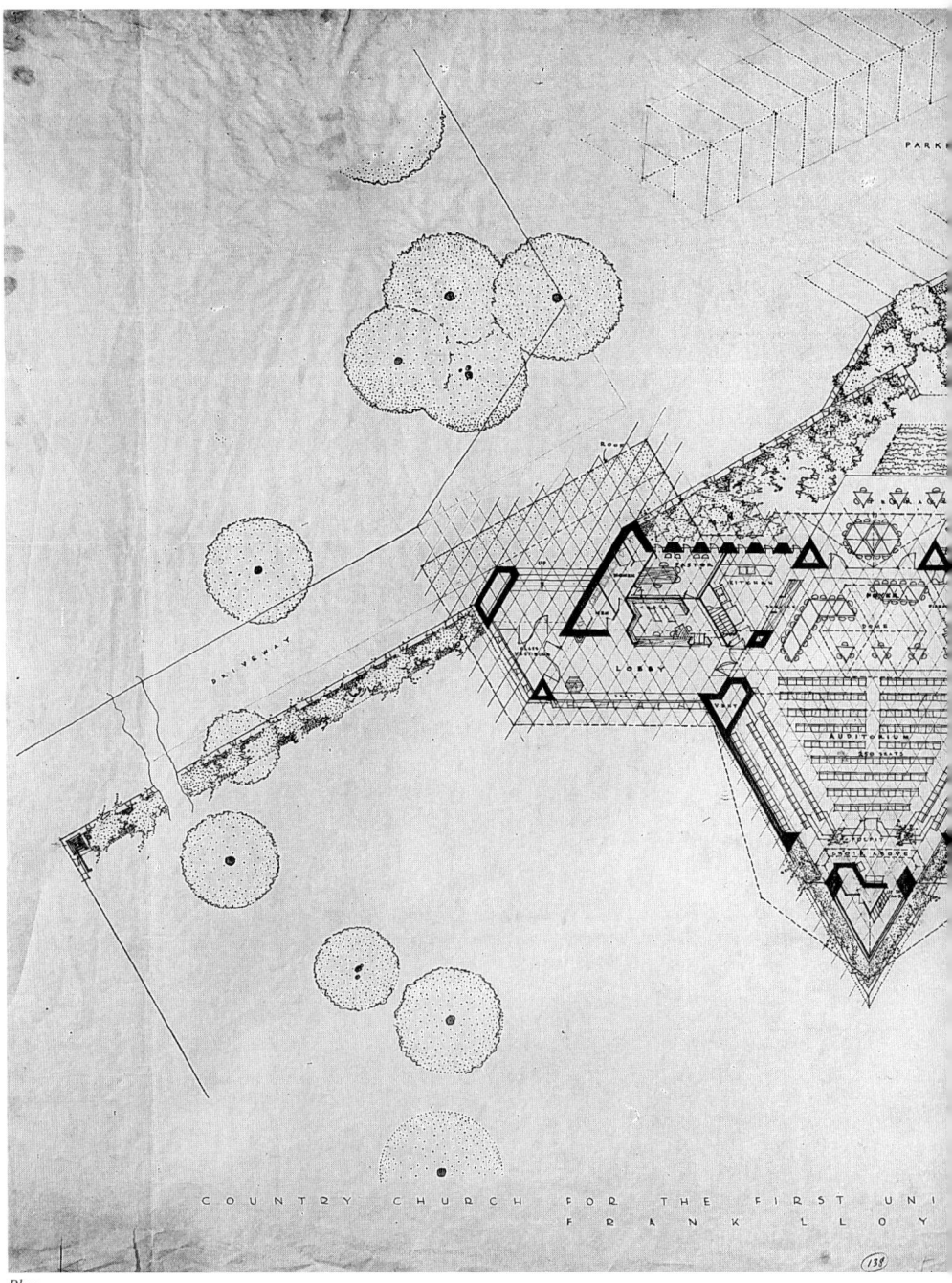

Plan

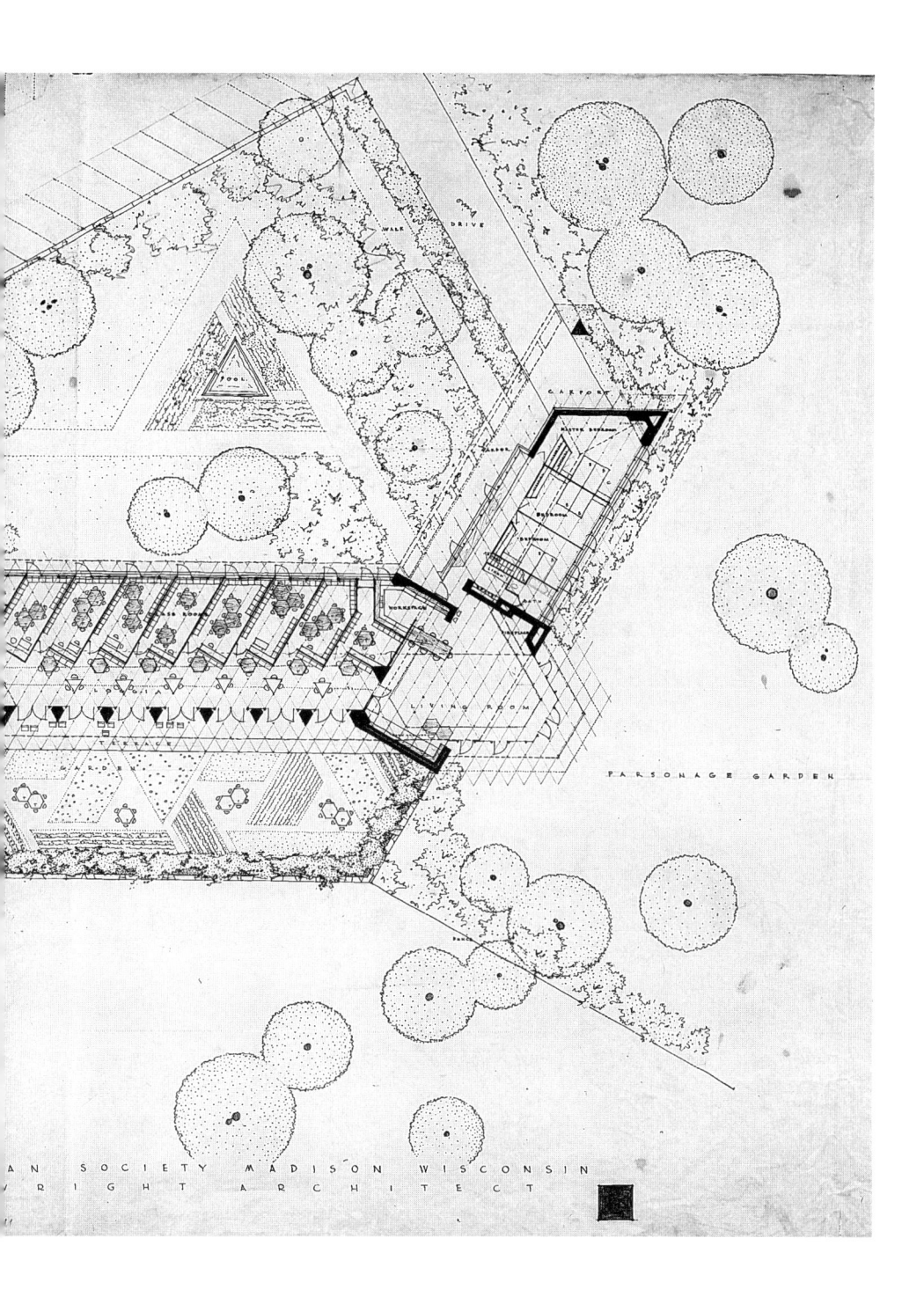

UNITARIAN SOCIETY MADISON WISCONSIN
WRIGHT ARCHITECT

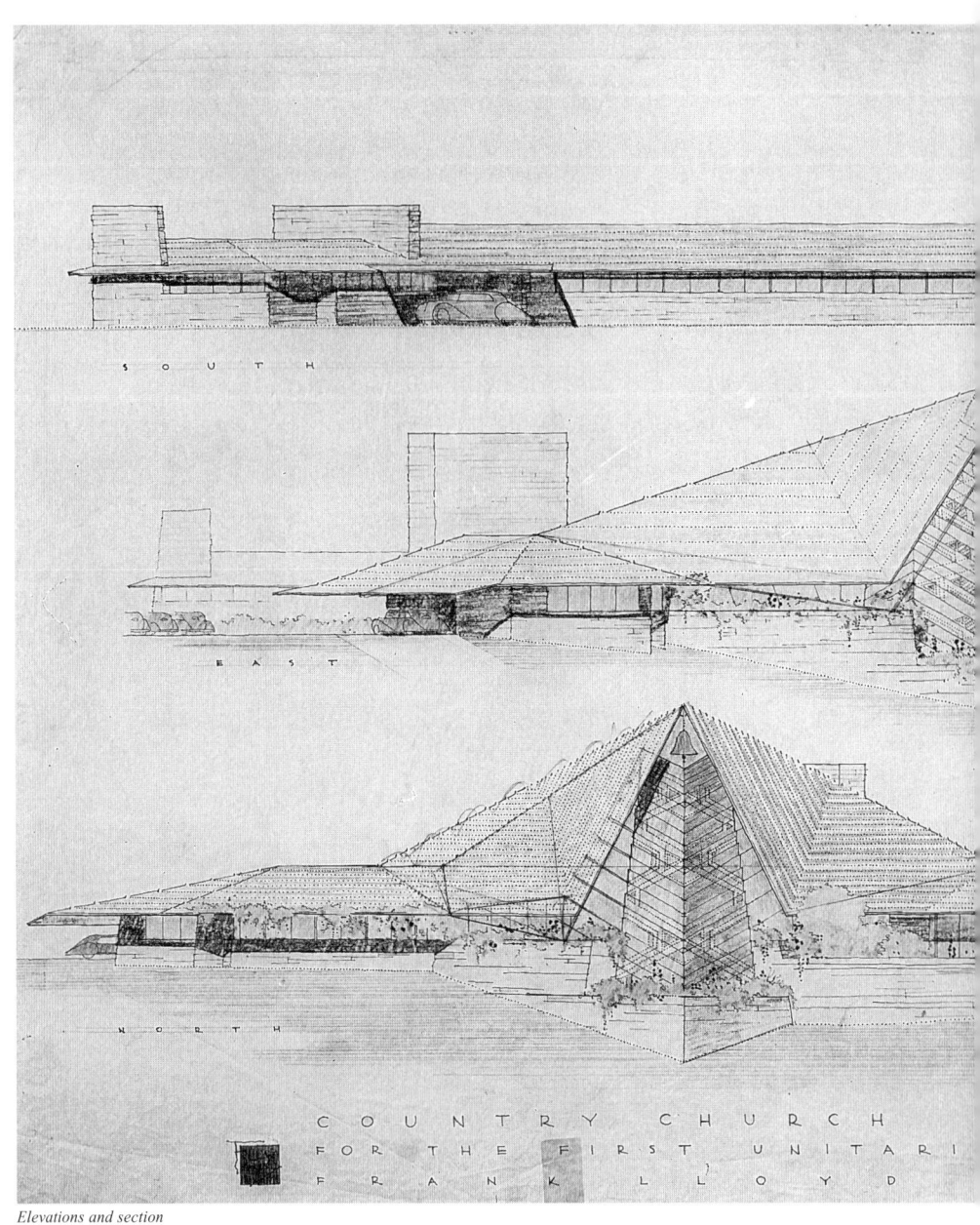

Elevations and section

SECTION ON CENTER LINE

ELEVATIONS   SCALE ⅛"=1'-0"
SOCIETY   MADISON   WISCONSIN
...IGHT   ARCHITECT

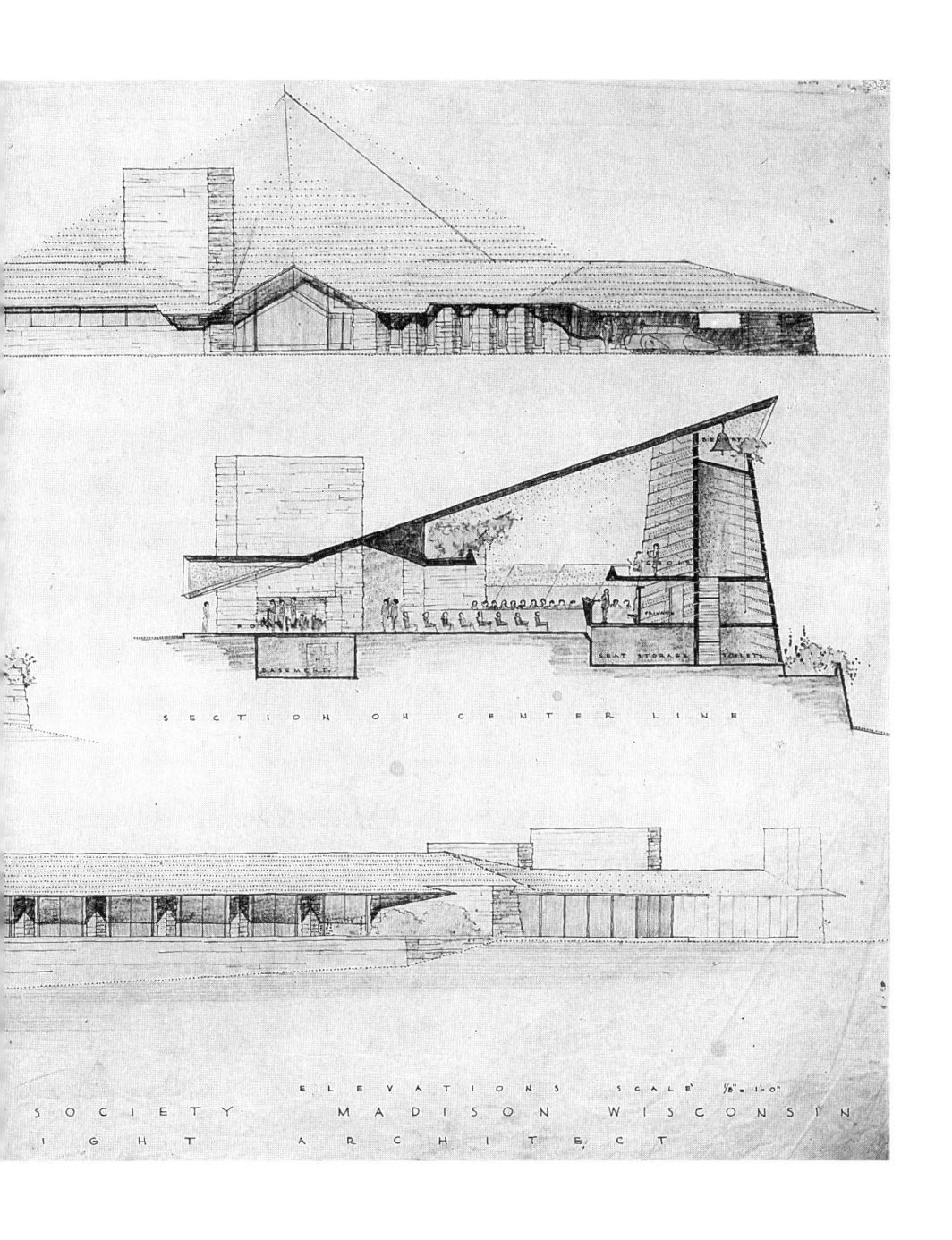

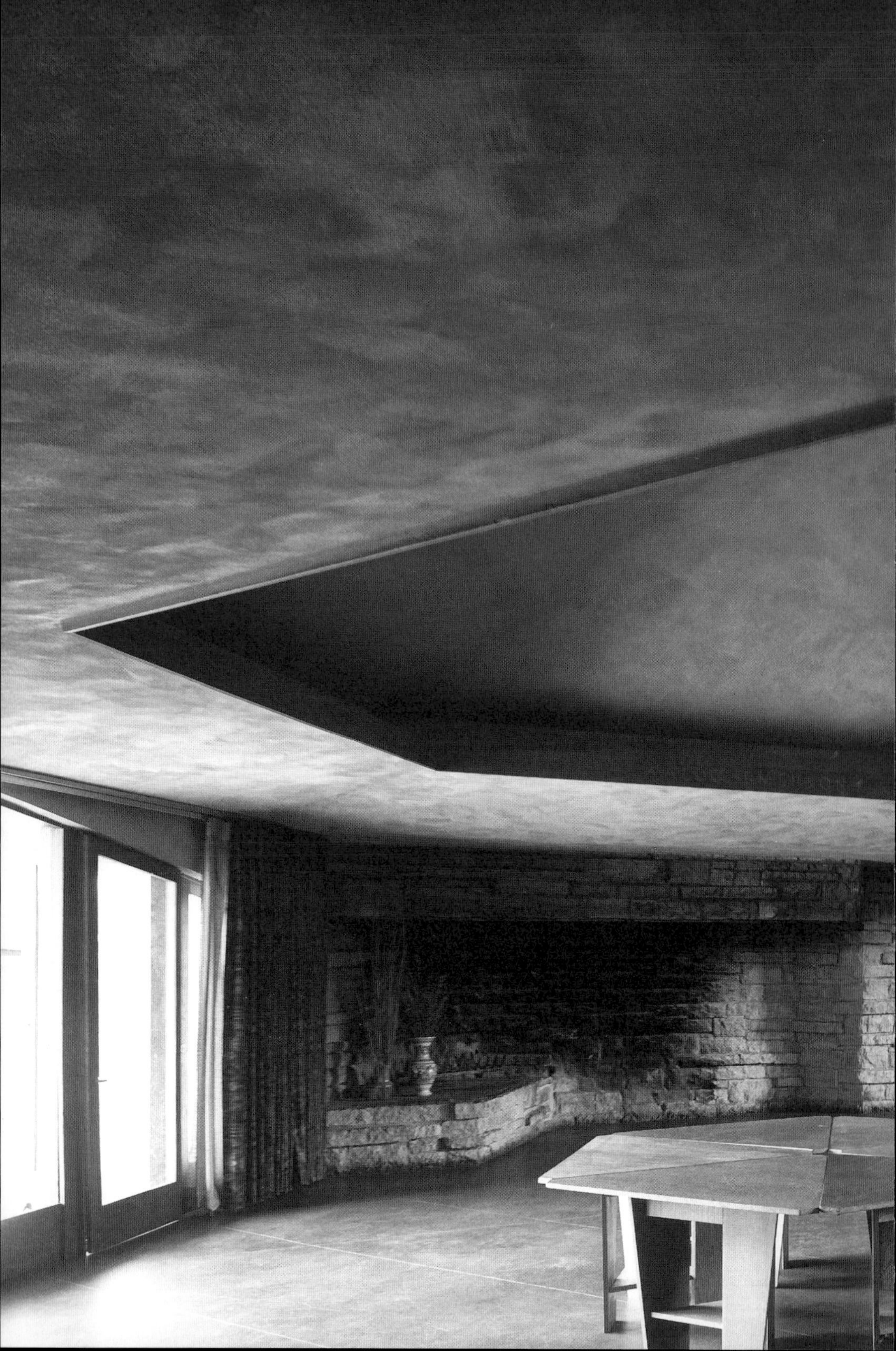

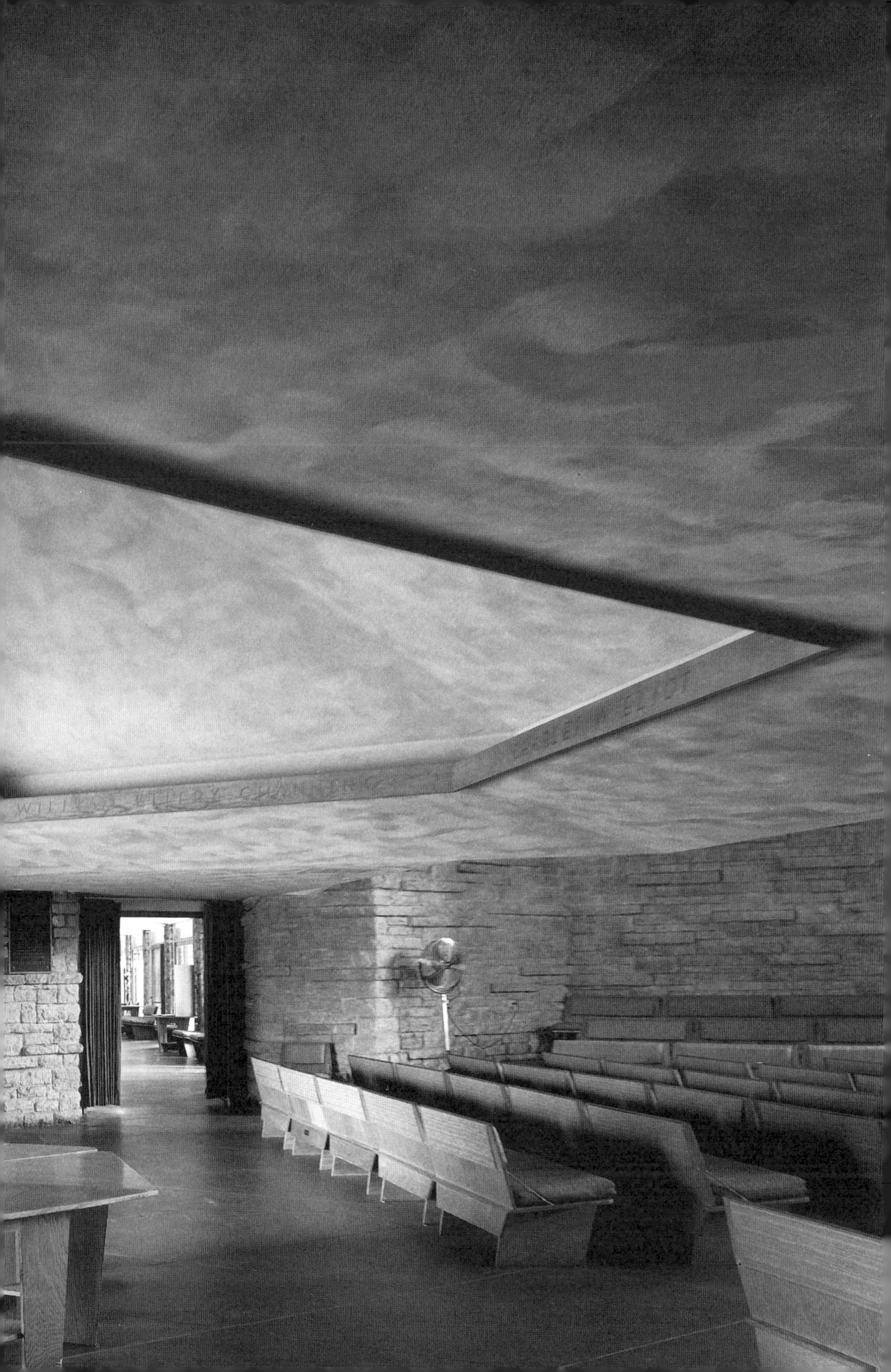

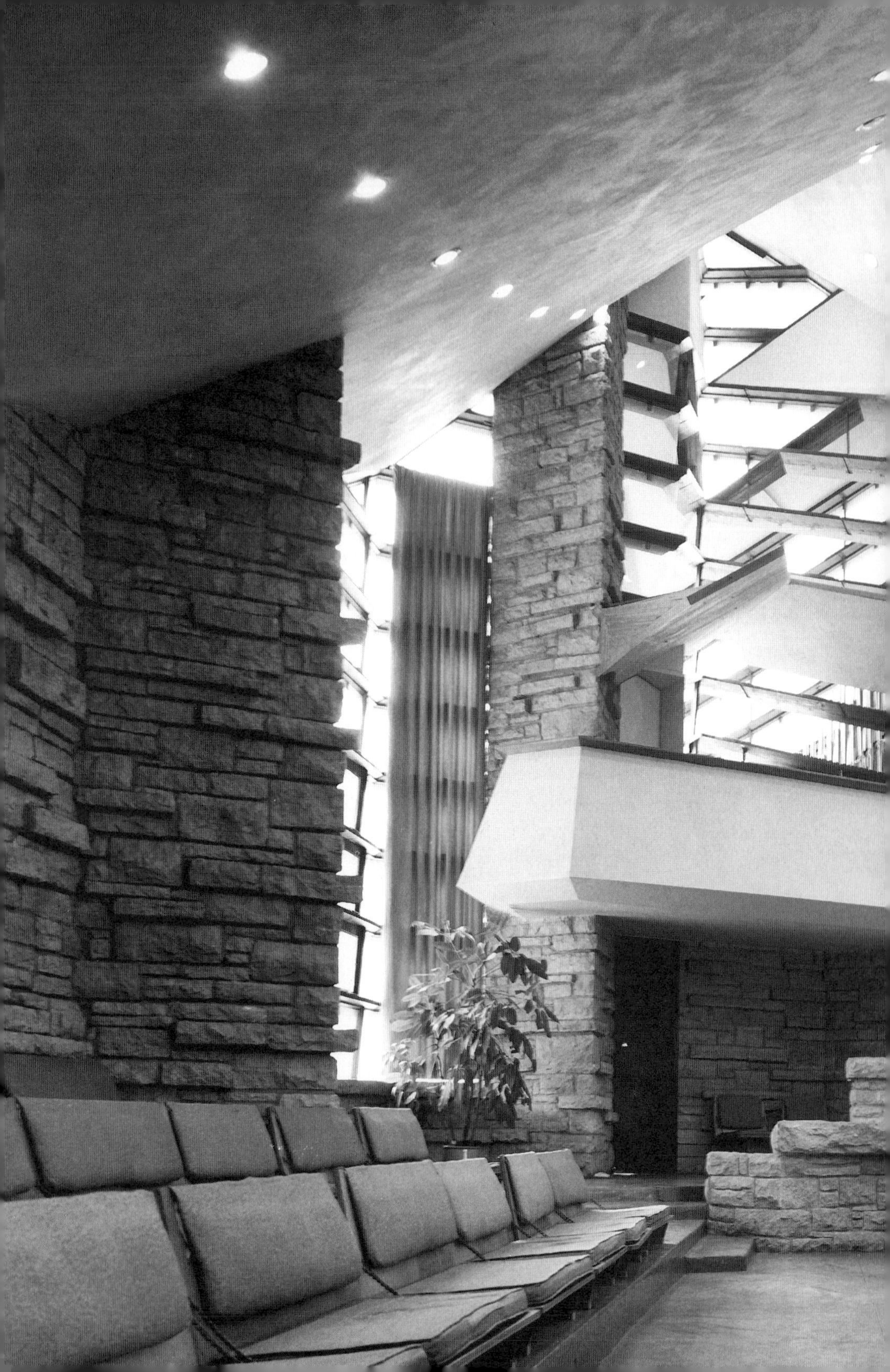

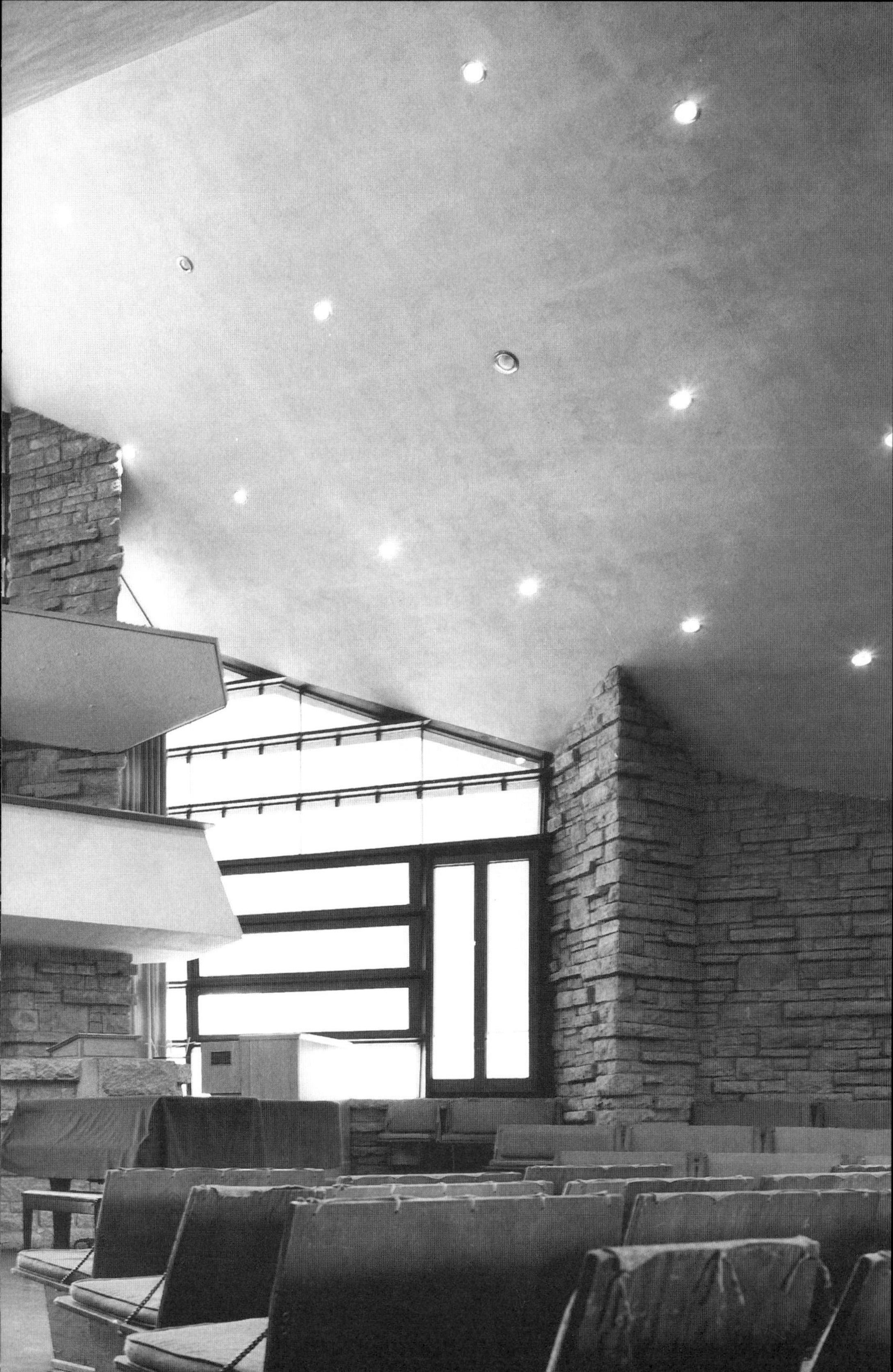

DO YOU HAVE A LOAF OF BREAD BREAK THE LOAF IN
HALF FOR SOME FLOWERS

NARCISSUS FOR THY BREAD FEEDS THE BODY INDEED BUT THE FLOWERS FEED THE SOUL

REAK THE LOAF IN TWO AND GIVE

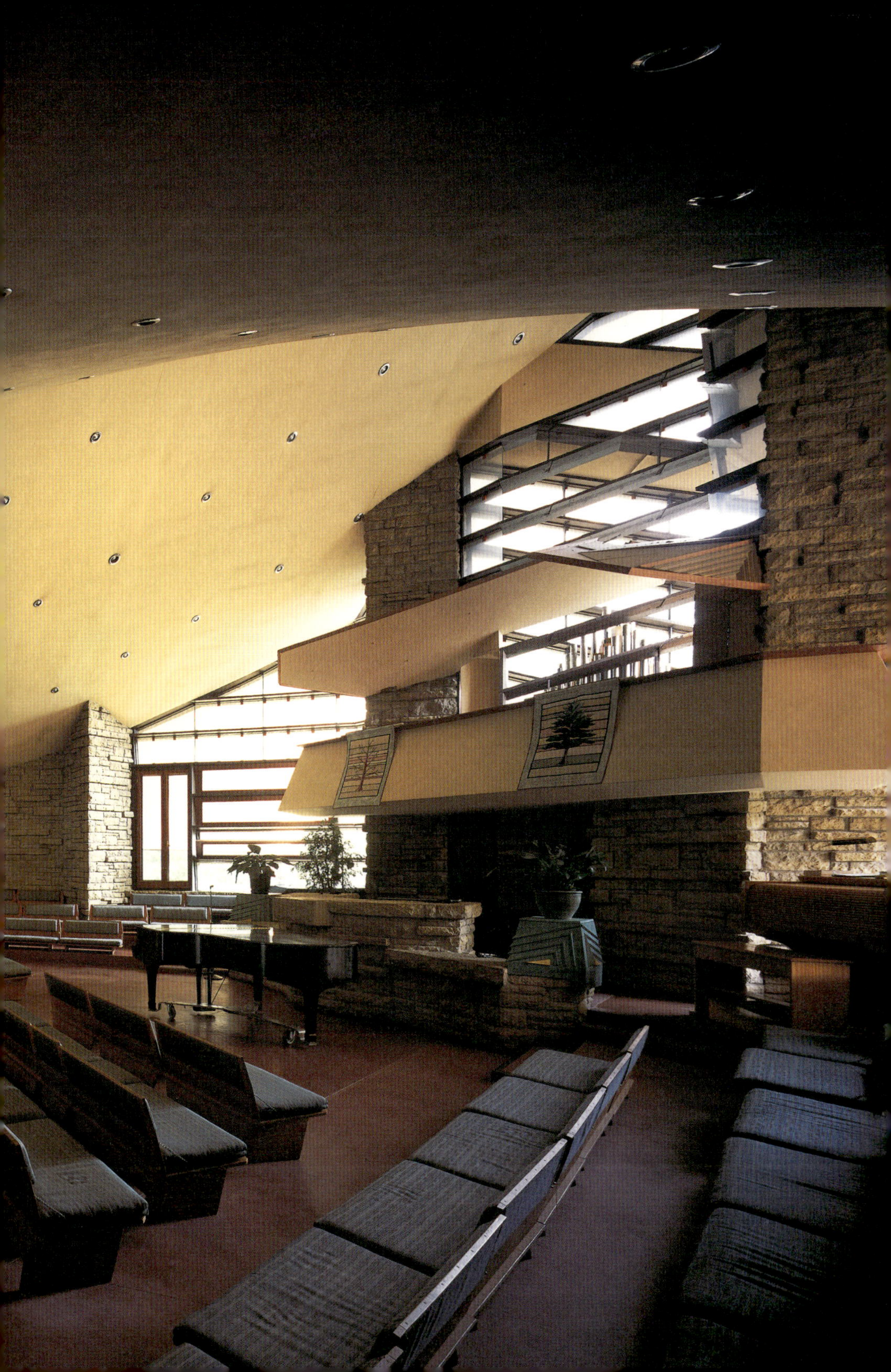

Beth Sholom Synagogue
Elkin Park, Pennsylvania, 1954

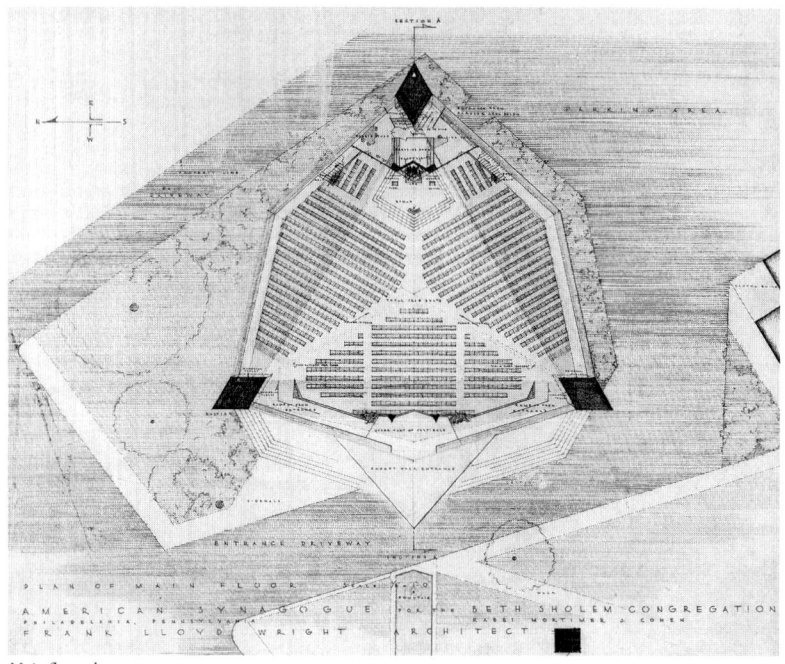

Main floor plan

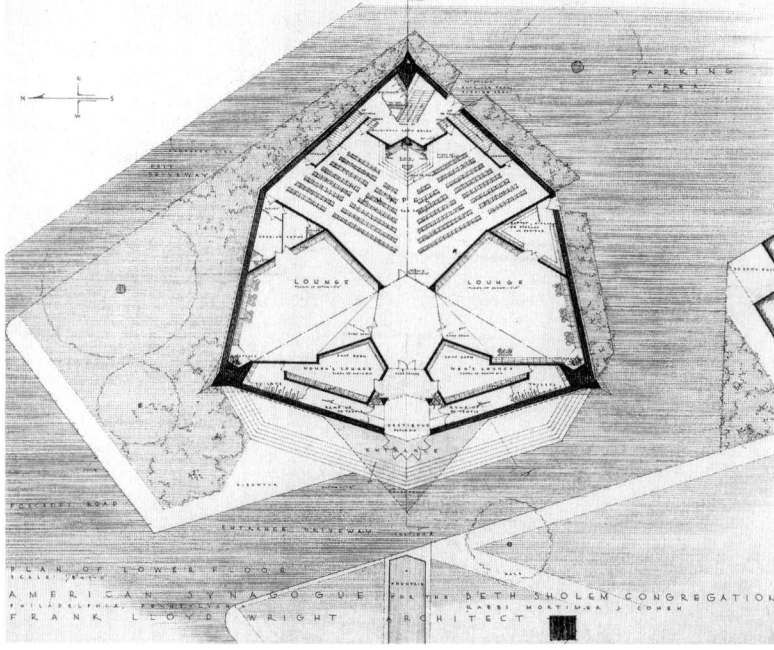

Lower floor plan

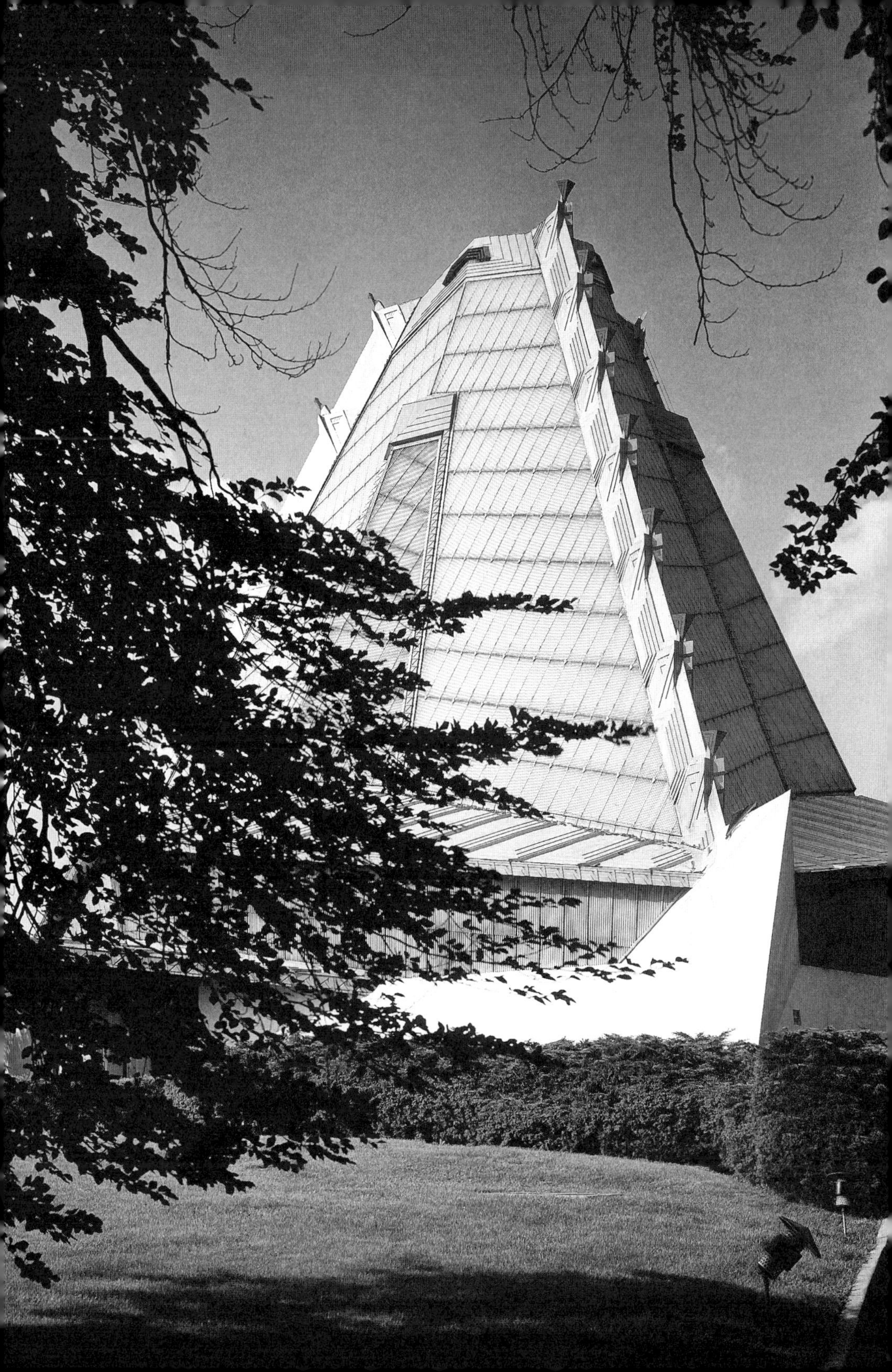

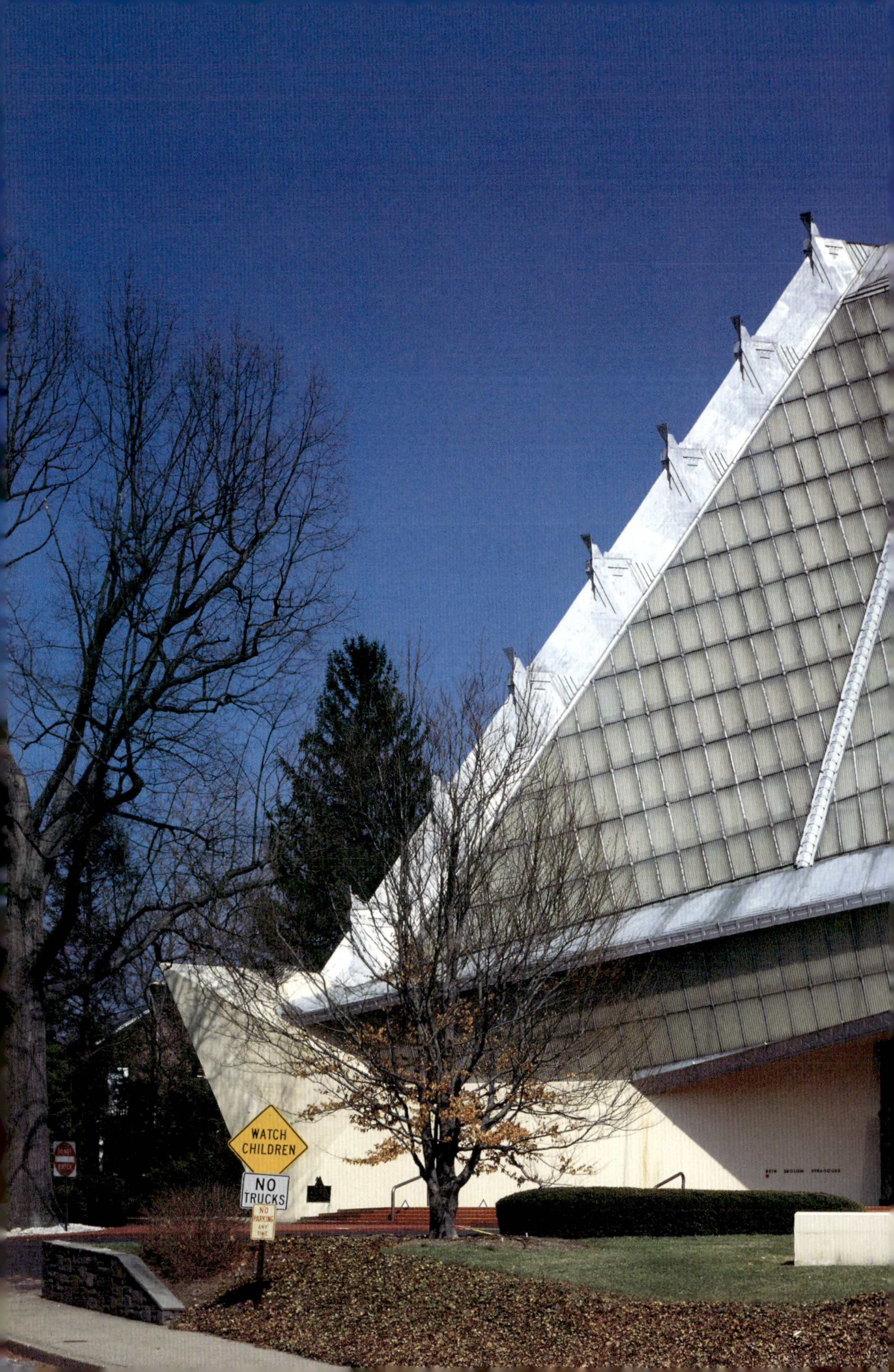
WATCH CHILDREN
NO TRUCKS
NO PARKING ANY TIME

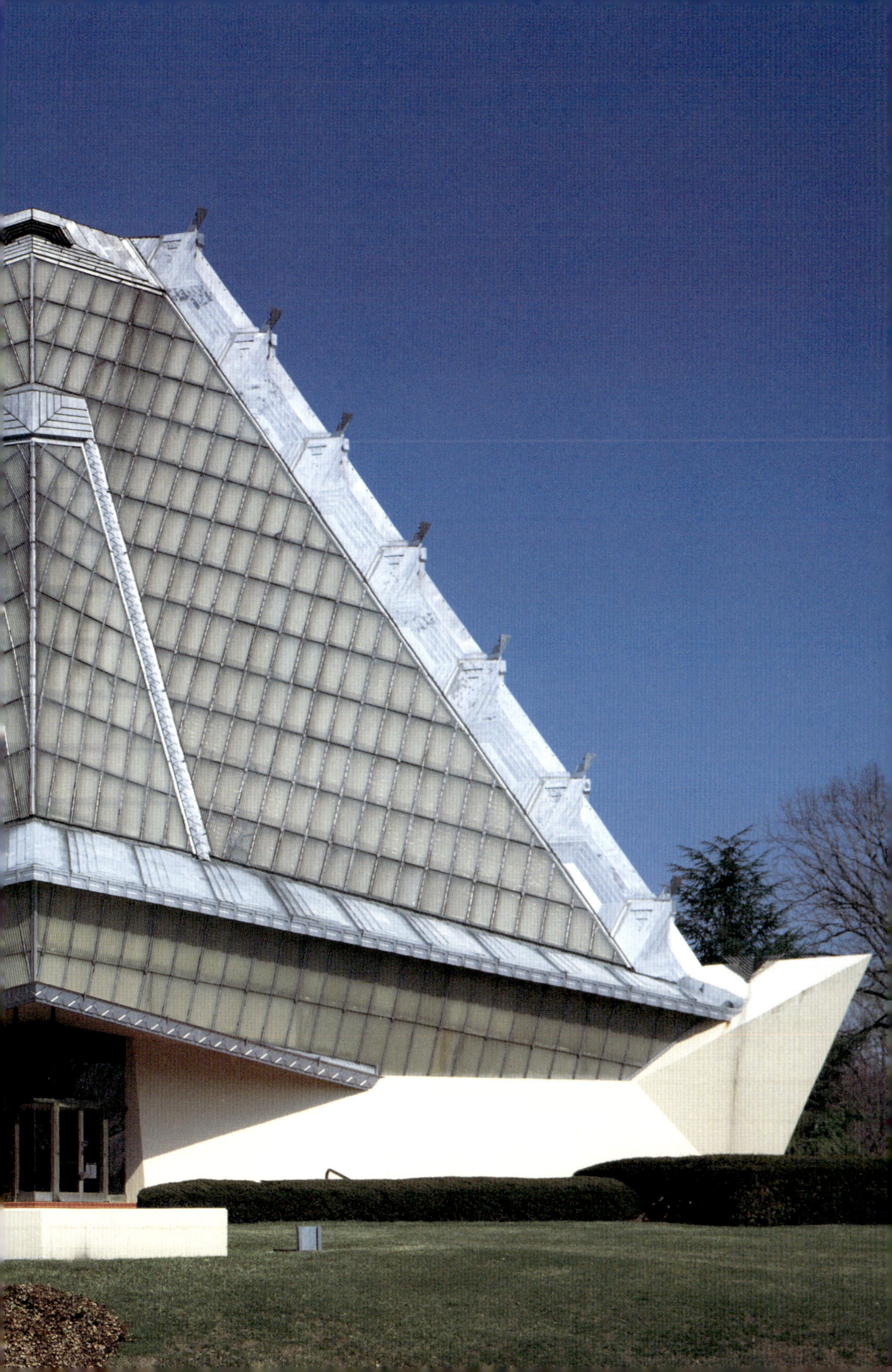

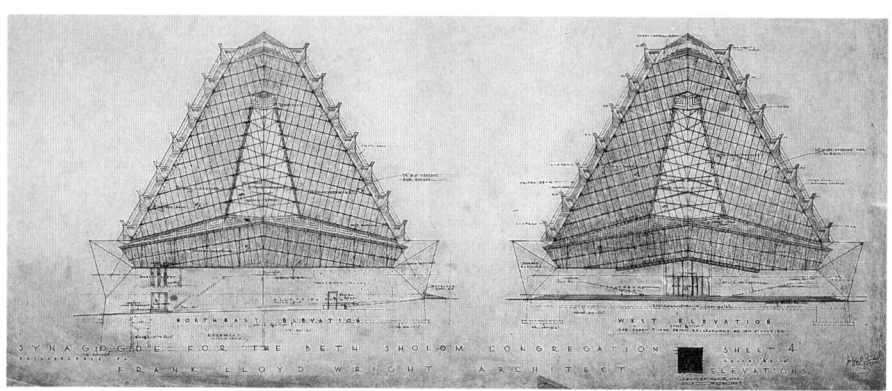

Elevations

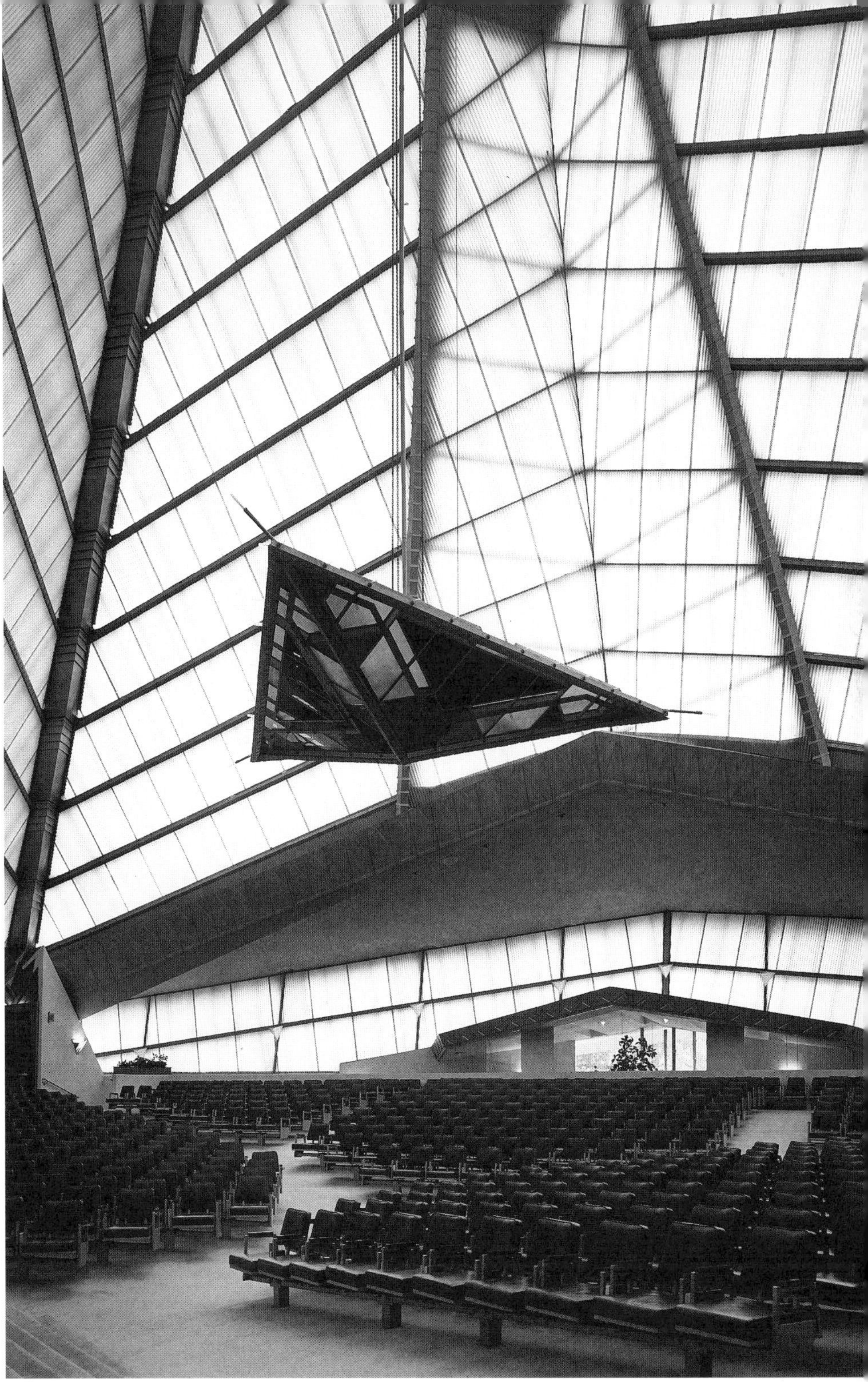

קדוש

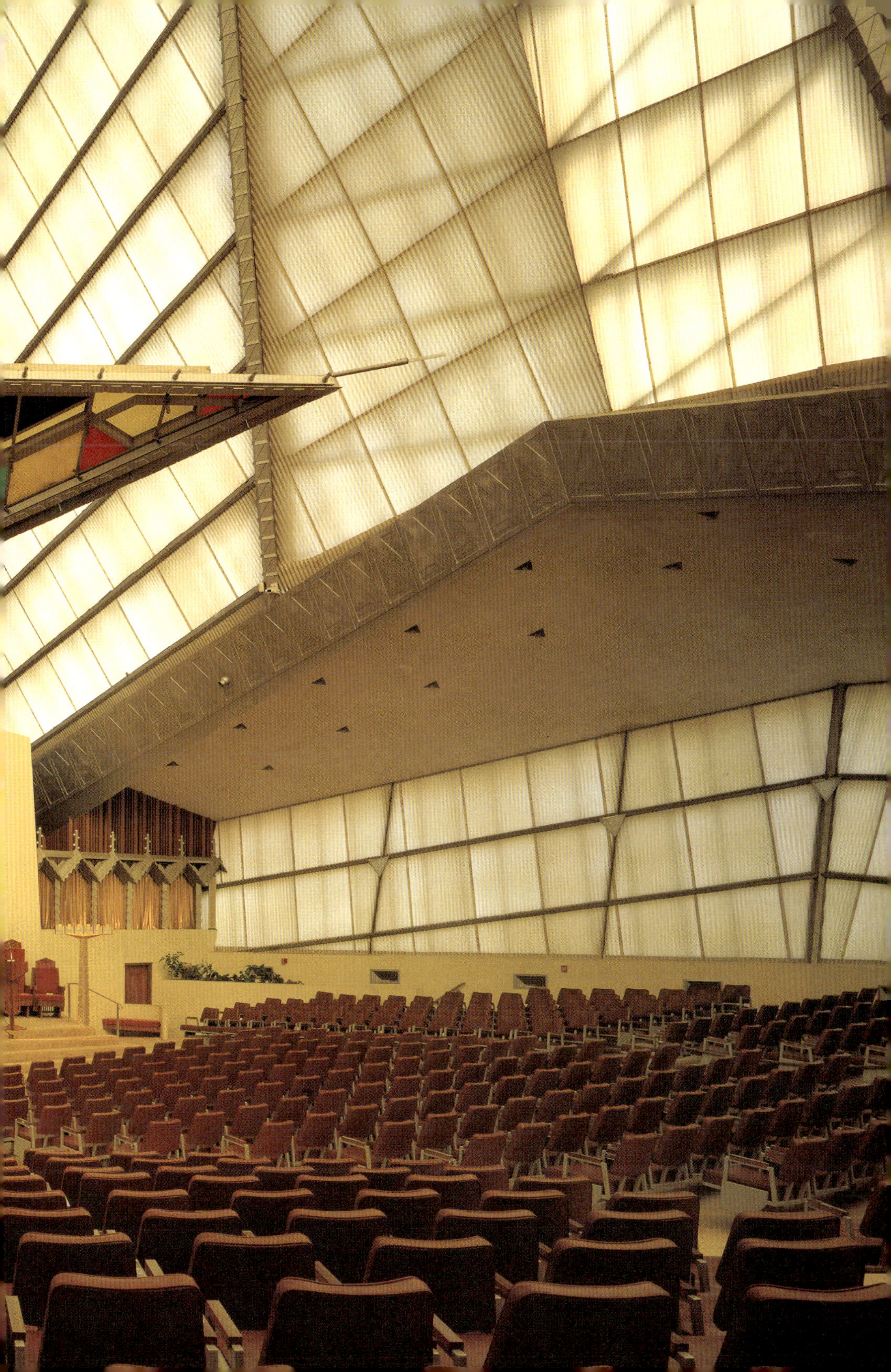

Annunciation Greek Orthodox Church
Wauwatosa, Wisconsin, 1956

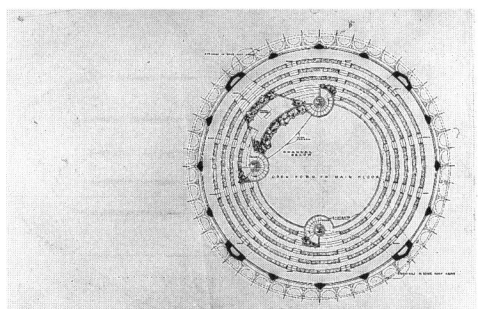

Balcony plan

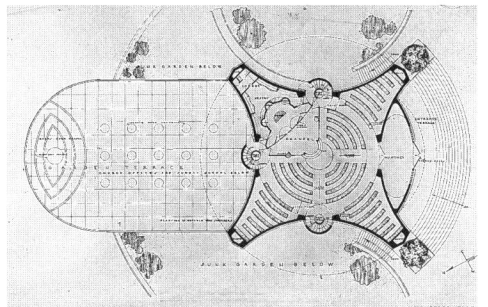

Main floor plan

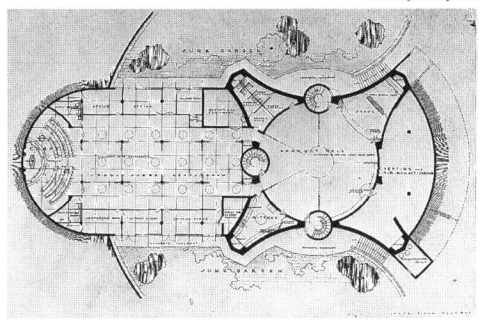

Lower floor plan

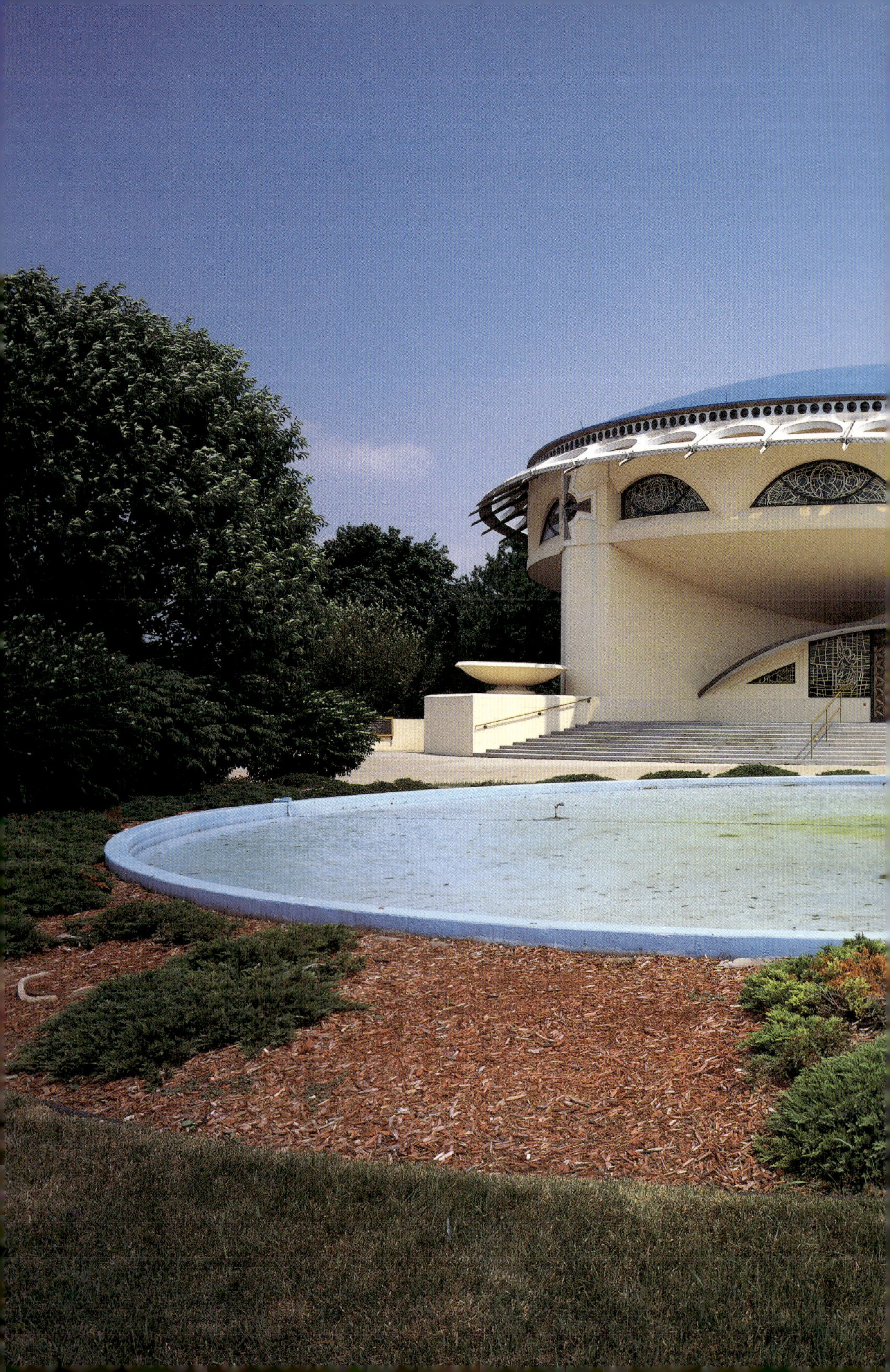

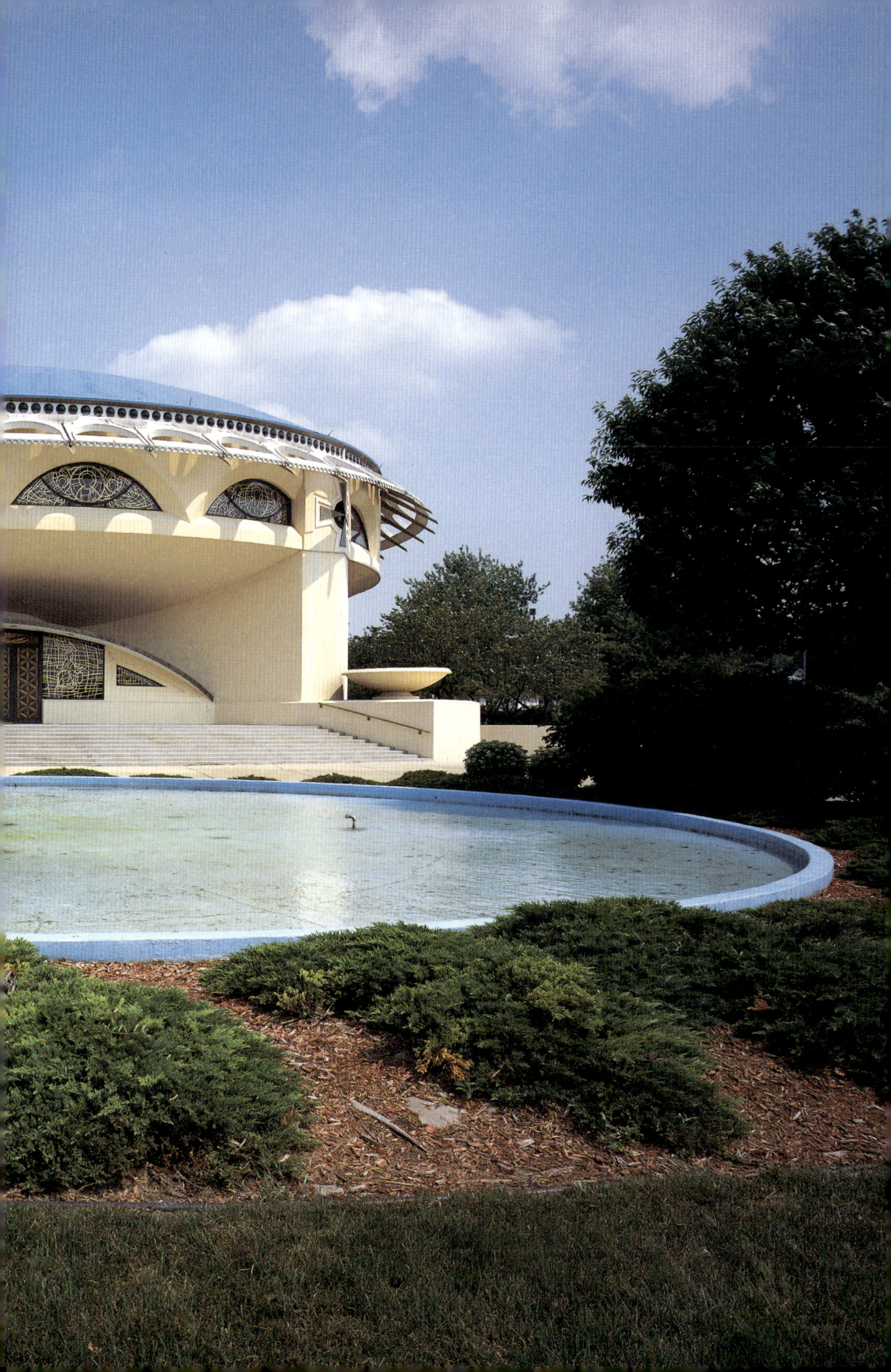

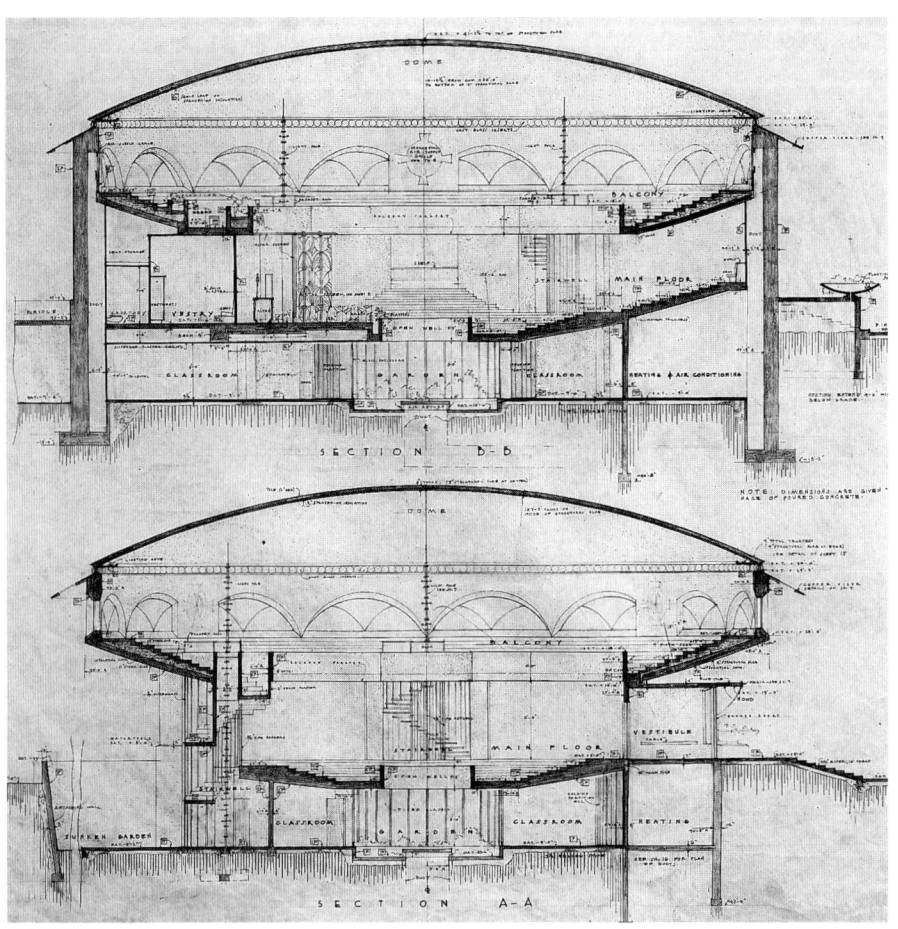

Cross sections

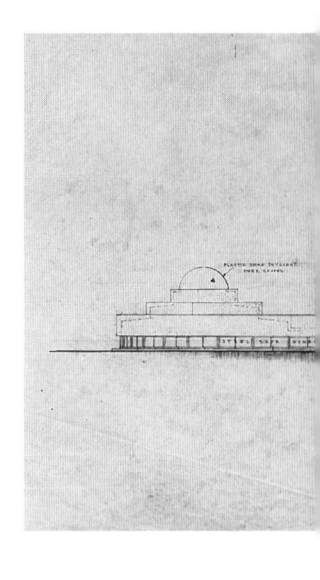

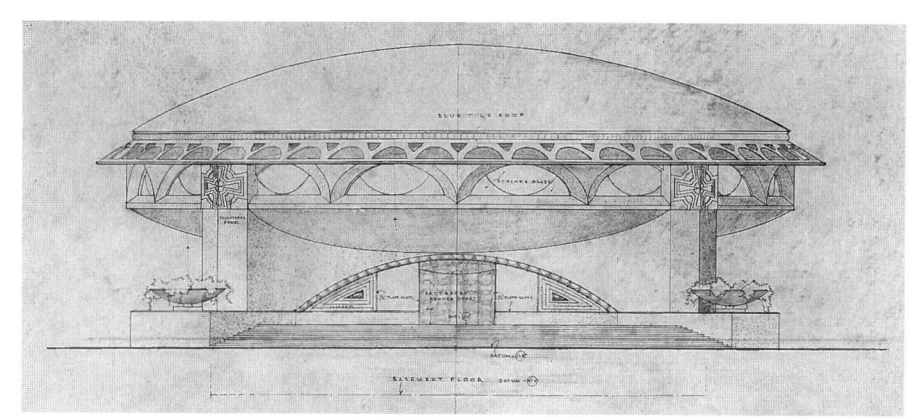

Southwest elevation

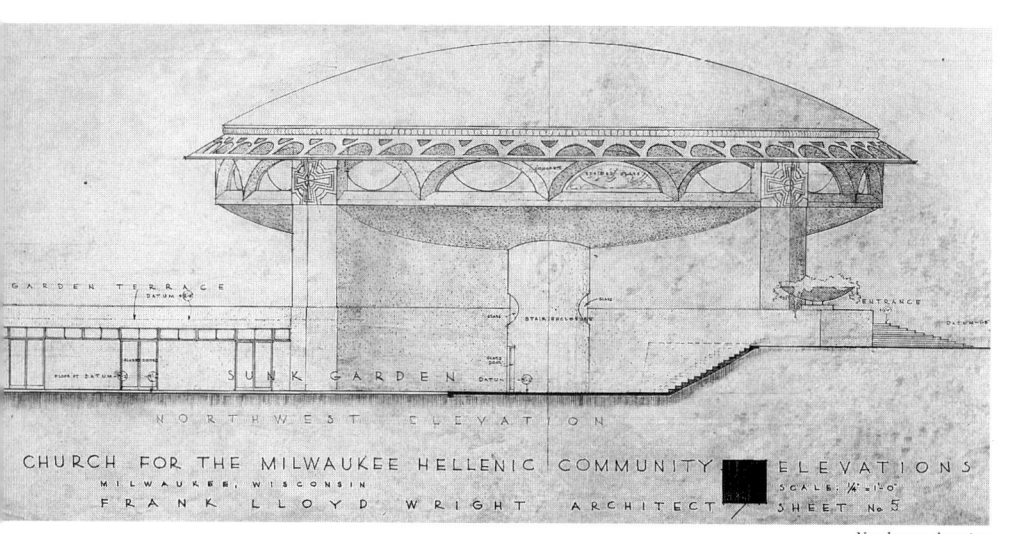

Northwest elevation

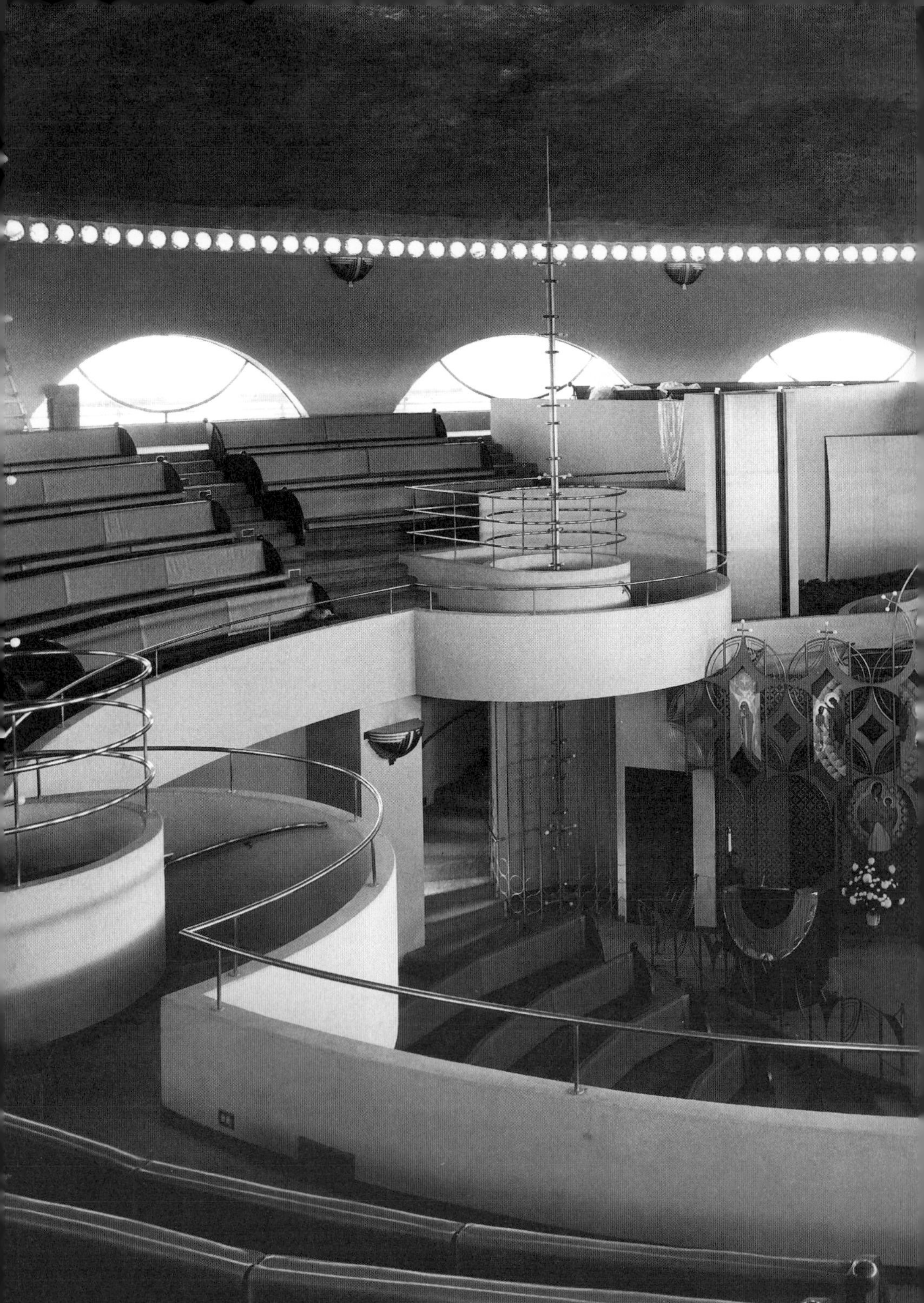

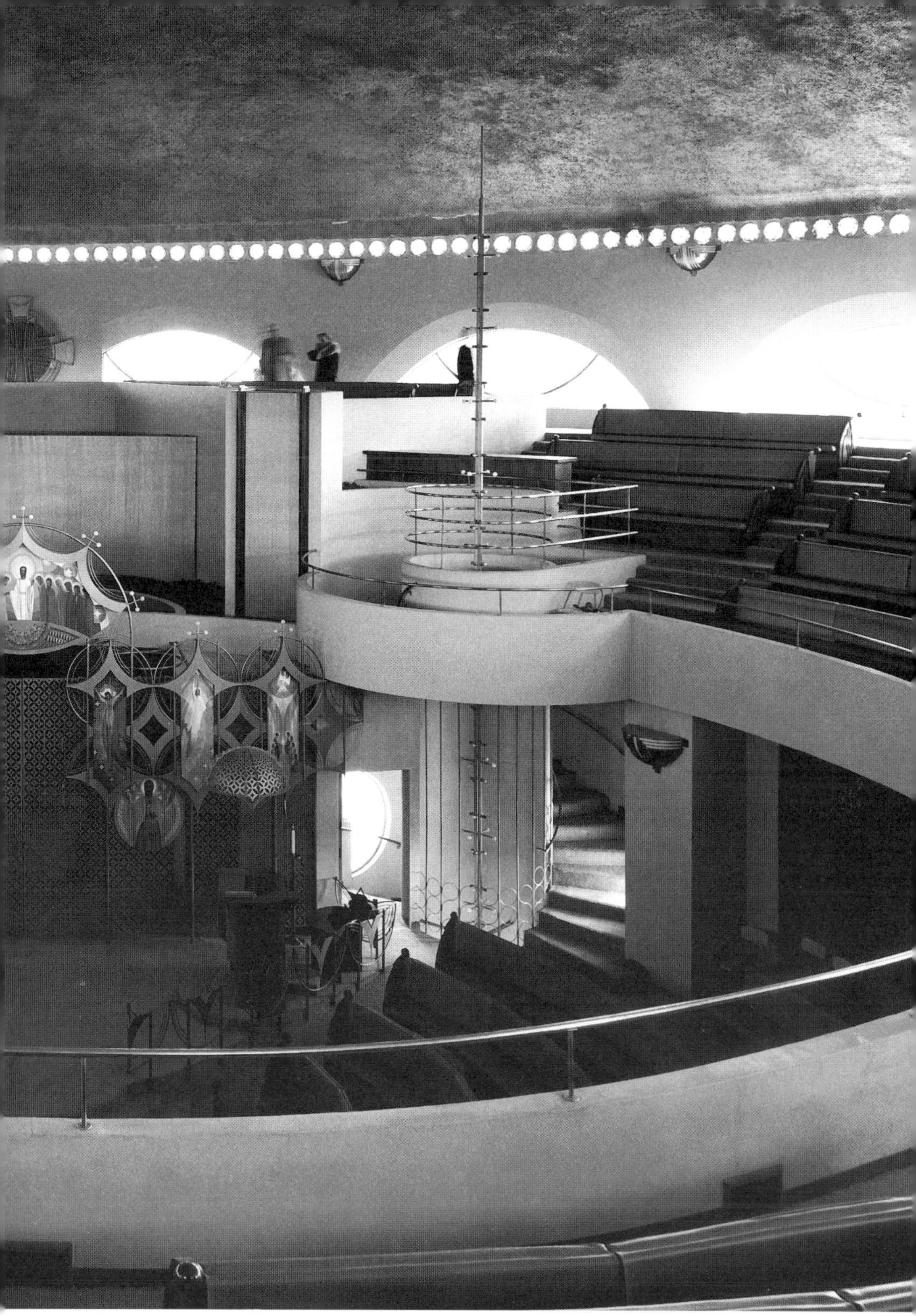

p.42-43

Administration Building for S. C. Johnson & Son Company: overall view

p.44-45

Administration Building and Research Laboratory

p.46-47

View from Franklin street

p.48-49

View toward main entrance from carport

p.50-51

Dendriform columns

p.52-53

*Entrance drive:
main entrance on right, carport on left*

p.54-55

*Entrance lobby:
view of revolving door and glass tubing*

p.58-59

Main entrance

p.62-63

Columns in carport

p.64
p.65

*Column and glass tubing Glass tubing:
view from entrance lobby*

Entrance lobby: view from bridge — p.66

Entrance lobby — p.67

Bridge at mezzanine level — p.68-69

Entrance of Great Workroom — p.70-71

Columns — p.72-73

Great Workroom: overall view — p.74-75

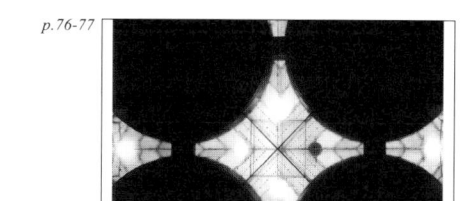

Detail of glass tubing skylight  — p.76-77

Detail of glass tubing high-side light   — p.78-79

Entrance to theater (now dining room)  — p.80-81

Theater (now dining room)  — p.82-83

Office on third floor — p.86-87

p.88-89

Detail of glass tubing partition

p.90-91

Domed ceiling of reception area in Research Laboratory

p.94-95

Research Laboratory for S. C. Johnson & Son Company: overall view

p.99

Research Tower: upward view

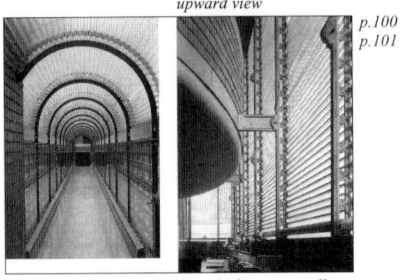

p.100
p.101

Bridge *Detail of interior wall*

p.104-105

Three Seminar Buildings, Florida Southern College: esplanade

p.106-107

Classrooms attached to esplanade

p.110-111

Roux Library, Florida Southern College: overall view

p.112

Entrance

p.114-115

Circular reading room

p.116-117 *p.130-131*

View toward Roux Library from esplanade roof *View toward Science and Cosmography Building*

p.118-119 *p.134-135*

Reading room *Esplanade of Science and Cosmography Building*

p.122-123 *p.136-137*

Industrial Arts Building, Florida Southern College: view from esplanade *Physics and mathematics wing*

p.126-127 *p.138-139*

Administration Building, Florida Southern College: office of bursar *Esplanade of Science and Cosmography Building*

p.128-129 *p.140-141*

Science and Cosmography Building, Florida Southern College: observatory *Detail of roof*

Solomon R. Guggenheim Museum: overall view p.142-143

View from Fifth Avenue p.145

Exterior of main gallery p.146-147

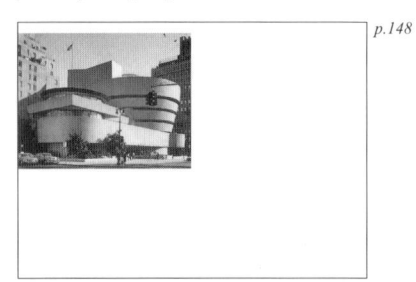

Overall view from Fifth Avenue p.148

Main gallery: downward view from sixth level p.150-151

Main gallery: upward view of glass dome p.152-153

Curved balustrade *Ramp: ground level to first level* p.154 / p.155

Main gallery: grand ramp p.156-157

Main gallery: view from third level p.158-159

Tower for H. C. Price Company: upward view *Overall view* p.162 / p.163

312

p.166-167 *p.176-177*

Upward view of tower

Living room of apartment: view from entry

p.168 *p.178*
p.169 *p.179*

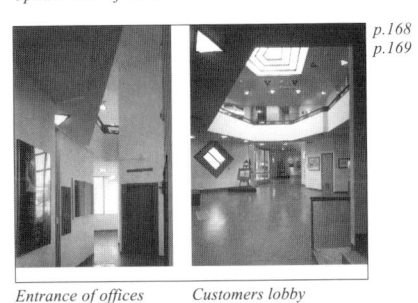

Entrance of offices   *Customers lobby*

Living room of apartment: *Center of tower*
master bedroom above

p.170-171 *p.182*
p.183

Mezzanine floor

Office   *Mr. Price's office*

p.173 *p.184-185*

View toward staircase

Marin County Goverment Center: aerial view

p.174-175 *p.186-187*

Living room of apartment

Overall view

313

p.190-191   p.202-203

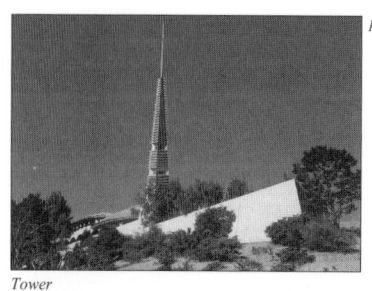

Tower   Mall with skylight

p.194-195   p.204-205

Arched underpass   Library

p.196-197   p.206
                                     p.207

Arch and skylight   Upward view of roof   Tower and pool

p.198-199   p.228-229

End of Administration Building   Unity Temple: overall view

p.200   p.232-233
p.201

Detail of window   Mall   Entrance

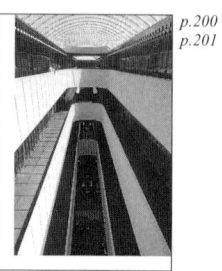

p.234-235

View toward pulpit

p.238-239

Skylight ceiling

p.240-241

View toward north

p.242
p.243

Stairs up to auditorium  *Pulpit and organ*

p.244
p.245

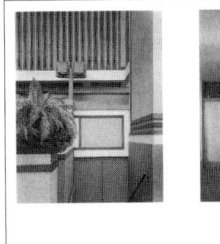

Detail of *Staircase at*
southwest corner *northeast corner*

p.246
p.247

View toward *Detail of*
northwest corner *southwest corner*

p.248-249

Downward view toward pulpit

p.250-251

Anne Merner Pfeiffer Chapel, Florida Southern
College: Danforth Chapel on right

p.254-255

West elevation

p.256-257

North elevation

315

p.258-259 
Entrance on southwest corner

p.260-261 
Auditorium: ground level

p.262-263 
Auditorium: balcony level

p.264-265 
Interior view of lantern tower

p.266-267 
Upward view of lantern tower

p.268-269
William H. Danforth Chapel, Florida Southern College: overall view from west

p.270-271 
Southwest elevation

p.272-273 
Interior view from balcony

p.274-275 
View toward altar

p.276-277 
Unitarian Meeting House: overall view from northeast

p.278-279

Triangular glass window and roof

p.284-285

Foyer: hexagon dome above

p.286-287

Auditorium: view toward pulpit

p.288-289

Auditorium: view from pulpit

p.290-291

Auditorium: overall view

p.293

Beth Sholom Synagogue: view from southwest

p.294-295

Overall view from west

p.296 *p.297*

View from northwest   *Detail of superstructure*

p.298-299

View toward ark

p.300-301

*Annunciation Greek Orthodox Church:
statue of cross and church beyond*

p.302-303

Southwest elevation

p.306-307

View toward chancel from balcony

GAトラベラー　007
フランク・ロイド・ライト
〈アーキテクチャー〉

2003年7月23日発行

企画・編集・撮影	二川幸夫
文	ブルース・ブルックス・ファイファー
翻訳	菊池泰子
ロゴタイプ・デザイン	細谷巖
発行者	二川幸夫
印刷・製本	図書印刷株式会社
発行	エーディーエー・エディタ・トーキョー
	東京都渋谷区千駄ヶ谷3-12-14
	TEL. (03) 3403-1581 (代)

禁無断転載

ISBN4-87140-617-2 C1352